D1521055

HIGHER EDUCATION IN POST-MAO CHINA

For our parents

— The Editors

HIGHER EDUCATION IN POST-MAO CHINA

Edited by
Michael Agelasto and Bob Adamson

香港大學出版社
HONG KONG UNIVERSITY PRESS

Hong Kong University Press
14/F Hing Wai Centre
7 Tin Wan Praya Road
Aberdeen, Hong Kong

© Hong Kong University Press 1998

ISBN 962 209 450 3

Cover photos by Jia Wenyuan

Printed in Hong Kong Caritas Printing Training Centre

Contents

Contents

Acknowledgements

The editors are grateful to Stanley Rosen, Hon Man Shan, David Goodman, Melody Ma Lai Ying, Wong Wai Yip and Jia Wenyuan for their help, as well as the editorial staff of Hong Kong University Press. The World Bank kindly gave permission for the inclusion of the Executive Summary from *China: Higher Education Reform. A World Bank Country Study* (1997). The production of this book was supported by a grant from the Sik Sik Yuen Education Research Fund.

About the Contributors

Michael AGELASTO is an independent scholar specializing in Chinese education and culture.

Bob ADAMSON is Associate Professor in the Department of Curriculum Studies and an Executive Committee member of the Comparative Education Research Centre at the University of Hong Kong. He teaches and publishes in the fields of English-language teaching, curriculum studies and comparative education.

CHENG Kai-ming is Chair Professor of Education and Pro-Vice-Chancellor at the University of Hong Kong. He is currently also Visiting Professor of Education at the Harvard Graduate School of Education.

CAO Xiaonan is a doctoral candidate in administration, planning and social policy at Harvard University. He publishes in the areas of social context of effective schooling systems, and the relationship between education and globalization. He has worked for the State Education Commission in the PRC and the World Bank.

Wenhui ZHONG obtained his Ph.D. from the University of Toronto in 1993. His main research interest is the participation of Chinese academic scholars in the world community. He works in the field of international communications and is now based in Hong Kong.

Michele SHORESMAN is Associate Director, International Studies and Director of Overseas Programs at Washington University in St. Louis. She has a Ph.D. from the University of Illinois at Urbana-Champaign. She wrote *Shao Nian Gong — A Children's Palace* with Roberta Gumport (1986) and *Tanoshii Gakushu — Learning with Enjoyment* with Waunita Kinoshita (1981).

Cong CAO is Research Associate in the Center for Asian and Pacific Studies at the University of Oregon, Eugene. He completed his Ph.D. at Columbia University in 1997 and is now studying social and economic transition in China, and the changes in the Chinese scientific community and their implications.

LIU Yingkai is Associate Professor in the Foreign Language Department of Shenzhen University. He has authored 8 books and over 100 articles, and has won numerous prizes for his teaching and research on rhetoric and translation theory. He serves as a member of the council or standing committee of four national academic associations.

Greg KULANDER has a Ph.D. in Chinese Studies from the University of Aarhus in Denmark. His recent research has concentrated on the agricultural extension system and higher agricultural education in China. His current interest is the impact of changes in the economic sphere on educational developments.

XIAO Jin is Assistant Professor affiliated to the Department of Educational Administration and Policy, at the Chinese University of Hong Kong. She has a Ph.D. in adult and continuing education from Michigan State University. Her research interests include human resource needs and economic development in China, and adult education.

Vilma SEEBERG is Assistant Professor of International-Intercultural Education in the Graduate School of Education of Kent State University, Ohio. She holds a Ph.D. from the University of Hamburg. She is the author of *Literacy in China* (1989) and articles on Chinese higher education, as well as multicultural education in the USA.

ZHANG Minxuan is a Ph.D. candidate at the University of Hong Kong and Associate Professor/Deputy Dean of the School of Educational Sciences, Shanghai Normal University. He has been a visiting scholar at the universities of East Anglia, Leicester and Oxford in the UK.

MOK Ka-ho is Director, Asia Pacific Social Development Research Centre, and Assistant Professor of the Department of Public and Social Administration, City University of Hong Kong. He holds a Ph.D. from London School of Economics and Political Science. His publications include *Intellectuals and the State in Post-Mao China* (1998).

David CHAN is Associate Professor, Department of Applied Social Studies, City University of Hong Kong. He obtained a Ph.D. from the University of Nottingham. He researches and publishes in the fields of sociology of education, educational policy studies and intellectuals in China.

Carol C. FAN is Associate Professor at the University of Hawaii. She has a Ph.D. in East Asian History from UCLA, her research and teaching focusing on gender across cultures, Chinese women, Asian American Studies.

Maria JASCHOK is at present a Visiting Fellow at the Centre for Cross-Cultural Studies on Women, Oxford University. She is the author of *Concubines and Bondservants* (1988), co-editor of *Women & Chinese Patriarchy* (1994), and has contributed to numerous edited volumes in the area of Chinese Women's Studies.

Chuing Prudence CHOU is Associate Professor, National Cheng-chi University, Taiwan. Her research interests include Chinese higher education and women, and secondary teaching in cross-cultural settings.

Flora Chia-I CHANG is Vice President and Associate Professor, Tamkang University, Taiwan. She has been working on educational policy issues and university cultural exchange programmes between Taiwan and overseas.

Gay Garland REED is Associate Professor of Educational Foundations at the University of Hawaii. Her research interests include moral/political education in the PRC, values education policy in Korea and the USA, the socio-cultural construction of identity, and the social and cultural contexts of education.

Teresa WRIGHT is Assistant Professor of Political Science at California State University, Long Beach. She holds a Ph.D. in political science from the University of California, Berkeley. Her research interests include comparative studies of political protest and political liberalization in East Asia.

Abbreviations

ACWF	All-China Women's Federation
BdAU	Beida Autonomous Union
CAS	Chinese Academy of Sciences
CCP	Communist Party of China
EFL	English as a foreign language
FBIS	Foreign Broadcast Information Service
FLD	Foreign Languages Department
HAE	higher adult education
ISTIC	Institute of Scientific and Technological Information of China
JPRS	Joint Publications Research Service
MoA	Ministry of Agriculture
MoEd	Ministry of Education
NAS	National Academy of Sciences
NGO	non-governmental organization
NPC	National People's Congress
PLA	People's Liberation Army
PRC	People's Republic of China
SAU	Shenyang Agricultural University
SdAU	Shida Autonomous Union
SEdC	State Education Commission
UNESCO	United Nations Educational, Scientific, and Cultural Organization
USSR	Union of Soviet Socialist Republics

PART 1
THE SCOPE OF REFORM

PART 1
THE SCOPE OF REFORM

PART 1

THE SCOPE OF REFORM

1

Editors' Introduction[1]

Michael AGELASTO and Bob ADAMSON

The People's Republic of China (PRC) is home to the single largest indigenous population in the world. The sheer size of the PRC's natural and human resources has enabled the country to occupy an increasingly important position internationally as a socio-economic and geopolitical force. After the death of the nation's founding father, Mao Zedong, the PRC's growing stature as a global power has accelerated since the government's shift from isolationist, politics-oriented policies to open door, economics-oriented policies. This shift was accompanied by major reforms in higher education, which was ascribed a key supporting role in the drive to modernize the nation. Although economics-oriented policies had featured in earlier stages of the PRC's development and although China has a long history of education, the reforms of the post-Mao era have taken the country's economic, social, political and higher education systems into unexplored terrain.

For China, the modern enterprise of 'higher learning' is a century-old foreign import and has been influenced to a large extent by Western philosophy and models during its development.[2] Later influence, shaped by both the international and domestic political environment in the 1950s and early 1960s, came from the former Union of Soviet Socialist Republics (USSR) for mainly ideological reasons, most notably the failure of the United States to recognize the PRC and the latter's need for a socialist role model. When the Chinese Communist Party (CCP) came to power under the leadership of Mao Zedong in 1949 and set about transforming the institutions left by the Nationalist Government, the central concerns of higher education remained unchanged — political order and rapid economic development. These concerns, especially the former, were reinforced during the period of close imitation of the Soviet experience because it 'held promise for an economic modernization that proceeded within a hierarchical and authoritarian political order'.[3] Such political order, plus a planned economic system under the control and scrutiny of the central authority, dominated all aspects of life in the PRC, including the higher education sector, during that era. Order was incrementally consolidated by disastrous back-to-back political movements in the country — the Anti-rightist Campaign, the Great Leap Forward and the decade-long Great Proletarian Cultural Revolution.[4] During these movements, education played an instrumental role in supporting the policies of the national leadership.

The Cultural Revolution, from 1966 to 1976, left the political, economic and social scenery of the PRC looking like a bomb-site. The nation had been torn by factional fighting and nowhere was this more evident than in education. Indeed, throughout the turmoil, students provided the fundamentalist vanguard of the movement. Teachers were vilified, defenestrated, rusticated or murdered, as the Confucian bond of loyalty between students and mentors was ruptured. Campuses became the focal point for revolutionary action with proletarian politics in command; classrooms were abandoned for a number of years. University entrance examinations were discontinued, with preference for admission given to those with a proletarian background. Academic pursuits were condemned as bourgeois and divorced from reality and students undertook farmwork and other labour.

In the two decades that followed the death of Chairman Mao in 1976, the principal architect of reform was Deng Xiaoping. Having outmanoeuvred Hua Guofeng (who claimed to be Mao's designated successor) and other pretenders, Deng initiated policies designed to stimulate economic growth. In 1978, the National People's Congress adopted a long-mooted policy, the Four Modernizations programme, which identified agriculture, industry, national defence, and science and technology as key areas for reform and investment. In economic terms, the targets were threefold: to double industrial and agricultural outputs from their 1980 levels; to quadruple the 1980 GNP by the year 2000; and to achieve economic parity in GNP per capita with middle-income developed countries by 2049.[5] To achieve this, Deng rejected previously favoured Stalinist models of economic development for their negative effect on the people's standard of living and for their overemphasis on heavy industry.[6] Instead, four major shifts were envisaged:

1. the development of a socialist market economy from a socialist planned economy;
2. the replacement of the Stalinist model of investment, imported during the fifties, with an indigenous model;
3. the loosening of state control of production to allow producers to enjoy greater autonomy; and
4. the establishment of the Open Door policy to enable participation in the international economy.[7]

Higher education was accorded a new task: that of supporting the modernization drive through developing the requisite human capital, as articulated by the CCP in 1985:

> Education must serve socialist construction, which in turn must rely on education. Our massive socialist modernization programme requires us not only to give full rein to the skilled people now available and to further enhance their capabilities, but also to train, on a large scale, people with new types of skills who are dedicated to the socialist cause and to the nation's economic and social progress into the 1990s and the early days of the next century.[8]

In the final quarter of the twentieth century, the nation's reforms in higher education have progressed in leaps and bounds along with, as this volume will demonstrate, stumbles and — in the case of the ill-fated événements of 1989 — calamitous misadventure. To date, three phases are discernible. Picking up the pieces after the Cultural Revolution and training human capital for national economic modernization were the initial and enduring challenge for higher education. The qualified staff and appropriate curricula, resources and facilities were not immediately available. One approach to this problem was through the Open Door policy, which encouraged foreign investment in the PRC in the form of joint ventures with Chinese companies, a measure designed to facilitate the transfer of technological expertise. In education, communication was two-way: teachers were brought into institutes of higher education from overseas to provide Chinese staff and students with access to foreign learning, while thousands of Chinese students went overseas to study for higher degrees.

This interflow had historical precedents and Deng was cognizant of the political and cultural tensions that this policy could produce. In a statement at the Twelfth Congress of the CCP in August 1982, he stated:

> We will unswervingly follow a policy of opening to the outside world and actively increase exchanges with foreign countries on the basis of mutual equality and benefit. At the same time we will keep a clear head, firmly resist corrosion by decadent ideas from abroad and never permit the bourgeois way of life to spread in our country.[9]

His caveat reflects the guiding principle of *zhongxue weiti, xixue weiyong* (adapting Western practice to suit Chinese conditions) that had been adopted by pragmatists in China since the Self-Strengthening movement in the middle of the nineteenth century.

Also in the first reform phase, the adoption of a new economic model, which involved a change from planned economy to socialist market economy, had important implications for higher education. In a *planned economy,* critical economic processes are largely determined not by market forces, but by a central economic planning body which implements society's major economic goals. A *market economy,* on the other hand, manifests extensive private ownership of capital and allocates goods and services by the price mechanism with government supervision, in the absence of omnipresent government intervention. This latter type of economy is characterized by volatility, competitiveness, openness and information network. It requires a large supply of trained professionals and technical personnel who are practical, flexible, versatile, international and innovative. Since the market fluctuates quickly according to the principle of supply and demand, the society constantly needs people who are well-trained in a certain speciality or a combination of specialities quickly. A market economy not only requires trained personnel speedily, it also needs a large number of them.

The first set of massive market economy reforms launched in the PRC around 1980 brought on startlingly rapid growth forcing the quick formulation of educational policy to deliver new types of human resources. These plans not only specified the mission of educational reform as improving the quality of the Chinese nation while training more and better qualified personnel, but they also emphasized the reform of existing educational structures, as well as the reallocation of responsibilities within each educational sector in the system. As reforms were actualized, tertiary industry (the service sector) increasingly outpaced primary industry, but in both sectors, knowledge-intensive and technology-intensive jobs grew most quickly.

The second phase of Dengist educational reforms started in 1985 and are described in detail in Cheng Kai-ming's chapter in this volume. They were signalled and legitimated two years previously when Deng wrote the 'Three Orientations' (*sange mianxiang*) inscription for Jingshan Secondary School in Beijing, which stated that education should be 'oriented towards modernization, the future and the world'. The focus of government concern was on aspects of the education system which were considered to be flawed, either because previous reforms had failed to address these particular issues, or because the modernization programme had created problems that the

current education system was not equipped to handle. The following areas of higher education were viewed as particularly problematic:[10]
1. the slow development of vocational skills;
2. the mismatch between jobs and tertiary graduates' specializations;
3. the inability of institutes to keep pace with modernization;
4. students' lack of independent thinking and study skills; and
5. over-centralized and over-rigid educational administration.

A number of problems arose from the fact that, for its size, the PRC has a small tertiary education sector. In the 1980s, graduates of conventional higher education institutes and secondary speciality (short cycle) schools totalled 1.7 million, which was only 10% of the population entering the workforce. In state-owned enterprises and industries, only 2.5% of the country's workforce were qualified technicians and engineers. Meanwhile, more than 4.5 million employed personnel required continuing education for in-service training or professional development. State officials estimated in 1987 that, by 1990, the number of technical and engineering personnel would have to be increased to 4.7% of the workforce of 105 million. At the same time, 3.5 million new teachers would have to be trained.[11] By 1994, in fact, total student enrolment in regular full-time higher education institutions had increased to 2.51 million from 1.02 million in 1980. Rapid economic growth in the reform era had certainly stimulated demands for higher education.

The reforms of the second phase placed emphasis on local responsibility, diversity of educational opportunities, multiple sources of educational funds, and decentralization of power to individual institutions' authorities in the governance of their own affairs.

Until recently the PRC had a tightly controlled labour force. Since the early 1950s, Chinese college graduates could get jobs only through state assignment, leaving no choice to the employers or employees. The *danwei*, or work-unit, is an administrative term referring to the organization of almost all urban workers under the authority of the central government. It is through the *danwei* that housing, jobs, goods and services are distributed to people. Until reforms allowed local experimentation in different systems, including the right of individuals to find their own jobs, assignment to the *danwei* was a decision made by the state.

In order to fulfil the need for professional knowledge and trained personnel for national modernization, the state allowed different types of educational institutions to flourish so as to create more educational opportunities. The state, therefore, provides only the framework necessary for educational development in the mainland and has deliberately devolved responsibility and power to local governments, local communities and other non-state sectors to increase educational provision. Local educationalists and scholars thus have begun to take the lead in developing initiatives to cater for the evolving market needs and people's pressing demands for better education.

At the turn of the century, the PRC is entering a new phase of its reform of higher education. One of several major initiatives is the 211 Project, which seeks to create an élite body of 100 institutions that, with private and state funding, can become centres of academic excellence. The revolution from the hyper-political, anti-intellectual, non-élitist policies of the Cultural Revolution is complete.

In the post-Mao era, therefore, the landscape of China has changed dramatically, both literally and figuratively. Modernization has brought about a building boom, a diversification of industry, a rise in the standard of living and a loosening of many controls on daily life. Likewise in higher education, reforms have sought to produce high-quality personnel and to gear the curriculum to the needs of modernization; to restructure the financing of higher education and the job assignment process as part of the market economy; to decentralize policy-making and to strengthen local autonomy to cater for the disparate needs of different regions.

These reforms have not taken place in a vacuum. During the period, the veterans of the Long March passed away — most notably Deng Xiaoping on 19 February 1997 — and a new generation that lacks the revolutionary credibility of its predecessors has taken control of the CCP. Internationally, the demise of the USSR and its communist satellites has provided salutary lessons to the PRC's leadership on the dangers of economic reforms, which domestically have had critical moments. There have been many outcomes that were unforeseen at the time of formulation. An example is the profound effect that the depoliticization of education has had on students' aspirations. Attitudes and behaviour of teachers and students within higher education have changed. Interactions with other countries, particularly those once anathema to the socialist PRC, have produced cultural tensions and a serious brain drain. Reforms have affected the participation of women, minorities and the disadvantaged in higher education. The purpose of this volume is to reach beyond the articulated goals of reform and their accomplishments and to explore the actual impact, both intended and unwitting. While not diminishing the successes already achieved, the chapter authors take a critical and analytical view of the gaps between Chinese planning and Chinese reality.

Despite China's size and importance, knowledge of the contemporary PRC is limited both inside and outside the country. The closed and often xenophobic policies of the Chinese political leadership made quantitative and qualitative research regarding many aspects of Chinese society, including education, difficult to carry out. However, since the leadership embarked upon the Four Modernizations drive and the concomitant Open Door policy, the PRC has permitted educational research by both domestic and foreign scholars. Still, much that was published on Chinese higher education in the initial reform period lacked a strong empirical and theoretical basis. Writings were often based on observers' 'impressions', with data coming from state-arranged interviews with educational leaders and policy-makers. From the 1980s onwards, many new scholars have chosen Chinese topics for their dissertation research, reflecting the growing domestic interest in research and the growing international interest in the PRC fostered by the reform era. This volume is composed mostly of thesis-based case studies that provide a wealth of data, new insight and fresh empiricism.

The book comprises 20 chapters, divided into 7 sections. The first section, of which this introduction forms a part, presents an overview of the reforms. The second section looks at the PRC's tertiary educators and is primarily concerned with the goals of the initial reform period. Cao Xiaonan analyses faculty development initiatives and identifies the age gap and brain drain issues as crucial concerns. Next, Wenhui Zhong looks at the participation of Chinese scholars in the world community. Barriers to presenting scholarship in an international forum include funding, language barriers and editorial standards. Then, Michele Shoresman presents a case study of the visiting scholars programme. From 1978 to 1988 mid-career professionals from the PRC undertook advanced training abroad. The author focuses on the University of Illinois which trained over 200 PRC scholars. Finally, Cong Cao examines the Chinese Academy of Sciences. He describes recruitment into this élite group through collective biographical analysis.

The book's next section presents case studies regarding the changing curricula in various institutions, which seek to serve the new economic order. They offer very different perspectives. A view from within, an *emic* view, comes from Liu Yingkai, an associate professor at Shenzhen University. Liu's chapter deals with the reorientation of curriculum to meet local needs, but also describes how the university coped with being a part of, and not just training personnel for, a socialist market economy. As a former 'foreign teacher' and outside observer on the inside, Bob Adamson looks at the education of language teachers at Taiyuan Teachers College. He focuses on two elements: the pragmatic solutions that were adopted to solve tensions arising from the reforms aimed at improving the quality of teacher education, and the problems faced by a middle-stratum institute to implement them. Next, Greg Kulander discusses agricultural universities, presenting detailed data for Shenyang Agricultural University. He shows how the reform era has caused the role of agricultural institutions to change and he analyses the reforms they have undertaken to meet the changing needs of rural society. Xiao Jin's study of higher adult education then explores an area that is often neglected in the literature, which mostly focuses on regular institutions of higher learning. The rapid expansion of higher adult education during the reform period has brought with it issues of efficiency, quality and relevance.

The fourth section examines the subject of economics of education, which has been a central issue in the second phase of reform. Vilma Seeberg's study of stratification trends in technical-professional enrolment focuses on the urban-rural divide and shows that families are pursuing maximum flexibility and mobility even at a high cost of tuition. Zhang Minxuan looks at changes in tuition policy. He relates changing equity conceptions with student financial support policies. Michael Agelasto surveys the changes in graduate employment, as the PRC moves away from manpower planning towards a market-oriented system that provides both students and employers greater choice. Mok Ka-ho and David Chan discuss the phenomenon of private higher education in southern China and conclude that it is, as yet, peripheral and that quasi-marketization has yet to be fully realized.

The next two sections address key social issues that were not on the original reform agenda, but were affected by the educational reforms. The first looks at how women fare in Chinese higher education. This question has received increasing attention, particularly with the PRC's hosting of the International Women's Conference in Beijing in 1995. First, Carol C. Fan presents an overview of the situation of female teachers and students in both the PRC and Taiwan. She discusses various causes of gender inequality. Then Maria Jaschok presents an ethnographic study of the PRC's first institution of higher education with a women-centred programme. Having served as vice-president of the institute, the author offers valuable insights into educational administration, management and politics. Chuing Prudence Chou and Flora Chia-I Chang focus specifically on discriminatory practices in the hiring, rewards and promotion of faculty staff in Taiwan, and compare the situation to that on the mainland.

The two chapters in the sixth section focus on the tensions emerging from economic liberalization and the determination of the state to maintain control in other dimensions. Gay Garland Reed looks at values education. She asks whether Lei Feng, an ideological role model for university students before reform, is relevant today. The chapter by Teresa Wright looks at student politics. Specifically, she examines the events of the Beijing spring of 1989. These authors offer insight on state control of education: a continual struggle between political loosening and tightening that has characterized higher education during the reform era.

The final section offers some concluding comments. Successes and tensions of the higher education reform programme are identified and some of the unintended consequences are highlighted. It draws out a number of common threads that run through the diverse chapters in the book. An appendix contains the executive summary of the 1997 World Bank report on Chinese higher education, followed by a glossary of this volume's most frequently used Chinese language terms, which appear in the text and notes in *hanyu pinyin* transliteration.

These chapters were specifically commissioned for this volume. A book of this size and depth would inevitably have omissions. The editors were unable to include individual chapters on important areas (for example, higher education for ethnic minorities, pedagogy, overseas study, World Bank influence and radio/television universities) because potential authors were unavailable. Nevertheless, by presenting new data resulting from in-depth research, much of it obtained at the grass roots, the authors convey the experience of higher education reform as implemented. In doing so, this new scholarship provides a valuable contribution to the literature on Chinese higher education.[12]

NOTES

1. Vilma Seeberg, Cao Xiaonan, Fu Sin Yuen-ching, Michele Shoresman, Mok Ka-ho and David Chan contributed material for this introduction.
2. See, for example, Xiong, 1983; Hayhoe, 1996. (Full details are in the Bibliography.)
3. Hayhoe, 1989a, pp. 18–9.
4. For a history of modern education in China, see Pepper, 1996.
5. Lewin *et al.*, 1994.
6. Leung, 1995.
7. Lewin *et al.*, 1994.
8. CCP, 1985.
9. Hayhoe, 1984, p. 206.
10. For a detailed discussion see Lewin *et al.*, 1994.
11. Y. Zhao, 1988, p. 217.
12. Some of this literature is critically reviewed in Liu Xiuwu, 1996.

2

Reforms in the Administration and Financing of Higher Education

CHENG Kai-ming

INTRODUCTION

This chapter presents an overview of higher education reform in the PRC, focusing particularly on finance and administration. Finance is always a central issue in the PRC's education reform. Education reforms have started with the decentralization of the financing system; with it comes reform in many aspects in education. Higher education is no exception. However, while the reforms in basic and technical/vocational education are based on a localization of finance, higher education remains very much a central, or at most provincial, endeavour.

Much of education reform in terms of structure and scale is derived from the reform *Decision* of 1985.[1] There were three major components in this reform: institution of nine-year compulsory education, strengthening of the vocational sector in secondary education and granting of more autonomy to higher education. Compulsory education has seen remarkable success at the primary level (first to sixth grades), although there are pockets of population where universal attendance has proved difficult. Compulsory education at the junior secondary level (seventh to ninth grades) is less successful, though improving. In technical and vocational education, the enrolment at senior secondary level (10th to 12th grades) has passed the target of 50% of total enrolment at that level. However, the original design of reform in higher education has taken a different orientation as will be seen in the following sections, and this is very much affected by the political climate of the times.

HIGHER EDUCATION INSTITUTIONS

Higher education is highly competitive in the PRC. The overall enrolment in 1995 was 2.91 million in the formal higher education sector and 2.59 million in the non-formal sector. The formal sector accounts for slightly higher than 3.4% of the relevant age cohort. This means that, on average, formal higher education institutions admit about half of the graduates of general senior secondary schools (i.e. the academic stream). The overall figure, of course, does not reflect the enormous disparity between regions. In Shanghai, for example, two out of three graduates from general secondary schools are admitted into higher education. In Guangzhou, the figure approaches one in two.

Undergraduate studies

Classifications of programmes and institutions in the PRC are by no means straight forward. Different classifications are used on different occasions depending on the subject of attention. Normative terms which carry legal status are often mixed with terms which are used only as a matter of convention. The following attempts to provide a picture of the classifications.

There is a classification by programme duration. Universities are usually either three or four years in length. In exceptional cases for extremely prestigious programmes, five or even six years are permitted. Four-year programmes are known as *benke* (literally, the main programme) and three years, *zhuanke* (the specialized programme). In 1995, there were over 1.6 million students in four-year programmes as compared with slightly fewer than 1.3 million in three-year programmes.[2] Until recently, there has been a general tendency for an increase in the latter. However, in developed cities, such a trend is complicated by employers' preference for four-year graduates over those from three-year programmes.

The institutions themselves are *not* normally classified by the duration of programmes. For example, of the total of 1080 institutions in 1994, three-year programmes were available in 1070 institutions, four-year programmes in 645 institutions. In reality, most of the 645 institutions which offered four-year programmes also offered some kind of three-year programmes. Institutions which offer only three-year programmes are sometimes translated (for example, by the World Bank) as polytechnic universities, but there is no such corresponding category in Chinese.

Credentials (*xueli*) from 1057 out of the 1080 (1994 figures) institutions are officially recognized as from institutions 'qualified to admit students for credential education'. In other words, upon graduation, students receive from these institutions diplomas which are officially recognized. For the first time, the list of such institutions was announced in 1995,[3] with the purpose of publicly disqualifying low-quality institutions which existed. In addition, a third category included 64 cases that represented approved extensions of formal institutions. In the announcement, an *asterisk* (*) was placed before some institutions as a warning that such institutions were 'slightly lower than what is required by the state'. Such an announcement has become an annual exercise.

Four-year programmes often, but not necessarily, lead to a Bachelor's degree. In the PRC, the status of a degree is still dubious. While a degree-awarding programme is usually seen to reflect higher standard, the degree itself plays a less significant role in employment than as a prerequisite for further studies. In 1994, there were 627 institutions which were officially recognized as *universities* (*daxue*). They conferred degrees. Another 453 were non-university institutions.[4] The degree system in the PRC is still very young. Despite attempts to set up a degree system during the 1950s and 1960s, it was established only after the Cultural Revolution (1966–76) and first implemented on 1 January 1981.[5] Thus, none of the graduates in the PRC from 1949 to 1981 were conferred any degree.

Postgraduate studies

The enrolment of Master's and doctoral students in 1995 was about 116 000 and 28 800 respectively. This total of less than 145 000 demonstrated a substantial increase of 13% over 1994.[6] In 1994, only 401 institutions offered accredited Master's programmes; 198 offered doctoral programmes.[7] Institutions, however, may offer postgraduate programmes which do not lead to degrees. Students in these programmes are still known as research students and they receive a diploma upon graduation. Such programmes are mostly at Master's level.

Master's studies, normally full-time, last for three years with heavy coursework in the first two years and a dissertation to follow. Doctoral studies are also normally full-time over three years, again with substantial coursework. It was only in the 1990s that institutions began to accept postgraduate studies in a part-time mode.

Non-formal higher education

There is an elaborate non-formal education system in the PRC which extends
from adult literacy programmes to higher adult education. Seven types of
higher adult education exist: radio/television universities, workers colleges,
peasants colleges, institutes of administration (formerly known as cadre
institutes), institutes of education, correspondence colleges, and the
correspondence/evening components of formal institutions. The modes
of non-formal higher education range from in-service full-time (a kind of
sabbatical), in-service release (for example, a day or two per week) to in-
service evening. As mentioned, in 1995, the enrolment in the non-formal
sector of higher education was 2.59 million, which is not far from the
enrolment in the formal sector (2.91 million).

Non-formal higher education is largely three years in nature, for the
most part following the curricula for formal higher education in
corresponding disciplines. Entrance to such programmes usually requires
passing the Adult Higher Education Entrance Examination, which is a
national public examination. Until recently, approval and recommendation
from the candidate's work-unit were required. With the deterioration of
state enterprises and their management systems, employees have had more
freedom to attend adult programmes, but it has become increasingly
difficult to secure sabbatical leave from the employer. Students in the three-
year programmes constitute 90% of the non-formal higher education
enrolment. Only exceptional programmes of higher adult education award
degrees and such degrees have to be awarded by approved formal
institutions.

In addition to institutional non-formal higher education, open learning
through the Self-study Examination has attracted many candidates, 4.8
million in 1993 alone.[8] The Self-study Examination is offered twice each
year. Candidates may enrol in individual subjects and may accumulate
their credentials over time. Unlike in other forms of non-formal education,
there is no entrance requirement for the Self-study Examination, which
perhaps contributes to its growing popularity. In the first examination in
April 1995, enrolment reached a record 3.65 million. Of these candidates,
50% were students of adult education institutions in one form or another;
the other 50% had undertaken private study.[9]

ADMINISTRATION OF HIGHER EDUCATION

The administration of higher education institutions follows the 'vertical'
and 'horizontal' patterns of general public administration in the People's

Republic. There are institutions all over the country which are administered, in the 'vertical' system, by ministries of the central government. Another system is the 'horizontal' system where institutions within a locality are administered by the local authorities, in this case the provincial government. In Chinese, the combined system is vividly described as 'columns and planes' (*tiaotiao kuaikuai*). The 'columns' are vertical lines of command; the 'planes' represent horizontal control.

The actual situation is complicated. While the horizontal system is relatively straight forward, the vertical system is almost unique to the PRC. A typical case is the Ministry of Railways, a gigantic nationwide enterprise which is self-sufficient in almost all respects, including manpower supply. For example, the Ministry runs its own systems of finance, health and education. This means the Ministry has to train its own personnel in all its subordinating units. It has to train its own accountants as well as medical doctors and nurses. For this reason, the Ministry of Railways operates its own medical university and its own university for finance and accountancy. It runs its own schools for children of its staff and hence has its own teacher training institutes in order to maintain the staff in such schools. Since the Ministry of Railways has subordinate units all over the country, its systems of universities and schools also extend over many parts of China. The same happens for many other ministries. These 'columns' have developed into serious departmentalization which is known as 'feudal partitioning' (*fengjian geju*), reflecting little coordination or cooperation among the departments.

All in all, in terms of accountability, institutes of higher education in the PRC are divided into four categories (see Table 2.1):

1. those under the direct administration of the SEdC;
2. those under the non-educational central ministries;
3. those under provincial and other local authorities; and
4. private institutions.

Among the four, (1) and (2) belong to the vertical system; (3) and (4) to the horizontal system. Institutions such as those under the Ministry of Railways belong to (2). The SEdC as the virtual ministry of education also takes on its own institutions, those in (1). Institutions in (3) are provincial institutions and are part of the 'planes'. Private institutions in (4) are administered by local authorities, hence they are also part of the horizontal system.

The reduction in number of public sector institutions is a result of the general policy to amalgamate smaller institutions in order to achieve a better economy of scale. The process has been slow. In 1995, the average size of a

Table 2.1
Distribution of institutions by governance

Administration	1993	1994	1995
State Education Commission	36	35	35
Central Ministries	325	325	323
Provincial	704	713	696
Private (*minban*)	na	7	na
Total (Excluding private)	1065	1080	1054

Sources: 1993 figures extracted from *Educational statistics yearbook of China 1993*,
                p. 18;
                1994 figures were released by Zhu Kaixuan, Chairman of the SEdC in a
                report in *Zhongguo Jiaoyu Bao*, 29 December 1994;
                1995 figures from Department of Planning, SEdC, cited in Min Weifan,
                1997, Table 1.
Note: In 1994 private institutions were first publicly recognized in the statistics,
                in keeping with the endorsement of private schools through legislation.

higher education institution was 2757 students, an improvement over the
1919 in 1990. Of the institutions, universities are usually larger; non-
universities are smaller. For example, in 1994, the average size of a university
was 3418; a non-university, 1338. Another area of general concern is the
samll staff-student ratio. In 1995, this was 1:7.3, comparing favourably with
1:5.2 for 1990.[10]

The term *key university* appears often in the literature outside the PRC.
The notion of *key* universities (*zhongdian daxue*), sometimes mistranslated
as *key point* universities, often arouses confusion. *Key universities*, similar to
key schools, follow the philosophy of paying special attention and giving
preferential treatment to institutions with good performance. Given the
resource constraint, the PRC sees this 'key' concept as a fundamental
strategy in educational development. From many Westerners' point of view,
however, this reflects overt bias towards the prestigious, making the
outstanding more outstanding, the better even better.

The concept of *key universities* was first introduced in 1954 when six
universities were identified as pilot institutions to pioneer some of the new
policies and reforms. These institutions — understandably those with better
performance — were given preferential treatment in terms of resources
and personnel. This evolved into a tier of privileged institutions which
were formally distinguished from the others. The notion of *key schools* and
key universities was totally abandoned and condemned during the Cultural

Revolution, not because it fostered inequality, but because it honoured the most 'bourgeois' institutions. After the Cultural Revolution, the concept was revived in the very first days of economic reform as a way for the state to nurture selected institutions when resources were scarce. The last formal list of key universities, 89 in number, was announced in 1981.[11]

Deng Xiaoping's doctrine of 'allowing a few to become rich first' assumes that since resources were not adequate, they should be given to the few who could make the best use of them. Such an assumption, which belongs very much to the ideology of a centrally planned economy, has faced challenges of another kind with the emergence of market economy and its respect for competition with equal opportunity.[12]

Although there has been no post-1981 nomination of *key universities*, the 89 institutions continue to call themselves key universities, quite legitimately. However, not all of them are under the SEdC, nor are they all under central ministries. In the meantime, while most of these institutions may preserve much of their prestige, the nomination released in 1981 is no longer an accurate indicator of their performance in the 1990s. In practical terms, with the reform in the financing system, these institutions are no longer protected by preferential resource allocations. Nonetheless, the notion of *key university* remains in discussions which refer to distinguished institutions. Most recently, there is a new move to improve the quality of institutions. This is Project 211 which will be discussed later.

FINANCING HIGHER EDUCATION

Before the reform, financing of higher education was characterized by a number of features. First, institutions were almost totally supported by state appropriation. In 1978, for example, 96.4% of higher education expenditures came from public coffers. Not only were students not required to pay, they were supported by the government with meal stipends and free accommodation. Second, the central government was the only controller of the education budget. Funds were channelled through the Ministry of Finance to various ministries and local governments, with the endorsement of the then Ministry of Education (MoEd). All funds were allocated for earmarked expenditures. Third, funds were calculated by 'basic number plus development'. The 'basic number' referred to the student enrolment and staff size as dictated by the national plan. Development referred to the incremental changes, again as required by the national plan.[13] Unspent funds were all returned to the government.

The reform in finance and administration takes place in one of the globe's most rigid systems of higher education. The PRC was the rare case where manpower planning in its strict sense was put into practice. Higher education was no more than an instrument to prepare manpower for the nation and hence was seen as an integral part of the state's manpower plan.[14] There was a nationwide unified system of student admission, unified curriculum structure, unified system of programmes, syllabi and textbooks, and a unified system of job assignment for graduates. Everything that happened in an institution was but part of the national plan. The centralization was very much the consequence of Soviet influence under which higher education was seen as a governmental endeavour taken care of by the respective government departments. It was also in the Soviet tradition that academic curricula were seen as manpower training programmes and thus were highly specialized and rigid.

Financial reform has been a critical dimension of economic reform in the PRC since the 1980s. In place of centralized incomes and expenditures, local authorities were allowed to retain part or most of their incomes and to decide their own spending plans. Local authorities may refer to enterprises (in the case of economic ministries), institutions (in the case of non-economic departments) or local governments. In practice, since 1980, there has been a demarcation between central and local control of incomes and expenditures. Within the territories of local control, the local authority has been given fairly significant autonomy in the management of resources. This is known in the PRC as 'eating in separate kitchens' (*fenzao chifan*) as a contrast to 'eating from the common pot' (*daguofan*). Most local authorities carried out similar reform among the subdivisions under their control. The demarcation between different levels of authority, however, was a matter of negotiation and was contingent upon circumstances.

Since 1994, there has been a further reform: taxation. The net effect of the reform, which is known as establishing a 'system of tax classification' (*fenshuizhi*), is to demarcate between legitimate authorities of taxation, so that both local and central governments have their legitimate sources of income. For the first time in the country, a difference between local and central taxes emerges. This reform, which is still ongoing, will reduce arbitrariness in the central-local negotiation.

In higher education, the reform was initially intended to increase the autonomy of institutions. The consequences have been quite significant in the realms of curriculum and teaching and particularly in fund-raising.[15] The *Outline for Reform*,[16] which was announced in 1993, has identified the reduction of centralization and government control in general as the long-term goals of reform. The objective is to achieve a situation where the government plays the role of 'macro-management through legislation, allocation of funding, planning, information service, policy guidance and essential administration', so that 'universities can independently provide education geared to the needs of society under the leadership of the government'. Such an orientation is further confirmed by the *Education Law* enacted on 18 March 1995.[17]

The present system of higher education finance is somewhat evolutionary in nature as the reform started back in the 1980s. The two major sources of income that an institution receives are state appropriation and other non-state income. The former is known as 'budgeted' (*yusuannei*); the latter, 'unbudgeted' (*yusuanwai*, extra to the budget). 'Budgeted' funds are almost synonymous to state appropriation.

State appropriation[18]

Since the early 1980s, the state has adopted the principle of 'he who manages, pays' (*suibanxue, suifuqian*). This is a direct consequence of the reform in the financial system. Since the local governments retain a considerable part of the income, they are also responsible for the local expenditures, which include education. The local governments, however, are still part of the 'state'. Hence the state still appropriates resources to higher education, but the actual actors which compose the 'state' have changed locations from the central to the local governments.

In theory, the state provides funding for salaries and the general operation of the institutions. The state also provides partial funding for capital investments. The principle for the management of government appropriation is 'one-line budget, retention of surplus' (*yusuan baogan, jieyu liuyong*). This is to provide incentive for institutions to economize on the resources available.

Unbudgeted incomes

Unbudgeted incomes are incomes which are not on the books of the government accountant. They became possible only because of the reform; previously, receiving funds from outside the government was improper. The 1985 reform *Decision* encouraged 'diversification of funding' (*duo qudao chouji zijin*). The five principal sources of unbudgeted income that have emerged in the past few years are: (1) university-run enterprises; (2) services; (3) commissioned training; (4) endowment/donations; and (5) student fees.

The largest sources of income for most institutions are commercial or industrial activities which are operated by the institution. The most successful ventures are found among well-known science and engineering universities in major cities. Almost all institutions operate some form of economic activity. However, some activities are more profitable than others. Success in such activities depends a lot on the location; universities in poor areas are at a great disadvantage. Some of these activities are related to research in relevant disciplines, but most of the other activities often have little to do with the institution's academic endeavour. Such activities are known as 'work-study programmes' (*qingong jianxue*) and are more recently known as 'university-run enterprises' (*xiaoban chanye*). Most institutions see such activities necessary, but unwanted. These ventures are encouraged by the state, enjoy preferential treatments in terms of taxation and are now provided for in the *Education Law*.[19]

Income is also generated from research, development and consultancy. Again, there is great disparity in the capacities of institutions in making profit out of such activities.

Commissioned training (*weituo peiyang* or *daipei*), sometimes also translated as contract training, is considered the second largest source of revenue in unbudgeted income. Commissioned training allows for an institution to offer courses for the training of personnel upon request, for a fee. The fee normally covers all of the recurrent expenditures and often part of the implied capital investment. The fee then becomes an extra income which the institution can use freely. Most of the income thus generated is retained by the academic or administrative department which delivers the course, and the institution extracts a certain percentage for overhead. The amount retained by the department is spent according to regulations specific to the institution. Often, part of the income goes to the improvement of facilities, the remaining to staff benefits. Commissioned training provides an institution with unprecedented discretion in expending the money.

In contrast to the income from commissioned training, donations are mostly used for the construction of buildings. The beneficiaries tend to be prestigious universities and small local colleges rarely obtain donations. Tuition fees are another source of unbudgeted income. This will be discussed in detail below.

As reforms have progressed, higher education institutions have tended to receive less money from the central government and indeed less from all levels of government. In 1996, for example, it was common for an institution to receive less than half of its income from the government. The state still pays for salaries, but staff of higher education institutions receive an increasingly large portion of their incomes from non-salaries (for example, bonuses, awards, supplementary stipends and allowances).

RECENT REFORMS IN HIGHER EDUCATION

The scene in higher education in the PRC has changed rapidly over the years. Four most recent reforms may further change the scene. They are the

1. introduction of student fees;
2. abolition of job assignment;
3. renewed selection of élite institutions; and
4. localization of institutions.

Introduction of student fees

One of the crucial moves in higher education reform is towards fee-charging. This is related to the system of university entrance. University entrance is very much controlled by the nationwide Unified Examination for University Entrance, which is often conveniently referred to as *gaokao*. This is the most significant screening throughout the entire education system in the PRC. Shanghai was the first place which opted out from the national system. It set up, in the early 1980s, its own system and today still admits students through results of its own examination system. Some other places have plans to follow suit.

Institutions which work under the auspices of the SEdC or other central ministries recruit students from all over the country. Their graduates are also assigned jobs in different parts of the country. As mentioned earlier, these institutions belong to the 'vertical system' and are virtually national institutions. The other institutions, in contrast, are local institutions. They recruit students from the local province or local municipality and their graduates are expected to work for the local province or municipality. Before the reform, the planned economy which practised manpower planning allowed little room for student choice and hence the system worked. Institutions were not allowed to admit students outside the state plan.

In practical terms, students are admitted according to two factors: their scores in the unified examination and the quotas of enrolment in specific institutions and specific majors/specialities. The quotas are assigned to an institution according to a national plan. Students obtain an average score in the *gaokao*,[20] in a range that permits choices of specialities in institutions. The students' ranked choices lead to a virtual 'cut-off' score (*fenshuxian*) specific to each institution. A prestigious university may require a score of 850 out of 900 for entrance. A second-rate institution may require only 600. The cut-off point for each institution is often called the 'score mark' (*fenshuxian*) for that particular institution.

Reform has motivated institutions to admit candidates below the cut-off point and hence outside the state plan, in order to increase income. Fee reform emerged in the early 1980s. The *Decision* in 1985 affirmed the admission of 'self-supporting students' and 'commissioned training students' as a way of 'funding diversification'. This means institutions could admit students outside the state plan (*jihuawai*). In 1989, institutions were allowed to collect fees for accommodation and sundry items. Starting in 1993, 30 institutions participated in a pilot scheme whereby all students, whether in the state plan or not, were required to pay fees. The standard rate was ¥1000–1800 per annum.[21] However, institutions are given the discretion to fix their own fees. Some charge as much as ¥3000. In practice the fee levels are fixed not according to costs, but rather by the market — according to what students can afford and according to the prospective returns to the graduates. Hence, universities in prospering Guangzhou charge fees higher than those in Beijing, which are in turn higher than those in Xi'an in the less developed west. Meanwhile, contrary to conventions, fees for science students, for example, are often much lower than those for students studying foreign languages and business studies which, with higher returns, are more popular disciplines.

A reform initiative known as 'merging the rails' (*binggui*) started in 1995. This has unified the admission criteria and fee levels for those students within the national plan with those outside it. In practical terms, this attempts to eradicate the admission of students with very poor performance but who can afford the fees, a practice which is viewed as scandalous in the Chinese community. The long-term implication, however, is that this policy virtually allows institutional plans to prevail over the national plan. The national plan would soon become insignificant. A recent report shows that in 1996, 661 (out of the total 1056) institutions and two-thirds of the overall intake were in the fee-paying mode.[22] Anyway, from 1997, all higher education institutions have started charging students fees.[23]

The general tendency in Chinese higher education is to charge a fee which is less than 25% of the recurrent unit cost.[24] Coupled to this tendency is the necessity to establish a student loan system.[25] Student subsidies were removed in 1987 and have been replaced by scholarships either as an award for excellence, as incentives into hardship areas (teaching, mining, agriculture), or to attract students to work in difficult regions after graduation.

Abolition of job assignment

As a direct consequence of the socialist planned economy, graduates of higher education were assigned jobs according to state plans. Under strict manpower planning, graduates were regarded as an anticipated input to the production machinery and were obliged to follow job assignments made by the state. There was an enormous exercise every year when graduates from the entire country were matched with posts in the entire country. In a socialist context, higher education was free to all students, who were also given free room and board. The returns to higher education were realized only in the state's production, but not on the individuals.

Job assignment faced challenges in the mid-1980s when graduates began to opt for alternative jobs with stronger economic incentives. In those days, graduates who opted out of the state allocation system were asked to compensate the government for disturbing the state plan (or to repay what the state had spent on them). The policy changed in the early 1990s, when students' free job-seeking became a matter of social demand. Institutions started to practise what is known as 'two-way selection' whereby activities were organized to allow potential employers and prospective graduates to understand each other and do some mutual matching. By the mid-1990s, most institutions practise 'two-way selection'.[26]

The national policy seeks to abolish state job assignment altogether by the year 2000. The policy is likely to be successful because of the small graduate output vis-à-vis the expanded demand following economic developments.

Quality selection: Project 211

Announced in 1993, the purpose of Project 211 is to identify for the twenty-first century 100 institutions of 'world standard'. The state has put aside a sum of incentive money to facilitate such a move.[27] The movement has already caused competition among institutions. Effects include the merger of prestigious institutions to increase their competition capacity. The most famous mergers involved five universities in Hangzhou, Zhejiang province and eight institutions in Yangzhou, Jiangsu province. There were even proposals to merge the most prestigious Beijing University with the Beijing Medical University, so as to become a real comprehensive university with all major disciplines represented. The net effect of the merger trend is that the total number of higher education institutions dropped from 1056 at the end of 1996 to 1034 in the first half of 1997.

The intended competition in Project 211 is, however, compromised by administrative interference, because the institutions were selected and nominated by the provincial authority before undergoing accreditation and validation. Some of the mergers mentioned above were really tactics to win accreditation for Project 211 rather than an effort aimed to improve excellence or efficiency. The final selection, though, is done after rigorous visits by an impartial and high-powered panel comprising prominent academics.

The drive for excellence has prompted the state to adopt preferential treatment to institutions as a policy of meritocracy. Such policies will inevitably change the relationship between the state and the institution and will further increase the disparity among institutions.

Localization of institutions

There is also a significant policy of localization of higher education institutions. This takes a number of forms. First, provincial authorities are invited to participate in the sponsorship and management of central-controlled institutes. In what is known as *gongjian* (collaboration in building the institution), there is now a central-local collaboration in institutions which used to be run solely by the SEdC or other central ministries. Such a mode of operation is attempted in almost all central-run institutions.

The second mode of localization occurs when some of the central ministries were dismantled because of administrative restructuring or were reduced in size as a measure to enhance efficiency. A typical case is the former Textile Ministry, which was converted into a corporation. Universities which were under the Ministry had to look for someone to 'adopt' them.

Transfer is a third option of localization. Transfer signifies a complete change-over from central ownership to provincial ownership. This occurs infrequently and is successful only when the institutions themselves are relatively successful.

Joint sponsorship is a fourth mode of localization. Here, joint ventures are established between the government and the non-government sector. The non-government agents, often commercial or industrial enterprises, may have different degrees of involvement in the financing and management of institutions.

Related to localization is the emergence of private institutions. The notion of a 'private' institution is a complex one in the Chinese context. However, there is a mushrooming of higher education institutions which are neither run by the government nor by a community; they are run by private individuals or non-government enterprises. The actual significance of this trend is yet to be appreciated. Estimates hint at a total of over 1230, about 100 of such are offering recognized certification.[28]

The movements in localization and privatization have further changed the role of the state, have increased the individuality of the institutions and will increase the disparity among institutions.

CONCLUDING REMARKS

Although the enrolment ratio of higher education in the PRC is by no means impressive, the nation has nonetheless one of the world's largest systems of higher education. The reforms mentioned above were all well thought-out and well-intentioned and appear to serve the anticipated purposes. Still, a number of issues arise.

First, disparity. While the general tendency of decentralization is crucial in yielding all the positive results of the reforms, it has brought about regional disparity which is now intrinsic to the reforms. In 1992, for example, the actual unit cost for higher education students varied from ¥5651 in Hainan to ¥2642 in Jiangxi.[29] The autonomy to mobilize local resources, the reliance on local taxes and the income-generating activities in institutions all render the institutions dependent on the local economy. Institutions benefit from the reforms if they are situated in a prospering region. They suffer from the reforms if there are few promising economic activities in their vicinity.

Second, inadequacy of funding. State appropriation is usually adequate to cover teachers' salaries, but apart from that, almost everything else is uncertain. To start with, teachers' salaries no longer represent their entire incomes. Teachers' incomes also rely on benefits and subsidies which, in turn, rely on the institutions' capacity to generate income.

Third, institutions are becoming 'independent legal entities', as stipulated in the newly enacted *Education Law*. The past ten years witnessed changes in the relationship between universities and the state. The proportion of government funds in institutional revenue has gradually reduced and institution-generated income has risen. The relationship is not yet defined; policy in this area remains to be implemented. Reform in Chinese higher education has just begun.

NOTES

1. CCP, 1985.
2. *Zhongguo Jiaoyu Bao*, 29 March 1995.
3. *Zhongguo Jiaoyu Bao*, 15–16 May 1995.
4. *Zhongguo Jiaoyu Bao*, 15–16 May 1995.
5. *Regulations concerning academic degrees of the People's Republic of China*, enacted by the National People's Congress, 2 February 1980. Details for implementation

were approved by the State Council, 20 May 1980. See *Provisional measures for the implementation of the regulations concerning academic degrees in the People's Republic of China* in SEdC, 1989a, pp. 19–27.

6. See documents cited in note 5.
7. See documents cited in note 5.
8. *Zhongguo Jiaoyu Bao*, 19 March 1994.
9. *Zhongguo Jiaoyu Bao*, 18 May 1995.
10. *Zhongguo Jiaoyu Bao*, 29 March 1995.
11. For details, see *Book of major educational events in China, 1949–1990*, pp. 1174–6.
12. In 1982 the then MoEd implored educationalists to stop using the term 'key primary schools'. This received only nominal support, for key primary schools are still maintained under different names: experimental schools, central schools, demonstration schools. Key secondary schools also remain. There are further hierarchies within key schools. For example, 'municipal key schools' and 'city-district key schools' are actually given more resources, enabled to provide higher standards of facilities, assigned better school buildings and allocated better students. In the end, key schools produce the best results in university entrance examinations and most of their graduates are admitted to higher education.
13. For a detailed historical review of the funding system for higher education, see S.M. Wang and W. Zhou, 1993.
14. The implications of such a system beyond finance are analysed in Cheng Kai-ming, 1994e.
15. Reforming the CCP's role, however, has not been successful. The reform, known as the 'President's Accountability System', intended to reduce the influence of the university Party Secretary in administration, but the initiative was curtailed by the political incidents of 1989. For details, see *Book of major educational events in China 1949–1990*, pp. 1095–6.
16. CCP and State Council, 1993.
17. *Education Law of the People's Republic of China*. For full text, see *Zhongguo Jiaoyu Bao*, 22 March 1995.
18. Much of the discussion in this section is based on S.M. Wang and W. Zhou, 1993.
19. This refers to Clause 58: 'The state shall adopt preferential measures to encourage and facilitate work-study programmes, social services and school-operated enterprises, provided such activities do not adversely affect the normal teaching in schools [and institutions].'
20. In Guangdong province, senior secondary students in the arts take exams in history, English, maths, politics, Chinese and geography. Each is scored on a 900-point basis and the average of the scores becomes the final mark. Science track students substitute physics and chemistry for geography and history. This system is generally practised throughout the PRC but varies in detail, province by province.
21. US$1 = ¥8 by the April 1995 exchange rate.
22. *Zhongguo Jiaoyu Bao*, 21 January 1997.
23. With the exception of institutions for teacher education, i.e. the normal universities.
24. See, for example, Min and Chen, 1994.

25. See Chapter 12 by Zhang Minxuan in this volume.
26. See Chapter 13 by Michael Agelasto in this volume.
27. Starting in 1995, the identified '211' schools each received ¥35 million for developments.
28. Interview with Shao Jinrong, Education Department, Committee on Education, Science, Culture and Public Health, NPC, August 1997. A *Regulation on school sponsorship by social groups* has recently been enacted. See *Guangming Ribao*, 11 August 1997 and Chapter 14 by Mok Ka-ho and David Chan in this volume.
29. SEdC and Shanghai Institute for Human Resources Development, 1993, p. 120. The comparison here excludes Tibet which is highly subsidized by the central government.

PART 2
ENHANCING SCHOLARSHIP

3

The Strategic Role of Faculty Development and Management

CAO Xiaonan

INTRODUCTION

Since the mid-1980s, the focus of educational reform in the PRC has not diverged (at least in theory) from the goal of producing more and better qualified people to meet the demands of the Four Modernizations.[1] This mission is especially evident in higher education — in particular, at the top echelons of the 'training-ladder' of qualified personnel (*zhuanmen rencai*). Faculty members have become the centre of attention due to their crucially important role in the modernization process. Indeed, since educational reform aims to raise both the quality and level of education in the population, university faculty members are charged with the task of helping other educators in all sectors within the system. However, the restructuring of higher education presupposes that university faculty membership must be restructured first. Moreover, if the modernization of the PRC is to catch up and surpass that of more advanced countries, then university faculty members must first be armed with updated knowledge and skills before they can train hundreds and thousands of needed high-level personnel. The importance of faculty members is also apparent in the political context. If the government wants qualified people to embrace a socialist ideology in order to maintain the current political system, university staff must first hold these values before inculcating them in their students.

The central government has been anxious whether university faculty members are able to fulfil these roles. Fifteen years after the restitution of formal higher education in 1977, the percentage of faculty members with advanced degrees was only about 19% of the country's entire faculty population,[2] still far behind industrialized nations (for example, in 1992, 54.5% of the full-time faculty staff in the USA held doctoral degrees).[3] The government's anxiety is manifested in its focuses on aspects of faculty quality and structure.[4] Consequently, faculty development and management have served as the main instruments for staff improvement.

Chinese views on the quality (*su zhi*) and structure (*jie gou*) of university faculty are quite different from prevailing definitions in the West.[5] While they share more or less the same definition of 'faculty structure' (i.e. such areas as faculty members' age, rank, salary and so on) for the purpose of administrative decision-making, Chinese see 'faculty quality' in a somewhat different fashion. This term is basically an extension of Mao's 'red-and-expert' (*hong yu zhuan*) conception, viewed in a contemporary light. In the current Chinese context, quality has two major components. The political aspect emphasizes the faculty staff's 'insistence on socialist consciousness' and 'willingness to make contributions to the construction of socialist modernization'.[6] The professional aspect simply focuses on teaching and research. Together with other political, cultural, economic and administrative factors, this difference in the meaning of faculty quality has distinguished Chinese policies and practices from faculty development and management in the West.[7]

Although the quality and structure of university faculty members in the PRC remain insufficient for any planned expansion of higher education, this chapter argues that the creation of semi-decentralized faculty development and management systems has already played an important strategic role in improving educational infrastructure. It starts with a brief description of university faculty under the 'old system' prior to reform. It then explores the strategic concerns of the central government that were behind some major policy decisions in this area, and identifies strategies and methods that have been developed for transforming those concerns into policy and practice. The chapter concludes by summarizing progress to date and suggesting areas for further improvement.

TRADITIONS AND CONDITIONS PRIOR TO REFORM

The strategic role of faculty development and management in Chinese higher education prior to current reforms was marked by a pattern of developmental instability due to the maelstrom of political events in the country. Because the early concern of the CCP regarding higher education was political order and rapid economic development, a close imitation of the Soviet model was adopted. The Soviet influence on university faculty development and management centred on organization and administration. The model for faculty training, which was attractive to many Chinese administrators at that time, was a hierarchical, centralized and well-organized network, and was characterized by the creation of specialized departments for faculty staff training in key universities. It was designed to fulfil government-planned training programmes for all faculty staff in the country.[8] With help from Soviet experts, the Chinese established a similar centralized network for their own faculty development programmes. One result was educational and cultural exchange between China and other socialist countries in the 1950s. During this period, 864 foreign (mainly Soviet) experts worked in higher education in China,[9] and about 1000 Chinese faculty staff went to the USSR and other socialist countries for advanced studies. These educators later became key figures in many subject areas.[10]

From 1950 to 1965, faculty development acquired goals, strategies and methods. When the CCP took power in 1949, its immediate political agenda was to carry out 'socialist transformation' (*shehui zhuyi gaizao*). While other sectors in society were undergoing major changes, such as land reform in agriculture and nationalization in industry, the government simply re-employed all faculty staff and maintained their status. It declared ownership of all higher learning institutions and launched a movement of *yuanxi tiaozhen* (faculty reorganization and readjustment).[11] From 1950, all faculty staff had to participate in political study sessions on Marxism, Leninism and Mao Zedong Thought to raise their 'socialist consciousness'. The MoEd also sent a handful of selected faculty staff to take advanced courses in selected universities such as the Northeast Revolution University and Harbin Industry University.[12] And, more importantly, a 'dual training requirement' — political correctness and professional improvement — originated at this time and later developed into one of the unique characteristics of faculty development in the PRC.

A major problem in the 1950s was the inability of some institutions to offer required courses due to a lack of qualified instructors. The MoEd instigated a series of policies to guide, regulate and advocate faculty training.[13] The goals were 'to train those from newly established institutions to be able to offer courses with confidence; and to give those with some teaching experience the ability to do research that would further improve their teaching'. The strategy was to use relatively well-equipped universities and their senior faculty staff as well as Soviet experts to undertake the training, through mentoring, in- and off-service courses, internships at teaching units and short-term seminars in the Soviet style. The training was administered by the MoEd. Sending institutions took charge of selecting candidates, and receiving institutions were responsible for designing curricula, organizing study activities and assigning supervisors. These detailed regulations served to strengthen the decision-making power of the central government. Despite the interruptions caused by the 'Anti-rightist Campaign' and the 'Great Leap Forward' political movements,[14] about 17 000 faculty staff (20% of the total force) received training during this period.[15]

Higher education experienced a significant expansion in the first half of the 1960s as the country enjoyed relative political stability. The number of institutions of higher learning doubled and the faculty workforce increased almost eightfold.[16] To cope with this expansion and the industrial growth under the Second Five-Year Plan (1958–62), the improvement of faculty staff was addressed primarily by two government policies. In the document pertaining to the establishment of national key universities, the government not only emphasized the role of these universities in faculty development, but also spelt out the decision-making and administrative procedures to be implemented. In the eighth item, for example, it stated: 'plans of national key universities on receiving faculty students must be decided and arranged by the central Ministry of Education in coordination with other government departments and local authorities'.[17] This created a highly centralized administrative framework for faculty development. Under this policy, between 1960 and 1965, the government arranged for about 22 000 faculty staff (16% of the total force) to be trained in 72 selected universities. Today, this teacher training is considered to be one of the major contributions that national key universities have made to the development of higher education in the nation.[18] Another document dealt with the structure of faculty staff in higher education by regulating the academic ranks, the criteria for promotion and other relevant procedures. Four academic ranks were defined: professor (*jiaoshou*), associate professor (*fujiaoshou*), lecturer (*jiangshi*) and teaching assistant (*zhujiao*). Promotion depended upon political as well as academic criteria and had to be approved by different levels of authority. For example, an associate professorship was authorized by the provincial authority and a professorship by the MoEd.[19] This represented a further lever for control by the central government in faculty administration. The policy resulted in promotion for 3506 professors, 4382 associate professors, 29 200 lecturers and 89 417 teaching assistants in all institutions of higher learning by September 1965.[20] The criteria for promotion were a chief motivation for staff's participation in training programmes, either political or professional. These two documents had such an impact on faculty life that they became the centre of the reform in the 1980s.

In the first 17 years of the PRC, the higher learning sector expanded from only 16 059 faculty staff in 205 institutions in 1949 to a total of 138 116 faculty staff in 434 institutions in 1966 and produced about 1.6 million graduates during that period.[21] However, this promising development was scuppered by the Cultural Revolution, which halted almost all activities in university faculty development and management, apart from organized political studies. Many staff were forced to leave their institutions and were sent to 'grass roots units' (*jiceng danwei*) or labour camps to receive 're-education' (*zai jiaoyu*). By the end of 1976, only 5819 professors and associate professors were left in academia.[22] One official reckoned she lost 1218 professors along with an entire generation of faculty staff over those ten years.[23] This devastation would confront later reformers.

Thus, the PRC's system of university faculty development and management was initially created by a political agenda, developed under Soviet influence, and later formalized with its own distinctive characteristics prior to the Four Modernizations and the Open Door policy. Higher education development reacted to the changing needs of the national political and economic agenda during different historical periods. Most programmes were state-mandated and a highly centralized mechanism was established for its operation: the MoEd as the final authority, in consultation with governmental departments and local authorities, and implementation at key universities followed by universal implementation in higher learning institutions nationwide. This pattern of development confirms the notion that policy in China is shaped primarily at the top and serves specific political agenda.[24]

CONSENSUS AND CONSISTENCY

The structure of authority in the PRC usually requires that major policy initiatives gain the active cooperation of many bureaucratic units that are themselves nested in distinct chains of authority.[25] This process has three characteristics. First, issues tend to rise to higher levels in the system (such as the State Council Standing Committee), since a single ministry or province usually lacks the clout, alone, to launch or sustain a major new initiative. Second, elaborate efforts are needed at each stage of the decision-making process to create and maintain a consensus to move the issue forward. Third, one or more of the top leaders must enthusiastically support a major policy in order to overcome the bureaucratic impasse at lower levels. Generally, analysts conclude that consensus building is central to the Chinese policy process.[26] These characteristics are manifested in the policy processes relating to the strategic role of faculty development and management in higher education during the reform period.

Since the late 1970s, the PRC's leaders have forcefully and consistently argued that the goal of modernization rests in part on education and its reform. They further maintain that the improvement of the country's educational system depends on its teachers and teaching methods.[27] Deng Xiaoping's statement at the National Education Conference in 1978 was arguably a milestone in this regard. In addressing education and its reform-related issues in general, Deng indicated his vision for the role of teachers: 'whether a school is successful in training qualified personnel for the construction of socialism — personnel who are developed not only morally, intellectually and physically, but also with a socialist consciousness and culture — depends upon its teachers'.[28] He further emphasized that 'the Party's committees at all levels should help teachers' political and ideological progress ... the task of education is getting tougher ... all levels of educational authority must make efforts and employ effective methods to increase teacher training for improving their teaching ability and overall quality'. This, together with his earlier speech at the National Science and Education Conference and a talk with senior officials at the MoEd in 1977,[29] demonstrated his enthusiasm in advocating educational reform and raising public awareness of teachers' roles. Similar comments were also made by other top leaders (such as Hu Yaobang, the former General Secretary of the CCP) on different occasions.[30] Given the domestic political environment at that time, these top leaders' words were soon interpreted as the central government's mandate for educational change. It thus became possible to restore major policies with regard to faculty management (such as promotion) in 1978 and to faculty development (such as the responsibilities of the key universities) in 1980.[31]

University faculty development and management were strengthened by the central government's *Decision* on educational reform in the spring of 1985. In addressing higher education, the document stressed that high-level qualified personnel should receive training within China, and that reforming the teaching system and improving teaching quality were urgent tasks for higher learning institutions.[32] It asked university faculty staff to improve the level of their teaching and research, as well as to assist in the expansion of nine-year compulsory education and vocational education through faculty development programmes. It suggested the establishment of a sabbatical-leave system for senior faculty staff for their professional development.[33] A similar theme appeared in the speeches of top leaders (such as Wan Li, the former Chairman of the NPC) and in commentaries of major newspapers (such as *Renmin Ribao*, *Guangming Ribao* and *Wenhui Bao*).[34] Also in 1985, the first International Symposium on Faculty Administration in Higher Education since the founding of the PRC was held at Fudan University and attended by Chinese officials, educators and overseas scholars. The National Association of Faculty Administration in Higher Education, a semi-autonomous professional organization, was established shortly afterwards to facilitate the exchange of information and promote the study of this subject.[35]

The leadership's perception of the role of university faculty staff experienced a significant shift after 4 June 1989. While its strategic role was still discussed in the media, the emphasis moved from a focus on academic/ professional improvement and administrative change to one of political correctness. This reflected the government's concern over the ideological purity of people trained by the system during the reform period. The government feared losing political and ideological ground if higher learning institutions produced qualified personnel with counter-socialist thoughts who were, nevertheless, desperately needed for national economic development. In his speech at the National Higher Education Conference in July 1989, Education Commissioner Li Tieying made the CCP's position very clear: 'Higher learning institutions play a very important role in the peace and stability of our society as well as in all aspects of the construction of our socialist modernization.'[36] He pointed out that 'education must maintain its socialist orientation' and that 'correcting faculty members' political perspective was the most urgent task of campus leaders'. Faculties of social sciences were particularly targeted as they were believed to be more liable to introduce 'bourgeois liberal thoughts' to their students, a view shared by some university administrators.[37] The central government believed that restressing the 'social practice' (*shehui shijian*) component in faculty staff development programmes especially aimed at junior faculty members was an effective way to educate teachers about socialism.[38] In the meantime, aspects of faculty management received a lot of attention as the leaders realized that issues such as low salary, poor working and living conditions and inflexible personnel systems contributed to recent campus unrest.

In the early 1990s the top leaders began to advocate strategic policies for moving the country into the twenty-first century. The strategic role of university faculty development and management was emphasized over political correctness with the publishing of the 1993 reform *Outline*. This document is considered a new blueprint as its opening states that '[this programme] guides the nation's educational reform and development for the 1990s and the beginning of the next century in order to make education better serve the country's socialist modernization'.[39] It emphasized again that 'the vigorous development of our nation depends on our education and the vitalization of our education relies on our teachers ... educational reform and development raise new and higher challenges to our teachers'.[40] The document suggested that faculty development in higher education should diversify its programmes, strengthen its social practice component, maximize the role of key universities and increase exchanges among institutions. In particular, a mechanism for identifying and cultivating promising junior faculty members was recommended.

The central government's views regarding faculty development and management were shared by local higher education authorities and senior university administrators who integrated them into their policies and practices.[41] With regard to local authorities, such a consensus was buttressed by the pressure of growing demands for high-level qualified personnel due to the rapid development of local economies. In Jilin province, for instance, the 1985 human resource development forecast estimated that, from 1984 to 1990, the numbers of professionals needed in the fields of finance and law would increase by 7.2 and 12.8 times respectively, in order to cope with the needs of local economic development. But there were only five institutions and about 100 senior faculty members in these fields.[42] With regard to universities, increased competition in teaching and research among their peers, both domestic and international, consolidated opinion on the need for reform.

From this, a clear pattern emerges in relation to university faculty development and management over the course of the reforms. Although the perception of its strategic role has been widely shared by people at different levels, both internal and external to the education system, the building of consensus was hierarchical. The initiative originated in the top leaders' speeches and the central government's proclamations on national development or educational reform. The issue was then addressed in specific sectors within the education system (such as teacher education and higher education). The consensus was strengthened gradually by internal support among these players and by constant repetition. Such a consensus resulted from a combination of rational choice, dictated by the demands for economic and educational development, and conformity to the political agenda pursued by the top leaders for the maintenance of socialism and of their own power. This unified perception of the importance and strategic role of faculty development and management formed a necessary foundation for higher education reform policies and their implementation.

STRATEGIC CONCERNS BEHIND MAJOR POLICIES

For some time the PRC has been seeking an adequate system for faculty development and management in higher education. In fact, as early as 1963, the MoEd issued a document asking all higher learning institutions to make a ten-year plan for improving the quality of faculty members.[43] Although the plan was aborted due to the Cultural Revolution, the idea became a legacy for later reformers. At the beginning of the reform period, strategies were built primarily upon prevailing conditions, such as age and qualification profiles, which were perceived as indicators of the faculty staff's capacity to meet the demands of the country's economic reform.

In industrialized nations, faculty qualifications and academic improvement are usually not considered agenda items for reform of higher learning institutions. A well-established degree training system and a competitive job market mechanism obviate the need for institutions to provide training programmes. Faculty development programmes focus mainly on improving teaching methods and skills.[44] This was so even in the USSR in the 1950s, although with a more centrally organized training network.[45] The basic conditions regarding faculty development in the industrialized world are very different from those in the PRC, where the formal degree training system was established only in 1980,[46] and most faculty members in higher education are still unlikely to have a qualification beyond a Bachelor's degree. As a result, their knowledge base and research ability are insufficient for the tasks they are expected to perform, especially in an era of rapid development in science and technology. Thus, the PRC has had to develop a system to provide training for staff's academic as well as professional growth. This concern was reflected in government documents and officials' speeches.[47]

'Age' was at the root of all the problems facing university faculty staff — the age distribution, academic qualifications and the distribution of academic titles. As the 1983 data show,[48] the average age of professors and associate professors was 68 and 56 respectively. Professors made up only 1.5% of the entire faculty workforce; the proportion for associate professors was 9.4%. In addition to the fact that only a small number of faculty members had advanced degrees, most staff had grown rusty in their subjects due to the isolation caused by the Cultural Revolution. The central government and higher learning institutions have addressed these unfavourable conditions through a two-fold strategy: improving quality by providing more faculty training programmes and adjusting unbalanced internal structures by modifying an inflexible administrative system.[49]

During the reform period, policies on faculty improvement have focused on two groups: young staff members (*qingnian jiaoshi*) under 35 years of age and core faculty members (*gugan jiaoshi*), who are good at both teaching and research. Young staff members determine the future of higher education in China. However, there has been a big gap between their expected performance in the future and their current abilities. The influx of young faculty members peaked twice during the reform period (see Figure 3.1).[50] The first peak (1982–83) reflected the urgency of restoring higher education after the Cultural Revolution. The second peak (1985–86) was caused by the government's 1983 expansion initiative. Each brought about 60 000 fresh graduates into the profession.[51] By 1988, there were 132 300 young faculty members in total, representing about 47% of the nation's entire faculty staff. In spite of their vitality and formal training, only 15% had received advanced degree training.[52] Both the central government and higher learning institutions in the PRC recognized that it was inappropriate to recruit college graduates to teach undergraduates, as the quality of teaching was unlikely to be improved in that way. However, the annual admission of postgraduate students in the PRC stayed around 40 000 with few part-time students allowed. Meanwhile, undergraduate enrolments steadily increased. Since the possibility of taking long-term off-service training was limited for young faculty staff, it would have taken years to give all newly recruited young staff some kind of postgraduate training. This prompted the central government to seek alternative ways to improve the qualifications of young faculty staff.

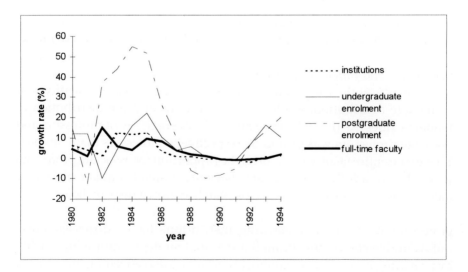

Figure 3.1   Annual growth rates of some indicators in higher education in the PRC, 1980–94[53]

In 1984, the MoEd launched a campaign that offered young faculty staff non-degree postgraduate-level training.[54] It allocated grants to some key universities to run special training programmes (*zhujiao jinxiu ban*). The central government anticipated that this, together with formal postgraduate training, would significantly improve the qualifications of young faculty staff. However, four years later, the country's urban economic reform began to show an adverse effect on higher education. For example, enrolment of postgraduate students began to decline and, simultaneously, young faculty staff started to leave the profession. In order to retain them and use the opportunity presented by declining postgraduate enrolment for increasing young faculty staff training, the SEdC (the former MoEd) began, in 1988, to encourage institutions to send selected young faculty staff members for commissioned postgraduate training in key universities.[55] This strategy, the SEdC claimed, was 'an alternative method for improving young faculty staff. It will lead to structural adjustment, improvements in quality and greater faculty stability'.[56] These policies, in addition to the recruitment of more graduates with advanced degrees into the profession, have played a very important role in improving the qualification profile of young faculty staff during the reform period.[57]

Towards the middle of the 1980s, traditionally stressed political allegiance was gradually eroded in favour of financial considerations and the acquisition of material wealth. The Open Door policy spontaneously brought in Western values and democratic ideas through cultural and educational exchanges with the West. 'Ideological liberalization' grew, particularly in the intellectual world. Institutions complained that traditional values and political consciousness were weakening among young faculty staff. After the student democratic movement in December 1986, the central government realized that traditional political pressure was no longer working in China's new environment. Any effective means of arresting the erosion of political belief among young faculty staff must be tied to their professional development. Thus, in 1987, the SEdC began to require universities to demand a one-year field experience programme from their young faculty staff. Its avowed purpose was to 'encourage young faculty to serve the community with their knowledge, learn the nation's reality, understand the Party's policies, establish a good work ethic, and increase the sense of responsibility for the construction of the socialist modernization in the country'.[58] As an incentive, some institutions made such field experience a requirement for promotion for junior staff. Besides loosely organized political studies, this was the only policy that specifically addressed the 'red' aspect of faculty improvement during the reform period.

The emphasis of the central government on core faculty members emerged from a deep concern about the limited number and advanced age of senior faculty members. In 1985, 85% of the professors and 47% of the associate professors in the country were over 61 and 56 years old respectively.[59] In Qinghua University, for example, advisers for doctoral candidates across all disciplines had an average age of 71.[60] Among 649 formal higher learning institutions, each institution averaged only four professors and eight associate professors.[61] The middle-aged faculty members (age 35–45), the natural successors of senior positions in academia, represented a small proportion in the workforce, only about 15%.[62] In addition, the traditional centralized approach of faculty staff recruitment — i.e., institutions recruiting mostly their own graduates — had resulted in 'several generations under the same roof'. Both the central government and universities became concerned about the successors to the senior faculty staff and the general intellectual health of the universities. In the early 1980s, the central government relied on international exchange programmes for training badly needed core faculty members. It also encouraged universities to select and send promising young and middle-aged faculty members abroad for short-term advanced studies or for international conferences and workshops.[63] Despite the demonstrated success of such exchange programmes, the high costs and growing number of students staying abroad called for alternative ways to train core faculty members. The central government's attention began to shift from foreign exchanges to domestic policies. By 1985, 1501 academic units granted doctoral degrees across discipline areas with 2786 authorized doctoral supervisors. There were 65 post-doctoral workstations and some national laboratories located in the country's higher learning institutions.[64] In addition, there were a few thousand returnees already working in key universities.[65] Using their strengths to train core faculty members, therefore, became the new focus of attention. In 1986, the SEdC asked key universities to accept 'internal visiting scholars' (as opposed to overseas visiting scholars) (*guonei fangwen xuezhe*).[66] The goal was to allow them to participate in research activities and update their knowledge. In the meantime, the SEdC issued a series of policy documents on faculty management issues, such as early retirement, selecting and cultivating excellent young and middle-aged core faculty members, rewards and promotions for young staff, and funds for returnees.

Strategies for faculty improvement over the course of the reform period had a strong element of élitism as illustrated by the emphasis on key universities and core faculty members. This was different from the traditional worship of élitism, influenced by Confucian values, in the Chinese intellectual world. System-wide quality and efficiency were apparently the major concerns of the central government in this regard.[67]

Key universities were expected to help lower-level institutions to raise standards, and core faculty members were expected to take the lead in improving teaching and research.[68] And, purely in economic terms, the money spent on a single 'internal visiting scholar' amounted to only one-eighth of the estimated cost of sending the scholar abroad.[69] This élitist approach often generated tensions among the different players over their share of the limited resources and their growing responsibilities.

CHANGES IN THE STRUCTURE OF AUTHORITY

The increased responsibilities and demands brought by these policies challenged the capacity of the old administrative system. The regulations restoring the faculty training system in 1980 declare:

> 1) The MoEd assigns to each key university the annual number of faculty students. 2) Each key university should file their curriculum for faculty students and submit it to the MoEd. The MoEd then publishes this information and allocates a certain number of faculty students to all provinces, autonomous regions and cities, and other government departments. 3) Each province, autonomous region and city, and government department allocates this number to its affiliated higher learning institutions. According to the allocated numbers, these institutions then select their faculty members and recommend them for off-service training at key universities. 4) Each province, autonomous region and city, and government department collects these applications and recommendation forms and then submits them to the MoEd. The MoEd holds an annual meeting with representatives from these parties and key universities in order to make the training arrangements. Key universities then give an acceptance notice to sending institutions.[70]

This hierarchical and highly centralized decision-making system was established under China's planned economy system and was incorporated within the administrative structure of higher education, especially in terms of governance and finance. In the early 1980s, three new challenges appeared. The old decision-making system lacked flexibility and prevented the meeting of urgent training needs brought about by the introduction of new subjects.[71] Although the old system apparently performed well in terms of planning enrolment, deciding who would take advanced study, in what subject area and at which key university, external efficiency suffered. The subject areas for which an institution was assigned were not always the ones it actually needed. The result was a waste of the limited resources.[72] Also, the administrative process involved in completing one cycle of admission was overelaborate and time-consuming. As demands increased, daily administrative tasks mounted at the MoEd. Meanwhile, the success of delegating decision-making power to lower levels of authority in other sectors such as agriculture was gaining more publicity. All these pressures forced the MoEd to consider changes in administering faculty training programmes.

The real incentive for change arose from a concern to reduce paperwork within the MoEd. While the MoEd was afraid to loosen control over raising the quality of faculty staff, it also wanted a decentralized system, in which it could rely on others to carry out the tasks of faculty development, while reducing its own administrative burden. Using a loan from the World Bank's second university project in the PRC in 1985, the MoEd established two national faculty development centres. This attempted to shift the administrative and coordinating work from the MoEd to the two centres and then build on them to form a nationwide network. The criteria for choosing the centres included geographic and subject coverage, the potential needs of higher education development, and the demands of other educational sectors such as teacher and vocational education. The two sites selected as the National Centres for Faculty Development in Higher Education were at Beijing Normal University and Wuhan University. Both schools were well-equipped and comprehensive key universities, the former mainly providing for faculty development needs in teacher education and liberal arts colleges, and the latter focusing on the remaining tertiary institutions.[73] With this development, the 25-year-old system of administering faculty development in higher education was formally abandoned. Nevertheless, the SEdC put the centres under its direct supervision. Soon after this change, six key normal universities in each autonomous region were chosen as the faculty development bases for teacher education in response to the requirement of improving basic education mandated in the 1985 government's educational reform *Decision*. The SEdC also called for each provincial educational authority to establish its own faculty development base to meet growing domestic demand. A three-level nationwide faculty development network for teacher educational institutions was thus in place by 1986. Under this new system, most activities relating to faculty development operated in a kind of free market fashion. Key universities now had authority to decide what programmes to offer, in which areas and how many trainees to take, so long as they fulfilled the annual obligation assigned by the SEdC (in this way the SEdC felt that it could maintain a degree of control). Sending institutions had free choice in deciding whom they sent to which institutions for advanced studies, based on their prioritized needs. The centres and training bases in the network were required to collect information on this 'free trade' process, study the market, give feedback to contributing institutions and coordinate programmes. They were required to make recommendations to the SEdC on policy changes related to university faculty development. The change of authority structure in the area is illustrated in Figure 3.2 (the dotted lines in the chart refer to possible direct interactions between the two relevant parties).

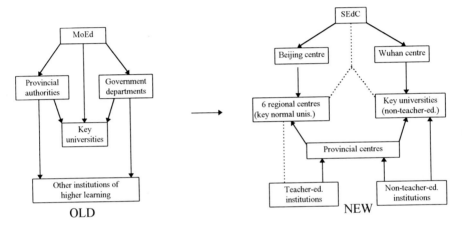

Figure 3.2   Change of authority structure in university faculty development in the PRC

The establishment of the faculty development network has, to some extent, changed the structure of authority. This might not have happened if an environment conducive to changing authority structure had not existed in the PRC at that time, especially in the higher education sector. In the 1985 *Decision*, the government called for a change in the governing structure of higher learning institutions. It advocated the 'President Responsibility System' to replace the 'Party's Committee In-Charge System'.[74] Institutional leadership was now supposed to be in the hands of experts rather than individuals chosen for their political beliefs. Other reforms within the higher education sector also influenced these changes. Many institutions were allowed to offer more flexible programmes and accept more self-supporting or commissioned training students in order to cope with increasing demands for continuing education. The changes, which were also reflected in the secondary education sector, exhibited four distinct elements. First, authority was delegated to lower levels of decision-making. Second, administrative decision-making belonged to experts, as opposed to CCP bureaucrats. Third, an increasing emphasis was placed on efficiency and accountability. Fourth, market influences and their incorporation into Chinese social relations were rising.[75]

While the structural change of authority in faculty development was effected, a similar change in faculty management also took place. Under the old system, faculty staff were assigned by the government to a particular higher learning institution, regardless of whether the individual was willing to work at that institution or the institution actually needed that particular person. Institutions did not have the authority either to recruit qualified individuals or to promote existing faculty staff to senior positions. Power remained in the hands of higher-level educational and personnel authorities. Faculty staff, like state employees elsewhere in the country, lived with a secure but inflexible personnel system. Growing pressure on three fronts demanded a change in this system. First, the job contract system appeared in other sectors of society, such as in small enterprises, due to urban economic reforms. Labour relationships were changing. Second, universities began to implement the new 'President Responsibility System'. Their presidents asked the central government for the power to appoint staff. Third, a growing number of faculty members complained that the system provided 'a common pot' (*daguofan*) limiting incentives and competition. As a result of these pressures, the SEdC began, in 1985, to experiment with a new system, called the 'Faculty Appointment System'. This first appeared in eight key universities and, one year later, expanded to include all institutions in the country.[76] Its design reflected the employment model in a free market. University presidents would have authority to recruit staff. In practice, however, authority over appointing senior faculty staff was still controlled by the SEdC. Concerned over 'quality control', the SEdC gave appointments authority only to those institutions that met its requirements.[77] By 1988, out of 1075 higher learning institutions in the country, only 80 were granted the autonomy to appoint professors and 158 to appoint associate professors.[78] Today, appointments to senior positions in most institutions of higher learning still have to be authorized by at least one higher level of authority (for example, ministries, provincial or municipal departments) in their affiliated administrative systems.

The changes in the administration of faculty development and management in the PRC's higher education system have had both positive and negative effects on faculty improvement. Given the country's culture, tradition and history, it is unlikely, in the near future, that the central government will relinquish all the power it has enjoyed. To date, the structural change of authority has mostly consisted of reallocating responsibilities to different levels. Some basic authority still rests with the government. For instance, the number of senior faculty staff an institution can hire has to be authorized jointly by its affiliated government agency and the SEdC. Unlike private institutions of higher learning in the USA, for instance, the majority of Chinese higher learning institutions are funded by the government and the government wants to retain oversight.[79]

STRATEGIES, METHODS AND RESULTS

During the reform period, two basic strategies have been employed by the central government in its effort to improve faculty quality in higher education. As mentioned above, one was to improve quality by creating and increasing training programmes. The other was to adjust the internal structure of faculty staff by introducing into the system competition and structural changes of authority. Both have been guided by a traditional philosophy of combining *dian* (key points) with *mian* (entire field) in practice,[80] which means that key universities and core faculty members, as opposed to average institutions and average teachers, are given priority in policy considerations as well as in their implementation.

The application of this élitist philosophy to the area of faculty development has produced five principles for its programme design. First, faculty development should integrate self-study approaches with needs-based institutional considerations. Second, in-service and on-campus training should be considered prior to off-service and off-campus studies for selected faculty members. Third, training curricula should combine theory with practice. Fourth, priority should be given to promising or core faculty members. Finally, overseas studies should be supplementary to domestic programmes for selected core faculty members.[81] In the faculty management area, this élitist philosophy has been embodied in two priorities: to promote young and middle-aged core faculty members to important positions and to guarantee the quality of faculty staff in key universities. Besides these initiatives from the central government, many universities and local educational authorities have initiated effective policies addressing their own developmental needs. For instance, based on the institutional plan for core curriculum development, Nanjing University has been working on the 'echelon formation' (*ti dui jian she*) of its faculty staff by introducing various types of competition.[82] Dalian Municipal Government initiated exchange and cooperation programmes among its 22 higher learning institutions in order to share the limited resources.[83]

In general, the approaches to faculty development include in-service training, practical training, off-service studies and academic exchange. By 1983, only in-service training and off-service studies had been applied to cope with the need for updating faculty staff's knowledge and the faculty shortage in some subject areas. According to one estimate, almost every faculty member in the country received some kind of training between 1980 and 1983. Key universities alone trained about 31 000 teachers from other higher learning institutions across the country under the MoEd's arrangement.[84] Such vast training across the *mian* created a foundation for later programmes geared to specific groups (*dian*). However, as the number of young faculty staff grew and more middle-aged faculty staff were promoted to senior positions, these two methods were no longer able to meet the increasing demands from teachers and institutions for further improvement. Over the course of the reform period, seven major domestic programmes were developed. They were:

1. professional training for newly appointed young faculty staff in psychology, professional ethics, higher education and teaching methods;
2. single subject training for those assigned to teach new courses or wanting to improve their teaching in a particular subject;
3. knowledge-updating workshops for middle-aged faculty staff;
4. postgraduate training for improving the qualifications of young faculty staff who did not have an advanced degree;
5. research training for middle-aged faculty staff who had taught extensively but had little research experience;
6. internal visiting scholar programmes and research seminars for core faculty members and promising leading figures in their discipline areas; and
7. social practice and community service for young faculty staff who lacked work experience outside academia.

Since the mid-1980s, the focus of these programmes has shifted from large-scale training for all faculty members to training young staff and core faculty members.[85]

The implementation of these strategies and methods has produced positive outcomes. During the reform period, about 5.7% of the entire faculty staff in the PRC's higher education system participated annually in various training programmes.[86] By 1991, 170 000 faculty members had received training at key universities. About 85% of young faculty staff had taken off-service training, 17 000 of whom attended 970 postgraduate-level training programmes offered at 140 universities.[87] Some 100 universities had accepted about 1000 internal visiting scholars. Most of them were promoted to senior positions.[88] In the meantime, about 60 000 faculty members had been promoted to senior positions through the new faculty appointment system. Special institutional policies for promoting exceptional junior staff had produced 60 professors and 1500 associate professors, all under 35 years of age.[89] More graduates with advanced degrees had been recruited into the teaching force, for example, about 5000 in 1992.[90] All of these measures have changed faculty profiles for age and academic title. Table 3.1 illustrates these changes. Compared with the situation in 1983, the faculty staff in 1992 are younger. In particular, the average age of professors dropped about ten years and the percentage of faculty staff with senior positions increased by about 17.4%. The structure of the faculty staff looks healthier than before. Although the percentage of faculty staff who had received formal postgraduate training improved by about 12% during those years, it was still quite low.[91] Given past performance, it will take a long time to change this condition with only the existing faculty development programmes.

Table 3.1
Comparisons of the age and academic title profiles of university faculty members in the PRC between 1983 and 1992 [92]

	Year	All Groups	Professor	Associate	Lecturer	Assistant
Average age (years)	1983	42	68	56	48	32
	1992	39	58	53	38	28
Percentage in the force (%)	1983	100	1.5	9.6	45.4	43.5
	1992	100	5.1	23.4	43.1	28.4

Perhaps the most significant contribution of faculty development and management concerns the improvement of teacher education. Between 1986 and 1990,[93] about one-third of the teaching assistants in teacher training institutions received postgraduate training, and 25% (about 30 000) of the faculty staff in those institutions received training at key universities. This was about 30% of all teachers trained by key universities during that period. The number of faculty staff with senior positions and with postgraduate education increased by 14% and 5% respectively. This achievement was made possible by the effective organization of the newly established three-level training network. Teacher training institutions of higher learning were traditionally perceived as the 'maternal institutions' (mu jie) of the teacher education sector in the PRC. The improvement of faculty staff has helped implement the nation's nine-year compulsory education scheme launched in 1985.[94]

In order for the PRC to learn the latest developments in science and technology and to raise the standards of higher education in the country, international exchange has become an important component of university faculty development and management. During the reform, more than 40 000 state-supported university teachers took advanced studies abroad and by the mid-1990s, according to official estimates, about half of them had finished their studies and returned.[95] This approach is particularly crucial in improving the quality of faculty staff in key universities; by one estimate, about one-third of faculty members have had the opportunity to spend time abroad for advanced studies.[96] Additionally, more than 11 000 faculty staff have participated in international conferences overseas in various academic disciplines. In the meantime, some 2000 foreign staff have worked in Chinese universities.[97] One of the major benefits derived from these international exchanges is that returnees and foreign staff have contributed to faculty improvement programmes in higher education. In addition to contributing to computer and foreign language training, they have brought in up-to-date subject information to their colleagues, established new disciplines and laboratories, developed new curricula, and introduced new teaching methods. These activities have benefited teachers from lower-level institutions, who have fewer opportunities to study abroad than their colleagues in key universities. Because of this work, returnees have been promoted and recognized as core faculty members.[98] Some have been appointed to important leadership positions. For example, in 1991, 17 out of 36 presidents at the SEdC-affiliated universities had advanced-study experience overseas.[99] These percentages were much higher for leadership positions at the departmental level. The interplay between international exchange and faculty development and management has to some extent facilitated both the improvement of faculty staff and changes in higher education as a whole.

Data on the development of higher education in the reform period further confirm the strategic role of faculty development and management. Figure 3.1 supports this assertion. The number of higher learning institutions and their full-time faculty staff have almost doubled. College and postgraduate enrolments have increased by 2.5 and 8 times respectively.[100] A total of 17 000 subject units in 185 higher learning institutions have been authorized to offer doctoral degrees. About one-third of the National Awards for the Natural Sciences[101] came from, and 54% of the research projects in the national '863' Hi-Tech Development Scheme[102] were undertaken by, the higher education sector.[103] In addition, universities accomplished about 7000 research and development projects annually and generated a profit of several billion US dollars during the Seventh Five-Year Plan (1986–90).[104]

The PRC's continuing reforms and economic growth since 1985 have made fundamental changes to society. Broad social changes, however, have simultaneously had some negative impact on faculty development and management in higher education. Increasing competition, for instance, has made cooperation among universities and between individual departments more difficult for faculty development programmes. Competition for the limited resources has led to redundancy in some training programmes as well as disappointment in some creative programmes.[105] Also, the social fashion of 'having a professional title' (zhi cheng feng) in the 1980s caused corruption in faculty promotion. Some members were promoted to senior positions on the basis of seniority rather than qualifications. Critics have charged that 'title' was linked to social welfare systems and was beyond the control of educational institutions. This, to some extent, demoralized faculty staff and diminished efforts towards quality improvement.[106] In addition, the growth of commerce along with the low income associated with teaching has driven faculty staff to more lucrative activities, such as part-time jobs.[107] Faculty development programmes appear less appealing now than in the early 1980s.

Two new strategic issues have attracted considerable attention in recent years: the 'faultline' (duanceng) or age gap and the 'brain drain' (liushi) of university faculty staff. The 'faultline' resulted from the Cultural Revolution. The brain drain of young faculty staff has become more severe than ever before. Despite the improvement in the faculty age profile, an insufficiency of faculty staff aged 35–45 remains. They made up only about 15% of the entire force in 1992 (Figure 3.3). In addition, almost 95% of professors and 78% of associate professors were over 50 years old. By the end of this century, most will have retired from senior positions.

The age gap particularly affected key universities and key discipline areas, as a 1991 SEdC survey showed.[109] In the early 1980s the MoEd's strategy was to fill the gap with a group of promising young faculty staff by establishing special policies for their training and promotion. To a certain extent, this special treatment worked,[110] but the unexpected brain drain of young faculty staff, especially the 'promising ones', subverted the strategy. From the mid-1980s, various factors resulted in the instability of young faculty staff. The appeal of going abroad (chu guo re) and working for foreign-funded joint ventures (wai qi re) attracted young faculty members. Given that their incomes had been among the lowest in society for quite a few years,[111] and that opportunities for postgraduate education were very

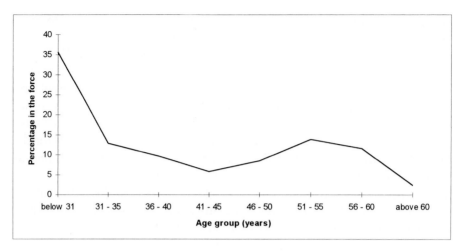

Figure 3.3   The age distribution of faculty staff in higher education in the PRC in 1992[108]

limited (annual admission was only about 40 000 people), they had concerns over their economic and professional future. Working conditions were poor, workloads heavy and obtaining research funds and promotion tremendously difficult. Only a few lucky ones benefited from the special policies. Indeed, the consequences of the brain drain of junior staff have been severe. About 27% of the young faculty staff recruited since 1981 (many of them seen as 'promising' or 'core' members in their departments) had left their institutions by 1991.[112] Among them, 51% went abroad for advanced studies and had no intention of returning soon; 49% joined foreign or joint ventures or other private companies. The situation was exacerbated at key universities and institutions in coastal areas.[113]

The brain drain of this group of promising young faculty members demoralized the entire staff, partly because the central government saw political education as a solution to the problem. Having realized the ineffectiveness of this approach, higher learning institutions and authorities have applied different ameliorative strategies, such as tightened procedures for applications to study abroad, special research funds for young faculty staff, improved working and living conditions, favoured treatment to returnees and so forth. The outcome of these approaches, unknown at present, does not look very promising. In sum, both the 'faultline' and the brain drain issues have been the subject of many studies.[114] Despite differing opinions on the subject, there is a general agreement that these problems are the inevitable products of reform and that their complexity goes beyond the domain of faculty development and management policies.

CONCLUSION

Recognition of the pivotal role that faculty development and management play in higher education was revived in many countries in the late 1970s and the 1980s. In contrast to the situation in the West, where the conception developed significantly during periods of demographic change and financial retrenchment,[115] the PRC has given considerable attention as well as resources to this issue during years of higher education's expansion and reform. The PRC's experience enriches our understanding of the role of a university faculty in a society in transition.

The Chinese experience shows that consensus building and structural change in authority are essential to what has been achieved in this area. Structural changes in authority consist of the reallocation of administrative responsibilities at different levels within the system. But the hierarchy of the structure remains basically unchanged. The three-level national training network for teacher education demonstrates this point. Although the central government has gradually loosened control and moved away from micro-management of institutions, it still remains the central government. Tensions caused by this, coupled with increasing institutional and local responsibilities, have generated some confusion in the implementation of policies and plans originating from the central government. For example, indications suggest that coordinating the SEdC-assigned training programmes among non-teacher-education institutions within the national training network has become more difficult in recent years. The fundamental question becomes: to what extent should higher learning institutions be treated as independent entities with a corresponding legal status? By the mid-1990s, legislation in this area was the topic of speculation.[116]

The emerging age gap and brain drain issues illustrate the interplay between policies and social changes. Faculty development and management are not only an engine for change in the reform of higher education but also a carrier of processes and outcomes of the overall reforms in the country. This dual character suggests the importance of viewing the work of faculty development and management as social engineering during a period when a society is in transition. Segmented, uncoordinated initiatives are less likely to produce desired outcomes than a set of comprehensive and coherent policies. The failure to resolve the faculty 'faultline' issue in the PRC reveals the weakness of the central government in coping with a changing environment. Simply stated, the government was behind the times. Rather than inventing solutions, it confined itself to traditional strategies such as emphasizing ideology and shaping policies in the context of a closed system.

The act of combining *dian* and *mian* in faculty improvement strategies has promoted academic élitism by artificially promoting the role of key universities and core faculty members. Given the growth and popularity of democratic ideas in the PRC,[117] the continuing emphasis of the central government on *dian* has been challenged recently. Criticisms have focused on the artificially created environment for core faculty members' growth, especially for promising juniors, instead of allowing open competition. On many occasions, intellectuals and educators have raised the importance of 'critical mass' in research and subject development.[118] Ironically, the contributions that key universities and core faculty members have made during the reform have strengthened the central government's idea of expanding higher education by the efficient utilization of the limited resources in the country.[119] Recently, the government launched several national projects, such as '211 Engineering' (*211 gong cheng*), 'Hundred, Thousand and Ten-Thousand Engineering' (*bai qian wan gong cheng*) and 'Across-Centuries Leading Scholars Project' (*kua shi ji you xiu ren cai ji hua*), which continue the practice of investing heavily in a handful of carefully selected universities and core faculty members.[120] In the state's view, these leading institutions and experts can help the PRC make its mark on global competition through advanced science and technology. But these initiatives involve unresolved issues, including traditional élitism, the concerns for efficiency and equity, and the growing appeal of democratic progress.

In sum, faculty development and management in Chinese higher education face a new set of challenges which are very different from those presented at the beginning of the reform period. As educational reform grows, the importance of faculty development and management will be enhanced. The government has outlined a new vision for educational reform in the nation:

> Global competition is fundamentally competition in science, technology and national quality. To this extent, a nation can win this competition in the 21st century only if she equips her educational system to meet all developmental needs of that century. China has to strategize her education now to confront those challenges.[121]

Once again, faculty development and management in higher education will continue to play a strategic role in this enterprise. But what will be their next agenda?

NOTES

1. See, for example, CCP Central Committee, 1985; SEdC, 1990a, pp. 1, 55; CCP Central Committee, 1994.

2. *Educational statistics yearbook of China 1993*, pp. 32–3.

3. National Center for Education Statistics, 1995, p. 231.

4. See, for example, *Jiaoyubu guojia jiwei guanyu jiasu fazhan gaodeng jiaoyu de baogao* (Recommendations for accelerating higher education development in China) issued by the MoEd and the State Planning Commission, April 1983, cited in SEdC, 1985, pp. 78–82.

5. See, for example, Altbach, 1977; Clark, 1987; Clark and Neave, 1992, pp. 1318–29, 1596–1658.

6. MoEd, *Gaodeng xuexiao jiaozhi zhize ji kaohe de zanxing guiding* (Regulations on responsibilities and evaluation of university faculty members) issued in November 1979, cited in *China education yearbook 1949–1981*, pp. 363–4.

7. 'Faculty development and management' is used here rather than the term 'faculty administration' for two reasons. First, the term 'faculty development and management' is closer to the commonly used phrase *shizi peiyong he guanli* by Chinese educators and administrators. The Chinese tend to view the word *guanli* (administration) as not being able to fully cover the meaning of *peiyong* (a mixture of training, cultivating and development). Second, many Chinese agree that there is a difference between *peixun* (training) and *peiyong*. In the late 1970s, a conceptual debate (staff training vs. staff development) took place in Britain. Scholars there preferred the word 'development' as it reflected broader needs for faculty improvement than did the word 'training'. This conceptual understanding of staff development by British scholars is similar to the Chinese concerns for the quality of the faculty, though social and cultural differences do indeed exist between the two nations. For detailed information, see, for example, Piper and Glatter, 1977, pp. 19–31; Cao Xiaonan, 1987, pp. 66–73.

8. Cao Xiaonan, 1991a, pp. 63–9.

9. *Jiaoyu duiwai jiaoliu huodong* (Educational exchanges with foreign countries), in *China education yearbook 1949–1981*, pp. 665–7.

10. Cao Xiaonan, 1991a, p. 63. Some well-known experts who studied in the USSR are, for example, Gao Jingde, a professor in mechanical engineering and the former president of Qinghua University; Zhang Qixian, a professor in precision instrument at Beijing Institute of Aeronautics and Astronautics; and Wu Zuqiang, a professor in composition and the President of the Central Music Conservatory.

11. *Quan ri zhi gaodeng jiaoyu* (Regular higher education), in *China education yearbook 1949–1981*, pp. 233–6.

12. *Gaodeng xuexiao jiaoshi* (Faculty staff in higher education), in *China education yearbook 1949–1981*, pp. 359–67.

13. See, for example, MoEd, *Gaodeng xuexiao jiaoshi jinxiu zanxing banfa* (Tentative regulations on faculty staff training in higher education) issued in November 1953, and *Guanyu jiaqiang gaodeng xuexiao jiaoshi jinxiu gongzuo de tongzhi* (Recommendations on strengthening faculty staff training in higher education) issued in July 1959, both cited in *China education yearbook 1949–1981*, p. 361.

14. Little information is available on how exactly faculty training was affected by these two political movements. Given the circumstances, some interruptions probably occurred. However, from the CCP's viewpoint, faculty members' participation in the movements was part of their training, i.e., the 'political

correctness'. In fact, such indirect comments can be found in CCP leaders' speeches during that time.

15. See *China education yearbook 1949–1981*, p. 361.

16. *Achievement of education in China: statistics 1949–1983*, p. 50.

17. *Jiaoyubu guanyu quanguo zhongdian gaodengxuexiao zanxin guanli banfa* (Tentative regulations for key universities) issued by the CCP Central Committee, October 1960, cited in *China education yearbook 1949–1981*, p. 786.

18. See *China education yearbook 1949–1981*, p. 360.

19. *Guowuyuan guanyu gaodeng xuexiao jiaoshi zhiwu mingcheng jiaqi queding yu tisheng de zhanxin guiding* (Tentative regulations on the academic rank and promotion procedures for faculty staff in higher education) issued by the State Council, February 1960, cited in *China education yearbook 1949–1981*, pp. 364–5. A fifth rank, instructor, also exists (see Chapter 15 by Carol C. Fan in this volume) but is just a transitional title for those awaiting formal appointment to a specific rank.

20. See *Achievement of education in China: statistics 1949–1983*, p. 102.

21. *Achievement of education in China: statistics 1949–1983*, p. 50.

22. *Achievement of education in China: statistics 1949–1983*, p. 102.

23. Cao Xiaonan, 1991b, pp. 103–15.

24. See Lieberthal and Oksenberg, 1988, chapter 1.

25. For recent studies, see, for example, Lieberthal, 1995, part three; Lieberthal and Oksenberg, 1988, chapter 1; Fewsmith, 1994.

26. Lieberthal and Oksenberg, 1988, pp. 22–3.

27. Paine, 1992a, p. 183.

28. Deng Xiaoping, *Zai quanguo jiaoyu gongzuo huiyi shang de jianghua* (Speech at the National Education Conference), April 1978, quoted in *China education yearbook 1949–1981*, p. 62.

29. Deng Xiaoping, *Jiaoyu zhanxian de boluan fanzheng wenti* (Issues in correcting mistakes in the field of education), September 1977; and *Guanyu kexue he jiaoyu gongzuo de jidian yijiang* (Comments on Science and Education), August 1977, quoted in *China education yearbook 1949–1981*, pp. 51–3, 46–51.

30. Hu Yaobang, *Wei shenme dui zhishi fenzi bu zai ti tuanjie, jiaoyu, gaizao de fangzhen* (Why do we no longer mention the policy of uniting and educating intellectuals?), October 1978, quoted in *China education yearbook 1949–1981*, pp. 63–7.

31. See *China education yearbook 1949–1981*, pp. 359–67.

32. See *China education yearbook 1949–1981*, pp. 10, 12–3.

33. See *China education yearbook 1949–1981*, p. 13.

34. See *China education yearbook 1949–1981*, p. 13.

35. National Association of Faculty Administration in Higher Education, 1985.

36. Li Tieying, *Gaodeng jiaoyu bixu jianchi shehui zhuyi fangxiang* (Higher education must maintain its socialist orientation), July 1989, quoted in *Zhongguo Gaodeng Jiaoyu* 95, no. 9, 1989, pp. 2–5.

37. See, for example, Zhou Xincheng, 1989.

38. See Li Tieying (note 36 above), p. 4.

39. CCP Central Committee and the State Council, 1993, pp. 8–17.

40. SEdC, 1993b, p. 1.

41. See, for example, Xin, 1992; Xu Tingguan and Ye Jun, 1991, pp. 22–5.

42. According to the forecast, the required numbers of professionals in finance and law in 1990 were 34 057 and 14 049 respectively. In 1986, there were only about 800 faculty members in these fields and no one single professor in law. See Ren Zhong, 1987.
43. *Jiaoshi de peiyang yu tigao* (Faculty staff development), in *China education yearbook 1949–1981*, p. 361.
44. See, for example, Elton and Simmonds, 1977; Teather, 1979; Clark and Neave, pp. 1757–9; Wang Wenyou, 1988.
45. See Clark and Neave, p. 651.
46. Postgraduate education on a small scale existed in China previously, but the formal academic degree system was not introduced by the National Academic Degrees Committee until 1980.
47. Besides those mentioned in note 1 above, see the MoEd document *Quanguo zhongdian gaodeng xuexiao jieshou jinxiu jiaoshi gongzuo zanxing banfa* (Tentative regulations on receiving faculty students in key universities) issued in July 1980, cited in *China education yearbook 1949–1981*, p. 818, for the rationale from the official viewpoint on this subject.
48. See *Achievement of education in China: statistics 1949–1983*, p. 103; Cao Xiaonan, 1991b, p. 106.
49. See *China education yearbook 1949–1981*, p. 360.
50. Since 1982, the majority of faculty staff recruited by higher learning institutions in China have been college graduates. Therefore, it is reasonable to assume that the annual growth rate of full-time faculty staff reflects the change of recruiting young faculty members in each year. This is supported by the actual numbers released from the SEdC (see note 52 below).
51. See *Achievement of education in China: statistics 1949–1983*, pp. 50, 113; *Achievement of education in China: statistics 1980–1985*, pp. 20, 42; *Education statistics yearbook of China 1987–1993*, the summary parts; *China statistics yearbook 1995*, pp. 585–9.
52. See *Achievement of education in China: statistics 1949–1983*, pp. 50, 113; *Achievement of education in China: statistics 1980–1985*, pp. 20, 42; *Educational statistics yearbook of China 1987–1993*, the summary parts; *China statistics yearbook 1995*, pp. 585–9.
53. Cao Xiaonan, 1990, pp. 162–4.
54. For this campaign, the MoEd issued the document *Gaodeng xuexiao juban zhujiao jinxiuban de zhanxin guiding* (Tentative regulations for running training programmes for Assistant Lecturers) in March 1984. See Cao Xiaonan, 1991a, p. 67.
55. The SEdC issued a special document *Guanyu zhuzhi gaodeng xuexiao qingnian jiaoshi baokao dingxiang peiyong yanjoushen he tianbao diaochabiao de tongzhi* (Organizing junior faculty members for commissioned postgraduate training programmes) in August 1988. See Cao Xiaonan, 1990, p. 163.
56. See Cao Xiaonan, 1990, pp. 162–4.
57. All those programmes were funded directly by the central educational authority after negotiations with the Ministry of Finance and the State Planning Commission. The receiving universities had a budget for every trainee equivalent to postgraduate level.
58. Shu, 1989, pp. 236–8.

59. See Cao Xiaonan, 1991a, p. 68.
60. See Cao Xiaonan, 1991b, p. 108.
61. See note 13 above.
62. Sun Xiaobing, 1991.
63. The MoEd's 1980 document on sending students abroad emphasized that 60% of government scholarships should be used for training university teachers. See, for example, *Jiaoyu duiwai jiaoliu huodong* (Educational exchanges with foreign countries), in *China education yearbook 1949–1981*, pp. 667–8, 672–3.
64. See Cao Xiaonan, 1991a, and Chapter 5 by Michele Shoresman in this volume.
65. *Education statistics yearbook of China 1991*, p. 16. According to the statistics, there were 9276 returnees between 1981 and 1985. About half of them returned to higher learning institutions.
66. In January 1986, the SEdC issued a special document *Gaodeng xuexiao jieshou guonei fangwen xuezhe de shixing banfa* (Regulations for accepting internal visiting scholars in universities). See Cao Xiaonan, 1991a, pp. 68–9. In the document, it was specified that only authorized doctoral training units (*bo shi dian*) were eligible to undertake this task and only authorized doctoral advisers could supervise these visiting scholars.
67. See, for example, note 1; Deng Xiaoping, *Jiaoyu zhanxian de boluan fanzheng wenti* (Issues in correcting mistakes in the field of education), September 1977, in *China education yearbook 1949–1981*, pp. 51–3; Li Tieying, 1992a; Zhu Kaixuan, 1992.
68. See, for example, Ji, 1994; Xue Huanyu, 1986; Zhou Pichuang and Chen Nailing, 1988.
69. Cao Xiaonan, 1991a, p. 69.
70. See *China education yearbook 1949–1981*, pp. 361–2.
71. This type of criticism did not appear in the media but was circulated (both in writing and orally) among university administrators. See, for example, Chen Hao, 1984, pp. 12–4.
72. See, for example, Chen Hao, 1984, pp. 12–4.
73. The SEdC issued a circular for the establishment of these two centres. It outlined their tasks, responsibilities and governing regulations. The document also clarified their relationships with the central authority and other key universities, and their role in national faculty development in higher education.
74. CCP, 1985, p. 15.
75. Delany and Paine, 1991.
76. Zhang Bingliang, 1990. Those eight experimental universities were Beijing University, Qinghua University, North China Jiaotong University, Beijing Polytechnic University, Fudan University, Shanghai Jiaotong University, Shanghai Normal University and Shanghai Machinery University.
77. In the 1988 document on reforming the academic rank system (*zhichen gaige gongzuo*) and improving the faculty appointment system (*jiaoshi zhiwu pinren zhi*), the SEdC required higher learning institutions to decide the size and posts of faculty based on the tasks derived from their institutional development plan. Theoretically, institutions that accomplished this requirement and demonstrated their managerial capacity should be given autonomy in faculty staff appointments. In practice, however, the decision of granting such autonomy was subjective. The SEdC seemed to trust certain key universities

more than others. For more information, see Zhang Bingliang, 1990, and Shi and Xiao, 1988.

78. Zhang Bingliang, 1990, p. 166.
79. In recent years, institutional finance has been diversified in the higher education sector. The proportion of government funds in the budget has declined in many institutions, especially large universities like Beijing University and Qinghua University. However, the majority of higher learning institutions in the country are still the property of the government.
80. This relates to the tradition of élitism in Chinese culture. For discussion see Taylor, 1981.
81. Cao Xiaonan, 1991a, p. 66.
82. See Xu Tingguan and Ye Jun, 1991.
83. See, for example, Dalian Shi Wei, 1986.
84. Cao Xiaonan, 1991b, p. 107.
85. Cao Xiaonan, 1991a, p. 67.
86. Cao Xiaonan, 1991a, p. 64.
87. Cao Xiaonan, 1991a, p. 68.
88. Wei and Chen, 1991.
89. See *Education statistics yearbook of China 1993*, pp. 32–3.
90. *Education statistics yearbook of China 1993*, pp. 34–5.
91. The percentage of faculty staff with formal postgraduate training in 1983 was about 7%. See Wang Wenyou, 1988, p. 114. As mentioned at the beginning of the chapter, the figure in 1992 was about 19%.
92. Cao Xiaonan, 1991b, p. 110; SEdC, 1993.
93. Ren Gaoshi, 1991.
94. Ren Gaoshi, 1991, p. 29.
95. He Jinqiu, 1992, pp. 8–9; Cao Xiaonan, 1991a, p. 64.
96. The estimation is based on figures from the section of *Duiwai jiaoliu* (Foreign educational exchanges) in *China education yearbook*, 1994.
97. Zhu Kaixuan, 1992, p. 7.
98. Data at the national level in this area is unavailable, but articles have appeared in journals and newspapers. See, for example, Hua, 1987; Yuan Wei and Xu Yi, 1988; Zhang Wei, 1988; Hayhoe and Sun, 1989; Ren Shi Bu, 1990; Croizier, 1993; Chen Yangjin, 1994, p. 6.
99. Li Tieying, 1992b.
100. *China statistics yearbook*, 1995, pp. 586–7, 589.
101. This award together with the National Innovation Award and the National Science and Technology Progress Award are the top three awards for outstanding research achievements in China.
102. This big project was launched in March 1986 to bring China up to the international forefront of science and technology, especially in seven fields including biological technology and information technology. For more information, see the interview with Zhu Lilan, the Vice-Chairman of the State Science Commission in *Renmin Ribao*, 9 January 1996, p. 3.
103. See Zhu Kaixuan (note 67 above), p. 7.
104. Ou Qing, 1991.
105. See, for example, Xin, 1992; Yuan Guanghui, 1992; Gao Yi, 1993.
106. No actual figure exists for the number of such cases in the country. However,

the criticism received wide attention in academia. See, for example, Chen Hao, 1988; Shi and Xiao, 1988.

107. The nature of the issue and the political climate in the country do not allow for aggregated data in this area. However, an unpublished 1988 SEdC survey on faculty staff income in higher learning institutions in Beijing showed that more than one-third of the faculty force had part-time jobs. Most of them taught at adult education institutions. Numerous studies have discussed teachers' low income. See, for example, Educational Fund Research Group of the SEdC, 1988, chapters 3 and 4 in Part One.

108. See note 2 above.

109. Of 600 doctoral training units in 20 SEdC-affiliated universities, 46.6% were led by professors over 66 years old. Only 10.1% had doctoral advisers aged 55 or below. Results of the survey are reported in Cao Xiaonan *et al.*, 1991.

110. This strategy was commonly practised in key universities. For example, East China Normal University appointed two full professors under the age of 35 in 1988. For more information, see Zhang Bingliang, 1990, p. 165.

111. See Educational Fund Research Group of the SEdC, 1988.

112. See Cao Xiaonan *et al.*,1991, pp. 54–5. Survey data on these items covered 96 institutions.

113. The survey reported that about 35% of the young faculty staff recruited in 30 SEdC-affiliated universities since 1981 had left their universities by 1991. This situation was echoed in Shanghai. See Hayhoe, 1989b.

114. See, for example, Hayhoe, 1989b; Hayhoe and Sun, 1989; Sun Xiaobing, 1991; Orleans, 1989; Hua, 1989; Yuan Xiangwan and Mao Rong, 1991; Broaded, 1993; Bai Zhou, 1993.

115. See, for example, Chait and Ford, 1982; Baldwin and Blackburn, 1983; Finkelstein, 1985; R. Beck, 1985.

116. Li Zhenping, 1994. Also see, for example, Wang Xiaoquan, 1993.

117. See, for example, Hayhoe, 1990; Link, 1992.

118. See, for example, Hua, 1989; *Kua shiji de Zhongguo xuyao kua shiji de rencai* (China needs talented people for the 21st Century), in *Shen Zhou Xue Ren* 56 (no. 10, 1994); Kinoshita, 1995.

119. See, for example, Li Zhenping, 1994.

120. For more information on these three national projects, see, for example, Wang Zhongli and Wu Zhenrou, 1993; Wu Fanghe, 1994; Bai Yu, 1994; *Renshibu tuichu 'Bai qian wan gongcheng' jihua* (The Ministry of Personnel launches 'Hundred, Thousand and Ten-Thousand Engineering' project), in *Shen Zhou Xue Ren* 55 (no. 9, 1994), p. 15. In 1994, the SEdC selected 42 young faculty members as the first group of Across-Centuries Leading Scholars. Each of them received an annual research grant of ¥150 000 for three years. See the news section in *Shen Zhou Xue Ren* 47 (no. 1, 1994), p. 5.

121. CCP Central Committee and the State Council, 1993, pp. 8–17.

4

Chinese Scholars and the World Community

Wenhui ZHONG

INTRODUCTION

This chapter analyses the participation of Chinese scholars in the world community since the PRC opened up to the world in the late 1970s. The first section presents a statistical overview of Chinese scholarly publishing in the international context in order to highlight the progress made in increasing the visibility of Chinese scholarship. The second section offers a critical analysis of the problems which Chinese scholars face in their effort to become full members of the international community. The first part is based on bibliometric studies which compare the output of scientific publishing between different countries, while the second relies on testimonies of Chinese scholars. Key issues discussed include patterns of scholarly creativity in the PRC, cultural difference affecting editorial standards in academic journals, language barriers to international publishing and strategies adopted to overcome them, and policy implications for the further integration of Chinese scholars into the global community.

EMERGING VISIBILITY OF CHINESE SCHOLARSHIP

Due to the Cold War and the policy of self-reliance (which led to isolation),

Chinese scholarship was almost completely unknown internationally during the period from the founding of the PRC in 1949 to the late 1970s, when Deng Xiaoping started the modernization programme of reform and opening up to the outside world. One useful measurement of scholarly productivity and influence is a bibliometric study of publications and citations. This type of study indicates the relative strength of a particular discipline, or a particular country's scientific power, or the relationship and development among disciplines.[1]

A huge gulf exists between the dominance of Western industrialized countries (the centre) and the minuscule share of Third World (the periphery) participation in scientific publishing. By almost any criterion, the Third World (even when aggregated into a single unit) consistently lags far behind the world powers.[2] Third World articles occupy a much smaller share of the world scientific output, are less likely to catch the attention of colleagues worldwide, and therefore are presumed to have a lower impact on the transformation of the knowledge system.

The lack of infrastructure for scholarly publishing in Third World countries results from the small market there or scholars' needs for high profile abroad, the short supply of skilled experts in the publishing field (for example, editors, designers and distributors), and language barriers.[3] However, peripheral voices can be heard, with limited success, if they choose to publish in journals in the First World countries of the West.

Although relevant statistics for the PRC during the 1960s and 1970s are incomplete, available data show that among the Third world's meagre 2% of the world share in scientific publishing of 1973, only two Third World countries are visible: India ranked 8th and Argentina ranked 25th for scientific productivity.[4] Moreover, within the Third World, a clear division between centres and peripheries can be seen from the fact that 60% of all Third World scientific articles in 1977–78 came from India, with another 20% from Argentina.[5] These two countries, particularly India, could be regarded as the centres of the periphery in international scientific publishing.

Since the PRC's reopening to the world, information about its scholarly publishing has become more available. The first public statistics in 1988 presented the results of bibliometric studies by the newly established Institute of Scientific and Technological Information of China (ISTIC), and drew the attention of the leadership and the general public to the dismal condition of scientific publishing.[6] For the first time, élite institutions in the PRC were ranked according to the number of publications they produced in internationally reputable journals. These citation studies by ISTIC have now become a normal part of the institute's functions in the annual report.

According to the initial statistics, the PRC not only trailed far behind the great scientific powers, but also did not achieve parity with a small country like Hungary in scientific publication in 1978–80, the first three years of the PRC's open door policies.[7] That the adjustment from isolation to open-door would require more than three years for the scientific community to mobilize its potential is supported by more recent statistics from the *Science Citation Index (SCI)*, which provided an updated country comparison (see Table 4.1). Except for the PRC all countries, as would be expected, showed a larger figure for the three-year period of 1978–80 than for the one-year period of 1990. In 1990 the PRC more than tripled its number of scientific articles of the earlier period. The rapid ascent of the PRC's representation in the international scientific community in the last decade is also demonstrated by the rise in its ranking of scientific publishing from 38th in 1979, to 23rd in 1982 and to 15th in 1989.[8] By that time the PRC had surpassed Argentina and East European countries, and together with India (ranked tenth), represented one of two major Third World countries among the predominantly Western scientific powers.

Table 4.1
Number of publications in SCI by selected countries

Country	Articles in Journals		Number of Journals
	1978–80[a]	1990[b]	1990[b]
USA	407 726	265 918	1 250
Britain	100 051	55 331	661
USSR	87 999	29 835	128
Japan	70 794	56 922	77
F.R. Germany	69 524	40 517	248
France	58 015	49 838	92
Canada	45 608	29 240	44
India	35 322	10 327	13
Czechoslovakia	9 900	3 995	18
Hungary	6 495	2 947	9
PRC	2 457	7 607	9
Taiwan	N.A.	2 550	3

[a] data from *Guangming Ribao* (25 January 1988)
[b] author's estimate based on Institute for Scientific Information, 1990

The inclusion of indices other than *SCI* reduces dependence on a single index. Figure 4.1 includes data from three additional scientific citation indices: *Index to Scientific Reviews (ISR)*, *Index to Scientific and Technological Proceedings (ISTP)* and the *Engineering Index (EI)*. The first two of these together with SCI are oriented towards basic science publishing, whereas the last focuses on the applied sciences, in particular, engineering. According to 1989 data, each index ranks the PRC differently: 15th on *SCI*, 28th on *ISR*, 13th on *ISTP* and 8th on *EI*.[9] At 15th (the average of the four indices), the PRC is competitive with Spain, Switzerland and Sweden in the hierarchy of international scientific powers.

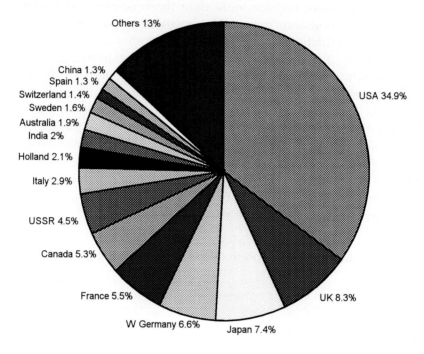

Source: ISTIC, 1990, p. 50

Figure 4.1 Scientific publishing in the top 15 countries

Criticisms of the biases and limitations of using citation indices to make judgements on Third World science are numerous.[10] A large part of Third World science — called non-mainstream science because it is missed by the major citation indices — has gone unnoticed by the international science community as a whole. This is the case for Chinese science, as it represents only 1.3% of all the world science in number of publications: out of a total of 3192 journals as the database for SCI in 1990, only 9 were published in the PRC. It is clear that the portrayal of Chinese scientific research from citation indices provides an incomplete picture. It alone does not represent the entire state of affairs of scientific research and communications in the PRC.

Bibliometrics exposes the formal relationship between scholars by providing a structural outline of productive scholars, authorities, etc. But it does not describe how the informal networks (the so-called invisible college, critical mass or inner circles) among scholars that lead to the final products actually work.[11] A good understanding of the multifaceted phenomenon of scholarly communication has to go beyond an examination of the product (number of publications and their impact), which can be measured quantitatively to a certain extent. It should also examine the process of communication, which can be best expressed qualitatively.

PROBLEMS OF LOW VISIBILITY

A common problem which a Third World country such as the PRC faces is the stratification of scientists into two main groups: one with an orientation to internationally visible research areas and the other working in areas with only local significance. The bibliometric study carried out by ISTIC points out this difference as represented in two types of scholarly journals: domestic and international.[12] The top three domestic research areas shown in domestic journals are health/medicine/pharmaceutics, agriculture/forestry/animal husbandry, and machinery/instrument, while the top three international research areas are physics, electronics/communications technology, and chemistry. Thus, physicists and researchers in electronics/communications technology tend to orient themselves to the international community, whereas researchers in agriculture-related fields and in machinery and instruments tend to concern themselves with issues and problems of national significance. Research in health-related fields is well represented in both the national and international scenes, although with different degrees of prominence: number one at the national level, number four at the international level.[13]

Language

English dominates international scientific publishing. According to world indices, English remains the medium for about 60% of all scientific documents and papers, compared with French at 17%, German and Russian both at 10% and Japanese at 3%.[14] Without competence in English, Chinese scientists are handicapped; they will be unable to keep up with the international literature or make their work known to colleagues outside the PRC.

The language barrier is substantial given the size of the PRC and the proportion of scientists relative to the total world number. Although the PRC ranks second in the world in the number of scientists and engineers

(8.3 million) after the former USSR (14.5 million), with Japan third (7 million) and the USA fourth (3.4 million), scientific publications in Chinese in international indices represent less than 1% of the total.[15]

Standards

In an attempt to find ways of improving the visibility of Chinese research in the global community, ISTIC conducted a survey of the internationally accepted editorial standards of the 1227 Chinese journals included in the 1989 Chinese citation studies. These standards, which may be taken for granted in Western industrialized countries, still pose obstacles for Chinese journals and their editors (see Table 4.2). Taken individually, each editorial standard may be too minor to preclude a journal from inclusion in international citation indices on the basis of form (rather than content). But if a journal fails to comply with several of these basic standards, regardless of content, then the chance of being visible in the world community immediately diminishes. The ISTIC report points out that only about 60% of Chinese journals have met all seven standards.[16]

Table 4.2
Editorial standards of 1227 Chinese journals

Editorial standard	Yes	(%)	No*	(%)
Volume & Issue Number	822	(67.0)	405	(33.0)
English Titles	1001	(81.6)	226	(18.4)
English Abstracts	838	(68.3)	389	(31.7)
Information about Authors	778	(63.4)	449	(36.6)
Papers with References	690	(56.2)	537	(43.8)
Scholarly Papers in Majority	825	(67.3)	402	(32.7)
Having ISSN	805	(65.6)	422	(34.4)

* No standards or incomplete fulfilment

Source: ISTIC, 1990, pp. 98–9

The 'papers with complete references' standard obtained the lowest achievement level (56.2%) among Chinese journals. In Western industrialized countries where modern science was born and has developed to the present state — which is generally considered to be at a higher level than elsewhere in the world — this requirement is consistent with the analytical precision held dear by scientific methodology. It is also compatible with increasingly efficient library and information retrieval and storage systems. But in a Third World country like the PRC, where a cultural tradition that has dominated for centuries now faces modernization, the road chosen for future development, there appears to be a different appreciation of the values of precision. For example, if the medical classic, *The Yellow Emperor's Classic of Internal Medicine (Huangdi Neijing)* is referred to or quoted, it is unnecessary to list details such as the exact page(s), edition and publication year because it is such a well-known work. China's long history has left the nation with a rich literature that touches upon almost all aspects of human life, so that there is sometimes the perception that whatever needs to be said has already been said in the classics. Indeed, traditional knowledge seems to be a collective ancestral legacy; the job for individuals is only to reinterpret and reapply it in appropriate situations. By contrast, modern science with its own set of norms has been in China for a much shorter period than in Western industrialized countries. Thus, China has to reconcile the conflict between the inertia of traditional cultural norms and modern scientific values. The debate over whether the Chinese tradition and historical legacy are a hindrance or a strength in the present modernization effort is very important if China is to pioneer a new path for development that has unique Chinese characteristics.

The non-compliance of editorial standards, such as the failure to provide volume numbers, English titles and abstracts, complete information about authors, and registration for ISSN, is a hangover from the recent closed-door era that oriented most journals towards unique Chinese practices. For example, the current ethos requires that a paper be specified as written by an individual or individuals — rather than by an institution — a shift in practice in the PRC reflecting a national adjustment from collective ascription to individualism. The transition from the PRC's besieged isolation to its place in a world of open interdependency renders secrecy in research unnecessary. In almost all research fields, giving the author's real name and contact address is unlikely to lead to the leak of state secrets.

The PRC's low participation in world scientific publishing relates to the number of citations an average paper uses. SCI reported this figure in 1988 to be 20.[17] But based on the 1227 Chinese journals in 1989, an average Chinese paper cited only 5.4 other items, a slight increase from 5.38 in 1988. More than a quarter (26.3%) of all papers had no citations at all.[18] The big difference in citation habits between Chinese and international writers is not only due to cultural legacy but also to the fact that Chinese institutions lack journals and papers.

Funding

Another related issue in scientific publishing concerns funding for research.

While the PRC's private or state-run companies may have financial resources to fund research in their own fields, little of their research has appeared in scientific publications. The 1990 ISTIC report estimates that publications in Chinese journals with research support by companies represented only 0.11% of all funded research in the PRC.[19] Much publicized research is either underfunded or not funded at all. For example, scholars in universities and research institutions of the Chinese Academy of Sciences carry out research largely because it relates to their teaching work or their assigned duties, and for this they do have some institutional financial support.

Expedient explanations for the non-compliance of seemingly simple editorial etiquette of scholarly journals may also be related to financial considerations. If paper is expensive and a journal has to cram in as many articles as possible, then the long tail of references or bibliography at the end of an article may be the first place to be cut. Moreover, if the information retrieval and storage system is poor and library materials are outdated, listing references is unnecessary when many Chinese colleagues do not have access to them.

In order to encourage scholars to initiate and carry out more research, in 1982, 89 high-level scientists proposed a science fund very much akin to those in industrialized countries where the most competent bidders get resources for their research. This proposal was adopted and put in place in 1986, when the single biggest research fund — the state Natural Science Funds — was established.[20] The Natural Science Funds is the main financial source for scientific publishing in the PRC, supporting almost 80% of all funded papers.[21] Other types of funds are beginning to emerge, for example, funds from foreign bilateral and multilateral cooperation, from local initiatives and from industry. Still, in 1989, among the 86 419 papers in 1227 select journals of Chinese science and technology, 5670 were supported by some kind of funding, representing 6.6% of all papers, a 49.4% jump from 4.4% in the previous year.[22]

PUBLISHING IN THE SOCIAL SCIENCES, ARTS AND HUMANITIES IN THE PRC

The natural sciences dominate the present knowledge system, including the output of research, human resources, funding, number of institutions and so on. The prevalence of science and technology is an accepted fact of life in the high-technology era and is regarded by many as the key to progress and modernity, although some would think otherwise.[23] Thus, bibliometric studies of scholarly publishing have focused mainly on the natural sciences and technology, treating the social sciences, arts and humanities as an afterthought. The growth and development of bibliometric services such as the Institute of Scientific Information in the USA demonstrate this kind of bias. Given the characteristics of communication among scholars in the social sciences, arts and humanities, the bias seems to be justified. Compared with the natural scientists, these scholars tend to communicate on a smaller 'orbit' because of the more varied ideologies, paradigms and discourses inherent in their fields. Added to these barriers is their higher dependency on language rather than laws, symbols, formulae and other signs to convey their meaning. Communication across linguistic barriers is more difficult than in the natural sciences.

Despite the lack of bibliometric data available on the scholarly publishing in the social sciences, arts and humanities, some issues discussed earlier — such as editorial standards of journals and citation habits of authors — are also applicable to this area of scholarship. Here, the major sources of data are the annual statistics of 1986–90 in the *Social Sciences Citation Index (SSCI)* and the *Arts and Humanities Citation Index (A&HCI)*, both published by the Institute for Scientific Information in the USA.

Based on data from *SSCI* and *A&HCI*, few papers were published by Chinese scholars in the five-year period of 1986–90 for social sciences (880) and arts and humanities (306). A major channel through which Chinese scholarship in social sciences and humanities is made known to the world is through a small number of English language journals with high international visibility. The *SSCI* includes four such journals, on economics, education, law/government and sociology/anthropology. They are all published by a Western academic press that selects and translates what are considered important papers from existing Chinese journals.[24] Similarly, the A&HCI includes three English language journals that are translations of existing Chinese journals in literature, history and philosophy. Only one — *Chinese Literature* — is published by a Chinese press. The important role of these English language journals is thus quite evident not only in crossing the language barrier, but also in bridging the intellectual gap between Chinese scholarship and non-Chinese readers. These translated journals usually have as chief editor a scholar from a Western industrialized country, who is a China expert in the field. They invite a Chinese colleague to be either co-editor or a member of the editorial board for selecting and translating worthwhile papers on a related theme.

This joint effort of involving Western and Chinese scholars to publish journals of Chinese scholarship seems to result in higher visibility for Chinese research in the social sciences, arts and humanities. The most prestigious journal among Chinese social scientists, *Social Sciences in China*, has an English edition, which is edited and translated by Chinese scholars, but it is not considered important enough to be included in *SSCI*. Thus, a big gap exists between what the Chinese regard as worthwhile scholarship and what interests the predominantly Western readers in the international scholarly community.

WHAT CHINESE SCHOLARS SAY ABOUT SCHOLARLY COMMUNICATION[2 5]

The participation by Chinese scholars in international exchange has increased tremendously since 1978. Such exchange takes place in many forms. The reciprocal forms of foreign contact mentioned by scholars themselves include:
1.   publishing in international scholarly journals;
2.   going abroad to attend academic conferences;
3.   going abroad as visiting scholars or as students;
4.   maintaining personal contact through correspondence;
5.   hosting international conferences in the PRC;
6.   conducting joint research projects; and
7.   joining or serving on international scholarly organizations.

Only a few extremely active senior scholars with foreign educational background have experienced all these forms of scholarly communication with the world community. In most cases, Chinese scholars typically encounter only one or two of these interactive channels. The limited number of two-way channels for active academic exchange fails to make scholars feel like full members of the international scholarly family.

Two important barriers — deficiency in foreign languages and lack of funding — most hinder the participation of Chinese scholars in the world academic community. Another barrier is the Chinese government's lack of interest in certain social sciences and humanities research topics because of their potential threat to existing power legitimization. Also, foreign scholars sometimes perceive that certain Chinese scholarship is inferior or too parochial.

INTERNATIONAL PUBLISHING

Most scholars who publish internationally (as well as nationally) have had prior overseas study or research experience. In fact, this early overseas exposure to the scholarship of a larger world outside the PRC after the door was opened in the late 1970s was the most consistent indicator of the scholars' high performance in Sino-foreign scholarly communication. Their sojourn abroad had somehow transformed their outlook and ethos and had set them apart from others. They are often referred to as 'returned scholars', and all have published at least one article in an international scholarly journal, either as a single author or as co-author with a foreign colleague.[26] Scholars with the longest foreign publishing record tend to be in high-technology frontier research at prestigious universities or research institutes who have extensive foreign networks due to their frequent trips abroad. The language barrier, as mentioned above, posed less of a problem to them than to scholars in the social sciences and humanities.

After the ideological split with the USSR in the 1960s, the Chinese government changed its foreign language policy to make English rather than Russian the major foreign language. Many science scholars switched languages with relative ease, whereas academics in the social sciences and humanities found the change impossible. The ones who had spent some time in another country as visiting scholars or students might have minimum command of the local language, but this level of linguistic competence is not sufficient for writing or publishing in a foreign language. Many scholars have dealt with this problem (especially in their first foreign publication) by co-authoring with foreign colleagues or supervisors. In some cases, the actual co-authoring process reflected a shared contribution among two or more authors in the conceptual development, experimentation or writing of the paper. For example, a Chinese and a foreign scholar would discuss the topic and arrive at some common viewpoints before the former wrote a paper and the latter revised it. In other cases, reported as a more common practice, the Chinese scholar contributed to the content (such as providing data) while the foreign scholar provided the form (and often the analysis). Typically, a Chinese academic identified the topic, carried out the research and wrote the paper in English with substantial Chinese influence. Then the paper was heavily edited by the foreign counterpart (often a supervisor) so that it conformed to the style and manuscript requirements of the intended journal. As their research experience, analytical experience and language abilities matured, Chinese scholars gradually became less dependent on a co-author and wrote papers as single authors. The opportunity of foreign sojourn, however short, seemed to correlate with a higher number of international publications and reflected the relationship in which Chinese scholars were placed. Often their foreign host was a colleague or supervisor with whom they could discuss research problems, on a one-to-one basis, in the local linguistic and cultural contexts.

Such constant contact over time fermented into Chinese-foreign co-authoring, which could not occur if the Chinese scholars had remained in the PRC. Moreover, a foreign visit broadened a Chinese scholar's vision (*kaiyanjie*), so that firsthand knowledge of intellectual currents and of the nature of some important international scholarly journals was acquired or enhanced, as well as developing professional relationships with journal editors.

In contrast, 'local scholars' have never been abroad and are active in the national rather than the international academic scene. They share three characteristics. First, they tend to work in the disciplines of the social sciences, arts and humanities, which render them more parochial than scholars in the natural sciences and technology. Second, they are likely to be younger scholars. And third, their institutions belong to the lower echelon of the national research community. While local scholars see language deficiency and the lack of easy access to current information on research in the world community as the major barriers preventing them from publishing internationally, returned scholars are more aware of the cultural differences between publishing in the PRC and abroad. Both groups consider mastering a foreign language to be a prerequisite for international publishing, but the ethos of Western scholarship (which most international scholarly journals reflect) is difficult for local scholars to grasp. Returned scholars sometimes follow up their concerns with action, as illustrated by the professor in humanities who persuaded the editorial committee of a respected Chinese journal to tighten up its citation requirements. In particular, she pointed out the unacceptable practice, according to Western scholarship, of attaching a bibliography at the end of a paper without precise references in the paper.

Returned scholars who serve on editorial committees of reputable scholarly journals in the PRC are able to compare Chinese and Western editorial practices.[27] In the natural sciences and technology, these practices are reported to be more universal, where the principle of peer review is followed with vigour. Some scholars report it is sometimes more difficult to publish in Chinese journals than in international ones because of the limited number of journals in their individual specializations in the PRC. When they look for an international outlet, they find more choices and they can get a faster response for publishing. The editorial policies in Chinese social sciences and humanities are purportedly based also on the principle of peer review, but Chinese scholars report instances where papers were commissioned. When occasionally papers were not up to standard, quality was compromised by accepting them to save the face of the authors. On this last point, one Chinese scholar related a personal anecdote for contrast. After he had written a scholarly paper under the aegis of his Canadian supervisor, he gave it to the supervisor for revision. He then submitted it as a co-authored paper to a reputable international journal for publishing. Two months later, the paper was returned with a note requesting them to do more substantial language editing. Clearly, the supervisor had done a sloppy job and he would have lost face in the Chinese context. What was remarkable, according to the Chinese scholar, was that the matter of saving/losing face was irrelevant in that case. His supervisor matter-of-factly acknowledged his neglect and promised to do a better job in the second revision.

A final difference between publishing in the PRC and abroad concerns financial compensation. Scholarly publishing in the PRC, in whatever field, usually pays authors for articles. With the present reform, however, some journals in natural sciences and engineering actually require financial contributions from authors. The amount can be as much as ¥200 for each paper, about the average monthly salary of scholars in some institutions. To compensate for the financial burden of the contributor, the fee is reimbursed if the paper is accepted for publication. In some cases, the publication cost may be taken from research funds. In most cases scholars at least break even financially. Journals with theoretical orientations usually do not require publication fees and most journals of social sciences and humanities continue to pay for articles. While Chinese scholars say that the small royalties are not an incentive for publishing in the PRC, the real and potential financial burden from foreign journals (postage, fax, photocopying, word processing, etc.) — small as it may seem to Westerners — does sometimes dissuade them from publishing in certain foreign journals.

INTERNATIONAL CONFERENCES

Most international conferences are held in major industrialized countries, but recently Chinese educators have been successful in hosting smaller-scale international conferences, symposia, seminars and workshops in the PRC. Many international scholarly organizations, such as learned societies and associations, hold annual or biannual conferences. International conferences abroad are considered extremely important to a Chinese scholar's professional life for several reasons, as indicated in these comments taken from interviews:

> This is the time to meet face-to-face scholars, whose works you have got to know quite well, but haven't had a chance to talk to.

I get inspiration when listening to other scholars of high calibre. Sometimes their topics are not necessarily directly related to my work. But their new concepts and ideas are heuristic to my thinking ... Once, I transplanted such an idea to my research in chemistry, which won me funding from the National Science Funds.

The very newest developments and ideas in the field are not reflected in scholarly journals. Even if they were, they got published six months later. And then there is probably another year or so of delay before we can read them because current foreign journals are notoriously slow in coming to our library.

At the conference, we know what's in a scholar's mind. We can hear about the circumstances surrounding the research being reported ... what problems were plaguing them ... how they got around them, and so on. You don't get that kind of information from a journal article; it mainly reports the results.

At these conferences, old personal friendships are renewed and new contacts are established. Most scholars from the PRC attending international conferences abroad are senior researchers who have benefited from professional networks established during earlier overseas visits or studies — the Saint Matthew's Effect in action.[28]

Many of the most active participants in international exchange are among the first group of visiting scholars or students sent by the government in the late 1970s and early 1980s. A year or two after their return, they were invited to present a paper at an international conference abroad. At that time the Chinese government provided the scholars with return airfare to the conference while the conference organizers covered the expenses incurred in the host country. The success of the first conference would then bring in invitations for the second, the third and so on. In later years demands for government funding for international travel and conferences escalated due to easier access to information about the outside world, and government funding by the late 1980s covered only limited travel expenses. An average university might be able to support only a few scholars a year by providing them air tickets to overseas conferences. Many scholars were thus unable to attend international conferences since most conference sponsors did not provide financial assistance unless the invited scholar was a special guest or served on an important committee of the organization. Consequently, only a few high performers who served on such committees could avoid the overcrowded competition for limited government resources.

Hosting international conferences in the PRC can offset the Saint Matthew's Effect. In the mid-1980s early participants of international exchange became more knowledgeable about the technical and practical aspects of organizing such affairs and developed the expertise and infrastructure to host conferences in the PRC. Dealing with the institution's bureaucracy caused frustrations; mobilizing and coordinating a large contingent of support personnel went beyond the power of an individual scholar. A Chinese academic who organizes an international conference must provide long in advance a well-justified plan to the superior administrative level detailing the programmes and foreign attendees. Once the plan is approved, the scholar must persuade relevant people in the academic affairs unit (that controls meeting rooms), the campus housing authorities, catering department, transportation department, and foreign affairs office to help prepare. Coordinating such a conference needs more than the authority of a scholar; usually the wholehearted support of the university president and Party secretary is demanded. Since the Chinese university or research institute is often a self-contained community providing a whole range of daily life services for staff, only the top leaders have the power to mobilize all units. In Western countries, most non-scholarly logistics such as travel arrangements, accommodation and catering are delegated to private agencies outside the campus. But in the PRC, every detail comes to the attention of the organizing scholar, who exhaustingly uses his/her network of connections to solve conflicts over jurisdictional turf in order to produce results.

If international conferences that attract enough high calibre scholars are held in the PRC, with adequate funding from the Chinese government and other external agencies, the returns of intellectual growth of large numbers of Chinese scholars should outstrip the costs. The amount of government money that can fund a few scholars to go abroad for a conference could benefit far more Chinese scholars if the conference were held in the PRC. The maximum benefit of conference attendance occurs when the participants, upon their return to their home institutions, share their experiences with their colleagues. Unfortunately, there is as yet no systematic mechanism or convention among Chinese scholars to share conference proceedings and papers.

COOPERATIVE PROJECTS

Joint research projects face the same difficulties experienced in writing collaborations. Foreign and Chinese scholars often lack mutual interests due to the 'non-mainstream' nature of most research done in the PRC (i.e., most research topics relate to national or local issues in the PRC rather than to universal theory development). Prospective joint projects are cancelled when the Chinese side feels that it does not have a sufficient share in ownership rights of the research results.

An example of a successful project is one between a Chinese scientist and a Canadian. They first met when the Canadian visited the university and laboratory where the Chinese scholar worked. They both shared interests in developing frontier research in their own specializations, and they were aware of their respective strengths and weaknesses, which were complementary to each other. That is, the Chinese had good instrumentation (thanks to World Bank aid) but no high-quality solvent for the experiment. The reverse was true for the Canadian. By combining forces, they carried out the experiment and jointly published the results in an international paper.

On the institutional level, cooperative projects are more common. Some involve the exchange of scholars to teach and learn at each other's institutions on an equal number of person/year basis. For example, for two years, an Australian university sent four scholars (for six months each) to a Chinese university to teach English and/or learn Chinese in exchange for two Chinese scholars (one year each) to teach Chinese and/or learn English. Other joint projects involve bilateral and multilateral aid to upgrade certain aspects of the PRC's human resources. For example, the British Council and the SEdC run postgraduate English language teacher training programmes at several foreign language institutes in the PRC. Also, UNICEF supports a project at a provincial teachers university to improve both the infrastructure and human resources in preschool education research and training.[29]

RESEARCH AND FUNDING

The issues Chinese scholars most often complain about concern funding and time off from teaching to do research. The stratified structure of Chinese higher education gives a relative advantage to research-oriented scholars in the national echelon of key institutions in terms of securing funding and time for research. The establishment of various research funds (at national, provincial and local levels) and the principle of peer review and fair competition have brought positive results. Wastage in repetitive research and lack of communication among scholars have been somewhat reduced and resources have been put to use more efficiently. Now Chinese scholars have little problem rejecting the Maoist egalitarian policies about resources distribution in favour of Deng Xiaoping's more élitist doctrine. In fact, they regard the stratified system as necessary and fair for resources utilization. Some scholars become quite innovative once they accept their place in the strata. They initiate research by networking with factories and enterprises to get funding.

The practice of allocating research funds based on open, fair competition, which to a large extent has replaced the personal distribution of resources by institutional leaders, started in the 1980s. With the establishment of ISTIC and the various foundations that award research funding to the best qualified bidders, funding and research competence are more in agreement. Now, the responsibilities of participants in a research project are more clearly delineated: the principal researchers and other participants in a research project are specifically identified rather than being anonymously represented by the name of an institution. No longer is a book written by an editorial committee or working group, but by real people with real names. The clouds of secrecy and myth surrounding some research work have dissipated because research results must now be known before an objective peer review may be conducted. The peer review process has given scholars some power and autonomy to guard against a certain amount of political and ideological interference. It has also enhanced the status of senior scholars.

During the 1990s, concern over economic development has brought research closer to addressing practical problems. At the same time, basic and theoretical research is being eroded because of neglect as manifested in a shortage of funding. Since the overall development level across all sectors in the PRC is still low, only low-technology research is likely to attract financial support from industry. The long-term goal of catching up with the world's scientific and technological powers is dependent upon the stable supply of funding in both basic and frontier research, and has resulted in the establishment of funds such as the Natural Science Fund, the National Social Science Fund and the High-technology Development Plan (also called the '863 Plan' after its date of adoption, March 1986).

The development of such funding mechanisms, along with the introduction of peer review, has brought the PRC's intellectual ethos more in conformance with the dominant world scholarly culture. Scholars report that they treat research proposals much more seriously now because they directly relate to funding. The minimum requirement for promotion to associate professor includes the publication of two scholarly papers in national-level journals or of one scholarly book. Some veteran university lecturers interviewed who claimed that the Cultural Revolution wasted their prime years for scholarship have found this requirement difficult to meet. Now, however, they have been forced to undertake research in order to stay in the system.

CONCLUSIONS

Both bibliometric studies and testimonies by Chinese scholars have identified recurring issues related to research and publishing, such as funding, language barriers and editorial standards.

Over two decades of educational reform, a rise in international visibility of Chinese scholarly publishing, especially in the natural sciences, has moved the PRC from virtual non-existence to being ranked 15th in the number of scientific publications. Yet, given the size of the PRC and of its large scientific contingent, its research output and international recognition still lag well behind those of Western industrialized countries. One significant trend is the acceptance of international conventions, particularly from Western academic culture, as sources of legitimization. The peer review system, the research funding mechanism, open and fair competition, and division of labour for efficiency are embraced as good for the PRC's reform in the research community. New two-way channels of scholarly communications — sponsoring international conferences and cooperative research projects — are encouraging. Yet, in sum, solutions to improve the PRC's scholarly research and publishing cannot escape from the need for better funding and the upgrading of the research infrastructure.

NOTES

1. For a more detailed discussion on the use of bibliometric studies for scientific productivity, see Price, 1986; MacAulay, 1985; Garfield, 1987, p. 9; Eisemon and Davis, 1989.
2. Garfield, 1983, p. 114. At the time the author was president of the Institute for Scientific Information, which issues the most frequently used annual citation indices.
3. Altbach, 1978, 1987a and 1987b.
4. Garfield, 1983.
5. Garfield, 1983, p. 117.
6. Zhao Hongzhou, 1988. See also Institute of Scientific and Technological Information of China (ISTIC), 1990.
7. Si, 1988.
8. Si, 1988.
9. ISTIC, 1990, pp. 51–4.
10. For example, Eisemon and Davis, 1989; Frame, 1985; Moravcsik, 1985a and 1985b.
11. Lievrouw, 1990.
12. ISTIC, 1990, p. 4.
13. ISTIC, 1990, p. 4.
14. ISTIC, 1990, p. 4.
15. *China statistics yearbook*, 1988, p. 1026.

16. ISTIC, 1990, p. 99.
17. ISTIC, 1990, p. 35.
18. ISTIC, 1990, p. 36.
19. ISTIC, 1990, p. 27.
20. Song and Kong, 1991.
21. ISTIC, 1990, p. 74.
22. ISTIC, 1990, p. 27.
23. Habermas, 1984.
24. The publisher is M.E. Sharpe, Armonk, N.Y.
25. This section is based on the author's three-month research trip to the PRC in 1991 that obtained testimonies from 86 Chinese scholars interviewed in seven cities (Beijing, Shanghai, Nanjing, Guangzhou, Xi'an, Lanzhou and Guilin).
26. See Hayhoe, 1990; Hua Xue, 1987; Lin Guojun *et al.*, 1988.
27. Scholarly journals in China are classified into first grade (the national), second grade (provincial) and third grade (local), indicating descending prestige.
28. 'For whosoever hath, to him shall be given, and he shall have more abundance; but whosoever hath not, from him shall be taken away even the little he hath.' (Matthew 13:12, The Bible, King James Version).
29. For other bilateral and mutlilateral projects, see *China Development Briefing 1* (no. 1) (http://www.hku.hk/cerc/china/cdb), retrieved 1996.

5

Returns to Education — The US/PRC Visiting Scholars Programme — 1978–88

Michele SHORESMAN

INTRODUCTION

This chapter examines the impact of the US/PRC Visiting Scholars Programme which allowed mid-career professionals from the PRC to undertake advanced training abroad. The academics discussed in this study were in their forties or fifties and spent at least one year in the USA between 1978 and 1988 at the University of Illinois, a comprehensive, multi-campus state university with strengths in engineering, physical and life sciences, and computer science. These are the disciplines in which approximately two-thirds of all PRC scholars sponsored by the Chinese government have studied.[1] Almost 400 universities in the USA had five or more visiting scholars annually during the decade of this study.[2] The visiting scholars did not enrol in degree programmes. Rather, the purpose of their stay was to learn new research techniques, catch up on developments in their fields and to become acquainted with the broader scientific community. They were nominated by their home institutions and their stay was supported in equal parts by the Chinese government and USA universities.[3]

This study compares the productivity of two groups of scholars: those who went abroad and those who did not have a foreign educational experience. Two hundred and forty-four government-sponsored visiting scholars studied at Illinois in the decade of this study. Of these, 191 returned to the PRC immediately after their Illinois study (a 78% return rate). From this group of returned scholars, a random sample of 125 was drawn proportionately from Shanghai, Beijing, Nanjing and the rest of the PRC.[4] In 1988 the researcher visited members of this alumni group in the PRC and questioned them about the impact of their stay at Illinois on their academic life. Data was collected either by personal interviews or by post. In total, 64 visiting scholars completed the questionnaire — 48 through face-to-face interviews — and these will be referred to as the sample.

In addition to the sample, a group of scholars who had not had overseas educational experience was obtained by asking each sample scholar to identify a scholar most comparable in age, rank and academic field who had not been abroad to study. This 'comparison group' was given a questionnaire which excluded those questions that pertained to the foreign educational experience. Comparison group data were collected from 45 scholars who had not had an educational experience abroad. The sample and the comparison group were similarly educated, close in age and a similar gender ratio was found.[5] Of all those surveyed, the vast majority of the sample and of the comparison group reported having the equivalent of a Bachelor's degree, fewer than one-fifth a Master's degree and fewer than 4% a Ph.D.[6]

Several productivity measures were used to evaluate the differences in academic productivity between the visiting scholars and their peers who had no foreign educational experience:
1. numbers of publications (journal articles, books and chapters in books);
2. numbers of new courses developed;
3. numbers of conference papers given;
4. numbers of lectures given outside the scholars' own institutions;
5. numbers of research awards;
6. numbers of joint research projects;
7. numbers of Chinese and international patents applied for and held; and
8. numbers of consulting contracts.

These productivity indicators were analysed and differences were tested for statistical significance. The sample and comparison scholars' productivity was compared over their entire careers. The results appear in Table 5.1. In addition, the sample scholars' productivity since their return to the PRC was measured against the comparison group's productivity over their entire careers. See Table 5.2 for these results.

Table 5.1
Average productivity: sample's and comparison
group's entire career

Variable	Sample	Comparison group
Conference papers*	4.22	2.23
Courses developed*	2.80	2.20
Consulting contracts*	3.45	1.89
Lectures	2.33	2.09
Journal articles	17.08	12.98
Books published	1.97	2.35
Chapters	2.81	5.67
Joint research projects**	1.98	1.02
Research awards**	4.22	2.23

*   Significant at the 0.05 level
** Significant if comparing the entire career of the comparison group and the work
     of the sample only since their return to the PRC

Table 5.2
Productivity: sample since their return to the PRC versus
comparison group's entire career

Variable	Sample	Comparison group
Research awards*	1.94	0.667
Joint research projects*	1.98	1.02
Conference papers	2.58	2.23
Lectures	2.05	2.09
Courses developed	1.59	1.22
Chinese patents applied for	0.109	0.022
International patents applied for	0	0.022
Chinese patents held	0.063	0
International patents held	0	0.022
Consulting contracts	0.969	0.755
Journal articles	8.67	11.82
Books	1.97	0.889
Chapters	0.797	1.889

*   Significant at the 0.05 level

SELECTION INTO THE PROGRAMME

Scholars were either self-selected or encouraged to study abroad by the
leaders of their institutions. In the latter case the dynamics of academic
politics surely played a role; however, the role of *guanxi* or connections in
the choice of scholars who were chosen to study abroad cannot be
ascertained from this study. One scholar described the process at his

university in this way, 'We took an English exam and gave a lecture to a committee about our research and teaching work. All department members and leaders attended this lecture. Cooperation, high-level research and teaching work as well as English were the basis of selection.'

One-quarter of the sample group were self-motivated and wrote to Illinois professors and asked to be invited. One scholar related that his university had to approve his going abroad to study. However, once approval was given, it was up to him to find a place to go. 'So I wrote some letters and Illinois was the first to respond.' Personality factors such as risk-taking were likely to have been important in the self-selection of scholars. In addition, some academics were encouraged to study abroad by their university's leadership. 'The leaders of our university informed the departments of the number of persons who could go abroad to study,' according to one scholar.

Administrators at the various institutions of higher education in the PRC might try to maximize the chances of showing positive programme effects by choosing scholars who, from their academic track records, were known to be more likely to embrace the new technologies offered by the visiting scholars programme.

TECHNOLOGY TRANSFER AND IMPROVED TEACHING

The Open Door policy brought the opportunity for a massive transfer of technology to the PRC during the decade of 1978 to 1988. Unlike students in degree or post-doctoral programmes, the visiting scholars, as the subjects of this study illustrate, were older. They planned to return to jobs they had held for as many as 20 years prior to coming to the United States for retraining. The visiting scholars' rate of returning home was thus far greater than that of younger students who had no jobs and in some cases no families (spouses and children) to return to in the PRC.

Most visiting scholars went abroad to learn advanced technologies. Prior to their Illinois experience, they had only 'textbook knowledge' and they felt they needed hands-on experience that could only be gained with study abroad. Often, the fields of knowledge they studied in the USA were either weak or non-existent in the PRC at the time they went overseas. Moreover, little advanced equipment was available in the PRC when educational reform began after the Cultural Revolution. Indeed, study abroad reflected an acknowledgement at that time by intellectuals of the poor quality of education and research. As one scholar put it, 'It is difficult to improve your research work here [in the PRC] because knowledge and teaching is narrow, so it is necessary to go abroad.' In coming to Illinois, they became aware of the level of international work in their field. They had the opportunity to meet international scholars and to discuss their work in a collegial atmosphere. One scholar summarized, 'It was necessary to go abroad to open my mind, open my eyes, to broaden myself.' Consequently, international contacts were made and cooperative research resulted.

Visiting scholars who left the PRC for study and training were expected to serve as the advance guard in two new policies initiated after the Cultural Revolution — the establishment of postgraduate-level education and the incorporation of research into universities. In the 1980s, postgraduate schools were inaugurated within Chinese institutions of higher education at both universities and research institutes. Previously, given the lingering Soviet influence, the PRC had supported research institutes separate from universities; little research was conducted at most universities. Overseas, scholars would gain both the confidence and the ability to train their students. Study abroad was expected to help scholars, upon their return, set standards for their postgraduate students.

More than half of the visiting scholars reported that their US experience had changed the way they thought about their teaching style or methodology: 'Teaching methodology is important for modernization'; 'for education to further China's modernization goals, teaching must be transformed to become itself not "mimetic" but "transformative"'.[7] However, the idea that knowledge resides in texts is a deeply rooted cultural concept. Traditional Chinese teachers were viewed as transmitters of this knowledge and students were rewarded for mastery of the texts. 'The passive learning that commonly results denies positive or significant educational opportunities to large numbers of students, and offers little in the way of skill development, independent inquiry and creative learning to the mass of China's young people.'[8]

Exposure to other methods of teaching resulted in scholars' rethinking of their own pedagogical style. One scholar stated, 'Before I came to the USA, I used traditional teaching methods. After I came back, I wrote a new book on how to use computers. I put together a microcomputer lab for students. Hands-on practice is necessary with computers.' Another scholar said, 'I want my students to ask more questions and to have more discussions in class.' Yet another said, 'I ask my students to memorize less and go to the library and read new journals more so that they know about the advances in our field. They also do a lot more lab work now.'

One scholar noted the difference in expectations for students, 'In the USA, students do independent research and solve problems by themselves. They use equipment and set up the lab themselves. In China this is not the case. The teacher gives more help to the students. This is not good for the students and causes them to depend too much on the teacher. I have changed my teaching style to make my students more independent.'

Reflecting on the influence of the Soviet system, a scholar said, 'I thought that the way we educate students in China is very good — the "Soviet way". Here I saw another way — more active learning. Before, we gave students no choices — no electives. I believe we should give students more choices now. The Soviet style is good for low-level students because they can't direct themselves. But it is not good for high-level students.'

Others found it more difficult to implement changes in their teaching style and in their institutions. Some found it difficult to overcome their students' passivity: 'Students are active in the USA, but in China students are used to just listening. This is difficult to change.' Others found that philosophical differences with administrators became a barrier for change. 'I had many ideas from the USA, but the leaders of my university did not agree with me. I wrote an article comparing Chinese and American advisors. I like the way an American advisor helps students to do research and gives support to the student.' One scholar reported, 'I can make no drastic changes; the social systems are very different. Many things are not transferable, yet it was a helpful experience.'

According to the sample, scholars reporting both research and teaching responsibilities jumped from 52% before going to the USA to 61% immediately on their return. For instance, 14% of the sample reported teaching postgraduate students, whereas they had previously taught only undergraduates. One scholar noted the importance of this preparation, 'My Illinois experience helped to establish standards for our postgraduate programmes. I gained ideas for the administrative work of our department.' The number reporting only research duties before coming to the USA was 28%; this figure dropped to 19% after returning, as research institutes moved into postgraduate education. The US-trained scholars felt well-prepared for these changes. One scholar declared, 'I really know how to teach students now — how to assign problems beyond using textbooks only.' Updated in their disciplines and armed with new research methodologies and ideas, they felt quite confident about their subject areas and could practise the new ways of teaching they had experienced. This confidence is reflected in the following comment, 'I now know how to train scientists and how to organize research.'

An important transfer of technology may occur in the teaching of undergraduate and postgraduate students who embody these new technologies and upon graduation take them into the workplace. The development of new courses might be one way of transferring the scholars' updated knowledge to their students. One scholar found that course creation can be facilitated if the department chair has had a similar overseas experience. 'The head of our department also had a US educational experience, so we made a lot of changes in our department. We moved US courses to China and even used US textbooks.'

Once these new ideas are accepted, the courses and textbooks can be adapted to the Chinese situation. This process hastens the transfer of knowledge and saves time and money on course development.

More than three-quarters of the sample reported having current responsibilities for either teaching or both research and teaching. In sum, while some respondents reported frustrations in implementing their new ideas, others seemed to have little difficulty transferring their American experience to the Chinese situation. As one scholar noted, 'I knew China needed this technology and I have been able to adapt and apply my knowledge to the Chinese situation.'

Transfer of technology often goes beyond scholarship into practical applications. Since his return, one professor had published papers on the Morrow Plots (the oldest long-term, unirrigated experimental corn fields in the USA). He then approached the Ministry of Agriculture with a plan to establish the first long-term agricultural experiment station in the PRC, using the same plot of land year after year. He was awarded the money to carry out his plan. As a consequence, nine experiment stations in the PRC are based on the Illinois model. In another case, during his two years at Illinois, a scholar investigated a new line of high oil-content corn. Upon his return to the PRC, his research continued in collaboration with three major American seed companies — Northrup King, Pioneer and Pfizer.

As many as seven years may pass before students of overseas-trained faculty staff enter the labour market and contribute to the national economy.[9] This lag, along with other factors such as antiquated laboratory facilities, inadequate funding, lack of time allocated for research and university politics, all contribute to the delay in transfer of learned technologies. Although a full assessment of the Visiting Scholars Programme is premature, early indications suggest positive returns.

ADVANCING RESEARCH SKILLS

Nearly 60% of the returned scholars reported that they were using new research methods, many involving computers. Almost 50% recognized that their training had changed their research methodology. One scholar commented, 'My advisor was very good. He did both experimental and theoretical research work. Before I came here, I only did experimental work, now I try to do both.' Another stated, 'I use new instruments for new subjects and have new ideas for research.'

One-third of the participants believed that newly acquired research methodologies were the most important benefit of their stay in the USA. One reported:

> I learned how scientists organize their scientific work. This gave me ideas of how to catch up with the world in science. US scientific instruments are very advanced. China is behind — even now we don't have many computers. Before and after the Cultural Revolution we did not do good work — our scientific level was low in research. After I returned, I learned how to design scientific research and how to put a research programme into practice. This helped me professionally a lot.

More than 15% of the returned scholars thought that new ideas for research were the most important outcome of their Illinois experience. Related to these newly acquired research methodologies were new ideas for research. 'I learned a new field, Artificial Intelligence [AI]. This was helpful in establishing a new research group when I returned. Now we have undergraduates as well as postgraduate students working in this field and we offer courses in AI.'

Others mentioned that their Illinois experience gave them confidence, stating that they were now willing to take risks and to fight for better working conditions and better equipment. Related to this boost in self-confidence is the fact that on return to the PRC, almost three-quarters of the scholars reported improved job performance and satisfaction after their experience abroad.

The lack of equipment and materials for use in research and teaching in the PRC was mentioned most often by respondents as preventing them from carrying out the research they began at Illinois. About 13% reported that they were unable to use the same research methods in the PRC as they had used in the USA. A technology gap between universities in the two countries was attributed to lack of equipment and materials. Some scholars were able to overcome equipment deficiencies by building their own equipment or borrowing another institution's laboratory. One teacher, for example, built himself a microcomputer based on a similar one he used at Illinois. Another secured support to go to Italy for six months so he could run a large software programme that computers at his own university could not handle.

The technology gap was in a large part the result of insufficient funding for basic research. From 1986 to 1988 research funding in the PRC was cut from US$26 million to US$13 million.[10] One scholar lamented, 'I have new ideas about hyperthermia, but our library is poor and there is no money for this research.' Another related, 'I don't have the money or equipment in China to complete the work I began at Illinois. We don't have lab animals like rabbits for experimentation in China. In the USA the results are tested by repeating the experiment. In China we don't have the conditions to repeat the experiment.'

The technology gap remains in some fields such as energy production, petrochemicals and technologies to protect the environment.[11] But the PRC has begun to close the gap in other areas such as textile production and telecommunications.[12] Until 1986 research institutes and universities in the PRC received funds from the government for research activities. These funds were distributed to department chairs, who in turn gave the money to their faculty members to do their research. With the establishment of the Natural Science Fund (*Guojia Ziran Kexue Jijin*) and the Social Science Fund (*Guojia Shehui Kexue Jijin*) in 1986 and the initiation of a peer review process, the research climate in the PRC is far more competitive today than in the past.[13]

Former visiting scholars were able to compete more successfully than their peers who lacked a foreign educational experience for rather scarce research funds, reported in 1987 to be worth ¥50 million earmarked to fund 34 key projects. The ability to win research awards is important not only for the scholar's own research, but for their universities and institutes as well. For example, Qinghua University reported that money earned from these projects had not only made up budgetary deficits but had also increased individual salaries, with staff members receiving bonuses up to ¥1000.[14]

That visiting scholars were able to win more research grants is consistent with the sample's responses to questions regarding the most important outcome of their stay in the USA. Almost 60% of the visiting scholars reported that they were using these newly acquired research methods, and nearly one-third said that new and improved research methods were the most important outcome of their visit. Thus, spending their time at a major research institution enabled them to win more research awards and have more joint research projects than their peers in the comparison group, in part because of the excellent role models for research they had encountered.

Visiting scholars conducted more joint research than their peers with no foreign educational experience. Scientists interviewed indicated that breakthroughs in science today are not likely to be made by any one individual working alone in a laboratory. At the time of this study, the PRC had few state-of-the-art facilities, so joint research provided a mechanism to maximize results. No one person has all the interdisciplinary skills needed, nor is all the equipment necessary for a comprehensive study usually found 'under one roof'. Therefore, joint research is important for the efficient use of both human and material resources.

PUBLISHING

Although publication of many journals was halted for the years of the Cultural Revolution, by 1979 the PRC was publishing 1200 journals, magazines and periodicals for national distribution. Nine hundred of these related to science and technology, 130 to literature and the arts and the remainder to the social sciences. In addition, another 610 were published locally.[15]

The dissemination of new knowledge through publishing was an important dimension of the scholars' newly acquired knowledge. Several scholars mentioned that they had published more since their experience abroad. One scholar described his experience as follows:

> Before coming to the USA all my papers were published in domestic journals — therefore, not accessible to the world community. Only after studying in the USA did I publish in international journals. I published six papers while in the USA. It was a milestone of my academic life. It changed my life and that of my colleagues as well, as I encourage them to publish in international journals, too.

Although the visiting scholars won more research awards and had more joint research projects than their peers who did not go abroad, the former group's publishing record was not significantly better than the latter's. Publishing over their entire careers shows no significant difference between the groups in terms of numbers of articles, books, or chapters of books published. In fact, the comparison group published more books and more chapters in books on average than the visiting scholars (though this was not statistically significant).[16] Presenting a paper at a conference is another means of disseminating new knowledge. The visiting scholars did give significantly more conference papers than their peers.

New knowledge can be protected by patenting. More than three-quarters of the visiting scholars were in science-related fields, and patenting is a recognized indicator of productivity in the sciences. However, China has no long-standing tradition of patenting. Although the PRC has had a patent law since the early 1950s, there was no patenting activity during the Cultural Revolution. Only in the last 20 years has patenting been encouraged. In 1984 the China Council for the Promotion of International Trade opened the country's first patent agency.[17] The Patent Law, which became effective in April 1985, protects the rights of inventors and creators.[18]

In addition, the Chinese have the right to monetary payments for their inventions and the right to disclose those inventions.[19]

Just 9% of the sample and 2% of the comparison group reported applying for one or more Chinese patents. There was not a significant difference between the sample and the comparison group with respect to patenting activity for Chinese or international patents applied for or granted.

REWARDS FOR PRODUCTIVITY

Rewards for productivity come in several forms. The most obvious are salary and promotions. Chinese academics are paid in other ways that include non-monetary perquisites such as work-related travel and housing allocation. Table 5.3 summarizes these data.

Table 5.3
Rewards: sample versus comparison group

Variable	Sample	Comparison group
Salary*	¥154	¥136
Promotions**	1.72	1.11
Work-related travel**	2.08	2.71
Housing**	2.56	3.05

Notes: The above figures are means. T-tests indicate that these variables were: * significant at the 0.05 level or **significant at the 0.005 level. Respondents were asked the number of work-related trips — domestic or international — that they took per year, from 0–2 trips to more than 6 trips. They were asked to rate their current housing on a scale from one (very good) to five (very poor).

Salaries

On average, the visiting scholars reported higher salaries, but the differences were not statistically significant.[20] The wage system in the PRC, however, is of crucial importance when looking at earnings. Jiaotong University is an example of wage reform in academia in the PRC. The major aim of the reforms at Jiaotong was to smash the 'iron rice bowl' and eliminate the practice of 'everyone eating from the same big public pot',[21] the egalitarian system of wage distribution which ignored performance. The university drafted new rules for promotion and pay raises. Before implementation there were 54 associate professors, each earning ¥133 per month. After implementation, these 54 had different salaries ranging from ¥160 to ¥208 per month.[22] Rewarding faculty according to the principle of 'each according to his/her work' allows wages to begin to reflect productivity.

A major problem of using earnings as a proxy for productivity in the PRC is that observed market wages frequently do not fully reflect the social benefits of education because wages are set by nonmarket forces such as the government. Nevertheless, the average salary rise for visiting scholars' *danwei* was one step on the salary schedule every two years. However, a person with outstanding research work could jump two or three steps on the salary schedule in a single year. For the visiting scholars, multivariate regression analysis revealed that none of the productivity indicators contributed significantly to variance in salary. However, the salary regression for their peers revealed two variables that contributed significantly to variance in salary: research awards received and the number of books written.

Professors who want to work for another university or for industry must have the permission of their current university and, of course, the permission of the *danwei* to which they want to transfer. Moving cities requires governmental authority to approve change in permanent residence registration (*hukou*). In general, the more skilled the employee, the more difficult it is to gain permission to change jobs. Each work-unit holds the employee's personal file (*dang'an*), and without its release the employee cannot get another job — with a Chinese or foreign enterprise — nor can he/she get a passport.[23] If a person leaves his/her job without the permission of the work-unit, his/her personal file is held, virtually blocking other employment for that employee.[24] In sum, these various factors — housing, *hukou* and *dang'an* — make changing jobs very difficult.

Human Capital theory asserts that education and on-the-job training rather than just age account for the life cycle earnings of individuals. Age is an important factor in promotion in the PRC and therefore, in salary. Also, since public income is more equally distributed than private income, and the larger the size of the public sector, the lower the inequalities, the differences in academic salaries were expected to be more narrow in the PRC than in capitalist countries.

The wage system for civil servants and urban factory workers in the PRC fails to reflect the productivity they acquire either through education or experience.[25] This holds true for academics as well. The determinants of income from sideline activities in the PRC show the impact of schooling: a 10% increase in income from sideline activities for every extra year of schooling for the head of household, according to one study.[26] As initiative and entrepreneurship have become important enough to take advantage of the emergence of free markets in the rural area, education seems to play a very significant role. Similar outcomes would be expected for academics in the PRC because they are now allowed to contract with industry, engage in consulting work or hold patents — all of which offer some monetary rewards to the individual as well as the work-unit. Differences in income would be expected due to these rewards for increased productivity.

Relatively high return rates to the PRC and lack of labour mobility mean that the transfer of technology effected by a visiting scholar is likely to accrue to the workplace that originally sent the scholar abroad to study. The relative lack of labour mobility paired with a very small private sector means that for scholars in the PRC there are no significant market factors affecting professorial salaries. Average salaries for social science and humanities professors in both the sample and the comparison group were lower than those in the 'hard' sciences, and this reflects more the political value placed on disciplines that are seen to enhance economic development (such as engineering) than the relative market value.

Academic salaries are very low in comparison to other wages in the PRC. In 1988, a taxi driver in Beijing could make as much as five times the monthly salary of a full professor per month (as much as ¥1000).[27] A peddler can earn even more — as much as ¥3000, whereas the mean monthly salary for a full professor in the sample was ¥211.[28]

Scholars were asked to report their base salaries without bonuses. At the time of this study, various bonuses were appended to salaries in the PRC in order to subsidize food, to alleviate some of the effects of inflation and to cover other living expenses. Bonuses could add an extra ¥30 to ¥60 per month to the base salary. One scholar reported the following monthly salary ranges for the various ranks at her university in 1988:

Lecturers/assistant professors   ¥80–¥130
Associate professors   ¥121–¥150
Full professors   ¥160–¥356

There have been no regular adjustments to salaries over the past 20 to 30 years in the PRC. One scholar reported that her salary was the same from 1956 to 1979. For these years there was little inflation compared to the 1980s and 1990s. As part of the 1986 salary reform, academics were given increases. Several scholars reported lower salaries because they were abroad in 1986 and thus not eligible for the increase.

One way to raise income is to engage in consulting. Indeed, the entrepreneurial spirit that has touched other parts of the Chinese economy has had an impact on the university campus as well. An increasingly important source of external income for both individuals and institutions is the contract mode of research and development. Contract research is seen as a means of disseminating scientific knowledge throughout the nation. The financial benefits of this activity accrue to both the institutions and the individuals involved. Payment for university-based research commonly comes through a fee per service, a percentage based on results or a service charge.[29]

Since 1986, researchers have been permitted to do work outside of their research institutes and many people, educators and scientific personnel included, have been taking second jobs. More than 1.39 million people employed in specialized fields in the PRC now have second or part-time jobs. These people account for about 14% of the country's total number of 'specialized and technical personnel' — a term that refers to college graduates who are now working in technical fields, scientific research and education. They are engaged in technological development, consultancy and other services.[30]

Visiting scholars would be expected to have greater consulting income than their peers because the former had been exposed to the latest technology and would therefore be in greater demand. Indeed, when comparing the two groups' entire career, the visiting scholars had more consulting contracts than their peers. Policies regarding outside contracts and consulting vary from institution to institution. One scholar related, 'At my university, 20% of the contract money is divided among the project team.' Another stated, 'You can keep 20% of your income from consulting, 80% goes to the university.' Yet another said, 'Our team has several contracts, but the money is used for equipment or travel, none is personal income.' A number reported that much of their consulting was purely service and that no remuneration was expected. According to one academic, 'The amount of consulting I do depends on myself. I want to concentrate on my research so I'm not so active in getting consulting income.'

Monetary reward was not the most important criterion for accepting a consulting contract. Rather, a contract would be accepted if the consulting opportunity would extend or enrich the scholar's current research. In some consulting situations money is not involved. One scholar in the sample described a barter situation, where he teaches his daughter's violin teacher English in exchange for his daughter's violin lessons. Values played a large part in the decision to accept or not to accept outside contracts. One scholar noted, 'I like to do research on high-level projects, not on low-level work, though it will bring in money.' Another related, 'Three or four enterprises have approached me, but I am too busy. I don't want to do that.'

The visiting scholars and the comparison group are very close in age. The values of their generation still reflect more of a 'serve the people' attitude than those of the younger generation. For full and associate professors, this translates in a preference for teaching over consulting. Their younger peers, the assistant professors, earned more from outside activities (see Table 5.4). No female assistant professor reported consulting income; however, the data for female full professors and female associate professors also indicate that the associate professors reported more income from consulting than their full professor colleagues.

Table 5.4
Average monthly income from outside contracts/consulting
by rank and sex

Rank and sex	Sample	Comparison group
Full Professor		
male	¥41.67	0
female	¥26.65	0
Associate Professor		
male	¥31.46	¥43.80
female	¥49.98	¥14.04
Assistant Professor		
male	¥66.66	¥65.78
female	0	¥35.42

Note: Exchange rate in July 1988 was ¥3.71 to US$1.

Promotions

For the decade preceding the initiation of the Visiting Scholars Programme, there were no promotions at universities in the PRC. When the scholars arrived at Illinois, the majority (almost 55%) were in the lowest professorial rank — that of assistant professor. An additional 30% of the sample held the title of associate professor and none held the rank of full professor. Immediately after their return to the PRC, there was little change in rank. However, there were major changes reported in job responsibilities, especially in the area of postgraduate student education, because the decade since the Cultural Revolution saw the inauguration of postgraduate schools within Chinese institutions of higher education — both universities and research institutes.

Since their return, 91% of the visiting scholars have received promotions and have had significantly more promotions in the past ten years than their peers without overseas experience. As discussed earlier, the visiting scholars' productivity was significantly greater and a higher promotion rate resulted.

While there was not an immediate change in most of the scholars' titles upon their return to the PRC, there was a significant change in their duties. More than 60% reported having new duties of teaching and research compared to 52% before going to the USA; 14% reported that they taught postgraduate students whereas before their Illinois experience they had taught only undergraduates. As noted earlier, the percentage reporting having only research duties dropped from 28% prior to attending the University of Illinois to 19% after their return.

Scholars also assumed administrative duties upon their return. Before going to the USA only 8% of the sample reported having duties other than teaching and research, which included administration. Immediately upon their return, 17% reported assuming administrative duties. At the time of the study 38% reported having administrative duties compared with 18% in the comparison group. These new duties included leadership positions with titles such as vice-chair of department, directorships or headships of centres, programmes, labs, and research and teaching groups. Several scholars, however, did not appreciate the move into administration. One expressed his frustrations at being assigned as a full-time administrator when what he wanted to do was to teach history. Another, who was a department chair, lamented that paperwork was taking him away from his research, which in turn was nullifying the effect of the Visiting Scholars Programme.

Non-monetary perquisites

Academics with foreign exchange experience were more productive than their counterparts who had not had this opportunity, and this productivity could be rewarded in non-monetary ways (perquisites), such as housing or work-related travel, especially if salary was not an available means for reward.[31]

Even though a number of visiting scholars believed that domestic travel in the PRC was indeed no reward (sometimes even a punishment), they were in fact travelling more than their peers. The difference between the groups in the number of research awards and joint research projects could account for some of the difference in the amount of reported travel.

Foreign travel is coveted as university money for foreign travel is scarce in the PRC. Many scholars indicated that they had papers accepted at international conferences but could not attend because they lacked travel funds. However, several had joint research projects that necessitated travel — one had been to England twice and another to Italy. One reported going abroad every year. That sample scholars were more successful at obtaining travel funds and were allowed to travel more than their peers is an indirect benefit of the Visiting Scholars Programme, as many scholars reported that while in the USA they had made international contacts in their fields that were potentially helpful in getting other invitations.

Housing was another non-salary perquisite that institutions used to reward scholars. Housing was assigned on the basis of seniority — a professor's age, number of years teaching, rank and the number of people in his/her immediate family. Scholars perceived housing allocation as unrelated to productivity and rank appears to be the main factor determining housing quality.[32]

CONCLUSION

Despite impediments to implementing change, most Chinese scholars who returned from the University of Illinois used in their current jobs the skills they acquired overseas. The Visiting Scholars Programme is an example of an educational policy that paid high returns.

Returned scholars were more productive than their colleagues who had not gone abroad for training. The former gave more conference papers than their peers, developed more new courses, had more consulting contracts, participated in more joint research projects and received greater numbers of research awards. Compared to their peers, the visiting scholars had significantly higher salaries, received significantly more promotions, did significantly more travelling, and rated their housing as significantly more satisfactory. In comparing the entire career of the comparison and the work of the visiting scholars only since their return to the PRC, the sample was still more productive than the comparison group in two areas: the number of joint research projects and the number of research awards received.

One-third of the sample reported that newly acquired research methods were the most important outcome of their stay at Illinois; a majority of the sample reported that their US experience changed the way that they thought about their teaching style or methodology. As a result, they now encouraged their students to be more active learners, assigned students to memorize less and read more, and assigned more lab work and more hands-on computer problems.

Transfer of technology took place despite the lack of state-of-the-art facilities, equipment and adequate financial investment in education. This transfer resulted because scholars brought home from the US research areas that were new to the PRC (such as artificial intelligence), new research ideas (especially in the fields of agriculture, engineering and computer science), and new teaching methods and materials.

Simple quantification fails to do justice to the far-reaching impact of the research contributions of the returned scholars. Investigations into new varieties of corn, for example, could change the eating habits of millions of Chinese consumers. The introduction of computer networking could help establish a service and information industry in the PRC. Moreover, since the time lag for investment in higher education may be as long as seven years, the full effects of the Visiting Scholars Programme may only just now become evident. The power of investing in educators potentially yields a multiplier effect on each of the hundreds of students whom each educator teaches. Updating knowledge, learning new research techniques and observing new teaching methods all make a scholar a better teacher. Most returned scholars felt that their Illinois experience changed the way they thought about their teaching style or methodology. Further research, however, is required before educators fully understand how different teaching techniques encourage students to be active learners and independent thinkers. Nevertheless, returns from the Visiting Scholars Programme have enabled the PRC to produce a better educated workforce who substantially contribute to the nation's modernization and economic development.

NOTES

1. Lampton, 1986, p. 18.
2. Lampton, 1986, p. 2.
3. Lampton, 1986, p. 52.
4. This research was undertaken for the author's Ph.D. dissertation, Shoresman, 1989. The sample approximates the geographical representation of scholars at Illinois from the PRC:

Location	All scholars		Sample	
Beijing	65	34%	41	33%
Shanghai	32	17%	19	15%
Nanjing	12	6%	8	6%
Other	82	43%	57	46%
Total	191	100%	125	100%

5. The sample's average age is 50.5 and is 87.5% male; respective figures for the comparison group are 49.1 and 60%. By rank:

	Sample		Comparison Group	
Full Professor	15	23.4%	0	0
Male	13	86.7%		
Female	2	13.3%		
Associate Professor	41	64.1%	32	71.1%
Male	36	87.8%	18	56.3%
Female	5	12.2%	14	43.8%
Assistant Professor	8	12.5%	13	28.9%
Male	7	87.5%	9	69.2%
Female	1	12.5%	4	30.8%

6. Data for the groups by undergraduate degree area:

	Sample		Comparison Group	
Engineering	18	28.1%	10	22.2%
Physical Science	15	23.3%	8	17.8%
Agriculture	9	14.1%	9	20.0%
Computer Science/Maths	9	14.1%	7	15.6%
Biological Science	4	6.3%	4	8.9%
Social Science	5	7.8%	5	11.1%
Foreign Languages	4	6.3%	2	4.4%
Total	64	100%	45	100%

7. Jackson, 1986, p. 121.
8. Paine, 1992a, p. 201.
9. McMahon, Yates, *et al.*, 1987, p. 23.
10. Smith, 1988, p. 16.
11. Y.H. Song, 1996.
12. Rehak and Wang, 1996.
13. See Chapter 4 by Wenhui Zhong in this volume.
14. *China Daily*, 1 July 1988, p. 4.
15. 'Publication', *Beijing Review* 22, no. 47, 23 November 1979, p. 31.
16. The comparisons between the groups are based purely on the quantity of publications; no attempt was made to determine qualitative differences.
17. 'China launches patent agency', *Beijing Review* 27, no. 32, 6 August 1984, p. 7.
18. Hu Mingzheng, 1984, p. 23.
19. Gale, 1978, p. 34.
20. T-tests were performed to determine whether there were statistically significant differences between the two groups in any of these measures. Pearson Correlation Coefficients were used to determine whether any of the reward measures (salary, travel, housing and promotions) correlated with any of the productivity measures. Finally, regression analysis was used to determine the amount of variance in salary due to each productivity measure.
21. Li Yongzeng, 1984, pp. 19–20.
22. Li Yongzeng, 1984, p. 20.

23. 'Technicians list complaint', *China Daily*, 26 July 1988; also an interview with a visiting scholar in Shanghai, June 1988.
24. Interview with a visiting scholar in Shanghai, June 1988.
25. Jamison and Van Der Gaag, 1986, p. 4.
26. Jamison and Van Der Gaag, 1986, p. 5.
27. 'Invest in scientific research', *China Daily*, 1 July 1988, p. 4.
28. *China Daily*, 26 July 1988, p. 5.
29. Cleverley, 1987, p. 6.
30. *China Daily*, 12 July 1988, p. 4.
31. For a discussion of non-monetary perquisites, see Bian, 1994.
32. When asked to rate their housing, visiting scholars reported significantly greater satisfaction with their housing conditions than their peers, even though the sample had been abroad and could compare their own housing conditions in China to those available elsewhere.

6

Modernizing Science Through Educating the Elite

Cong CAO

INTRODUCTION

In embarking on the Four Modernizations, the PRC placed intrinsic importance on science. Following the chaos of the Cultural Revolution, the nation's leadership decided to emphasize scientific research and to increase the number and quality of scientists. This endeavour was undertaken through many strategies, including the developing of the scientific élite.

The making of scientists is affected by several factors, among which education and performance serve as the two defining criteria for the status of scientists.[1] Of course, the relationship between the two criteria is not causal: a higher educational level does not necessarily guarantee better career performance. The effect of scientists' completed education may indeed operate through their performance. This chapter, based on theories explored by Western sociologists of science, examines the relationship between educational attainment and the formation of an élite group of scientists in China — academicians (*yuanshi*) of the Chinese Academy of Sciences (CAS, *Zhongguo Kexueyuan*).

International research on the educational attainment of scientists has reached two major conclusions. First, education plays an influential role as scientists begin their careers.[2] Second, the education institution itself is important, with prestigious educational institutions turning out more productive scientists than non-élite academies.[3] Research on the influence of education on the formation of the US scientific élite — Nobel laureates and the members of the National Academy of Sciences (NAS) — reveals that a large proportion of the élite have trained at a very small number of élite institutions.[4] Studies have concluded that 'recruitment into the élite involved their early concentration within the social and educational structure',[5] and have found a 'relationship between early location in the stratification system and ultimate success'.[6] If there is indeed a universalism in science,[7] education should be one of the universal criteria for the status of scientists. This chapter examines the extent to which this is the case for the PRC.

This study mainly uses the method of collective biographical analysis, with data coming from biographies of CAS academicians.[8] In testing for universalism of education in the fostering of élite scientists, it explores whether the experience of Western capitalist countries can be extended to the PRC, a socialist system. In particular, it examines the undergraduate and postgraduate origins of élite Chinese scientists, compares election cohort characteristics of these scientists in their educational attainment patterns, and looks at whether mentor-student relationships play a part in scientists' election as CAS members. First, the CAS membership system is described.

THE CHINESE ACADEMY OF SCIENCES AND MEMBERSHIP SELECTION[9]

The CAS was established on 1 November 1949, exactly a month after the new CCP government proclaimed the People's Republic. It was created out of the two academies run by the former Guomindang (Nationalist) government, the Academia Sinica (*Guoli Zhongyang Yanjiuyuan*) and the Peiping Academy (*Guoli Beiping Yanjiuyuan*), both of which dated back to 1927.[10] The CAS, being at the pinnacle of the Chinese scientific community, is headquartered in Beijing and is now composed of 132 research institutes scattered throughout the country.[11] Designed to assume 'academic leadership' through its different academic departments (*xuebu*),[12] it is empowered to 'attract prominent scientists from across the country to take part in its academic direction'.[13]

The CAS establishment of academic departments in 1955 followed the model of the Academy of Sciences of the former USSR.[14] It began with four academic departments: Physics, Mathematics and Chemistry; Biological and Earth Sciences; Technical Sciences (such as electrical engineering, mechanical engineering, civil engineering, architecture and other applied scientific fields); and Philosophy and Social Sciences. After selection by scientists and approval by the CCP according to three criteria — academic achievement, promotion of the disciplines and loyalty to the people's cause[15] — the first academic department membership (*xuebu weiyuan*) was awarded by the State Council to 233 scientists, three-quarters of whom were natural scientists.[16] In 1957, 21 additional members (18 from the natural sciences) were selected jointly by scientists and the CCP, bringing the total to 254, and one department was divided into the Department of Biological Sciences and the Department of Earth Sciences.[17] During the Cultural Revolution decade (1966–76), not only were the activities of the CAS academic departments completely disrupted, but also several members lost their lives to political persecution.[18]

Since 1977, in pursuit of the Four Modernizations, scientific research in the PRC has boomed. In early 1979, the activities of the 'smashed' CAS academic departments were formally resumed and the reputation of denounced academic department members was rehabilitated.[19] The Department of Philosophy and Social Sciences split off into the Chinese Academy of Social Sciences in 1975.

Because of a shrinking and ageing membership — the average age in 1979 was 73 — the first election of CAS membership in 22 years was held in 1979–80, in which 117 members cast anonymous ballots, electing 283 new members. At the same time, the Department of Physics, Mathematics and Chemistry was split into a Department of Mathematics and Physics and a Department of Chemistry.[20] The injection of new members reduced the average age to 66;[21] more importantly, this election marked the formalization of electoral procedures. Contrary to the 1955 and 1957 elections in which the Party was deeply involved, this was the first time when Chinese scientists engaged in an élite election which was merit-based, peer-reviewed, academically democratic and without interference from the CCP and the government. Existing CAS members decided the number of new members to be elected and set the criteria for election as those who 'support the Party and socialism and have made important achievements in and contributions to our country's research in science and technology'.[22] Candidates were recommended by two or more academic department members, or CAS-affiliated institutes, research institutions under governmental ministries, institutions of higher education, science commissions of provinces, municipalities and autonomous regions, or scientific societies. Institutional nominees had to be first screened by units at a higher administrative level. CAS members then evaluated all candidates for their respective academic departments, a process which yielded a final candidate list. After anonymous voting by current CAS members, the State Council gave a *pro-forma* approval.

No new members were selected during the 1980s, but in 1991, 210 scientists were elected to the academic departments through a similar procedure as in the 1980 election. Elections have since become a biennial event. In January 1994, the Chinese title changed from 'academic department member' (*xuebu weiyuan*) to 'academician' (*yuanshi*), the latter now being the highest lifetime academic honour given to distinguished Chinese scientists. The first CAS by-laws, adopted in 1992 and amended in 1994, make eligible for membership those 'scientists with research fellow, professor or similar academic titles and Chinese nationality (including overseas residents and the residents of the regions of Taiwan, Hong Kong and Macao) who have made systematic and creative achievements and major contributions in the fields of science and technology and who are patriotic and honest and upright in their style of learning'.[23] By 1996, a total of 801 Chinese natural scientists, including 36 women, had been elected (see Table 6.1).

Table 6.1
CAS academicians and election cohorts

Department \ Cohort	1955	1957	1980	1991	1993	1995	Total	Female
Mathematics and Physics	28	7	51	38	10	10	144	9
Chemistry	20	0	51	35	10	9	125	9
Biological Sciences	60	5	53	34	11	12	175	6
Earth Sciences	24	3	64	35	10	10	146	4
Technical Sciences	40	3	64	68	18	18	211	8
Total	172	18	283	210	59	59	801	
Female	1	0	14	12	3	6		36

Sources: *Renmin Ribao*, 3 June 1955, p. 1; 31 May 1957, p. 1; 30 March 1981, p. 4; 4 January 1992, p. 3; 30 December 1993, p. 3; 4 November 1995, p. 4.

Surveys conducted in the PRC on occupational prestige and on Chinese public attitudes towards science and technology find that the occupational status of scientists is very high (natural scientists hold the top rank), as in other countries.[24] For a long time, due to the absence of regular elections and the continual debate on whether academic department membership should be considered a working title or an academic honour,[25] the CAS academic departments never achieved the status equivalent to that of Western academies or royal societies. However, CAS academic department membership elections have always given a significant amount of weight to achievements scientists have made. Members have achieved renown, nationally if not worldly, and they have a reputation similar to that enjoyed by their counterparts who hold academicianship in other countries, and have formed a unique group of scientists in China. Current CAS academicians, who numbered 576 as of the end of 1995, are élite among about 380 000 Chinese scientists and engineers.[26]

EDUCATIONAL ATTAINMENT OF CAS MEMBERS

Undergraduate origin

Nearly all CAS members underwent undergraduate education. Other than several members who were self-educated,[27] members graduated from institutions of higher learning in mainland China, Hong Kong, Taiwan or abroad. The few exceptions include three practitioners of traditional Chinese medicine elected in 1955 who had acquired medical knowledge from their progenitors, something common to the discipline. Table 6.2 lists names of PRC institutions that have contributed ten or more CAS members.

These institutions may be categorized as either comprehensive, polytechnic or specialized. Comprehensive institutions, accounting for 50% of the total CAS members, offer courses in a broad spectrum of disciplines in the natural sciences, social sciences, humanities and even engineering. Polytechnic universities, known for their training programmes in the natural sciences and engineering, make up 29%. Some of these, such as Qinghua, Dongnan, Zhejiang and Jiaotong, were formerly comprehensive universities before their colleges of arts and sciences were moved so they could concentrate on engineering instruction.[28] The third category represents single speciality colleges, such as medicine and geology, which account for 15% of the élite membership.

Research outside the PRC discusses the accumulation of advantage in the more prestigious universities. For North America, a relationship exists between students, who acquire prestige from these universities, and universities themselves, which receive further prestige from their students as they become eminent.[29] In Britain, '[s]cientists trained at the more prestigious universities are exposed to a socialization process which helps them get a head start in becoming successful scientists'.[30] In both places a selective recruitment of students occurs at the more prestigious universities, where superior facilities and faculties are available. Do these explanations fit the situation in the PRC?

Table 6.2
Tertiary education of CAS academicians

University / College	1955-57*	1980	1991	1993	1995	Total
Comprehensive University						
Beijing University[a]	31	42	23	9	11	116
Nanjing University[b]	25	43	29	3	5	109
Southwest Associated University[c]	0	29	5	1	0	35
Fudan University	4	0	10	1	5	20
Wuhan University	1	5	10	1	0	17
Xiamen University	4	11	1	1	0	17
Zhongshan University[d]	4	10	1	0	0	15
Other key universities	5	8	4	7	1	25
Others	9	22	11	5	6	53
Subtotal						406
Polytechnic University						
Qinghua University[e]	27	39	20	4	2	92
Zhejiang University	2	24	10	2	2	40
Jiaotong University	7	14	11	1	1	34
Tianjin University[f]	8	12	4	1	1	26
Tongji University[g]	4	7	4	2	0	17
Other key universities	0	5	8	4	1	18
Others	0	0	3	0	1	4
Subtotal						232
Speciality College						
Beijing Geology College	0	0	6	3	2	11
Shanghai No. 1 Medical College	0	3	5	2	0	10
Other key universities	5	0	13	4	7	29
Others	11	4	11	2	6	34
Subtotal						84
Outside Mainland China	39	7	16	3	2	67
Unfinished Tertiary Education	2	1	1	0	0	4
Unknown	0	0	0	0	2	2
No Tertiary Education	4	2	1	0	0	0
Total	190	283	210	59	59	801

*   As the 1957 election provided only a small number of members — those who had failed to be elected in 1955 and recent returnees from abroad — it is combined with the 1955 election as one cohort.

[a]   Includes Beiping University and Yenching University

[b]   Includes Dongnan University, University of Nanking (*Jinling University*), Zhongyang University (Nanjing and Chongqing)

(Table 6.2 to be continued)

c   Southwest Associated University, located in Kunming from April 1938 to May
      1946, amalgamated Beijing, Qinghua and Nankai universities during the Anti-
      Japanese War
d   Includes Zhongshan University Medical School and Lingnan University
e   Includes Qinghua School
f   Includes Beiyang University, Beiping Engineering College, the Tangshan Institute
      of Technology, the Tangshan Institute of Railroads and the Hebei Institute of
      Technology
g   Includes Tongji University Medical School

Sources: *Elite in Chinese science*, 1985, 1988; *Academic department membership
           of the Chinese Academy of Sciences 1991*; *Kexue* (Science), vol. 46,
           nos. 5–6, 1994, vol. 47, nos. 1–3, 1995; *Zhongguo Kexue Bao* (China's
           Science News), overseas edition, 26 February, 1996, p. 6.

The universities listed in Table 6.2 represent part of China's key
(*zhongdian*), or prestigious, component of higher education.[31] Key
institutions usually have a longer history than their non-key counterparts,
which means that their prestige has been accumulating over a long term.
For example, Beijing University was founded in 1898; Jiaotong University
dates back to 1896. With their higher prestige, Beijing University and
Qinghua University claim to be China's equivalents of Harvard and the
Massachusetts Institute of Technology (MIT) in the hierarchy of US higher
education. For a long period, key universities have received support from
either the Nationalist or Communist government and have been able to
recruit superior faculties, maintain strong libraries and facilities, and make
outstanding academic achievements. Recently, Nanjing University, Beijing
University, and the University of Science and Technology of China, a
polytechnic institution, were ranked as the top three universities in science
and technology in the PRC based on publications and citation analysis.[32]
Able to recruit nationwide, these key educational institutions have also
placed a very high value on their role as a route of upward mobility for
students. As shown in Table 6.2, 15 key universities have produced a total
of 559 CAS members — about four-fifths of the élite with Chinese
undergraduate origins (722), and key universities have collectively reared
631 élite scientists, or 87% by the same measurement. In sum, access to the
nation's prestigious universities has become the primary path to scientific
élite membership in the PRC.
    The institutional origin of CAS members represents the uneven
geographical distribution of university education.[33] In imperial times, China
recruited its best scholars to study in its capitals. Centralization of academic
research provided China's capitals with significant status in higher

education. Nanjing, in which Nanjing University and Dongnan University are located, and Beijing, which houses Beijing University and Qinghua University, have served as the capitals of the Nationalist and Communist governments respectively. As a legacy of urban orientation, prestigious universities were also set up at such cities as Shanghai, Tianjin, Xiamen, Wuhan and Guangzhou. Although the demands of socialist construction have created regional centres of excellence, the role of metropolitan key universities has not been replaced.[34] Place of study is also related to discipline. In the case of geology, Beijing University alone has produced 45 CAS members.[35] At the turn of the century, industrial development in China necessitated the exploration of natural resources. Young students were sent abroad to study mining and geology. When they returned in the 1910s and 1920s, they worked in the Department of Geology at Beijing University, in turn training more geologists.[36]

Missionary education

Foreign missions had an impact on the development of China's higher education during the period from the mid-1850s to around 1950. Three of the earliest established Chinese universities — Beiyang, Jiaotong and Beijing — invited US missionaries as the Dean or the Director of Western Studies.[37] Before 1949, famous missionary higher educational establishments included Peking Union Medical College (*Beijing Xiehe Yixueyuan*, founded by missions from USA in 1906), West China University (*Huaxi Daxue*, USA and Britain, 1910), Hsiang Ya Medical College (*Xiangya Yixueyuan*, USA, 1914), Fuchow Union University (*Fuzhou Xiehe Daxue*, USA, 1915), the University of Nanking (*Jinling Daxue*, USA, 1917), Yenching University (*Yanjing Daxue*, USA, 1919), Fu Ren Catholic University (*Furen Daxue*, USA, 1929), among others.[38] However, during the educational institution adjustment in 1952, foreign missionary universities were all abolished.[39] Table 6.2 lists graduates from these former foreign missionary universities under the names of existing universities into which they were amalgamated. If counted separately, however, missionary universities produced a total of 88 (11%) CAS members — 24 from Yenching, 17 from Nanking and so on. The fact itself suggests a positive function of foreign missionary universities in nurturing élite Chinese scientists. Nevertheless, the role of missionary education in China is still controversial, and recent Chinese publications on the history of education in China continue to criticize the educational invasion by foreign countries.[40]

Postgraduate origin

Postgraduate training is an important process through which young scientists obtain training in theories and methodologies; it also provides them research experience. Many élite Chinese scientists have followed this pattern of pursuing postgraduate study. Among them, however, only 139 (17%) had postgraduate training in China.[41] In contrast to the small proportion of Chinese élite scientists who were trained at home, 423 (53%) earned Master's or doctoral degrees from foreign universities or research institutes. As indicated in Table 6.3, 29% of CAS members pursued postgraduate study in US universities. Universities in the USA also awarded more doctoral degrees (179) to CAS academicians than all other countries combined (165).

Many élite Chinese scientists received their degrees from élite foreign universities. Chinese scholars have come from US Ivy League universities such as Harvard (18), Cornell (16), Columbia (9), Yale (9), Princeton (7), Pennsylvania (4), and other prestigious universities, such as MIT (21), California Institute of Technology (Cal Tech) (19), Illinois (16), Chicago (15), Michigan (11), the University of California (8), Purdue (7), Carnegie Tech (6), Wisconsin (6) and so on. The Chinese scientific élite also have held degrees from famous universities outside the USA, including London (14), Cambridge (11), Paris (9), Berlin (8) and Munich (5).

The large number of foreign postgraduate degree holders among élite Chinese scientists from a particular school often corresponds to the strength of the field in that school. For example, Princeton has been well-known for its programme in mathematics; consequently, three out of the seven élite Chinese scientists who graduated from Princeton studied mathematics there. Columbia, which has been strong in chemistry and chemical engineering, has produced four of the Chinese élite in these areas. As the cradle of future élite Chinese physicists, Cal Tech has turned out 12 CAS members in the fields of physics, electronics and aerospace engineering. Cornell was the *alma mater* of 11 élite Chinese biologists in agronomy, ecology, entomology, genetics, mycology and zoology. Chinese scientists also studied under famous professors, including Nobel laureates Max Born, William L. Bragg, Arthur H. Compton, Archibald Hill, Richard Kuhn, Thomas H. Morgan, Linus Pauling, Ernest Rutherford, Erwin Schrödinger and Heinrich Wieland. In order to pursue excellence, the future Chinese scientific élite, if possible, tried to select the best programmes and best teachers. Through the processes of self-selection of students and social selection by institutions and teachers, the Chinese scientific élite had access in their formative stages to some of the greatest minds in world science.

Table 6.3
Foreign-trained postgraduate origins of CAS academicians

Country	1955-57	1980	1991*	1993	1995	Subtotal	Total
USA							
Doctoral	59	98	17	3	2	179	
Others	22	24	5	2	1	54	233
Great Britain							
Doctoral	16	29	5	0	0	50	
Others	4	5	2	0	0	11	61
Germany[a]							
Doctoral	20	9	2	0	0	33	
Others	0	1	0	0	0	1	34
France							
Doctoral	12	2	0	1	1	16	
Others	0	1	0	0	0	1	17
Japan							
Doctoral	4	0	3	0	0	7	
Others	3	1	0	0	0	4	11
Other Western Countries							
Doctoral	6	5	3	2	2	16	
Others	0	1	1	0	0	2	18
Former USSR							
Doctoral[b]	0	10	17	5	5	39	
Others	0	2	3	3	3	8	47
Eastern European Countries[c]							
Doctoral	0	0	2	0	0	2	
Others	0	0	0	0	0	0	2
Others							
Doctoral	0	1	0	0	1	2	
Others	0	0	0	0	0	0	2
Total							
Doctoral	118	154	49	13	11	344	
Others	29	35	11	2	4	81	425

[a] Includes the former West Germany
[b] Includes holders of candidate degrees (*fuboshi*)
[c] Includes those from the former East Germany
*   One member who holds two Master's degrees — one from UK and one from Australia — is counted twice. Another member who holds two Master's degrees — one from Australia and one from Germany — is also counted twice.

Some Chinese scientists received their degrees in the former USSR and Eastern European countries during the 1950s and early 1960s before the relationship between China and the USSR deteriorated. The former Soviet Academy of Sciences alone produced 18 CAS members. This tendency towards skewing to certain countries, either Western countries or the Eastern bloc during specific periods, reflects the influence of foreign policy on the training of scientific manpower in China.

Estimates suggest that about 1500 Chinese natural scientists who obtained doctoral degrees and candidate degrees (*fuboshi*) from abroad during the period from 1850 to 1962 have returned to China.[42] As indicated in Table 6.3, 344 CAS members are returnees. In other words, one-fifth of all returned foreign doctoral degree holders were elected to CAS, which indicates the significant effect of returned scientists in the élite group. This influence becomes more significant given that some foreign doctoral degree holders had already died when membership elections were held, and that few Chinese scientists either went or returned from overseas between 1962 and 1978.

MENTOR-STUDENT RELATIONSHIP: THE CASE OF ELITE CHINESE PHYSICISTS

Along with prestige of an educational institution, the presence of a mentor is an important determinant for CAS membership. Mentoring, of course, is not unique to China. Research on US Nobel laureates finds that '[t]he presence of great teachers accounts in part for the differential distribution of prizewinners among universities by field of work'.[43] The relationship between mentor and student also explains to some extent career advancement of students. The recruitment of Chinese physicists into CAS accords with the US findings.

A total of 110 physicists have been elected as CAS members in the Department of Mathematics and Physics (and its precursor the Department of Physics, Mathematics and Chemistry). They studied at universities in mainland China, Taiwan, the USA and the USSR (see Table 6.4).

Most of these physicists graduated from China's key universities. Besides those who graduated from colleges in Taiwan (two), the USA (four) and the USSR (three), only five élite Chinese physicists came from non-élite undergraduate institutions. Below, the cases of three universities — Qinghua, Beijing and Southwest Associated — will be examined.

Returned scientists from abroad have had a great influence on the training of Chinese scientists.[44] On their return to China, they usually taught at prestigious universities, where they guided one generation after another of Chinese scientists. Physicists Rao Yutai, Ye Qisun and Wu Youxun are generally recognized as the first-generation Chinese physicists, major figures who introduced modern physics into China. Rao and Ye obtained Ph.D. degrees from Princeton and Harvard in 1922 and 1923 respectively, and Wu studied under A. H. Compton, a 1927 Nobel Prize winner, at the University of Chicago, where he received a Doctorate in 1925. When the

Table 6.4
Undergraduate institutions of the Chinese élite physicists

University/College	1955-57	1980	1991	1993	1995	Total
Qinghua University	9	6	6	0	1	22
Beijing University[a]	3	7	7	3	1	21
Nanjing University[b]	4	8	7	0	1	20
Southwest Associated University[c]	0	7	0	0	0	7
Fudan University	0	0	4	1	1	6
Zhejiang University	0	2	1	0	1	4
Jiaotong University	1	2	0	0	0	3
University of Science and Technology of China Technology	0	0	3	0	0	3
Other Key's	4	4	0	2	0	10
Others	1	2	0	1	1	5
Outside Mainland China	4	2	1	1	1	9
Total	26	40	29	8	7	110

[a]   Includes Beiping University and Yenching University
[b]   Includes the University of Nanking (*Jinling University*), Nanjing Higher Normal College, Zhongyang University (Nanjing and Chongqing)
[c]   Southwest Associated University combined Beijing, Qinghua and Nankai universities during the Anti-Japanese War.

three scholars returned to China, they taught at Qinghua University and Beijing University, the most important training centres of Chinese physicists. Ye served as the chair of the Department of Physics and later as dean of the School of Sciences at Qinghua. He recruited into the Qinghua faculty scholars including Wu, Zhou Peiyuan and Zhao Zhongyao, the latter two both with Cal Tech Ph.Ds. (and being second-generation Chinese physicists). Similarly, at Beijing University Rao and his student Wu Ta-you, with a 1930 Ph.D. from Michigan, played important roles in building their faculty. Wu Ta-you, an accomplished Chinese physicist of the second generation, is now the president emeritus of the Academia Sinica in Taiwan.[45] When the Anti-Japanese War broke out in 1937, Qinghua and Beijing had to move to Kunming where they combined with another university, Nankai, into Southwest Associated University.[46] During that difficult period, scholars mainly from Qinghua and Beijing physics faculties made great efforts in training a generation of Chinese physicists. When the war was over, Qinghua and Beijing universities returned to Beijing. The educational institution readjustment of 1952 merged the basic science departments of Qinghua University and Yenching University into Beijing University, which has in turn taken top spot in educating Chinese physicists. Figure 6.1 depicts mentoring at Qinghua, Beijing and Southwest Associated universities before the readjustment when students had more autonomy in choosing their mentors.[47]

EDUCATIONAL ATTAINMENT PATTERNS AND THE RECRUITMENT OF THE ELITE

Undergraduate study at China's key universities, postgraduate study in foreign countries, and study with great mentors are factors that affect the recruitment of Chinese scientists into the élite. How have educational attainment patterns of the Chinese scientific élite changed over time? Levels of attained education may be categorized into the following patterns:
1. undergraduate study in China;
2. both undergraduate and postgraduate training in China;
3. undergraduate and postgraduate study in China, with final postgraduate degrees from a foreign university;
4. undergraduate study in China and postgraduate study abroad;
5. undergraduate study abroad; and
6. both undergraduate and postgraduate degrees abroad.

Table 6.5 depicts these attainment patterns for each of the five election cohorts of CAS membership. The data suggest that educational attainment patterns are directly related to election cohorts. Scientists with domestic undergraduate education and foreign postgraduate education dominated the first two elections. This mirrors the history of higher education in China.

China's modern higher education developed as Chinese students returned from abroad. Under the suggestion and supervision of Rong Hong, the first Chinese who was awarded a Bachelor's degree from Yale University, the first batch of Chinese teenage boys was sent to America in 1872 with the hope of absorbing Western academic thought and contributing to China's future. Students were also sent to European countries and Japan. They returned with Western science and technology and they became the Chinese élite in various fields.[48] However, it was the students who studied in the USA under the Boxer Indemnity Scholarship Programme (*gengzhi peikuan jiangxuejin*)[49] who became the driving force of China's efforts in advancing modern science. Among the CAS members elected in 1955 and 1957, 39 (20%) held foreign undergraduate degrees and 34 continued for postgraduate study, most being Boxer Indemnity beneficiaries. Upon their return to China in the early twentieth century, they helped stimulate and

	Qinghua University (1920-37)	Beijing University (1920-37)	Southwest Associated University (1938-46)
First Generation	Ye Qisun* (Harvard, 1923)	Yutai Rao* (Princeton, 1922)	
Second Generation	Zhou Peiyuan* (Cal Tech, 1928)	Wu Youxun* (Chicago, 1926) Zhao Zhongyao* (Cal Tech, 1930)	
Third Generation	Wang Ganchang (1929)* Zhou Tongqing (1929)*# Fu Chenyi (1929)# Gong Zhutong (1930)** Wang Zhuxi (1933)* Zhao Jiuzhang (1933)*# Lu Xueshan (1933, graduate)* Weng Wenbo (1934)** Zhang Zhongsui (1934)* Peng Huanwu (1935)* Qian Weichang (1935)* Qian Sanqiang (1936)* Wang Daheng (1936)* He Zehui (1936)** Ge Tingsui (1937)* Zhang Enqiu (1938)**#	Guo Yonghuai (1935)* Ma Dayou (1936)*	Li Yinyuan (1943)** Huang Kun (1944, graduate)* Deng Jiaxian (1945)** Zhu Guangya (1945)**

	Qinghua University (1946-52)	Beijing University (1946-52)	
Fourth Generation	Wang Zhuqia (1948)** Li Deping (1948)*** Zhou Guangzhao (1951)** He Zuoxiu (1951)** Hu Renyu (1952)*** Pu Fuke (1952)*** Huang Shengnian (1952)*** Guo Zhongheng (1952)***	Yu Ming (1949)**	

*1955-57 election cohort   ** 1980 election cohort   *** 1991 election cohort
physicists who were not in the Department of Mathematics and Physics

Figure 6.1 CAS members who had physics training in Qinghua, Beijing and Southwest Associated universities

Table 6.5
Educational attainment patterns and election cohorts

Patterns \ Election Cohort	1955-57	1980	1991	1993	1995	Total
1. Home Undergraduate	31	69	103	38	31	272
2. Home Undergraduate / Home Postgraduate	2	21	40	4	11	78
3. Home Undergraduate / Home Postgraduate / Foreign Postgraduate	19	28	6	3	5	61
4. Home Undergraduate / Foreign Postgraduate	93	155	45	11	8	312
5. Foreign Undergraduate	5	2	7	2	0	16
6. Foreign Undergraduate / Foreign Postgraduate	34	5	8	1	2	50
No Tertiary Education	4	2	0	0	0	6
Others and Unknown*	2	1	1	0	2	6
Total	190	83	210	59	59	801

* Includes traditional Chinese medicine practitioners, those who received undergraduate education in Taiwan or Hong Kong, and those whose educational attainment patterns are unknown

develop undergraduate education. In fact, 145 (76%) of the 1955–57 elected members attended higher education institutions in mainland China, and some of them were selected in the same election cohort as their mentors. In the 1920s and 1930s, an undergraduate degree was the highest pursuit for the élite-to-be unless they went abroad. During the early 1930s, postgraduate education was established at prestigious Chinese universities, such as Jiaotong, Qinghua and Beijing, and formal postgraduate study became institutionalized as a virtual prerequisite for admission into the ranks of scientists. However, some students still used Chinese undergraduate or postgraduate training as the springboard for obtaining a higher degree abroad. This contributed to the higher numbers of the third and fourth categories in the first two membership elections. Since 1978, with China reopening its door, many scientists have been dispatched to developed countries in the West, resulting in a significant impact on the development of their fields.[50] In fact, among 73 of the 1991–95 elected CAS members with foreign doctoral degrees (see Table 6.3), 13 were from Western countries (three each from Japan and West Germany, two from the USA, and one each from Austria, Australia, Denmark, France and Sweden) in this new wave of studying abroad. Western-trained scientists, especially with doctoral degrees, will more likely appear in greater numbers in future CAS elections.

The number of élite scientists with home undergraduate training increased from the year 1955 to 1995. This does not mean that undergraduate education was sufficient or that postgraduate education was unnecessary for élite Chinese scientists. Instead, this reflects the change in China's higher education system after the CCP accession to power. Between 1949 and 1969, only about 8000 Chinese finished their postgraduate studies at key universities or research institutes.[51] During the decade of the Cultural Revolution, higher education was virtually destroyed. From 1956 to 1978, apart from graduates sent to USSR satellite countries in Eastern Europe, almost no students were dispatched to Western countries for advanced training and few returned from the West. Since scientific research was again in demand after Dengist reforms started, college graduates with academic calibre were reinstated. This explains why over half of those elected between 1991 and 1995 had only undergraduate education in China. And this situation will not soon be changed until scholars with post-Cultural Revolution Doctorates both from abroad and at home mature, which means that in the near future, scientists with only domestic undergraduate degrees will continue to be elected to the élite group.

As indicated above, new returnees with foreign Doctorates have emerged as the élite; recent elections have also witnessed an increase in the number of CAS members who received advanced degrees from China's higher learning and research institutions. This corresponds with the development of China's postgraduate education. In the 1991 election, among the 40 domestic Master's degree holders, 35 were awarded their degrees after 1949, when the PRC was established. Postgraduate training has been flourishing since the late 1970s and doctoral degrees have been granted since 1982. In fact, three scientists who received Chinese Doctorates in the 1980s were elected in 1995. It is therefore expected that scientists with domestic postgraduate credentials will have more chance to be elected to the élite group in the future.

THE UNIVERSALISM OF EDUCATION IN THE PRODUCTION OF THE SCIENTIFIC ELITE

China fits the global pattern in that education plays a visible role in rearing the scientific élite. On the other hand, a leading US theorist has suggested that 'science is afforded opportunity for development in a democratic order which is integrated with the ethos of science'.[52] In other words, the circumstances of democracy are suitable for the development of the universalistic ethos of science. The PRC is generally considered less democratic than Western countries, and the US situation described in the quotation above does not appear to exist in the PRC's sphere of science.

Education alone, of course, could not and should not be used to evaluate a scientist for élite membership. More important criteria are academic performance, scholarship and scientific productivity, as well as administrative experience and characteristics particular to the field in which a scientist works. In the case of the PRC, scientists working in military or national defence-related fields might be more likely to be elected to CAS as a way for the state to show its appreciation of their achievement.[53] The political attitude of scientists can be a critical criterion.[54] Also, the election to CAS membership might also depend on who one knows or what kind of *guanxi* a scientist has in the Chinese scientific community,[55] although social relationships through mentoring and collegiality are found elsewhere and are certainly not peculiar to China. The PRC is not unique in having its own criteria for membership of the élite: in other countries, 'there are also particularistic elements in the evaluation and reward systems of science'.[56]

The formation of the Chinese scientific élite has been closely connected with the élite's educational attainment and this reflects to some extent the mechanism of universalism, rather than that of particularism. Even the 14 CCP members elected to CAS in 1955 had college or more advanced degrees, except for two who had abandoned their studies to join the Party.[57] Education has played a continuous and consistent role in the formation of the Chinese scientific élite, despite changes in China's social and political environment and education system over the last forty years. These changes have not longitudinally caused a major shift in the pattern of producing élite scientists (attending a prestigious university, having a postgraduate education, or studying under an élite mentor).

Nurturing the best at prestigious institutions is, of course, particularistic, not universalistic. Those graduating from non-élite institutions of higher learning might not be afforded the same chance of being elected as those with élite institutional origins, despite similar academic performance. However, in both less developed and industrialized societies, education functions as a funnel through which capable and talented young students are selected. Higher education in China, regardless of variations in institutional quality and prestige, has been largely meritocratic, since entrants are selected according to unified examination scores, except during the Cultural Revolution period. Key Chinese universities have simply creamed off the most talented among them. Thus, prestigious higher education is universalistic, in contrast to direct inheritance of occupational status from parent to child. Achieved factors explain more about selectivity to higher education than ascribed family background factors. If higher education is a necessary requisite for the Chinese scientific élite, then selective admission of students into élite universities is not relevant to the composition of the élite. Since educational attainment as measured by institutional prestige is a process in which universalistic factors are used, as an intermediate factor, it should at least be viewed as weakly universalistic in selectively producing the scientific élite. In another sense, educational attainment may be viewed as strongly universalistic since it has a consistent role over different social settings.[58]

In sum, the relationship between educational attainment and the formation of the Chinese scientific élite lends support to the universalism hypothesis of the production of élite scientists in terms of their educational background. This universalistic value found in the capitalist social system also occurs in the PRC.

NOTES

1. See Zuckerman and Merton, 1973.
2. For a discussion of the influence of education on a scientist's career, see Crane, 1965; Zuckerman, 1970 and 1977.
3. Crane, 1969; Gaston, 1970; and Hargens and Hogstrom, 1982.
4. Zuckerman, 1977, pp. 84–95.
5. Zuckerman, 1977, p. 82.
6. Cole and Cole, 1973, p. 72.
7. This claim is set forth in Merton, 1973 (originally 1942), pp. 267–78.
8. Data were obtained from the following sources: *Elite in Chinese science*, two volumes, Beijing: Popular Science Press, 1985 and 1988; *Academic department membership of the Chinese Academy of Sciences 1991; Kexue* (Science), 1994, vol. 46, nos. 5–6, 1995, vol. 47, nos. 1–3 (1995); *Zhongguo Kexue Bao* (China's Science News), overseas edition, 26 February 1996, p. 6; *Kexuejia Zhuanji Dacidian Bianjizu* (Editorial group of *The Biographical Dictionary of Scientists*), 1991–94.
9. This section is based on Cao Cong, 1996.
10. For a history of the CAS in its early years, see Suttmeier, 1969, pp. 110–58; Yao Shuping, 1989; and Yao Shuping, Luo Wei, Li Peishan and Zhang Wei, 1994.
11. For a complete list of current CAS-affiliated research institutes, see Qian and Gu, 1994, vol. 3, pp. 676–88.
12. Suttmeier, 1969, pp. 130–3.
13. Yao Shuping, 1989, p. 453.
14. Suttmeier, 1969, pp. 69–81 and 120.
15. Yao Shuping, 1989, p. 453. However, the CCP was intimately involved in the selection of academic department members of the Department of Philosophy and Social Sciences by judging whether candidates applied Marxist ideology in their research.
16. Academic department member was a working title of academic leadership. Rather than actually changing their *danwei*, CAS members stay in their institutions to undertake research, promote scientific efforts and consult for other government units.

17. Song Zhenneng, 1990.
18. Those who either were killed or committed suicide include Deng Shuqun, a fungus scientist; Liu Chongle, a biologist; Rao Yutai, a US-trained, first generation physicist; Xu Baolu, a mathematician; Ye Dupei, a metallurgist; Zhang Zongsui, a mathematician; Zhao Jiuzhang, a meteorologist and space physicist who had made outstanding contributions to the development of artificial satellites; others died after 1976 as a result of the persecution during the ten-year calamity, such as Ye Qisun, a US-trained, first generation Chinese physicist. Yao Shuping, Luo Wei, Li Peishan and Zhang Wei, 1994, p. 155.
19. *Zhongguo Kexueyuan guanyu huifu xuebu de tongzhi* (CAS Circular on the Restoration of the Academic Departments), 24 January 1979, reproduced in *Chinese Academy of Sciences yearbook 1982*, p. 198. In January 1967, leftists within the CAS decided to 'smash' the academic departments which they denounced as the product of learning from Soviet revisionism. In fact, they did physically smash the seals of the academic departments, according to a retired CAS cadre (interview, Beijing, 1996).
20. Song Zhenneng, 1990, pp. 278–9.
21. Yao Shuping, Luo Wei, Li Peishan and Zhang Wei, 1994, p. 189.
22. *Guanyu zengbu Zhongguo Kexueyuan xuebu weiyuan de tongzhi* (Circular on the enlargement of CAS Academic Department Membership), May 1979, reproduced in *China Academy of Sciences yearbook 1982*, p. 210.
23. *Zhongguo Kexueyuan Xuebu Lianhe Bangongshi* (Unified Office of the Academic Departments of the CAS), 1994, pp. 30–5.
24. Lin Nan and Xie Wen, 1988, p. 809; Zhang Zhongliang, 1991, pp. 311–7.
25. See Cheng Chu-yuan, 1965, pp. 25–6; Suttmeier, 1974, pp. 52–5 and 1969, pp. 119–33; and Li Zhenzhen, 1992.
26. *China science and technology yearbook 1995*, p. 65.
27. Hua Luogeng, a world famous mathematician, who was then a research fellow in the Institute of Mathematics, CAS; Shen Hong, a self-taught expert on mechanical engineering; and Jia Lanpo, a palaeontologist, who received on-the-job training from his mentors.
28. For a discussion of the 'readjustment of colleges and departments' (*yuanxi tiaozheng*), see Hayhoe, 1996, pp. 77–83.
29. Zuckerman, 1977, p. 63.
30. Gaston, 1970, p. 719.
31. See Hayhoe, 1996, p. 95, especially note 67. For further discussion of key universities, see Chapter 2 by Cheng Kai-ming in this volume.
32. *Guojia Kewei Zonghe Jihuaju he Zhongguo Kexuejishu Xinxi Yanjiusuo* (Comprehensive Planning Bureau of the National Science Commission and the Institute of Scientific and Technical Information of China), 1995; *Yijiujiusi nian Zhongguo keji lunwen tongji yu fenxi* (News release on China's scientific and technical papers in 1994: statistics and analysis), also published by the Comprehensive Planning Bureau.
33. The issue of unbalanced distribution of China's universities is discussed throughout Hayhoe, 1996.
34. Taylor, 1981, p. 11.
35. The number, obtained from an exhibition held by the Department of Geology, Beijing University, includes those who were first enrolled in Beijing University but graduated from Southwest Associated University.

36. For example, Zhang Hongzhao came back from Japan and Ding Wenjiang from England in 1911, Li Siguang from England in 1920 and Weng Wenhao from Belgium in 1922.
37. Li Peishan, 1993, p. 605.
38. See Li Peishan, 1993, pp. 605–6; Feng Kaiwen, 1994, p. 30; and Lutz, 1971, pp. 531–4.
39. Li Peishan, 1993, pp. 603–18; Lutz, 1971, pp. 473–84; and Qu Shipei, 1993, pp. 642–6.
40. Feng Kaiwen, 1994, pp. 29–32 and 181–3; and Qu Shipei, 1993, pp. 359–61.
41. See Table 6.5 on page 113. The lower percentage of Chinese élite scientists with a Chinese postgraduate degree is in part due to the underdevelopment of postgraduate education in China during the period when the élite received education.
42. Cheng Chu-yuan, 1965, pp. 123, 199 and 223. The years varied from country to country, for example, the USA and Canada, 1850–1953; Japan, 1901–39; UK, 1911–49; France, Germany and other Western countries, 1907–62; the USSR and Eastern European countries, 1950–62.
43. Zuckerman, 1977, p. 29.
44. Cheng Chu-yuan, 1965, pp. 222–42; and Schnepp, 1989, pp. 175–95.
45. Dai Nianzhu, 1982; and Dai Nianzhu and Wang Bin, 1993, pp. 1–16.
46. Qu Shipei, 1993, pp. 522–30.
47. Besides those CAS members who were under the direct guidance of Ye, Wu Youxun, Rao and the later generation, some other students who were sent by the Nationalist government to study abroad in the 1940s (for example, Wu Xuelin, Gu Gongxu and Qian Xuesen) also sought and received advice from the first two generation physicists on where to study and whom to follow. Also included in the Southwest Associated training period were C. N. Yang and T. D. Lee, two Chinese-American physicists who won the Nobel Prize in Physics in 1957.
48. Liu Dachun and Wu Xianghong, 1995, pp. 154–9.
49. In 1900, the allied army of eight nations occupied Beijing after putting down the Boxer Rebellion (*Yihetuan Yundong*) and forced the government of the Qing Dynasty to sign a treaty, which required China to pay these foreign countries an indemnity. In 1908, since the indemnity — $24 million — exceeded its loss during the war, the US government earmarked $11 million to train Chinese students. This included both establishing a preparatory school, the forerunner of Qinghua University, and supporting Chinese students who continued their studies in the USA. Approximately 3500 Chinese students took part in the scholarship programme. Later, Britain and other countries adopted the US model, supporting Chinese students' studies in their own countries under similar scholarship programmes. See Li Peishan, 1993, pp. 607–8; and Liu Dachun and Wu Xianghong, 1995, pp. 209–13.
50. Schnepp, 1989. Also see Chapter 5 by Michele Shoresman in this volume.
51. The number is based on a table in *China education yearbook 1949–1981*, p. 964. Between 1949 and 1965, 16 397 Chinese students finished postgraduate training, 6454 (about 40%) of whom were in the fields of science, engineering, agronomy and medical science. The table does not collapse the annual figures across disciplines from 1966 to 1969, which total 4546. Supposing that students who

majored in science-related disciplines had the same percentage in total student body as before, the number would be 1818.

52. Merton, 1973, p. 269.
53. Complete data on this are difficult to collect. However, of 283 scientists elected in 1980, in addition to scientists from the CAS-affiliated research institutes who contributed to national defence-related scientific research, 30 (10.6%) were elected from the Second to Seventh Ministries of Machine Building and the Science and Technology Commission for National Defence which are believed to be involved in national defence-related research. See Yao Shuping, Luo Wei, Li Peishan and Zhang Wei, 1994, p. 190.
54. For political reasons, several scientists were not selected in 1955. During the Anti-Rightist Campaign of 1957, CAS academic department members Cai Liusheng, Lei Tianjue, Liu Sizhi, Meng Shaoying, Qian Weichang, Sheng Tongsheng, Xie Jiarong, Yu Ruihuang, Yuan Hanqing, Zeng Zhaolun and Xiang Da (a social scientist) were labelled 'rightists' and deprived of membership. Feng Zefang and Tang Feifan committed suicide during the campaign, the former was on the verge of being labelled, while the latter died before being purged. These 'rightists' were later rehabilitated and by 1980, their memberships were reinstated (interview, Beijing, 1996). Fang Lizhi, a 1980-elected Academic Department Member, had his membership revoked for his alleged involvement in the student movement of 1989.
55. For a general discussion of *guanxi* in China, see King, 1991, pp. 63–84; Walder, 1986; and M. Yang Mei-hui, 1994. Interviews with CAS academicians in the PRC indicate that personal connections can have either a positive or negative impact on a scientist's being elected.
56. Zuckerman, 1977, p. 251.
57. Party members included seven with Doctorates, three with Master's and five with Bachelor's degrees. According to an informant, being a CCP member has not been an issue in evaluating a candidate for CAS membership since 1991. A 1955 member who is also a Party veteran reported that there were less Party members than non-Party members (interviews, Beijing, 1995).
58. For a discussion of the strong and weak universalism hypotheses, see Xie Yu, 1989, pp. 11–2, and 1992, pp. 259–79.

PART 3
MODERNIZATION AND THE CURRICULUM

7

Educational Utilitarianism: Where Goes Higher Education?

LIU Yingkai

INTRODUCTION

Throughout history, Chinese people have been characterized by their utilitarianism. In traditional culture, utility was put above everything else, as illustrated in the expression, 'Gear one's study to the art of government and practical use (*jingshi zhiyong*).' The purpose of study was not personal academic development but 'cultivating oneself, administering state affairs and ensuring national security (*xiushen qijia zhiguo pingtianxia*)'. The goal of education was not to create thinkers and theorists of the exploring kind, but instead, people 'to order and regulate the affairs of the state (*jingbang jishi zhe*)'.[1]

In the 1950s the value of utility began to find new expression. The PRC's educational policies 'vacillated between two seemingly totally opposing views, one emphasizing its political significance too much and the other stressing its economic significance too much'.[2] In the mid-1950s the state began to stress that 'education must serve proletarian politics', reducing education to being a servant girl of politics. Thus, quite often education was besieged by politics and was sometimes even replaced by physical labour, which was once said to be the most important kind of education. The Cultural Revolution (1966–76), in particular, wreaked a great catastrophe on education, bringing it to the brink of destruction with the slogan and practice of education serving the 'class struggle between proletariat and bourgeoisie'. This was the quintessence of education serving politics.

With the Four Modernizations and related reforms, including opening up to the outside world, a form of market-oriented economy has been replacing the rigid planned economy in the PRC. The Chinese people's material life has greatly improved. But an income disparity between brain workers and brawn workers has emerged since the middle of the 1980s. A striking example is that high school students who failed to gain entry to tertiary education have become moneybags overnight; they dress in conspicuous fashion, spend money like water and take pride in their obviously advantageous position in society. In contrast, intellectuals — even the most outstanding ones — cannot conceal their wretched and shabby appearances. Popular sayings reflect this social spectacle of income disparity: 'The one who works with the scalpel is inferior to the one with the hair-clippers' (*Na shoushu dao de buru na titoudao de*), and 'The researchers on guided missiles are inferior to tea-egg sellers' (*Gao daodan de buru mai chayedan de*).[3]

While the status of money in the PRC is constantly rising, that of knowledge is declining unceasingly. The belief that studying is useless, which was quite rife when education served politics, is gaining ground again. The number of primary and secondary school students' quitting school is surprisingly great. By the end of 1988, the attendance rate of children aged 6 to 14 was 76.7%; i.e., 40 million school-age children had quit school or had not been to school at all.[4] Illiterate Chinese number over 229 million, ranking first in the world.[5] Even among college students, postgraduate students and Ph.D. seekers, there are quitters. In recent years the number of applicants for postgraduate courses has declined. In a university in Jiangsu province the standard rate of enrolment of doctoral students had been one in 30–40 applicants, but in 1988 the total number of places (80) in fact exceeded the total number of applicants.[6]

Why does education in the PRC seem to be losing its value? The answer is complex, but utilitarian trends can be explicated through a case study of the English language curriculum at Shenzhen University (Shenda). The school is located in the PRC's most economically developed area, the Shenzhen Special Economic Zone, which leads the nation in market reform. The approaches to learning found at Shenda could well provide an alternative future for Chinese higher education.

ENGLISH-MAJOR CURRICULUM, SHENZHEN UNIVERSITY

Background

Shenda was established in Shenzhen, southern China, in September 1983. As a special economic zone and a shop-window of economic reform, this city puts development of the economy above everything else. It has long been proud of its high speed of economic development, something praised as 'Shenzhen speed'. The city is also a shop-window of opening to the outside world, taking the lead in establishing foreign links. It is said to be in the top three cities in the PRC most visited by foreign government leaders. It is safe to say that an international orientation is of importance, immediately next to the city's economic development.

Shenda, being the only university in Shenzhen, has been characterized since the first day of its establishment by its efforts to accustom itself to the development of the economy and foreign-concernedness. It is natural for Shenda to 'increase its sensitivity to the economic zone' and to attach particular attention to the practicality, suitability and applicability of its curriculum. To adapt itself to the development of the economy, this university has set up many nationally new economy-related specialities such as bonds and securities, real estate development, special economic zone accounting, as well as courses already established in other universities such as enterprise management, accounting and economics. The less directly economy-related departments or specialities have successively changed their names by adding 'applied' to their original names, such as Applied Chemistry and Applied Physics, so as to impress people that their departments or specialities are less theoretical and more applicable in nature. Those departments that are least concerned with the economy, such as the departments of Chinese Language and Literature, and Mathematics, adopt fuzzy names. The former changed its name to the Department of International Cultural Communication and the latter to Soft Science. To indicate that it is closely related to the policy of opening to the outside world, Shenda has set up such foreign-related specialities such as courses in Chinese/English Secretarial Skills, Tourist Culture, International Finance, International Trade, International Accounting and International Economic Law.

This instant-success tendency of meeting the needs of economic reform and opening to the outside world can also find expression in students' preferences in entering college, as indicated in Tables 7.1 and 7.2. Table 7.1 shows that the average scores of the students majoring in International Finance and in International Trade are much higher than those in other

Table 7.1
Maximum and average College Entrance Exam scores for Shenda freshmen by speciality

Speciality	1992		1993		1994	
	max.	average	max.	average	max.	average
International Finance	849	772/762	809	751/730	801	746/701
International Trade	822	727/721	782	696/726	741	715/671
Computer Science	745	680	727	683	746	677
Architecture	756	676	723	661	758	665
Applied Chemistry	714	638	681	630	634	611
Applied Physics	711	649	675	633	685	632
Chinese	700	678	724	687	687	663
English	784	694	722	670	739	671
International Economic Law	720	704	719	691	717	668
Laws of Hong Kong, Taiwan & Macau	742	687	706	688	710	672

Source: Shenda Academic Affairs Office
Note: Finance and Trade majors admit secondary graduates from both arts and science tracts. The scores are separated by a slash: arts preceding science. Intertract comparisons should be avoided because scores are not fully comparable. Arts tract includes English, Chinese and Law.

Table 7.2
Maximum and average College Entrance Exam scores in Maths and English for Shenda freshmen by department

Department	Mathematics			English		
	1992	1993	1994	1992	1993	1994
International Finance & Trade	877	801	793	851	840	822
Economics	784	768	821	788	872	778
Management	701	735	752	733	765	798
Electronics	784	788	829	750	785	778
Mathematics	803	687	696	788	726	726
Architecture	735	734	784	788	808	798
Applied Chemistry	701	689	610	733	744	672
Applied Physics	745	741	667	733	744	651
Chinese	755	742	764	750	840	726
Foreign Languages	724	705	752	767	785	778

Source: Shenda Academic Affairs Office

specialities. Besides, the maximum score winners are also the students majoring in these two foreign-concerned specialities. Table 7.2 shows that the student with the best score in mathematics was not in the departments of natural sciences nor even in the Department of Mathematics, and that the student with the best score in English was not in the Department of Foreign Languages. The best score winners both in maths and English were in the Department of International Finance and Trade. This appears to be true for the whole country, especially in prestigious universities such as Beijing University. The reason is that the general situation of economic reform and opening to the outside world in the whole country creates a dire need for this kind of personnel, and the much higher salary offered by this sector of employment attracts the best and brightest.

Broadly speaking, education aims at producing qualified personnel. Nevertheless, institutions of higher learning are different from elementary and secondary schools in that they have dual purposes. One is to produce qualified personnel and the other is to carry out academic research. But in Shenda there is not much atmosphere of academic research. A journal editor from Anhui University went to Shenda in 1991. His striking impression was that in Shenda, few people were willing to write articles. In Anhui, he had to select and reject papers from the many that were submitted for his consideration, but in Shenda he sometimes had to wait for papers or plead for them. According to him, some full and associate professors in Shenda had been occupying their posts without writing anything for some five years and accepting much higher salaries than others with a very easy conscience.[7]

Research is the key to ensuring the leading role of theory and science in educational policies and is also the prerequisite for running a college successfully. Nevertheless, Shenda's Higher Education Research Institute has long been subject to a shortage of funds and up until now can only do some compilation work. It has yet to fulfil its proper functions of a consultant and an innovator. Shenda's Scientific Research Office, whose task is mainly to supply financial support to the various departments and academics, has also been sharing the same destiny of fund shortage. Due to the lack of atmosphere of academic research and shortage of financial aid and even spiritual encouragement, quite a few young and middle-aged academics with research potential and promise have decided to abandon their pursuit — especially those in the humanities and social sciences.[8] More than half of them just make last-minute efforts in writing, solely for the purpose of getting academic promotion. This percentage is even considered to be too conservative. Some say two-thirds of the academics belong to this category.

The English-major curriculum

In the core English courses many utilitarian elements appear. For instance, aspects of commerce, tourism, job-hunting, customs-checking and catering services infiltrate the foundation courses of Oral English and Oral Interpretation. Situations using practical expressions are repeated so often that they quickly lose their novelty in content and fail to arouse the students' interest. Less attention is given to the basic functional aspects of language such as sequence of time, attitudes and measurement. Consequently, students sometimes cannot express themselves well in some situational cases and sometimes commit errors in register or pragmatics. This latter error type is illustrated in the following short dialogue between a student and a foreigner:

> Foreigner: Thank you!
>
> Student: It's my duty to do so.

The student's response represents a pragmatic mistake as it hints that if not for duty, the student would not have come to the foreigner's help.

Most utilitarianism is much more covert. Table 7.3 presents the four-year undergraduate curriculum for Shenda English majors. Courses called English for Foreign Trade, English for Travelling and Financial English are included in the freshman or sophomore curriculum and substitute for hours that could guarantee a more solid foundation in basic language skills of listening, speaking, reading and writing.

Courses absent from the curriculum

Humanities or foundation courses such as literature and linguistics are considered by most students to be too 'ivory tower' because they don't directly teach skills needed in the workplace. Students' dislikes greatly influence the leadership; such courses remain in the curriculum in name only. For example, linguistics was offered only once, in 1988. Only five students took the course that semester and this so greatly discouraged the teachers of linguistics that the course was not offered again. Teachers in the department often complain that there is too little idealism in the curriculum. Ironically, the faculty staff themselves majored in literature or linguistics and their knowledge is not much used in the classroom. They experienced non-utilitarian education where literature courses promote philosophical, aesthetic and humanitarian values. Particularly, great books and poems can foster moral concepts and develop critical thinking. This occurs elsewhere in the PRC.

Table 7.3
Timetable for English majors, Shenda (weekly hours)

Course	Type	Year One		Year Two		Year Three		Year Four	
Term		1	2	1	2	1	2	1	2
Intensive reading	r	6	6	6	6	4	4	2	
Phonics	r	2							
English grammar	r		2						
Extensive reading	r	2	2	2	2				
Listening comprehension	r	4	4	4	4				
English for travel	e		2						
Oral English	r	4	2	4	4				
English for foreign trade	e			2	2				
Video watching	e	3	3	3	3	3	3	3	
Typing	e	3							
News listening comprehension	e					4			
English writing	r	2	2	2	2	2	2		
Sketches about UK & USA	e			2	2				
Oral interpretation	r		4		2	2	2	2	
Translation	r					2	2	6	4
Financial English	e			2					
Practical English writing	r					2	2		
Guidance on English Exams	r				2				
English usage	e			1	2				
British literature	r					2			
Japanese	r				4	4	4	4	
Selected modern essays	e					4	4	4	
TOEFL listening	e						2		
American literature	r						2		
English lexicology	e			2			2		
World history & geography	e						2		
Selections from English literature	r							4	
English newspaper reading	e							4	
Anglo-Chinese culture comparison	e							2	
TOEFL training	e							4	
Graduation thesis	r								10
College Chinese	r	2							
History of Chinese Revolution	r	2							
Physical training	r	2	2	2	2	2	2	2	
d-base language	r	4							
Military training	r	4 weeks							
Military theory	r	2	2						
Moral training	r	2	2	2	2	2	2	2	
Principles of philosophy	r	2	2						
Political economics	r			2					
Chinese socialist construction	r			2					
Theory of politics	r				2				
Introduction to public relations	r						2		

r = required (*bixiuke*) e = elective (*xuanxiuke*)

Beijing University, with its long tradition of humanitarianism, attaches great importance to literary courses in the Department of English. Surveys of English and European literature are both obligatory courses. Many courses that do not directly relate to future employment are nonetheless offered. Optional offerings, at least eight of which must be taken over the four academic years, include Greek and Roman Legends, Introduction to Literature, Selected Readings of Short Stories, Western Culture, Selected Readings of Poetry, Selected Readings of Classic Essays, Analysis of English Movies, British and American Poems of the 20th Century, and Introduction to the Literary Genre. Other optional courses include Literary Appreciation, Selected Readings of English Plays, History of English Literary Criticism. Moreover, Russian Literary History and Contemporary History of Chinese Literature, which seem to have nothing to do with English, are taught in English as elective courses. This picture contrasts with that of Shenda's English Department, which consistently offers only one linguistics course — Lexicology — that has been taught steadily. In literature, no substantial course is offered, although expatriate teachers sometimes include literature in their classes. Courses by foreign teachers, however, are inconsistent and are not a substantial part of the curriculum.

In order to help students lay a solid foundation, the state syllabus stipulates that the course of English Phonetics be divided into two parts, which are to be offered separately in the first two years.[9] Beijing University arranges this sequence in the freshman year. At Shenda this course is offered only in one semester; only 50% of the required teaching hours are completed. The state syllabus stipulates that a course in English Grammar also be divided into two parts to be offered in the first two years. At Beijing University this course may be selected among a group of required courses in the second semester of the first year and the first semester of the second year. After a semester of study, the students, having proceeded from overestimating their grammar competence to obtaining a cool-headed self-appraisal of their ability, tend to conscientiously select this course which is at different levels of difficulty at its different periods. Nevertheless, at Shenda, the grammar course is a requirement for all, regardless of individual ability; the single course is placed in one semester and, therefore, only 50% of the teaching hours stipulated by the state syllabus are offered.

In some Chinese institutions every teacher has a copy of the syllabus; while in others, both teachers and students have copies. Before 1993 no one at Shenda had a copy, not even the department chairperson. The syllabus's objectives, requirements, course structure, testing and evaluation were not relevant concerns to teachers or management. For over five years, lopsided and unbalanced arrangements of teaching content, the abandonment of particular courses, and the arrangement of courses before students had the necessary skills to master them commonly occurred. Since 1993, faculty members have begun to appreciate the state syllabus and have begun to follow it more faithfully.

UTILITARIANISM AT SHENDA

Inattention to research

The annual funds for supporting the research of Shenda academics have been set at around ¥200 000 (US$25 000). The university library receives ¥700 000 (US$87 000) for acquisitions. Both of these amounts are much lower than the levels of advanced universities in the PRC. For example, the figures for research spending at Chongqing University and Zhejiang University are ¥40 million (US$5 million) and ¥100 million (US$12.5 million) respectively.[10] Money aside, Shenda boasts an impressive teaching staff, according to their credentials. Although established only in 1983, by 1996 it maintained a staff of 31 full professors and 152 associate professors; 53 had Ph.Ds and 175 had Master's degrees. As of 1993, this contingent had altogether published 214 books, 805 research papers in the social sciences and 252 in the natural sciences. They had completed 163 research items, 103 of which had won national, provincial or municipal awards; 19 patents had been issued by the state; and numerous research projects had reached international standards.[11] A closer examination of these figures, however, indicates they are not impressive, when compared to other Chinese universities.

In 1992, there were 522 institutions of higher learning (including *zhuanke* programmes) that offered majors in the humanities and social sciences. For that year altogether, 3486 research papers were published with the average for each institution being 105, but Shenda teachers and staff members published only 63 research papers in these fields. For the same year, research papers in science and technology published in international journals or presented at international conferences by PRC scholars numbered 15 466; those published in domestic journals numbered 98 575. A total figure of 114 041 means an average of 114 for each institute of higher learning that has science specialities. The corresponding figure for Shenda was only 60. In research, therefore, in both the social and natural sciences, Shenda lagged behind the average Chinese higher learning institution.[12]

In many Chinese tertiary institutes, the research atmosphere is very thin.[13] The lack of attention paid to research is manifested in the Shenda

English Department, where no more than 4 of its 39 teachers are dedicated to research. Their colleagues spasmodically undertake research only because it is a requisite for promotion. The status quo of English teachers' research is reflected in the following general statement on English language teaching in the PRC:

> Quite a number of teachers are not capable of doing research. Those capable cannot afford the time and energy. Those with the time and energy do not have sufficient reference materials and tutors guiding their research. Even though you may achieve great research after tremendous effort, it is hard for you to have articles published today when publications are so commercialized.[14]

Emphasis on spare-time work

Teachers in almost all Shenda departments are engaged in spare-time teaching in order to supplement their regular incomes, which are lower than those of their children who have just graduated from college and work in local banks or companies. About 40% of the teaching staff have a second occupation, such as being part-time lawyers, accountants, teachers, designers or researchers.

Across the PRC, teachers in almost all departments and institutes of foreign languages are engaged in spare-time teaching. This practice is considered acceptable, understandable and necessary by both the leadership and staff. It occurs at Shenda where English teachers instruct not only English majors, but also all students in other departments of the university.[15] In addition, teachers are called upon to provide instruction for several international exchange programmes.[16] English teachers are also needed for adult education and non-degree English courses run by the department itself. The department has 39 regular teachers, but the number of teachers needed to maintain average teaching loads of 12 hours per week would be 58. This shortfall of 19 teachers means that 20% of the faculty staff have to teach over 20 hours a week. Some of the teachers have to teach five different English courses during a single semester. In such an understaffed department, all the teachers are overworked. They cannot concentrate on a course or two so as to be professionally proficient, neither can they find much time to do research.[17]

Absence of teacher training

Given heavy teaching loads, it is not surprising that teachers find little time to hone their teaching skills or just to discuss their teaching methods with their colleagues. There is no peer review or comment; teachers work independently and not in groups, in contrast with elsewhere in the PRC. Departmental management is preoccupied with schedules and teaching arrangements and devotes little time to issues of pedagogy. Curriculum development is given scant attention, except when forms are required by the university's Academic Affairs Office. Both long-range plans and short-term arrangements are wanting. In the absence of a system of awarding and rewarding research achievers, quite a number of teachers are content with teaching the same courses, in some cases for ten years, without making any changes. There are few opportunities for an English teacher to go off-campus for further study and foreign study is not encouraged.

The ultimate disengagement

From Shenda's early years, many teachers and staff members, all who have transferred from the interior of the country, have switched to enterprises or other trades. Some have gone and not returned. Shenda's English Department has lost about 25% of its teachers for these reasons. For the entire university, the corresponding number in the past 12 years is 180, accounting for 29% of the total faculty. Nearly all those who left were young and middle-aged teachers and most hold Master's or Ph.D. degrees.

What forms a thought-provoking contrast with students' being tired of studying is that teachers are fed up with teaching. Quite a few teachers are ashamed of their profession. Lots of them have embarked on business careers after deserting their teaching work; others are engaged in other trades while they are still making do with their teaching; and still others have landed better jobs but have suspended their salaries while on perpetual leave. One of the leaders of the Foreign Language Education Section of the Higher Education Department of the SEdC said that some of the foreign language teachers 'have aimed at companies and foreign-funded enterprises', 'since from the angle of material benefits, working in colleges and universities are [sic] really inferior to working there'. This leader followed with '[s]ome teachers, though still teaching, are engaged in their second jobs which have nothing to do with their foreign language knowledge, e.g. starting companies or doing business'.[18]

INSTANT-SUCCESS TENDENCIES

Utilitarian tendencies on the part of students are manifested in various forms. They are most apparent in students' selection of majors. Around the time high school seniors take the college entrance exam in July, they list their choices for post-secondary education. Schools admit incoming freshmen according to these exam scores, with the most prestigious majors in the most prestigious schools getting students with the highest scores. In a comprehensive school such as Shenda, the popularity of majors is reflected in the entrance exam scores (see Tables 7.1 and 7.2). Data indicate a ranking of majors, with Foreign Trade and Finance at the top and English, Chinese and Law at the bottom. In 1994 the Foreign Languages Department was nearly reduced to begging for students. The lowest student scored only 600, 21 points lower than the average of all specialities. Thus, through their choice, students express their preference for utilitarian subjects. This phenomenon is not unique to Shenda. It occurs elsewhere in the PRC:

> The current trend is that the number of the students who enter themselves for such specialities as economy, foreign trade, foreign affairs, tourism, etc., is far larger than those [sic] for pure foreign language/literature specialities; therefore, institutes and departments of foreign languages have to take students' demands into consideration, or they will have trouble enrolling good students.[19]

Students also stress utility in choosing courses. Their mentality is greatly influenced by the values of society. The ideals teachers tried to foster in students during primary and secondary schooling begin to waver in the worldly environment of their college years. Lack of respect for education is implied in such heart-rending bywords like 'as poor as a professor and silly as a doctor (*qiongde xiang jiaoshou, chunde xiang boshi*)'. In their colleges and universities, students are swept away in torrential tides of the society's commercialization; the consciousness of commodities pokes its way into every nook and cranny. Consequently, the haloes around the teachers' profession have been lost, the brilliance of academic degrees has been dampened while the sense of mystery and sacredness has faded. Lots of students are resolved to desert the road to high accomplishments in their academic pursuit. Lots of them speculate in stock market shares; others are engaged in business and still others while away their time. If a course such as English for Foreign Trade is deemed useful, they choose it and study with interest. Only because such fast food-type, applied courses take less time and energy and can be put to immediate use after graduation, a large number of students are head over heels in love with them, as shares speculators are keen on landing the go-go stocks. Sometimes, however, courses in theory are required. Forced to take them, they just drift along, content with obtaining a passing grade. Their slogan is 'Long live 60 (*liushi fen wansui*)' as 60 points is the passing grade. As for the students lower down, their only dream is to get a passing mark in all the courses they take. If they think they will fail, they cheat.

Education's utilitarian nature is reflected in the types of jobs students take after graduation. In Shenzhen, students have never been assigned jobs. Instead they have to look for jobs themselves. That university students go to work in the business sector is becoming common in the PRC. Prior to Dengist reforms, students were assigned jobs with state enterprises or government bureaux. Now, students are free to choose and many choose business. Of the graduates of the Foreign Languages Department, for instance, 92% work in enterprises and banks. Almost a decade ago, the Guangzhou Foreign Languages Institute (Guangwai) found that upon graduation, most of the students hoped to work in enterprises. Those who wanted to work in foreign trade, where opportunities for earnings are good, accounted for 50% of all the graduates. Those who preferred to be assigned to work at the alma mater represented only 1%.[20]

Graduates, especially at Shenda, have little interest in advanced studies. Many graduates of the English Department have gone abroad and some study business in postgraduate courses in North America. Excluding these graduates who have emigrated, however, almost no alumni pursue postgraduate study.[21] This situation exists elsewhere in the PRC. For example, only 10% of the undergraduates from the Guangwai 1987 study went on with advanced studies.[22] This figure has probably dropped considerably in the past decade; according to a faculty member at Guangwai, only 6% pursue a higher degree. Finding a job upon graduation is more in line with students' instant-success considerations.

ENGLISH-TEACHING REFORMS TO MEET THE MARKET ECONOMY'S NEEDS

With the PRC's market-oriented reforms, there is a greater demand for English teaching. At the same time, more and more employers require that graduates of English should not only be good at English, but also have professional knowledge related to their fields of business. As a result, foreign language institutes and departments of foreign languages in universities have been reforming their English teaching. They have jettisoned the system of language/literature and have added special fields and applied courses. In this respect, Shanghai International Studies University (Shangwai) took the lead. Early in 1989, Shangwai proclaimed:

> Our target is to develop from the present-day monistic institute concentrated on foreign language/literature teaching into a foreign language university featured by its applied disciplines of a plural nature.[23]

Specialities were set which have a direct bearing on economics, including

International Economy and Trade; International Economic Law; International Accounting; Foreign Affairs Management; Dissemination and Technology of Education.[24]

Following the example of Shangwai, language teaching units in Beijing, Guangzhou, Chengdu, Xi'an, Dalian and Tianjin began to offer new fields of study. There, foreign languages and foreign-related applied disciplines such as English for foreign affairs and for foreign trade are combined to a varying extent. Other institutions changed in basic character. The Beijing Second Foreign Language Institute has now specialized in training personnel in the field of tourism. The Beijing Foreign Affairs Institute and the Beijing Foreign Trade Institute are characterized by their utilitarian nature. Other departments of foreign languages of comprehensive universities and teachers' colleges have adopted a major-minor system, which means that an English-major student should also minor in applied disciplines, such as those related to economics, trade, finance and tourism. This is expected to increase their graduates' competitive edge in the job market.

Which orientation: theoretical versus practical knowledge?

There is a view that a foreign language is a tool, rather than a vocational field of study and that it must be attached to a particular speciality.[25] Yet, this is not the case in other countries where language study continues to survive, despite market pressures for utilitarianism. In European countries and North America especially, institutions emphasize general education; language study and studying other cultures are important parts of general education. Also, research using primary sources requires foreign language knowledge. Sociologists, anthropologists and other social scientists need to know foreign languages. Yet, the PRC does not pay much attention to the social sciences; minimal research is done in other cultures.

Specialization

Especially troubling is the increased amount of attention that is paid to the establishment of special fields of study, in addition to the development of practical courses within the existing curriculum. In the process of reform in Chinese higher education, insufficient consideration has been given to whether a particular field of study is actually needed when it is set up. The speciality of International Economic Law at Shangwai, for example, is a very narrow field of study. Would not most jobs in the field be taken by law graduates? Can graduates in this English speciality find employment after graduation? Even in cases of a perfect job match between the field of study and workplace demands, have graduates acquired a sufficiently broad base of knowledge to enable them to change jobs or fields in the future? In contrast to the period of job assignments under the planned economy, the emerging market system will likely be characterized by frequent job and career shifts. Education needs to be broad enough so that graduates are well-prepared to change jobs. The PRC's educational system in the 1950s adopted the Soviet model, which was characterized by overspecialization. The separation of liberal arts from sciences and engineering — and even sciences from engineering — and the creation of many sub-specialities contributed to the narrowing of fields of study. This development contrasts with the contemporary trend in education which advocates interdisciplinary teaching and research and the mutual infiltration between liberal arts, sciences and engineering.[26] Nevertheless, the Chinese market economy seems to be replicating Soviet overspecialization, although ironically overspecialization can indeed limit education's adaptability to the constantly changing society caused by market movements.

Over-attention to being adaptable to the changing society can cause departments to neglect laying a solid foundation for language studies. The teaching of basic knowledge and theories and the training of basic skills are a fundamental part of language study. During the first two years the students develop the four basic skills of listening, speaking, reading and writing. In the third and fourth years, according to the national syllabus, particular attention should be given to the development of comprehensive English skills, imparting of cultural knowledge and improvement of communicative abilities. Communicative skills require a mastery of grammar as well as sociolinguistic, textual and tactical abilities.[27] Courses related to these four skills should be common to specialized courses.[28]

The instant-success tendencies oppose the basic principle of laying a solid foundation. But one scholar notes, 'The demands of society for foreign language learners are all-round while the types of specialized knowledge are numerous.'[29] For very practical administrative reasons, syllabus reform of foreign language units cannot afford to include many types of specialized knowledge. First, too few language teachers (most of whom specialize in literature or linguistics) are available to teach specialized courses. To co-opt a linguist or literature scholar is likely to produce a course that is little more than vocabulary instruction, for the scholar is unlikely to have a thorough grounding in the speciality to be taught. Second, a plethora of hastily arranged, *ad hoc* courses will generate administrative chaos, with ever-changing schedules and room assignments. Third, numerous catalogue additions present students with a smorgasbord of offerings, which even when all taken do not provide a nourishing meal. As one Shenda student reported, 'We don't need the teacher. We can buy the book and learn it ourselves.' Education that makes the teacher unnecessary suggests, at the very least, a severe misallocation of resources.

A foreign language institute or department revolves around foreign language study. Its *raison d'être* is its comparative advantage. To change the very nature of the unit reduces its advantages. In other words, why cannot English be taught in each speciality, so that architecture students, for example, study architectural English and physics students begin with 'English for Physics'? This situation is the logical extension of the present trend towards utilitarianism. A study by the Beijing Foreign Studies University (Beiwai) notes:

> A student who learns English well faces no big problem no matter what specialized field he is engaged [sic] in the future... On the contrary, if he acquired only a superficial knowledge of a specialized course at the cost of developing English, he will experience a kind of 'congenital deficiency'... Establishment of specialized courses of a utilitarian nature affects students' studies of English; therefore, it is hard to bring about highly accomplished learners.[30]

Meeting workplace needs

The hiring practices of foreign banks and accounting firms in Shenzhen illustrate the comparative advantage of English study. These firms' speciality is finance/accounting, but they recruit large numbers of foreign language graduates, as well as graduates in other non-finance-related fields. The firms believe that it is better for an employee to have a good command of English, the language of training and a major language used daily in the workplace, than to know the minutiae of finance. The details of accounting or banking can be acquired through on-the-job training. One international accounting firm with a branch in Shenzhen puts its recruits into a month-long, intensive, off-site training programme. For three consecutive years, the company recruited the top Shenda English student to be an accountant. In sum, the basics of accounting can be taught in four weeks; the basics of English require a substantially larger investment, which universities, rather than firms, are able to make.

If too much stress is laid on fast food-type courses, foundation courses themselves will become neglected. The Beiwai study reported: 'Four years is not sufficient time for an English Student if occupied by many specialized courses rather than his/her major courses. As a result, the student's basic language skills are not ideal at all. Some students' spoken and written English are both poor.'[31]

Pedagogy

Courses in theory are demanding and challenging to students. They are high-powered courses which emphasize theory, basic knowledge, structure, the standard and the difficult. They reflect the essence of things and, therefore, can help to form a theoretical frame and conceptual system of a discipline. They help a student to deduce and learn by analogy. Learning must be difficult, challenging the student's intellect and arousing more interest in further studies.[32] Education advances in 'degrees of difficulty', along which students proceed. Horizons are constantly expanding and students are encouraged to overcome difficulties to develop their intelligence.[33]

One of the teacher's tasks is to help students cultivate a strong desire for study and a spirit for exploration, to achieve the ability to teach themselves and to foster the initiative in studying and applying knowledge. A famous saying concerns education in ancient China: 'It is better to teach people how to fish than just to give them fish (*Shou ren yiyu buru shou ren yi yu*).' Helping students to cultivate their abilities to study on their own is more productive in the long run than the fast-food fish of applied courses. In order to be able to do this, teachers must delve into their profession and actively take part in research, so that they themselves can develop professionally.

Another important job of the teacher is to impart correct social values. This aspect of education transcends a moment's ongoing utility and immediate interests. At the initial stage of vigorous growth of a commodity economy, the inclination of people's mentality to money and material benefits, the loss of idealism, the deformation of values and moral concepts may hold sway for a certain period of time.

CONCLUSION

Since the effects of educational reform show themselves slowly, educators and educational policy-makers need foresight. The general trend in foreign language teaching is towards seeking instant successes and immediate benefits, at the expense of laying strong foundations. A balance should be maintained between theory and practice.

Now, more and more people have come to realize that the gap between advanced and backward colleges chiefly finds expression in the gap in research work between them. Harvard and other internationally high-ranking universities enjoy their prestige chiefly because of their research achievements. Therefore, scholars with a breadth of vision in Shenda have begun advocating that equal stress should be put on research and teaching, instead of attaching sole importance to teaching.[34]

A guiding principle of foreign language reform is the function of strengthening humanitarianism. Both teachers and students should be concerned about the ultimate value of education and bring into play its pioneering nature and foresight. Campus culture is duty-bound to enhance the culture of society by way of guiding the social ideal and even opening up new vistas. Universities and colleges should maintain their independence and should persevere in introducing new civilization and other kinds of spiritual wealth. They should influence society with their excellent cultural and spiritual elements and lead society with their constructive and creative ideas rather than submit to the pressure imposed by the productive system of society. If the imperative to strengthen humanitarianism in education is constantly weakened, universities and colleges will inevitably be reduced to vocational training centres which are aimed at giving people a livelihood. This is just a dark reality in higher education.

Higher education should stick to its own humanitarian, pioneering nature with foresight, purity and independence and guard against its fast secularization, pragmatization and commercialization. Idealism accounts for the very difference between campus culture and culture of society. A stress on idealism should not be considered a bookish approach or a pedantic view. Its immediate practical significance may influence the policy-deciding processes of the central and local governments and the leadership at the levels of the institutions and the departments. It may have a bearing on the correct choice of life on the part of teachers and students.

To enable tertiary institutions to give impetus to a healthy development of the whole society, government at all levels should be aware of the strategic position of education, so as to create material conditions for the healthy growth of education and furthermore of the whole society. This entails increasing investment in education. Encouragingly, some measures have been taken in the last few years to improve the economic status of teachers and to improve conditions for education's development.

If idealism is stressed in an academic unit, importance will be attached to the education of moral concepts among both teachers and students, as a result of which, their material desires will not influence them as much as they used to, and their glorious feelings as an embodiment of the social conscience will be enhanced so as to exercise their influence over the whole society. Then senior secondary school students might discard the currently-prevailing utilitarian considerations when they apply for entrance to universities and colleges. Consequently, the situation in which the special fields of a more humanitarian but less utilitarian nature find difficulty in recruiting students will be greatly changed. And the leadership at the levels of departments and universities will not have to get accustomed to meeting passively the temporary needs of society and students. When the tide of utilitarianism is turned, teachers will resume their mission of being a guide in the spiritual homes of students. They will foster a kind of pride in their profession so that they will love their work, endeavour to gain professional proficiency, take an active part in research, and accept the responsibilities of imparting knowledge as well as cultivating people.

NOTES

1. But there is also another tendency: placing classic books, benevolence and righteousness in such a high position has evolved in the contemporary age to dogmatism and doctrinairism which pay little attention to effectiveness and usefulness.
2. Stanley Rosen, cited in Liu Xuehong *et al.*, 1991, p. 141.
3. Tea-eggs are eggs stewed in tea, often sold by illiterate hawkers. In Chinese the second character in both words *egg* and *missile* are homophones, thus producing a kind of black humour. Other expressions are: 'A professor is poorer than a peddler of sweet potatoes (*Dang jiaoshou de buru mai hongshu de*).' and 'Three masters of mind like Zhuge Liang are inferior to a cobbler (*Sange Zhuge Liang buru yige choupijiang*).' The original saying is 'Three cobblers with their wits combined can defeat Zhuge Liang, the master of mind.' Zhuge is a character in the novel *Romance of the Three Kingdoms*.
4. Yao and Liu, 1993, p. 276.
5. Shao, 1995, p. 438.
6. Liu Xuehong *et al.*, 1991.
7. Wu Zhong, 1994b.
8. Liu Yingkai, 1994.
9. *Gaodeng Xuexiao Yingyu Zhuanye Jichujieduan Yingyu Jiaoxue Dagang* (Syllabus of the English Major Foundation Stage in Chinese Institutions of Higher Learning), Beijing Waiyanshe, 1988; and *Gaodeng Xuexiao Yingyu Zhuanye Gaonianji Yingyu Jiaoxue Dagang* (Syllabus of the English Major Advanced Stage in Chinese Institutions of Higher Learning), Beijing, Waiyanshe, 1990.
10. Figures cited in Wu Zhong, 1994a.
11. See Zhou Shizhen, 1995.
12. Zhou Shizhen, 1995. These figures are not based on per capita output, but as Shenda is an average-sized university, the data appear basically correct.
13. Liu Runqing *et al.*, 1989, p. 3.
14. Liu Runqing *et al.*, 1989, p. 3.

15. Currently, there are 160 English majors, among whom 116 are undergraduate students and 44 are two-year certificate students (*zhuankesheng*). Non-English majors are required to take a two-year sequence of foundation English and may take optional courses provided by their departments.
16. One programme is co-run by Shenda's computer department and its counterpart at Lancashire Central University in the UK. Shenda's Department of Chinese has a joint programme with Edmonds Community College, Seattle, Washington, USA.
17. Chen Dongcheng, 1995, p. 48.
18. Zhang Xuyi, 1993.
19. Liu Runqing *et al.*, 1990.
20. Guangzhou Foreign Language Institute, 1987, p. 18.
21. Some graduates are hired by university departments. Since 1983 only two students of the Shenda English Department have continued on as faculty members.
22. Guangzhou Foreign Language Institute, 1987, p. 18.
23. Hu Menghao, 1989, p. 3.
24. Dai Weidong, 1993, p. 5. Dai is president of Shangwai.
25. Liu Runqing *et al.*, 1990.
26. Yuan and Wei, 1991, p. 361.
27. Richards and Rogers, 1986, p. 71.
28. Yang Qinghai, 1993.
29. Yang Qinghai, 1993.
30. Liu Runqing *et al.*, 1990.
31. Liu Runqing *et al.*, 1990.
32. Liu Jiannan *et al.*, 1992, pp. 115, 139–40.
33. Liu Jiannan *et al.*, 1992, pp. 115, 139–40.
34. Wu Zhong, 1994a.

8

Modernizing English Language Teacher Education[1]

Bob ADAMSON

INTRODUCTION

This chapter examines the consequences of the Dengist educational reforms for English language pre-service teacher education. It focuses on contentious topics (*viz.*, that the English language embodies foreign influence) and on key aspects of modernization — teacher education plays an important role both in upgrading the quality of teaching and in supplying sufficient personnel to support the expansion of basic education. The central theme of the chapter is a case study of a teacher education college from the initiation of reforms in the late 1970s. It charts changes in the English language curriculum and discusses related issues, such as staff development and deployment, as the college grappled with the problems of implementing the reforms.

In the past two centuries, the status of English in China has shifted from that of a scorned pariah to one of high prestige today. In the early days of the Canton settlements only the despised 'linguists', social outcasts to a man, were permitted to learn the barbarians' tongue.[2] In contrast, English is nowadays a prerequisite for both academic development and, as it would appear from the growing numbers of competent English speakers among top-ranking leaders in the CCP, political advancement.[3] The increasing globalization of English in the nineteenth and twentieth centuries means that English now

... is situated in many contexts that are specific to that globalization: to use English implies relationships to local conditions of social and economic prestige, to certain forms of culture and knowledge, and also to global relations of capitalism and particular global discourses of democracy, economics, the environment, popular culture, modernity, development, education and so on.[4]

Naturally, not all of these relationships are particularly attractive to a nation which prides itself on its distinct cultural identity and avowed antagonism towards imperialism and capitalism, but the PRC's determination to be accepted with respect as a member of the international community necessitates acquiring competence in the major international language. Indeed, English has always appeared to be a double-edged sword, posing a major threat to the rulers of China. First, in imperial times, the Emperor ruled as a sovereign godhead in a rigid, hierarchical social system that combined politics and religion; erosion of power threatened the very fabric of the state. The system was built around the notions of harmony and benevolent government, which included the observance of religious rites.[5] English represented very different values: it was the language of missionaries who preached alien religions; of philosophers who propounded alternative, subversive social systems; of governments who pursued aggressive foreign policies; and of peoples who lacked the sophistication and refinement that China's history bequeathed its own population. The demise of the Qing Dynasty was hastened by the controversies over how to deal with the foreign powers and their technology. Many believed that it was imperative for the Chinese to learn English in order to gain access to foreign know-how so that China could strengthen herself to resist further humiliations. The resistance of the emperors (and the powers behind the throne)[6] to these views fostered disharmony and contributed to the undermining of the imperial system. Four decades of turbulence preceded 1949, when the CCP established the PRC. As a nation with a communist leadership, the PRC was placed in a position of political conflict with many Western powers, most notably the USA, for whom English served as the mother tongue.

Two distinct policies towards the English language have emerged historically. The first is to try to batten down the hatches, shun any form of contact or even react violently, such as during the Boxer Rebellion or the early phases of the Cultural Revolution, when teachers of English were vilified and beaten.[7] The other school of thought perceives English as potentially beneficial for national development, particularly if damage to the social and political fabric can be minimized through a process of synthesis, labelled *zhongxue weiti, xixue weiyong* (Chinese essence, Western practice). Thus the study of English could be undertaken for purely functional rather than cultural goals. According to Wen Ti, a scholar at the time of the Hundred Days' Reform:

> If we wish to receive the benefit of Western methods, we must first acquire a knowledge of Confucius, Mencius, Ch'eng and Chu [i.e. Neo-Confucianism], and keep it as the foundation to make people thoroughly familiar with filial piety, younger-brotherhood, loyalty, sincerity, ceremony, righteousness, integrity, a sense of shame, obligations and the teachings of the sages and moral courage, in order to understand and demonstrate the foundation, before we can learn the foreign spoken and written languages for some practical use.[8]

The Open Door versus Closed Door lines have been discernible in many facets of the relationship between the PRC and the West since 1949. At times, the CCP has supported the policy of strengthening the nation through Western-style 'modernization' (albeit with Chinese characteristics), whereby the study of English is seen as necessary for acquiring technological expertise and for developing international trade. Alternatively, Chinese leaders have preferred to turn towards the more politically sympathetic foreign countries, such as the former USSR, for partnership, and the study of English has accordingly been relegated to a position of less importance than the study of Russian.[9] At other times, campaigns have been waged in an attempt to restrict the importation of any values that leaders perceive as detrimental to Chinese society, resulting in the virtual isolation of the country.[10] A further conflict thus arises with educators who believe that the study of English should include broad cultural content, so that, for instance, the literature component is not restricted to authors portraying class struggle or similarly politically correct themes. These tensions surrounding English has resulted in its status being described as a 'barometer of modernization'[11] in that its position in the PRC has been more enthusiastically endorsed by top leaders at times when national economic considerations have prevailed over views reflecting a more isolationist or anti-capitalist agenda.

Since 1978, the Four Modernizations programme has represented a sharp divergence from the 'politics to the fore' ideology of the Cultural Revolution. The end of the PRC's political and economic isolation renewed awareness of the value of English for technology, commerce and international diplomacy. English as a foreign language (EFL) became an essential requirement for study overseas and an asset in securing lucrative employment; consequently, it enjoyed a renaissance among Chinese students. Educational authorities interpreted the implications of the modernization programme for English language teaching by shifting the intended pedagogy and content towards a focus on communication skills and cultural awareness. Three syllabi for English in junior secondary schools were introduced in 1977, in 1982 and in 1993, all of which emphasized the communicative aspects of language learning.[12] Native-speaker teachers were recruited from overseas by teacher education institutions to help develop the language skills of teachers and, in some cases, to introduce new pedagogical practices. In 1988, foreign textbook publishers[13] were contracted to collaborate on the production of English courses for secondary schools nationwide.[14]

The expanded provision of basic education envisaged by the *Nine-Year Compulsory Education Law*[15] places an onus upon teacher education institutes to produce larger cohorts of teachers, a challenge which is intensified by the profession's lack of attraction to new recruits, because of poor salary, conditions and social status, as well as the availability of more lucrative employment to competent English speakers in commerce or tourism.[16] In many respects, the unattractive nature of teaching is a problem of long-standing in China. Teaching bears the stigma of failure. Scholars who failed to make the grade in the competitive examinations for the imperial civil service found in teaching a means of earning a daily crust and the respect of one's students, but little else. In the PRC, education has often been seen by the CCP as an ideal tool for propaganda, and the classroom was the front line of several political movements. The Cultural Revolution, in particular, included a move to break, often violently, the traditional bonds of loyalty between teachers and students.[17] Along with other intellectuals, teachers were also placed in the 'stinking ninth' social category — basically the lowest of the low.[18]

Besides recruitment, another problem facing the institutes concerns the requirement to upgrade quality. In 1987, the then Premier Zhao Ziyang commented:

> Basically, the development of science and technology, the revitalization of the economy and indeed the progress of the whole society all depend on improving the quality of the workforce and training large numbers of competent personnel.[19]

The issue of quality raises a number of questions. What kind of competence in English language may be considered to be of appropriate quality? What is the measure of quality in English language teaching? How can these standards be achieved, particularly at a time when the institutes are also expected to produce ever higher numbers of teachers? In search of a solution, educationalists within the state policy-making agencies turned overseas in the time-honoured maxim of *zhongxue weiti, xixue weiyong,* an approach facilitated by the Open Door policy:

> We should make further researches into all the pedagogic schools, rejecting the dross and assimilating the essence, and make them serve us according to our national conditions.[20]

However, grafting Western techniques in English language teaching and teacher education onto existing Chinese practices necessitates bridging a number of divides. Not least is the distance between the centre and the periphery. The implementation of policy is a long and winding road that journeys through different government departments at various levels (provincial, county, municipal) before reaching individual institutes, by which time the distance from the centre allows institutes to enjoy considerable autonomy, as the principle of *shan gao huangdi yuan*[21] comes into play.

The actual grafting is problematic, given the differences between Chinese and Western cultures of language teaching and language teacher education. Formal teaching of English at tertiary level in China, at least prior to the modernization drive, stressed the teacher-centred, literary-based, grammar-translation methodology,[22] while Western practice was moving towards student-centred, multi-media, communicative-competence models.[23] The Chinese conception of teacher education appeared to differ from the Western conception in its emphasis on language competence, rather than pedagogic competence.[24] These divides have often led to tensions when foreign teachers, who often bring their own agenda and cultural baggage, have been employed in the tertiary sector in the PRC. The differing views of language learning — the traditional Chinese view of language as a fixed body of knowledge versus the Western view of language as a dynamic, evolutionary phenomenon — pose a key contradiction, and the experiences of foreign and Chinese teachers as they mutually adapt or fail to resolve these tensions are well documented.[25]

The Chinese practice of English language learning was initially shaped by views of its own language and the pedagogy employed by the missionaries and other foreign teachers in the nineteenth century. The Chinese language served as a vehicle for cultural transmission, which is reflected in the choice of resources for teaching it. The canons of classical literature formed the principal corpus of texts,[26] which were learnt through rote memorization — sometimes even backwards.[27] One underlying assumption of this technique was that the subtleties of the literary content were beyond the comprehension of young minds, which did, however, possess the ability, under the guidance of the teacher-scholar, to memorize the corpus for later contemplation and enlightenment. This approach dovetailed with the pedagogy of the first foreign teachers of English, who likewise used books of literary texts as the main form of instructional resource.[28] More recent language pedagogy in the West has stressed the importance of oral competence, as well as reading and writing skills, and included a shift away from concentrating upon discrete grammatical rules, to a view of language as a holistic, multi-faceted, dynamic entity that is strongly influenced by sociocultural factors. Language learners were no longer to be passive acquirers of rules, but, instead, were expected to practise and produce language according to their individual needs and ability. The exposure of the PRC to these views of language and language learning before 1978 was limited by political considerations. In the 1950s, reference was made to teaching methods in the USSR, which mirrored the grammar-translation approaches already favoured in China, while, in the early 1960s, there was a brief flirtation with behaviourist audio-lingual techniques, imported from the USA.

The shift in conceptions of language learning also brought about changes to the role of the teacher. Traditionally, the Chinese teacher-scholar served as the fount of knowledge and as a role model for students, who would respond with respect and lifelong devotion.[29] As teaching was considered to be the direct transmission of knowledge and culture, little attention was paid to pedagogic skills: students were expected to memorize whatever they were presented. It was sufficient that the teacher-scholar had a solid grasp of the subject matter and led a respectable life. Any move, as occurred in some Western countries, towards a less teacher-centred approach which required a high degree of pedagogic competence could therefore be construed as threatening the authority and status of the teacher in China. The implications for teacher education are serious; whereas the training of a teacher in the traditional mould would concentrate on subject knowledge, the new Western ideas would require a shift in focus to incorporate pedagogic competence. Which teacher educators in the PRC would possess the expertise to carry out this change, or, given the self-undermining nature of such an initiative, would be motivated to do so?

The tensions engendered by the reforms since 1978 in EFL teacher education were felt by many institutes, especially those employing foreign teachers. The case study which follows demonstrates how one institute, Taiyuan Teachers College, where the author worked as a teacher at the college for four years in the mid-1980s, handled these tensions. The first part of the case study outlines the context: a brief history of the college, its facilities, courses, students and the staff of the Foreign Languages Department (FLD). The second part describes and analyses the changes to the curriculum and practices for EFL teacher education after 1978 and includes a discussion on the role of foreign teachers in this period. The final part extrapolates and generalizes the findings of the individual case study.

THE CASE STUDY

The college

Taiyuan Teachers College opened in 1958. Taiyuan, the capital city of Shanxi province in north central China, was developed as a base for heavy industry in the 1950s, fired by the coal from the major coalfields in the province. Under the Dengist economic reforms, light industry expanded. Geographically and economically, Taiyuan is located in the middle stratum; as part of the industrial heartland of China, it is poorer (and Shanxi province as a whole is much poorer) than the seaboard areas where the Special Economic Zones have been established, but it is richer than rural areas. Similarly, Taiyuan Teachers College is not as prestigious as teacher education institutes located in major cities, but the college, serving the municipality of Taiyuan and surrounding countryside, is larger than institutes located in county towns. Hence, it occupies the middle stratum of teacher education. The college has been able to employ native speakers as teachers since 1981 and it established academic links with a British university in 1987.[30]

The history of the college reflects national experiences. Initially, it offered vocational training in three subjects: Chinese, mathematics and biology. Lacking trained staff and experiencing low student intakes, the college did not flourish and closed in 1962. It reopened with a wider range of courses than previously offered, in May 1978, the year of Deng Xiaoping's keynote speech[31] that set out the new direction for education. The college is sited around the courtyards of the Hou family ancestral estate and it includes the original building of Shanxi University, constructed in Western style, financed by indemnities exacted from the imperial government by the Western powers following the Boxer Rebellion.[32] Since 1978, extensive building projects have been carried out to cope with curriculum expansion, increasing student numbers and the need to upgrade the accommodation provided to senior members of staff. Considerable investment has been made in educational hardware, with the establishment of science and language laboratories (the latter being state-of-the-art when purchased in the early 1980s), an electronics workroom and a library that contains, according to official figures, nearly a quarter of a million books.[33] At the same time, many of the decaying historical buildings have been razed.

The college has 11 departments, offering 12 subjects at *zhuanke* certificate level: Chinese, politics, history, foreign languages, mathematics, physics, chemistry, biology, geography, physical education, and arts and craft (which includes music). Since 1986, the Chinese Department and the FLD have been authorized to confer *benke* degrees. The FLD also provides in-service *zhuanke* courses of two years' duration for teachers who do not possess a teaching qualification. In 1986, in response to public demand and a government directive permitting colleges to raise money through marketing extramural courses, the FLD opened a night school. Profits were used to upgrade equipment in the FLD and to provide supplementary income for members of staff.

Students

The majority of students entering the college come from within Taiyuan, a city with a population of around two million. However, the college reserves a small number of places for students from nearby rural areas and from cities within Shanxi province which do not offer teacher education of a commensurate standard. Except for a few generally older students who choose teaching as a career, most students attend the college on the basis of their results in the municipal examinations for senior secondary school graduands. Shanxi University and other institutes of higher education take priority over the college in creaming off the students with the best results. This system effectively prevents the vast majority of the college's students from having much say in the kind of vocational training that they are to receive. In fact, many students have no specific desire to become teachers, despite accepting a place at the college after the *gaokao*.[34] Another consequence of the creaming process is that the students entering the FLD are not usually highly competent in English. Furthermore, their inability to achieve a place at university leaves them with a strong sense of failure, an opinion generally shared by society.[35] As noted above, the association of failure with the teaching profession has deep historical roots in Chinese culture.

Dormitory accommodation is provided for students where required and a regimented timetable for boarders was initially put in place, commencing with compulsory morning exercises before breakfast and ending with 'lights-out' at 10:30 p.m. Over the years, enforcement of the timetable has become less strict as students have been allowed greater liberty; for instance, morning exercises have been replaced by an optional recreation session.

The Foreign Languages Department

The FLD recruits approximately 60 students a year for the *zhuanke* course. Two parallel classes exist; unstreamed academically, they are composed according to the geographic origin of the students. The FLD is principally concerned with training teachers of English, although it does also teach courses to students studying other majors. Russian, French and Japanese subsidiary subjects are taught only to *benke* students. The staff responsible for teaching *zhuanke* and *benke* courses in the FLD number around 20 Chinese and 2 foreign teachers. Of the 19 local teachers employed by the college in 1989, 1 was a retired professor who still offered some courses, only 3 were associate professors, 8 were lecturers and 7 were teaching assistants (*zhujiao*). The 'faultline' caused by the Cultural Revolution is evidenced by the absence of a generation of teachers with 15 to 30 years of experience.[36]

The FLD is led on the academic side by the department head, who is appointed by the college leaders and is usually an associate professor. There is also a CCP Secretary attached to the FLD who was originally responsible for liaising with the head[37] (although this role declined over the reform period) and for supervising political aspects relating to the FLD's work.[38] The staff of the FLD were recruited in three phases. When the college reopened in 1978, the first staff hired were experienced teachers of English in secondary schools or evening classes, some trained before 1949. The second group were recruited from among the first graduates of the college in the early 1980s. Later, with the upgrading of teacher education nationwide and the higher numbers of students being trained, the college has been able to recruit university graduates. Significantly, only two of the local staff (those at teaching assistant rank) recruited in the two later phases had any secondary school teaching experience, other than participating in Teaching Practice as student teachers. Staff were selected on an academic, rather than a professional, basis.

The methodologies employed by the staff to teach English may be divided into two orientations: Grammar-Translation and an eclectic approach. The Grammar-Translation Method is favoured by the most experienced group of teachers in charge of 'Intensive Reading' courses. Students prepare for each lesson by combing the text to be studied, parsing each sentence and learning any new vocabulary. In class, the teacher calls upon students to explain, in Chinese, the meaning of difficult passages and to elucidate grammatical points. These are then practised in exercises. When, in 1986, the head of the department decreed that the medium of instruction should be English as much as possible, the teaching method shifted to more of a Grammar-Paraphrase Method, with explanations of difficult passages being offered in English rather than Chinese. The two former secondary school teachers were allocated courses in Listening and Phonetics, which they taught intensively: word-by-word comprehension and imitation. This prescriptive methodology owes much to the Grammar-Translation Method that still holds sway in senior secondary schools and bears a close resemblance to the way that the Chinese language is taught in schools.[39]

Many younger lecturers in the department have been exposed to alternative approaches, as the possibilities for overseas training or learning from foreign teachers increased with the Open Door policy. Those who graduated from universities, such as Shanxi University or Shanxi Teachers University, had been taught, in part, by foreign teachers. Also, through the college's links with the University of Newcastle-upon-Tyne (the FLD offered Chinese courses to a small number of British students in the late 1980s and early 1990s), several members of staff attended a year-long EFL course in Britain. One lecturer gained a scholarship to the University of Florida (to study English literature rather than EFL). The majority of staff going to overseas institutes returned to the college, but some have remained abroad. Within the PRC, advanced in-service courses are offered at major institutes in Beijing, Shanghai and Guangzhou, often in collaboration with the British Council or another foreign agency. The members of staff from Taiyuan Teachers College who attended such courses, as a result of their training, tend to employ eclectic methods that combine grammatical explanation in English with activities in groups and pairs to develop the appropriate language skills. One lecturer attributes his methodology to foreign influence:

> When I was a university student, every time I had a lesson taught by a foreign teacher... I would note down their teaching method. Because each time I learned something from them, so I think my students might learn something from us... In my 'Intensive Reading' course, I tried almost every method I know, mainly British teaching methods.[40]

The EFL curriculum

In 1978, the college initially offered *zhuanke* courses of three years' duration. The curriculum for the FLD was divided into five areas: political theory, pedagogical studies, academic language, physical education and EFL studies. The curriculum stipulates the subjects to be studied and the contact time to be allotted to each subject. The same number of contact hours is stipulated for every *zhuanke* course in the college. Although the curriculum is formulated at provincial level in accordance with national guidelines, individual colleges have considerable autonomy in interpreting and implementing the curriculum. The FLD curriculum for English underwent two major revisions in the 1980s. In 1984, the first revision was concerned with the EFL studies component, responding to changes in the national English syllabus for junior secondary schools which took effect in 1982, and which stressed communicative skills as a central goal.[41] A revision in the following year saw the reduction of the *zhuanke* course from three years to two; it resulted from preparations for the forthcoming Nine-Year Compulsory Education Law, which was to be promulgated in 1986.

The initial curriculum (Table 8.1) had as its core subjects Intensive Reading, which concentrated on the linguistic analysis of texts, and Extensive Reading, which focused more on comprehension skills. Two new courses, Conversation and Writing Skills, were instituted on the initiative of the head in 1981 and 1982 respectively, although neither course appeared in the official curriculum.

Table 8.1
Three-year *zhuanke* course for teachers of English: subjects and contact time (1978)

Area	Subject	Hours
Political Theory	Marxism / Leninism	70
	History of the Party or Political Economics	72
Education	Psychology	54
	Education	54
Academic Language	Academic Chinese	105
Physical Education		142
English Language	Intensive Reading	712
	Extensive Reading	250
	Listening and Speaking	172
	Reading and Writing	142
	Translation	60
	Western Civilisation	60
	Phonetics	35
	Grammar	72
	Secondary English Materials & Methodology	60
	Subsidiary Subjects	90
	Teaching Practice (6 weeks)	

Grand Total 2150

A process of rationalization occurred in 1984, with the first major revision of the curriculum. The motivation for the revision was the shift in orientation of the junior secondary school English syllabus towards greater stress on communicative competence rather than grammatical knowledge. The provincial authorities allowed the FLD a free hand in redesigning the curriculum within the framework of the guidelines that called upon EFL teacher educators to adapt to the new orientation. The revised college curriculum (Table 8.2) removed 'Intensive Reading' from its core position. This course was combined with 'Extensive Reading' as the 'Reading' course, which was allocated the same number of hours (250) as 'Extensive Reading' in the old curriculum. A new core course, 'Integrated English', was established, combining 'Listening and Speaking', 'Reading and Writing', 'Conversation', and 'Writing Skills'. Room was also found for courses on the four individual communicative skills: 'Reading' (as noted above), 'Listening', 'Speaking' and 'Writing' (combined with 'Translation'). The emphasis was thus firmly placed upon communication, as the head explained:

> [O]ur Department adopted ... new courses in our curriculum so our students get a good chance to train themselves to be more effective in English language in a few ways: they can listen effectively, can listen to a native speaker's report, even they can listen to the BBC and they can speak fluently. They can talk without any shyness with the foreigners. I think that must be the effect of the change of curriculum.[42]

Table 8.2
Three-year *zhuanke* course for teachers of English: subjects and contact time (1984)

Area	Subject	Hours
Political Theory	Marxism / Leninism	70
	History of the Party or Political Economics	72
Education	Psychology	54
	Education	54
Academic Language	Academic Chinese	105
Physical Education		142
English Language	Integrated English	712
	Reading	250
	Listening	172
	Speaking	142
	Translation / Writing	60
	Western Civilisation	60
	Pronunciation	35
	Grammar	72
	Secondary English Materials & Methodology	60
	Subsidiary Subjects	90
	Teaching Practice (6 weeks)	

Grand Total 2150

The second major revision of the curriculum took place in phases between 1985 and 1988, as a result of the *Nine-Year Compulsory Education Law*. It became apparent that greater numbers of teachers would be needed in order to meet the requirements of the law. Shanxi Provincial Education Bureau, exercising its right of control over such policy matters, decided from September 1985 that the length of the *zhuanke* course should be reduced from three to two years. In obeying this directive, the FLD initially attempted to squeeze three years' material into the new course by pruning the chapters of individual books to be studied. This approach was rejected as impracticable in the revised curriculum of 1988 (Table 8.3), which sought to identify priorities for the course and to allocate contact hours accordingly. One area of considerable debate was whether or not to retain Teaching Practice, as some leaders felt that the time and logistical demands outweighed the benefits accruing to the student teachers. Although the final decision opposed cutting it from the curriculum, the fact that the possibility was even discussed indicates the low status given to pedagogy components.

The 1988 curriculum was organized so as to allow the students to follow a broad-based foundation year covering political theory, education, psychology and basic phonetics, together with the core courses. The study of junior secondary school EFL teaching materials and pedagogy precedes Teaching Practice. In the final term, a small amount of time is devoted to two subsidiary courses, but most attention is given to the core courses of 'Integrated English', 'Listening', 'Speaking', 'Reading' and 'Writing', which form the components of the final examination.

The shortening of the programme to two years raised questions about the quality of education that could be achieved in that time. One lecturer commented:

> The graduates can never be proficient enough to teach at a [secondary] school in their two years' study here; they will learn very, very little about what they're going to teach. So, in my idea, a three-year course is the least possible time for learning a foreign language... but, as the [Provincial] Education Commission says, as we don't have enough [secondary] school teachers we'll have to use this emergency measure.[43]

This emergency measure lasted until 1991, when the three-year course was restored on an experimental basis. The problem facing provincial education officials was how to abandon the system of two-year courses without appearing to admit that the system was unsatisfactory. The solution was to adopt a '2+1' structure, modelled upon a system operating in Sichuan, whereby the students spend the third year studying a second major subject. The FLD restored the three-year course by using the '2+1' scheme as a rhetorical cover. In reality, as a departmental document lays out,

> There will be no '2+1' in the English courses. The students' language knowledge and their skills of translation are both to be strengthened in the third year, so as to qualify them for future teaching and to enable them to assist local people in translation work, which will be important in promoting the modernization drive.

Table 8.3
Two-year *zhuanke* course for teachers of English: subjects and contact hours (1988)

Subject	Total hours per subject	Year One Term 1 (14 weeks)	Term 2 (18 weeks)	Year Two Term 3 (18 weeks)	Term 4 (12 weeks)
Principles of Marxism / Leninism	28	2			
Chinese Revolution and Socialist Construction	36		2		
Education	28	2			
Psychology	36		2		
Academic Chinese	64	2	2		
Physical Education	100	2	2	2	
Integrated English	496	8	8	8	8
Reading	184	2	2	4	4
Listening	124	2	2	2	2
Speaking	124	2	2	2	2
Grammar	72		2	2	
Pronunciation	28	2			
Writing	24				2
Secondary School Teaching Methodology & Materials	36			2	
Subsidiary Subjects	60			2	2
Unscheduled Activities	27				
Total	1467	24	24	24	20

In September 1994, after the experimentation period, the restored three-year structure was formally adopted. In the third year, students studied four courses: 'Technical and Commercial Translation', 'Western Culture', 'Western Literature' and 'Prose Writing', each being of 60 hours' duration.

Foreign teachers

The recruitment of teachers through the British organization Voluntary Service Overseas (VSO)[44] started in 1981. Under the terms of the agreement, these 'foreign teachers' (the official designation) work for two years in the college, with extensions and early terminations permissible by mutual consent. By 1994, 12 foreign teachers had worked in the college; 3 extended their stay, 1 (the first) left after 18 months. The teachers held teaching qualifications in modern languages or EFL from British or European universities.

The arrival of the first foreign teacher in September 1981 posed a problem for the FLD. In deciding which courses to allocate to her, the department head eventually asked her to teach classes in 'Conversation', as a peripheral, extracurricular activity. Likewise, the following year, when a second foreign teacher arrived, the newcomer was asked to teach an extracurricular course, 'Writing Skills'. Once again, this course was not listed in the official curriculum. The first foreign teacher, who had considerable teacher education experience and a Master's degree, eventually broke her contract, citing, among other reasons, failure to find satisfaction in her work. Another problem was the arrangements made for her living conditions: a careful control was placed on visitors by the college authorities, who appeared to have two objectives in mind, limiting contact between the foreign teachers and locals, and preserving the safety of the foreigners, for which the college felt responsible.

Initially, the foreign teachers believed that their role was ill-defined, as two of them wrote in April 1984:

> Our objectives are fuzzy; the Chinese position, however, appears to be simple: foreign teachers... are employed to work alongside Chinese teachers to provide an extra boost to the students' language level. They are peripheral to the core of the course, 'Intensive Reading', which is grammar-based, rote-learnt and conducted in Chinese.[45]

The presence of foreign teachers continued to concern some of the college authorities, particularly the Party Secretary in the FLD, who attempted to lay down strict guidelines for students in their relations with foreign teachers. This tension was summed up by the foreign teachers:

> We suppose [our] real use is to give the subject they are studying in this rather dreary way a human, if foreign, face... It is, unfortunately, not the view of some of the older Chinese leaders who, in a series of addresses to the students, have warned them against any but the most necessary contact with us.[46]

This report was written at the time of the national 'Campaign Against Spiritual Pollution' (*jingshen wuran*) that began in late 1983. The campaign tried to prevent what authorities perceived as the more undesirable elements of Western culture from entering the country. The foreign teachers at the college were discouraged from travelling outside the city and were requested not to use Western pop music[47] as teaching material. Students' music cassettes were confiscated and students were given guidelines on the approved topics (the discussion of language points, for instance) for conversations with their foreign teachers, although this stricture was widely ignored in practice. By the summer of 1984 the campaign had died out and the restrictions forgotten, if not formally lifted. Conditions improved with the lightening of the political climate, with the result that the foreign teachers were free to form friendships and to play a more active role in the academic and social life of the city.[48]

In 1983, the foreign teachers were assigned, for the first time, to teach two courses that appeared in the official curriculum: 'Reading and Writing', and 'Listening and Speaking'. Both foreign teachers would teach the same students. This proved to be an unwieldy arrangement, as VSO had supplied the college with a set of textbooks[49] which used an integrated skills approach, merging the four skills of reading, writing, listening and speaking. It was impractical for the foreign teachers to separate out the reading and writing sections from the listening and speaking sections without sacrificing the coherence of the textbook contents.

At the time of the 1984 curriculum revision, the foreign teachers proposed combining their courses as 'Integrated English'. The new arrangement allowed for one foreign teacher to be allocated to each class. As a counterbalancing measure to the holistic approach to language of the 'Integrated English' course, extra time was devoted to the individual language skills of reading, writing, listening and speaking, by assigning local staff to teach such courses. The 'Reading' course remained, principally, the preserve of teachers who favoured the traditional Grammar-Translation methodology. With 'Integrated English' replacing 'Intensive Reading' as the core of the curriculum, the foreign teachers were thus moved from the periphery to the centre of the FLD's courses. This move provided the foreign teachers with a clearer role. Next, they turned their attention to the realms of methodology training, despite, in some cases, their own relative inexperience in the field. Occasional demonstrations of methodological techniques (such as communicative pair work and role plays) were introduced into 'Integrated English' lessons, but this practice was viewed with concern by some local staff who believed that these methods were inappropriate for the 'Chinese situation'. Indeed, one student was criticized by his supervisor in November 1984 for adopting such techniques in Teaching Practice. Nonetheless, the foreign teachers in 1986 felt that their efforts had some value:

> [W]e personally see our presence here as justified by two main factors: we are native speakers; and, although pedagogic traditionalism is strong, we hope that the methodology we use and teach in class will in turn give our students some alternative ideas when they themselves become [secondary] school teachers.[50]

In 1987, foreign teachers were formally given permission to teach methodology as a component of the 'Integrated English' course. The head explained this decision as a result of the Open Door policy:

> The Chinese traditional methodology of teaching English is only Grammar-Translation... So, in the past, our students can read only: they cannot speak even a bit because they haven't any training in listening and speaking. When the Open Door policy was adopted in our country, we had more chance to have contact with the foreigners' new materials; we gradually got to know that our traditional methodology was backward, so we gradually changed to the new methods in our teaching.[51]

He said that he also found that students responded well to the teaching strategies used by the foreign teachers:

> Chinese teachers ... teach how to translate a text and how to remember a word, and how to alternate a sentence from a simple to a complex one, and how to teach the students to learn by heart, phonetics and so on. It is not so active, but ... our students like foreigners' methodology more, because it is more active. It is new, because they can learn, they can get their students to learn from play, talking and so on. But our Chinese teachers have only one book and one piece of chalk and the blackboard, nothing else![52]

One of the Chinese lecturers who was receptive to the new methodology felt that a process of synthesis was better than the direct adoption of foreign methods:

> We have learnt some new teaching methods from the foreign teachers, but we have also accumulated our own experience and developed some methods ourselves. If we want to teach the students efficiently, we'll have to sometimes create better teaching methods, but — and we all have this experience — to create a new teaching method is much more difficult than to introduce some new ones, and also to create a new one might not be successful. But by studying what is needed in [secondary] schools we can try to form a teaching method that would be very useful for our students.[53]

The pedagogy component concentrated on practical strategies to encourage communicative activities rather than on theories of language acquisition. It centred around techniques for teaching new language items, and for teaching listening, reading and communicative writing skills. As a result of the college's official approval of this work, from 1990, VSO started to recruit teachers with greater experience in both EFL teaching and teacher education.

The foreign teachers were evacuated from the PRC by VSO in the wake of the clearing of Tiananmen Square in June 1989, but the project resumed the following September. The 'Campaign against Peaceful Evolution' was instigated in the aftermath of the crackdown, with students being warned in speeches to guard against being corrupted by Western influences. Compulsory military training (mainly marching practice) received greater attention than in the past, but the work and daily life of the foreign teachers were largely unaffected by the campaign, which existed more on a symbolic and rhetorical level.

Links with secondary schools

As the college was established to provide secondary schools with teachers, links between the two parties have existed since 1978. The principal form of contact is through Teaching Practice for the students, which takes place towards the end of October in the second year of training, by which time the students have completed a course in teaching methodology lasting approximately seven weeks. The students are assigned to secondary schools in and around Taiyuan, with a typical English Department of a secondary school receiving six or seven student teachers for a period of six weeks. Each student is allocated a supervising teacher from the school staff and a tutor from the college. Since 1985, foreign teachers have also acted as peripatetic advisers. The students usually observe the supervising teacher during the first two weeks and then they share the teaching load among themselves for the remaining four weeks. An informal survey of students carrying out Teaching Practice in 13 schools in 1988 shows that they each taught a paltry average of 15 lessons (of 45 minutes each) in total.

The circumstances confronting a student teacher on Teaching Practice are far from ideal. The limited number of lessons available can lead to over-anxiety and exaggerated preparation. Furthermore, a large group of observers often congregate, comprising the supervising teacher, tutor, foreign teacher (possibly) and fellow students, who are encouraged to spend free lessons in observing their colleagues. In feedback after Teaching Practice in 1988, students criticized over-supervision and the lack of opportunities to practise. Typical suggestions included lengthening Teaching Practice to two or three months, reducing the amount of observation and allowing more practice inside the college. However, some secondary school teachers, concerned about the examination prospects for their pupils (by which they themselves are judged), are loath to entrust classes to a student teacher; indeed, it is not uncommon for the supervising teacher, dissatisfied with the quality of instruction that the class is receiving from the student teacher, to take over lessons allocated to Teaching Practice. Also, the orientation of the college towards language courses militates against finding further time for methodological practice, particularly when the training period was shortened to two years, and there is a lack of staff qualified to take such courses.

In October 1989, the Provincial Education Commission addressed the problem of the college staff's lack of secondary school experience by directing two teaching assistants or lecturers (selected on a roster basis) from every department in the college to be seconded to secondary schools for a semester. These teachers were not only to teach, but also to study teaching methods used by secondary school teachers and to assess the implications of the situation in secondary schools for the development of future teacher education courses. The new measure was implemented in the second semester of the 1989–90 academic year. Although most teachers and lecturers did not relish the prospect of teaching in a secondary school, at least one member of the college staff saw the benefits of the scheme:

> [C]lose contact should be very useful. The teachers in our College have been imagining what is needed in the [secondary] school. If we have more contact, it will prove what they do need and what we should do for our students.[54]

The policy addresses a noticeable gap in experience between secondary schools and teachers colleges. In the context of EFL teaching, it provides a bridge between the methodology of junior secondary schools (where the curriculum has become increasingly communication-oriented, particularly since the further revision to the national syllabus in 1993)[55] and the traditional environment of the college. In the long term, this measure, together with the opportunities for advanced study abroad or in prestigious domestic institutions, may allow local staff to take over the teaching of practical methodology from the foreign teachers. The policy also corrects a misapprehension that the college might have had over its primary function, following criticism by the SEdC in 1988 of a national trend:

> In the previous period [i.e. prior to 1988], there had been a tendency, in teacher education at the college level, of neglecting the purpose of training for college education and seeking to parallel that of university education; the curriculum and contents of teaching had tended to be hard-going and difficult, failing to establish a close connection with the related courses taught in junior secondary schools; the links in Teaching Practice had been weak and not enough importance had been attached to the training of the students' basic skills of instruction.[56]

CONCLUSION

The period since 1978 has been one of relative stability in the PRC, as the proponents of the Four Modernizations programme in the CCP have prevailed over political forces seeking either liberalization or intransigence.

Three specific challenges to education have been elucidated in this period: a reorientation of curricula towards academic, professional and vocational training; the assimilation of foreign ideas and expertise, and the broadening of mass education to a national norm of nine-year compulsory schooling.

As far as the reorientation of the curriculum is concerned, the case study demonstrates that a more holistic and communicative view of EFL has replaced the traditional literary bias of the Grammar-Translation method, with 'Integrated English' replacing 'Intensive Reading' and 'Extensive Reading' as the core element. While the directives from the national and provincial governments provided the broad guidelines for change, the realization of the reforms in the college involved elements of compromise and pragmatism. The availability of a set of textbooks and the previously unsatisfactory experience of the foreign teachers led to the institution of the 'Integrated English' course, which was the creation of the college. No such course existed in the provincial guidelines. At the same time, the Grammar-Translation methodology was not entirely jettisoned, as this would have created serious difficulties to senior staff who were more comfortable with this approach. The 'Reading' course provided a slot for these teachers. To improve the vocational quality of the college courses, links between the FLD and secondary schools evolved from tenuous beginnings in 1978 to well-developed cooperative activities. The place of Teaching Practice in the curriculum was questioned in 1988, and this suggests that the authorities either perceived Teaching Practice as having little merit in principle, or, more likely, believed that the opportunities for teacher education afforded by the contemporary format of Teaching Practice were negligible. Teaching Practice was salvaged, however, and there was a movement towards enhancing the methodological components in the curriculum and broadening the staff's experience of junior secondary schools.

The influence of foreign teachers in the college increased in various stages throughout the period under study. The foreign teachers were initially placed on the periphery of the curriculum, to their disgruntlement. However, after curriculum revisions and lobbying by the foreign teachers, they eventually took on the core language component and much of the practical methodology work. Local staff received increased opportunities to study overseas as more foreign links were established at college, municipal, provincial and national levels. Their contact with foreign ideas was also increased by the provision of advanced courses in teacher education within the PRC. By the mid-1990s, though, local staff had yet to reclaim the core courses in the college curriculum from the foreign teachers. This may arise from the 'foreignness' of the methodology and a reluctance, on the part of older teachers in particular, to embrace the new initiatives too boldly, given the historically fickle nature of the politics of EFL teaching in the PRC. In effect, it was safer to leave these courses to the foreigners. A further and much stronger incentive for the college staff to disinvest from mainstream work stemmed directly from the entrepreneurial ethos engendered by the modernizations programme and the need for staff to supplement their incomes: many of the staff became involved in lucrative private tutoring, television and publishing work and, as a result, were not anxious to assume extra burdens in their college workload.

The *Nine-Year Compulsory Education Law* proved a problematic reform, as far as the development of the college curriculum was concerned. The implementation of the policy in a province already short of teachers led to the reduction of the *zhuanke* course from three to two years. While the FLD reaffirmed its commitment to the communicative orientation of the 1984 curriculum, it had difficulty in finding a suitable way to shrink the course syllabi. Staff raised doubts over the two-year course, fearing insufficient time to train teachers effectively. The measure exacerbated existing problems of quality. The low standards in English of students entering the FLD created the need for remedial language work. Problems of motivation also existed, with teaching offering poor economic rewards and low social status, while English skills were sought in professions that offered better pay and conditions. At the same time, the FLD was under pressure to improve the pedagogical components of the course, and it needed to employ the foreign teachers in this area, as local staff lacked the necessary training and experience (although some of the foreign teachers were also novices).

This case study suggests that individual institutions in the PRC respond to national policies according to the resources, including personnel, at their disposal. For instance, when the modernizations programme required the qualitative development of ELT education, by moving towards a more communicative approach and more focused teacher education courses, the college maintained more traditional methods at the periphery and employed foreign teachers as agents of change. The fact that the college was unable to make the necessary adjustments with local staff alone also suggests that national policies are formulated somewhat ambitiously, without due regard for the resources at the disposal of individual institutions; it was somewhat fortuitous (such as in the timely arrival of the textbooks from overseas) that the college acquired the means to make a significant adjustment. This portrayal of localized policy-making points out the problems facing lesser institutes as they attempt to follow the lead of prestigious counterparts. It also suggests that policies made by the central agencies are reinterpreted and implemented by the peripheral agencies according to local conditions.

In the case study, the college achieved a reorientation of its curriculum to match the thrust of the reforms only by marginalizing senior staff and placing local teachers in a supporting role to foreign teachers. It should be stressed that this is an individual response by an individual institution to a complex and demanding situation, and that every institution's situation will vary within the parameters of the general thrust of reform. In many respects, the response of Taiyuan Teachers College, on the face of it, represents an unhealthy compromise, given the important role ascribed to foreign teachers. The local staff were not, however, entirely averse to this situation, as it freed them to earn supplementary income away from the college, and, particularly in the case of experienced teachers with long memories, shielded them from the vanguard of reform, which, as the history of EFL teaching in China has shown, could prove a vulnerable position should there be another dramatic shift in national politics. The provision of advanced language courses and EFL teacher education courses in the PRC and overseas, and the growing links between teacher education institutes and secondary schools represent key strategies in improving the quality of the courses provided by institutes such as Taiyuan Teachers College. The major obstacle, however, is the comparative attractions that lie elsewhere for competent linguists in the PRC. This disinvestment from the mainstream of education by talented personnel is a significant challenge to central authorities, who will need to review on a regular basis the attractiveness of the teacher education profession in terms of pay, conditions and social status.

NOTES

1. Parts of this chapter appeared in Adamson, 1995. The author is grateful to Taiyuan Teachers College and Voluntary Service Overseas for their collaboration in this research.
2. The 'linguists' acted as go-betweens to facilitate trade with foreign companies. See the essay by Feng Guaifen (1809–74) quoted in Teng and Fairbank, 1979, p. 51.
3. In recent years, leaders such as Jiang Zemin, Qian Qichen and Zhu Rongji have been competent in English.
4. Pennycook, 1994, p. 34.
5. See, for example, Confucius' comments in 'Great Learning' Chapter 5.
6. Such as the Empress Dowager, Cixi, at the turn of the century.
7. According to Chinese friends of the author, some teachers of English were murdered by their own students.
8. Translated by Teng and Fairbank, pp. 183–4.
9. Such as, for instance, during the mid-1950s, when Russian was taught as the main foreign language in secondary schools. See Adamson and Morris, 1997.

10. This occurred during the early stages of the Cultural Revolution.
11. Ross, 1992, p. 240.
12. Communicative approaches to EFL focus on active production of realistic language by the students, rather than just a knowledge of language systems.
13. Longman International (UK) collaborated with the People's Education Press (the curriculum development and publishing wing of the SEdC) on the 'Junior English for China' project funded by the United Nations Development Programme.
14. The materials are supposed to be adaptable to suit different teaching contexts throughout the PRC.
15. The target of the end of the century applies specifically to the richer seaboard areas and the industrial hinterland. The poorer rural areas are expected to provide nine-year schooling as soon as circumstances permit.
16. See Chaper 13 by Michael Agelasto in this volume.
17. A letter written by Huang Shuai, a fifth-grade primary student, was published in *Beijing Ribao* (12 December 1973) and *Renmin Ribao* (28 December 1973). In it, she asks, 'Are we children of the Mao Zedong era to be made to act like slaves under the "schoolmaster's absolute authority" created by the old education system?' Quoted in G. White, 1981, p. 194.
18. See Li Kwok-sing, 1995, p. 27.
19. Zhao Ziyang, 'Advance along the road of socialism with Chinese characteristics', report delivered at the Thirteenth National Congress of the Communist Party of China, in *Documents of the Thirteenth National Congress of the Communist Party of China*, 1987, p. 22.
20. Liu Daoyi, 1988.
21. Literally 'the mountains are high, the emperor far away'.
22. See, for example, Dzau, 1990.
23. See, for example, Harmer, 1985.
24. See, for example, Maley, 1990; Oatey, 1990; Sunderland, 1990; Yao Ruoguang, 1988. Yao's study of secondary school English teachers in Anhui province finds weaknesses in pedagogical training inherent in the teacher education system, as well as exaggerated stress on reading and grammar, to the detriment of communicative language skills.
25. See, for example, Scovel, 1983; Wu Jingyu, 1983; Yu Chenchung, 1984; Harvey, 1985; Bennett, 1992; Huang Yisi, 1992; Josselyn and Wang, 1992. For more on the relationships between Chinese and foreigners, see Chapter 16 by Maria Jaschok in this volume.
26. Chen Lifu, 1986.
27. The *beishu* (literally 'back to the book') method is described in the autobiography of the last emperor. See Pu Yi, 1964.
28. Pu Yi recalls that he studied English by reading extracts from *Alice in Wonderland*.
29. Chen Lifu, 1986.
30. The University of Newcastle-upon-Tyne. Newcastle and Taiyuan became twinned cities in 1986.
31. Deng Xiaoping, *Zai quanguo jiaoyu gongzuo huiyi shang de jianghua* (Speech at the National Education Conference), April 1978. See *China education yearbook 1949–1981*, p. 62.
32. The money for Shanxi University was requested by Timothy Richard, a Welsh

missionary. More than fifty missionaries had been massacred in Taiyuan during the Boxer Rebellion. For more on Boxer Rebellion indemnity funds, see Chapter 6 by Cong Cao in this volume, note 49.

33. The definition of a book in this respect is quite elastic: it includes, for example, pamphlets.
34. An informal survey carried out by the author in a class of 27 students in 1985 found that only 3 wanted to be teachers.
35. Lo, 1984b.
36. See Chapter 3 by Cao Xiaonan in this volume for a discussion of age gap.
37. The Party Secretary had equal status to the Department Head and had to be consulted on policy matters.
38. This includes conducting political education, recruiting new Party members and organizing their work.
39. Dzau, 1990.
40. Interview with the author, Taiyuan, March 1987.
41. People's Education Press, 1982.
42. Interview with the author, Taiyuan, August 1988.
43. Interview with the author, Taiyuan, March 1987.
44. Voluntary Service Overseas (VSO) is a charity based in London which recruits professionals in various fields to work in developing countries, usually with a two-year commitment.
45. Project report to VSO, 1984.
46. Project report to VSO, 1984.
47. Folk music, however, was acceptable. The author argued unsuccessfully that John Denver's songs, which were very popular with the students, could be classified as folk music. There was a dance competition held in the college at the time of the Spiritual Pollution campaign, in which the FLD students were disqualified, apparently for wearing jeans and dancing to disco music.
48. Taiyuan has a reputation as being conservative in outlook. In the mid-1980s, for example, interracial dating and marriage met with official disapproval.
49. The *Strategies* series, published by Longman.
50. Project report to VSO, 1986.
51. Interview with the author, Taiyuan, August 1988.
52. Interview with the author, Taiyuan, August 1988.
53. Interview with the author, Taiyuan, March 1988.
54. Interview with the author, Taiyuan, March 1988.
55. People's Education Press, 1993.
56. State Education Commission, 1990a, p. 20.

9

Agricultural Universities: Engines of Rural Development?[1]

Greg KULANDER

INTRODUCTION

Agricultural universities worldwide have always been more pragmatic than comprehensive or liberal arts universities. Their mission is clear: to systematize and develop agricultural science and technology for use in production by farmers, thereby improving both rural living standards and the national economy. This holds true for Chinese agricultural universities as well. 'Vitalizing Agriculture with Science and Education' (*ke jiao xing nong*) has been a popular slogan in the Chinese press since the early 1990s. It signals the general desire of policy-makers to increase the direct net social benefits of science and higher education, in order both to rationalize investments and to tie the work of scientists and educators more closely to existing problems in production. The PRC's agricultural colleges and universities are granted a key role in recent rural development policy statements.[2] They sit at the pinnacle of a large and growing vocational education system, with their mission expanding in recent years to include not only more research responsibilities (such as research and development of marketable products), but also — even more importantly — extension activities. Thus, the current proclaimed role of agricultural universities is to (1) educate high-level personnel according to the needs of agricultural and rural modernization (as reflected by market demands); (2) carry out basic (*jichu*), applied (*shiyong*) and developmental (*kaifa*) types of research[3] in a ratio of 6:2:2; and (3) to extend (*tuiguang*) research results (primarily from their own research projects) to farmers.

Agricultural colleges have undergone many of the same reforms as other tertiary-level educational institutions in the PRC, but with some notable exceptions. Due to both their importance for the national economy and their relatively low popularity, special measures have been taken to ensure their continued development. Preferential enrolment (i.e. lower entrance examination scores) of rural students linked to contingent job placement in rural areas was introduced in 1983 both to extend recruitment geographically and to secure high-level personnel for the poorer rural areas.

Based on a case study of Shenyang Agricultural University (SAU), a key agricultural university in Northeast China,[4] discussions with leading authorities, and available investigative reports, this chapter illustrates some of the successes of these policies as well as some of the difficulties experienced by agricultural colleges. It begins with an overview of the human resource situation in rural China, with particular emphasis on middle- and high-level personnel. The main section describes the Chinese tertiary-level agricultural education system, then briefly charts its historical development, and addresses the reforms initiated during the 1980s and 1990s. The chapter concludes with an account of the current status of Chinese agricultural universities and their future prospects.

RURAL HUMAN RESOURCES

Despite the PRC's rapid industrialization over the past 15 years, the agricultural sector remains by far the country's largest in terms of employed personnel. In 1992, agriculture employed 72% of the entire adult workforce.[5] The profile of agricultural production has changed substantially since 1980, however, and this has had important consequences for the make-up of the rural workforce.

Though the majority of the Chinese rural labour force still works in traditional crop farming, the areas of animal husbandry, aquatic production and agricultural sidelines are experiencing swift growth (Table 9.1). The share of traditional agriculture fell from 64% in 1980 to only 55% of the total agricultural production by 1992, while animal husbandry and sidelines doubled their respective shares and aquatic production increased fivefold (Table 9.2). The rural personnel structure reflects this changing make-up. By 1992, 43.5 million rural labourers were engaged in forestry, animal husbandry, fishery and the like, 10% of the total rural labour force and 13% of the rural agricultural labour force.[6]

There is a growing international awareness that an adequately trained human resource base is a necessary (though not sufficient) prerequisite for

Table 9.1
Breakdown of rural labour force (1993)

Rural* labour force	442 549 000	100.0%
Of which:		
Agriculture — forestry, animal husbandry, fishery	332 582 000	75.2%
Agricultural industry	36 590 000	8.3%
Construction	18 868 000	4.3%
Transport and telecommunication	7 994 000	1.8%
Small retail businesses	9 488 000	2.1%
Financial and insurance sector	311 000	0.1%
Others	36 716 000	8.3%

Source: *Agricultural yearbook of China 1994*, p. 294
*Rural = township or village level
Note: Total agricultural labour force is 456 817 000 (see Table 9.3).

Table 9.2
Share of total agricultural production (%)

Year	Agriculture — plant production	Forestry	Animal husbandry	Fishery	Sidelines
1980	64.3	3.1	14.2	1.3	3.4
1990	58.5	4.3	25.6	5.4	6.2
1992	55.5	4.6	27.0	6.8	6.1

Sources: *Agricultural yearbook of China 1982*, p. 26
          Agricultural yearbook of China 1991, p. 287
          Agricultural yearbook of China 1993, p. 247

rural development.[7] In the PRC, however, the agricultural workforce makes up the most poorly educated segment of the population. Of the 457 million employed in the agricultural sector, almost 23% are illiterate or semi-literate and another 45% have received only primary schooling. Just slightly more than 4% have attained a senior secondary level (*gaozhong* or *zhongzhuan*) certificate, and the college educated cohort numbers only 54 000 for the whole country[8] (see Table 9.3). This educational profile has important implications for future development of the agricultural sector.

Middle- and high-level personnel in the agricultural sector are employed in three main occupational areas: teaching, research and extension. The vast majority either work in the extension system or are connected in some way with it.[9] The modernization of Chinese agriculture is highly dependent upon how effectively new technology is transferred to rural areas, and the main conduit for this effort is the extension system.[10] The success of this system lies in turn with the quality of its personnel and the ability of farmers to absorb new technology.[11]

Table 9.3
Workforce educational profile

Education level	Entire workforce ('000)	%	Agricultural labourers* ('000)	%
Tertiary (*benke*)	4 301	0.7%	8	0.0%
Tertiary short-course (*zhuanke*)	7 818	1.2%	46	0.0%
Specialized secondary (*zhongzhuan*)	13 424	2.1%	321	0.1%
Senior high (*gaozhong*)	58 242	9.0%	18 879	4.1%
Junior high (*chuzhong*)	209 139	32.3%	126 915	27.8%
Primary school	244 834	37.8%	207 173	45.3%
Illiterate / partially illiterate	109 486	16.9%	103 475	22.7%
Total workforce	647 244	100.0%	456 817	100.0%

Source: *China statistics yearbook 1993*, p. 90
*Not including technical personnel or state employees

The agricultural extension system operates at four levels: province, prefecture (*diqu*), county (*xian*) and township (*xiang*), with the county-level agro-technical extension stations serving as the key link between rural areas and higher-level government. Although one million positions are available at district (*qu*)- or township-level extension stations, only 870 000 of these are filled. Of these current workers, 44.4% have only a primary school certificate and 19.4% even less than that. A mere 11.4% have earned a *zhongzhuan* certificate.[12] In 1990 there were only one college and two secondary school graduates working in agricultural extension per 10 000 agricultural workers.[13] Extension experts generally agree that there should be 10 to 30 graduates from secondary level or above per 10 000.[14] Moreover, the Ministry of Agriculture (MoA) has suggested that a suitable educational profile would be one to two college educated workers for every three to five specialized secondary school graduates (300 000–400 000 college and 600 000–700 000 secondary school graduates in all) employed at the city district- and township-level extension stations.[15] In sum, agricultural extension in the PRC is plagued by both quantitative and qualitative personnel problems.

The efficacy of the extension system, once considered to be an extremely effective administrative apparatus,[16] deteriorated during the 1980s due to changes among its target group, the farmers, and inappropriate extension methods.[17] Extension services continued to employ a strong administrative 'push' approach during the 1980s, with new technology centrally developed and then extended in a layer-by-layer approach to large areas. But with the introduction of the household responsibility system,[18] its target group changed: from 6 million production teams to 200 million rural households spread out over all of China with widely differing climatic, soil and water conditions as well as socio-economic levels. Extension by administrative fiat became obsolete, and the skills required of local extension agents, who previously functioned primarily as mere messengers, changed accordingly.

In addition to the general quantitative need for raising basic education levels, the entire qualification profile of extension workers has altered with the introduction of economic reforms. From basing their service purely on agricultural science, they now must provide comprehensive pre-, in- and post-harvest services based on principles of not only natural science, but social science as well.[19] Problems of supply and demand, pricing and profit must be addressed. In addition, the characteristics of the target group have changed. From having large organizations as their clients, extension agents today must instead concentrate their energies more on the individual farmer, which requires entirely different pedagogical and social skills.

Market reforms in rural areas have also opened up new sectors where high-level personnel is required. The phenomenal growth of township enterprises and the establishment of large numbers of rural cities have greatly increased the need for administrators and managers with higher education. Of the more than 50 million persons employed at the currently existing 1.5 million township enterprises, fewer than 300 000 have any kind of tertiary-level education, an average of only 1 college educated person for every 5 enterprises.[20] The scarcity of personnel in agriculture with higher education is aggravated by the flight of rural high-level personnel into metropolitan areas and into non-agricultural-related occupations. Official Chinese statistics show that 1.5 million people were educated in agriculture at either the tertiary or secondary level between 1949 and 1989, but only about one-third of this number were registered as agricultural technical personnel in 1989.[21] While some would have reached retirement age by 1989, a substantial number of those receiving secondary- or tertiary-level education in agriculture have left the official nomenclature of the agricultural sector.

Given this overview of the PRC's rural human resource problems, this chapter now examines the nation's tertiary-level agricultural education system. How well is it geared towards filling the human resource needs of the agricultural sector into the twenty-first century? In what ways does it contribute to rural development?

TERTIARY-LEVEL AGRICULTURAL EDUCATION

Scope

Currently 85 tertiary-level institutions in the PRC specialize in all agriculturally related fields (plus 11 in forestry) with a total enrolment of 173 000. Table 9.4 displays the different types of institutions by their specialization; 50 schools extend over comprehensive agriculture. Eighteen universities are administered (and funded) directly by the MoA in Beijing. The rest are provincially run, though the MoA retains the overall responsibility for their curricula. Eight of these 18 are designated key universities, a status which accords them additional funding and greater responsibilities,[22] and they are geographically spread out to each of the major regions of the PRC. They carry out most of the postgraduate training and are responsible for conducting region-specific research. The average enrolment for these key institutions in 1994 was about 3500 students. Provincial-level institutions are generally smaller, averaging approximately 2000 students, while those institutions offering only associate's degrees enrol just 1000 students on average.

Table 9.4
Breakdown of tertiary and senior secondary agricultural educational institutions by type (1993)

Type	Tertiary level		Senior secondary level	
	Schools	Enrolment	Schools	Enrolment
Comprehensive agriculture	50[a]	110 232	234	165 242
Water conservancy and hydropower	17	31 873	64	57 808
Land reclamation	7	13 089	15	9 405
Aquatic products	5	7 305	17	9 284
Meteorology	3	3 223	16	5 433
Agricultural mechanization	1	2 089	101	65 361
Agricultural engineering	1	3 041	–	–
Agricultural teachers college	1	2 311	–	–
Total	85	173 163	447	312 533

Source: *Agricultural yearbook of China 1994*, pp. 275–89
[a] includes 13 short-cycle colleges
Notes: Mean enrolment at tertiary level: 2037, at senior secondary level: 699
Table does not include forestry education

Previously offering exclusively agriculture-related specialities, these institutions branched out during the early 1990s. Today more and more students at agricultural colleges and universities do not major in agriculturally related subjects. Almost 135 000 were enrolled at agricultural colleges and universities in 1993, but only 96 000 were registered as having agricultural majors. At the national level only 3.8% of the total tertiary student enrolment majored in an agricultural subject in 1993 (see Table 9.5). This figure had fallen steadily from 5.6% in the early 1980s, reflecting the low priority given to higher agricultural education. Though its absolute enrolment increased during the 1980s, agriculture as a field of study was outpaced by all other major subject areas.

Table 9.5
Tertiary-level enrolment (1993) by type of institution and field of study

Type of institution / field of study	Enrolment by type of institution	Enrolment by field of study		
		Total	Normal programme (B.A. / B.S.)	Short-cycle programme (2–3 years)
Total	2 535 517	2 535 517	1 417 357	1 118 160
Engineering	928 552	934 039	605 015	329 024
Teacher training	566 552	594 053	225 842	368 211
Finance & economics	167 071	333 240	148 049	185 191
Medicine & pharmacy	224 936	231 375	155 143	76 232
Humanities	–	127 149	72 797	54 352
Natural sciences	–	98 964	78 637	20 327
Agriculture	134 802	96 196	61 601	34 595
Political science & law	33 341	51 831	30 969	20 862
Art	15 271	28 308	13 074	15 234
Forestry	21 024	23 289	14 922	8 367
Physical culture	15 572	17 073	11 308	5 765
Comprehensive	303 945	–		
Short-cycle vocational	79 909	–		
Nationalities	26 782	–		
Language & literature	17 760	–		

Source: *Education statistics yearbook of China 1993*, pp. 18–9, 22–3

There are altogether approximately 4000 postgraduate students in agriculture, one-half of whom came directly from their undergraduate studies, while the rest undertake in-service training. The latter are typically younger teachers at the universities. Thirty-four of the agricultural universities have Master's degree programmes (in altogether 75 different specialities) and 18 offer Ph.Ds (in 45 specialities).[23]

Agricultural colleges and universities typically offer two types of undergraduate programmes — a short-cycle (two- or three-year) course leading to a *zhuanke* and a regular (four- or five-year) course leading to a Bachelor's degree (*benke*). Much of the expansion in tertiary-level enrolment during the 1980s and 1990s has been in the short-cycle programmes.[24] This move has not been quite as pronounced in agriculture as in other fields, though by 1993, more than half of all students admitted were being enrolled in short-cycle programmes.[25] At SAU, for example, the percentage of short-cycle admissions rose from zero in 1982 to almost 43% in 1994. The emphasis on short-cycle programmes represents a policy both to increase output of tertiary-level graduates at a relatively low cost and to meet the demand of the rural job market for generalists with broader training.

The curricula provided at the agricultural institutions of higher education covered 55 specialities and 765 educational programmes in 1993.[26] Much of the emphasis is put on the traditional areas of crop and animal production. A typical undergraduate programme is made up of approximately 50% basic courses (*jichuke*), 30% basic speciality courses (*zhuanye jichu*) and 15% speciality (*zhuanye*) courses, with the remaining portion divided among army training, moral activities, social practice and work weeks. Basic courses include such subjects as foreign language, computer programming, chemistry, physics, biology, philosophy and agricultural economics. Around 25% of the curriculum involves laboratory work, and 25 to 30 weeks over the four years are spent on various sorts of practical training.

Tertiary-level adult education in agriculture is also available. Correspondence students are enrolled at schools attached to the regular institutions of higher agricultural education. In 1993, there were 15 804 students studying at these schools towards degrees by correspondence, 96% of whom took short-courses. In addition, independent cadre training and higher adult education institutions also provide tertiary-level agricultural education, with 1100 and 4300 students enrolled in 1993 at these

Table 9.6
Total tertiary-level agricultural enrolment by type (1993)

Educational type	Total enrolment	Normal course (B.A., B.S.)	Short-course (2–3 years)
Regular higher education	96 196	61 601	34 595
Attached correspondence school	15 804	676	15 128
In-service cadre training	1 118	0	1 118
Higher adult education	4 301	0	4 301
Total	117 419	62 277	55 142

Source: *Education statistics yearbook of China 1993*, pp. 23–5, 96

two types of institutions, respectively (Table 9.6 gives a detailed breakdown of the different types of tertiary-level agricultural enrolment).

Historical development

First set up at the beginning of the century, five agricultural colleges existed before the overthrow of the Qing Dynasty in 1911. They continued to expand and in 1937, 13 higher agricultural institutions enrolled 2590 students.[27] After the Communist victory in 1949, higher agricultural education has followed the general path of the rest of the educational sector in the PRC. In the 1950s, existing agricultural departments at comprehensive universities were consolidated into 15 independent institutions, altogether enrolling more than 10 000 students. These colleges and universities then underwent rapid and uncontrolled expansion during the Great Leap Forward, reconsolidation with emphasis on the development and propagation of scientific knowledge during the early 1960s, and closure during the Cultural Revolution. At that time universities were physically moved to rural areas and staff put to menial work. After 1978, reconstruction was followed by rapid but controlled growth during the 1980s and 1990s.

Chinese higher agricultural education was heavily influenced by the USSR during the 1950s and traces of this impact still exist in the 1990s. Under the Soviet system teaching and research were separated and carried out at two distinct types of institutions: teaching at colleges and universities, and research at institutes overseen by the Chinese Academy of Agricultural Sciences. Areas of study were fragmented into narrow specialities so that graduates became capable of working in only a single highly specialized field. Administration of higher education was extremely centralized with all decisions concerning personnel, funding, curriculum, enrolment and job placement made at the highest administrative level.

Still, in contrast with agricultural universities in many other developing countries, the Chinese institutions avoided Western influence in many areas. Often, developing countries, including India, have looked to the West for both material aid and organizational inspiration, adopting both curricula and teaching materials based on the environments, organisms and problems of Western countries with different climatic conditions and levels of economic development.[28] Due to the PRC's sustained period of academic isolation from the West, it evaded this uncritical adoption and did not experience negative aspects of academic colonialism such as human resource flight (brain drain), credentialism (diploma disease), dependence on expatriate staff, and inappropriate knowledge transfer. Though allowing for a certain indigenous development, this isolation has of course had its dark side as well — the absence of academic exchange and the resultant inhibition of Chinese scientific progress.

Current reforms in the PRC are to a high degree directed towards eliminating Soviet-inspired practices. The strengthening of research and the expansion of outreach activities are central components defining the future role of these institutions. Specialities are being broadened in order that graduates can better meet the needs of the job market. In the spirit of the economic reforms, educational administration in the PRC is being decentralized. More decision-making power is being delegated to the leaders of individual institutions.

REFORMS OF HIGHER AGRICULTURAL EDUCATION IN THE 1980s AND 1990s

Enrolment and job placement

Only 56% of agricultural university enrollees in 1992 had named agricultural universities as their first choice of schools. Undesired enrolment and poor career prospects, particularly in traditional specialities like agronomy and plant protection, are the principal causes of low student motivation.[29] A survey of graduating seniors at SAU found that only 28% chose 'interest in subject matter' as the most important reason for their studying at an agricultural university.[30] Of those surveyed, 72% had wanted to switch to a non-agricultural university or major. Not surprisingly, almost half of the teachers surveyed were either dissatisfied or extremely dissatisfied with their students' low motivation level.

Reforms in the enrolment and job placement systems were introduced in part to address these problems. Self-supporting (*zifei*), commissioned training (*daipei/weituo*), locally committed (*ding xiang*) and practically experienced (*shijian*) are new categories of students. The aim in introducing these new categories is to

1. enrol highly motivated students with an agricultural background and experience; and
2. ensure a steady supply of university graduates to rural areas and thus compensate for the high-level personnel flight from the agricultural sector.

These students, though preferentially enrolled, are all still required to take the unified entrance examination for admission, but do not have to attain as high a score as regular students.

Zifei and *weituo* students at agricultural universities are often identical, as many self-supporting students are in fact sponsored by their employers. *Weituo* students usually refer to a group from a particular locality or *danwei*, who are educated and sent back to their original work-units. Both groups pay tuition fees to the university; in exchange, they have the right to choose freely in which department they will study; they are not assigned a job upon graduation. *Dingxiang* and *shijian* students agree to return upon graduation to their home towns to work. The latter group refers to youths with a senior secondary education who did not pass the entrance examination for tertiary education and who have been in the workforce for a couple of years.[31] *Dingxiang* and *shijian* students are often from poorer areas, and education subsidies provide a type of development aid to these areas.[32] Because they do not have to attain as high an entrance examination score as regular students and are thus at a lower academic level, they are often taught in separate classes. From 1983 to 1994, almost 20 000 *dingxiang* students were enrolled by agricultural colleges and universities. According to a study of 12 universities enrolling *dingxiang* students from 24 provinces, 90% of the students were able to return to their places of origin.[33] Almost 10 000 *shijian* students were enrolled by agricultural universities from 1989 to 1994.[34] According to an MoA study, of a total of 2100 *shijian* students who had graduated from 11 universities, 98.8% returned to the county or lower level to work, and more than 98% of their employers reported satisfaction with the graduates' work.[35] Another survey covering 2600 students found that more than 88% of the students had gone to work at the township level.[36]

Following the lead of other types of tertiary-level institutions, agricultural universities and colleges began in 1987 to gradually introduce a job placement system whereby universities meet with prospective employers (*gongxu jianmian*) to discuss job placement of the graduates. This was followed by the two-way choice (*shuangxiang xuanze*) system whereby students directly meet with the employers. Actual job markets for high-level agricultural personnel have yet to evolve. All students are still guaranteed a job, and a county personnel department will find jobs within the county administration, most often in extension, for most of those unable to find employment by themselves.[37]

At SAU approximately 30% of the graduates end up at research institutes, 15% at educational institutions (mostly secondary-level) and 55% in the agricultural extension system.[38] At the postgraduate level, in contrast, very few end up in extension: national statistics show that 31% work at research institutes, 47% at educational institutions (mostly universities), and 20% work in management in either enterprises or government administration.[39] This illustrates a growing job hierarchy that is developing based on academic degrees. Previously, many of those hired by the universities had only an undergraduate degree, but as postgraduate programmes expand, so do the qualifications demanded by the universities and high-level research institutes.

Curriculum and instruction

Curriculum reform policy at agricultural universities has stated the need to reduce the number of specialities and to broaden course offerings to include more humanities and social science subjects as part of the basic programme. Yet little reduction in the number of specialities has actually taken place. Indeed, the number has risen over the past ten years despite declarations stating the need to increase the proportion of the curriculum made up of basic science courses. New specialities fill perceived needs in the fields of economics, management, environmental protection, food processing and storage, etc. Often, however, they seem little more than new labels on old bottles. The credit system, which is generally in place at most agricultural universities, especially key institutions, may widen the curriculum and increase its flexibility.[40]

The qualification profiles of high-level positions in the agricultural sector have changed radically with the introduction of a market-oriented economy. This has placed new demands on the content and methods of tertiary agricultural education. For example, the difficulties of transferring and promoting technology often lie in the consciousness of farmers, not in their technological prowess;[41] thus agricultural university graduates working in extension must possess strong social skills and understanding in order to perform their duties most effectively. However, the survey of SAU seniors indicates that a majority believe that in fact they lack sufficient social or creative skills for their future jobs.

Reform of teaching methods is a slower process than even curriculum reform. Rote learning is a respected pedagogy and the advantages of other forms of learning are just beginning to be understood. In particular, the Marxist adage of combining theory and practice is back in vogue and is used to promote a pedagogy that encourages students to be more actively involved in the learning process. Agricultural universities have always emphasized practical learning more than other forms of tertiary education, and student practice (*shixi*) is an integral part of the curriculum. Reality can be quite different however. The author witnessed many a class sitting on the roadside watching a few of their fellow students picking weeds, ostensibly attending *shixi* class.[42] Arranging student practice outside the campus has become very difficult since work-units have become more independent administrative and financial entities. Previously, both the universities and the work-units were part of the same administrative 'system' (*xitong*) and were obliged to cooperate. Now, many work-units are preoccupied with making money and have little interest in training students. Often they simply refuse to accept them or they demand economic compensation, payments which agricultural universities cannot afford.

Consequently, universities are establishing cooperative agreements with local areas in order to secure training sites for their students. A linkage may involve a township government, secondary schools and some enterprises or production units. In exchange for training the teachers of the local schools, the local government helps to find areas where students can carry out their student practice — both before and after graduation.[43]

University personnel administration and staff profile

Chinese agricultural universities and colleges are administratively divided between the national and provincial levels. This clear-cut division is changing, however, as many of the key universities under the MoA are beginning to establish closer administrative contacts with the governments of their provinces. SAU, for example, has introduced a one-school, multi-system (*yixiao duozhi*) administration, where the MoA still provides the basic funds, but Liaoning province takes care of most of the administration. According to policy statements, this movement from sole sponsorship to co-sponsorship (*danke — lianhe banxue*) is intended for all MoA institutions.[44]

Agricultural universities are experiencing increasing autonomy. The university president currently has the authority to hire and promote to all positions below the vice-president without having to consult Beijing. The MoA and the SEdC retain the right to appoint and/or approve presidential and vice-presidential candidates. Yet, the total numbers of professors and associate professors are still fixed at each institution according to the official staff size (*bianzhi*) authorized by the MoA. This restriction has led to the strict enforcement of the retirement age of 60 for men and 55 for women in order to make room for the next generation.

Personnel management is also under reform. The goal is to implement a system whereby teachers and staff are remunerated based on actual workload and performance. Starting in 1994, wages were supposed to be made up of two components: a 70% basic wage (seniority- and title-based) and a 30% bonus (*jintie*) to be contingent upon actual performance. At SAU, however, the bonus was still given equally to all, with the exception of some very special cases, where it might be withheld.[45] Having secondary employment (*jianzhi*) is a relatively new phenomenon. Moonlighting, at least in northeast China, has not yet posed a problem for personnel management; extra job opportunities are simply too few.

Table 9.7 provides the staff age profile of the agricultural and forestry colleges and universities. A so-called 'faultline' (*duanceng*) characterizes the teaching corps, with an absent generation, who should be in their 40s, missing due to the ravages of the Cultural Revolution.[46] Moreover, a large and important group educated during the 1950s and 1960s is rapidly on its way to retirement. In nationally run agricultural institutions, 98% of the professors and 91% of the associate professors will reach retirement age within the next ten years.[47] This group has been responsible for all postgraduate training and most of the important research projects carried out during the past ten years. Educators are concerned about upgrading the skill levels of younger staff so that they can quickly step into the positions being left vacant by the older generation.[48] Statistics for SAU reveal that this renewal process has yet to occur. Only 30% of the associate professors and 5% of the professors were under the age of 50.[49] Moreover, almost 90% of the professors had either already passed retirement age or would do so within only a few years, and the same was true for almost half of the associate professors. Faculty certified to advise Ph.D. and M.Sc. candidates represented a very aged contingent, with only 13% under the age of 50; all but two of those qualified to be Ph.D. supervisors were past retirement age.

Table 9.7
Age profile of agricultural universities' teaching staff

Age group	Teaching staff	Percentage	Percentage of all universities
< 31	9 000	36.6	33.1
31–35	3 800	15.4	15.0
36–40	2 500	10.2	10.9
41–45	990	4.0	6.0
46–50	1 200	4.9	7.8
51–55	2 700	11.0	12.2
56–60	3 700	15.0	12.7
> 60	710	2.9	2.3
Total	24 600	100.0	100.0

Sources: Interview with Higher Education Division Head, Bureau of Education, MoA, March 1995; *Education statistics yearbook of China 1993*, pp. 28–9

The educational profile of the teaching staff reveals that only a small proportion (16% of all institutions of higher agricultural education and 30% of key universities) possess a postgraduate degree (see Table 9.8).[50] Moreover, 'in-breeding' (*jinqin fanzhi*) is a common phenomenon, with most staff receiving all of their training at their home institutions. At SAU, for example, up to 80% of all teaching staff were 'home' educated, though this proportion is falling as only 60% to 70% of all new positions are currently being filled by its own graduates.[51] This results in a very shallow academic environment dominated by the research agenda of only a few strong individuals, who function as mentors for the rest.

The nurturing of new, scientifically competent teachers is inhibited by several factors. Real wages of university teachers fell drastically during the late 1980s and early 1990s. Particularly those graduates with other 'marketable skills' like foreign language ability, computer expertise and business acumen are finding more lucrative positions outside the agricultural universities — indeed, outside the agricultural sector altogether.[52] This human resource flight is abetted by the rapid rise in popularity (especially among self-supporting students) of certain subjects like agro-business, management and finance. Shortages of qualified teachers then arise in these subjects, something which further increases the workload of the remaining teachers, making them more apt to look for other job opportunities.[53]

Table 9.8
Educational qualification structure of teachers at tertiary-level agricultural institutions

	Total	Eight key universities	Provincial-level universities	Short-course colleges
Ph.D.	1.1%	3.5%	0.5%	0.2%
Master's	15.4%	27.6%	13.4%	2.4%
Undergraduate	74.0%	65.6%	77.0%	72.4%
Associate	9.8%	3.3%	9.0%	25.0%

Source: Yang Shimou, 1995, p. 70

Finances

Another important area of administrative reform is the distribution of financial resources. Until recently state appropriations have supported almost the entire budget for agricultural schools. Moreover, annual appropriations were based exclusively on an incremental approach with strict guidelines on their usage. Schools lacked motivation for increasing efficiency. This state funding system underwent important changes in the 1980s and 1990s.[54] An increasing amount of revenue is being generated by the universities themselves. The 1994 balance sheet for SAU shows that almost 30% of the available funds were self-generated (see Table 9.9). Tuition fees and research and extension income provided the two primary sources of income. In only two years, tuition fees[55] rose eightfold from ¥500 000 to more than ¥4 million and thus made up 13% of the operating budget in 1994. Income from extension was derived mostly from training courses for local governments. The incremental budgetary process has been replaced by a formula-based appropriation, where the most important parameter is the number of full-time equivalent students.[56] Furthermore, if internal efficiency generates savings, this money can be retained by the institution and does not have to be returned to the central government. Internal efficiency, though improving, remains a serious problem, however, as Chinese agricultural colleges and universities have a teacher-student ratio of only 1:5.6.[57]

Fund-raising initiatives by agricultural universities include university-run industries (*xiaoban chanye*), companies undertaking science and technology development (*keji kaifa*) and contract research. Although university-run industries or cooperatively-run enterprises provide an increasingly important source of income for other types of universities,[58] these mechanisms are generally not very lucrative for agricultural universities. The market for agricultural technology and agricultural products is limited. However, the development of new seed types, pesticides and fertilizers is an area in which agricultural universities, due to their laboratory facilities and high-level personnel, hold a competitive advantage. In an attempt to capitalize on this revenue-generating potential, most, if not all, universities have already formally established *keji kaifa* companies, operating on a semi-private basis. After substantial reinvestment, profits are divided between the university, the departments involved, the individuals actually doing the work. These profits remain quite small, and it is unlikely in the near future that they will contribute significantly to the income of agricultural universities. Likewise, contract research provides only a minuscule part of universities' incomes.

Research and extension

Partly due to Soviet influence during the 1950s, the main function of agricultural universities and colleges up to the mid-1980s was to produce high-level personnel. Research institutes received most of the available

Table 9.9
Balance sheet for SAU, 1994

Revenues		¥ ('000)	
MoA allocation		23 730	
Additional revenue			
Research and extension income	3 960		
University-run industries	220		
Tuition fees	4 300		
Other	700		
Total additional revenue		9 180	
Total income			32 910

Outlays			
Personnel expenses			
Basic salaries	6 650		
Wage allowances	2 150		
Welfare allowances	270		
Retirement benefits	4 955		
Scholarships / grants	1 317		
Food allowances	415		
Total personnel expenses		15 757	
Instruction-related expenses		2 385	
Operating expenses		6 526	
Equipment		272	
Repair and upkeep		469	
Other expenses		460	
Total expenses			25 869
Savings and construction			7 041
Total outlays			32 910

Source: Interview, SAU Finance Department Head, April 1995
Note: Reliable figures for Chinese budgets are rare. These data were provided
          by the school official responsible for SAU's budget, yet the figures do not
          correspond exactly to those in the SAU yearbook. Generally speaking,
          personnel expenses seem to make up approximately 60% of agricultural
          university budgets, and the 'additional revenue' share of the total budget
          is increasing every year.

resources for agricultural research.[59] Extension, while carried out to some degree by the universities in connection with their research, was never a declared goal of the universities. It has never been one of the components of their evaluation, either at the institutional level or at the individual level.[60] Indeed, despite the fact that a very large number of agricultural university graduates had been assigned jobs in the extension system, extension science was not even part of the curriculum until very recently.[61]

The implications for higher agricultural education of the measures proposed and implemented in the name of *ke jiao xing nong* are far-reaching. They range from the setting up of training programmes for grass roots-level extension technicians to the establishing of complex linkages with vocational schools, enterprises and local governments. While 90% or more of university staff will still be utilized in the education of high-level personnel and various kinds of research, the Vice-minister of Agriculture has declared that the development of specialized teams of extension personnel should be stressed and that their efforts sufficiently rewarded.[62]

One of the most visible programmes developed in the name of *ke jiao xing nong* involves the increasingly large-scale extension networks run by agricultural universities. For example, SAU has close relationships with 5 cities, 11 counties and 30 townships in Liaoning province, where it sends 20 to 30 teachers each year for long-term (over six months) stays and more than 200 teachers each year for short-term visits. They provide short training courses, coordinate research projects based on local needs, receive students for their practice periods and generally serve as a link between rural areas and the agricultural universities. Cooperative education ventures involving vocational secondary schools and/or enterprises often result from these linkages. In addition, university teachers are sometimes seconded to serve in administrative positions in a county for a period of three to five years. All of these linkages have led to noticeable improvements in agricultural production, especially in fruit and vegetable cultivation.

CURRENT STATUS AND FUTURE PROSPECTS OF CHINESE AGRICULTURAL UNIVERSITIES

The burden on Chinese agricultural universities is a very heavy one. The future livelihood of 72% of the workforce in part depends on the ability of agricultural universities to perform their educational, research and extension tasks in a way which satisfies the needs of agricultural modernization. Agriculture remains a vital, yet relatively underdeveloped, sector in the Chinese economy.

Higher agricultural education in the PRC suffers from many of the same difficulties found in other developing countries, the most important of which is simply the fact that it is attached to the weakest economic sector. Low status, low funding and few opportunities to generate additional income combine to make life very difficult for agricultural universities. One researcher characterized the position of agricultural education as being a 'disaster household' within a 'disaster area' (education).[63] His comments refer to the Cultural Revolution, but to some extent they apply today.

The universities' primary task of teaching has been made much more complex during the 1980s and 1990s by the rapidly changing demands being put on their graduates. Departmental dividing lines, speciality set-ups, curriculum content and teaching methods must all be altered if graduates are to meet the labour market demands set by the changing socio-economic and agro-production systems. The secondary tasks of research and extension have also become more difficult to accomplish due to poor financial circumstances and changing relationships with and among governmental offices.

To accommodate the new demands and adjust to the new circumstances, a number of important reforms of agricultural universities have been implemented. A strict job placement system has been replaced by a more open and flexible system that allows graduates more choices in job selection. New types of students are being preferentially enrolled to ensure that the more backward rural areas obtain needed high-level personnel. Curricula are also being altered to fit new labour market demands. A number of initiatives have been taken in the name of *ke jiao xing nong* to bring the world of academics and scientists closer to the realities of farmers, including the establishment of strong linkages with local areas, providing teaching, research and extension efforts a distinct target.

A number of problems remain, the most critical of which is inadequate finances. The marketization of the tertiary education sector during the 1980s and 1990s has not improved the relative status of agricultural universities. Their ability to obtain new sources of revenues is much more limited than other types of universities. The low level of development of agriculture makes agricultural universities less attractive for potential self-supporting students as jobs are generally located in poor rural areas where wage levels are fixed and opportunities limited. Commissioned research is restricted and relatively poorly compensated for. The development of marketable products is difficult and risky; agricultural research needs long-term and high levels of investment. Moreover, the market for agro-technology is blurred by the continued presence of state-run research and extension stations, which provide technology to farmers without charge. Without an adequate financial base, agricultural universities will be hard-pressed to complete their multifarious tasks satisfactorily.

Teaching staff face many problems. The new generation of scientists, many possessing postgraduate degrees, are expected to revitalize and raise the standards of agricultural universities. This depends on the universities' capacity to improve living and working conditions for the younger teachers so that they will no longer be tempted by job opportunities elsewhere. Teachers are genuinely interested in their work, but they are extremely dissatisfied with their low wages and poor living conditions.

Whether agricultural universities will become true 'engines of rural development' remains to be seen. Much progress has been made, particularly in the early 1990s. Schools are now in a transition period when policy statements and theoretical propositions are quite far from reality. The human resources possessed by agricultural universities, including their enormous personal and institutional networks, represent a vital link between the PRC's urban bases of scientific and technical knowledge and the nation's huge mass of farmers. Achieving the modernization goals set out by the Chinese leaders can only be realized through the prudent and extensive development of these human resources. Future research should explore the widening regional differences among agricultural universities and colleges, in terms of the resources available to them, the degree to which they have developed local ties, and the amount of adjustment made to their curricula and pedagogical practices. Marketization of Chinese education requires careful monitoring and continual examination to determine the impact of these changes on agricultural universities.

NOTES

1. This chapter is based on the author's Ph.D. dissertation in the Department of East Asian Studies, University of Aarhus, Denmark, financed in part by the Danish Council for Development Research and the Danish Social Science Research Foundation. Much of the research was conducted at the case study agricultural university which the author visited three times over a period of three years for a total of four months. Research included (1) interviews conducted with administrators, teachers and students; (2) questionnaire surveys of a representative sample of 81 teachers and 376 students drawn from the departments of Agronomy, Agricultural Engineering, Agricultural Economics and Animal Husbandry/Veterinary Medicine; and (3) structured and unstructured interviews with more than 50 alumni at their current posts. Other interviews included officials at the MoA, SEdC, various research institutes and other agricultural universities. Appreciation is expressed to the MoA for its support for the project and to the Foreign Affairs Office at Shenyang Agricultural University (SAU) for logistical and secretarial help.
2. See speeches made by Zhang Xiaowen, Vice-director of the SEdC, and Hong Fuzeng at the national general higher agricultural and forestry education working conference. Zhang Xiaowen, 1994; Hong, 1994; Sun Xiang, 1991.
3. Basic research is that directed towards fundamental theoretical problems; applied research attempts to solve specific problems in (agricultural) production; and developmental research refers in the Chinese context to that which develops products with a revenue-generating potential.
4. Located in Liaoning province, SAU is one of the eight national key comprehensive agricultural universities directly administered by the MoA. A total of 4230 undergraduates and 293 graduate students were enrolled in 1994, 39% of whom were female and 26% of whom were self-supporting. Of the

undergraduates 28% were enrolled in short-course programmes (two to three years). Out of a total staff of 1642, there were 657 teachers. Seven specialities were offered at the Ph.D. level, 26 at the Master's level, 22 at the Bachelor level and 17 at the Associate level.

5. *China statistics yearbook 1993*, p. 90.
6. *Agricultural yearbook of China 1993*, p. 239.
7. Variations in natural resources account for less of the difference in productivity between countries, while divergencies in human resource productivity explain more. See Ruttan, 1982, p. 40.
8. *China statistics yearbook 1993*, p. 90.
9. The term 'agricultural extension' refers to the systematic diffusion of technological innovations to farmers. In the PRC, both teachers and researchers usually conduct some extension-like activities as part of their work, and researchers contact extension centres directly when they have some new technology that needs to be disseminated. 'Technology' is used in this chapter in its broadest sense, to include both software (for example, information concerning pesticide use, cultivation methods) and hardware (new harvesting and planting equipment, new seed types, etc.).
10. Chinese agriculture is restricted by the low ratio of arable land to population. Thus any increase in agricultural production must come through higher yields. As manpower is abundant, the scarce land resource sets the technological agenda.
11. Currently, only 30–35% of national agricultural research results are being extended to the farmers. Yang Shimou *et al.*, 1992, p. 11.
12. Hong, 1994, p. 13.
13. Kulander and Delman, 1993, pp. 87, 122–5.
14. This number was agreed on as a 'tentative rule-of-thumb' at a Food and Agriculture Organization conference held in East Africa. Arnon, 1989, p. 744.
15. According to the Chinese Vice-minister of Agriculture at a 1994 national working conference on higher agricultural and forestry education, cited in: Hong, 1994, p. 13.
16. See Feuchtwang, Hussain and Pairault, 1989, p. 31. Evidence of the effectiveness of the Chinese extension system includes the incredibly fast dispersion of the high-yield rice variety beginning in 1964: within 13 years, the hybrid covered 80% of the rice-sown area, which is as rapid a distribution as any recorded in Asia.
17. Agricultural extension was still carried out based on bureaucratic missions, despite the introduction of the household responsibility system (see note 18), and farmers were coerced into accepting new technology. Delman, 1993.
18. This refers to the system whereby each individual household is given responsibility for its own parcel of land and is required to deliver only a certain quota of, for example, grain to the state; any surplus may be retained and sold. The changing of the basic economic unit from the production team to the household in the early 1980s initiated the reform period.
19. Zhao Longqun, 1995.
20. Hong, 1994, p. 14.
21. Kulander and Delman, 1993, p. 122.
22. Of the other ten, six are agro-reclamation colleges and four aquatic product colleges.

23. Interview with head of the Postgraduate Division, Bureau of Education, MoA, March 1995.
24. Its proportion of total tertiary admissions rose from one-third to two-thirds during the 1980s. Henze, 1992, pp. 125–6.
25. *Education statistics yearbook of China 1993*, pp. 22–3.
26. *Education statistics yearbook of China 1993*, p. 17.
27. Yang Shimou, 1995, p. 3.
28. Bunting, 1991, p. 8.
29. Wang Jingsong, 1994.
30. The survey is described in note 1.
31. Nationally, only approximately 25% of senior secondary school graduates are able to pursue tertiary education directly; the rest go straight into the workforce without further training. In rural areas, this amounts to a considerable waste of human resource talent, as the education received by these youths has been solely concentrated on the subjects of the entrance examination to tertiary education and thus is not very applicable to the type of jobs they are given in rural China. Giving these youths a chance to attend an agricultural university to further their education is an excellent way to exploit the latent potential of this resource.
32. Another kind of student similar to the locally committed student is one who receives 'job specific training' (*duikou*); they are usually graduates of secondary schools who are selected to be trained as teachers and are committed to return upon graduation to their original secondary schools and teach.
33. Wang Hongyi, 1995, p. 3. Wang Hongyi heads the Bureau of Education at the MoA.
34. Wang Hongyi, 1995, p. 4.
35. Wang Hongyi, 1995, p. 4.
36. Interview with head of Higher Education Division, Bureau of Education, MoA, March 1995.
37. In the survey of SAU seniors (see note 1), *guanxi* was considered the most important factor among potential variables that could influence employment (job placement system, employer initiatives, student initiatives, *guanxi*, teacher recommendation). Teacher recommendation was ranked next, with the other factors rated as equally important; in contrast, a majority of teachers in the sample believed the unified job placement system was the most influential factor.
38. Interview with Student Affairs Department Head, SAU, March 1995.
39. Interview with Postgraduate Division Head, Bureau of Education, MoA, March 1995.
40. The students at Beijing Agricultural University are now able to choose 30% of their courses as electives, while at SAU the figure is only about 15%. [Editors' note: The credit system is not always effective. See Agelasto, 1996c.]
41. Ma Chuanpu and Yang Siyao, 1995, p. 23.
42. For recent discussions of teaching reforms at agricultural colleges, see You *et al.*, 1992, and Ma Chuanpu, Liu Yan and Yu Changzhi, 1994. Numerous articles have been published extolling the virtues of student practice. The SAU survey of graduating students reported that their favourite teaching method was student practice, but more than half were either dissatisfied or extremely dissatisfied (23%) with the way it was run.

43. See, for example, Li Lianchang *et al.*, 1993; Liao, 1993; Liu Zhenhui, 1994, pp. 59–61.

44. CCP Central Committee and State Council, 1993.

45. Interview, Personnel Department Head, SAU, March 1995.

46. See *Zhe Nong Da Jiaoshi Duiwu Yanjiu Ketizu*, 1991; Li Zhongyun and Xia Hongsheng, 1991; Yang Qihe and Ruan Xiumei, 1990.

47. Yang Shimou, 1995, p. 70.

48. See, for example, Cai Jie and Deng Haiyun, 1992; *Bei Nong Gong Qingnian Jiaoshi Peiyang Ketizu*, 1990, pp. 18–21, 64; Liu Hongren, 1994.

49. *Shenyang Agricultural University yearbook 1994*, p. 195.

50. Interview with Wang Guangzhong (May 1993), head of the higher agricultural education research group at SAU and editor of *Gaodeng Nongye Jiaoyu*; and Yang Shimou, 1995, p. 70.

51. Interview with Personnel Department Head, SAU, March 1995.

52. The survey asked students the relative importance of courses in their future employment. Responses were evenly divided between their major field of study, foreign language ability and computer expertise, so awareness of the problem has certainly spread to the students.

53. An investigation of the working conditions for younger teachers at 17 agricultural and forestry colleges revealed that teachers under 40 in business/economic-related departments spent 80% of their work-time teaching undergraduates. Gong *et al.*, 1995, p. 24.

54. For details, see Chapter 2 by Cheng Kai-ming in this volume.

55. Include those paid by both self-supporting and commissioned training students.

56. Min, 1994, p. 116.

57. This ratio is that for all comprehensive agricultural universities in 1993 and is calculated from *Agricultural yearbook of China 1994*, p. 275. This figure is rising quite rapidly. As recent as 1990, the teacher-student ratio was only 1:4.5, *Agricultural yearbook of China 1991*, p. 237. In comparison, the ratio for all universities was 1:6.5 in 1993, *Education statistics yearbook of China 1993*, p. 18. This rose to 1:7.3 in 1995 according to Min Weifan, 1997b, p. 4.

58. For examples of the income-generating capacity as well as negative impacts of such cooperative ventures, see Yin Qiping and G.White, 1994.

59. Indeed, the universities' shares of total agricultural research expenditures and research personnel, though rising steadily throughout the 1980s, had only reached 8% and 15% respectively, by the late 1980s, showing the continued dominance of the research institutes. Fan and Pardey, 1992, p. 46.

60. Much of what agricultural university teachers did during the Cultural Revolution was extension work of sorts as they lived and worked in rural areas and in fact served an important role in the extension of basic technology.

61. It was not until 1987 that agricultural extension as an academic discipline was first offered at Beijing Agricultural University.

62. Hong, 1994, p. 17.

63. Ma Chuanpu and Yang Siyao, 1995, p. 24.

10

Higher Adult Education:
Redefining Its Roles

XIAO Jin

INTRODUCTION

Soon after the twin policies of the Four Modernizations and the Open Door were initiated in the late 1970s as the means for achieving economic transformation, demand for human resources soared. However, the education system revealed its incapability of rising to the challenge to produce well-trained personnel in huge numbers. To address this problem, the PRC government adopted a 'walk-on-two-legs' strategy to develop a large education system by expanding formal education enrolment and building up an adult education system.[1] This system, which represents a structural change in education, has been characterized by a fast, but uneven, expansion and diversified structure of the two parallel subsystems.

The national leadership especially viewed the post-secondary sector as contributing directly to research and development because they believed that the training of specialized personnel would improve the forces of production.[2] However, scarcity of resource allocation to formal higher education and its incapability of satisfying the large demand for higher education were recognized as long-term issues; higher adult education (HAE), therefore, was adopted as an alternative or complementary track. Its roles in socialist modernization became legitimate when the State Council announced the SEdC's Decisions on Reform and Development in Adult Education in 1981 and 1986.[3] Henceforth, the development of adult education was put on the national agenda as an imperative for human resources development (see Table 10.1).

Table 10.1
Enrolment in regular and adult education by level (in thousands)

Year	Regular Education			Adult Education		
	Higher	Secondary	Primary	Higher	Secondary	Primary
1949	116.5	1 268.0	24 391.0			
1950	137.5	1 566.0	28 924.0			
1951	153.4	1 964.0	43 154.0			
1952	191.2	3 145.0	51 100.0	4.1		1 375.0
1953	212.2	3 629.0	51 664.0	10.0		1 523.0
1954	253.0	4 246.0	51 218.0	13.0	946.0	2 088.0
1955	287.7	4 473.0	53 126.0	16.0	1 362.0	4 538.0
1956	403.2	6 009.0	63 466.0	64.0	2 799.0	5 195.0
1957	441.2	7 081.0	64 283.0	76.0	3 302.0	6 267.0
1958	659.6	11 998.0	86 403.0	150.0		26 000.0
1959	812.0	12 903.0	91 179.0	300.0	11 162.0	55 000.0
1960	961.6	14 873.0	93 791.0	793.0	19 740.0	76 160.0
1961	947.2	10 344.0	75 786.0	410.0	3 760.0	3 200.0
1962	829.7	8 335.0	69 239.0	404.0	3 480.0	2 052.0
1963	750.1	8 376.0	71 575.0	418.0	5 581.0	4 043.0
1964	685.3	10 195.0	92 945.0	445.0	8 480.0	7 904.0
1965	674.4	14 318.0	116 209.0	413.0	8 540.0	9 237.0
1966	533.8	12 968.0	103 417.0			
1967	408.9	12 545.0	102 443.0			
1968	258.7	14 051.0	100 363.0			
1969	108.6	20 253.0	100 668.0			
1970	48.0	26 483.0	105 280.0			
1971	83.0	31 494.0	112 112.0			
1972	194.0	36 167.0	125 492.0	16.6	809.7	
1973	314.0	34 947.0	135 704.0	145.8	1 235.1	
1974	430.0	37 137.0	144 814.0	213.7	2 395.8	46 976.1
1975	501.0	45 368.0	150 941.0	729.1	3 857.4	95 914.8
1976	565.0	59 055.0	150 055.0	2 628.6	3 251.9	127 302.4
1977	625.0	68 488.0	146 176.0	1 738.9	2 358.9	96 407.3
1978	856.0	66 372.0	146 240.0	1 408.3	2 989.7	46 605.0
1979	102.0	60 249.0	146 629.0	1 722.3	6 104.8	4 870.0

(Table 10.1 to be continued)

(Table 10.1 continued)

1980	1 144.0	56 778.0	146 270.0	1 554.1	8 044.7	4 251.7
1981	1 279.0	50 146.0	143 328.0	1 346.3	8 206.7	3 522.9
1982	1 154.0	47 028.0	139 720.0	1 173.0	10 804.0	7 566.0
1983	1 207.0	46 347.0	135 780.0	1 128.0	9 748.0	8 172.0
1984	1 396.0	48 614.0	135 571.0	1 384.0	5 987.0	9 322.0
1985	1 703.0	50 933.0	133 702.0	1 725.0	5 470.0	8,338.0
1986	1 880.0	53 223.0	131 825.0	1 856.0	8 066.0	12 614.0
1987	1 958.7	54 037.3	128 358.5	1 858.0	10 470.4	13 517.0
1988	2 065.9	52 468.2	125 357.8	1 727.6	12 311.1	16 095.0
1989	2 082.1	51 813.4	123 731.0	1 741.1	15 411.1	19 461.0
1990	2 062.7	52 391.9	122 413.8	1 666.4	15 294.4	22 820.0
1991	2 043.7	53 695.6	121 641.5	1 476.0	34 236.0	8 536.0
1992	2 184.4	55 104.9	122 012.8	1 478.7	39 344.5	8 288.9
1993	2 535.5	55 581.4	124 212.4	1 862.9	44 479.1	7 876.9
1994	2 798.6	58 947.0	129 226.2	2 351.8	50 822.6	7 613.4
1995	3 051.8	63 806.8	131 951.5	2 570.1	56 941.7	7 782.5
1996	3 183.4	68 281.5	136 150.0	2 655.7	60 185.9	6 731.4

Sources: 1949–81: *China statistics yearbook 1984*, p. 483; *China education yearbook 1949–1981*, p. 967
1982–84: *China education yearbook 1982–84*, pp. 61–4
1985–86: *China education yearbook 1985–86*, p. 3
1987: *China education yearbook 1988*, p. 26
1988: *China education yearbook 1989*, pp. 68–9
1989: *Education statistics yearbook of China 1989*, pp. 3–4
1990: *Education statistics yearbook of China 1990*, pp. 2–3
1991: *Education statistics yearbook of China 1991/1992*, pp. 2–3
1992: *Education statistics yearbook of China 1992*, pp. 2–3
1993: *Education statistics yearbook of China 1993*, pp. 2–3
1994: *Education statistics yearbook of China 1994*, pp. 2–3
1995: *Education statistics yearbook of China 1995*, pp. 2–3
1996: *Education statistics yearbook of China 1996*, pp. 2–3

Two years after launching national reforms in the formal education sector in 1985, the government released a reform and development plan in the adult education system.[4] This was the first major policy initiative in adult education since 1949. The plan targeted the whole workforce as its clients, asserting that skills, educational level and moral improvement were fundamentally critical to the realization of social modernization. Therefore, adult education was seen as a necessary condition for economic growth and technology advancement. The plan included three key components: formalization of adult education programmes, especially HAE; development of a complete adult education system with all levels of programmes through expanding enrolment; and finally, utilization of resources of all professions to run the adult education system. These reforms signified the Chinese leaders' intention to legitimize adult education and to develop a dual system to address the issue of a rising demand for education.

The development of adult education in the PRC before the reform era can be divided into two periods: the pre-Cultural Revolution period (1949–65) and the Cultural Revolution period (1966–76). This chapter will trace the development of HAE in both these periods. In particular, it will review national polices and contextual circumstances for the expansion of HAE and examine the functions of these HAE programmes in the post-Cultural Revolution period. Finally, it will critically assess the changing relationship between education and national development in the PRC and relate such an assessment to the international debate on adult education. It will also discuss implications of policy and research for improvement of higher adult education.

Western educators and those concerned with adult education for developmental purposes differentiate between the terms 'formal' education and 'non-formal' education. They attach to 'non-formal' education the connotation of a particular philosophy of teaching, learning and organization of programmes. Using these terms in the Chinese context serves to confuse rather than to clarify. The purpose of adult education in the PRC today is to address the huge rising demand for education by providing educational experiences as equal to the established formal path as possible. Naturally, the formalization of adult education has become part of the reform plan and is clearly related to nationally stated goals and to the levels of programmes, especially in higher education. Within the adult education system, both formal and non-formal programmes exist. In this chapter the term *adult education* refers to education provided to adults. It includes both formal and non-formal programmes.

HISTORICAL CONTEXT OF HIGHER ADULT EDUCATION

Pre-Cultural Revolution

The First National Education Conference was held in December 1949.[5] The Chinese leaders decreed that socialist construction would be the main initial task for the PRC and that education should prepare to launch a basic education campaign to eliminate illiteracy, which then encompassed 80% of the population. Literacy was to 'open the eyes' of all the people. To build a modernized socialist country required the eradication of 'illiteracy of reading, illiteracy of knowledge and illiteracy of science'.[6] Before 1978, education was essentially an ideological instrument. By raising literacy, the state could inform the people of the government's social and economic commitments as well as mobilize the masses to create political solidarity in pursuit of national goals.

Table 10.2
Literacy levels of population by education level[7]

Education level	Percentage of population (%)			
	1964	1982	1990	1996[b]
Illiterate / semi-literate	56.8	31.9	20.6	15.6
Primary	35.3	39.9	42.3	41.3
Junior secondary	5.8	20.0	26.5	31.5
Senior secondary[a]	1.6	7.5	9.0	9.4
Post-secondary	0.5	0.7	1.6	2.2

Source: *China statistics yearbook 1994*, p. 61. Literacy rate and education completion rate are calculated based on the 1964, 1982 and 1990 census data, for the age groups of six and above.
[a] Including both general education and vocational / technical education enrolments
[b] *China Statistics Yearbook 1997*, p. 78. Based on 1% sample.

For such a purpose, the National Association for Wiping Out Illiteracy was established on 15 March 1956 and great efforts were made by the government and various grass roots organizations to erase illiteracy. The Central Committee of the CCP and the State Council issued a Decision on Wiping Out Illiteracy on 29 March 1956.[8] It proposed eliminating illiteracy in government organizations in two to three years; in industry in three to five years; and in cities and in the countryside in five to seven years. Three Get-Rid-of-Illiteracy Campaigns were launched during 1952, 1956 and 1957. The standard for literacy was set at 2000 Chinese characters for employees and 1500 for peasants.[9] In implementation, these literacy campaigns adopted adult education programmes: spare-time education, on-the-job training and study on work-release. The goal set 1962 as the year by which 70% of the illiterate population should become literate through adult education programmes.

As the literacy rate increased through the expansion of primary education in the late 1950s and early 1960s (see Table 10.2), adult secondary general education and vocational/technical education programmes were implemented. The purpose of the policy was to train the workforce with job skills at the basic and intermediate levels, thus raising productivity.[10]

From 1956, at the same time secondary adult education programmes

Table 10. 3
Enrolment of employees in education (in thousands)

	1960	1961*	1962	1963	1964	1965
Total enrolment	22 570	4 790	2 310	3 000	4 143	4 002
Literacy education	7 720	280	2 860	263	536	562
Primary	1 792	693	693	567	942	832
Junior secondary	1 699	857	1 606	999	1 455	1 170
Senior secondary**	1 580	442	441	434	545	442
Post-secondary	470	164	164	190	245	165
% of workforce	53.7	14.4	9.34	9.1	11.9	10.8

Source: Zhang Yongchang, 1985, pp. 308–12
*   As a result of the Great Leap Forward and Anti-Rightist Movement, enterprises
    could not maintain large anti-illiteracy campaigns. Total employment in the PRC
    was cut from 50 million in 1960 to 32 million in 1963. Enrolment in education
    programmes dropped sharply in 1961.
** Including both secondary vocational and technical education enrolment

began, the MoEd started to develop higher education programmes for those
who had finished secondary education.[11] Spare-time and correspondence
courses were set up to accommodate the demands for higher education
among working adults. These courses were intended to upgrade the
education level of peasant and worker cadres and to prepare them for
leading positions in socialist construction. In 1965, the Higher Education
Department held a conference on the development of higher spare-time
and correspondence education as ways for promoting HAE.[12] The then
President Liu Shaoqi in particular advocated a dual education system to
carry out upgrading tasks. The policy reflected both an economic and
technical concern for improvement of the workforce in production by means
of an alternative form of education. In 1965, adult learners representing
11% of the workforce were enrolled in about 1000 higher spare-time
education institutions and 126 correspondence study institutions (see Table
10.3).[13]

Cultural Revolution

When the Cultural Revolution started in 1966, the plan for the development
of higher spare-time and correspondence education came to a halt, as with
all other formal education programmes. The radical wings, led by Mao
Zedong and the 'Gang of Four', believed that communism was to be
advanced by continuing a revolution that would effectively resist the

revitalization of capitalism. Higher education institutions were seen as the fortress wherein capitalist ideology was reproduced by intellectuals, most of whom had received bourgeois education in the capitalist era before 1949.[14] As a result, higher education institutions became the frontier (and target) of the Cultural Revolution. Masses at the grass roots were motivated to engage in the movement of eliminating capitalist and bourgeois ideologies. Teaching in all higher education institutions then stopped; students and staff were deployed to the countryside and to factories to receive re-education by peasants and workers with proletarian consciousness.

In replacing the 'capitalist type' of universities, the radicals created new models of universities for workers, cadres and peasants, namely 'July 21 Workers Universities', 'May 7 Cadres' Schools' and 'Chaoyan Agricultural Universities'. These types of universities sprouted everywhere. For instance, in the eight years from 1968 to 1976, 'July 21 Workers Universities' increased in number from 1 to 33 374 with an enrolment of 148.5 million. Cadres and university teaching staff were deployed to 'May 7 Cadres' Schools' across the country. The purpose of these institutions was to train people into a type of personnel with both political soundness ('red') and professional skills ('expert'). Raising proletarian consciousness through political indoctrination became everyday life. Only those assessed as 'red' could teach at universities or could be enrolled as students. Proletarian politics and communist ideology became the core curriculum.

Consequently, 106 of the PRC's higher education institutions were shut down and those which were permitted to operate admitted no new students. By the time admissions were resumed in higher education institutions in 1970, enrolment had decreased to 48 000 from 674 000 in 1965. Enrolment gradually rebounded to 565 000 in 1976. During the decade-long Cultural Revolution, higher education institutions only graduated one million students, 70% of whom were enrolled before the Cultural Revolution.[15] The whole country was engaged in wiping out bourgeois ideology and resisting capitalism revitalization.

Expansion of higher adult education (1976–80)

In 1978, the milestone event, the third Plenary of the Eleventh CCP Congress, formally signified the end of the Cultural Revolution and the beginning of the modernization era. Education, previously considered worthless, was proclaimed essential for economic growth, and higher education was especially viewed critical to the training of specialized professionals. Therefore, universities started to resume their normal operation and increased enrolment. In addition to the existing 392 universities in 1976,

Table 10.4
Dual system of higher education in China

Year	Regular Education		Adult Education	
	Institution	enrolment ('000)	Institution	enrolment ('000)
1949	205	116.5	1	0.1
1950	193	137.5	2	0.4
1951	206	153.4	3	1.6
1952	201	191.1	7	4.1
1953	181	212.2	27	9.7
1954	188	253.0	37	13.0
1955	194	287.7	49	16.0
1956	227	403.2	156	64.0
1957	229	441.2	186	76.0
1958	791	659.6	386	150.0
1959	841	812.0	869	300.0
1960	1 289	961.6	–	793.0
1961	845	947.2	–	410.0
1962	610	829.7	1 125	404.0
1963	407	750.1	1 165	418.0
1964	419	685.3	1 061	445.0
1965	434	674.4	964	413.0
1966	434	533.8	–	–
1967	434	408.9	–	–
1968	434	258.7	–	–
1969	434	108.7	–	–
1970	434	48.0	–	–
1971	328	83.0	–	–
1972	331	194.0	195	16.6
1973	345	314.0	280	145.8
1974	378	430.0	3 158	213.7
1975	378	501.0	10 836	729.1
1976	392	565.0	46 810	2 628.6
1977	404	625.0	34 919	1 738.9
1978	598	856.3	10 395	1 408.3
1979	633	102.0	6 289	1 722.3
1980	675	1 144.0	2 682	1 554.1
1981	704	1 279.4	1 525	1 346.3
1982	715	1 154.0	1 147	1 173.0
1983	805	1 207.0	1 196	1 128.0
1984	902	1 396.0	1 157	1 384.0

(Table 10.4 to be continued)

(Table 10.4 continued)

1985	1 016	1 703.0	1 216	1 725.0
1986	1 054	1 880.0	1 420	1 856.0
1987	1 063	1 958.7	1 399	1 858.0
1988	1 075	2 065.9	1 373	1 727.6
1989	1 075	2 082.1	1 333	1 741.1
1990	1 075	2 062.7	1 321	1 666.4
1991	1 075	2 043.7	1 256	1 476.0
1992	1 053	2 184.4	1 198	1 478.7
1993	1 065	2 535.5	1 183	1 862.9
1994	1 080	2 798.6	1 172	2 351.8
1995	1 054	3 051.8	1 156	2 570.1
1996	1 032	3 184.4	1 138	2 655.7

Sources: *China education yearbook 1949–1981*, pp. 965–7, 1036–7; *China education yearbook 1982–1984*, pp. 61–3; *China education yearbook 1985–1986*, p. 3; *China education yearbook 1988*, p. 26; *China education yearbook 1989*, pp. 68–9; *Education statistics yearbook of China 1989*, pp. 3–4; *Education statistics yearbook of China 1990*, pp. 2–3; *Education statistics yearbook of China 1991/1992*, pp. 2–3; *Education statistics yearbook of China 1992*, pp. 2–3; *Education statistics yearbook of China 1993*, pp. 2–3; *Education statistics yearbook of China 1994*, pp. 2–3; *Achievement of education in China: statistics 1949–1984*, pp. 20, 239; *Achievement of education in China: statistics 1980–1985*, p. 94; *Education statistics yearbook of China 1996*, pp. 2–3; *Education statistics yearbook of China 1995*, pp. 2–3.

312 new universities were set up by 1981; enrolment increased to 1.3 million in 1981 from 0.57 million in 1976. HAE at the same time experienced rapid changes after the Cultural Revolution over three periods: 1976–80, 1981–86 and 1987 to present.

The rising demand for higher education proved to be more than the regular system could satisfy. The demand came from those of college age as well as young adults who had missed out on educational opportunities because of the Cultural Revolution. In addition, the Four Modernizations demanded educated manpower. About 80% of the workforce had not finished junior secondary education; technicians in industry accounted for only 2.8% of the whole workforce; and managerial personnel did not have any management training.[16] An influential study on the PRC's educational needs for the year 2000 estimated the number of specialized personnel in 1983 to be 15.9 million and that there would then be a demand for a total of 34 million by the year 2000 (see Table 10.5).[17]

Table 10.5
Estimate in 1983 of human resource needs
for the year 2000 (in millions)

Education level	
postgraduates	0.7
four-year university graduates	8.7
two- to three-year university graduates	8.0
secondary vocational education graduates	17.0
Total	34.4

Source: Zhou Beilong and Zhou Chenye, 1985

In sharp contrast, the education system had produced only 4.11 million university graduates and 7.22 million secondary vocational students in the 35 years from 1949 to 1983.[18] The study suggested the development of vocational/technical training of all types and the inclusion in higher education of alternative delivery modes.

As formal higher education was incapable of meeting the anticipated demand, higher adult education expanded rapidly. For instance, in 1975, HAE enrolled about 0.73 million students. But the next year when the Gang of Four fell, HAE enrolment in various programmes grew to 2.63 million, about five times regular university enrolment. The demand for higher education soared. In the period from 1976 to 1980, local adult education institutions were allowed to develop their own programmes, teaching materials and expand enrolment according to their circumstances and with the resources available.[19]

As indicated in Table 10.4, the HAE system by the mid-1980s had become equivalent to the formal higher education system in terms of the number of institutions and enrolment size, and it offered diversified programmes to meet the rising demands of groups other than secondary school leavers. The central government in this period was preoccupied with post-Cultural Revolution re-evaluation of political issues and economic development and reform plans. Thus, adult education development took on a laissez-faire approach. There were no coordinated efforts among institutions and a parallel system developed.

Formalization of higher adult education (1980–86)

Seeing the potential of adult education and its flexibility, the government adopted the concept of 'walk-on-two-legs', a dual strategy,[20] and it started to harness HAE at the same time. The State Council and the MoEd issued several documents on the expansion of HAE with reference to radio/TV universities, employee and peasant higher education institutions, administrative cadre colleges, and correspondence and evening universities.[21] These documents called for a nationally coordinated effort in providing higher education. The policy's five key components were:

1. utilizing local resources to establish new HAE programmes;
2. administering open admission to working adults who had a senior secondary education diploma or equivalent;
3. developing curricula up to university requirement and quality and appropriate to meet local socio-economic needs;
4. recruiting qualified teachers and tutors; and
5. granting graduates certificates and diplomas upon completion of studies.

The government granted autonomy to ministries, local provinces, municipalities and key universities to formalize HAE under their administration. During this period, HAE became structured into departments arrayed at both local and higher administrative levels. At the national level, the Third Department of Higher Education, set up in 1984 under the then MoEd, was made responsible for HAE.[22] It was charged with formulating policies and guidelines, making strategic plans, developing core curricula, and coordinating adult education programmes with other central-level ministries. Other ministries (for example, Agriculture, Health, Industry, Energy, Communication) assigned these tasks to a corresponding section and office, such as the training and education section in the personnel office. These were responsible for the training and education of personnel in their ministries from the central level to the local level. HAE in these ministries was carried out in their subordinate institutions or universities.

As detailed in Table 10.6, higher adult education comprises six categories of programmes:

1. The Radio and Television University (RTVU) started to enrol students in 1980. It provides three-year university programmes in nationwide broadcasts. It operated 29 RTVUs in 1981 and now runs 46 RTVUs across the PRC. RTVUs have administrative centres in each province along with teaching and tutoring stations across provinces where students receive tutoring and examinations. Courses cover general university courses, science, technology, Chinese languages studies, economics study, management and administrative cadre studies. Among all the HAE programmes, RTVU has the largest enrolment.
2. Worker and peasant colleges are run by different ministries, or by

Table 10.6
Enrolment in higher adult educational institutions

Year	Radio/TV University		Worker's College		Peasant's College		Administrative Cadre College		Education Colleges		Independent Correspondence University		University Adult programme[a]	
	schools	enrolment	schools	enrolment	schools	enrolment	schools	enrolment	schools	enrolment	schools	enrolment	normal course	short-cycle course
1979	29	280 158	–	–	165	15 324	–	–	34	50 821	–	–	–	–
1980	29	324 372	1 194	236 388	72	4 578	–	–	31	49 268	4	14 890	162 134	–
1981	29	268 026	1 140	245 530	4	834	–	–	32	90 830	5	14 372	189 203	–
1982	29	347 167	820	143 674	4	781	–	–	290	474 000	4	14 890	154 862	197 000
1983	29	478 758	841	173 225	4	900	15	1 907	304	201 000	3	8 114	204 690	265 000
1984	29	599 000	850	192 000	5	900	54	15 000	218	164 000	2	2 708	243 595	319 000
1985	29	673 600	863	260 200	5	1 300	102	40 300	216	247 100	2	9 904	364 552	493 000
1986	29	604 400	952	339 400	5	1 104	165	55 600	262	259 900	7	32 000	–	563 100[b]
1987	39	565 948	915	337 906	5	700	168	55 768	268	251 203	4	33 266	176 255	450 038
1988	40	453 800	888	288 000	5	648	171	61 700	265	276 200	4	12 100	–	635 100
1989	39	417 522	848	254 229	5	353	172	63 039	265	280 379	4	13 884	34 622	567 310
1990	40	387 813	835	230 323	5	247	175	54 186	265	252 977	4	15 751	175 206	550 049
1991	42	282 374	776	219 142	5	263	168	51 868	254	185 591	4	13 070	143 254	580 385
1992	44	335 531	726	230 115	5	299	166	56 768	251	179 190	4	13 505	128 472	556 534
1993	45	437 895	714	275 246	4	694	170	93 093	249	216 865	4	12 139	138 557	713 621
1994	46	536 423	703	307 478	4	1 000	166	135 359	245	230 412	4	13 604	174 668	894 467
1995	46	541 600	694	313 900	4	1 000	166	147 700	242	213 700	4	13 500	200 347	1 138 322
1996	46	526 600	680	326 200	4		164	153 800	240	205 400	4	13 600	224 255	1 204 765

Sources: Achievement of education in China: statistics 1949–1984, pp. 240–5; China education yearbook 1982–1984, p. 63; China education yearbook 1985–1986, p. 12; Education statistics yearbook of China 1987, pp. 90–1; China education yearbook 1989, p. 69; Education statistics yearbook of China 1989, pp. 86–7; Education statistics yearbook of China 1990, pp. 90–1; Education statistics yearbook of China 1991/1992, pp. 98–9; Education statistics yearbook of China 1992, pp. 98–9; Education statistics yearbook of China 1993, pp. 94–5; Education statistics yearbook of China 1994, pp. 94–5; Education statistics yearbook of China 1996, pp. 96–7; Education statistics yearbook of China 1997, pp. 96–7.

a Including the divisions of correspondence, evening schools, regular short-cycle course and short-cycle course for cadres

b Total enrolment including normal course and short-cycle course ministry-affiliated enterprises which establish colleges for their employees. These colleges enrol employees who have a senior secondary education diploma. The purpose of these colleges is to upgrade employees' and peasants' knowledge and skills, with the expectation that continual upgrading would improve employees' productivity.

3. Administrative cadre colleges were started in 1983 and are run by ministries and provinces.[23] The central government upgraded ministry-run administrative cadre training institutions to provide HAE programmes or granted ministries the right to set up ministry-run administrative cadre colleges.[24] So far about 170 administrative cadre colleges have been put into operation. Provisions include short management training as well as university degree programmes to those personnel under the age of 40 in administrative positions.

4. Educational colleges were set up to offer continuing education programmes to primary and secondary school teachers. These colleges are usually under the administration of the respective local education departments. They provide teachers with short-term training courses as well as post-secondary degree programmes. In recent years, some also started to provide postgraduate courses to teachers.

5. Correspondence universities are administered under the SEdC. From the 1950s they have promoted higher degree education among working adults. They are intended to minimize the costs on educational institutions as well as the cost on work-units. Students enrolled are most likely technicians, administrative personnel and teachers with secondary education degrees. These universities provide curricula and learning materials appropriate for self-study. Upon completion of certain courses, students and teachers will meet for tutoring and examinations.

6. Regular universities also offer adult education programmes of various kinds. As long as a university satisfies its enrolment quota specified in the state plan, it can utilize its resources and offer adult education programmes. Universities retain the income generated from these two- to three-year evening degree programmes and short-term training courses.

IMPLEMENTATION OF HAE REFORM AND DEVELOPMENT PLAN SINCE 1987

Adult education in the seventh Five-Year Plan (1986–90) underwent another reform that redefined adult education objectives. The stated aims of national development were both material improvement and moral civilization (*wuzhi wenming, jingshen wenming*). Conceptually, the Chinese leaders believed that upgrading the knowledge, skills and morals of working adults was imperative for success in modernization. Adult education, therefore, was seen as an indispensable means of providing recurrent education to the workforce for the purpose of economic development and social progress. The central government then released the 1987 reform and development decisions in the adult education system.[25]

As economic reform got underway, adult education was assigned specific tasks to provide:
1. on-the-job training or recurrent education for the existing workforce to upgrade job skills;
2. basic compensatory education to those who had not finished secondary schooling;
3. degree education programmes for training intermediate-level technicians and cadres with academic qualification;
4. continuing education to update knowledge and skills for those who already had higher education degrees; and
5. entertainment programmes to meet adults' needs for personal enrichment.

In the early 1980s enrolment in HAE decreased as those who had missed schooling because of the Cultural Revolution were finishing their studies. However, in the mid-1980s enrolment increased again as the central government re-emphasized the goals of improving the forces of production through adult education. In addition, during the sixth Five-Year Plan period (1980–85), about 48 million adults were enrolled in secondary adult education programmes, 1.44 million working adults finished senior secondary adult education studies and 2.66 million finished adult secondary technical studies.[26] These groups created a new rising demand for HAE.

Strategies for implementing the reform and development plan

The reform and development of adult education since 1980 has had two distinctive features. One is the central government's commitment to formalizing HAE. The second is the link between adult education and the improvement of the workforce of production. In attempting to formalize and promote HAE, the government experimented with a number of strategies. These schemes, formally adopted nationwide since 1988, concern admissions, certification, personnel policies and finance.

First, the central government increased central control of HAE. Before

1981, admission was conducted by individual HAE institutions. Starting from 1982 to 1985, admission was brought under the control of the provincial government and ministries. After 1986, admission was placed under the direct control of the central government. HAE institutions were required to submit an intake plan to the Department of Adult Education, after which enrolment quotas were assigned. All candidates were required to take the HAE entrance examination, which was administered nationwide.[27]

Along with the admission reform, a certification system was implemented in 1988 to control the quality of HAE. Individual HAE institutions apply to the central government for approval of their qualification to issue graduate certificates. There are three kinds of certifications.[28] One is equivalent to a formal university diploma. Another is a vocation certificate certifying that the learner has finished a group of courses in a certain vocation and is able to practise in that field. The last is a single course completion certificate. Students can enrol in either a degree programme, a vocational programme or a single course.[29] Upon accumulation of sufficient course credits, a student can apply for a diploma[30] or vocation certificate.

In order to control HAE quality, the MoEd in 1983 set up the National Commission for Guiding Self-study and Examination. After a few years' trial in a few provinces, it started to operate nationwide in 1988. Having met course requirements, adult learners sit for the national degree examinations (which are equivalent to a university basic programme examination), special vocation examinations, or a four-year university degree examination.[31] Diplomas will be granted accordingly after the examination, and the degree has the same effect as the equivalent granted by formal universities. Adult learners who failed to pass an examination may retake it.

As an alternative, adults can enrol in higher education programmes at local adult education institutions which are unable to issue a university diploma or certificate. Or they can choose self-study programmes. In such a way, they enrol into HAE courses with no restrictions on the length of study. After they have fulfilled course requirements, adult learners sit for degree examinations.

The third strategy of reform and development concerns the personnel system. The state policy on staff promotion requires the evaluation of both work performance as well as training and education. It also requires that both job recruiting and promotion exercises should include the consideration of one's training and education.[32] This strategy attempts to ensure that employees have sufficient training to satisfy job requirements. It also pushes adult education institutions to develop programmes to upgrade employees' knowledge and skills. The government requests that an amount equal to 1.5% of the annual payroll of state-run enterprises be allocated for education.[33] In addition, all enterprises are encouraged to include employee training in their budgets and allocate additional resources from profits earned.[34] Workers' unions in work-units also spend 25% of the collected union fees on members' education.

ISSUES IN IMPLEMENTATION

Since the Cultural Revolution, HAE has contributed greatly to the provision of education to working adults, in terms of quantitative enrolment. However, this achievement should not distract attention from some of the problems in the development of HAE. A few key issues can be identified.

Enrolment and school size

An assessment of the efficiency of investment in education considers the utilization of resources. The internal efficiency of regular higher education is low by international standards.[35] Due to its uncoordinated provision, low internal efficiency is noted in HAE, too.[36] For instance, small enrolment is a problem. In 1988, among 1350 institutions, only 168 (about 12.5%) had an enrolment of above 800 students; 558 (41.3%) had an enrolment of below 200 students; 239 (18%) had an enrolment of below 100.[37] Among all HAE institutions, RTVU is the largest provider. Correspondence universities have an average enrolment of more than 3000 students per institution, but students are usually enrolled in a single course or certificate study (for example, accounting). Most other institutions have low enrolment, and many students enrol in short-time programmes or a single course.

Table 10.7
Enrolment and size of higher adult education institutions (1994)

Type of programme	Institutions	Average enrolment
Radio / TV	46	11 661
Worker College	703	437
Peasant College	4	173
Cadre College	170	769
Teachers College	245	940
Correspondence University	4	3 401

Note: Calculated from 1994 data from *Education statistics yearbook of China 1994*, pp. 94–5.

The original scheme of adult education sought to utilize local resources to provide education.[38] Resources in small amounts came from ministries and education departments at both the national and local levels and from various local groups.[39] Little coordination has existed among these institutions, and they have developed programmes with whatever resources were available. More than 1373 HAE institutions were operational in 1988, exceeding the number of universities. Often, several programmes in the same city provide identical courses, most with low enrolment and operating with limited resources. As a result, each institution strives to improve quality but lacks resources sufficient for the task. All these uncoordinated efforts spread thinly the resources for adult education.[40]

Quality of education

The quality of HAE programmes is affected to a large degree by the quality of the teaching staff, availability of teaching materials and equipment, and the teaching delivery mode.[41] Teaching staff include university lecturers and secondary school teachers who moved to HAE institutions, as well as pensioners or part-time teachers who work at universities. Some university lecturers moved into HAE because they graduated during the Cultural Revolution as worker-peasant-soldier students and were not qualified to teach at regular universities. In 1987, 350 of the 915 general HAE institutions and 113 of the 262 teacher training colleges had no associate professors or lecturers with Master's degrees.[42] The staff also lacked adequate training in teaching adults and planning programmes for adult education.

There is a lack of adequate financial resources to support teaching activities. Most adult education institutions provide only classrooms, with few instructional aids or lab equipment and often no libraries. Teaching is carried out solely in the lecturing mode with a blackboard and chalk. Reading the standardized textbooks is largely the only form of study for students. In addition, instructors have little access to updated information about theories and new developments in their fields. Little funding is available to carry out research on working adults' needs in the workplace. Consequently, the curriculum is merely a copy of that at university and fails to address the particular learning needs of HAE students.[43] Teachers' ignorance of students' life experiences and how to incorporate them into their pedagogy negatively affects teaching quality. Inattention to students' learning characteristics and their problem-solving needs is partly responsible for ineffective pedagogy.

Relevance

The mismatch between what is taught and its relevance in the workplace creates the problem of low external efficiency. Often, work-units find HAE programmes irrelevant to their practical purpose and find on-the-job improvement among their newly trained staff to be too limited.[44] As promotion requires educational credentials, many working adults have enrolled in HAE merely for the sake of obtaining a credential. This push for credentialism[45] benefits individuals, but enrolments can also generate income for HAE institutions. The issue of relevance becomes of secondary importance in consideration of programme development in HAE.

No evaluation of the effects of different adult education programmes on productivity has yet been undertaken. Current reports are often on quantitative expansion and general concepts of adult education. Few studies evaluate changes in learners' performance in the workplace or the improvement of organizational performance and productivity. Given different arguments for[46] and against[47] degree programmes of HAE as well as an absence of empirical data, how exactly different types of adult education programmes and delivery modes contribute to employee performance — i.e., productivity — remains unknown.

CONCLUSION

The history of HAE in China suggests it is important not only because of its scale, but also because it reflects changes in the country's perspective on education and national development. The Chinese leaders in the post-Cultural Revolution period mainly have seen education as an important contributor to economic development through providing recurrent education for the workforce. In particular, HAE prepares experienced employees for more complicated jobs that require advanced knowledge and skills. The application of technology by working adults is believed to contribute to an increase of productivity.

The leadership has assumed that the PRC's economic development would raise the demand for university-trained personnel. Given the limited government resources for regular higher education, an innovative strategy was adopted — 'walking-on-two-legs'. The best secondary school graduates enrol in formal higher education; the others choose various non-formal or HAE options. Two distinct achievements are addressed: the quality of workers is upgraded while the social demand for regular higher education is reduced, alleviating social pressure of expanding regular higher education. Therefore, the formalization of HAE may be viewed as a form of social control.

Internationally, adult education programmes meet a number of development needs, including vocational or occupationally related training, remedial basic literacy and civic/economic/political/community competence. They provide knowledge and skills in jobs, health, welfare and family life. In USA, interest in revitalizing the economies of the state governments through development of human resources proves to be one of the most substantial boosts to adult education of all public activities.[48] As economies advance to a more hi-tech era and globalized manner, human resource development is viewed as critical by learners, business and industry, and the nation. It also helps fill the education gaps caused by rising development needs as observed especially in less developed countries.[49] These gaps involve demand/supply, job skills, adaptability, cost and efficiency and equity — all that arise in the course of development. In the PRC, adult education expansion particularly satisfies the needs of meeting the demand/supply gap and job skill gap as economic development got underway. It, therefore, is accorded an important role in the overall human resource development of the country.[50] Across the globe, 'adult education is moving from a marginal position in relation to formal education systems to take a more crucial place in society's overall provision for education'.[51] Adult education in the PRC may likely increase its importance in the future because of changing human resource developments due to a technological redefinition of the workplace, increasing international competition and the high costs of formal education.

To cope with the financing problem while facing an increasing demand for education, the government decentralized education finance. Adult education institutions are locally financed.[52] Paradoxically, inefficiency has been noted because of the large number and small size of HAE institutions as well as programme duplication.[53] Unfortunately, there are few studies of cost and financing of adult education, and behaviour of education costs is known only from what has been observed in formal education. This internal efficiency problem is also critical in formal universities in the PRC.[54] International experiences show that unit costs decrease at larger institutions.[55] While keeping education provision sites close to learners, HAE could develop regional coordination among providers and avoid costs and duplication in the competition between providers. Local or regional planning, coordination, and information networks all could achieve such purposes with state aid.[56] Further studies are needed to provide evidence of increasing internal efficiency in the Chinese contextual situations.

Until now, attention to the quality of HAE has been reserved for admission control through entrance examinations and degree examinations which result in credentials. However, what 'quality' means in HAE is not addressed yet. Some have raised questions about the relevance of degree programmes to productivity increase and have proposed non-degree HAE programmes.[57] Unfortunately, few empirical studies examine how different types of adult education programmes contribute to improving employees' performance. International experiences show that learning is more effective when it relates to problems in the workplace and real life.[58] But a mismatch between educational experience and job skill requirements can lower productivity.[59] The first study on the impact of worker training in Shenzhen, in southern China, shows that the transfer of training relates to management in the workplace.[60] Further study of the impact of HAE on productivity is needed because improved productivity is a stated objective for national development. In sum, future studies need to examine (1) the productivity of graduates of different HAE programmes and (2) the impact of policy and management in the workplace on the transfer of learning.

NOTES

1. Ministry of Education, 1980.
2. CCP Central Committee, 1985, p. 193.
3. CCP Central Committee and the State Council, 1981, p. 2; Li Peng, 1986.
4. State Education Commission, 1987.
5. Zhang Yongchang, 1985, p. 239.
6. Zhang Yongchang, 1985, p. 286. The remark was by the then Vice-Premier Chen Yi.
7. The literacy rate and education completion rate are calculated based on the 1964 census data, for the age groups of six and above. See *China statistics yearbook 1994*, p. 61.
8. Zhang Yongchang, 1985, p. 278.
9. *China education yearbook 1949–1981*, pp. 578–82.
10. Lin Feng, 1958.
11. Higher Education Department, *Gaodeng jiaoyubu guanyu yeyu gaodeng xuexiao de xuexi shijian yu zhengdun, gonggu tigao jiaoxue zhiliang de tongzhi* (Announcement on spare-time higher education: scheduling and improvement of teaching quality), 21 February 1957, in *China education yearbook 1949–1981*, pp. 897–8.
12. Higher Education Department, *Gaodeng hanshou jiaoyu huiyi jiyao* (Excerpt of higher correspondence education meeting) in *China education yearbook 1949–1981*, pp. 898–900.
13. Zhang Yongchang, 1985, p. 312.
14. In August 1971, the CCP Central Committee issued 'A Memo on the National Education Working Conference' which proposed to evaluate the nation's education system. The memo concluded that (1) Mao Zedong's proletarian education line was not being implemented and (2) most teaching staff still held bourgeois ideology.
15. *China education yearbook 1949–1981*, p. 235.
16. CCP Central Committee and State Council, 1981, p. 2.

17. Zhou Beilong and Zhou Chenye, 1985, pp. 42–6. In 1983, the State Council's Institute for Economic, Technological and Social Development organized a research project on 11 issues faced by the PRC in achieving modernization by the year 2000. The effort resulted in 12 reports on population, employment, economy, national consumption, science and technology, education, national resources, energy, environment, agriculture, transportation, international relationships, as well as a master report. These reports estimated the current status and issues to be solved by the year 2000. Brief reports were also published in *Jingji Ribao* (*Economics Daily*) on 2, 4, 6, 9, 11, 13 and 20 November 1985. Specialized personnel include people who received secondary vocational education degrees and above.

18. *Achievement of education in China: Statistics 1949–1983*, pp. 24–5.

19. Education Department and Central Broadcasting Bureau, *Guowuyuan pizhun jiaoyubu zhongyang guangbo shiyeju guanyu quanguo guangbo dianshi daxue gongzuo huiyi de baogao* (Report on the national radio/TV university work meeting by the Education Department and Central Broadcasting Bureau, endorsed by the National Council) in *China education yearbook 1949–1981*, pp. 900–1.

20. 'Walking-on-two-legs' means educational provisions by both formal higher education institutions and adult higher education institutions. See Ministry of Education, 1980. This document claimed the legitimate status of adult higher education.

21. The MoEd issued a few documents to set up new higher education institutions and increase enrolment. To ensure the implementation of the dual strategy, the State Council also endorsed the documents and reissued them to the relevant departments. These documents, with date of SEdC endorsement, included: *Guowuyuan pizhun jiaoyubu, zhongyang guangbo shiyeju guanyu quanguo guangbo dianshi daxue gongzuo huiyi de baogao* (Report on the national radio and TV university meeting held by Education Department and the Central Broadcasting Bureau endorsed by the State Council), 11 January 1979; *Guowuyuan pizhun jiaoyubu guanyu juban zhigong, nongmin gaodeng yuanxiao shenpi chengxu de zanxing guiding* (Temporary regulations of establishing employee and peasant higher education institutions endorsed by the State Council), 8 September 1979; *Guowuyuan pizhun jiaoyubu, zhongyang guangbo shiyeju guanyu dierci quanguo guangbo dianshi daxue gongzuo huiyi de baogao* (The second report on the national radio and TV university meeting), endorsed by the State Council, 29 November 1979; *Guowuyuan pizhun jiaoyubu dali fazhan gaodeng xuexiao hanshou jiaoyu he yedaxue de yijian* (Suggestions on the development of higher correspondence education and evening universities endorsed by the State Council), 5 September 1980; *Guowuyuan pizhun jiaoyubu guanyu gaodeng jiaoyu zixuekaoshi shixing banfa de baogao* (Report on trial of higher education examination of self-learners endorsed by the State Council), 13 January 1981.

22. In 1989, the *Chengren Jiaoyusi* (Department of Adult Education) and the *Disan Jiaoyusi* (Third Department of Higher Education) were integrated as the Department of Adult Education.

23. As most cadres had no training in administrative affairs, six ministries proposed to the State Council plans for setting up cadre colleges under the administration of each ministry in 1983.

24. State Education Commission, 1993a, p. 39.

25. State Education Commission, 1987a, p. 1.

26. Calculation based on statistics in *Achievement of Education in China: Statistics 1980–1985*, pp. 18, 100–1.
27. State Education Commission, 1993a, pp. 37–8.
28. State Education Commission, 1987a, p. 6.
29. For worker and peasant university students, generally credits representing 2000 to 2200 hours of study for science and engineering students and 1800 hours of study for social study students could earn a diploma equivalent to a two-year formal university study. For RTVU students, 220 credits (each credit representing 20 hours of study) could earn a diploma equivalent to two years' university study in science and engineering programmes; 150 credits (each credit representing 20 hours of study) could earn a diploma equivalent to two years' university study in arts and letters. See *China education yearbook 1949–1981*, pp. 915–6; and *China education yearbook 1982–1984*, pp. 255–77.
30. The term *xuewei* (diploma) applies to a Bachelor's degree or above whereas *zhenshu* (certificate) is awarded for a single course and other education programmes. Adult learners could accumulate a set number of certificates for conversion to a diploma.
31. State Council, 1988.
32. State Education Commission, 1987a, p. 7.
33. CCP Central Committee and State Council, 1981.
34. State Education Commission, 1987a, pp. 9–10.
35. Tsang and Min, 1992.
36. Wang Yaonong, 1995.
37. Yin Fenghe, 1988.
38. Yu Bo and Xu Hongyan, 1988, p. 102.
39. Lin Sha and Zhang Zhenkun, 1988.
40. Yu Bo and Xu Hongyan, 1988.
41. Wang Yaonong, 1995.
42. Yin Fenghe, 1988.
43. McCormick, 1984.
44. Li Yuzheng and Zhao Zhenghua, 1987, pp. 32–5. The author's field visits to adult education institutions and factories in Guangdong, Sichuan and Yunnan provinces in the summer of 1988 revealed the problems of irrelevance. Often, this kind of problem was not reported, only 'good news'.
45. Shang, 1989; Li Yuzheng and Zhao Zhenghua, 1987.
46. Li Yanqing, 1995, pp. 10–3, 31.
47. Yi, 1993.
48. Cross and McCartan, 1984, pp. 90–118.
49. Hunter, Borus and Mannan, 1974, pp. 69–73.
50. Xiao, 1989.
51. Organization for Economic Cooperation and Development, 1977.
52. Xiao and Tsang, 1994.
53. Wang Yaonong, 1995.
54. Tsang and Min, 1992.
55. Brinkman and Leslie, 1986.
56. Cross and McCartan, pp. 119–30.
57. Yi, 1993.
58. Knowles, 1984.
59. Tsang, 1987.
60. Xiao, 1996.

PART 4
MARKETIZATION OF HIGHER EDUCATION

11

Stratification Trends in Technical-Professional Higher Education

Vilma SEEBERG

INTRODUCTION

This chapter looks at contemporary trends in Chinese society as it undergoes the transition from isolated bureaucratic socialist state to player in the global economy.[1] We examine whether, in the transitional times of the late 1980s, the advantaged social strata were passing on their status to the next generation by means of higher education of the technical-professional kind. Two types of research were used to examine enrolment patterns as predictors of social and economic changes in the PRC: qualitative analysis of interviews and statistical analysis of a stratified, random sample sociological survey.[2] The findings of the quantitative analysis are statistically generalizable to the national student population, but caution is warranted as Chinese institutions vary greatly one from another.[3]

The economic transition undertaken in all of the former socialist states has had an impact on their social structure, but the significance of that impact has been difficult to assess. What movement is taking place and how quickly? Which are the lasting trends, who is moving ahead and who is losing?

Educational trends provide useful insight into long-term social patterns. People 'flow through' educational systems over an extended period of time and educational decisions are made with long-term goals in mind. At the upper levels of the educational pyramid, the stakes are high and the competition fierce.

Reforms in the educational systems have accompanied the economic and political changes throughout the former state-socialist world. The changes have been tailored largely to respond to market needs. For example, redistributive admissions policies based on CCP politics largely have given way to examination-driven merit selection based on skills competition. Has this change made a difference in who is admitted into higher education? Under state socialism, a bureaucratic system of allocation and distribution had a monopoly hold on power, and political capital was the coin of the realm. In the deregulated economies of ex-socialist states, however, economic capital — indeed money — is the new coin. How has this impacted élite formation? Will the socialist political élite seize control, recasting itself as the new capitalist élite; will the pre-revolutionary financial élite re-emerge; or will new class groupings form?

Technical-professional higher education

The Thirteenth Party Congress proclaimed in 1987 that further economic growth in the PRC 'hinged' on the progress of science and technology and increasingly on the quality of education received by 'workers' and 'intellectuals'.[4] In response, technical-professional higher education was expanded to produce workers skilled in the processing of technology and information. For example, in industrial and agricultural production, such personnel serve as engineers, agronomists, food production specialists; in management, as middle-level managers; in medicine, as pharmacists, nurses or lab professionals; in commerce, as account executives, accountants or legal paraprofessionals; in education, as secondary school teachers. Though loosening state control over important sectors of the economy, the Chinese government, through the first phase of reforms, 1980–95, has kept a tight grip on education. It did, however, increasingly 'marketize' both the supply of students to education and the product of education. The previous redistributive socio-political aims of education became subsumed under national economic development goals. Hence, technical-professional education at the tertiary level assumed an unaccustomed importance in the educational system and it was expected to provide the engine of economic growth. Furthermore, the flow of youth through the technical-professional educational systems represents avant-garde trends in social patterns at the upper end of the social hierarchy.

Stratification

Post-reform China inherited a steep educational pyramid.[5] From the 1950s to the 1980s, 'upward access channels for the majority of [lower school] students were never significantly widened'.[6] Access to advanced skill and academic training and employment did not expand beyond élite population groups, higher Party members and the urban professional class.[7] In 1980, about 2% of primary school entrants made it to higher education.[8] Throughout the 1980s, the proportion of the age group enrolled in higher education remained at this level even despite the rapid expansion of higher education places.[9]

During the dramatic transition in the 1980s and 1990s, however, stratification in Chinese society was shifting rapidly in structure and composition.[10] Though the legacy of the bureaucratic rank order remained strong,[11] the transformation towards a money-based economy proceeded at a rapid pace. The complexities of the economy in the 1990s — partially marketized, partially state-controlled — defy conventional analysis, but many scholars have pointed out that stratification in the PRC came to resemble a class system replacing the socialist rank order.[12] The forming status groups were characterized by prestige, privilege, access to resources and power, and, increasingly, income, wealth and common political interests. This is the classic definition of social order.

Additionally, in dualistic economies where the modern world is sharply distinguished from the traditional, the urban and rural divide is paramount. A complete complement of social classes often exists within each sector. In China, the urban-rural gap has remained wide; the masses have lived and worked in the traditional rural economy, mired for generations at the lower echelons.

This stratification overwhelmingly defined education as well.[13] Even in the 1980s the single most important determinant of higher education enrolment was the geographical location of a student's home.[14] In 1982, higher education students were 84% urban and 15% rural, or a 5:1 urban-rural student ratio, whereas the total population ratio was almost the inverse, 1:4.[15]

The Chinese higher education system has always engaged in a systematic hierarchical ranking, with universities being ranked by prestige, level of administration and concomitant resources.[16] Programmes of study too were ranked by prestige and wealth. The 1985 higher education reform established 'affirmative action' as a tool for minority recruitment, with a maximum quota set at 25% of student population. These reforms labelled students by enrolment status, and these distinctions were reflected in the differing types and location of jobs offered to graduates. Public perception quickly congealed into a firm rank-ordering of the categories. Since the groupings mirrored existing social divisions, particularly the urban-rural divide, this new stratification in access quickly appeared in the social structure of higher education. The next section examines the enrolment categories and who was enrolled in them, in order to give a picture of social stratification.

Enrolment categories — definitions

The central government made available in rural areas a locally committed scholarship programme (*dingxiang zhaosheng*) as part of its general higher education scholarship funding under the central examination system (*tongkao shangxue*). The administration of the programme was turned over to county-level units of the relevant government ministry because local agencies could oversee better the selection and reassignment of students. The purpose was to ensure that rural students would study rurally relevant course work and return home to bring new skills to rural areas. In urban areas, a corollary policy was mandated; however, unlike in rural areas which lacked resources, local urban agencies or enterprises were expected to fund the scholarships themselves. Enterprises could set up contract scholarship study arrangements (*weituo peiyang*) for their employees. Students in both programmes accepted the scholarships in return for making five- to ten-year work commitments after graduation, warranted by signed contracts. Entrance examination score cut-offs were lowered for students from poor or rural districts.

A third type of enrolment, which in fact had existed prior to 1952, responds to the pressure of private demand for higher education. Students scoring slightly below the cut-off line could enrol as tuition-paying students (*zifei*) in the major of their choice. Considered private, these students fell outside the state enrolment and graduate assignment plans. They were considered 'profitable' by many institutions and some universities provided better accommodation and services — for a price. The high tide of private students occurred in 1993, after which time the government clamped heavy controls on enrolment quotas and supervised universities more strictly.[17]

The national unified-examination tuition-waiver scholarship (*tongkao gongfei* or *guojia fuwu*), initiated in 1953, continued to provide major student financial aid.[18] Students qualified through a highly competitive national examination for study in a certain major. Tuition-waiver scholarships existed for most degree programmes, but were expected to be phased out by the turn of the century. In teacher education and agriculture,[19] the national scholarship paid for room and board as well as tuition. Upon graduation, students in this group were assigned jobs in government offices somewhere in the nation through the unified job assignment system.[20] However, since 1989, increasingly larger proportions of students and employers had been authorized to initiate their own job search and placement (two-way choice or *shuangxiang xuanze*).

Students' career future was to a large extent determined by their enrolment category, as well as the university and major into which they were placed by virtue of their examination score. This new element added another dimension to stratification in the higher education system.

Perceptions of stratification and reproduction

The categories of enrolment were perceived by student families as leading to differential life chances. Families judged the categories by how likely they were to result in a good job or placement in a good labour sector or in an advanced economic market, such as a coastal city. Students jockeyed in the categories to get the most advantageous position for a mobile career future. The interviews present a complex picture where the future is judged correlative to background, where access to information strongly affects judgements and where systemic employment customs narrow decision-making options.

Interviewees perceived the following ranking (from least to most desirable) of enrolment categories in regards to the opportunities they offered.

1. locally committed recruitment-placement study (local);
2. contract scholarship study (contract);
3. self-supporting/private tuition enrolment (self); and
4. national tuition-waiver scholarship (national).

This rank-ordering reflects a strong conservative expectation but, also, a strong showing for money-driven changes in enrolment stratification.

The education reform policy continued the pattern of connecting enrolment and job assignment. Indeed, the categories of enrolment were perceived by student families as leading to differential life chances. Both educators and families saw life chances as the interaction between the type of employment and where the job was located. Families were looking for future mobility in high-return labour market segments and, perhaps more importantly, placement in an advanced economic market.[21]

The qualitative evidence below shows that, due to the dual economy and dualistic educational policy, different opportunities and categories of

enrolment were available to the two major segments of population. The
urban population chose between contract, self-supporting/private tuition,
and national scholarship study; the rural population chose between locally
committed and national scholarship study. The structural division created
by the policy was quite strong; few urban youths were found in the rural-
targeted locally committed category and few rural students in the urban-
targeted contract or self-supporting/private tuition categories.[22]

Local commitment

The locally committed recruitment-placement category was offered to rural
students and committed a student to fixed employment in a rural setting.
This commitment was seen as guaranteed employment in an advanced
labour segment for some time which was, however, located in one of the
poorest economic markets, in relatively harsh living conditions. The returns,
living conditions and socio-economic mobility, however, were expected to
be better than for other rural and county town occupational opportunities.
Urban students and entrepreneurial rural students saw this enrolment
avenue as less desirable than the other options. Many locally committed
students who entered university, though originally grateful for the chance
to enter at all, after some exposure, changed their outlook. Learning about
the greater opportunities of other tertiary students brought about a re-
evaluation of their own relatively limited future. Many such students
attempted to master strategies to circumvent the local commitment; some
were reported to have succeeded. Postgraduate studies were seen as one
of few avenues of escape from local commitment. This, it was believed,
accounted for the oft-mentioned studiousness of rural students.[23] Hence,
by the mid-1990s rural families' perception of the locally committed
category had improved. For many, particularly for those with lower tertiary
entrance examination scores, it offered the only path to higher education.
Thus, in the eyes of the majority of the rural population this enrolment
category provided access to relatively high-return opportunities. But for
the tertiary population as a whole, this category was ranked least desirable.[24]

Contract study

The contract scholarship study category guaranteed the students an urban,
steady, relatively high-return job in their employing unit. This was a
guarantee of an urban job and residence registration, both highly prized
commodities. Many of the contract scholarships were underwritten by the
most politically well-placed and most highly endowed state enterprises in

highly industrialized settings, or, in contrast, in rich ministry enterprises in hardship areas, for example, the mining and oil industries. In this latter case, the children of employees often used the contract system.

For an urban student, however, a contract required return to a position in a former enterprise and it represented low mobility and much job stress. Being favoured above others for a privileged place in higher education could mark the students; they could be subjected to acts of jealousy by colleagues. This kind of environment usually meant a stifled career and an assignment to a non-essential position. Often a unit would have reassigned the student's original position and would have no real use for skills acquired in higher education.

Children of employees in hardship postings, such as mining in Xinjiang, gladly accepted this rare opportunity to study. However, after getting into university, they wished not be posted back to the hardship areas. This mixed benefit picture tended to discourage demand for contract enrolment among the most privileged urban workers and some privileged rurally located workers.

Other urban youths made side-contracts with enterprises to recommend them as their employees while the students paid the enterprises tuition that the enterprises would forward to the universities, in exchange for no work contracts. The students would find their own jobs and the enterprises would be relieved of the difficulty of finding appropriate positions or disturbing the work climate of the units.[25]

For the average urban worker, without access to a free labour market, particularly those with lower higher education entrance examination scores, this category of enrolment was highly desirable, as evidenced by the subversion of the system through 'tuition-laundering'. But due to its limitations and forced reintegration into a given enterprise or administrative agency, this category was ranked second least desirable.

Self-supporting students

This category required the greatest financial investment in education and provided the greatest freedom of employment, practical only for well-off students with access to free-market regions, such as the metropolitan cities in the early to mid-1990s. Employment in coastal areas and metropolitan cities, even for mere high school graduates, was associated with high income and modern amenities. The most privileged families — those with sufficient income and extensive connections (*guanxi*) to help their children find employment after graduation — preferred this category. Almost exclusively, only children of the most privileged families benefited from this category of enrolment. In contrast, students without leads to well-paying jobs perceived no advantage from paying tuition that was sometimes as high as twice the annual local salary of a well-employed person. Lack of access to a national or urban job-assignment system was seen by some as a barrier to secure, élite employment. For less privileged and less urban families, the incentives in this category were perhaps out-of-reach. Even if feasible, this choice was risky, though better than nothing.

The assessment of this category is mixed but possibly highly desirable to a small élite. The preponderance of the evidence ranks it the second highest category. This is the most volatile of the categories, impacted directly by the most rapidly changing economic conditions in the PRC, and, within a short period of time, it may be the most advantageous enrolment category. Certainly by the year 2000, when almost all university study will be tuition-based, a re-evaluation will be necessary.

National tuition-waiver scholarship

Upon graduation, students with national tuition-waiver scholarships were guaranteed centrally assigned, lifetime employment as state cadres (*ganbu*). Historic considerations alone would certainly place this category at the top of the ranking. Until 1978, with the bureaucracy holding the monopoly in social mobility, higher education enrolment served as the only alternative to internal CCP mechanisms as the route to the upper social ranks.[26]

In contrast to pre-reform days, this category in the 1980s and 1990s was seen as a highly constrained employment channel and as most likely leading to a stultifying career in an uncertain, and increasingly more remote, location. However, the loosening of the job assignment system since 1989 has given growing numbers of students the right to find their own employment. This was a widely welcomed relaxation of constraints. Students who lived in advanced economic markets tended to believe that, if left to their own devices, they could find more rewarding employment than through the job assignment system (*fenpei*).[27] For those not located in advanced economic markets, this category guaranteed decent job security and possible high returns, while permitting some flexibility and mobility. This category was ranked the most advantageous.

THE MODEL OF STATE SOCIALIST STRATIFICATION

The sociological literature on China prior to the Dengist reforms, though sparse in empirical findings, showed a high degree of agreement in regard to the characteristics of the socio-economic order and what major factors determined the life chances of a Chinese citizen. The broad conclusion was that location in the dual economy, socio-economic status and political-cultural status together largely determined the kind of lives people lived. This model of bureaucratic state socialism and how it was defined in the field study are briefly described below.

Urban-rural location in the dual economy

During most of the twentieth century, the variation between rural and urban areas was generally cited for causing the greatest differences in life chances for the Chinese people.[28] Since the enforcement of the household registration system (*hukou*) in the late 1950s, city life and village life have constituted separate and different worlds. From its inception, the PRC has supported an economic policy that presented 'an allocational bias in favour of heavy industry over agriculture and personal consumption',[29] a view shared by many economists.[30] The rural/urban income gap increased over the next three decades — Maoist rhetoric to the contrary.[31] Over this time, the residence registration and ration coupon (*piao*) or 'unified purchase and supply' turned the farmer into a virtual captive to his village and village boss.[32] In 1982, even official Beijing acknowledged the rural/urban disparity as a 'potentially volatile' political situation.[33]

Socio-economic status

In the international literature, socio-economic status is commonly measured simply by the occupation of a person. However, in the PRC as a bureaucratic socialist state, social scientists have found that a more accurate measurement is occupational rank. In this case, rank refers to the enterprise or agency level, that is, the official administrative level which governs the enterprise. Occupation refers to the type of position held, for example, management or technical.[34] Some research on pre-reform urban China found administrative level to be a significant indicator of economic status which, when added to occupational status, substantially accounted for differences in employment gains and benefits over a lifetime.[35]

Administrative level or rank fundamentally measures whether the work-unit (*danwei*) or enterprise belongs to the formal state-run or the informal non-state sector. The state-owned sector offers salary, benefits and pension, rationing, and generally fits the concept of primary employment. The lower-level work-units constitute a much greater proportion of the economy and are engaged largely in farming, rural semi-manufacturing enterprises and similar low-skilled urban enterprises. Into the 1990s, enterprises in this sector were either borderline or wholly traditional in their means and ways of production.[36]

State-owned enterprises constituted almost the entirety of the modern sector of the economy and were mostly located in urban areas. Some large, modern-sector enterprises, for example, oil refineries, were located in rural areas and the lifestyle of their employees was much harsher. A rigid division between the state-owned and informal sectors was enforced through lifelong employment tenure and the residence registration system.

In sum, the literature regarding socio-economic status shows that occupation and mobility are not strong factors in determining life chances. But, as stated above, when added to rank, they provide a good measure. In this study, the indicator of socio-economic status is called the bureaucratic rank order, that is, the administrative level of one's work-unit combined with the occupational status of one's parents.[37]

Cultural-political capital

Another dimension of social stratification is cultural capital, which in Western social sciences is measured by parental educational level. Parental education data was unavailable for this sample, but data on secondary school preparation of the tertiary students was accessible. Whereas parental educational level indicates that the cross-generational cultural capital of the family is invested in the student, secondary schooling indicates cultural capital accumulated by the student himself/herself and the sociocultural status of the family.

In the PRC, secondary school assignment is based on residence registration. Schools are run on the same schema as the economy, by administrative levels, with the lowest level, village primary schooling, under 'collective' (*minban*) administration and largely unsupported by the state.[38]

Secondary schools are state-run and usually located in urban centres. Few secondary schools exist in rural towns. Rural secondary students usually attend boarding schools at their own costs in the regional district centres or county towns. Hence, a student's secondary school background represents widely varied cultural capital, depending on the rural/urban dichotomy and the administrative level of the school.

Students attend schools administered by the same level as their parents' residence registration, which is based on the parents' place of work. For collective farmers, the commune is the holder of the residence registration, and the student with sufficiently high test scores can attend boarding school in the district centre, a larger market town.

During some ideological eras, admission to a secondary school was primarily based on recommendation for either good political activism or high academic performance. In the 1980s, the parents' ability to pay the boarding school living and tuition costs was a major issue. Many students were ill prepared by their poor rural secondary schools and could not pass the increasingly rigorous high school entrance examination. Recommendation for good political behaviour was always necessary, and in the 1990s, it continued to provide privileged access to higher education enrolment (*baosong shangxue*). Hence, secondary schooling always reflected political status, and in the 1980s, both cultural and economic status.

In this study, the indicator of political-cultural status is the administrative level of a student's secondary school.

In sum, the state-socialist stratification model used in this study, as it relates to determining educational outcomes, consists of location in the dual economy, socio-economic status and political-cultural status. How the sample breaks up in terms of these variables is shown in Table 11.1. Figure 11.1 presents a graphic representation of the model.

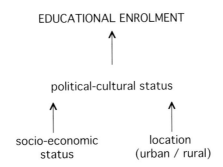

Figure 11.1 State-socialist stratification model

SOCIALIST STRATIFICATION OR SOCIAL CHANGE?

The quantitative aspect of the research was designed to measure the extent to which the state socialist model discussed above described the enrolment patterns in higher education between 1985 and 1990 and the variations from those patterns. The survey of nearly 1000 university students' records brought in enough data to draw statistically generalizable conclusions from the analysis. To the extent that the state socialist model did not explain the enrolment patterns, descriptive follow-up analyses were done. Thus, we can get a distilled, spare view of an older social structure maintaining its hold or new forces coming to the fore in Chinese society.

Table 11.1
Frequency distribution of variables

Enrolment Category	Number	%
Locally Committed	200	20.0
Commissioned Training	94	9.5
Self-supporting	63	6.3
National Scholarship	641	64.2
Total	998	100.0

Location of Family Home	Number	%
Rural		
Rural Town	255	25.9
Urban		
County Town	180	18.3
City*	194	19.4
Metropolitan City*	351	35.6
Missing	14	–
Total	998	100.0

* City refers to all cities other than the self-governed cities of Beijing, Tianjin, Shanghai, Guangzhou, herein called Metropolitan City.

Administrative Level	Father's		Mother's	
	Number	%	Number	%
Below county	231	24.2	310	33.3
County	482	50.5	432	46.4
Provincial City	163	17.1	131	14.1
Central Government	79	8.2	58	6.2
Missing	43	–	67	–
Total	998	100.0	998	100.0

Rank and Occupation	Number	%
Rural Managerial & Worker	320	33.4
Urban Worker	333	38.4
Urban Managerial & Professional	305	31.8
Missing	41	–
Total	998	100.0

Location of Secondary School	Number	%
Rural		
Vocational	31	3.1
Rural Town	57	5.7
Urban		
County	274	27.6
City	217	21.9
Provincial Key or Metropolitan	414	41.7
Missing	6	–
Total	998	100.0

Sex	Number	%
Female	338	33.9
Male	658	66.1
Missing	2	–
Total	998	100.0

The research methodology, though common in social science research conducted in many Western countries, is path-breaking in the China field. Given the paucity of empirical social science done in China, very little theory has been tested in the field, few concepts have been operationalized as testable variables, no instruments have been checked for reliability or validity.[39] For this research topic, the socialist stratification model was tested for 'goodness of fit' (logistic regression analysis) to the whole sample of students and the urban and rural sub-samples to see the extent to which it explained the current enrolment patterns. Then, chi-square analyses of two-variable relationships were done to look into the new enrolment categories in more detail and to fine-tune an understanding of emerging trends.

The first analysis showed that the socialist stratification model explained much of the enrolment pattern for the whole sample, but it accurately predicted only the old type of enrolment in the national scholarship category. It could not predict who would enrol in the reform categories. The socialist stratification model, though statistically significant, did not fit the current enrolment patterns very well, and it particularly lacked accuracy in distinguishing students in the reform categories from those in the national scholarship category.

Interestingly, the two factors in the socialist stratification model that contributed most towards the prediction were parental occupational rank — whether high, middle or low — and the location (urban or rural) of the secondary school attended by the student. The literature on bureaucratic socialism had proposed that the urban or rural *hukou* was the most important determinant of life chances. As far as determining the educational enrolment chances of a student in the late 1980s and early 1990s, the location of the secondary school was relevant; home location, however, was not. The parents' socio-economic rank, a semi-socialist semi-free market factor, was also a determinant (see Table 11.2).

The socialist stratification model better explained the enrolment patterns of the rural than urban samples. Indeed, for the urban sample, the analysis revealed an interesting reversal of the model. Though the socialist stratification model fit the urban students' enrolment pattern well, it did not explain the enrolment pattern in the reform categories at all. Unexpectedly, the prediction was negative. What was supposed to be a social advantage and lead to enrolment in the more advantageous category actually turned out to be a disadvantage. For example, students from metropolitan cities[40] were likely to enrol in higher education either as tuition-paying students or on a contract scholarship through an enterprise. These were preferred to attending on national scholarships. Such students were likely to have achieved a high enough score in the qualifying examination

Table 11.2
Logistic regression of enrolment status, on social status characteristics of students: national versus reform enrolment categories

| | Parameter Estimates | | | | | |
| | Model 1 | | Model 2 | | Model 3 | |
Effect	b	Exp(b)$^\Delta$	b	Exp(b)	b	Exp(b)
Intercept	-.99^b	...	-1.86^a	...	5.45^d	...
FamLocUR	-.23	.79	...	...	...	...
FamLocat	...	...	...	...	-.42^a	.66
OccAdvan	.36^a	2.42	.49	1.64	...	...
MFAdLev	NA	NA	...	...	.07	1.08
SchLocUR	1.20^d	3.32	1.07^b	2.91	...	...
SchLoc3	...	...	...	...	-1.18^d	.31
Model χ^2	42.09^d	...	11.92^a	...	50.41^d	...
df	4	...	2	...	3	...
R^2_L	.04	...	.04	...	.08	...
Predicted:						
Model	67.19%	...	68.28%	...	77.88%	...
L & C & S	15.72%	...	32.10%	...	.00%	...
National	95.50%	...	88.36%	...	100.00%	...
Accuracy λ_p	.08	...	.11	...	.00	...
Number N	906	...	168	...	663	...

^{a}p<.05 ^{b}p<.01 ^{c}p<.001 ^{d}p<.0001

FamLocUR	= Family Location: Urban/rural
FamLocat	= Family Location (three levels)
OccAdvan	= Occupational Advantage Status (three levels)
SchLocUR	= Location/type of Upper Secondary: Urban/rural
L & C & S	= Locally committed, commissioned training and self-supporting enrolment categories

Model 1 = whole sample   Model 2 = rural sample   Model 3 = urban sample
Exp(b)$^\Delta$ is a measure of the added proportion of the total prediction contributed by this factor beyond that of the previous factor(s).

to win a national scholarship, so the model would have predicted thus. Instead, they were not likely to accept a national scholarship. In sum, for the urban student population from the late 1980s to early 1990s, the socialist stratification model did not determine educational future and, by inference, life chances.

For the rural sample, the socialist stratification model fit somewhat more accurately, predicting some of the enrolment pattern in the reform categories and two-thirds of the pattern in the national scholarship category. The factor that contributed most towards the prediction was the urban versus rural location of the secondary schools; it was a strong predictor. Apparently urban schools are better at preparing graduates to achieve high qualifying scores than rural town secondary schools. Though rural town upper secondary schools were rare in the PRC in the 1980s, the government promoted vocational-technical secondary schools in these locations. The survey showed, however, that such schools were disadvantageous in terms of obtaining national scholarships for their students. This finding is a confirmation of the bureaucratic socialist stratification model and the cultural-political policy on secondary schooling associated with it. In the countryside, socialist stratification was replicating itself through the 1985 enrolment policies. Anecdotal evidence indicated increasing competitiveness in secondary schooling during the 1980s, with schools increasingly charging for tuition, for example. This is supported by the study's empirical data. Urban schools continued to privilege their graduates in terms of their educational future; rural schools did not.

In general, the socialist stratification model did not do well at predicting the enrolment pattern in the new reform categories. This finding is a sign of social change rather than an indication of old-line bureaucratic socialist stratification. Apparently new considerations, preferences and criteria were being applied to the evaluation of the opportunities presented by the various enrolment categories on the part of both urban and rural higher education-bounds youth and their families. Anecdotal data and economic conditions suggest that urban families evidence less old-line bureaucratic socialist behaviour than their rural counterparts, whose environment has changed much less.

EMERGING TRENDS: THE NEW ADVANTAGES

Descriptive data on the relationship between the significant predictor variables and the reform enrolment categories allows us to distinguish significant variation not detected in the above inferential statistical analyses. Looking into the relevant relationships that were found in the logistic regression analysis allows us to plot trends in the demographic distribution, even in the categories whose enrolment was purposefully limited to a small number, as was the case with the reform categories. If students of higher status, as measured by the socialist stratification model, were overrepresented in the less advantageous enrolment category, i.e., the reform categories, this would be an indication of new trends in social stratification behaviour.

The follow-up chi-square analysis of the sample as a whole, which represents the technical-professional student population of the PRC, provides some useful data on the background of the students in all of the reform categories. Parental occupational class and secondary school location accounted for a large part of the overall variance. As Table 11.3 shows, rural managers, staff and workers, who represent 33.4% of the sample, were overrepresented in the reform categories (47.1%) when compared to urban professionals, staff and workers (29.9%).

Table 11.3
Socio-economic status: whole sample and parental occupational class

		Rural Managers, Staff & Workers	Urban Workers & Staff	Urban Professionals & Managers	Row Total
Loc&ComSelf	Count	150	100	89	339
	Column %	47.1	29.9	29.1	35.4
National	Count	169	233	216	618
	Column %	52.9	70.1	70.9	64.6
Total Column	Count	320	333	305	957
	%	33.4	34.8	31.8	100.0

Pearson x^2 = 28.73632, df 2, $p<.000001$, missing: 41
Loc&ComSelf = Locally committed, commissioned training and self-supporting enrolment categories
National   = National scholarship enrolment category

The same pattern is repeated even more strongly for the other determining background factor, secondary school location (see Table 11.4). The rurally schooled, who represent only 8.8% of the sample, were overrepresented in the less advantageous reform categories (69.4%) when compared to the urban schooled (32.6%). Also, though 26% of the sample were from rural homes, only 8.8% came from rural secondary schools. The other 16.2% of the sample that were rural apparently were sending their children to urban boarding schools.

The urban-oriented, more privileged sector continues to subscribe to a higher valuation of the national scholarship and the rurally-oriented, least privileged sector is much more confined to the lower-opportunity categories. In general the socialist stratification model seems to be alive and well.

Table 11.4
Political-cultural status: whole sample and
location of senior secondary school

		Rural	Urban	Row Total
Loc&Com&Self	Count	61	295	355
	Column %	69.4	32.6	35.8
National	Count	27	610	637
	Column %	30.6	67.4	64.2
Total Column	Count	87	905	992
	%	8.8	91.2	100.0

Pearson x^2 = 47.03535, df 1, p <.000001, missing: 6
Loc&Com&Self = Locally committed, commissioned training and self-supporting enrolment categories
National   = National scholarship enrolment category

As is clear from the previous analyses, this overall look is too general to be very meaningful, as it hides several contradictions and phenomena. Separate foci on the urban and the rural populations are required.

Urban students

Home location, whether in a county town, an ordinary city or a metropolitan city, accounted for most of the variance in the enrolment category of urban students. But the results run in the opposite direction from that expected. As Table 11.5 shows, the proportion of students enrolled in the reform categories grows as home-city size increases. The socialist stratification model predicted the opposite — that the reform categories would provide less opportunity for mobility and more disadvantages than the national scholarship category. Students from the three metropolitan cities seemed to prefer less mobility; they were overrepresented in the contract and private tuition categories (31.7%) when compared to the total share of students (21.9%) in those categories (a slightly higher percentage than allowed by government quota). Also, 12% of students from ordinary cities and 9.5% of students from county towns were similarly enrolled. These findings clarify the logistic regression finding of a negative relationship between the socialist stratification model and enrolment status. In significant proportions, students from the most privileged home locations preferred the contract and private tuition avenues of enrolment.

The interviews found that people in metropolitan cities preferred putting their career future into their own hands, studying privately or being sponsored by a local government agency or enterprise, because any of these options was more likely to assure employment in their home metropolitan cities than the option of national scholarships. These modern city youths were maximizing their economic future by choosing a 'lesser' educational opportunity. Even at the cost of paying for tuition, the most privileged preferred a guaranteed metropolitan job to tuition-free study with only a possible chance of a metropolitan job.

For the students from ordinary cities, the calculation looked somewhat different. For them, the chances that a national scholarship might lead to a job assignment in a larger urban area meant possible upward mobility, hence a national scholarship was still a worthwhile risk. Thus, the more removed a city is from the major developed areas, the more appealing the national scholarship category became.

This was indeed a new trend.

Table 11.5
Socio-economic status:
urban sample and home location

		County	City	Metropolitan	Total
Contr&Self	Count	12	20	103	135
	Column %	9.5	12.0	31.7	21.9
National	Count	116	143	221	480
	Column %	90.5	88.0	68.3	78.1
Total Column	Count	128	163	324	615
	%	20.8	26.5	52.7	100.0

Pearson x^2 = 39.17777, df 2, p =.00000, missing: 110
Contr&Self   = Contract and self-supporting enrolment categories
National   = National scholarship enrolment category

Secondary school location, whether in an ordinary or metropolitan city, was another moderately strong and indirect predictor in the regression model. The same pattern as that for home location appeared in this analysis, as Table 11.6 shows. The larger the urban area of the secondary school location, the higher the proportion of students enrolling in the reform categories (9.7% and 32.4%). The most privileged students, who had attended metropolitan or provincial key schools, were overrepresented in contract and private tuition enrolment categories (32.4%) when compared to the total share of urban students in this category (21.8%).

On the other hand, those who had attended ordinary city secondary schools were overrepresented in the national scholarship category (90.3%) when compared to the total share of students in that category (78.2%).

This inverse pattern was a strong and highly significant finding attesting to the new trend (see Table 11.6).

Table 11.6
Political-cultural status:
urban sample and secondary school location

		Rural	City	Metropolitan	Total
Com&Self	Count	0	27	106	133
	Column %	6.6	9.7	32.4	21.8
National	Count	6	251	220	478
	Column %	93.4	90.3	67.6	78.2
Total Column	Count	7	278	326	611
	%	1.1	45.5	53.3	100.0

Pearson x^2 = 46.55891, *df* 2, *p* = .00000, missing: 114
Com&Self = Commissioned training and self-supporting enrolment categories

The urban sample showed an unexpected overrepresentation of families with higher background status selecting more risky opportunities through the reform categories in technical-professional higher education enrolment. The opposite trend occurred among families of middle and lower status. Apparently, the most privileged segments of the population, in terms of residence and political-cultural capital, responded to the new opportunities and changed their preferences accordingly.

Rural students

Of the students in the sample, 26% were from rural homes, an underrepresentation by a factor of three in respect to their proportion in the national population. Within technical-professional higher education, a larger share of rural (36.9%) than urban students was found in the policy-restricted reform categories which offered fewer opportunities and were hypothetically, at least here, also the less advantageous enrolment categories (21.9%).

As Table 11.7 shows, the rurally schooled were overrepresented in the locally committed category (58.7%) when compared to the total share of students in this category (36.9%). Families with a greater political-cultural capital, indicated by urban secondary schooling, were overrepresented, though not by much, in the national scholarship category (68.9%) when compared to the total share of students in this category (63.1%). This significant but moderate magnitude finding shows that among the rural sample, the socialist stratification model still holds sway and the next generation shows continuous behaviour. One-third of the rural young people pursuing technical-professional higher education would likely return to work in the rural areas, reproducing the urban-rural divide, though their status within the rural population would be higher than that of their parents.

Table 11.7
Political-cultural status:
rural sample and secondary school location

		Rural	Urban	Row Total
Local	Count	29	58	87
	Column %	58.7	31.1	36.9
National	Count	20	128	149
	Column %	41.3	68.9	63.1
Total Column	Count	49	186	236
	%	20.9	79.1	100.0

Pearson x^2 = 12.81262, df 1, p = .00034, missing: 23
Local   = Locally committed enrolment category
National = National scholarship enrolment category

The follow-up analysis showed quite clearly that a new trend was emerging among the urban population. The most privileged urban segment, those living and educated in the metropolitan areas of the country, was responding to new incentives in their areas and was exhibiting behaviour different from that described in the socialist stratification model. No similar change was visible in the rural population since the socialist stratification values seemed very much alive in the late 1980s and early 1990s.

Discussion and conclusion

The urban 'super privileged' and rural 'super underprivileged' both stayed in their places through enrolling in the reform categories, and the middle stratum, both urban and rural (64.2%), became mobile through enrolling in the national scholarship category.

Rural families were represented in significant proportions in both the national scholarship and the rural reform enrolment categories. Among rural background students, those with a higher status strongly tended towards the national scholarship category. Though this pattern seems to confirm the reproduction of the socialist model, it can be understood from a transitional perspective as well. For the rural population, the national category assured upward mobility, greater opportunity for individual advancement, and more reliance on individual resources than the locally committed reform category.

Thus, though it looks like the socialist stratification was being reproduced at the two ends of the social spectrum, this pattern actually represents social change. The élite was changing its behaviour in order to take advantage of the new channels to stay ahead, to maintain its status. The middle and lower strata were also responding to the new incentives embodied in the new system. They, however, could only respond to the changed socio-economic environment by using old behaviours and proven ways.

That, however, is the point of the reforms. They were instituted not to change the system but to given marginal groups access to the system. In this aspect, the reforms were successful. Rural students constituted a sizeable portion of enrolment (26%) and lower-echelon urban students, those from county towns, were also present (15%).

The single consistently significant and strongest predictor of enrolment variation was the political-cultural factor measured by secondary school location. This contradicts much that has been written in the sociological literature on the PRC, holding that household registration and bureaucratic rank were the strongest determinants of life chances. However, since this research concerns the area of higher education enrolment, it is perhaps least surprising that secondary education should be the outstanding predeterminant.

In the 1980s and 1990s, enrolment was synonymous with graduation, and tertiary graduation was still so rare (less than 5% of the age group) that it perforce lent élite status. We can draw some inferences from the findings of this study for the future technical-professional élite. In the early 1990s, outfitted with a key urban education followed by technical-professional higher education, young people were certain to have gained membership in the élite club of privileged urban technocrats, passing their life in the relative comfort of the boom towns of marketizing China. This represents a clear pattern of class reproduction and social continuity.

Farmer children and urban worker children, however, also had the chance to join the technological élite, though not necessarily in the boom towns but in still relatively comfortable smaller urban centres. A noticeable contingent of the technical élite would be engaged in the rural economy —

but it is doubtful that they would maintain lifelong residence in rural areas.

Finally, a comment on the participation of women in technical-professional higher education and the technical-professional élite. Female students participated almost equally as men, in technical-professional subject areas leading to urban opportunities, but in much lower numbers in rural programmes. Women were strongly underrepresented in all rural subject areas, except in teacher preparation. The higher the social status of a female student, the more likely she was to participate on an equal footing with male students regardless of subject area. Here also, the exceptions were teacher preparation, which women dominated, and agriculture, where women were severely outnumbered.

All in all, a picture of social class reproduction emerges with an economically upward trend, assuming continued economic growth and continued rapid technological development in both urban and rural areas. The picture shows some blurring of class lines and at least some inclusion of marginal social strata and women in the technical élite.

Postscript

The conclusion that families are pursuing maximum flexibility and mobility even at a high cost of tuition is underscored by data from the SEdC that show that higher education enrolment exceeded its limits by 21% in 1992 and 17% in 1993 as universities were overenrolling private tuition-paying students.[41]

The SEdC's 1994 enrolment plans allowed universities to enrol up to 25% of their students in the private tuition category, a fivefold increase from the previous policy. Included in the plan was an undetermined proportion (a very small number) of contract-scholarship students at Master's level, heretofore permitted only at the undergraduate level.[42] In 1994, a partial-tuition programme was instituted at 50 universities and in 1995 at 100 universities.[43] By the year 2000, national scholarships will be eliminated and all students will have to have to pay the same amount of tuition, either through their own resources or a sponsoring enterprise or agency (most likely restricted to government-owned ones). Annual tuition was to be set at ¥1000–1500 (US$118–$178) or somewhat higher, depending on the popularity of the degree. In any case, the minimium amount represents about a quarter of the annual income of an 'ordinary' Chinese family. At the same time the SEdC announced plans to offer partial and full scholarships as well as loans to financially needy and meritorious students by the autumn of 1995. In the meanwhile, universities were soliciting foundation funding, and student personnel (*fudao laoshi, banzhuren*) were raising small amounts of funding as students' needs arose.

The findings outlined in this chapter suggest that expanding private tuition enrolment will allocate more benefits to the already most privileged youths in the PRC. Relative to their urban cousins, rural students will have a harder time getting into higher education. This direction of reform will limit rather than broaden the nation's social mobility and will concentrate development using technical-professional skills in the already advanced areas. People in those areas will be continuously able to move further ahead, leaving those already lagging, further behind. The brain drain from the northwest to the southeast, already well underway, will be helped along by private tuition policies. Universities in advanced areas will have more local resources to draw upon to raise more scholarship funds than in poorer areas. Even socio-economic equity will be more likely possible in the advanced regions than in the poorer ones. Only a yet undocumented 'trickle effect' seems to run in the reverse direction, allowing some youths from rural areas to 'jump the village gate' and provide a role-model-by-mail to those left behind the gate.

NOTES

1. Data for this chapter were collected in an ongoing research project, Chinese Higher Education Research Project, at Kent State University, Ohio. Since 1990, the project has studied enrolment patterns and their relations to educational policy reforms and national economic development. Chinese partners include the PRC Ministry of Agriculture, Bureau of Education (MoA): Mr Yun Zemin, Deputy Director, Division of Higher Education and Mr Han Huipeng, Deputy Division Chief, Division of Research; the Central Institute of Educational Research, administered by the SEdC, Bureau of Planning: Meng Mingyi, Chief of the Division of Higher Education and Professor Zeng Zida, Deputy Chief of the Division of Technical-Vocational Education; Dr. Shi Jinghuan, Professor, Beijing Normal University, Department of Education; and Xin Fuliang, Senior Researcher, Shanghai Higher Education Research Institute.

2. Survey data were collected from a sample of students in Chinese technical and professional colleges who enrolled between the years 1985 and 1991. A stratified random sample (N = 998) was collected at 11 public and private tertiary institutions which granted certificates and degrees in various technical-professional fields. They are located in four of the six administrative regions of the PRC. Eleven data collection sites were visited between June 1990 and June 1991: Beijing Computer Institute (BCI); China Management and Administration University (CADU) in Shanghai; Jiaotong University (JU); Nanjing Normal University (NNU); North West Agricultural University (NWAU) in Yangling, Shaanxi; Shanghai Architectural College (SAC); Shanghai University College of Engineering (SUCE); Shanghai Light Industry College (SLICE); and South West Agricultural University (SWAU) in Beibei, Chongqing, Sichuan. For details, see Seeberg, 1993a.

3. The institutions sampled for this chapter average several thousand students, a

size indicating their higher than average administrative status. In 1989 there were 400 regular technical-professional higher education institutions with an average of 500 students each. Each institution is subject to particular structural constraints, further compromising generalizability. Dai Shujun, 1990.

4. Party Congress Report, cited by He Dongchang, 1988.
5. Seeberg and Wang, 1991.
6. Epstein, 1983, p. 78.
7. Seeberg, 1990.
8. Sun Jian, 1980.
9. Li Xing, 1990.
10. Yan Yunxiang, 1992.
11. Walder, 1986; Watson, 1984.
12. Yan Yunxiang, 1992; Nee, 1989.
13. Seeberg, 1990.
14. Lo, 1984a.
15. *Shanghai Wenhui Bao*, 3 November 1982, p. 1, cited in Rosen, 1984, p. 82, Table 4.7.
16. See Chapter 2 by Cheng Kai-ming in this volume.
17. Personal communication, 1996; survey data, 1996.
18. For more on financial support, see Chapter 12 by Zhang Minxuan in this volume.
19. The subject areas of teacher education, agriculture, forestry, mining and geography were in low demand and thus received greater government funding to maintain required student enrolment.
20. For more on job assignment, see Chapter 13 by Michael Agelasto in this volume.
21. Interviews, 1990.
22. Seeberg, 1993b.
23. Interview with Zeng Zida, Deputy Chief, Division of Vocational-Technical Education, Central Institute of Educational Research (CIER), Beijing, June 1990; interview with Ma Fuliang, Director of Academic Affairs, South West Agricultural College, Beipei, Sichuan, June 1990; structured interviews with five students each at Beijing Normal University, Northwest Agricultural University and Southwest Agricultural University, June-July 1990; personal communication, Shi Jinghuan, BJNU, 1992.
24. See Seeberg and Wang, 1991.
25. Interviews with Meng Mingyi, Chief of the Division of Higher Education, CIER, Beijing, June 1990; Wei Gang, Director of the Higher Education Planning Department, Shanghai City, Shanghai, July 1990; Xin Fuliang, Deputy Chief and Senior Researcher at the Shanghai Higher Education Research Institute (SHERI), Shanghai, July 1990; Yu Lulin, president of China Social University, Beijing, June 1990; interview with Zeng.
26. This was true except during the Cultural Revolution when mobility and enrolment were based on political correctness.
27. Interviews, Meng, 1990; students, 1990; Wei, 1990; SHERI, 1990, see note 25.
28. Klatt, 1983.
29. Howe, 1987, p. 113.
30. Dernberger, 1982; Ishikawa, 1967, 1983; Lardy, 1983; Tang and Stone, 1980.
31. Lardy, 1983.

32. Hinton, 1983. Some have argued that the urban/rural dualism in the economic structure was breaking down in post-reform China. See L. Song, 1990. Others continued to find evidence that 'rural and urban industries in China are essentially mutually exclusive systems with little movement of labour between them'. See Peng, 1992, p. 201.
33. Beijing Radio, 21 May 1981, cited in Klatt, 1983.
34. Whyte and Parish, 1983.
35. For the years 1949–79, see Lardy, 1983; and Seeberg, 1990. For 1972–78, see Whyte and Parish, 1983; Korzec and Whyte, 1981; and Walder, 1986. For 1976–90 see Lin Nan and Bian Yanjie, 1991; Parish, 1984; Walder, 1990.
36. Howe, 1987.
37. Such a combined variable was created from the official Chinese employment data (SSB). The categorical ordering of the variable was based on the International Standard Occupational Scale. See Treiman, 1977.
38. Cheng Kai-ming, 1991; Seeberg, 1990.
39. In this research project the researcher had to undertake some of this preliminary work within a very unsystematic research environment. However, the questionnaire used in 1990 has been tested in three different studies and the sociological input variables have been found reliably to predict the educational outcomes.
40. The three self-governed cities — Beijing, Tianjin and Shanghai — are considered to be three of the four most economically developed areas of China. Their secondary schools are considered among the best in the country.
41. Report from Agence France-Presse, 3 February 1995, cited in *China News Digest*, 3 March 1995. The on-line publication was found at URL: gopher://cnd.org.
42. 'Postgraduate enrolment takes new twist', *China Daily*, 9 September 1992, p. 1.
43. Reuter in *China News Digest*, 19 April 1995.

12

Changing Conceptions of Equity and Student Financial Support Policies

ZHANG Minxuan

INTRODUCTION

This chapter focuses on the transition from free higher education to a tuition fee-based system in the PRC during the reform period. The former was characterized by grants without tuition fees to all students while the latter may be described as conditioned aid with tuition fees — one with strings attached. By analysing the change in policies, this chapter explores the shift in the conception of 'equity' behind them. For data it relies on documents from 1950 to 1995, on limited but useful official statistics and on the author's survey of 420 students in four universities, two under the SEdC and two under provincial control. In total 73 administrators at the central, provincial and institutional levels were also surveyed.

In the past two decades the term *equity* has appeared internationally in most of the literature concerning student financial support policies.[1] Free higher education and grants in developed and developing countries have come under critical scrutiny, and efforts have been made in various countries, including the PRC, to institute fairer support policies. The PRC, as this chapter describes, has developed systems with its own features and approaches and as a consequence, encountered its own problems.

Conceptions of equity

Equity is a 'slippery'[2] and a 'normative'[3] concept. Linguists and philosophers have studied equity since Socrates and Aristotle, and the term is used broadly (and perhaps recklessly) in the economics, politics and social psychology literature. Equity is considered by some contemporary scholars as a synonym for 'justice' and 'fairness',[4] and dictionaries intermarry the definitions of 'equity', 'justice' and 'fairness'.[5] However, philosophers and economists have discerned a difference between 'equity' and 'equality'. Some writers have warned that 'Equity is more than equality'.[6] Generally, the conceptions of equity can be divided into two categories. One is 'horizontal equity'. This emphasizes 'equal treatment to equals'. In other words, attention is paid to the mathematical equality or egalitarian distribution among all the members in a certain community. All members are viewed as equal. The other type is 'vertical equity', emphasizing 'unequal treatment to unequals'. Here, distribution is unequal but 'deserved' according to set criteria.[7]

BEFORE THE REFORMS: FREE HIGHER EDUCATION IN THE PRC

In the early 1950s, free higher education was instituted in the PRC, as the working people were declared to be owners of the country (*laodong renmin dangjia zuozhu*) and were bestowed an equal right to employment, education and participation in state administration. Higher education was no longer to be a privilege of the ruling classes and all institutions were required to open their doors to workers and peasants.[8]

A financial support policy was instituted to guarantee the equal political right to higher education for the working class, with the People's Grant established in some regional policy documents[9] and in a national *Circular* endorsed by the then premier Zhou Enlai in 1952.[10] Although there were several piecemeal adjustments in the mid-1950s and 1960s, this policy remained in effect until the mid-1980s; and even during the Cultural Revolution it was thoroughly implemented. The policy specified:

1. Higher education is no longer to be the 'exclusive privilege of the wealthier classes'. The government will provide an 'equal opportunity for all young men and women in institutions of higher learning'.
2. All students in higher education institutions are free from paying for tuition and accommodation.[11]
3. College students are entitled to a People's Grant.
4. A uniform food and meal allowance shall be payable to all students.

5. Other living allowances are permitted, subject to 'democratic discussion'.[12]

Therefore, equal access to higher education was provided regardless of family economic background and all students received public support: in the 1960s over 75% of students received a People's Grant. This was quite different from support systems such as those operating in the USA and Japan, which required all students to pay tuition fees but provided needs-based support to the disadvantaged students. But it was similar to the systems operating in the USSR, UK and West Germany in the first three decades after the Second World War. The Chinese system of this time may be characterized as a 'horizontal equity' distribution approach giving 'equal treatment to equals'. The 'equals' here were not economic equals. Rather, they were whoever passed the college entrance examination. All students who passed the examination were regarded as in need of financial support and were consequently treated equally. Their different economic backgrounds were virtually ignored in this egalitarian distribution of financial support funding.

No student paid fees and everyone received similar financial support. Accordingly, they had to accept two preconditions in return for these private benefits. The first was that they should 'obey' the government job-assignment on graduation.[13] As the MoEd stipulated in the *Circular*: 'All college students will be assigned by the government to constructive work immediately after graduation ... so it is stipulated that the People's Grant be given to all of them.'[14] Through national manpower planning, administrative actions and the moral-political education in higher education institutes, the majority of graduates were prepared to 'go to the countryside, go to the factories and go to the most-needed places in the nation' (in the words of a popular song of the time).

The other condition was the acceptance of low and uniform salaries set by the government after graduation. From 1958 all graduates earned almost the same starting salary, regardless of the major they had studied or their jobs. From 1958 to 1978, most intellectuals received only one pay rise, in 1963–64. Egalitarianism had applied to the distribution of People's Grants, and similarly egalitarian was the fact that the average salary of graduates was almost the same as, or sometimes even lower than, that of their peers who had not received higher education. Official wage statistics for 1962–83 show that the average wage for the education, science, health and culture sectors, in which half of all tertiary graduates worked, remained below the national average and lower than that for many other sectors (Table 12.1).

Policy-makers and theorists advanced two main reasons for this low-

Table 12.1
Average wages in state-owned enterprises by trade

Trade	1962	1965	1970	1975	1980	1983
Industry	652	729	661	644	854	878
Construction	705	730	650	740	923	1023
Transportation	702	774	709	699	906	959
Public Utilities	631	687	660	639	789	876
Civil Servants	626	684	678	645	807	927
Science, Education, Culture and Health	540	598	555	574	741	873
Finance, Bank	559	624	588	609	760	820
Commerce, Service	494	579	553	562	723	764
Agriculture	392	433	419	460	636	713
National average	592	652	609	613	803	865

Source: Ministry of Labour, 1985

and-egalitarian-pay policy for graduates. The first reason was that it would be a 'bourgeois' privilege if people obtained higher income or extra benefits on the grounds of capability or education: this was anathema to the principles of socialism. The pool of graduates could become 'the breeding ground of new bourgeoisie and revisionists' and therefore 'should be strictly limited in the socialist society'.[15] This claim was taken to an extreme during the Cultural Revolution. The second reason was that, although graduates might contribute more to the society because of their education, they still could have no right to extra pay because the cost of their education had been borne by the people. Advocates of this line of thinking quoted from Engels' *Anti-Duhring*:[16]

> How then are we to solve the whole important question of the higher wages paid for compound labour? In a society of private producers, private individuals or their families pay the costs of training the qualified worker; hence the higher price paid for qualified labour-power accrues first of all to private individual... In a socialistically organized society, the costs are borne by society, and to it therefore belong the fruits, the greater values produced by compound labour. The worker himself has no claim to extra pay.

In this way free higher education was closely connected to the egalitarian *daguofan* salary policy. The underlying logic was:
1. All people had an equal right to higher education, therefore
2. All students who pass the entrance examination should be supported equally;
3. The support was provided by the people (through the state and government);

4. Students must study for the people and the state, therefore
5. Graduates should accept job assignments that meet the needs of the state and the people;
6. Graduates should 'repay' the financial support they received by making greater contributions to society and receiving the same income as non-graduates.

This system sought to balance private (personal) and social benefits and to maintain horizontal equity both inside and outside the support policy. Although there were unexpected side-effects, such as reducing the diligence of students and the productivity of intellectuals, policies based upon the egalitarian equity principle greatly contributed to a dramatic change in the family background composition of tertiary students in the 1950s, and to the rapid formation of a large contingent of cadres and intellectuals. Students of worker/peasant origin increased fourfold over five years in the early 1950s (Table 12.2). Nevertheless, in the 1980s both the policy and its underpinning logic were challenged and lost their legitimacy.

Table 12.2
Changing class composition of students 1952–58

School Year	Students of worker/peasant origin	% of all students
1952–53	40 000	20.46
1955–56	80 000	29.20
1957–58	160 000	36.49

Source: *Peking Review*, no.12, 1958, p. 16.

THE REFORM ERA: TOWARDS CONDITIONED AID WITH FEES

The move towards tuition fees and conditioned aid since the early 1980s occurred neither systematically nor quickly. Rather, the reform was incremental and by the mid-1990s still taking shape. It has followed the pace of the profound social and economic changes in the country.

In 1978, the Third Central Committee Session of the 11th National Congress of the CCP shifted the emphasis from political class struggle to economic modernization. The first reform initiatives appeared in rural areas with the household responsibility system with remuneration linked to output (*jiating lianchan chengbao zerenzhi*). Families as work-units were permitted to retain profits from production after handing in a fixed quota to the government. This system replaced the egalitarian distribution among members of a production team regardless of their individual productivity. In 1984 the CCP affirmed a policy of 'encouraging some people to get rich first'.[17] The latest reform wave emerged in 1992 and 1993 with the transition of the entire economic system from a planned economy to a socialist market economy.

Throughout this process the concept of 'distribution according to work' was redefined as the fundamental Marxist distribution principle and as 'the most important mechanism to improve productivity'.[18] The conception of equity began shifting from one mandating equal results (everyone gets the same) to one of equal opportunity with results based on ability. Slogans such as 'It is a misunderstanding that socialism means egalitarianism in distribution'[19] and 'Egalitarianism is not equity'[20] began to appear in newspapers, academic journals, textbooks and government documents. People started to legitimate the new principle: the more you work and contribute, the more you could get and the richer you could become.

The student financial support policy experienced a parallel reform, also breaking away from egalitarianism. It moved from the People's Grant to allotting a proportion of funds equally among all students, while reserving some money to reward students with superior academic achievement, with the rest set aside for the neediest. The formula used in 1980 in Nanjing College of Chemical Engineering was typical. The total grant amounted to ¥22 per student per month. An equally distributed part went to two-thirds of the students. The remaining one-third went to the best and neediest students, each categorized in three levels. [21]

In 1983 the MoEd established the People's Scholarship (*renmin jiangxuejin*) alongside the People's Grant with the intention that the former should gradually replace the latter as 'the main approach vehicle for financial aid'.[22] The MoEd argued that grants placed an undue burden on the government as the 'single standard applied to all students (*yi dao qie*) regardless of their academic major or the type of institution they attended'. In addition, the uniform grant had not achieved the original goal of helping students to study well. The MoEd acknowledged that 'the uniform grant failed to take properly into account student's performance'.[23] The SEdC, successor to the MoEd, agreed, 'Some students took the People's Grant as their due, but did not study hard or strive to make progress. Even students with a poor attitude towards study and poor performance could enjoy the grant.'[24]

These criticisms of the People's Grant policy raise two issues of equity. First, was it fair that the government/society should bear all the expenditures of higher education including the cost of instruction and students' living expenses? Should not students share at least some of the costs of their higher education? The government contended that the state was overburdened and implied that the students and their families did not meet enough of the expense. Second, what was the equitable way to distribute aid? The government did not give any clear-cut answers to these questions, nor did it set up any definite objectives or timetables. Instead, it cautiously groped its way. The first step was to continue to offer grants to all who reached a certain standard (judged according to examination scores), while a competitive scholarship would be used as the financial support mechanism. Although the government did not appear to have a clear strategy for the reform of financial support policies, it was obvious that gaining entrance to higher education would no longer be the only criterion for receiving support. Other criteria emerged as new schemes were set up according to new concepts.

Tuition fees

Tuition fees are an important component of student financial support policies. Change in this aspect began with divergent fees and scales for different students. Before 1980, all university places were allocated according to a government plan and all students were exempt from tuition and accommodation fees. In 1980, the Shanghai Municipal Government started a pilot scheme, approving 24 institutions to admit 1000 self-supporting students along with 'state-plan students' (*guojia jihua sheng*). The self-supporting students had to pay tuition and other sundry fees (including accommodation if they lived in a student dormitory). They had no public health insurance and had to compete for jobs in the labour market when they graduated.[25] Between 1980 and 1983, 4300 such self-supporting students were enrolled.[26] The CCP's *Decision on the reform of educational structure* in 1985 officially approved this approach, permitting a proportion of self-supporting students and those sponsored by enterprises (*weituo peiyang*) to be admitted besides state-plan students.[27] By 1994, self-supporting and commissioned training students comprised over 28% of the student population (Table 12.3). The SEdC regulated that the maximum payment was to be not lower than 80% of the real unit cost of higher education. The tuition fees paid by these two groups of students were called the 'cultivation fee' (*peiyang fei*).[28] Enterprises sponsoring students who were under contract to them also had to pay a 'capital fee'.[29]

As a result of these innovations there emerged a three-fold structure of student categories and fee scales (see Table 12.4). Different students paid different fees according to different scales based on the benefits accruing.

The two basic reasons for the divergent fees were:
1. the students were meeting their own educational demands and would
    obtain high private returns to higher education when they found their
    own jobs; and
2. the enterprises would acquire the extra personnel they needed outside
    the state plan.

Table 12.3
Undergraduate students by type in 1993–94

Type	1993		1994	
	number	%	number	%
State-plan students	1 926 451	75.9	1 993 500	71.3
Commissioned training students	372 032	14.6	482 400	17.2
Self-supporting students	231 668	9.1	318 700	11.4
Total*	2 535 517	99.6	2 798 600	99.9

*   As in-service teacher training degree courses are excluded from the statistics,
      totals do not add up to 100%.
Sources: *Education statistics yearbook of China 1994*, pp. 20–1; State Education
         Commission, 1995

Table 12.4
Categories of students and fees, 1984–88

Student category	Fee paid	Amount/rate	Paid by	Rationale
State-plan students	no tuition	–	state subsidy	state & social benefit
	sundry fee	¥100–¥200/year	student	
	accommodation fee	¥20/year	student	
Commissioned training students	cultivation fee (tuition)	¥700–¥1300/ year	enterprise	enterprise benefit
	capital fee	¥9500–¥15 000 (4 years)	enterprise	
	sundry fee	as for state-plan students	student	
	accommodation fee	as for state-plan students	student	
Self-supporting students	cultivation fee (tuition)	80%–100% of unit cost	student	student benefit
	sundry fee	as for other students	student	
	accommodation fee	¥100–¥150/ year	student	

Source: Shanghai Higher Education Bureau, 1992

The second step with regard to tuition fees required that state-plan students should also pay some of the costs of tuition, with the reasoning that these students, as well as the state, were beneficiaries of higher education. In the 1989–90 academic year, the SEdC permitted institutions to charge state-plan students ¥100 for tuition and ¥20 for campus accommodation every academic year.[30] In 1992 the SEdC, Ministry of Finance and State Bureau of Planning allowed provincial authorities and other ministries to raise the tuition scales of the institutions under their control according to local circumstances. The scale in Shanghai was set at ¥400 and accommodation at ¥40–¥160 for state-plan students. Thus the line between the state-plan category and the two fee-paying categories (which were increasing rapidly) began to blur. A debate now emerged, as to whether it was equitable to let low-scoring self-supporting students sit in classrooms alongside high-scoring state-plan students. One argument was, 'It is not equitable to buy examination scores with money.'[31] On the other side, it was argued that the majority of self-supporting students were not from rich families, but from quite poor families. Indeed, many were from the countryside and, arguably, had not received as good a basic education as their urban counterparts. Paying represented their principal means of access to higher education. Therefore, it was questioned whether it was equitable that these self-supporting students should pay several times as much as state-plan students simply on the grounds of their lower scores in entrance examinations.[32]

Partly as a result of this debate, and because of the rapid development of the socialist market economy, the third step came, known as 'merging the tracks' (*binggui*), with the rationale that 'Higher education is non-compulsory education, so, in principle, all students should pay tuition fees'.[33] High-ranking officials in the SEdC stood up against the phenomenon of 'buying examination scores with money' and were eager that all students and their families should bear a sufficient proportion of the unit cost. The new policy sought to merge the different scales of tuition fees for different categories of students.[34] In 1994, 40 pilot institutions adopted the merging mechanism, with all degree students paying ¥1000–¥1200. In 1995 about 200 institutions followed suit, although the tuition fees payable by students differed from province to province. The 36 SEdC-maintained institutions were asked to collect no more than ¥1800 per student, while individual provinces set the rate according to local unit costs and affordability. For instance, in Anhui, a middle-stratum province, the merged track scale was ¥1800, whereas in Shanghai the figure was ¥2500–¥3000,[35] and ¥3000–¥3600 in Guangdong province, an affluent seaboard province.

The government planned to merge the tuition-scale tracks for all freshmen in the autumn of 1997 and in all institutions for all degree and certificate undergraduates by the end of the century. All students would then be called 'tuition-paying students' (*jiaofei sheng*) and the terms 'state-plan students', 'self-supporting students' and 'commissioned training students' would disappear from official documents. The target tuition scale would be set at 25%–30% of the unit cost of an institution's recurrent expenditure.[36] In other words, all students would be paying tuition fees from the year 2000 onwards, but the amount would vary among institutions and courses. The tuition fees would reflect 25% of the cost of a course while the government would subsidize the remaining 75%. In the academic year 1996–97, students in SEdC-maintained institutions paid according to three scales reflecting different unit costs (Table 12.5).

Table 12.5
Tuition scales in 'merged-tracks' institutions, 1996

State Education Commission Institutions		Local Institutions in Shanghai*	
course	scale amount	course	scale amount
humanities/science/ engineering	¥1000–¥2600	general majors	¥2500
fine arts/advertising/ design	maximum ¥4000	special majors	¥3000–¥3500
performing arts	maximum ¥6000	fine/performing arts	¥5000

*   Institutions under the SEdC and other ministries in Shanghai had approval to charge tuition according to Shanghai's scale.
Sources: State Education Commission, 1996; Shanghai Education Commission, 1995, p. 1

Three types of scholarships

The government scholarships that were introduced in 1983 comprised three types, each based on different criteria. The 'excellence scholarship' (*youxiu xuesheng jiangxuejin*) was awarded for meritorious academic performance, in three classifications. The first-class scholarship (awarded to 5% of the eligible students) usually covered all tuition fees, the second-class (awarded to 10%) around half, and the third-class (10%) a quarter. There were small scholarships for special academic or social performance available to the remaining eligible students. In the event, between 35% and 60% of all students were awarded scholarships ranging from ¥50 to ¥2000.[37] For instance, Zhejiang University, a well-known key university, awarded first-class scholarships of ¥1500 to 5% of its students, second-class scholarships of ¥1000 to 12%, third-class scholarships (¥500) to 18% and other small scholarships (no more than ¥300) to 15% of its students in 1995–96. In that year, tuition and sundry fees amounted to ¥1500 for all 'tuition-paying students' under the merged-track system.[38]

The 'special-major scholarship' (*zhuanye jiangxuejin*) was intended for major courses which trained human resources considered urgently required by the state and included fields of study that brought a relatively low private return. Accordingly, most students in teacher education, agriculture and mineralogy were offered these scholarships.

The 'orientation scholarship' (*dingxiang jiangxuejin*) required graduates to relocate to remote areas or grass roots work-units, where conditions would be harsher than in cities. For instance, many graduates from medical institutions held such scholarships, as they were asked to work in remote or backward areas. Students holding special-major scholarships or orientation scholarships were estimated to comprise about 20% of all state-plan students in 1993.[39] In 1994, holders of these scholarships received an average of ¥500, as well as exemption from paying tuition fees.[40]

Student loans

The introduction of student loans was a totally new approach in Chinese higher education. The first circular on loans in 1986[41] specified that 30% of university students could obtain interest-free loans through direct application and a means test. The intention was that these loans would permit disadvantaged students to overcome financial obstacles during their studies. They would be able to repay the loans after graduation as their education would enable them to obtain better incomes than they would have otherwise. This approach was widely endorsed by administrators of higher education institutes (almost 90% of those interviewed for this research). Yet loan applications declined in the early 1990s. Most universities in the survey reported that loan applicants represented only around 10% of their students. However, the administrators expected the rate would probably rise once all the students have to pay substantive tuition fees in the future.

Support for the exceptionally disadvantaged

Another development in government financial support for students was the establishment within all institutions of the Special Subsidy Fund for Exceptionally Disadvantaged Students (*tekun buzhu jijin*). Given the disparities between regions and between city and rural areas, as well as high inflation, each institution was asked to set up and maintain a fund to ensure that no students would drop out for reasons of financial hardship.[42] The criterion of need was given top priority, but the number of these 'exceptional students' proved quite low, around 10%–15% of all students and inclusion was determined in various ways by institutions. For example, in Shanghai many institutions took ¥150 per month for living expenses as the threshold. A student who lived below that level in 1994 would be treated as an 'exceptional student'. In Anhui province, in contrast, some institutions simply counted the poorest 5% of the students as the 'exceptionally disadvantaged'. In one university in Xi'an with a student population of 11 000, only 20 students were treated as 'exceptionally disadvantaged'.

Work-study

A recent development has been the Campus Work-Study Programme, established in 1993 with a Premier Foundation fund of ¥150 million allocated to the 36 SEdC-maintained institutions. Other institutions received similar support from the ministries or provinces responsible. All students were entitled to join the work-study programme (the government financed part-time jobs on campus); but if the work places were limited, the economically disadvantaged students would be given priority. In some universities, such as Qinghua, disadvantaged students would receive double pay when they joined the work-study programme.

In sum, six public financial support schemes existed in the PRC, with at least two available in each of the over 1000 Chinese tertiary institutions (Table 12.6). In terms of equity considerations, these schemes reflect at least five criteria, namely 'performance merit', 'higher social return', 'means-tested and higher private return', 'exceptionally disadvantaged' and 'needs-based and work'.

The right of job choice

Before the reforms, all students had to accept the work assigned to them after they had received free higher education and People's Grants. Now, because most students share some of the costs of instruction (although this amounted to less than 9% of recurrent expenditures for state-plan students in 1994)[43] and various government financial support schemes are available, the students' right to find their own jobs has increased. Since 1985, self-supporting students have always had to find jobs (*zizhu zhiye*) and most were initially concerned about unemployment. Except for special-major and orientation scholarship holders, most other students have had a more

Table 12.6
Support schemes and their features

Scheme	Target student	% of all students	Amount	Features
Excellence-based Scholarship	Excellent students	30%–35%	¥50–¥2000 (yet only 5%–10% get over ¥1000)	Performance merit
Special-major Scholarship	Students in teacher education, etc.	about 14%	Tuition + living allowance	Social return & need
Orientation Scholarship	Students to work in assigned areas	less than 5%	Tuition + living allowance	Social return & need
Student loans	Disadvantaged	35% entitled	¥300–¥1500	Needs-based & private return-based
Special Subsidy	Exceptionally disadvantaged	5%–10%	Case by case	Needs-based
Work-study	All; disadvantaged given priority	various	minimum ¥1.50/hour	Needs-based & work

Sources: Ministry of Education, 1983; State Council, 1986; State Education Commission, 1993b; State Education Commission, 1994b; Qinghua University, 1994

limited right, called 'two-way choice' (*shuangxiang xuanze*). In this system, every graduate is guaranteed some sort of a job so that no one will be unemployed, but students are limited to selecting from the government's list. Work-units, in contrast, have the right to raise their requirements and even refuse graduates in certain cases.[44] Nevertheless, the approach is overwhelmingly welcomed by students, especially those in well-known institutions and in popular majors, for whom the job hunt is a buyers' market. Unrestricted free choice is less than half as popular as two-way choice (Table 12.7). Some students feared that unrestricted free choice would lead to unemployment. The right of job choice makes it possible for graduates to choose jobs with better pay (students' primary consideration), better living conditions, higher status and more chances of career development. In sum, students overwhelmingly choose job choice, complemented by tuition and loans, over the former policy of free education, work assignment and low pay (Table 12.8). The government's objective is 'Students pay for a part of their cultivation expenditure, and in turn, the majority choose their own jobs upon graduation'.[45]

Table 12.7
Student job choice approaches

First choice	Number of students	%
Two-way choice	246	58.6
Free self-choice	101	24.0
Postgraduate study	44	10.5
Job assignment	19	4.5
Missing	10	2.4
Total	420	100.0

Source: Author's survey

Table 12.8
Student preference of the two groups of policies

Preferred policy	Number	%
Free higher education + grant with work assignment and low wages	40	9.5%
Fee-paying higher education + loans with free job choice and higher wages	364	86.7%
No response	16	3.8%
Total	420	100%

Source: Author's survey

As the new policy was being developed and implemented, educational administrators and students were increasingly concerned about the expected income of graduates (Table 12.9). In fact, the private economic return of higher education was becoming more and more obvious. The monthly income of the surveyed students' fathers indicates a significant difference[46] between the income of the fathers with higher education and those with senior secondary education. The average monthly income in 1994 of the fathers with higher education was ¥787; with senior secondary education, ¥690; with junior secondary education, ¥575; with primary education, ¥447. For the illiterate or those with only basic literacy, it was ¥418.[47]

Statistics also showed that the national average wage was ¥4538 in 1994, while the average wage in the health sector was ¥5126, the education sector ¥4923 and the science sector ¥6162.[48] Official statistics for selected provinces

Table 12.9
Attitudes towards graduates' salary

Item	Administrators' attitude		Students' attitude	
	Totally agree	Strongly agree	Totally agree	Strongly agree
The average starting salary of the new graduates was higher than that of others in the same age group after 1990.	14.5%	37.4%	12.5%	21.0%
The average life income of this generation of graduates will be markedly higher than that of others in the same age group.	31.9%	40.6%	28.2%	31.2%

	Students' attitude			
	same as others	a bit higher	much higher	the higher the better
How high do you expect your starting wage to be?	3.2%	35.6%	24.5%	36.7%

Source: Author's survey

in the early 1990s suggest that the average wage for education/science/culture/health workers exceeded that for other paid labourers (Table 12.10). Even given inflation, this was a marked improvement, both in absolute terms and relative to other workers, from earlier times, as reported in Table 12.1.

According to a study out of the Chinese Academy of Social Sciences, the rate of marginal private return for different types of education shows that tertiary schooling provides the highest return (Table 12.11), although the private return in the PRC is still very low from an international perspective.

Table 12.10
Average wage in five provinces, 1993

Province	Provincial average*	Average in education and culture sectors*	% above provincial average
Heilongjiang	2661	3153	18%
Zhejiang	3932	4090	4%
Anhui	2770	2826	2%
Shaanxi	2890	3038	5%
Gansu	2902	3093	7%

* unit = yuan (¥)
Sources: *Statistics yearbook of Heilongjiang 1994*; *Zhejiang yearbook 1994*;
          Statistics yearbook of Anhui 1994; *Statistics yearbook of Shaanxi 1994*;
          Statistics yearbook of Gansu 1993

Table 12.11
Private return on education by level

Education Level	%
higher education	4.5%
senior secondary education	3.9%
junior secondary education	3.4%
primary education	2.7%

Source: Zhao Renwei, 1994

UNRESOLVED EQUITY ISSUES

An old Chinese saying — 'Without destruction there can be no construction'
— aptly applies to the change in financial support policies in China. At
every step some destruction of the old horizontal equity concept has
occurred. Destroying the old, however, has not automatically caused its
replacement to materialize spontaneously.

The former policy, based on horizontal equal equity, was simple. Its
replacement, based on vertical deserved equity, is much more complex and
thus must be much more sophisticated. Horizontal egalitarian equity could
be constructed with mathematical precision, while vertical deserved equity
relies much more on judgement and even 'subjective preference' within
and even outside a community.

Different support programmes now are derived from different 'deserved
equity' criteria and they have different functions. In choosing one over
another, policy-makers must evaluate the programmes' roles, advantages,
effective aspects and limitations. For instance, the excellence scholarship

encourages students to study hard, and as such it is closely linked with personal qualities such as intelligence, diligence, creativity and motivation. It is the most popular support programme among students and has the strongest support from teachers and administrators as well. Almost one-third of the students surveyed preferred this type of scholarship to be the main government support system. Yet, as Table 12.12 indicates, among 420 students, those from peasant families are underrepresented among scholarship winners (the average rate was 34%, but the rate of scholarship winners from peasant families was 22.2%). However, children of intellectual and cadre families are well overrepresented (33.5% and 38.8% respectively). Among the 17 top prize winners (over ¥1000) there were none from peasant families. Meritorious performance is still heavily impacted by factors beyond a student's control, such as family background and the quality of basic education in the home area. Excellence scholarships, therefore, cannot be relied upon to solve the financial support problems of rural students, who are often the neediest.

Another matter concerns the balance in subsidies between students in higher education and school pupils. The subsidy for each tertiary student is much higher than the government support for each pupil in free and compulsory primary and secondary education (Table 12.13). Now in the PRC, the enrolment in higher education institutions represents only about 3.5% of the age cohort and 1.5% of the national enrolment in primary and secondary schools.[49] Yet the public budget appropriation to higher education is over 21% of the total expenditure on public education.[50] Is it equitable to allocate so much public funding to higher education? The SEdC believes that the proportion of public support for higher education is still too high.[51]

An intellectual confusion over the equity issue characterizes documents on student financial support systems. The issue is virtually never discussed in an analytically sophisticated way. As a result, there is no clear plan or timetable at the central government level for the development of a policy on equity. Support programmes designed at the institution level are often extemporaneous, given the absence of guidelines from above. As one policy-maker put it, 'At present the aid programmes and schemes in the country are still in chaos: many of them were designed to cope with emergent situations or out of some wishful assumptions, so that they were neither efficient nor effective.'[52] The PRC still has a long way to go if a systematic and effective financial support policy is to be set up on the basis of a multi-deserved equity conception.

Table 12.12
Scholarship winners and their fathers' careers

Father's career	Number of students	% of all students	Number of winners	% of father's career group	% of winners	No. of top prize winners	% of top winners
Cadre	117	27.9	48	41.0	33.5	4	23.5
Intellectual	85	20.2	33	38.8	23.1	7	41.1
Manager	34	8.1	12	35.2	8.4	2	11.8
Worker	50	11.9	20	40.0	14.0	2	11.8
Peasant	108	25.7	24	22.2	16.7	0	0
Others	16	3.8	6	37.5	4.1	2	11.8
Missing	10	2.4	0	0	0	0	0
Total	420	100.0	143	34.0	100.0	17	100.0

Source: Author's survey

Table 12.13
Distribution of public appropriation among students by educational levels

Educational level	Primary	Secondary	Higher education
Distribution of 1994 public education budget appropriation (million ¥)	303.4	343.58	184.69
% of the whole public education budget in 1994	34.58%	39.16%	21.05%
Unit cost of public education recurrent expenditure	¥236	¥678	¥5048
Tuition and sundry fees equal to % of the unit cost			
in 1992	12.2%	12.9%	5.1%
in 1994	10%	10%–31.8%	14.7%
Times of unit cost of primary education			
in 1992	1	2.21	28.70
in 1994	1	2.87	21.39
Unit public expenditure as % of GNP per capita 1994	6.3%	18%	133.7%

Sources: Finance Department, State Education Commission and SIHRD, 1994, 1997; *China development report 1995*

NOTES

1. See, for example, Department of Education and Science, 1988; Wran, 1988; Woodhall, 1993; Ziderman and Albrecht, 1995.
2. Barr, 1989, p. 10.
3. Le Grand, 1991, p. 11.
4. Le Grand, 1991, p. 8.
5. Le Grand, 1991, p. 11.
6. Alexander, 1982, p. 195.
7. McMahon and Geske, 1982, pp. 14–6.
8. Zheng Shaolun, 1953.
9. North China People's Government, *Guanyu yijiuwuling nian Huabei diqu guoli daxue xuesheng Renmin Zhuxuejin de zanxing tiaoli* (Provisional regulations for the People's Grant for national tertiary students in the North China region, 1950). In State Education Commission, 1992.
10. Government Administration Council, *Guanyu tiaosheng dazhongxuesheng Renmin Zhuxuejin de tongzhi* (Circular on the adjustment of the People's Grant to tertiary and secondary students), 1952. In State Education Commission, 1992.
11. Zheng Shaolun, 1953; see also the Government Administration Council document (note 10).
12. See the Government Administration Council document (note 10).
13. Government Administration Council, *Guanyu fenpei quanguo gongsili gaodengxuexiao bennian shujia biyesheng gongzuo de tongling 1950* (Circular on job assignments of graduates in all public and private higher learning institutions in the summer vacation 1950). In State Education Commission, 1992, pp. 127–8.
14. See the Government Administration Council document (note 10), p. 106.
15. Yue, 1975.
16. Anti-Duhring. In Engels, 1975, p. 187.
17. CCP Central Committee, 1984, p. 18.
18. Deng, 1993.
19. CCP Central Committee, 1984.
20. Zhang Chenxiang, 1995, p. 13.
21. Nanjing College of Chemical Engineering, 1980.
22. Ministry of Education, 1983.
23. Ministry of Education, 1983.
24. State Council, 1986.
25. Hu Ruiwen, 1982.
26. Hu Ruiwen, 1982.
27. CCP Central Committee, 1984, p. 12.
28. State Education Commission, 1990b.
29. Shanghai Higher Education Bureau, 1992.
30. State Education Commission, 1989b.
31. Miao, 1994, p. 156.
32. Miao, 1994, pp. 156–64.
33. CCP Central Committee and the State Council, 1993.
34. Student Affairs Department of State Education Commission, 1994.
35. Shanghai Financial Bureau, 1995.

36. Cheng Kai-ming, 1995b.
37. Finance Department, State Education Commission, 1995, p. 47.
38. Zhejiang University, 1995, p. 27.
39. State Education Commission, 1994a.
40. Finance Department, State Education Commission, 1995, p. 64.
41. State Council, 1986.
42. State Education Commission, 1993b.
43. Ziderman and Albrecht, 1995, p. 43.
44. State Education Commission, 1994a.
45. State Education Commission, 1994a.
46. df 163, 2-tail sig. .0029.
47. Author's survey, carried out in four universities in Shanghai and Zhejiang, sampling 420 students.
48. *China statistics yearbook*, 1995, pp. 114–5.
49. State Education Commission, 1995, p. 2.
50. Financial Department, State Education Commission and Shanghai Institute of Human Resource Development, 1997.
51. Financial Department, State Education Commission and Shanghai Institute of Human Resource Development, 1997, p. 16.
52. Zhao Zhongjian, 1994.

13

Graduate Employment: From Manpower Planning to the Market Economy

Michael AGELASTO[1]

INTRODUCTION

As the PRC moves away from a socialist redistributive economy and towards something that resembles a market-driven system, many aspects of central planning are being replaced with market mechanisms. For most of the past 25 years, a continuously evolving planning process controlled the placement of university graduates into jobs with state-run firms or governmental bureaux. Now, as a consequence of a general trend towards marketization, graduate allocation (*biyesheng fenpei*) is being rapidly phased out and replaced by a system that allows students, tertiary institutes and employers more choice. Such a system is usually labelled two-way choice or mutual selection (*shuangxiang xuanze*).

After a brief description of the history of manpower planning around the globe, this chapter describes the PRC's *fenpei* and discusses the continuing relevance of certain manpower planning issues in the quasi-market economy the PRC is developing. The chapter employs the term *manpower planning* in its broad sense to refer to macro-economic planning at the national level where the objective is to change employment patterns towards desired goals. Here, manpower planning includes *inter alia* a body of literature, quite prevalent in the 1960s and 1970s, that advocated hooking together education with employment needs. These theories were applied in a number of countries over this period; its chief proselytizers were several well-funded multi- or non-government organizations.[2] While other countries attempted to plan for their human resource requirements, the PRC went a step further: it allocated individuals to their places of employment. This feature makes the PRC case special, if not unique. Now, the PRC has followed most of the rest of the globe in abandoning manpower planning in favour of more market-oriented forms of human resource development that involve less state control.[3]

MANPOWER PLANNING — THE GLOBAL PERSPECTIVE

There seems to be broad agreement around the world that the human resource aspects of education need some degree of planning. This is because 'various imperfections in the economic system, and the lack of a pricing system in education, prevent the educational system from reaching the point of maximum efficiency without some external interference'.[4] The bottom-line question here is rather basic: how many graduates, in what fields, does/ will the economy need? Over the past 30 years, various perspectives and strategies involving economic theories have been developed to answer this question. The major approaches to educational planning include: manpower planning or the manpower requirements model, social demand (or demand-for-education), and rate-of-return.[5] All these are found to have severe limitations, both theoretical and practical, which lead educational planners to arrive at a 'synthetic' model that includes aspects of all three theories.[6]

The manpower planning approach puts forth a reasonable assumption: since education precedes employment, for the sake of efficiency the two activities should somehow be linked. Yet, when one starts collecting data from the past and projecting it for the future, the planning process breaks down. Thus, in its implementation stage, manpower planning generated considerable criticism and became a favourite whipping boy of educational economists.

It is no wonder that manpower planning got bad press in the academic community, as well as among manpower planning's practitioners.[7] It was doomed to failure. In the process of forecasting labour needs, a projection of a current trend (for example, for number of engineers) is linked with certain assumptions to form a forecast. UNESCO materials for training future manpower planners list seven key assumptions:[8]
1. estimates of growth rates during period;
2. estimates of the distribution of growth by sector;
3. assumptions on the evolution of productivity by sector;
4. assumptions on the evolution of the employment structure by sector;

5. assumptions on the evolution of training-employment relations;
6. productivity functions by level of training; and
7. assumptions on manpower replacement (mortality, retirement).

Even if the planner were able to assume and estimate correctly, the data collected would be likely to be far from perfect, due to imperfections in the data collection process. Nevertheless, the planning process was elaborate, as illustrated by the 764-page manual that the World Bank prepared for users.[9] Although such a semi-futile exercise can taint the overall desirability of planning, this is not to say the exercise was totally worthless. It forced on decision-makers an awareness of rational planning and raised the level of awareness among policy-makers for the need of educational planning. Much was gained from the process, even if the products themselves were destined for the rubbish bin (or the bookcases of educational planners).

Manpower planning is useful for developing countries because it can straighten out manpower and educational 'bottlenecks' that result from rapid economic growth and educational expansion.[10] Manpower planning is also seen as relevant to countries where 'the basic purpose of education is to prepare people for quite specific jobs in order to meet the needs of the economy ... and individual choice is secondary to meeting the needs of the economy...'.[11] Thus, it would seem that manpower planning fitted the needs of China in 1949, when the CCP came to power and started to introduce the concept of a centrally planned economy.

Critical historical overview of manpower planning in the PRC

A detailed survey of the PRC's manpower planning programme identifies certain themes: concerns over geographical imbalance, anxieties over the mismatch between education curriculum and the needs of the workplace, the use of experiments in designing programmes, and the mix of plan and market.[12] Government-issued documents on employment allocation,[13] an official history of higher education[14] as well as an account edited by individual educationalists[15] suggest that the PRC's manpower planning policy was characterized by constant changes in policy design and in administrative authority over policy implementation.

Starting in the 1950s, the most populous nation on earth rose from millennia of feudalism and a recent half-century of destruction from war and revolution to create an industrial base, a viable national political framework, a transportation network and a socialist economy. The PRC was helped by Soviet models, technical assistance and financial support, in education as well as in other fields.[16] The centralized graduate job placement scheme reflects this help and it was retained long after Soviet planners were sent home. Then, during the 1960s and 1970s, while planners for multi- and non-governmental organizations were assessing manpower needs around the globe, the PRC was undertaking socialist reconstruction, a stop-and-go process that moved forward despite interruptions by political mobilizations and movements. For such a large country, the PRC's rapid development in a relatively short period is unrivalled in the history of mankind. This progress can be attributed, in no small part, to the fact that the PRC was able to produce skilled manpower. Chinese educationalists acknowledge that *fenpei* played an essential role in meeting the special needs of the country's key construction projects and the remote regions. It was seen as suitable for the PRC's development at that time. In addition, the importance of manpower planning also lay in its value as one of the key tools the state used to guide an individual's career[17] and control his/her behaviour.[18]

The earliest form of manpower planning, in 1952 after the CCP had sufficiently consolidated its power and established its rule over the country, focused on geographical needs in the distribution of educated personnel. The mismatch between curricula in higher education institutions and the skills needed on the job was a grave concern to planners, but later, inadequate supply also dominated the discussion. An extreme example occurred in a particular chemical specialization where demand for graduates was 71 times the available supply.[19] In general, the planning procedure went like this:[20]

> The year before students were to graduate, university and colleges reported to the provincial departments that were in charge concerning the number of graduates and other relevant information. [For example, tertiary institutions under the Ministry of Mines would report to the local branch office of the Ministry.] Provincial departments then reported to the departments in charge at the central level. They, in turn, gave information to the national-level planning department which then sent it back down to the provinces. At the local level the work-units reported to their overseeing department on their needs for students and these data got reported up to the state planning department which developed a draft for state council approval. When settled, plans were distributed to local level. The university decided assignments according to the plan and reported the list to local government for its approval. After the approval, the tertiary institution sent students to the work-units.

This up-and-down-the-hierarchy type of decision-making was characterized by negotiations which resulted in modest revisions in the plans as they were handed from office to office. The top agency for planning frequently changed. In 1950 the State Council and the Education Committee were in charge. Responsibility shifted in 1951 to the Personnel Committee. The Higher Education Ministry took over in 1954, the State Planning Committee in 1955, the State Economic Committee in 1957 and the State Council's Personnel Bureau from 1959 to 1961. The constant change may reflect the bureaucratic jockeying for position one would expect to occur in a newly established state. Each year, the State Council made the final political decision on whose turf manpower planning should be placed.

Finally, in 1962 Zhou Enlai, head of the State Council, reported that education and job assignment were not being properly coordinated and, on behalf of the Council, ordered the Ministry of Education to take charge of both manpower training (education) and job assignment. The issue of mismatch continued to be the hot topic in manpower planning circles, to the point where one policy document even bemoaned the fact that tertiary institutions were concerned only with educating people, not with the needs of society.[21] In addition, the problem of students' refusal to obey their allocation also became a worry to policy-makers.

The Great Proletarian Cultural Revolution (1966–76) severely affected manpower planning. In 1968 the Central Committee of the CCP ordered all graduates to go to the countryside, the frontier or the 'grass roots' areas where they were to work with peasants, workers and soldiers. In 1979 the policy returned to what was in place before the Cultural Revolution.

The years following the Cultural Revolution saw the beginnings of Deng Xiaoping's reform policies. From 1983 onwards the job allocation system came under constant reform. In the late 1980s public criticisms of manpower planning first started appearing, criticisms from both government officials and academics. Before the introduction of Dengist reforms, however, manpower planning had received no public criticism in the PRC. Several reasons explain this lack of critical public comment. First, discussions over policy, and especially criticism, are generally not aired publicly. Of course, this does not mean there is no dissent, but rather that dissent takes place in an arena that is closed to the public. In the PRC's system of 'democratic centralism' and 'people's dictatorship', the public are involved through their Party representatives, not through participation by average citizens. The policy process involves negotiations at various levels and these meetings are often not reported in the press. Second, in the early days of the PRC, manpower planning had the overwhelming approval of both academics and practitioners. It was considered to be a system that worked well.[22] Qualified graduates were assigned to jobs and this resulted in national economic development.

Manpower planning reforms had their origins in a local 1983 experiment that was being carried out initially by Shanghai Jiaotong University (JiaoDa),

Xi'an Jiaotong University and Shandong Marine Institute, Qinghua University and later by other tertiary institutes.[23] The experiments, which called for a greater role for institutes, allowed students and work-units to contact each other in a 'demand-meet-supply' arrangement. The experimental procedure at JiaoDa for getting a job is described like this:

> Work-units send in a needs description; tertiary institutions form an opinion on allocation, then present a plan to higher bodies or allocating units for reference. This calls for examination of some graduates by prospective work-units for jobs. Employing work-units give a twelve-month probation; they can return some students, who can then find jobs by themselves, if approved by relevant departments.[24]

Since 1983 human resource development has been 'reformed' (*gaige*), a term used for the first time in this context and one which would thereafter form part of the manpower policy vocabulary.[25] Universities were given more autonomy and allowed to give suggestions about job allocation. They now had authority to prepare a list of graduates; tertiary institutions could take back graduates who were found to be mismatched and then reassign them. Also, at the tertiary institution's discretion 20% of the students could be assigned out of the plan. At this time the state was still taking a certain percentage of the graduates and all the rest would be assigned at the local or provincial level.[26]

The important educational *Decision* issued in May 1985 devotes several paragraphs to discussing tertiary job allocation.[27] According to this carefully developed and politically massaged policy,[28] enrolment should be designed in accordance with the state plan and '[a]fter-graduation job placement for students so enrolled will be made under a system which takes into account the graduates' inclinations, the recommendations of colleges and the employers' requirements'. In giving limited autonomy to tertiary institutes, the reforms moved towards establishing an educational market, and indeed, self-supporting university students and those sent by employers or other clients such as municipalities are excluded from the state job allocation plan.[29] Students from vocational high schools were also not subject to rigid job planning.[30] The state would no longer attempt to solve the problem of mismatch through job allocation or clarify the vague connection between enrolment and employment. However, a state allocation plan was still in effect. The stated goal of policy was 'to rationalize, not eliminate, *fenpei* ... [not to] retreat from planned allocation...'.[31] In the actual 1985 plan, however, the state made assignments for only 10%–20% of the graduates covered by the state plan. Assignments for the remainder were made by tertiary institutions.[32] Some tertiary institutions were being allowed to 'recruit independently' of the state plan;[33] many were encouraged to try out 'contract training' as a substitute for the recruiting system that fostered mismatch.[34] This avenue allowed for companies to contract directly with tertiary institutions for the training of their employees.

The 1987 allocation plan, coming on the heels of a nationwide student protest movement in the previous December, saw the central government taking only 12% of tertiary graduates.[35] Regulations, which were subsequently omitted from the official document compilation published in 1992, required graduates to spend one probationary year at the grass roots level, rather than be directly assigned to state organs.[36] Here, the term *grass roots* perhaps may be liberally interpreted to mean all work-units except those high in the central government. Grass roots also connote jobs where graduates 'directly participate in productive labour and come into direct [contact] with the working masses'.[37] Sending graduates to the countryside can be seen as the way the state took revenge on the students for having protested the previous December.[38]

The year 1988 marks the first appearance of the term 'two-way choice/ mutual selection' (*shuangxiang xuanze*). Cities around China also started establishing labour exchanges and job markets. These were quite literally where supply meets demand, in other words, where students discussed job prospects with prospective employers.[39] In these supply-and-demand interviews (*gongxiao jianmian*), students and employers entered into standard job contracts (tersely worded and non-negotiable). The tertiary institution then reviewed (and almost always approved) the arrangement and 'allocated' the student. Not only in Beijing and Shanghai, but in cities as varied as Xi'an, Shenyang, Guiyang and Wenzhou, large turnouts of graduating seniors checked out jobs. A job fair in Guangdong, for example, attracted 42 000, with 20 000 coming from outside the province.

The reform process that had been building for most of the decade culminated with a policy that was approved by the State Council in March 1989.[40] In this document, known as the draft mid-term reform scheme (*zhongqi gaige fang'an*) because it fit conceptually between immediate short-term actions and long-term goals, the government offered the strongest statement to date, what it called an 'open-minded approach' to job allocation. The draft mid-term report declared that the state would not play an important role in assigning jobs.[41] Companies, instead, would choose the best students for the available jobs.[42] Students not hired through this method would be sent back to their home towns to find their own jobs.[43]

A significant feature of these reform documents was their continued groping for the appropriate system. A wide range of approaches was being suggested, including 'assigning jobs a year before graduation ... and stepping up lateral adjustment [changing jobs] to promote exchange of talented people'.[44] During this time, the first six months of 1989, experiments and suggestions for change characterized an open intellectual environment in many areas of Chinese life. This extent of open debate and dialogue had rarely occurred to such a degree in the PRC's history. It was a time when politicians were holding open and frank discussions with the public. Zhu Rongji, then mayor of Shanghai, had one such meeting with a group of Shanghai natives who studied in Beijing. Calling themselves 'abandoned children', these students complained that Beijing employers would not hire them because they were not Beijing natives, and that Shanghai employers would not hire them because they did not go to local tertiary institutions.[45] Job placement, just as other elements of the political economy, was subjected to much critical and creative thinking. Policy experiments and innovations reflected this.

Then came the *événements* of 1989. SEdC documents thereafter showed a noticeable change in rhetoric. Whereas in the years leading up to the 1989 reforms, policy writers had enthusiastically called for an expansion of the system of two-way choice, the November document detailing the next year's plan failed even to mention the term,[46] although the description was the same. It repeated a call made in earlier documents for provinces and localities to choose one or two tertiary institutions to replicate the Jiaotong/Qinghua model. Also, penalties for students who disobeyed allocation were increased. Previously, students who refused assignments could be asked to pay back all scholarships received and even some tuition, *peiyang fei* (cost of development). Graduates who wanted to work in Party or government departments above the provincial level were now required to undergo one or two years in low-level 'grass roots' jobs.[47] Graduates would have to transfer their *hukou* (residency permit) to the local area, and those already assigned to Party or government jobs would have to give them up and take lower-level work providing more 'practical' experience. One of the rationales behind 'tempering' graduates at the grass roots was that fresh college youths lacked the 'power of independent judgement and the ability to tackle practical problems'.[48] Such tempering helped to nurture better cadres.[49] The application of these regulations, which were not reprinted in the SEdC's official documentary history, was less than universal, a case that resembled the situation of punitive regulations following the 1986 student protests.

For the next several years allocation went on without substantial change. The state continued to assure and secure jobs for graduates according to the 1991 plan because the SEdC considered completely free competitions for jobs 'still not a suitable option' because the state needed to place graduates in areas of greatest need.[50] Two-way choice had come back in style.

The next major manpower planning initiative came in late 1992 as new directions for higher education were being proposed.[51] The policy included 19 points on higher education reform and represented the first attempt at comprehensive educational reform in higher education in China's modern history, for it articulated policy directions involving the scale, rationale and structure of higher education, as well as enrolment, pedagogy, financing and employment. The earlier 1985 policy overhaul had not touched on many of these topics. The 1993 reforms addressed student recruitment in the same section with job assignment. The policy came just short of declaring assignment dead. It argued that the system of guaranteed jobs and cadreship must be changed because of the adoption of a market economy. Recommended to use two-way choice, tertiary institutions and work-units should meet to discuss plans for job arrangement (*jiuye*). Policy no longer used the term 'allocation', *fenpei*. The state's participation was limited. It should still assign and assure some graduates for important state projects, national defence, education, basic and high-tech research, and certain difficult professions (*jianku hangye*) that remained undefined. The proposals implied that these government assignments were to be given priority. For a viable policy, it suggested that tertiary institutions must recruit students from remote and rural areas. Also implied was that the government might have to assign people to areas they did not want to go to and that students who worked harder (as shown by better results) would get the better jobs.

National policy would now tie tertiary recruitment more closely with employment. According to the policy, the state would no longer pay students' tuition for higher education. Post-secondary education was not compulsory; thus, those who wanted to get the rewards of going to university should be expected to pay for their tertiary schooling.[52] Loans and scholarships should be made available. Students who took up 'difficult' jobs (still undefined) could be given incentives and financial inducements. The proportion of fee-paying students and those sponsored by work-units was to be increased and was referred to as 'adjustive', as in 'adjusting' the system to include them. It would take time for the move from *fenpei* to *jiuye* — job allocation to job arrangement, but the trend appeared unmistakable and observers did not expect a return to yesteryear.[53] Most importantly, the multi-faceted aspect of reform was recognized.[54] Input (admissions) and output (employment) were sharing space in the same journal articles.[55]

The 1994 job arrangement encouraged all tertiary institutions to adopt two-way choice and students to work at the grass roots. Experience from 1993 showed that only 30% of Shanghai graduates found jobs in key work-units (state companies or bureaux under central or provincial administration) in Shanghai, with the others going elsewhere.[56] The SEdC still was to guarantee manpower for large- and medium-sized companies and for military and national priority purposes.[57] By 1995, 90% of the graduates were reported to have found their own jobs.[58] Now, reform was being seen as a set of interrelated components, although how the components fitted together was not clear.[59] The official press continued to praise graduates who volunteered to work in remote areas.[60] The Beijing Education Department set up a special fund which allocated ¥1000–¥5000, as an encouragement, to each graduate who chose to work in remote and less developed regions.[61] The new policy on paying tuition and fees, for example, needed to be linked with the nation's geographical development needs, but planners were uncertain how to do this within the newly adopted market framework.

As the economy slowed down in the early 1990s, some college graduates found urban jobs scarce and they settled for working in township enterprises. One graduate from Foshan in Guangdong province reported that he went to a factory and was assigned to the production floor because the factory was short of skilled labour to operate the parts assembly machines. At first, this was explained as part of the training process. Several years later he still operated the machines because no office jobs had opened up.[62]

The foregoing analysis of the PRC's manpower planning has identified certain features that run through its development. First, *fenpei* lacked administrative consistency. Allocation was handled by various administrative agencies, whose mandates frequently changed. The policy did not progress in a straight development and the move towards market economics was not gradual. The second characteristic of job assignment was a general concern that education be connected with national needs. This consideration materialized in the various campaigns that forced students to work at the 'grass roots', local levels of government. It was also reflected in the government's worries over 'mismatch', an issue which relates to the match between graduates' education/training and the use of their skills on the job. Through the years several surveys had reported mismatches of 10%–20% and most commentators considered figures in this range to be unacceptable. The use of experiments to develop policy initiatives was the third feature present in the evolution of graduate assignment reform. Certain key institutions, notably Qinghua and Shanghai Jiaotong, were permitted to develop alternatives to *fenpei*. These experiments provided models for other tertiary institutions and eventually evolved into the system that was developed to replace mandatory allocation. The fourth element characterizing Chinese manpower planning was the saturating role that politics played in all phases of policy. One can functionally break down the educational policy process into (1) policy framing, (2) policy adoption and (3) policy implementation.[63] The first of these functions is handled by planners, the second by politicians and the latter by higher education institution administrators. In many Western countries, the middle part of the process involves politics. For the PRC, political considerations were of tantamount importance in all three stages. Finally, throughout its history, manpower planning has been seen as a panacean means to manipulate the labour market in order to achieve desired goals. In the early days of centralized planning, job assignment was used as a relative simple solution to the problem of connecting education and employment. In the later stages of manpower planning, the free market has become the cure-all.

ANALYSIS OF MARKET-ORIENTED MANPOWER PLANNING REFORMS

The PRC's educational community, both administrators and academic researchers, view the market-oriented reforms favourably. Despite methodological shortcomings,[64] journal articles reflect current attitudes of Chinese academics towards state policy. Although not free to criticize new policy directions in the direct way that characterizes Western publications, writers on manpower planning are not just parroting 'the Party line'. They share with state policy designers the philosophical underpinnings of the new policy. In addition, they provide the basis of support for policy reforms and shape policy opinion at the local level, where state policy must receive approval if it is to be fully carried out. Chinese policy, contrary to a common misconception in the West, does not flow down through the hierarchy with obedient implementation at all levels. Lower-level bureaucrats have a *de facto* veto power.[65] Such is the case with educational policy. For example, bureaucratic opposition may be credited with delaying for over a decade the implementation of a student loan programme and a fee-paying tuition scheme.[66] Another example is the 1989 decision to have all graduates refresh their ideological commitment with a year in the countryside which also ended up in non-implementation. Thus, it is important to note the views of academics on the particular aspects of policy reform they approve, for this can suggest the level of support that policies will receive from those at the lower levels of hierarchical decision-making.

The nexus between input (enrolment) and output (job assignment) must have been informal, at best. A fictitious example can serve to illustrate. Ms Zhou's unit is responsible for enrolling students in the Department of

Stomatology in the Zhejiang University of Medicine, run by the provincial government. How many students should she enrol? The provincial education commission will issue her a directive on which she may have formal or informal influence depending on her relations with officials in the appropriate office. How will that office know the number of graduates needed? The National Planning Commission and its lower-level affiliates in coordination with the SEdC and its lower-level affiliates work out the job assignments and these are passed down to a Mr Zhang, who is in the job placement office of the medical university. If Mr Zhang talks with Ms Zhou, some informal planning might result. If Mr Zhang tells Ms Zhou that there is a large surplus of stomatologists, will Ms Zhou pass along the word that enrolment should be lowered? In theory, at least, these informal networks may have affected manpower planning issues.

From the planning perspective, Chinese manpower planning was not the unified system it pretended to be. It is referred to as an 'arrangement in different levels under the unified plan of the government with a percentage for redistribution'.[67] This translates as economic sectoral planning, with the Ministry of Mines, for example, educating its technical workforce, then assigning them to jobs. The same was done by the Ministry of Agriculture and a score of other ministries (Culture, Public Security, Diplomacy, Industrial Chemistry, Light Industry, Sanitation and Hygiene, etc.). Many ministries had provincial-level counterparts, such as bureaux and administrations. In addition, the SEdC, provincial education administrations and some municipalities ran their own higher education institutions. The result was an unplanned planning bureaucracy cut by both economic sector and level in hierarchy. The only unifying element in the system was the prime directive: assign graduates to jobs. Cadres (administrators) assigned to planning could build their own niches, but these were never secure for long, given the continuing rule changes. Local practitioners — such as placement officers in tertiary institutions and those in work-units taking in fresh graduates — found the system bureaucratic and chaotic. Thus, it was hardly surprising that reform was welcomed.

The favourable review the reforms received at the local level may be attributable to several other sets of factors: the practical and the theoretical. First, those who had to implement state directives became fed up with allocation. The rules and procedures changed constantly and the local-level bureaucrats bore the brunt of complaints from higher education officials, employers, students, parents and government cadres. One can suppose that administrators were constantly under pressure from friends and relations to help secure good jobs for them or their children. Many no doubt considered the system a dinosaur from the Soviet era. The second reason the reforms received support was simply that practitioners agreed with the initiative. Job allocation was seen to have major shortcomings, each of which could be solved through a supply-demand system based on market economics. The problems were seen as inefficiency, participants' irresponsibility and lack of competition. The reforms, as seen by Chinese observers, addressed each of these issues.

Efficiency through flexibility

Initially, allocation was extremely rigid at all levels. It was unduly inefficient. Once students got jobs they were just like paired birds — mated for life. This rigidity, so the argument went, caused considerable inefficiency, including work-unit (*danwei*) overstaffing and employee-employer mismatch. Talents were being wasted in the *fenpei* system. Throughout the PRC, graduates were not able to use their acquired skills on their jobs. Tertiary institutions were turning out graduates in specialities that were no longer needed by society. Mismatch was illustrated by the oft-told anecdote of the nuclear physicist who must serve as a secretary in a factory because that was where she was assigned. Little statistically reliable data, however, backed up the mismatch perception. It was merely assumed that the reformed system would be more efficient — manpower would be better utilized. If students contacted work-units directly, they would have a better idea how to evaluate themselves. A new principle would be employed: 'good students better use'. Better match between speciality of study and job would result because jobs that deal with specialized subjects would have a better chance for promotion. There would be no advantage in going to a political *danwei*, such as a municipal bureau, because future political reforms would mean that power would not be guaranteed for life.

A general feeling persisted among observers that the former system's rigidity did not fit with the PRC's contemporary economic reforms. The reformed system was intended to develop, not impede, students' creativity and spirit by treating them as individuals. A reformed market would require labour mobility and graduates would be required to be versatile. The concept of flexibility also extended to the university curriculum which many educators in the PRC saw as too specialized, a hold-over from the Soviet-inspired era. *Fenpei* was partly to blame for curriculum stagnancy because it did not force specialities to evolve.

Allocation hampered the market's ability to influence course content and it prevented education from meeting society's needs. Many majors were outdated and required adjustment to meet the needs of the market. Students often enrolled in their majors 'blindly' and the education they received paid too much attention to theory, too little to practical applications. In other words, graduates were 'unable to use their hands', not employing what they had learned (*dongshou nengli cha*). Teaching only emphasized book-learning and students lacked broad knowledge.

Two-way choice is understood to be an interim measure between allocation and free market. Just as the designation of the 1989 reforms as *mid-term* suggests, manpower planning in the PRC is in transition. Eventually, the invisible hand of the market should be controlling labour flow, which was impeded in *fenpei*. In the past, tertiary institutions were isolated from society. Implementing these reforms will generate closer relationships between tertiary institutions and the workplace. At this stage, tertiary institutions play a key role in arranging supply to meet demand. Tertiary institutions should take a more active role in supervising two-way choice.

Responsibility through accountability

The state was fully responsible for designing and executing *fenpei*, and the three major participants — tertiary institutions, students and work-units — had little more to do than to follow directions. They were dependent on taking orders from higher authorities. Students, especially, became dependent, not active. Critics argued that *fenpei* bred irresponsibility and that the reforms would create a system which required the participants to be responsible for their actions. Thus, it would produce accountability.

Tertiary institutions

Under the old system, tertiary institutions were not responsible for judging the relevance of their curricula against the needs of society. Teaching quality was never examined. In contrast, two-way choice could accelerate educational reform because tertiary institutions would be forced to adjust their majors to society's needs. The burden could now fall on tertiary institutions 'to educate in order to fit society's needs'. Given the 1985 reforms that provided tertiary institutions with institutional autonomy, institutions could move from being 'closed' to being 'open'. They could decide on their own how many students should take particular majors and could determine the length of training. Tertiary institutions would become accountable. Good institutions would get good students. Bad ones would not be able to survive.

Employers

Work-units were not required to be responsible under allocation because employers had to passively accept assignees, and they often had no choice but to put them in inappropriate positions. This system has been equated to an 'arranged marriage'; what is called for now is the 'freedom of love'. In the future, companies will hire according to need. They will have to compete among themselves for the most talented graduates. Previous to the reforms, companies lacked autonomy in selecting personnel. Now, they have it.

Students

The allocation system was associated with the *daguofan*, an entitlement given to all workers in the socialist system. Getting into university meant automatic allocation to a job. Students did need to do well in their studies. The *daguofan* encouraged them to strive only for the passing mark, usually 60 in the PRC, and thus become *liu shi fen wan sui* 'Long Live 60' worshippers. Since jobs were not allocated on the basis of achievement, students lacked motivation and were under no pressure to perform well. In short, they lacked 'creative spirit'.

In sum, the PRC's manpower reforms are expected to bring competition into higher education and prod students into being active, not passive. In terms of job assignment, students will begin to face choices. The reforms will enact the 'good graduates better jobs' principle.

Equity through fair competition

The third major area of concern involved competition (*jingzheng jizhi*), something which *fenpei* prevented and which the reformed system is expected to provide. The reforms would create a system that encourages competition among the principal players. This is more in line with the PRC's move from plan to market. Through the continued forces of competition, the best students would go to the best tertiary institutions, where they would study diligently. They would get the best grades and would be chosen by the best work-units through the fair competition of a job market (*rencai shichang*). This would be made possible by the free flow of information, which two-way choice would encourage. Thus, students would compete among themselves to be the best. Work-units would compete to gain the reputation as the most desirable place to work. The allocation system had lacked competition. Graduates were wanted everywhere, like an emperor's daughter who never had to worry about getting married (*Huangdi de nü er bu chou jia*). In the same vein, tertiary institutions could take advantage of the competitive environment to improve teaching quality. Good teachers would be rewarded and bad students would be eliminated (*taotailü*) in a survival-of-the-fittest scenario. Feedback from work-units would allow tertiary institutions to improve their curricula.

These three propositions — that the reforms would ensure efficiency through flexibility, responsibility through accountability, and equity through fair competition — are the crux of the initiatives. This utopian vision is somewhat obfuscated by the reality that the PRC's labour market system is not yet developed. By 1995 work-units did not yet have the power to make hiring decisions and fair competition is yet to be achieved.

CHINESE MANPOWER PLANNING IN A GLOBAL CONTEXT

In many Western countries, manpower planning was more successful as an exercise that developed planning than as a forecasting tool. It met severe criticism on theoretical grounds. An historical analysis of the PRC's manpower planning indicates that after adopting the Soviet model, planners have not relied on foreign economic models, but rather have developed ones better catered to the nation's political, economic and organizational structure. Yet, Chinese planners during *fenpei* did not appear to profit from Soviet experience, which included lessons on mismatch, assignment refusals by graduates and refusals by work-units.[68] During the reforms, lessons from outside the PRC have not been recognized. None of the 68 articles in Chinese journals reviewed for this chapter studied experiences outside the PRC. The popularity of reforms within Chinese academia and bureaucracy indicates little relationship between manpower planning inside the PRC and what has occurred outside.

In some countries, manpower planning was often initiated by, or at least greatly influenced by, planners of non-governmental organizations. In contrast, the PRC's policies grew endogenously. Both the policy-makers and the systems they developed were indigenous, not imported. Nor is there evidence that the PRC has been influenced by Asian examples, such as Taiwan[69] and South Korea,[70] which retain strong graduate employment systems (but without job assignment). To frame the PRC's manpower planning in a global context is more an interesting intellectual exercise than a useful one. For the PRC, globalization is real, but as far as manpower planning is concerned, globalization has remained relatively unimportant. But might it become important? The following scenario seems likely.

The current politically correct attitude in the PRC which sees market as

a panacea may well give way to an eventual realization that a stronger
state role in human resource development is required to address issues
such as mismatch, regional disparities and various items on political
agendas. In this scenario, the PRC's desire to return to a stronger central
planning approach would not match global trends. Chinese policy-makers
would have to choose between cross-national trends that move in one
direction and national needs that suggest another.

With little influence from the outside world, the PRC decided to abandon
the job allocation system that constituted its own version of manpower
planning. It did so because there was general agreement that *fenpei* did not
fit appropriately into the concept of market economy that was being
developed. The problem of mismatch — not using what you study in your
job — that had troubled the PRC's planners for decades, suddenly vanished.
The 'invisible hand' of the market would put people where they needed to
be. As one of the PRC's planners explained, 'Mismatch is not a problem.
The market takes care of it, just like in America. We can learn from the
United States.'[71]

For Chinese planners to look to the USA for inspiration is problematic.
Employment in many free-market societies is characterized by frequent
career change and by a fairly high level of mismatch. Another major
difference is that most US university students receive general education.
Graduates are often hired not so much for their specific skills as for their
problem-solving abilities, communication and organization skills, the ability
to think creatively and critically.[72] Another difference is that a quarter of
the US population over 25 have a college degree, compared with only about
2% in the PRC. Around 50% of the college-age cohort in the USA have
some post-secondary education. Even with the expansion of non-formal
education such as TV universities, the comparable group is small in the
PRC.[73] In free-market economies, much technical training is acquired on
the job as companies are willing to make investments in human resources.

Emerging research in the Shenzhen Special Economic Zone, where the
market economy has existed longer than elsewhere in the PRC, suggests
that the US model will not prove instructive for Chinese planners. In
Shenzhen there is high mismatch, but the compensating factor — a liberal
education — does not exist. Graduates of Shenzhen University, for example,
get little general education and for the most part they do not use their
acquired technical skills in their jobs. There is little evidence of human
resource development by employers, except for some foreign-capitalized
companies. At present, several factors are preventing true marketization.
There is such a high demand for college-educated youths that qualifications
and individual abilities are not especially relevant. Second, jobs in certain

sectors — notably in governmental bureaux and state-run companies —
are not filled through formal procedures in the market-place, such as
recruiting, advertisements or recommendations from tertiary institutions.
An inefficient information system means that job seekers must resort to
informal networks for finding jobs. In the mid-1990s, almost all jobs in
these sectors are landed through informal networks and this is one of the
reasons mismatch occurs. Even when graduates enter through the
employer's front door, the lack of an effective rules-driven bureaucracy
has removed meritocracy as an element of the job search in the state sector.

The PRC's abandonment of manpower planning was a political triumph
for reformers under the spiritual guidance of paramount leader Deng
Xiaoping. It was a defeat for the conservative 'radicals' who were reluctant
to see the socialist redistributive economy convert into a capitalist consumer-
oriented economy. Manpower planning's demise can be viewed as a
political decision.

The *fenpei* system in the PRC was administratively unwieldy. This is
one of the major reasons its death sentence was applauded by academics
and bureaucrats. The new reforms, however, were initially greeted with
more scepticism than enthusiasm. When lower-level bureaucrats do not
like a policy, they can sometimes exercise some *de facto* veto. The enrolment,
tuition and job assignment reforms which were first announced in the late
1970s have continually met obstacles in implementation.[74] Reforms in higher
education have been the rope of a political tug-of-war between the reformers
and the leftists in the Chinese political scene. Educational policy reform
resembles a pendulum whose swing is regulated by the ups and downs of
the radical and moderate groups.[75] For manpower planning, this is
illustrated by the 'send graduates to the grass roots' campaign which was
introduced after the student disturbances of December 1986. The emphasis
on dispatching graduates to backward and developing regions certainly
served a political need to get troublesome intellectuals out of the cities
where, as a mass, they could cause problems. But this policy was not
accompanied by ideological rhetoric as politically inspired policy usually
is. Moreover, the administrative changes discussed above actually lessened
state control. Although politics sometimes has a negative influence on
educational policy, in this instance, politics seems to have permitted a
general policy shift in a particular direction for a whole decade. For only a
brief period educational reforms virtually ceased after the events of 4 June
1989.

The change from unified job assignment to a free labour market did
not result from marketization, but rather provided the major *rationale* for
scrapping the system, a *post factum* rationale. The central government's

departure from manpower planning can also be seen as part of a larger disinvestment package from tertiary education. Components of this strategy include giving decision-making autonomy to tertiary institutions and removing state subsidies for students. All in all, even after Dengist reforms, the PRC's manpower planning was politics-driven and budget-driven. It did not resemble the type of manpower planning that has existed in free-market economies. In the latter, policies addressed economic rather than ideological issues. Until the 1993 reforms, manpower planning had never been contemplated, let alone effected, in the PRC. State policy had not combined enrolment with job placement. The two had remained separate functions, as they have in the USA.[76]

The PRC's affair with manpower planning might be best described as a 'fling' — brief but intense — the love object disposed of when a more suitable partner came along. The 'two-way choice' replacement, which involves graduates, employers *and* tertiary institutions, has generated much fantasy, but it is doubtful whether it will materialize according to the planners' designs. Graduates looking for jobs in Shenzhen, which never experienced *fenpei* and where the freedom to choose has characterized the job search for 15 years, rely heavily on *guanxi* (personal connections) for jobs in the state sector. Tertiary institutions do little to guide students into the workplace. Superficially, the college-to-work system that is emerging in the PRC may appear 'globalized', but if a case history of *fenpei* serves to enlighten us about the future, it is highly unlikely that the new system will mirror the practices of other economies. Past experience in human resource development suggests that the PRC can be synchronized with a global trend, but apparently not influenced by it.

NOTES

1. The author greatly appreciates the help of Yang Tao, Zhang Jiafeng and Zhang Jian in translation and interpretation for this chapter.
2. See, for example, Youdi and Hinchliffe, 1985; G. Williams, 1987.
3. *Manpower planning* (MP) as a term has also fallen in disregard worldwide as a politically incorrect gender-biased term. It is often replaced by *human resource development* (HRD). In this chapter MP refers to China's *fenpei* system while HRD refers to both MP and the experiments and programmes brought about by reform.
4. Cohn and Geske, 1990, p. 234.
5. Cohn and Geske, 1990, pp. 212–23; Rogers and Ruchlin, 1971.
6. Psacharopoulos, 1979, pp. 159–69; Blaug, 1967; Muhammad Shamsul Huq, 1975.
7. Psacharopoulos *et al.*, 1983.
8. UNESCO Division of Educational Policy and Planning, 1983, p. 26.
9. Serageldin and Li, 1983.

10. Sheehan, 1973, p. 97.
11. Vijaykumar, 1978, p. 143.
12. Agelasto, 1996b, chapter 2.
13. Zhang Jianhua, 1992.
14. Zhao Qindian, 1993, pp. 36–44.
15. For example, *Book of major educational events in China, 1949–1990*, pp. 1531–45.
16. Orleans, 1987. See also Matthews, 1982, pp. 169–74.
17. This point is made by L. White, 1978, p. 207. He concludes: ' ...government policies in the form of educational programs, patriotic rustication plans, employment procedures and residence registration all had effects on individuals' career motivations in Shanghai...'.
18. 'The most important decision of most students' lives was that relating to job assignment at the end of their university years as it has usually been a once-in-a-lifetime decision, and departmental Party personnel have had the most important jurisdiction over it. They determined how individual students were to be fitted into the job assignments offered to the department by the state planners. This has meant a very strong incentive for conformity on the part of students and even various kinds of ingratiation with those controlling this all-important decision.' Hayhoe, 1991, p. 126.
19. Zhang Jianhua, 1992, p. 56.
20. *Book of major educational events in China, 1949–1990*, p. 1534.
21. Zhang Jianhua, 1992, pp. 87ff.
22. Du Ruiqing, 1992, p. 8.
23. The Jiaotong experiment is described in detail in *China education yearbook 1988*, pp. 217–20. Sichuan University was added in 1984. Zhejiang University copied the experiment in 1987. The Shandong experiment called for *yufenzhi*, arrangement before graduation. This was a pre-allocation system in which work-units participate in education. When admitted to university, students know where they will be working. A similar pre-allocation was carried out by Zhejiang University, called 3–1–1, where students studied for three years, went to work for one year and returned to study for the final year.
24. Zhang Jianhua, 1992, pp. 242ff.
25. *Book of major educational events in China, 1949–1990*, p. 1543.
26. Zhang Jianhua, 1992, p. 262.
27. CCP Central Committee, 1985. Cheng Kai-ming, 1986a, pp. 255–69; Cheng Kai-ming, 1986b. See also, Lewin *et al.*, 1994.
28. The *Decision* followed several years of policy discussions and negotiations at various levels of the government and was pre-sold to 'comrades at the basic level' in a series of local symposia before the document's formal release. For one such meeting, see Xu Guangchun, 1985.
29. This is known as commissioned enrolment. See Cheng Kai-ming, 1986a, p. 265.
30. For further discussion see Cheng Kai-ming, 1994a.
31. Davis, 1990, which cites articles from *Renmin Ribao*, 15 July 1985, p. 3 and *Zhongguo Jiaoyu Bao*, 16 July 1985, p. 1.
32. 'Report on job placement for college graduates', Xinhua, 14 July 1985, translated in FBIS-CHI-85-137, 17 July 1985, pp. K13-K15; 'Colleges given more placement power', Xinhua, 14 July 1985, translated in JPRS-CPS-85-084, 20 August 1985, p. 46.

33. Zhuang, 1985.
34. Gao Baoli and Zhang Tiegun, 1985.
35. Zhang Jianhua, 1992, pp. 326–7.
36. 'Probation measures for graduates issued', Xinhua, 31 August 1987, translated in FBIS-CHI-87-169, 1 September 1987, pp. 26–7. The policy was earlier reported in *Wen Wei Po*, the Hong Kong paper which is believed to receive both financial support and inside information from the Chinese government. See Juan, 1987.
37. 'Responsible person of the State Education Commission answers *Liaowang* reporter's question on the assignment of jobs to college graduates this year', *Liaowang* Overseas Edition, no. 20, 14 May 1990, p. 17, translated in FBIS-CHI-90-108, 5 June 1990, pp. 33–5.
38. Cherrington, 1991, p. 93.
39. FBIS-CHI-88-098, p. 28; Li Chao, 1988; see also Li Ping, 1990.
40. 'Report on job assignment for graduates of colleges and universities', SEdC document 19, 1989, in Zhang Jianhua, 1992, pp. 367–76; *China education yearbook 1990*, pp. 189–92.
41. Zhang Jianhua, 1992, p. 376.
42. Zhang Jianhua, 1992, p. 373.
43. Zhang Jianhua, 1992, p. 374.
44. 'State Council approves report on job assignment', Xinhua, 4 February 1989, translated in FBIS-CHI-89-024, 7 February 1989, pp. 27–8.
45. 'Shanghai mayor, students discuss job assignments', *China Daily*, 3 April 1989, p. 3, in FBIS-CHI-89-064, 5 April 1989, pp. 53–4.
46. Zhang Jianhua, 1992, pp. 385–9.
47. Tam, 1989; 'College graduates undergo grassroots training', Xinhua, 7 November 1989, in FBIS-CHI-89-214, 7 November 1989, pp. 21–2.
48. 'An important measure for China to bring its cadres: university graduates going to the grassroots level — official of the Organization Department of the CPC Central Committee answers questions', *Liaowang* Overseas Edition, no. 47, 20 November 1989, pp. 6–7, translated in FBIS-CHI-89-232, 5 December 1989, pp. 17–20.
49. Mi and Hong, 1989.
50. 'State to secure jobs for all college graduates', Xinhua, 10 January 1991, in FBIS-CHI-91-008, 11 January 1991, p. 25.
51. A mimeographed document from the SEdC in November 1992 appears to be an earlier draft of a proposal to speed up reform in higher education. This latter document was formally approved by the SEdC on 8 December and published as *Guanyu jiakuai gaige he fazhan gaodeng jiaoyu de yijian* (Some opinions about speeding up reform and developing higher education), *Zhongguo Jiaoyu Bao*, 29 January 1993. This new thrust was repeated in the comprehensive reform of education issued by the State Council in which higher education was only a small part of the national policy initiative. See CCP Central Committee and State Council, 1993; also, State Education Commission, 1993d.
52. Xu Xiu, 1992; Zhou Runsun, Mo Huilin, Xu Zhenhua and Tu Yaqin, 1992.
53. Zhao Qindian, 1993, p. 42; Cheng, 1994a, p. 70.
54. Zhu Wenqin, 1994.
55. Ou Fangqing; Xu Xiu, 1992.
56. Zhang Jianhua, 1992.

57. *Jinnian gaoxiao biyesheng jiuye banfa queding* (This year's university graduates' job procurement process), *Renmin Ribao*, 19 January 1994, p. 3, reprinted in *Gaodeng Jiaoyu* no. 2, 1994, p. 34.

58. 'Ninety percent college graduates to find jobs on their own', China News Digest (an on-line service), Global News, 7 July 1995, referring to a report in *China Youth Daily*.

59. Zhu Wenqin, 1994.

60. Xia, 1994.

61. 'University graduates face good job opportunities', Xinhua, 4 April 1994, translated in FBIS-CHI-94-065, 5 April 1994, p. 15.

62. Similar stories were related to the author by several university graduates from medium-sized cities in Guangdong.

63. Robinsohn, 1992, p. 18.

64. See Cheng Kai-ming, 1994b; and Rosen, 1987.

65. See Shirk, 1993.

66. See Pepper, 1990, pp. 155–60, for the tuition controversy, and Li Shouxin and Bray, 1992, pp. 375–87, for a description of the 1987 pilot loan programme which, seven years later, has still not been established despite numerous state documents advocating its implementation.

67. Zhou Yuliang, 1990, p. 394.

68. Matthews, 1982. More flexibility was built into the post-Stalin Soviet graduate employment system, pp. 170, 173–4.

69. See Young Yi Rong, 1995, pp. 105–24.

70. See Chon, 1995, pp. 125–148.

71. Interview, Shanghai Institute of Human Resource Development, March 1994.

72. These and other qualities are discussed in Green and Seymour, 1991.

73. See Chapter 10 by Xiao Jin in this volume.

74. Pepper, 1990, pp. 155–63.

75. Shen Jianping, 1994, pp. 1–13.

76. J. Smith, 1982.

14

Privatization or Quasi-Marketization?

MOK Ka-ho and David CHAN

INTRODUCTION

Since the founding of the PRC, education has been under government control, characterized by the notion of 'bureaucratic centralism'.[1] In the mid-1980s the CCP began to diversify education, allowing and encouraging the establishment of schools run by the non-state sector. In recent years, private education has been undergoing rapid development, particularly in China's big cities. Reductions in state regulation, provision and subsidy in education have already indicated that the PRC's recent educational development marks a move towards privatization and quasi-marketization.

Instead of relying upon the state's financial support, educational funding has been diversified with other resources, such as overseas donations, financial support from local government taxes and subsidies, as well as tuition fees.[2] One of the strategies being adopted by the CCP to reduce costs and increase efficiency and effectiveness in educational service delivery is the introduction of the 'fee-charging' principle in higher education.[3] Early in the 1980s, the plan for having fee-charging students was regarded as the 'ultra-plan', implying that the intake of these self-supporting students was beyond the state plan.[4] But the fee-paying principle has become more prevalent in the 1990s in the educational sphere. In 1993, 30 higher learning institutions were selected for the pilot study for the *binggui* ('merging the tracks') scheme, whereby students were admitted either because of their public examination scores or because they were willing and able to pay a fee, though their scores were lower than what was required. In 1994, more institutions entered the scheme and the fee-charging principle was thus legitimized.[5] A study conducted by the World Bank reports similar findings, that the state has devolved the responsibilities of education planning and financing to provincial governments.[6] In this policy context, it is not surprising that in the past few years commissioned training (*daipei*) students, self-supporting, and TV university and correspondence university students have taken a bigger share of the total student population in China.[7]

This chapter examines how the flourishing market economy and the policy of decentralization adopted by the post-Mao leadership have affected educational development. It commences with a history of private education, especially higher education, in China. It then reviews current developments, which include reductions in state regulation, provision and subsidy. The next part considers the concepts of privatization and marketization to determine whether the PRC's developments fall under these rubrics. The final sections discuss the Chinese experience in the global context and define educational privatization with Chinese characteristics.

THE DEVELOPMENT OF PRIVATE HIGHER EDUCATION

Private education has existed in China since the Spring and Autumn periods and it especially flourished in the Han Dynasty. While higher educational institutions were run mainly by the government, private academies of learning (*shuyuan*) started to grow by the late Tang Dynasty and persisted all the way through the late Qing period.[8] About 1200 such academies existed in the Ming Dynasty and over 1900 in the Qing Dynasty.[9]

After the Opium War in the mid-1800s, private missionary schools and universities gradually sprang up all over China. By 1917, 80% of higher degree students attended missionary universities, putting them very much in control of China's higher education.[10] Even in 1950, a year after the nation's founding, 39% of the total of 227 universities were private.[11] However, following the Soviet model, in 1952 all private institutions of higher education were made public.

The rise and growth of private higher education (1978–86)

Modern China's development of private higher education began in 1978, the year when the CCP officially announced its Open Door policy and its ambitious pursuit of the Four Modernizations. With the nation's emphasis on economic development, the impetus for manpower training greatly facilitated the growth of education, particularly higher education. Exactly 30 years after the closing of all private educational institutions, in March 1982 the first *minban* (literally, people-run) higher educational institution opened — Zhonghua Zhehui Daxue (Chinese Social University) in Beijing. At this time over 100 such *minban* higher educational institutions were established across the country.[12]

Minban schools are those run by the non-state sector, including private and community-run schools. The difference between *minban* and *private* educational institutions is not always clear; the terms are often used interchangeably. Privately-owned schools are normally labelled *minban* instead of private, because the socialist state is perceived as uncomfortable with the notion of *private*. Regardless of the nomenclature, these schools are not supported by the state, but mainly rely upon social donations, individual contributions, student tuition fees and local support.

The Constitution of 1982 stipulates that 'the state encourages collective economic organizations, governmental enterprises and other social forces to initiate and administer various kinds of educational activities according to laws'.[13] These words gave formal and legal recognition of what had already been occurring.[14]

The rectification of private higher education (1987–91)

In 1987 the SEdC promulgated a document called *The Provisional Regulations on Social Forces Running Schools*, requiring local governments and educational administrative authorities to solve certain problems, such as disorders in the governance of *minban* schools as well as irregularities in their conferring of diplomas.[15] Central educational authorities became more prudent in handling private higher educational affairs and the regulations and provisions as implemented were not conducive to the development of private *gaoxiao*.

The very people who ran *minban* institutions felt that these new governmental policies were unreasonable. Thus, in order to promote their interests in a public forum, they held the first national conference on *minban* higher education in Wuhan in January 1989. More than 70 *minban* higher educational institutions were represented. Educators pointed out that the authorities were providing too little support and imposing too many restrictions. Furthermore, they argued that the management of *minban gaoxiao* was not as disorderly as the authorities suggested.

The 1989 meeting produced a platform of five concrete suggestions:
1. programmes and admission should serve social needs;

2. evaluation of education quality should be based on social effects;
3. non-governmental *gaoxiao* must rely on themselves for most of their expenditures, yet the government should grant some kind of subsidy;
4. non-governmental *gaoxiao* should employ retired teachers, experts or cadres; and
5. graduates of both public and non-governmental schools should be entitled to equal job opportunities.

At the same time, the forum called for the educational authorities to liberate their thinking, to open themselves to new ideas and to strengthen their commitment to reform.[16]

New development of private higher education (1992 to present)

The year 1992 marked the advent of a 'second spring' for private higher education. The presidents of some 50 *minban* higher educational institutions met in Beijing in February and their policy proposals were submitted to the SEdC.[17] Thus, on 17 August 1993, the SEdC issued the *Provisional regulations for the establishment of people-run schools for higher education*, which for the first time specified the governance of *minban* higher education on a legal basis.[18]

Seven chapters of the 1993 Regulations cover the legal status of *minban* higher education, the criteria for their establishment, the formal application procedures, and the evaluation and approval process by the SEdC. They also concern the administration and governance of these institutions.[19] By 1994, more than 800 *minban* higher educational institutions existed across the nation, with 18 of them authorized by the SEdC to grant *benke* diplomas.[20]

The National Minban Higher Education Commission, under the auspices of the China Association for Adult Education, was established during a conference meeting from 25 to 27 May 1995 in Beijing. More than 150 representatives from over 106 localities attended. Forty representatives were elected to form a Standing Committee with formal officers and a bimonthly magazine called *Minban Jiaoyu Tiandi* (People-run Education Forum).[21] They intend to assert their professional autonomy to the SEdC by gaining the right to accredit *minban gaoxiao*. The exact number of private *gaoxiao* in the PRC remains a mystery; government statistics report the number at 1230.[22]

Current developments

Independent of state subsidy, private institutions are relatively free to design their own programmes, which respond to students' needs by adopting a practical orientation. Being sensitive to market needs, private *gaoxiao* offer mainly vocational and technical courses, as well as classes in business and commerce. They provide in-service training for upgrading workers' specific skills and knowledge, as well as offering basic training.

Zhitong Private University, a privately owned educational institution in Guangzhou, offers a variety of courses. Students take these courses either by correspondence and self-study or by attending classes. Zhitong University, approved by the Guangdong Higher Education Bureau in the 1980s, was the first private tertiary institution to offer tutorial classes at the provincial level. In 1993, Zhitong was widely regarded as providing quality distance learning. The most prominent features of this university are its courses in humanities/social sciences, vocational/technical training, and business/commercial studies. Practical courses cater for different market needs in English communication, international business and trade, etc.[23]

Nanhua Commercial and Industrial College and Hualian Private University, both in Guangzhou, view students' interests and needs as the 'guiding principles' for the design of curricula and courses.[24] Treating students as 'consumers', these private colleges offer courses unavailable in regular institutions.[25] Hualian, for example, consists of five departments which offer a total of nine majors, each designed to provide a curriculum incorporating multi-disciplinary courses. Furthermore, the university has taken positive measures to run programmes jointly with similar universities both at home and abroad.[26]

Beijing's Haidian University, founded in March 1984 by retiring faculty members of various universities in Beijing, has since 1987 recommended its graduates to various employing units, which pay the university for each graduate it hires. In 1987, the university recommended 227 graduates and received ¥510 000; in 1988, it recommended 370 graduates and received ¥850 000. Compensation averaged about ¥2300 per graduate and the total it received made up almost 75% of its total expenditures. This policy reflects the market value of its graduates, which in turn indicates the value of *minban gaoxiao* in the changing labour market. This type of *minban* university requires less investment, yet has yielded relatively good benefits to society. They evidence relatively good educational quality, a highly efficient operation, and adaptability to social and economic environments.[27]

Sanda University in Shanghai, founded in 1992, received SEdC permission in 1994 to issue its own diplomas. Its board of directors gives the president broad decision-making responsibilities. The specialities are designed to meet market demands for both the Pudong Economic Development Zone in East Shanghai and the whole nation. It has also undertaken exchanges with other *gaoxiao* both at home and abroad in order to raise its academic standards.[28]

Like Sanda, Hualian University is privately endowed, governed by a board of directors, and practises the president responsibility system, receiving recommendations from an advisory committee. The university has over 80 faculty members, with departments headed by professors who had worked in public *gaoxiao* before reaching mandatory retirement age. Hualian has exchanges with several universities in Guangdong and invites overseas academics and appoints language experts from abroad as visiting professors. It has branches in other provinces where it works with local institutions. Its long-term goal is to manage a continuous stream of education, including kindergarten, primary school, secondary school, college and university. Institution officials believe that the teaching experience and scholarship of its faculty members compare favourably with those in the major public universities in Guangdong.[29]

RATIONALES FOR PRIVATE EDUCATION REFORM

The resurgence of private educational institutions suggests that the PRC's education has shifted from state monopoly to a mixed economy of education. There are several different forms of privatization in education.[30] The educational system might be dominated by the mass private and restricted public sector. Or it may be a mixed system, with both the private and public sectors playing a role in providing educational services. A third possibility is that the private sector plays a very limited role, characterized as a 'peripheral private sector'.[31] The following discussion examines the nexus between the PRC's private and public higher education systems.

Private higher education's re-emergence is closely connected to the CCP's encouraging the market to create more educational opportunities. Decentralization in the PRC's educational realm has allowed far more flexibility and diversity in the delivery of educational services in the mainland.[32] Unlike in the Mao era when the state held primary responsibility for the provision of educational services and uniformly maintained them, the new educational market in the reform period can complement the state-run educational system as well as offer an alternative to it.

Devolution of responsibility and power to localities

In 1985 the CCP initiated structural reforms at the institutional level. The central government affirmed the importance of professional knowledge and technical know-how to the success of the PRC's modernization, and admitted that the state alone could not provide sufficient educational services to satisfy heightened social aspirations and parental expectations. Acknowledging that overcentralization and stringent rules had killed the creativity and spontaneity of individual institutions, the CCP thus partially handed over management responsibilities to local leaders and educationalists. In order to reduce its rigid control over schools, the Party decided to

> ...take resolute steps to streamline administration, devolve powers to unit at lower levels so as to extend the schools' decision-making power in the administration of school affairs... [33]

In 1993, the CCP reiterated its support for decentralization and diversification of educational services. It declared that the

> Government has to change its function from direct control to managing schools through legislation, funding, planning, advice on policies and other necessary means.[34]

> [T]he national policy is to actively encourage and fully support social institutions and citizens to establish school according to laws and to provide right guidelines and strengthen administration.[35]

Consequently, local initiatives, particularly with the support of local governments, became a crucial force in educational development in the PRC. The state encouraged 'people in all walks of life' to run schools and even invited 'international cooperation' to provide more educational opportunities for the Chinese citizens.[36] Centralized control over *gaoxiao* further devolved into greater autonomy and flexibility for individual institutions to govern their affairs, with more control over student enrolment and job assignments.[37] As a result the SEdC has maintained only macroleadership, offering general guidelines rather than direct management.[38] The 1995 *Education Law* has further revitalized local communities and encouraged private support to education.[39] Educational institutions are required to conduct their affairs in accordance with the respective ordinances and regulations.[40]

Multiple channels of educational funding

Encouraged by state support, local governments have explored different channels for financing education. Local governments now provide about 80% of higher education funds.[41] Intake of self-supporting and commissioned training students increased dramatically between 1986 and 1989.[42] For example, in Zhejiang province, the recruitment of self-supporting students in higher educational institutions jumped from 404 in 1986 to 2549 in 1989.[43] Similarly, university admissions of self-supporting students in Shanghai jumped from 829 in 1987 to 13 438 in 1994. As a result, institutions like Huanghe University of Science and Technology in Zhengzhou, Henan, rely mainly on donations and tuition fees for income.[44] In the past few years commissioned, self-supporting, TV university and correspondence university students have taken a bigger share of the total student population.[45]

All in all, the state has progressively rolled back from the frontier of social provision, leaving the responsibilities to local governments and individuals.[46] Local educationalists in the Pearl River Delta are well aware of the state's disengagement from financing education. In response, they foster educational development through providing diversified educational services and seeking multiple sources of funds.[47] Consequently, a significant proportion of educational funds is being drawn from the non-state sector.[48] Hualian Private University runs a computer shop and is opening a farm to provide additional income to finance its educational programmes. Without receiving any public funds, Nanhua Commercial and Industrial College, one of the only two Guangdong private universities with SEdC recognition, depends heavily upon tuition fees and support from trade unions in the province.[49] In general, many educational institutions run their own businesses such as computer shops and consultancy firms to get more money to finance their programmes, and such developments are also popular among key universities.[50] Being better off financially, parents living in the Pearl River Delta are able to pay for tuition and quality education for their children, unquestionably creating a favourable environment for the rise of private educational institutions in the Delta. At the end of 1992, there were already 125 private schools ranging from primary to tertiary levels.[51] In 1993 alone, 45 additional schools were established in Guangzhou to provide post-secondary vocational training.[52] From 1993 to mid-1995, there were about 690 *minban* and private schools mushrooming in Guangdong province.[53]

Autonomy and flexibility in school governance

Against a liberated policy context, local educationalists in both the public and private sectors now have far more autonomy, exercising their discretionary powers to chart the course of educational development in the PRC.[54] In the Mao era, the Ministry of Education tightly controlled student enrolment. Now, schools enjoy flexibility in recruiting students. This is especially true in Guangdong, where even in the public sector local governments enjoy a certain degree of autonomy to implement a policy before it is formally approved by Beijing.[55]

The adoption of a policy of decentralization has allowed more autonomy and flexibility for local educational practitioners in school governance. During various field visits to schools and colleges in Guangdong province in recent years, the authors were repeatedly told by the local educationalists that they had enjoyed far more flexibility and autonomy in school management. After the initiation of educational reform in the mid-1980s, the SEdC has given only general policy guidelines, instead of detailed regulations to direct educational development in the mainland.[56] The first *Education Law* of the PRC promulgated in April 1995 stipulated that more autonomy and discretion would be given to local educational practitioners, so they could design appropriate programmes and reforms to enhance educational standards and to create more learning opportunities for the people living in their regions.[57] The devolution of financial responsibilities from the central to the local governments and other sectors of the community has not only diversified financial resources to support education, but has, in fact, given local educationalists more autonomy in school administration and management. This is particularly true among *minban* and private schools and colleges.

No matter what managerial structure *minban* schools/colleges adopt, the principals and presidents — *lingdao* (leaders) — have far more autonomy in school governance. The financial independence of *minban* schools and colleges has indeed given *lingdao* more discretionary power in deciding matters regarding recruitment of teachers, student admission and even the design of curricula and courses.[58] Differing from public schools in terms of administrative structure, most of the non-governmental schools and colleges have a board of directors or trustees, which supervises the principal or president. *Lingdao* of non-governmental *gaoxiao* have more power to hire and dismiss personnel, utilizing the competition mechanism.[59] Shanghai's Sanda University appointed 15 associate professors from Beijing University, Qinghua University and Shanghai Jiaotong University.[60] Like Sanda, Hualian University in Guangzhou recruited teachers from not only Guangzhou but also the whole nation.[61] No doubt, enhanced financial ability of these non-governmental schools/colleges has allowed leaders to adopt a more innovative approach in educational development. With a flexible operational mechanism, *minban* and private schools and colleges are more sensitive to emerging market needs, and are able to develop special courses to meet the needs of the market economy. In turn, more parents are willing to send their children to study there.[62]

CONCEPTS OF PRIVATIZATION AND QUASI-MARKETIZATION

Determining whether the PRC's educational development has really been going through processes of privatization and quasi-marketization first requires scrutiny of these two concepts. The initiation of privatization and quasi-marketization must be understood in view of the socio-political context in which these strategies were initiated. In recent years critics around the globe have questioned the state's role in the welfare sector.[63] After the Second World War, the expansion of state activities and state intervention in the public domain has produced both fiscal and political crises.[64] A growing political debate ensued over the ongoing ability and propriety of large-scale state intervention in public life. In the 1970s, the consensus on the welfare state commonly shared in the West since the Second World War came under increasing challenge. The more prominent concerns surrounded the slow-down of economic growth, supposedly uncontrollable public budgets, inefficient state enterprises and public services, and insatiable social demands. At the ideological level, big governments were accused of usurping the proper role of markets and the ability of individuals to run their own affairs.[65] Having realized the importance of productivity, performance and control, governments began to transform their management.

Views on privatization are too diverse to permit a simple dictionary definition. The concept is best understood as an approach to social policy rather than a policy itself.[66] No matter how diverse the definitions, privatization is closely associated with a reduction in state activities, especially in terms of provision, subsidy and regulation.[67] In very broad strokes, privatization concerns the transfer of responsibility from the state to the non-state sector.[68] To enhance effectiveness, economy and efficiency, market criteria such as profit and affordability serve as operational principles in rationing or distributing social services.[69] In addition, user charges ensure cost-effectiveness.[70]

Markets within the public sector are still at an early developmental stage because for most cases, they are, at best, 'quasi-markets'.[71] Although competition is introduced in enterprises and service suppliers, quasi-markets are different from conventional markets because the former do not aim to maximize profits. The customer's purchasing power and purchasing decision are not the same as in conventional markets, in which customer purchasing power is normally expressed in money terms. Purchasing power in quasi-markets takes the form of an earmarked budget or 'voucher' restricted to the purchase of a specified service allocated to users, or it is centralized in a single state purchasing agency. Purchasing decisions in quasi-markets are not made by direct users but instead by a third party, such as government departments, on behalf of the users.[72] In spite of such differences, the introduction of quasi-markets to run public services aims to enhance customers' choice and ultimately improve the performance of the public sector.

The introduction of quasi-markets can clarify the responsibilities between purchasers and providers, effect better service management and provide an efficient service delivery against a relatively competitive market setting within the public sector. Clearer responsibilities between principal and agent should increase the degree of transparency in public services, resulting in accountability.[73] With efficiency, responsiveness, choice and equity determining a better delivery of public services, quasi-markets are being experimented with in many parts of the world.[74]

PRIVATIZATION IN EDUCATION WITH CHINESE CHARACTERISTICS

The CCP has gradually forsaken its monopoly over the provision of educational opportunities, thus fostering the growth of various types of schools run by the non-state sector. Re-emphasizing the importance of individual responsibilities and encouraging local communities and social organizations to create additional educational opportunities, the state is continuously reducing its educational subsidy, provision and regulation. Multiple channels of financing include educational surcharges,[75] local government subsidies, tuition and miscellaneous fees, and funds raised from overseas Chinese and compatriots in Hong Kong and Macau.[76] The developments show a shared responsibility between the state and the non-state sector in providing educational services.[77] Above all, the emergence of private education reveals that the PRC's education is going through a process of privatization and marketization. This is similar to the trend in the PRC's welfare sector that has re-emphasized individual responsibilities and local initiatives, lessening the importance of the state in welfare provision. The recent changes in the PRC's educational provision clearly indicate the retreat of the state in terms of provision, regulation and subsidy. The boom in private higher education and the increasing number of self-supporting students suggest that a quasi-market is evolving.

Even though the state has not deliberately set out to promote private education, the PRC's persistent call for decentralization and diversification of educational services has created ample room for the growth of private education. Refocusing curricula towards a more practical orientation and emphasizing the importance of vocational training, together with the flourishing of private education in the 1990s and the emergence of the fee-paying system, manifest a response to the new market setting.

Despite privatization and quasi-marketization, internal markets in Chinese higher education have not fully evolved. The split of purchaser and provider is unclear. The strategy of privatization or marketization adopted by the CCP is highly instrumental, intended to improve administrative efficiency and effectiveness, rather than to make a fundamental shift of value orientation. The CCP has never committed itself theoretically or ideologically to public choice theory, the philosophical basis of marketization and privatization. The emergence of private education in the post-Mao era has not seen much variation. Only one kind of privatization has emerged: the private sector plays only a very limited, peripheral role. Moreover, the public sector in higher education is starting to look private. Public universities run businesses, charge tuition and orient courses for newly emerging work sectors. In this regard, a discussion of privatization of higher education in the PRC would seem to include not only schools that call themselves private, but also public schools that in many ways appear to be private, thus making the distinction between private and public problematic. Private education has indeed become more popular in the PRC, but its development is likely to play only a supplementary, not dominant, role in the PRC's education. The mainstream still lies with the schools run by the public sector.[78] The growth of private learning institutions in socialist China implies that the conventional system has somehow been broken. The newly emerging private educational institutions may pose a challenge to the traditional system, especially when these new schools show they are more responsive to emerging market needs.

The principle of marketization 'denotes a process whereby education becomes a commodity provided by competitive suppliers, educational services are priced and access to them depends on consumer calculations and ability to pay'.[79] Regardless whether terminology such as 'marketization', 'commodification' and 'socialization' is used by the CCP, the role of the state in the social policy arena is declining. The growth of private *gaoxiao* suggests the mainland is moving towards a similar, though not exactly the same, global process of privatization in education.

TOWARDS A GLOBAL TREND: EDUCATION AND THE MARKET-PLACE

The Chinese experience of marketization and privatization fits into the global context of 'small government and big society'. Privatization of education has been underway in Britain since the 1980s in the belief that the process would make the public sector more effective, efficient and responsive to the changing demands of the public.[80] The introduction of the Assisted Place Scheme (APS) is designed to transfer high-ability pupils from low-income families from the maintained sector to the private sector. In addition, the former conservative government privatized the cost of education by encouraging charities to sponsor or donate funds to private schools with tax exemption.[81] In recent years, the British government has implemented a scheme called 'Local Management of Schools' (LMS) — decentralizing budgets to schools which pushes/encourages schools to look for industrial or commercial sponsorship.[82] As well, universities are urged to make good the reductions in government funding by raising research money from trusts or from industry, by securing sponsorship for particular activities and so on.

Intending to improve educational services offered by the public sector, the US government has tried to give more choice and open statewide public school options to students. By introducing competition to education, together with the adoption of a 'customer-oriented approach', US citizens nowadays experience considerable choice in educational services.[83] In recent years, different measures such as Total Quality Management, Statistical Processing Control, Employee Involvement, Process Re-engineering and Just-in-Time Production have been adopted in both the private and public sectors to assure service quality. Other major reforms involve school choice, teacher education and certification, curriculum, and site-based decision-making empowering teachers and school authorities to govern school affairs.[84] Increasing educational options to students and nationwide recognition of the importance of competition have begun to gain momentum as reflected by the growth of educational choice programmes throughout the USA.[85]

To make schools more responsive to the needs of both parents and students (customers of services), decentralization permits school authorities to enjoy more flexibility and autonomy in deciding administrative, recruiting, programmatic and personnel matters.[86] All these measures have invoked heated debate and discussion. Advocates say this transformation would not only increase competition, but also improve educational services and save public expenditure. Sceptics argue that education is different from hard services or commodity-oriented products because of its human service nature. Despite the controversy, the importance of 'value for money' and the emphasis on 'accountability' have fostered privatization of public education. Bringing 'market elements' into the public sector gives people more choice and many believe that eventually better-quality education will result. No matter how diverse the views on this issue are, different experiments in contracting out, franchising, using vouchers, and even selling assets and load shedding continue to be undertaken in the USA and UK.[87]

Under labels like 'New Public Management' in the UK and 'Reinventing Government' in the USA, different market mechanisms have been introduced in an effort to enhance efficiency, accountability and consumer choice. As quite a significant number of higher educational institutions are publicly funded in Britain, Australia, Holland and Sweden, higher educational development is significantly affected by the similar tide of 'public sector re-engineering'.[88] Despite the fact that there has not been a conventional 'market' system formed in the educational sphere, somehow 'quasi-markets' have been evolving in the educational sector in these countries. In recent years, educational development in Britain, Australia, Holland and Sweden has been under great market pressure. Coupled with constrained state budgets, governments in these countries have adopted more market-type mechanisms in running higher education. Nowadays, universities in these countries have to go through different types of assessment exercises to get sufficient financial support. Central to all these control mechanisms is a performance-related funding system, which is primarily concerned with quality assessment in terms of research output and teaching quality. Under such circumstances, universities find themselves living in a more competitive external environment; thus they have to improve their performance in order to secure adequate funding. Within universities, more discretionary power has been given to vice-chancellors, deans and heads of units and departments at all levels to reward those with 'outstanding' performance and, at the same time, penalize those with 'poor performance'. The formation of independent audit or quality assessment bodies seems to suggest that there is a split between 'providers' and 'purchasers' in educational endeavour, under the system of which the state becomes the major purchaser, through the independent funding assessment bodies, buying services offered by different universities (providers).[89] Not surprisingly, the introduction of market principles in higher educational development has affected not only the systems which have been adopted, but also planning, funding, evaluation and regulation of educational development in these countries.[90] The reintroduction of student fees in the UK and Australia, and the experiment of educational vouchers in the USA and other developed countries have demonstrated how educational development has been affected by market forces.[91] A globalization process has been influencing educational development, linking education more closely with the needs of 'the economy' and, in turn, giving rise to corporate managerialism.[92]

The tide of marketization and privatization is popular not only in the developed countries but also in the developing world.[93] For example, private schools challenge public-dominated schools in Latin America.[94] Many countries, regardless of their levels of development, have a varied public/ private mix of educational services.[95] In a wide range of countries the majority of students attend private rather than public schools.[96] In some countries, privatization of education is one of the ways to transform the traditional public/private boundary in education.[97] The share of the private sector is becoming more significant than that of the public or state-run education. The tradition in which education was dominated by the public sector is giving way to the quasi-market concept. This is a global feature of educational development.

SUMMARY

This chapter has discussed how the flourishing market economy and the policy of decentralization adopted in the post-Mao era have affected the PRC's higher education. Recent years have seen reductions in state regulation, provision and subsidy, suggesting that the PRC is part of the global trend of privatization. Yet, a close scrutiny reveals that quasi-markets have not yet evolved. The split between purchasers and providers is not clear. The strategy of privatization or marketization adopted by the CCP is highly instrumental, intended to improve administrative efficiency and effectiveness, rather than to enable a fundamental shift of value orientation. The emergence of private higher education indicates a very limited role for the private sector, which remains only peripheral, under the dominance of public institutions. Nevertheless, the growth of private learning institutions in socialist China reveals that the entire system is changing. The public/ private boundary is becoming a blur, as public *gaoxiao* adopt market principles and mechanisms to improve their performance and accept fee-paying students outside the state plan. The Chinese experience of privatization and marketization differs from what occurs elsewhere, but Chinese higher education has similarly been affected by the strong tide of the market economy.

NOTES

1. 'Bureaucratic centralism' emphasizes central planning for social and economic development under the influence of ruling groups and administrative or professional elite. For details, see Lauglo, 1995.
2. Mok, 1996. See also Chapter 2 by Cheng Kai-ming in this volume.
3. See Chapter 12 by Zhang Minxuan in this volume.
4. Cheng Kai-ming, 1996b.
5. Cheng Kai-ming, 1996b.
6. World Bank, 1991.
7. Bray, 1996; Pepper, 1995; Hayhoe, 1996.
8. Ding and Liu Qi, 1992; Yang Busheng and Peng Dingguo, 1992.
9. Chen Yuanhui, *et al.*, 1981.
10. China National Institute of Educational Research, 1995, p. 4.
11. China National Institute of Educational Research, 1995, p. 5.
12. China National Institute of Educational Research, 1995, p. 10.
13. National People's Congress, 1982.
14. Article 19, contained in China National Institute of Educational Research, 1995, p. 55.
15. SEdC, 1987b.
16. Wei Yitong and Zhang Guocai, 1995, pp. 7–8.
17. The meeting was held in Beijing from 20 to 26 February and reported by the Central People Broadcasting Station three times on 25 February.
18. SEdC, 1993c.
19. Wei Yitong and Zhang Guocai, 1995, p. 10.
20. China National Institute of Educational Research, 1995, p. 11.
21. *Minban Jiaoyu Tiandi*, no. 3, 1995, pp. 5–6.
22. *Zhongguo Jiaoyu Bao*, 1 November 1996.
23. Zhitong University, 1995; Mok, 1997b.
24. Interviews with Niu Xianmin and Hou Defu, presidents of Nanhua and Hualian respectively, July 1995.
25. Interview, Niu, July 1995.
26. Interview with Professor Hou Defu, president of Hualian University, Guangzhou, July 1995.
27. Interview with Professor Chen Baoyu, vice-president of Haidian University, Beijing and vice-director and secretary-general of the National Minban Higher Education Commission, Xiamen, October/November 1995. Other private Beijing *gaoxiao* are discussed in: 'Beijing starts non-government education institute', *Beijing Ribao*, 31 July 1993, p. 1, in FBIS-CHI-93-161, 23 August 1993, p. 58; Yang Zhihan, 1988.
28. Interview with Prof. Qiang Liangqing, vice-president of the Board of Directors of Sanda University and professor at Fudan University, Shanghai, Xiamen, November 1995. Other Shanghai private *gaoxiao* are examined in Xinhua, 'Shanghai opens more nongovernmental colleges', FBIS-CHI-93-219, 16 November 1993, p. 50; and 'Non-state colleges approved in Shanghai, Guangzhou', *China Daily*, 5 June 1995, p. 3, in FBIS-CHI-93-108, 8 June 1993, p. 31.
29. Interview with Hou Defu, July 1995.

30. Tilak, 1991.
31. Geiger, 1987.
32. Cheng Kai-ming, 1994a.
33. CCP, 1985.
34. Policies and Law Department, SEdC, 1993, p. 6.
35. CCP Central Committee and State Council, 1993.
36. CCP Central Committee and State Council, 1993, Article 16.
37. Pepper, 1995.
38. This has been reported by several local education officials during the authors' various field trips in 1995–96.
39. Article 19 and article 25, *Education Law of the People's Republic of China*, April 1995.
40. Christiansen, 1996; Cheng Kai-ming, 1995a; Lamontagne and Ma Rong, 1995.
41. National Centre for Educational Development Research, 1996, p. 13.
42. Lewin and Xu Hui, 1992, p. 5.
43. Yin Qiping and G. White, 1994, pp. 10–2.
44. Interview with Hu Daibai, president of Huanghe University of Science and Technology, November 1995.
45. Interview with Hu Daibai, November 1995.
46. Cheng Kai-ming, 1996b.
47. Mok, 1996.
48. Cheng Kai-ming, 1996a.
49. Interview, Niu and Hou, July 1995.
50. Kong, 1993.
51. *Guangdong yearbook 1994.*
52. *Guangdong yearbook 1994.*
53. *Guangzhou Ribao*, various issues, March 1995; Liang, 1993.
54. Mok, 1997a; Mok and Chan, 1996.
55. Cheung and Iu, 1995.
56. Observation during field visits conducted in Guangdong province, 1995 and 1996.
57. Articles 19, 25 and chapter 7, *Education Law of the People's Republic of China*, April 1995.
58. Zhu Yimin, 1996.
59. Qu Tiehua, 1996.
60. Qu Tiehua, 1996, p. 34.
61. Interview with Hou, November 1995.
62. Interview with Hou, November 1995.
63. Le Grand and Robinson, 1984.
64. O'Connor, 1973; Castells, 1978.
65. Habermas, 1976; Offe, 1982; Seldon, 1990; George and Wilding, 1994.
66. Wilding, 1990.
67. Le Grand and Robinson, 1984.
68. N. Johnson, 1990.
69. Walker, 1984.
70. Le Grand, 1983.
71. Le Grand and Bartlett, 1993. This concept is similar to that of 'internal markets'. See Walsh, 1995; Ranson and Stewart, 1994.

72. Le Grand and Bartlett, 1993.
73. Walsh, 1995; Le Grand and Bartlett, 1993.
74. Williamson, 1975; Glennerster, 1991, 1995.
75. Nowadays, Chinese enterprises are required to contribute some portion of their income as educational surcharge to support educational development.
76. Mok, 1996.
77. Cheng Kai-ming, 1994c; Yuan Zhengguo, 1995.
78. Hayhoe, 1996, pp. 225–6.
79. Yin Qiping and G. White, 1994, p. 217.
80. Walford, 1990.
81. D. Johnson, 1987; Hannagan, 1992; Walford, 1990.
82. Bridges and McLaughlin, 1994.
83. Beers and Ellig, 1994; Feeney, 1994; Sontheimer, 1994.
84. Brown, 1995.
85. Hakim, Seidenstat and Bowman, 1994.
86. Beers and Ellig, 1994; Feeney, 1994; Sontheimer, 1994.
87. Brown, 1995; Bridges and McLaughlin, 1994; Pring, 1987.
88. Niklasson, 1996.
89. Niklasson, 1996, pp. 10–1; Bartlett, 1993.
90. Niklasson, 1996, pp. 10–9.
91. DeAngelis, 1996; Sontheimer, 1994; Menge, 1994.
92. Dudley, 1996.
93. World Bank, 1988.
94. Levy, 1986.
95. James, 1992; Tilak, 1991.
96. James, 1992; Tilak, 1991.
97. Edwards *et al.*, 1985; James, 1986; Naismith, 1994.

PART 5
WOMEN IN CHINESE HIGHER EDUCATION

15

Mixed Blessings: Modernizing the Education of Women

Carol C. FAN

INTRODUCTION

This chapter examines the roles of higher educational institutions in shaping women's lives and the influences women have had on education in the PRC. It will analyse women both as students and faculty staff by considering the characteristics and development of the gender gap in higher education within historical and cultural contexts. Through an empirical analysis based on recent national surveys and other data, it will investigate the political and economic, as well as social and cultural factors, that inhibit the participation and achievement of women in Chinese higher education.[1]

Education has been a central focus of Chinese women seeking to improve their condition, to find alternate roles and to raise their status. Higher education, an international indicator of status for women, imparts skills that create options for women economically, socially and politically. Globally, women's professional advancement is more closely linked to their educational attainment than it is for men's. Men use their educational credentials for entry to jobs and then rely on experience and connections for advancement. For women, formal credentials remain critical throughout their working lives. Women's access to higher education was one of the most dynamic forces for social change in China. It directly challenged the existing social structure and widely accepted ideas about the roles, careers and status of women. Education affects women's opportunities in work.

Women do not get the same salary, rank and promotion based on their education as men. If women's credentials are not as good as men's, they can suffer even greater inequality in work.[2]

After the 1949 revolution and women's rights movement, women were described as 'holding up half the sky' in the PRC. CCP leaders politicized women's issues, which helped the Party gain wide support and power. Its ideology was one of a patriarchal socialist body politic in spite of a strong commitment to gender equality.[3] From its inception in 1921 the CCP has included the liberation of women from traditional forms of oppression as part of the CCP agenda in building a socialist society. However, in the revolutionary process, women's liberation was often subordinated to class contradictions. The CCP prioritized class struggle far above the accomplishment of gender equality. It reconstructed a patriarchal family economy and patriarchal consciousness to facilitate the construction of a socialist society. This family solidarity further inhibited prospects for the development of feminist consciousness. Accordingly, 'socialism has not liberated women because a socialist model of production has proven to be compatible with a patriarchal sex-gender system'.[4]

The PRC's transition from a centrally planned economy to a market economy results in complex socio-economic developments in which women face many problems, such as restricted employment opportunities forcing them to stay at home (*funü huijia lun*),[5] the kidnap and sale of women and the reappearance of prostitution.[6] Female tertiary graduates are being turned away from jobs for which they are qualified. There is a marked decrease in women's participation in politics. The 'one child per family' policy instituted by the PRC government in 1979 ushered in a dramatic rise in female infanticide. The growth of the global market has benefited a few urban educated women, but the majority of rural Chinese women continue to be impoverished.

WOMEN AS STUDENTS

According to the 1990 PRC census, only 1.4% of the total population were tertiary graduates (13.6% for Taiwan). Chinese women in the PRC are underrepresented in higher education, accounting for only 30% of the tertiary students, 29.7% of the faculty staff and only 11% of the professors.[7] In Taiwan, 49% of all higher education students and 32.2% of the faculty staff are female,[8] but the more advanced the level of work, the fewer the women.

In 1990 the National Women's Federation in the PRC was given the authority and the funding to undertake a national survey on the position of women. The survey, conducted jointly with National Bureau of Statistics, was based on home interviews with 41 556 subjects — 20 770 (49.48%) men and 20 786 (50.26%) women between ages 18 and 64 — divided equally between urban and rural residents. The questionnaire examined education, occupation, social mobility, opportunities for new jobs and promotion, political participation, marriage and family, family planning and gender identity. The results show that gender inequality exists both in and between urban and rural areas (Table 15.1). Urban women between ages 18 and 64 constituted 7.1% of tertiary graduates, but only 0.4% in rural areas.

Table 15.1
Percentages of men and women who received higher education in the PRC

	URBAN		RURAL	
	Men	Women	Men	Women
College	13	1.9	0.9	0.2
College-plus	6.6	0.5	0.4	0

Source: Tao *et al.*, 1993

Table 15.2
Percentages of male and female students in universities and junior colleges in Taiwan

	Men	Women
Associate	50	50
Bachelor's	55	45
Master's	73	27
Doctor's	84	16
Total	54	46

Sources: *Education statistics of Republic of China, 1994; UNESCO statistical yearbook, 1993*, p. 70

When the PRC was first established, it emphasized education as a vehicle to promote socialism, and the goal for education depended upon state policy. The reform era has led to the decentralization and autonomy of industries, the establishment of private enterprises, and the elimination of the cradle-to-grave state-insured employment system. The issues of gender and class intensified. Rural women were underrepresented in higher education (Table 15.1 and Figure 15.1). The enrolment of female students in higher education first rose from 19.8% in 1949 to 25.3% in 1953, then declined to 22.6% by 1959, but recovered to 26.9% in 1965. During the Cultural Revolution, when universities and schools were closed down for two year or more, there was no record of enrolment from 1963 to 1973. Educational policy changed in 1977 when national entrance examinations were reinstituted. The number of female students dropped slightly, but enrolment slowly recovered to about one-quarter of the total in 1981. It further increased to about a third of total enrolment in 1984. This percentage has not changed much for over two decades, although total university enrolments have expanded by two and a half times since 1980.[9] In Taiwan, however, higher percentages of women are enrolled in all post-secondary programmes (see Table 15.2).

Table 15.3 shows the composition of the freshman class of Beijing University from 1988 to 1992, with almost the same percentage of women every year. The year 1989 saw a lower total enrolment and the percentage of women as high as 35%, because the government declared after the events of 4 June 1989 that students in this particular university needed more political instruction, amounting to an extra year of study. Some high school graduates stayed away from this university and as a result total enrolment dropped that year, but the percentage of women increased.

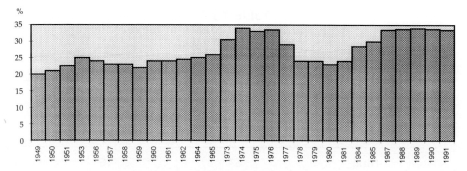

Sources: *Zhonghua Quanguo Funü Lianhehui Yanjiusuo*, 1991, p. 168; *China statistics yearbook* 1992, p. 719

Figure 15.1 Percentage of women's enrolment in higher education in the PRC, 1947–91

A 1991 survey of 'The Status of Women in Contemporary China' initiated by the United Nations Fund for Population Activities and conducted by the Chinese Academy of Social Sciences provides useful data on political participation, access to education, labour participation,

Table 15.3
Proportion of female freshmen entering Beijing University

Year	Total no. of freshmen	Women	%
1988	2260	699	31
1989	737	260	35
1990	1535	521	33
1991	1770	571	32
1992	1810	557	31
Total	8112	2608	32

Source: *Jinri Beida*, 1994, pp. 138, 340–78

occupation, health care, social norms, marriage, family, and decision-making on domestic matters.[10] The data on educational attainment (Tables 15.4 and 15.5) indicate the percentages of urban and rural women who have received undergraduate or postgraduate education. According to the study, the gender gap among undergraduates is obvious in urban areas, but less clear in rural localities. Educational achievement for the age cohorts of 20–24 and 50–54 is lower for both genders. There are more female tertiary graduates, especially rural women, among the 30–35 age cohort (educated during the Cultural Revolution period); the numbers decreased thereafter. The recent drop in enrolment in higher education for both genders suggests that perceived social and economic returns to education may be smaller than before the reform period.

Table 15.4
Percentages of urban men and women who received
higher education in the PRC

Age	College		College-plus	
	Men	Women	Men	Women
20–24	0.28	0.22	0.08	0.13
25–29	3.28	2.20	1.73	1.08
30–34	2.93	1.55	1.56	0.48
35–39	4.39	2.95	1.17	0.54
40–44	3.40	1.70	0.89	0.36
45–49	1.87	1.04	1.58	0.44
50–54	1.49	0.61	1.62	0.79
55+	0.70	0.00	0.92	0.00

Source: Institute of Population Studies, 1994, p. 52

Table 15.5
Percentages of rural men and women who received
higher education in the PRC

Age	College		College-plus	
	Men	Women	Men	Women
20–24	0.04	0.05	0.00	0.00
25–29	0.07	0.08	0.08	0.00
30–34	0.03	0.13	0.00	0.04
35–39	0.12	0.23	0.00	0.04
40–44	0.04	0.09	0.00	0.00
45–49	0.05	0.09	0.01	0.02
50–54	0.00	0.17	0.00	0.01
55+	0.00	0.00	0.00	0.00

Source: Institute of Population Studies, 1994, p. 53

Reasons for gender inequality among students

A cultural explanation offers insight into the gender disparity in higher education enrolment. In spite of a century of revolution, traditional attitudes towards daughters persist — a woman's role is defined in terms of her being a wife and a mother. The birth of a girl was not a happy event, because a daughter could contribute little to her family in terms of material resources or care for her parents in their old age. Thus, parents tried to ensure that their daughters married well. Education for a daughter was deemed irrelevant and even dangerous in that it could jeopardize her chances of a good marriage. This tradition remains strong and the Chinese language continues to structure, constrain and reflect the way Chinese see and express gender. Phrases such as 'men respected, women despised' (*nanzun nubei*), 'when husband calls, wife follows' (*fuchang fusui*) and 'a wife should seek fortune through her husband' (*qiyi fu weigui*) reinforce the superiority of the husband and inferiority of the wife in the family. Furthermore, 'women without talent are virtuous' (*nuzi wucai bian shi de*). A good and capable wife is described as a success arising from inside assistance (*xian neizhu*), but a man's achievements fail to give credit to the assistance and sacrifices of his spouse. Marriage was considered the single most important event in a woman's life because it was her career or livelihood. Once married, a woman becomes the property of her husband's family and is relegated to the world of household and community. A common description of a daughter is 'a commodity on which money has been lost' (*peiqian huo*) and 'a daughter married is like spilled water' (*jiachu de nüer pochu deshui*).

Therefore, some parents were reluctant to invest their resources in someone who eventually would become a member of another family.

There is a powerful pull of marriage and motherhood on college-age women. Chinese girls, like those in other cultures, are socialized into the notion that it is natural and normal for everyone to marry and have children. Some women wish to marry men who are older, better educated and who have better jobs; they worry that too much education may jeopardize their chances of a good marriage. Recently there has been a revival of traditional social values that encourage men to choose marriage partners who are less educated than themselves and who will make sacrifices for their careers. It prompts many young women, especially tertiary students, to seek physical attractiveness and the image of a 'good wife and wise mother' (xianqi liangmu).[11] A recent survey conducted in Hangzhou University asked male and female students about their attitudes towards a dual-career family. Only 28% of the male students but 68% of the women agreed with the statement: 'No matter how successful a woman's career is, she must be a good wife and a wise mother at the same time.' In response to the statement, 'A happy family life is most important to me', an overwhelming majority of both male (91%) and female (89%) students agreed. In addition, 91% of the women hoped their husbands' careers would be more successful than their own. In the same survey conducted in Beijing, 76.5% of female students recognized a contradiction between being successful in their profession and being able to have a happy family life.[12]

Admission policies provide another reason for female enrolment's levelling off for the past 20 years. In recent years, female applicants to institutes of higher learning have also experienced institutional discrimination. There are reports that women are less likely to be admitted even if they are as equally qualified as men. Women who are admitted need higher scores than the men.[13] In one investigation, Henan, Hubei and Hunan provinces all reported a policy of adding two to four extra marks to the scores of female candidates in the National Higher Education Entry Examinations as a form of positive discrimination. Some administrators in tertiary admissions justified this affirmative action by pointing to the career barriers for female graduates.[14] Some senior secondary school teachers counselled female students not to major in science or engineering and to apply to those universities where the expectations placed upon female students were low. Postgraduate admission rates show that preference for men in postgraduate education is even stronger, because university selection committees argue that 'females need no more than a stable job after graduation'.[15]

In the reform era, state-centralized admission and job assignment procedures have been modified to allow for greater autonomy in recruitment on the part of the employer. One result is that the long-standing problem of making full use of the talents of female graduates has further intensified. In 1985, a third of Fudan University graduates who were assigned by the state were rejected by potential employers.[16] The situation has been exacerbated by the fact that the preference for male employees led to adjustments in the enrolment of women in tertiary institutes, rather than confronting the causes of gender discrimination in employment. One cause is the so-called 'distinctive female characteristic'. Female intelligence is considered to be fundamentally different: verbal and intuitive rather than analytical and technical, so not suitable for managerial or other decision-making positions. The other cause is a woman's biological difference and her family roles.[17]

Inflation, which has accompanied economic reform, has resulted in a decline of the real value of education budgets and incomes. To make ends meet, universities must rely on their own money-making efforts, and this affects admission policy. For example, Beijing University's Department of Genetic Engineering admitted only students who paid tuition fees (60 in total).[18] The move towards students' paying their own tuition fees[19] may adversely affect female participation. Recent data suggest that the proportion of rural students in universities is dropping and that the emphasis on self-supporting students is likely to reinforce this trend. It is likely that 'some of the gains of affirmative action over the years would be eroded, particularly for rural students'.[20]

In Chinese rural society, where 70% of the population lives, gender inequality remains most entrenched. Today, most rural Chinese women suffer from poverty, lack of health care, and illiteracy. According to the 1993 census, illiteracy rates for girls in western China are shockingly high: Guizhou, 62.28%; Gansu, 81.48%; Qinghai, 79.30%; and Ningxia, 64.88%.[21] They have no access to good health care, professional training or higher education. Most rural women in the transition period of economic reforms are burdened with increased work as men move away from farms and into industrial work. Furthermore, many rural women participated in the development of industry and enterprises with the privatization of communes to individual families (*baochan daohu*), which in turn would pay tax to the government for the right to cultivate land. To help their mothers shoulder these increased burdens, young daughters drop out of school. In fact 71% of illiterates over the age of 12 are female; of these, 88% are rural women.

State policy since 1949 has decreed equal educational opportunities for men and women, but, until the reform era began, it was the provision of family support — in the form of fewer chores or more private tutoring for sons than daughters — that was the major factor affecting educational opportunities. Survey data of 1991 explain why daughters do not pursue higher degrees. The problem of not being admitted to post-secondary schools and the inability to afford the cost of education apply in urban areas to both men (19.86%) and women (20.62%). But women (3.13%) are three times more likely than men (1.13%) to report that they were also required to take care of younger siblings, while 0.26% of the men and 0.89% of the women did not receive parental encouragement. In the rural regions, 40.7% of the men and 39.9% of the women cite economic reasons; 28.5% of the men but only 14.7% of the women failed the entrance examination. Five times more women than men dropped out of school in order to provide care for siblings; and three times more women than men did not continue schooling because they lacked parental support.[22] One scholar found that 'institutions with high rural enrolments tended to have lower percentages of female participation.... These figures reflected a situation in rural lower secondary schools where girls were not encouraged by their families to enter upper secondary schools and where many dropped out due to the pressures of family needs ... and boys were almost certain to receive greater family support for higher education than girls'.[23] This results in a smaller pool of female applicants for post-secondary schooling and may provide a major explanation of the gender imbalance in university enrolment.

For the urban area, the 1987 One Percent Population Survey examined the presence and persistence of the gender gap in education, employment and occupational attainment.[24] The survey proved the hypothesis that sons receive a larger share of resources than daughters, contributing to the higher probability of a son's enrolment. A related hypothesis is that daughters who have no brothers receive greater encouragement to continue in school than those who do have. The not-so-surprising finding of this empirical study is that a father's education and profession have a strong influence on his daughter's/daughters' chances of receiving tertiary education: the gender gap in enrolment being narrower among students whose fathers are more educated and in professional occupations. It could be that education influences fathers to treat their children in a more egalitarian way. This survey concluded that women's disadvantage is most evident in their severe underrepresentation in powerful positions.

Even when admitted to higher education institutions, women face obstacles. Gender discrimination exists within the institutions. Female students are often streamed into traditional female studies and professions, and they often receive less attention from teachers than male students do. According to a sample survey conducted by the National Women's

Association in five engineering universities in Beijing, 36.9% of the answers from 622 female students point to the fact that professors pay more attention in the classroom to male students.[25] 'In both rural and urban cases, the belief that girls were intellectually, physically and emotionally inferior to boys — an old belief newly clothed in scientific garb — helps to legitimize the limiting of educational and career opportunities for girls.'[26] One explanation for these institutional barriers is the lack of role models. Because there are few female faculty staff members, female students generally lack the interaction, identification and support that their presence could otherwise promote.

RETURNS TO EDUCATION

Leaders of both the women's movement and the CCP have long argued that the most important step for women's emancipation is the reintroduction of the entire female population into the labour force. CCP leaders believed that the establishment of socialism would inevitably result in the liberation of women and, following Engels' theory, predicted that improvement in women's status would surely follow their participation in production. Simone de Beauvoir, in a criticism of historical materialism, argued that gender inequality was an eventual outcome of co-option between feminism and socialism. She explained that Engels had tried to reduce the antagonism between the sexes to class conflict and she concluded that this thesis was simply untenable. 'For one thing there is no biological basis for the separation of classes... What is still more serious, woman cannot in good faith be regarded simply as a worker; for her reproductive function is as important as her productive capacity, no less in the social economy than in the individual life.'[27] For Chinese women the reproductive function is the single most important role assigned to them by traditional Chinese culture. Confucian tradition emphasizes ancestor worship as an expression of the continuity of lineage. This emphasis on the continuity of the family line led to the placing of great value on producing sons.[28] The paramount importance of lineage constructed politically the single most important identity for Chinese women, transforming all social and economic relationships associated with it, and generating cultural practices that have had an adverse and even deadly impact on Chinese women, including many closely successive pregnancies, the practice of polygamy, child marriage and female infanticide.

Educational attainment, especially a university education, has the most substantial effect on employment. For 30 years, the policy of low wages and high employment gave urban women quantitatively the same access to employment as their male counterparts. According to the 1990 census, the number of women in the industrial labour force increased from 610 000 (7% of the total work force) in 1949 to 56 million (38%) of the total employed population.

However, economic reform has led to decentralization and autonomy of industries and elimination of the state job assignment system. Enterprises are now expected to be responsible for their own profits and losses, and work-units exercise their discretion in hiring. This often results in increasing discrimination against female tertiary graduates in spite of their academic qualifications.[29] A decrease in the number of female cadres, and difficulties in female tertiary graduates being allocated jobs, became major problems for urban women.[30] Compared to men, female workers are seen as less productive and cost more in labour protection expenses. There is not too much difference in salaries between men and women or from one level to another. But differences exist in other non-cash incentives, such as housing, food, child care, medical service, bus passes, funeral support, bathing facilities, sports, entertainment activities, libraries and the education of children in better school districts. There is no national health system, the employing unit being responsible for its own employees' health and maternity provision, labour insurance and welfare benefits.[31]

It was the female workers who bore the brunt of the drive to reform the labour structure. Women have constituted 62.5% of redundant workers, which amounts to 21% of all female workers.[32] Many managers felt that the system of protective benefits for female workers constituted an example of the *daguofan* and should be abolished.[33] Women are the first to be fired by struggling state firms and the last to be hired by the vibrant private sector. State figures show that women make up 70% of the 20 million workers made idle by enterprise reform. 'It's clear that there's been a great reversal with the reform era. Things are going backwards,' said Wang Xingjuan who runs the PRC's only nationwide women's hot line. She said that as government supervision wanes, employers — who are mostly men — are reverting to traditional, patriarchal ideas that women should not work and fear that female employees will quit to marry or cost money for maternity and child care.[34] The All-China Women's Federation, which has conducted studies on the attitudes of enterprise officials towards hiring female managers, reports a factory manager's reasons for not accepting female tertiary graduates:[35]

1.   Female graduates are too pampered and proud. If you displease them, they are likely to make trouble. It is better to hire temporary help, since they are obedient and easy to handle.

2.   Both married and single women have many bothersome demands: married women want housing, then there is pregnancy, childbirth ... and child care. The unmarried ones have a high opinion of themselves, but they still expect you to find them a marriage partner.
3.   If she is talented and you promote her, there is always the suspicion that you are attracted to her. When the personnel bureau last asked me if I would accept a woman, I finally conceded by saying, 'Okay, but send me an ugly one.' When the comrade at the bureau laughed and said, 'You then have to assume the responsibility when you fail to find her a husband.' I also laughed and said, 'In that case, you'd better not assign any woman to our factory.'

Class and geographic origins are other factors for job assignment for graduates. As a vice-president of a tertiary institute in Beijing observed, most undergraduate students now originated from urban senior secondary schools and it was only the children of cadres and intellectuals who could go to college. Because of their origins, he said, his students all wanted provincial jobs at least, and were not interested in openings at the county level or below, where needs were now great.[36] At Beijing University, one middle-ranking official complained that she found it increasingly difficult to place female graduates who studied philosophy, history or Chinese. Although many work-units such as factories, secondary schools and county offices needed staff with skills the women possessed, the Beijing University graduates had higher expectations and refused to take jobs with lower-level units. In order to train more marketable graduates, the university started a new 'secretarial class' run by the Chinese Department to produce graduates with clerical skills. Students majoring in foreign languages such as Spanish and Japanese were required, at the same time, to study English, a language more in demand by employers.[37]

WOMEN AS FACULTY STAFF IN HIGHER EDUCATION

Women constitute about one-third of the tertiary faculty staff in the PRC (Figure 15.2), an almost threefold increase from 11% in 1950 to 29.1% in 1990. In China, teaching has historically been considered an appropriate calling for women, and the state system of job assignment provided female graduates with relatively equal opportunities with men.

The representation of female faculty staff in Chinese higher education is higher than other Asian countries like Japan and Korea,[38] but lower than in Taiwan (Figure 15.3 and Table 15.6). In Taiwan, the number of female professors increased fourfold from 7.88% in 1950 to 32.99% in 1994.[39] In the PRC, women are better represented at the lower ranks, but the discrepancies between men and women in the posts of professor and associate professor are comparable. Female faculty staff comprise about 18.7% of full professors in humanities, 15.7% in social sciences, 6.3% in sciences and technology; and for the rank of associate professor, 36.5% in humanities, 25.4% in social sciences and 13.2% in sciences and technology. The rank of instructor in humanities and social sciences has an almost equal number of men and women, but this is not the case in science and technology. The only position in which women outnumber men in humanities and social sciences is that of teaching assistant. Women's lower participation in science and technology contributes to their disadvantaged status, as will be seen later in this section.

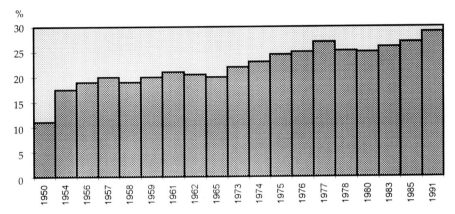

Sources: *Zhonghua Quanguo Funü Lianhehui Yanjiusuo*, 1991, p. 174; *China statistics yearbook* 1992, p. 719

Figure 15.2 Percentage of female faculty members in higher education in the PRC, 1950–91

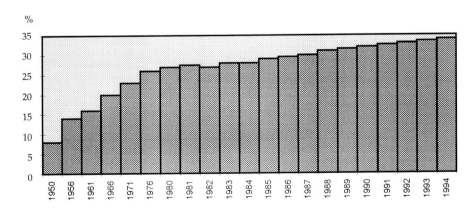

Source: *Education Statistics of the Republic of China 1994*

Figure 15.3 Percentage of female faculty members in higher education institutions in Taiwan, 1950–94

Table 15.6
Number of full-time staff in universities and colleges in Taiwan, 1994–95

		Humanities	Social Sciences	Science and Technology
Professor				
	Male	972	558	23285
	Female	224	104	154
Associate Professor				
	Male	1391	1011	3433
	Female	801	345	524
Lecturer				
	Male	5	2	4
	Female	3	0	0
Instructor				
	Male	969	373	1073
	Female	908	358	588
Teaching Assistant				
	Male	384	132	720
	Female	652	522	679
Others				
	Male	612	3	6
	Female	243	0	0
Grand Total				
	Male	4333	2079	7521
	Female	2831	1329	1945
	Total	7164	3408	9466

The representation of women in a faculty varies conversely with their rank. Their presence does not necessarily mean empowerment as they are still distant from decision-making. For example, in 1988, when women accounted for 28% of all faculty in China, they made up 34% of the teaching assistants, 36% of the instructors, 29% of the lecturers, 19% of the associate professors and only 11% of the full professors. They served as only 8% of the advisers for Master's students and 3% of the supervisors for doctoral students.

Data for 1991 suggest that more women are found among younger faculty staff — 37% of those under 30 and 30% of those between 31 and 40.[40] The overwhelming majority of female professors were appointed after the economic reforms began.[41] The increase in female faculty staff in part results from a process of default, in that many male staff have left for more lucrative careers in business or have gone abroad for further studies.[42] However, the women's future is insecure because relatively few of them have higher degrees compared to their male counterparts.[43] They are expected to take on heavy teaching loads and assume middle- and lower-rank administrative work. These factors deter them from competing with male colleagues on an equal basis for promotion. A sample survey in Shanghai on preferred occupational categories found that teaching received a very weak endorsement — way behind the first choice of managerial positon. In traditional China, however, scholars and officials were much respected, while merchants were the lowest on the social scale. So the survey suggests that the social status of teachers had dropped to a new low and that their financial plight is worse after economic reform.[44]

Beijing University, the PRC's most prestigious academic institution, illustrates the pattern of female participation in higher education (Figure 15.4). Founded in 1898, it became in 1920 the first national university to admit female students.[45] At present none of the top-rank administrators are women. Women number 109 out of the 718 full professors. Female faculty staff show a strong presence in traditional female fields, representing 57% in the English Department, 49% in Russian language, 46% in Marxism studies, and 51% in library science. There are 36 physicians on campus: 31 are women; the chief is a man.[46] The higher the academic rank, the fewer the women and most women, are clustered on lower levels such as research assistant, assistant specialist and lecturer.

In pursuit of economic reform, higher learning institutions are encouraged to supplement their state budgets with private income, the proceeds of which are to be shared among faculty staff in the form of bonuses.[47] Staff have to conduct research and publish, generate income-producing services and serve as consultants. Male colleagues are in a better position to meet the new demands and women are usually assigned supportive roles in teaching and research. Many female staff are in the humanities, which, except for English language, have very limited scope for marketable and profit-making projects. A preliminary sample survey in three national key universities — Beijing University, Beijing Normal University and Qinghua University — in 1986 provides valuable statistics on the distribution of rank and degree of marketability of female faculty members. Beijing University is a comprehensive university of arts, sciences and the humanities; Beijing Normal University focuses mainly on teacher education; and Qinghua University is renowned for engineering and sciences. Beijing University had 38.6% female teaching staff, 11.6% female full professors and 24.7% female associate professors. Beijing Normal University had 34.7% female teaching staff, 11% female full professors and 37.4% female associate professors. By contrast, at Qinghua University, with its highly marketable orientation towards science and technology, only 2.6% of its professors and 16.8% of its associate professors were female.[48]

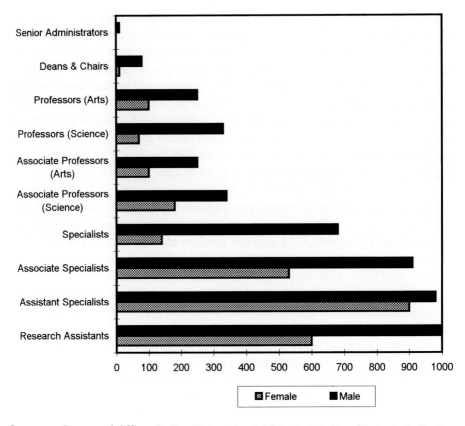

Sources: Personnel Office, Beijing University, 1994; *Jinri Beijing* (Today's Beijing),
          1994, pp. 138, 340–78

Figure 15.4 Faculty members of Beijing University, 1994

Science and technology is one of the Four Modernizations, and the educational reforms that were designed to maximize economic productivity completely reversed the former institutional separation of science and technology and of research and teaching in the institutions of higher learning.[49] New interdisciplinary studies among the natural sciences, the applied sciences, and technology arose, accompanied by free competition for research funding. But various surveys indicate the underrepresentation of women in influential posts in this field.[50] For decades the prestigious and powerful Chinese Academy of Sciences resisted admitting women as members. A number of renowned female scholars were finally elected in 1980: among them was Xie Xide, a professor of physics and president of Fudan University — the only female president of a tertiary institution in the PRC.[51] In 1994, the Chinese Academy of Sciences selected only 30 women (5.3%) as members (*xuebu weiyuan / yuanshi*).[52]

Overall, as a leader in women's studies in the PRC laments, economic reform and modernization have suddenly intensified women's problems. Women's progress seems to have reversed and women's liberation is in a state of crisis.[53]

Reasons for gender inequality in faculty staffing

Statistics around the globe indicate that women in academia are in positions with heavy teaching loads and high administrative demands. As faculty members, they are segregated in the tasks they perform, the places they teach, the fields they occupy and the ranks they hold. Across all dimensions, women receive lower compensation. They are located not only in less prestigious tertiary institutions, but also in less powerful fields and disciplines.[54]

Advancement in the hierarchy of a university requires a major commitment of time, effort and an insider's insight into the formal and informal rules and regulations of the academy. Many women find difficulty in meeting these conditions. Understanding and manipulating the informal norms require initiation into the powerful collegial networks that control the profession. Women are less likely than men to be sponsored by influential, established scholars who can help them in powerful collegial networks.[55] This lack of *guanxi*[56] adversely influences the career growth of academic women and deters Chinese women even more.[57] Compounding the situation in the PRC is the lack of support groups for women. The PRC has virtually no autonomous female faculty groups, as organizations are closely monitored by the CCP.[58]

While female faculty staff are found to be competent in teaching, they lag behind in research and publications. Since these latter two categories hold much weight in promotion decisions, women, despite their competence in teaching and lower-level administrative work, do not advance as quickly up the academic ladder as men.[59] Their participation remains contingent upon the ability to find adequate arrangements for the family and child care. Men fulfil their family responsibility by doing well in their career. Most Chinese take on little of the housework or child care. Women's roles have expanded, but traditional duties to family and home have not diminished. As one observer noted, Chinese female academics felt that ' ...men in the same ranks ... tended to be promoted first, partly because they had more time for research and writing, and partly due to a general bias in favour of male faculty'.[60]

Likewise, accommodation causes dissatisfaction, as female faculty members have to attain the rank of associate professor before being given housing on their own campus, whereas men only have to be teaching assistants.[61] Married female faculty staff are often not considered as individuals; instead, they are expected to get housing through their husbands. This often means a long commute from the apartment in the husband's work-unit to their own institute, further complicating child care arrangements. The expression 'two persons to guarantee the success of one'(*er bao yi*) refers to the idea that the success of the husband is ensured by sacrificing the wife's career. Now it refers to an academic couple who must concentrate on the husband's career development, as his (not her) promotion would improve housing conditions.

There are other discriminatory policies against women which hinder their full participation in higher education. As noted above, many women are assigned to support services and administrative work. Also, the low proportion of academic women is partially due to the early retirement system. In 1996, the compulsory retirement age, except for those in the top positions, was 60 for men and 55 for women.[62] Another reason is that the majority of women in the PRC do not evidence an interest in politics nor voice a consciousness of women's rights. Because female faculty staff generally lack an awareness and knowledge of, as well as an interest in women's issues, there is a lack of scholarly attention paid to women's studies. This is in sharp contrast to the USA, for instance, where women's studies 'is at the centre of a revolution whose aim is nothing less than the transformation of the university'.[63] In the 1980s, women's studies sprang up into existence all over the Chinese intellectual landscape to reconstruct the significance of women as a social category. In 1995, 61 'Women's Studies Institutes' were serving as research centres to promote research on women's issues by providing organizational support, and, as a result, exerting some influence in the PRC and abroad. However, only the International Women's Institute in Zhengzhou University, founded in 1993, offered an undergraduate curriculum on women's studies.[64]

CONCLUSION

From the end of the nineteenth century until the present, Chinese women's education has been the construction of men — mostly privileged intellectuals and high officials. As women have gained access to formal education they have been exposed to a systematized view of themselves, first as inferior, then as different. Current state policy, male perspectives in education, the dominance of men in faculty staff and administration, conflicts between gender role and career, and the stereotyping of women's intelligence and ability are all factors that conspire to allow women on campus a mere physical presence, not intellectual power or full participation.

Chinese state policy in theory provides equal educational opportunities for men and women. However, Chinese academic women continue to lag behind men in overall participation, status and rewards. Rapid economic growth and its side-effect of inflation have since 1980 forced many institutions of higher learning to search for profitable programmes. This marketization has widened the gap between men and women, between urban and rural and between coastal and inland areas in the PRC.

In 1992 the NPC passed a law to protect women's rights in education and work. It specified that 'educational institutions and pertinent departments should ensure that females and males are treated with equality when it comes to starting school, progressing from a lower-level school to a higher one, assigning jobs on graduation, awarding academic degrees, and selecting people for overseas study'.[65] Yet, another section of the law offers the escape clause: 'except for certain work categories or positions that are unfit for women'.[66] With the reforms in job assignment procedures since the 1980s, educational institutions have little control over the employment of their graduates. Therefore, many female students and graduates face discrimination in employment. The Programme for the Development of Chinese Women 1995–2000 Plan promulgated in 1995 by the NPC attempts to develop women's education by wiping out illiteracy among young and middle-aged women; starting universal nine-year compulsory education by the end of the century; increasing the participation of women in political affairs; and improving women's institutions.[67] Other steps include raising women's status by abating job discrimination, eliminating female infanticide, and stopping the buying and selling of girls and women. Now the challenge is not in enacting laws but in implementing them, so that they take effect in the daily lives of women. Chinese women have been struggling for equal access to various levels of education for over a century. The development of higher education for women has made considerable progress. Yet there is still a long way to go for women's full participation and true equality between men and women in education, employment, housing, retirement and other benefits.

Improvement in the system of child care and child care leave is most urgent as well as fundamental changes in traditional attitudes pertaining to women and their roles as wives, mothers and workers. A woman should not be forced to choose between the child she loves and the work she needs.

In higher education, networks and mentors can help female faculty staff connect with other female academics, so as to facilitate information exchange, collaboration, career planning and strategizing, professional support, and access to upward mobility. The mainstream curriculum in key universities and colleges needs to be transformed to include women's studies, an extended academic arm of the contemporary movement for women's liberation.[68] Faculty staff in women's studies can help female students to become aware of the changes in society and in women's lives, and help them plan their careers and prepare them for their future by counselling and advising them. Further, women's studies can provide the necessary energy, enthusiasm and intellectual leadership for equal access to higher education in the PRC.

NOTES

1. Main sources of data are *Zhonghua Quanguo Funü Lianhehui Yanjiusuo* (Institute for Research on Women, All China Women's Federation), 1991; Tao *et al.* 1993; Institute of Population Studies, 1994, pp. 52–3; *Jinri Beida* (Today's Beijing University), 1994, pp. 138, 340–78; *Education statistics of the Republic of China, 1993*, p. 111; *Index on education statistics of the Republic of China, 1994*, p. 34; with additional data provided by Personnel Office, Beijing University, 1994.
2. Fox, 1984, p. 239.
3. C.C. Fan, 1996, p. 2.
4. Stacey, 1983, p. 266.
5. Tan, 1994, pp. 65–73.
6. *Beijing Review* 38, no. 36, 4–10 September 1995, pp. 6–13.
7. Han, 1988, p. 41.
8. *Education statistics of the Republic of China 1994* and *UNESCO statistical yearbook 1993*, p. 70.
9. *Education statistics yearbook of China 1989* showed that the number of students enrolled in higher education increased from 284 816 in 1980 to 705 345 in 1988.
10. The Institute of Population Studies conducted a survey on 4509 sample households from urban areas and 4524 from rural communities of couples living together with the wives' age ranging from 20 to 54 in Guangdong, Jilin, Ningxia, Shandong, Shanghai and Shaanxi in 1991. Both the wives and the husbands were asked the same questions except for an additional section on fertility for the women. Specific data examined women's access to public resources, their age when they first went to school, length of schooling and educational level, age at first employment, reason for hire, type of occupation and salary.
11. Tan, 1994.
12. Xu Min, 1993. For career-minded tertiary students, there seems to be a growing trend to defer marriage. A 1987 survey of ten Shanghai higher education institutions revealed that about one-third of female graduate students did not have a potential spouse, even though they had reached the age of 25–35. See Hooper, 1991, p. 362.

13. *Zhongguo Funü Bao* (China Women's News), 22 September 1986, p. 1.
14. Hayhoe, 1996, p. 156.
15. Sheng *et al.*, 1990.
16. Chen Ziju, 1984.
17. Hooper, 1991, p. 359.
18. *Renmin Ribao,* overseas edition, 21 February 1993, p. 3.
19. See Chapter 12 by Zhang Minxuan in this volume.
20. Hayhoe, 1991, p. 226.
21. Zhou Wei, Zhang Tiedao and Liu Wenpu, 1994, p. 15.
22. Institute of Population Studies, pp. 73–4.
23. Hayhoe, 1996, pp. 179–80.
24. Bauer *et al.*, 1992, pp. 347–9.
25. Sheng *et. al.*, 1990, pp. 39–40.
26. Honig and Hershatter, 1988, p. 20.
27. De Beauvoir, 1974, pp. 64–5.
28. According to Mencius, '[t]here are three things which are unfilial and to have no posterity is the greatest of these', (translated in Legge, 1935, p. 313). Chinese classical scholars interpret this to mean that the most important goal of every man is to have a male heir. Mencius does not specify the other two unfilial things.
29. *Zhongguo Funü Bao* (China Women's News), 27 February 1985 , p. 1.
30. Chen Shaoxiong, 1990. See also Jiang, 1988, pp. 12–3.
31. Since 1987, there have been six types of wages: basic wages (time-rate and piece-rate) 67.7 %, bonuses 14.9%, supplementary wages 3%, subsidies 14.3 %, overtime, and other wages (the latter two accounting for only 3%). See Bian, 1994, pp. 13, 48–9 and 145–75.
32. Women's Work Department, All-China Federation of Trade Unions, conducted a survey that examined 660 enterprises from the end of 1988 through the beginning of 1989 in *Jingji Cankao* (Economic Reference), 22 March 1987, p. 1.
33. Rosen, 1992.
34. Reported by Reuters, 'Repressed women in China fighting back' in *Honolulu Star Bulletin*, 11 August 1994, pp. A-7.
35. *Funü* (Women) 1988, no. 5, pp. 12–3.
36. Pepper, 1990, p. 154.
37. See Reuter's report (note 34).
38. According to *UNESCO statistics yearbook 1993*, in 1989, only 15% of higher education faculty members in Japan were women and 18% in Korea.
39. *Education statistics of the Republic of China*, 1993, p. 31.
40. *Education statistics yearbook of China* 1991–1992, pp. 32–3.
41. *Education statistics yearbook of China* 1991–1992, p. 54.
42. See Chu and Ju, 1993, p. 112.
43. Ruth Hayhoe and her team discovered this fact in their interviews with 38 female scholars who had returned from abroad. See Hayhoe, 1996, p. 131.
44. Chu and Ju, 1993, p. 112. The survey was carried out in a stratified probability sample of 2000 respondents in Shanghai, China's largest metropolis with a population of almost seven million, and Qingpu, a rural county outside Shanghai, with a population of 440 000 in 1985. On the special choices of ideal jobs, the survey asked the respondents to select only one preferred occupational category among eight. The results: 'managerial position' received the highest

endorsement and 'political, party cadre' the lowest. 'College/high school teacher' constituted only 5.2%, ranked the sixth.

45. In 1920 when Beijing University admitted three female students, someone asked President Cai Yuan-pei, 'Did you get approval from the Ministry of Education?' President Cai replied, 'There is no rule to keep them out of the University, I don't see any reason to check with the Ministry of Education.' See C.C. Fan, 1992, p. 129.
46. *Jinri Beida* (Today's Beijing University), 1993, pp. 363–73.
47. Henze, 1992; Yin Qiping and G. White, 1994.
48. Sheng *et al.* 1990, pp. 14–64.
49. See Law, 1995.
50. A survey of 1342 scientists and technical workers covering 12 provinces and major cities, conducted in 1991–92 by the Education Bureau of Chinese Academy of Sciences, showed 68.3% of female scientists had college or graduate degrees. But only 3.1 % occupied the highest rank, 28.1 % the second highest rank and 41.2% middle-rank positions in government and research institutes. *Woguo nukeji rencai de tanshuo* (A study of women in science and technology), in *Funü, yanjiu luncong* (Collection of women's studies), 1994, vol. 1, pp. 24–34. A survey of 4800 female scientists and technical workers covering nine provinces and major cities conducted in 1985 also indicated that the higher the position, the fewer the women: the majority being engaged in supporting roles, with the exception of the health sector. See Rosen, 1992, pp. 263–4.
51. Human Resources Research Institute, State Science and Technology Commission, 1986.
52. *Beijing Review*, 4–10 September 1995, p. 9.
53. Li Xiaojiang, 1994, pp. 377, 380– 2.
54. Fox, 1984, p. 230.
55. O'Leary and Mitchell, 1990.
56. *Guanxi* could include a friend, a neighbour, a former teacher, a relative, a former superior, or any relationship one may find useful someday. The more key government offices and social sectors one's network covers, the more social influence one has at one's disposal and the more easily one can get things done. See Chu and Ju, 1993, pp. 150–1. Also see M. Yang Mei-hui, 1994; Yan Yunxiang, 1996.
57. Davis and Astin, 1990.
58. Faculty members who return from studies abroad admitted that they had never known of a female college faculty group in China to discuss common concerns of women. See Hayhoe, 1996, p. 239.
59. Hayhoe, 1996, p. 131.
60. Hayhoe, 1996, p 242.
61. Hayhoe, 1996, p 242.
62. Sheng *et al.*, 1990, p. 61.
63. E.T. Beck, 1990.
64. See Chapter 16 by Maria Jaschok in this volume.
65. 'Law protecting women's rights interests', Beijing Xinhua Domestic Service in Chinese, 7 April 1991, translated in FBIS, no. 92, 14 April 1992, p. 18.
66. 'Law protecting women's rights interests'. See note 65.
67. *China Daily*, 6 September 1995, p. 1.
68. Stimpson, 1987.

16

Chinese Educational Reforms and Feminist Praxis: On Ideals, Process and Paradigm

Maria JASCHOK

INTRODUCTION

This chapter discusses the birth, life and closure of China's first institution of higher education with a women-centred programme, the Zhengzhou International Women's Institute.[1] The Institute closed in March 1995, 22 months into its existence, due to larger political issues to be discussed below, but also due to internal dysfunction and ultimately insurmountable contradictions among the parties which established it. Situated in Henan province, the heartland of China, the Institute was set up in 1993 in the provincial capital Zhengzhou by a group of women who were inspired by Ren Hua, a well-known voice among intellectuals in Chinese women's studies, to devote themselves to the purpose of 'education of dedicated women, in the nurturing of their maturation and growth, and in the facilitation of a public career-oriented competence and confidence'.[2] As a result of national educational reforms, the Institute was able to establish itself as an independent, *minjian* (non-governmental) school. This status allowed for contract hiring of staff and for independence in financial management. It made possible a most avant-garde experiment: a women-centred Institute combining calls for raising female subjective consciousness with the honing of technical and cultural skills, run independently (*duli*) of but within the educational system. Here features of the *xin tizhi* (reformed system) were combined with the *jiu tizhi* (traditional university and women's educational system) in a constellation of power, authority, idealism and ambition which was to prove as a source of inspiration, but also ultimately of destructive tension.

Participant — Observation

Between September 1993 and March 1995, the author participated in the creation and administration of the Institute. Nearly two years of experience, observations and lengthy conversations resulted in daily journal entries, something which was actively encouraged by colleagues to the extent that they even initiated some conversations in order to ensure their voice in the documentation. This ethnography records the establishment and presence of a radically new women's institute and its vanguard role in bringing education to women and women into education.[3] I expected to be documenting course outlines and curricular blueprints, but in the end, I found myself recording the problematic issues of *fenli* (separateness).[4] These issues encompassed separation as a dialectical relationship between traditional ingrained dependency and the clarion call for a new era of self-determination. It became a new educational text and an educational process carried by enduring authority patterns; and it was tempered by the constraints and structures of power embedded in the culture of a *danwei*, the Chinese work-unit.

The establishment of the International Women's Institute permitted the study of change in a specific ideological space and over a period of time sufficiently long to allow for the documentation of adversities of change. This experiment also brought together into a single *danwei* representatives of different parts of the women's movement — the Maoist-sponsored women's education carried out by the All-China Women's Federation (ACWF) as official executive organ, and, in contrast, the Institute as leading the new era of *minjian* institutions.

Establishing an academic and political space in which women's education could be revolutionized was made especially difficult by the conservative environment of Henan, at that time only just beginning a process of 'opening up' to economic investment opportunities. Strong pro-market forces were battling a predominantly native and past-oriented value system, and an unwavering tight control by the state over ideological and political sites of friction and dissent.[5]

ON MODERNIZATION AND WOMEN'S EDUCATION: MULTIPLE VOICES

To place the birth and development of the Women's Institute, it is first of all necessary to present leading Chinese reflective voices and the emergence of a revisionist periodization of women's history. The much hailed and lauded modernization of the PRC's economy has brought women only uneven benefits.[6] Disadvantaged by a womb-centred culture and patriarchal expectations of women's place in the domestic sphere, women are ill-prepared for the newly competitive pressures from a growing market society. Their predicaments have been recognized to require separate and systematic attention.[7] Matters are made worse by a worrying trend in education, as discussed elsewhere in this volume.[8] A strong interventionist role for the government to counteract undiscriminating market forces through strong affirmative actions and education in raising cultural and technical skills has been advocated as imperative by the leadership of the ACWF and independent scholars alike. The development of the many women's colleges, women's studies departments, and women's vocational classes inside and outside the ACWF structure over these last years testifies to an astonishing enterprising spirit and rapid growth of independent and semi-independent organizations.[9]

But the debate over education became politicized when independent gender activists challenged the official functional educational paradigm to insist on the reappraisal of education, through a conscious rejection of past educational models and their underpinning political culture. Calls for the nurturing of female self-awareness (*zijue*) and for a subjectivity unfettered by traditional dependency (*yilaixing*) attest to the absence of former models in current education. The argument that women can assume their rightful place only in modernity requires continued theoretical advances (beyond the confines of orthodox Marxist class analysis) and official tolerance of new educational structures to facilitate 'collective female development'.[10]

Reconstructing a history of dependency

The defining criterion of women's dependency, *yilaixing*, has become the critical measure by which a new periodization of Chinese women's history is challenging the historical framework of an orthodox scholarship.[11] Marxist-Leninist historians, in whose thinking women's liberation can only be the outcome of national liberation and state-sponsored organization, see the victory of the CCP in 1949 as the historical turning point for women. The time before Liberation is characterized as steeped in feudal and patriarchal oppression, and the time after 1949 as the realization of the liberation of women through appropriate legal instruments and socio-political movements and campaigns.

In contrast, the revisionist historians place the turning point in 1978 with the beginning of a liberalization of Chinese society under Deng Xiaoping. In terms of this framework of reference, state monopoly over goals and means of liberation before 1978 resulted in a state of collective female dependency and acquiescence to a series of official implementations of sexual egalitarianism from the top, spearheaded by the ACWF. In this phase, undoubtedly fundamental legal and social rights for women were achieved, but at a price. In an exercise of patriarchal prerogatives, sources of domination and control over women merely shifted from family and husband to the state and its various executive organs, but left women's essential nature, *suzhi*, intact.

After 1978, during the early phase of the New Era (as distinct from the preceding era of women's liberation in the wake of the May Fourth Movement of 1919), the dependency of women was questioned as its consequences for women collectively and individually were beginning to be explored in women's literature. As *nuxing kunhuo* (the perplexed state of women), these new insights were incorporated into a newly emerging body of theoretical work by Chinese gender scholars in women's studies.[12] Important advances by scholars contributed to a crucial trend in the women's movement of the New Era, namely to *bentuhua* — understood to mean indigenization, not nationalism — and a conscious separation from universalist trends in Western feminist scholarship.

A spontaneous (*zifa*) women's movement developed in the 1980s in a symbiotic relationship with scholarly research and theoretical advances. In 1985 the first women's research centres were set up at Beijing University and Zhengzhou University. In the sphere of publishing, in the organization of interest groups as *minjian* (independent grass roots) structures, and in organizational work at all levels of rural and urban societies, a marked tendency towards pluralism was seen by some scholars as the first signs of a gradual undermining of the monopoly of the 'official flagship of the CCP', the ACWF. Despite the fact that as early as 1984 the ACWF had sought to retain credibility by setting up women's research departments at all levels of its organization, it began to lose its pre-eminence with the growing dichotomization of women's political culture. During this period spontaneity overcame planning; *duli*, independence, foiled dependency on Party and State; pluralism conquered centrally steered women's politics.[13]

While the women's movement of the New Era was created on the basis of the comprehensive legal and social *gaizao* (transformation) effected after

1949 under a socialist system, the new women's movement is not a natural continuation of the early state-sponsored women's movement. Rather, it is rooted in specific social circumstances and is representative of specific interests and viewpoints voiced by women themselves. The discourse on the nature of *jiefang*, liberation, is becoming one of multiple voices. With this the question of legitimacy of representation of women's interests and of means of furthering these interests (importantly, through education) arises — making the state *one* of the parties, not *the* defining party, in a potentially deeply challenging political debate.

THE INSTITUTE: CREATION AND CONFLICTING AGENDA

The Institute owed its existence to opportunities granted under the liberalization of the educational system and owed its *de facto* closure 22 months into its operation, in March 1995, to vacillations between centripetal and disintegrative forces in the system. Structural changes necessary to meet demands of a modernizing and increasingly diverse consumer society met impediments from within a recalcitrant culture. Insecurity over personal consequences along with support generated for reform as implemented through the system of *guanxi* were complicating the progress of reform.

Ambiguities intrinsic to the dismantling of an authoritarian state structure and culture were exacerbated in the course of 1993 and 1994 by a politicization of 'women's issues' in the run-up to the 4th International Women's Conference (in September 1995) in Beijing. The government's fears over control of the 'non-governmental organizations' (NGO) of the Conference, as well as concerns over internationalization of domestic issues pertaining to women's rights, made the Women's Institute suddenly a sensitive and suspect enterprise; its proponents became subject to attentive surveillance.

The founders of the Institute created a highly dynamic and gendered space of activism in which were fused political, educational and economic concerns. Dissonance, fissures and uncertainties that surfaced in the course of the Institute's history are reflected in the different, often conflicting, agenda of the parties at the Institute's founding. They mirrored the wider disparities which constituted the culture in which educational change was taking place.

The Remaking of a *danwei:* agenda and obligations

The parties involved in the setting up of this *minjian* ultimately failed to develop it into an alternative site of educational learning. To ensure a site and economic footing for the Institute, agreements were reached between activists and the Provincial Women's Federation Cadre School (*Sheng Funü Ganbu Xuexiao*), subsequently approved by Zhengzhou University, to set up the Institute on the campus of the Cadre School, in a suburb of Zhengzhou, about four kilometres from the main campus of the University. The Women's Institute would, however, coexist within the structure of negotiated semi-autonomy that accommodated the University's numerous other institutes.

Agenda of the international women's institute

Establishing the new *minjian* Institute inside the university system through a merger of sorts with a governmental (ACWF) structure applied pragmatism to the long-term goal of creating a separate (*fenli*) institution. This merger was expected to enable the Institute to influence both mainstream higher education and ACWF education through contributions to curriculum, teaching methodology and teaching content.

University affiliation would instantly legitimize the Institute as an institution of higher education and permit student as well as staff intake. The Cadre School would provide essential facilities — such as classrooms and language laboratory — and basic administrative and teaching staff. It would also provide an initial financial infrastructure until other sources of income materialized. Its status as a semi-independent institution promised a certain degree of financial and administrative autonomy (particularly in contracting and appointing personnel, independence in the creation of a women-centred curriculum, and authority over pedagogy).

In an introductory speech to the first intake of students, Shi Dongliang, the academic dean of the Institute, stressed the school's unique features, including its independence from higher authority in building a streamlined administration, and its ability to monitor faculty staff quality through regular review. The students, all fee-paying (*zifei xuesheng*), would be drawn from a wider than usual spectrum of society, recruited through advertisement and private recommendation, so-called *shehuizhao xueshengmen* (students admitted through informal channels). This was made possible by a flexible admissions policy which paid less stringent attention to academic performance as the sole criterion of admission. Therefore, students with barely average high school grades could be considered as candidates, so long as they passed a comprehensive interview conducted by Institute staff. Unlike ordinary students (who had passed the provincial-level entrance examination), these students would not receive a Bachelor of Arts degree, *wenping*. They would be given only a certificate, *zhengshu*, issued by the Institute upon completion of their studies. Whereas degree candidates were eligible for job assignment and a *hukou* (residence permit) in the provincial capital, *zhengshu* students fended for themselves. This admissions policy gave a chance to applicants with low test scores, largely a result of attending low-quality, rural secondary schools.[14] The policy also generated much needed income. More students brought more tuition fee payments — about ¥3000 each annually — at a time when the Institute had scarce economic resources.[15] In a few instances, poorly educated students attended the Institute more for status than education, primarily only because their families could afford tuition.

The Institute's independence permitted it to develop an international character: a Western vice-president, a research programme for international scholars and postgraduates, and student exchange through which Chinese students would be sent abroad and Western undergraduates would come to Zhengzhou.

Agenda of the Cadre School

The Cadre School leadership's support of the Institute was based on its desire to reverse its waning influence and recapture lost prestige. The leaders wanted to set an academic direction for attracting more students and qualified teaching staff, thus in turn generating desperately needed income. Formerly, the Cadre School had trained young women for positions within the Federation when the Federation was unchallenged as the sole provider of women's social, educational and ideological needs. This had brought access to financial subsidies and social status. The waning credibility of the CCP and thus of its executive arm, the Federation, had brought on the crisis in individual grass roots-level units. Now, the central government was no longer willing and able to provide funding.

Thus, the negotiations to place an institute of higher education for women on its campus were born out of a financial crisis. Also, Cadre School staff felt uncertain over the school's future and many doubted that the leadership was capable of effective management in a time of change. It is not surprising that the cautious style of the old Cadre School leadership later found itself at odds with the expansive approach to institution building that was favoured by the Women's Institute leaders.

ACWF agenda

In 1993 Liang Hui, the chair of the provincial Women's Federation, was nearing the end of her working life with the Federation and was eager to depart on a triumphant note. In order to facilitate her entry into a new position in Beijing with another organization, she needed a prestigious, locally based programme to contribute to the programmes that were to be organized around the Beijing International Women's Congress in 1995.

Initially, Liang Hui knew little (or as she maintained, nothing) of the agreements reached between Ren Hua and her group of independent scholars and the Cadre School leadership. Although not cognizant of the arrangements, she was keen to keep the productive activists and their projects in the province. Not only were these well-publicized projects conducted on a large scale, but their funding came from prestigious foreign funding institutions, most prominently the Ford Foundation.

University leadership

The president of Henan Provincial University was in his last year of office, weighed down by criticisms of ineffectual leadership and at odds with his successor, a much younger and more ambitious man. His decision to support the Institute culminated in official approval (*pizhun*) from the Provincial Educational Affairs Bureau and the University leadership in May 1993, after the leadership made a hastily arranged inspection visit (*jiancha*) of the Cadre School campus and its facilities.

The president wanted to keep Ren Hua, whom he called Henan's *guojia baoku* (national treasure), because of her talent, enterprising spirit and contacts with important institutions and scholars at home and abroad. His support was probably motivated by his *guanxi* obligation to support the daughter of an old and good friend, but he also wanted to retain Ren for his own institution, which was struggling to gain academic recognition as a centre of learning and research. The University could ill afford to lose the driving force behind women's studies in the province. Ren Hua had won national and international fame when she founded the first women's studies research centre in the country. She had been the first to organize national and international women's studies conferences in the PRC. Her continued presence, albeit somewhat controversial, was a useful addition to the portfolio of a university seeking key (*zhongdian*) status (a designation which assured access to state resources and nationwide recognition). Also, Ren Hua had threatened to remove herself to a university outside Henan should an institute not be created for her. This threat and the demonstrations of loyalties by her group of supporters, who promised to leave the Cadre School for Ren's new destination, were thus successful.

While the current president had strong personal ties of loyalty with the future head of the Women's Institute, the Institute actually received almost no institutional support from the University. There was no official acknowledgement of the Institute until 4 September 1993, three days after its official opening, when the President and Party Secretary, bowing to personal pressures, arrived for a perfunctory tour of the brand-new Institute. The president's successor expressed no interest in the project as he was locked into a relationship of implacable mutual animosity with the current office holder.

Less than three months had elapsed between the initial conceptualization of the Institute and the official stamp of approval by the relevant authorities. Only the liberalization of the educational system could account for such a fast establishment of an institution of higher learning, women-centred and with features of *minjian* status. But, in the final analysis, *guanxi* and the paying of old debts to cherished friends had paved the way for the new, alternative institution of learning.

The start-up of the Institute carried with it an implicit commitment by University leaders and provincial authorities to core women activists around Ren Hua, as well as to staff and teachers of the Cadre School, which was promised economic expansion, higher salaries and better housing. There were, however, unresolved tensions, such as over financial arrangements and the Institute's lack of candour to the provincial Federation leaders. Moreover, the ACWF in Beijing was resentful over the perceived affront to its leadership role. Strongest reservations over lack of consultation came from their *lao dajie* (oldest and leading members of the Federation) who saw the Institute's approval as an act of provocation designed to undermine the establishment of their own pet project, a richly funded women's college in Beijing. This college was to serve as a visible sign of the ACWF's resurrected official importance in the run-up to the Beijing International Women's Conference, and the Zhengzhou Institute was viewed as unwanted competition.

Thus, women's education in this context acquired a symbolic value of political import that was to make the issue of education one of secondary importance to the question of legitimacy of representation. The real questions concerned who controlled education, power struggles played out at personal and political levels.

THE INSTITUTE'S LIFE AND CLOSURE

In the Institute's first week, its academic dean, representing the absent president, gave a group of nervous, somewhat disorientated women students a long and detailed exposure to the origins, objectives and uniqueness of the experiment of which they were to be a part. She laid the psychological basis for subsequent discussions: the students were asked to *fengxian jingshen* (be prepared to take risks) with an Institute with no history, a skeletal staff and an as yet incomplete pedagogical design. Additionally, most students were to graduate without a *wenping* and they would not have claim to a Zhengzhou *hukou*, something highly desirable, particularly for girls from the countryside.[16]

The heart of the Institute's pedagogy, according to the dean, was to be students' societal development (*shehui fazhan*) in conjunction with individual development (*geren fazhan*). Two streams of education were to supply academic training: a degree in Applied Sociology for the most academically promising; and a General Education degree for those who wanted a more general education to prepare themselves for careers in the public and private sectors of industry, or as a foundation for possible further specialized education. Academic subjects were to be supplemented by classes in speech, deportment and physical education. Internships with relevant work-units were to be as important as classroom education. But at the heart of it all was to be a women-centred approach, preparing students through individual self-disclosure and collective consciousness-raising for upwardly mobile careers and social vanguard roles.

The women-centredness of the Institute was to express itself in five areas.

1. Theoretical research projects (*lilun yanjiu*) were largely to be conducted by Ren Hua through continued emphasis on her scholarship.
2. Women's studies research (*funü yanjiu*) would invite scholars and postgraduates from abroad to do research and fieldwork.
3. An oral history project on various aspects of women's lives in modern Chinese society (*lishixue yanjiu*) would be utilized as demonstration material for students' education.
4. The women's museum, located on the premises of the Institute, would facilitate cultural research (*wenhua yanjiu*) in women's artistry, creativity and culture.
5. The health and reproductive health project investigating rural women's fertility and birth control patterns would illustrate a women-centred way of conducting research (*fangfalun yanjiu*).

These elements were to constitute the building materials for the new women's education, its new didactic methods and teaching resources.

Placing a central emphasis on the coupling of self-development with academic standards and expectations was complicated by putting an equal emphasis on the nurturing of deportment and decorum. The expectations for the Institute and its students as agents of change and their potential for altering mainstream education were pitched high.

Fenli — reforming the educational danwei

The Chinese *danwei* is not only a site of employment, but also the central source of authority over all aspects of its members' lives, 'designed to control and to meet needs'.[17] It is thus also the dynamic building site of political control — what Foucault calls 'fields of force' — that reflects the durability and adaptability of an authoritarian state even in change.[18]

The implementation of the ideals of the Institute as a catalyst of educational (therefore social and gender) change within the organization of a *danwei* raises questions of what happens as the ideals and visions of gender activists are put to the test of daily institution building. How much change is possible or even desirable at a grass roots level (as opposed to Beijing-dictated decrees of change), and what compromises are dictated by local configurations of power and situated interest?

Relationships

The comparison of a work-unit to a patriarchal family is instructive. 'The unit leader has all the powers of a patriarch; you oppose him at great risk and you can't change families.'[19] Maintained by deeply ingrained socialization patterns, such as deference, loyalty, allegiance and gender socialization, education has to reconstruct its own social processes by addressing itself to the imperative of changing these patterns. Thus, the way the Institute was structured, organized and maintained had to be revolutionized.

The most important relationship in the Institute occurred between the president and her closest confidante, Shi Dongliang, the academic dean (*jiaoyu zhang*) who combined this position of trust with duties which ranged from secretarial support and research assistantship to serving as the Institute's acting head during the president's frequent absences. It was a relationship of mutual dependency, which also affected relationships within the institution, and structured perceptions of allegiance owed by *all* to the institution, and that meant to its president.

Shi Dongliang, a middle-aged married woman who had been a traditional *xianqi liangmu* (virtuous wife) dedicated to serve her husband, children and mother-in-law, had been a serious if uninspired teacher at a technical college. She had discovered meaning when she listened in 1985 to a lecture Ren Hua gave to a class of women cadres. She was so moved that she wept. For the first time she realized that her fate was shared by other women and however pitiable, it was a fate capable of being changed. After the lecture, she went to Ren to offer unconditional service. She has always seen Ren as the thinker, the leading light of the women's movement and viewed herself as the loyal foot-soldier whose reward lay in serving a great mind. A distinct cultural pattern, the servitude of intellectuals — 'the subservience [in intellectual production and political action] to a higher object that characterizes the relation that Chinese intellectuals have to the authoritarian state'[20] — reproduced itself also in the Institute's microcosmic world of entangled sentiment and sublimated yearning for personal meaning.

The lecture that changed Shi Dongliang's framework of intellectual and emotional orientation caused her to follow her idol through political battles and ideological skirmishes. Each new obstacle inspired her to be of even greater service. She also discovered in herself a capacity to use the springboard of Ren's flights of intellectual activity for the manufacturing of popular and accessible lectures and speeches for the masses of women she would learn to carry with her on the wings of her own passion. Thus, Shi Dongliang, who had previously taught at an orthodox educational site, the Women's Cadre School of the ACWF, became one of the most seasoned speakers, untiringly bringing Ren's ideas to country women, Federation cadres, intellectuals and workers.

Out of these classes and lectures, outside the Federation structure and university lecture halls was born a new paradigm of womanhood that would infuse the ideology of the Women's Institute, the *xiandai nuren*, but it also cornered sentiments of loyalty to the leadership. When Shi Dongliang was appointed academic dean of the Institute, she continued to dedicate herself to unconditional service to the cause. Ironically, this relationship of selfless devotion to the creator of the new paradigm of womanhood reflected contradictions between, on the one hand, the message of *duli*, independence, of the president in her role as an ideologue and, on the other, the authoritarianism that characterized the president as an educational leader. These features had their roots in enduring dimensions of institutionalized hierarchy and personal dependency.

Structural tensions

The personnel and financial problems that showed up early in the relationship between the Women's Institute and the Cadre School leadership illustrate how structural constraints can undermine a strategy of collaboration between proponents of reform and representatives of the status quo. For example, despite dissatisfaction with the director of finances, the Institute leadership saw no way to fire her. There were no provisions to retire or sideline this high-level cadre as she was securely locked into an administrative and political structure (the ACWF), supported by *guanxi* (connections from her powerful times), that she could seemingly activate at will.

The Institute's income-generating schemes did not match the school's needs. An abundance of *minbande* (privately founded) institutions had already begun to offer evening language classes, computer literacy and similar courses at an earlier time when it was still possible to cash in on an eager clientele searching for ways to increase their knowledge. The Institute faced a much more wary, experienced public which sought quality, experience and competitive tuition fees. Enrolments did not materialize and the Institute faced a financial crisis, which sparked disagreement over feasible solutions as well as accusations over the proper apportioning of blame and incompetence.

Staff started to lose the optimism that characterized the founding days. As different interpretations of the financial prospects began to circulate, each version demanded adherents and professions of loyalty. A power struggle over final authority and fate of the Institute's independent course commenced. A gulf opened up between the group around the president and the group around the Cadre School president. The Institute downsized from a small but compact campus with a basic institutional infrastructure to a small site of two offices and a few classrooms and dormitories for the students. Basic requests for teaching materials or even hot water turned relations among a deeply divided campus population into a minefield of accusations and counter-accusations.

A more intrusive policy of political and intellectual surveillance began to affect relationships, work style and the earlier atmosphere of openness. Very quickly the initial advantages brought by the fusion with the Cadre School created friction. Work in an educational *danwei* had provided a livelihood of little excitement with few prospects for promotion for the Cadre School staff, but it had granted unquestionable security. Thirty-two senior teachers and families, 40 staff and a number of junior teachers and their families, 15 retired teachers (teachers recently forcibly retired because they were considered unsuitable by the Institute leadership) and a number of part-time staff became involved observers and sometimes vocal participants in the evolving events.

The Cadre School: supporting the leader's cause

At the first signs of financial crisis, the Cadre School leadership separated legitimate members (insiders) from intruders (members of the Institute). Meetings were held to announce plans for economic retrenchment and denounce the Institute for having been the cause of the crisis. Demonstrations of loyalty to the leader were demanded — and, by most of the staff — given. Self-preservation — preserving one's stake in a home, rights to old-age benefits, financial security, as well as resentment on the part of those who felt pushed aside when the Institute entered the Cadre School — all came into play. Even retired teachers, disgruntled at the state of affairs or anxiety-ridden at a potential political fallout, attended meetings and signed a petition to banish the Institute.

Protected by this mass-line support, the Cadre School leadership moved to 'educate' the 'disloyal' or 'ambivalent' elements in their midst, those who were absent from the meetings, those who did not sign and those who kept silent. House visits, persuasive talks and promises of favourable consideration in future allocation of a flat (a long-awaited event) created an atmosphere of omnipresent tension.

In the midst of hostile exchanges, the old system could be seen to serve the ambitions of the Cadre School leaders, but also protect the interests of dissenting staff. For example, four teachers who followed the Institute had their salaries reduced by 30%, but were never seriously threatened by loss of income. These 'rebels' were threatened with loss of housing, but they still continued to live in the Cadre School housing complex from where they cycled to work at the main campus, the new home of the Women's Institute.

Loyalties and allegiances

At the same time, the Institute held meetings to affirm loyalty and hear pledges of commitment to the president. Tearful accounts of *chiku*, past sufferings, reflected an 'imperative of optimism': a deeply-held conviction that the deprivations of today will be followed by a full life tomorrow.[21] For most of the activists, this collectively willed optimism effectively cancelled out any doubts as to the wisdom of the course taken or the quality of leadership and style of decision-making — pointing to the fragility of institutionalization which clearly magnified the importance of strong or charismatic leadership.

External pressures started to intensify towards the end of the first semester, a measure of the provincial authorities' unrepentant distrust of a perceived systemic anomaly. Mounting disagreements within the Women's Institute leadership had begun to filter outwards, in turn compounding official fears over the potential political repercussions from an institutional experiment beset by instability and interpersonal antagonism. Routine relations with provincial educational authorities, the provincial foreign affairs department, the University leadership and the provincial Women's Federation acquired the dimensions of daily struggle, *douzheng*. The sense of crisis deepened and with it a need for clearly defined boundaries around the Institute staff. This brought in time an increasing contraction of transparent administration, on the one hand, and a small clique that began to form around the president, on the other.

The external pressures produced concomitant pressures and changes in, for example, personnel policies. Whereas initially *hege* (professionally qualified) faculty staff were hired, over time this priority gave way to criteria of proven trustworthiness, loyalty, and the capacity to *chiku* (suffer). The increasingly embattled institution allocated less time to evolve a coherent praxis of alternative education in the selection and training of teachers.

Trustworthy allies are not always the most constructive collaborators in a project which demands by necessity openness, competence, frank exchanges and mutual respect. In other words, the leader's personal political needs took priority over the interest of the Institute (which was being reworked constantly and often unpredictably to cope with threats, fictional or real). In all these shifts that occurred, the activists grouped themselves around the leader in conformity to imperatives of loyalty similar to those demanded of the Cadre School staff.

As a result of these developments, a large part of the inner circle was made up of Federation teachers, well-tempered in mass-line conduct and trials by fire. Instead of the Institute's changing the Federation's orthodox educational praxis from within, it was the Federation, through its teachers (still on Federation payroll), which began to exert influence on the work style among colleagues and relations between faculty members and students. Didactic presentations came slowly to replace the relatively open exchanges of early weeks.

One of the outstanding features of a *minjian* institution is contract-based faculty staff, giving the institution the chance to select the most suitable candidates for a competitive salary, but without the package of benefits (the iron rice bowl) which a traditional *danwei* provides. Because of the marriage of convenience with the Cadre School, these features could only be partially present because the perceived financial burden from a large percentage of retired staff was an important constraint.

During the second and third semesters, after the Institute's separation

from the Cadre School and relocation to the main campus, an atmosphere
of embattlement permeated staff and classrooms. At meetings loyalty was
demanded from the hired staff through old patterns of persuasion and
pressure. Whereas the traditional *danwei* institution holds the very
livelihood of their members as leverage, *minjian* variations may make
promises of rewards or their withholding. The basis of new sources of
control included participating in international meetings, visits abroad to
attend conferences, meetings with foreign dignitaries — all scarce
opportunities for many Chinese intellectuals, particularly those tied to
mediocre institutions. These constitute new weapons wielded in the old
authoritarian ways, or operated in a practised fashion of hierarchical,
unquestioned leadership style.

The brief history of the Institute reveals the crucial part individual
agency plays in initiating change against the forbidding presence of Chinese
provincial bureaucracy. However, the same qualities needed to change
conduct, perceptions and allegiances may — because of the sluggish pace
of system reform — bring about its negation. The unavoidable personal
conflicts and accommodations that played out in constant meetings,
assemblies and work reports were familiar work style, but they drew energy
and attention away from the innovative and creative aspects of work.

PEDAGOGY OF CHANGE

From the commencement of the first academic semester, a full programme
of initiation meetings introduced visions of change to come, of distinctive
differences of the school and thus uniqueness of its students (*women shi
dutede nüren*), and set a tone of optimism and affirmation. This programme
was evolved by the academic dean, Shi Dongliang. But in the frequent
absence of Ren Hua, who was preoccupied with other research projects
and often called upon to attend conferences and meetings abroad, Shi had
no choice but to assume the leadership and responsibility for formulation
of the promised fresh approaches to pedagogy and work style which were
to lay the foundation of the new paradigm of education.

As a part of university education, the curriculum needed to balance
obligatory elements (military training, political philosophy, Chinese and
foreign languages, and world history) with a women-centred emphasis.
Right from the start, official speeches and internal staff workshops stressed
the alternative model of modern womanhood (*xiandai nüxing*) which the
Institute was to nurture. Its advocation was tied up with the critique of
existing education, seen as unquestioningly incorporating and reproducing

gender bias. But how a systematic implementation of this model could be translated into a viable culture and structure of education was not a subject matter of institutional, professional discourse. Such discussion was obviated by the lack of appropriate pedagogical resources and faculty staff's inexperience in women-centred teaching pedagogy.

Many student complaints related to the Institute's failure to appreciate the difference between issue-specific educational campaigns (something which in particular Cadre School staff had experience in, such as education of women on sexual health and reproductive rights) and the design and implementation of an academic university-level programme. Concerns addressed how to incorporate as well as critique existing bodies of knowledge, and how to meet official examination requirements while at the same time not compromising women-centred classes and projects.

The initial phase of consciousness-raising and the creation of an ambience of security and support for young and intimidated women were successful. The first-year curriculum developed as its core course a 'know thy sex' theme through participants' personal accounts, self-disclosure and 'speak bitterness' sessions. Also included were sessions on elementary psychology and on female anatomy and life cycle. The teacher started by sharing her own history of growing into adulthood, going to great pains to discuss culturally taboo subjects such as first menstruation. The students felt encouraged to reveal their own fears and their parents' ignorance and neglect of this key event in their maturation process. The aim was to bring the young women to realization rather than denial of their difference as members of the female sex (*lixing zixing*). This contrasts with the Maoist egalitarian treatment of sexual difference as entirely a matter of bourgeois lifestyle. Developed, even thriving, on this foundation of difference, with all its associated biological and psychological features, a nurturing education could empower women to demand equality on their own (female) terms. In this course, the teacher's function was a vital one; she served both as a role model and as the guarantor that consciousness-raising would take place within certain 'correct' parameters rather than as individualistic expression.

The impact of collective initiation rites resulted in near identical statements on the part of students, whose earlier learning process had involved recital. Now extensive repetitions of the canons of revolutionary intent were to remodel educational culture, as much as educational priorities and methodologies. In consequence, old boundaries were not so much redrawn as renamed: students' work progress, leisure pursuits, social activities and *nan pengyoude shi* (the boyfriend factor) were the targets of an ever-watchful maternalistic regime, represented by zealous student instructors who all came from the Cadre School background — *dang mamabing* (mothering complex) activists with years of experience in execution of thought reform.

Students' bodies and minds were put through the wringer of daily all-day schedules of the tightest discipline. The military training at the beginning of the opening semester set the tone for subsequent routines of early rising and early sleeping times (when lights were switched off). This inscribed itself on students' minds in one vital message: do not forget who you are and who tells you who you are. Unruly impulses and thoughts on the part of individual students were quickly put down to mould a personhood expressed at the collective level and in collective harmony. Individualism had a difficult stand in this environment.

Within weeks the collective transformation was worn like an Institute badge. Students wrote in their essays about how they were awakened from 'sleep' to believe in themselves as women; they would not replicate their mothers — dependent and mute. The world was theirs to take on, as successful career women and as *nüqiang ren*, women who would be successful in their competition for careers and in their creation of domestic contentment through love nurtured from a position of strength and a knowledge of women's rights. The master text supplied by educators was faithfully reproduced by students and regurgitated to the last word. The new mode of thought was taken to a collective level in the ritualized meetings that punctuated learning periods. Self-determination understood as an oath of allegiance to the writers of the educational text celebrated its absence in the carefully steered enactment of the text.

Authority and attendant prerogatives remained intact. That the patterns of dependency and hierarchical decision-making were not themselves being questioned was illustrated once when students practised *zifa* — spontaneous, collective self-expression — and neglected consultation procedures with their instructors and the leaders of the Institute. This event generated a severe reaction from those who had earlier held forth on new defining characteristics of *xiandai nüren*, modern women. There was unanimous consensus among Institute leaders that the students had failed to act in a mature way. They had been disloyal to the leadership (by abandoning its texts), a quality more important than the students' trying to understand issues on their own. However, despite being criticized, the students walked the streets, as they said, proud and with their heads held high. When in the second semester the Institute was moved to the main campus, Institute students were perceived by their fellow students as visibly different, more proud, more self-assertive, more talkative and more opinionated. When the Institute was closed in early 1995, the students were criticized as dangerously out of control and negatively influenced by *nüquan zhuyi*, the women's rights movement.

Education at the Institute had been less influenced than in other schools by political studies, labour activities and participation in the many patriotic movements that took place during this time. An example is the 'Learn from Han Suyun' movement (which had a strong impact on the Cadre School activities). A nationwide campaign in 1994–95 presented and propagated an officially approved model, the peasant and soldier's wife, Han Suyun, for women to emulate, as a construct of a femininity which signalled the virtues of self-sacrifice to the point of near self-destruction, for the country, Party and family (in this order).[22] The public narrations of Han Suyun's sacrifices as patriotic love*fests* constituted the combined labour of the ACWF, the Guangdong Women's Federation, the CCP's propaganda apparatus and the People's Liberation Army — supported by the mass media. Han Suyun-inspired groups of *junsao* (army officers' wives) soon appeared all over the TV screens and magazine covers, urging emulation of wifely devotion and loyalty. In its embodiment of femininity *in extremis* and in its valourization of faith in the Party and the state (*funü wei guojia*, women stand up for their country), this construct is not in total opposition to the gender activists' ideal *nüren* as it might first appear. The two paradigms are related through underlying patterns of socialization which establish their origin in the same hierarchical culture.

Despite gender activists' oppositional critique of state appropriation of women, the case study of institution building under discussion suggests how difficult it is to dismantle shared assumptions of privileged voice and power of command, '...a circuit of productivity that draws its capital from others' deprivation while refusing to acknowledge its own presence as endowed'.[23]

The alternative paradigm of education attempted to facilitate the entry of women into market society as competitive, skilled and self-determined. Underlying this ideal is a discourse on women's legacy of dependency. But by failing to dismantle socialization patterns of dependency and deference, not least due to external pressures, the Institute merely displaced one set of hierarchical leadership patterns with another.

ALL THAT IS INSIDE IS NOT CENTRE[24]

From the beginning of my work with the Institute, the very provincial and educational authorities which had approved my appointment as vice-president continually questioned the legitimacy of this appointment.

Meetings were convened and *baogao* (reports) requested to dispute the appointment process and my status — which in post-1949 China was unprecedented (foreign scholars may be appointed as visiting instructors and so-called 'foreign experts', but they do not become administrators and are never major participants in the educational system). Opposition came mainly from the University Party secretary, who was supported by the Cadre School head. My person became a symbolic battleground among those who had approved the Institute as a *minjian* institution. My position as a controversial foreign element in the body of the Chinese educational administration symbolized the extraterritorial rights which the University president had granted Ren Hua to choose a 'foreign' vice-president.

In relation to other members of the faculty and staff, I was automatically slotted into a space which had been pre-defined for me: *waiguo* (the other country). Assumptions about *waiguo*, its inhabitants and ways of life and morality overpowered personal encounters and confirmed rather than helped to dispel *a priori* projections. *Waiguo* was defined as everywhere outside China; differences and diversities were flattened into one mass of rigid otherness referred to as 'the foreign country'. Daily work routine and interaction at the closest, spontaneous level initially produced only friction. Yet in time, my unwillingness to accept being 'othered' by the *waiguo ren* (foreigner) label along with my colleagues' admirable patience resulted in our developing daily, mutually enlightening conversations about differences between *waiguo* (the world as one country which is the result of particular projections) and *guowaide guojia* (countries outside China as representing differing histories and civilizations). The concept of *waiguo* often serves as a blanket term which calls forth instant associations: decadence, loveless family life, alienation and an inability to understand the mystique of *Zhongguo* (China). Often, my critical substantive comments were dismissed with the devastating retort, *'dangran, bu tai xiguan Zhongguo shenghuo'* (of course, she is not familiar with the Chinese way of life). But, over time, our conversations helped to shift our positions and perceptions, so that we could start taking into account subject positions different from one's own. This process spilt over into more creative approaches to classroom teaching, and into an opening up of its core discourse on nation-specific women's histories, differing experiences of patriarchal cultures, and women's movement projects of liberation and self-definition.

Towards the second semester, students, had replaced references to *waiguo* and *waiguo ren* with more specific nationality or ethnic identifiers. The older staff found this development difficult to emulate or commented on it with amusement. But many of us were beginning to practise 'cultural openness', a process derived not from 'a passive immersion in [others'] cultures, but ... a striving to understand what it is that [other] voices are saying'.[25]

Another kind of 'othering' involved my usefulness as a *mingpai* (signboard) for the Institute. I came to signal certain qualities of the Institute, such as emphasis on internationalism of academics and a raised level of intellectual aspirations.

The heated disputes over 'the international character' of the Institute here serve as instructive readings for its provocation of political controversy, eventually fatal, as well as for its promise of cultural challenge to educational orthodoxy.

CONCLUSIONS

How representative is the case of the International Women's Institute? Its location in Henan is significant; the region's political conservatism accounts for the intensity of inhibitions and resistance to change. The province's reputation as ideologically firmly in control brings forth issues more starkly than might be the case elsewhere in the PRC. This factor, however, does not render it singular or totally unrepresentative.

As of 1996 the Institute remained closed, but it was still continuing on as a political factor. None who was involved was left unaffected. Even its most negative adversary has realized that women's education, while heavily contested, has an important role to play in shaping Chinese higher education.

The education in self-worth has left its mark on former students. Dispersed to several academic departments, they are seen as too '*ziyou*' (independent-minded) and as '*hen youyijiande*' (very self-opinionated) young women. They claim a mental space for themselves, something which the Institute's demise cannot erase.

In retrospect, it may seem that the Institute was a daring act of imagination and invention in a fruitless search for a space outside state powers and Party controls, defeated when its host organizations turned on the reformers. But an act of a collectively shared-in imagination may engender a political space which, by its very creation, became an important force in education in the province. What determines its fate, however, is bound up more by political and cultural issues than by questions of intrinsic educational import.

A product of the ongoing reform of the educational system, the Institute case illustrates the contradictions which lie at the heart of the restructuring of education: enduring political imperatives for tight control over values and value-makers, education and educators. These are the underpinning and maintenance mechanisms of a monopolistic one-party state. Erosion of central CCP control in the economic and financial sphere of the government has compounded the sense of insecurity over survival felt by both the core leadership of the Party and by bureaucrats and cadres at different levels of administration. In this dialectic between the forces of decentralization — economic in their roots but cultural in their most controversial manifestations — and an enduring bureaucracy whose legitimacy stands little to gain but much to lose from outsider challenges to sources of authority, a powerful discourse has emerged over the role of education. That discourse does not die with the demise of the Women's Institute. Rather, it is continuing as part of the powerful political processes that transpire in the daily business of making society work, adapt, change and endure in Henan and elsewhere in the PRC.

NOTES

1. Names of institutions and persons connected to the case study have been changed.
2. Institute brochure, February 1994.
3. Existing women's centres are representative of Women's Federation educational policies and share certain key features. They work within the state's paradigmatic gender definitions. They are assigned social spheres of gendered responsibilities and influence, and thus offer no challenge to a compartmentalized educational system and its underpinning values. Examples include the traditional, semi-independent, vocational Women's College in Fuzhou, the more recent Women's College established in Nanjing in response to pressures to offer up-to-date education, and indeed the Provincial Women's Cadre School in Zhengzhou.
4. At issue is the concept of women, understood as conscious oppositionality to patriarchal control and simultaneous establishment of a sphere of self-determination as selfhood. In terms of Barlow's post-structuralist analysis of gender discourse in post 1949 China, *nüren* has come to represent the aspirations of the New Era gender activists, as opposed to *funü*, the term appropriated by the All-China Women's Federation to denote the Maoist construct of an appropriately liberated female gender. See Barlow, 1994.
5. The French sociologist Gabriel Tarde distinguishes between two kinds of consumer societies: (1) societies in which the rule of tradition or customs, of the native and of the past, prevail; and (2) societies which are subject to frequent change and at the mercy of fashion. Qu in R. Williams, 1982, p. 357.
6. This case is put forward by a social scientist from the Beijing Academy of Social Sciences. See Gao Xiaoxian, 1994.
7. See also Du Fangqin, 1990; Rosen, 1994; Zhao Weijie, 1995; Liu Bohong and Sung Rong, 1995; Jaschok, 1995.
8. See Chapter 15 by Carol C. Fan and Chapter 17 by Chuing Prudence Chou and Flora Chia-I Chang in this volume.

9. For a historical outline of Chinese women's formal education, see Gu, 1995.
10. Li Xiaojiang, 1994.
11. This section is based on the work of the most representative voice of New Era gender activism, Li Xiaojiang.
12. Also, see Zhu Qi, 1990; Du Fangqin, 1990.
13. For a description of women NGOs, see Liu Jinxiu, 1991.
14. Even the brightest and most motivated students have little chance to go to university if they come from remote districts and poor rural areas with a weak and underfunded educational schooling facility. About half of the students admitted in 1993 came from rural townships in Henan province; the rest were equally divided between the countryside, that is, small villages, and Zhengzhou.
15. Speech by the academic dean to students, 20 September 1993.
16. This spirited attack so frightened a number of peasant families present at the ceremony that they left the same day, taking their daughters with them.
17. Pye, 1988, p. 155.
18. For a lucid discussion of the importance of Foucault's work to feminism, see Scott, 1990, reference to Foucault quotation on p. 136.
19. Link, 1992, pp. 68–9. Also, see the seminal study of the political culture of work-units in Walder, 1983 and 1986.
20. Chow, 1993, p. 80.
21. Pye, 1988, p. 153.
22. Han Suyun supported, nursed and took responsibility for an extended family in the absence of her husband who pursued his career in the army. Neither ill health nor concern over material survival weakened her resolution not to interfere with her husband's life and work. Her sacrificial service to the cause of family, army and country, and her near death as a result of her silent, unaided labour were celebrated in meetings (organized by ACWF cadres and attended by the national leadership), study sessions, and frontcover pages and editorials in the daily press, most prominently in the *Renmin Ribao*.
23. Chow, 1993, p. 14.
24. Quoting from the title of an article by Harlow, 1989, p. 162.
25. Lugones and Spelman, 1990, p. 33. See also Bulbeck, 1991.

17

Gender Differences in Taiwan's Academe — Implications for the PRC

Chuing Prudence CHOU and Flora Chia-I CHANG

INTRODUCTION

Throughout the world teaching in higher education has traditionally been a male-dominated profession. Women have been a minority of instructors and professors at colleges and universities, even in countries where women represent over half of the students in higher education. As a minority, women have been segregated into the lower ranks, into part-time teaching and into the less lucrative and 'female' fields. Discrimination against women has occurred with respect to hiring, reward, promotion and granting tenure. Women have not been sponsored into the academic profession in the same ways as men have.[1]

This chapter draws from two empirical studies on female faculty members in Taiwan.[2] Women's participation in Taiwan's higher education serves as a good indicator for the modernization in the PRC's education system, and the findings of Taiwan studies therefore are relevant to the PRC. The purpose of this chapter is to analyse how and to what extent gender differences exist in the measures of hiring faculty staff, rewards and promotion in Taiwan, and to relate these findings to the PRC.

STATUS OF WOMEN IN TAIWAN

As in many patriarchal societies, Chinese women have suffered from being treated as an inferior group and deprived of access to political power and economic independence.[3] The patrilineal descent principle operates as a major source of women's subordination. A strong preference for male children permeates Taiwan's society, as sons are seen as a potential source of support for their parents in old age, while helping to continue the family name. The general attitude towards women is reflected in common Chinese maxims, such as 'Male superior, female inferior' (*zhong nan qing nü*) and 'Husband masters the public domain and wife masters the home' (*nan zhu wai, nü zhu nei*). These traditional gender roles have been legitimized as stabilizers of both family and society in Taiwan's ideology.

Unlike their Western counterparts, Chinese women in the past were not organized to fight against their disadvantaged situation. As a result of the political revolution in 1911 and the May Fourth Movement in 1919, women started to play a more active role in the society and struggled to liberate themselves from the traditional value system.[4] In education, women gained some privileges such as admittance to national universities and more opportunities in higher education.

Prior to 1895, the beginning of Japanese colonization, the position of women in Taiwan and the Mainland was quite similar in regards to lack of education, rigid kinship ties and absence of legal rights. Women were confined to their families before marriage and to their husbands afterwards.[5] Under the colonial policy from 1895 to 1945 when Taiwan was occupied by Japan, girls were allowed to attend primary schools to become literate, but were prevented from pursuing higher education. In 1945, when Taiwan returned to mainland China, many laws prevailing in mainland China were extended to Taiwan. A notable example is the 1947 Constitutional Law, which stated that all citizens of the Republic of China were equal in law, regardless of gender, religion, race and political party. Despite Taiwan's economic modernization that has expanded women's access to education and economic participation in the labour force, Confucian beliefs still prevail, and Taiwanese society remains strongly patriarchal. Persistence of traditional values and socialization processes perpetuate traditional sex-role differentiation.[6] This traditional ideology and social role of women were rarely questioned until the 1970s, when a 'new generation' of Taiwanese emerged.

ECONOMIC PARTICIPATION OF WOMEN IN TAIWAN

Despite the traditional Chinese view of women as tied to home, several factors have given rise to new role expectations. These include a rise in women's overall educational level, technological advances that simplified housework, and a decline in fertility rates. As a result, women have entered the labour market in increasing numbers. The female labour force's participation rate in Taiwan increased from an average of 34% in the 1960s to 45% in 1993.[7] The share of female employment in total employment increased from 28% in 1951 to 38% in 1992.[8]

With respect to salary differentials, women in Taiwan earned 42% of men's annual income in the labour market in 1964 and 57% in 1978.[9] In 1991, on average, women earned less than 68% of the wages paid to men.[10] According to the 1982 Survey of Family Income and Expenditure, women with graduate school education were paid about 88% of salary paid to men with comparable education and 77% in 1991.[11] In 1988, the female/male earnings ratio for those with undergraduate education was about 2:3 and about 1:2 for those with primary education. In 1991, it was 7.8:10 and 5.9:10 respectively.[12] Thus, the discrepancy in salary between men and women decreases as education level rises.[13]

The earnings differential is attributed to differences in the employment structure. Female workers engage in relatively less attractive and less lucrative occupations, or at the lower end of production with less pay and less job security. Due to their responsibility for the family and their disrupted employment, women have less opportunity for promotion and are more likely to be concentrated at the lower levels of the occupational ladder.

With respect to hiring, women face discrimination and unequal opportunities. In the government sector, women have faced relatively fewer barriers because the National Public Service Examination is open to both sexes. The proportion of women passing this examination has increased dramatically, from less than 4% in 1950 to more than 50% in 1992. For example, in 1992, of the 6995 people passing the examination, 59% were women in the Higher Level Examination; 81% of the 6018 people who qualified in the Ordinary Level Examination were women. Although women do not face formal obstacles in either examination, after passing the examinations they need to wait longer for a job assignment than men since the government often classifies the candidates. Moreover, equally qualified men have more opportunity to be assigned jobs in the government sector. Also, many private-sector employers and firms formulate unreasonable policies to keep out women. In private companies women are often forced to resign upon marriage or pregnancy. Employers sometimes set quotas to protect the numbers of men in the various jobs and to keep the number of women low.[14]

In sum, increased access to education has had an important impact on female economic participation, female employment structure and female earnings. Continued expansion of educational opportunities for women would further expand their socio-economic participation and improve their social status. However, even after entering the job market, women face discrimination in training and promotion.[15] Equal opportunity in hiring, training and promotion for women is a prerequisite for the attainment of equality across gender. How to overcome the subtle gender bias in work and cope with personal life and career is one of the greatest challenges that women around the globe encounter today.

EMPIRICAL RESEARCH ON HIRING FACULTY STAFF AND THE ACADEMIC REWARD SYSTEM

This section first reviews the process for hiring faculty staff and the academic reward system in Taiwanese higher education institutions. Then, it presents the results of two empirical studies.

Hiring faculty staff

Hiring, evaluation and certification of faculty members are closely regulated by the Ministry of Education. All new faculty members start at the same rank and salary level in accordance with their qualifications.

The recruitment of personnel in a department is usually handled by its chairperson, who screens the applications and nominations, then submits his or her selection to an *ad hoc* committee for further evaluation. In recent years, with an increasing push for academic democratisation, the *ad hoc* committee has started playing an important role in the first step of the hiring process by reviewing all the applications. However, the chairperson still remains very influential in the decision process in the department. The *ad hoc* committee, in turn, submits its recommendation to the dean of the college for final approval. Finally, the dean's decision is submitted to the university senate for endorsement. Once the senate approves the hiring decision, the Ministry of Education sets the rank and grants the newly hired faculty member a teaching certificate.

The screening criteria (such as qualifications) are based upon the subjective judgement of the chair and the *ad hoc* committee. Their perceptions may be distorted, for example, by personal prejudice against women. The chair may be authoritarian and monopolistic, and may exercise personal favouritism and nepotism in hiring. Thus, departments may recruit not simply on the basis of qualifications, but also according to gender preference. To determine the extent to which this practice occurs, this study looks at the attitudes of both the department chair and the *ad hoc* committee members in the hiring process.

In 1995, a survey was conducted among current and former department chairs and professors who were on *ad hoc* hiring committees in the 11 fields of study in 33 higher institutions in Taiwan (N = 283). They were given ten fictitious job résumés describing the applicants and were asked to complete a questionnaire.[16] According to the survey, the most important stated criteria in hiring faculty staff in Taiwan were the candidate's publications and education. The second and third important criteria were work experience and age respectively, followed by familiarity and alumni status. The marital status and gender of the applicant were not reported as very important.

To determine whether gender in fact made a difference in the hirability ratings for each candidate, a summary rating of the four measures of applicant's hirability (competency, attractiveness as colleague, general desirability and the reviewer's inclination to hire the candidate) was calculated for each candidate. No significant difference appeared when candidates were represented as women or men. No personal characteristic — for example, rank, educational background, country of earned degree, teaching and administrative experience, age, department, institution — showed a consistent pattern of strong gender preference in hiring faculty staff .

Income and promotion

The remuneration paid to full-time university teachers in Taiwan consists of salary and allowances. Salary corresponds to position, concurrent administrative work and professional experience. Allowances apply to food, housing and research.[17] Outside income is also an important form of academic reward, as many faculty members serve as paid-consultants to outside business enterprises.

The four ranks in the faculty hierarchy in the early 1990s were teaching assistant, lecturer, associate professor and full professor. Given a teacher's good record and specialized publications, the minimal number of four years of service is required for a teaching assistant to become a lecturer; at each step at least three years are needed before a lecturer can become an associate professor and then be promoted to a full professor. Ideally, promotion should be based on performance in teaching, research and service. In reality, however, teaching performance is difficult to measure; research productivity is usually evaluated by only one representative work; and the priority given to service during an academic career varies over time. Consequently, seniority has become a surrogate for performance and the major criterion for rank promotion.

In 1990, a survey with interviews collected various data, including academics' personal attitudes towards the academic reward system.[18] Female faculty members had a lower total income than their male counterparts, even after demographic, educational and work variables were taken into consideration. Not surprisingly, the survey found that those who held a higher academic rank assumed higher-level administrative positions, published more books and articles, worked in a public institution or engaged in community service, and were more likely to have a higher total income.

Concerning promotion, academics who either (1) did not have a doctoral degree, or (2) had earned their degrees from domestic institutions, (3) majored in non-natural sciences, or (4) were not in administration took more time to advance to the rank of professor. Women tended to spend more years before being promoted to the rank of professor than to that of associate professor. Women encountered fewer chances to be promoted at the senior stage than at the junior rank.

The reward system (income and promotion) appears to be fair and objective. Women's lower achievement was very much shaped by forces from different directions, family influence in particular. Men and women experience different career patterns and treatment in academe. Marriage facilitated men's academic career while inhibiting women's achievement in academe.

Results

Gender differentiation is entrenched in income and promotion in the academic sector. As compared to their male counterparts, female faculty members tend to spend more years before achieving the professor rank and earn a lower total income. Male faculty members have more publications, more access to higher administrative positions, community services and social networks. Consequently, men are more visible in the field, receive more recognition and allowances from institutions and have more presence in the decision-making process. Social networking in academe results in more outside income for male than female faculty members. Whether there is gender discrimination in Taiwan's academic reward system is still a question to be answered. Nevertheless, female faculty members, on the average, are promoted slower and earn less.

Women often lack the encouragement and opportunities to tap into the social and information networks which are vital for occupational attainment, especially in a society like Taiwan where much information tends to travel through informal channels. In academe, as in other sectors of society, success is often affected by not only what you know but whom you know; not only by hard work, but also by guidance, support and advocacy from those who are already established in the system. The exclusion of women from the information network and their underrepresentation in faculties contribute to unequal opportunities for women, who cannot translate their educational attainments into gains in the academic market-place.

COMPARISON BETWEEN TAIWANESE AND MAINLAND UNIVERSITY WOMEN

Since 1950 female graduates in the PRC have had relatively equal job opportunities under the socialist job assignment system. This is also the case in academe where female professionals are relatively well represented compared to their counterparts in other Asian countries.[19] Returnees from study abroad working in northwest China, for example, reported they experienced no career barriers caused by their gender.[20] Similarly, the Taiwanese women in the faculty study discussed above reported being aware of no discrimination in the hiring process. To date research has been limited in scope and the data in both cited studies are by no means representative. They nevertheless raise the question: are the interviewees just too successful to have experienced gender discrimination in their career? How aware of discrimination are the faculty members? For both Taiwan and the PRC, true gender equality in the hiring of faculty staff has yet to be established. As Stanley Rosen and many others have critiqued, the reforms in the post-Mao era have created a context unprecedented since 1949 which legitimated not only the traditional attitudes against women, but also the explicit gender discrimination in employment and education.[21] A lot of survey data suggest that the economic reforms have in fact contributed to gender inequality in the PRC.[22] Women continue to be excluded from employment and education as Chinese modernization proceeds.

The PRC *Education Law* issued on 18 March 1995 reimposes gender equality in education. '...Citizens under the law should have equal educational opportunities regardless of ethnicity, race, gender... (item 9) and '...schools and related departments should ensure that females and males are treated equally when it comes to school admission, further studying, job employment, awarding academic degrees, and selecting people for overseas study' (item 36).[23] The passage of the law, of course, does not guarantee its effective implementation or cause an attitude change in the society to reverse the perceived inferior position of women. Despite family obstacles and traditional values that work against women, the current social structure and public policies on economic reform in the PRC also appear to have a negative impact on women's employment opportunities. In fact, many reports show that Chinese college women have experienced increasing discrimination in employment since the 1980s. As a result of the recent modifications in the centralized job assignment system, coupled with increasing enterprise autonomy, more and more employers tend to hire male graduates rather than their female counterparts.[24] College women are considered by many employers to be less creative, more arrogant and hard to deal with. An investigation conducted in Shanghai in 1988 shows that more than 50% of female graduates were rejected by their prospective hiring units.[25] Younger women also consider the increasingly explicit gender inequality as a serious social issue.[26] With respect to academic women, the case can also be applicable to their profession. Many surveys conducted in the PRC reveal that women are less likely to be hired in the profession, have less opportunity to be promoted to the top positions, are underrepresented among those with the highest degree, and tend to cluster in more female-traditional fields.[27] For example, among members selected for the Academic Degrees Committee of the State Council, women accounted for only 4% (26 out of 644) in 1985.[28] Another example is that the recruitment of female scientists in the Chinese Academy of Sciences declined in the mid-1980s (to less than one-third); so did women recruits in other state-owned scientific and technical departments.[29] Statistics also show that the higher the position, the greater the discrepancy between men and women.[30] The percentage of female professionals declines as one moves up the career ladder. Although there is no direct evidence to show that women face gender discrimination in faculty hiring, it is obvious that, in the post-Mao reform era, more and more female graduates have been less likely to be hired by the work-unit — let alone develop their career in academe.

Though no actual statistics show that Mainland female faculty members earn less than their male counterparts, the increasing pressure from market reform has a great negative impact on female professionals. For example, from the 1980s, many Mainland universities have struggled to make extra income to improve faculty members' salaries. In addition to a fixed institutional salary, faculty members now receive benefits from other sources, such as fees from self-supporting students, research contracts with enterprises, and profit from school-run factories. Men tend to have a greater network for outside opportunities and are more likely to engage in research projects with outside sources. While achievements are necessary for academic reward, women are not put into a position to demonstrate their abilities. Female faculty members are expected to take up much of the teaching, lower-level administration and household and parenting chores.[31] The latter activities are not as well rewarded as the former ones, and income discrepancy between male and female academics in the PRC is visible, if not statistically definable.

Housing is also an important issue in the academic reward system. In many Mainland universities, female faculty members qualify for on-campus housing only after they reach the rank of associate professor, whereas men are provided with accommodation at the rank of teaching assistant. This double standard reflects the value that men's career development carries more weight than women's in Mainland academe.[32] Another example shows the unequal treatment of men and women. The retirement age is 60 for men and 55 for women. As one approaches retirement, opportunities become fewer and fewer for women than men, while pressures increase. Consequently, women do not move up as much as their male counterparts.[33]

For both Taiwanese and Mainland female faculty members, a graduate degree is crucial to promotion. In Taiwan, a doctoral degree is essential for female professionals in academic employment, research, high-level administrative positions, and for rank advancement.[34] Compared to their Taiwanese counterparts, Mainland female faculty members also face difficulties in promotion. As the current criteria for promotion emphasize formal graduate degrees and research productivity, women are disadvantaged because they are less likely to hold a graduate degree or to publish. Consequently, women's rank promotion tends to be slower than their male counterparts.

CONCLUSION

Gender differences exist in the measures of academic rewards and promotion in Taiwan. Although empirical studies do not show a consistent pattern of strong gender preference in the résumé-evaluation stage of hiring faculty members, due to the imperfection of this evaluation technique, discrimination possibly exists; more comprehensive research is needed.

Regarding the status of female faculty members in Taiwan and the PRC, both groups share commonalties in their academic careers. The status of contemporary Taiwanese and Mainland women reflects a mixture of traditional values coupled with modified ideas about women and their role in society. Although female faculty members are generally highly educated, better informed and represent the élite levels of the society, many of them are still confronting traditional gender prejudice or discrimination at work.

In terms of educational achievement, the progress of women in Taiwan and the PRC has increased at all levels of education over the past four decades. Specifically in higher education, Taiwan's female participation increased almost fourfold, from 11% in 1951 to 43% in 1994. The attainment rate of Mainland women started at a higher level than in Taiwan and increased by only 12% in the last 40 years (see Table 17.1).

Table 17.1
Percentage of female educational participation in Taiwan and the PRC

	Year	Taiwan	PRC
Primary Education	1950	39	–
	1951	–	28
	1971	48	–
	1973	–	40.7
	1994	48	47.1
Secondary Education	1950	28	–
	1951	–	27.8
	1971	40	–
	1973	–	33
	1994	47	41.6
Higher Education	1951	11	22.5
	1971	37	–
	1973	–	30.8
	1994	43	34.5

Sources: *Education statistics of the Republic of China 1950, 1951, 1971, 1995;* Hsieh, 1995; *Essential statistics of education in China, 1994; Achievement of education in China 1949–1983,* 1984.

Likewise, the representation of Taiwanese women in faculties started lower than in the PRC but caught up in the 1990s. The current proportion of female academics is similar in both societies; about one-third of academics are female (see Tables 17.2 and 17.3).

With respect to the hiring of faculty staff, research for both Taiwan and the PRC reports that discrimination does not exist. Yet, the lack of social/informal networks coupled with a biased evaluation of female applicants could indicate gender discrimination. The current revised job placement

Table 17.2
Percentage of female faculty members
in Taiwan and the PRC

	Taiwan	PRC
1949	–	20.6
1950	7.88	–
1965	18.13	25.8
1990	31.06	29.1
1994	32.99	32.0

Sources: *Educational statistics of the Republic of China 1995; Educational statistics yearbook of China 1994; Achievement of education in China, 1949–1983*

Table 17.3
Percentage of female faculty members at different ranks, 1994

	Taiwan	PRC
Professor	11.2	13.6
Associate Professor	22.3	23.2
Lecturer	43.4	34.4

Sources: *Educational statistics of the Republic of China 1995; Educational statistics yearbook of China 1994; Achievement of education in China, 1949–1983*

system reveals a renewed discrimination against women at university.[35] To substantiate whether there is true equality in faculty staff employment requires further investigation.

In terms of rewards, income discrepancy between male and female faculty members prevails in Taiwan. Although no data exist to indicate that Mainland female faculty members earn less than their male counterparts, recent market reforms are theorized to have a negative impact on women's income.

For both Taiwanese and Mainland female faculty members, a graduate degree is of great importance for rank promotion. In both societies, female academics spend more time on teaching and lower-level administration than on research publication. Despite career pressure, female faculty members in Taiwan and the PRC are still expected to assume full responsibility for family and child care obligations. As a result, female faculty members take a longer time than men for advancement to a higher rank.

In sum, gender differences exist with respect to hiring, reward and promotion in Taiwanese and Mainland academic sectors. Women have had more barriers and have not been sponsored into the academic profession in the same ways as men have. The status of Taiwanese female academics is found to be comparable to that of their Mainland counterparts.

NOTES

1. Kelly, 1991.
2. F.C.I. Chang, 1995; Chou, 1992.
3. M.B. Young, 1973; E. Shu-shin Lee Yao, 1983; Sheridan and Salaff, 1984.
4. E. Shu-shin Lee Yao, 1983. Ono, 1989.
5. S.N. Robinson, 1975.
6. Chiang and Ku, 1985.
7. *Statistical yearbook of the Republic of China 1994.*
8. *Statistical yearbook of the Republic of China 1993.*
9. Fei, Tsau and Lai, 1982, pp. 159–85.
10. Chang, 1994.
11. Chin-fen Chang, 1995, p. 155.
12. Hsieh, 1995.
13. Ben, 1985.
14. K.C. Chen, 1993.
15. Chin-fen Chang, 1995; Kuo, 1993.
16. In the study, a stratified random sampling by the tri-category of departments (humanities, social sciences and sciences/technology) and universities was used. These résumés closely approximated those usually submitted by applicants for faculty positions in Taiwanese colleges and universities. The ten applicants were shown as having varying academic qualifications, such as education, publications, work experience and personal characteristics (such as age, gender and marital status).
17. In addition, a research subsidy fund was set up under the National Science Council of the Executive Yuan for those who wished to conduct specific research projects. The pay scale for public institution teachers is fixed according to the salary scale for public functionaries and based on 12-month employment. See *Education statistics of the Republic of China 1991*; Lu, 1986.
18. The subjects were full and associate university professors from a national data-set in Taiwan. All women in the data-set, totalling 827, were included in this study and a comparable number of men were also selected. Two major instruments were developed for data collection in August 1990: a survey questionnaire and an in-depth interview. The survey returned 740 valid responses (45%). In addition, 23 faculty members took part in the in-depth interviews.
19. Hayhoe, 1996. Thirty-eight female faculty were interviewed for this study.
20. Hayhoe, 1996.
21. Andors, 1983, pp. 101–49.
22. *Zhongguo Funü Bao* (China Women's Newspaper), 26 April 1989, p. 2.
23. *Zhongguo Jiaoyu Bao*, 22 March 1995, p. 1.
24. Jiang, 1988; Rosen, 1992.

25. Su, 1989.
26. *Zhongguo Funü* (China Women), no. 1, January 1989, pp. 18–24.
27. Educational Research Institute of Sichuan Normal University, 1986, p. 17; Rosen, 1992, pp. 267–70.
28. Human Resources Research Institute, State Science and Technology Commission, 1986, pp. 3–5.
29. Lilu, 1988.
30. Lilu, 1988.
31. Hayhoe, 1996.
32. Hayhoe, 1996, pp. 242–3.
33. *Zhongguo Funü Bao* (China Women's Newspaper), 31 March 1986, p. 3; 22 September 1986, p. 1.
34. Chou, 1992.
35. Hayhoe, 1996, p. 242.

PART 6
VALUES AND ASPIRATIONS

18

Is Lei Feng Finally Dead?
The Search for Values in a Time
of Reform and Transition

Gay Garland REED

INTRODUCTION

Periods of dramatic economic and social change are inevitably unsettling;
they force upon society unanticipated cultural adjustments which can
threaten traditional values and patterns of interaction. This observation,
which applies to segments of Chinese society at almost any point in the
last century, is especially relevant to the post-Mao era and is manifested in
moral education at Chinese universities.

The title of this chapter — 'Is Lei Feng Finally Dead?' — is derived
from some common sayings heard on the streets of China since the mid-
1980s. It refers to the perception that the socialist values which the hero/
role model, Lei Feng, represented have disappeared.[1] According to
propagandists, the People's Liberation Army soldier lived an exemplary
life and died in the line of duty. In 1963, Chairman Mao wrote a famous
piece of calligraphy urging the nation to follow in Lei's footsteps. Over
subsequent decades he served as a political tool to inculcate socialist values
and promote 'spiritual civilization'. But given the reforms in higher
education since 1978, is Lei Feng still a viable role model for tertiary
students? Are the socialist/communist values that he represented obsolete
and incompatible with 'commodity socialism'? Has Chinese society
undergone such drastic change that Lei Feng is now an unwelcome remnant
of the past?

Common sense suggests that a unidimensional model like Lei Feng would not be relevant to young people in the context of rapid social, economic and political change. The introduction of competing notions of what it means to be 'successful' in China at the end of the twentieth century makes the virtue competition that promoted models of the Lei Feng-type a phenomenon of the past.[2] Traditional and socialist notions of asceticism and frugality have been replaced by a pattern of increasing consumerism.[3] Nevertheless, analyses of newspaper articles, commentaries, and political statements, coupled with personal interviews and data drawn from a number of country-wide surveys suggest that rumours of Lei Feng's decease are exaggerated. The demise of Lei Feng that seemed to be a *fait accompli* a few years ago is not so certain as China moves towards the twenty-first century. A new wave of nostalgia, a revival of patriotism and a growing concern about the negative effects of money and individualism have breathed new life into Lei Feng and his message of 'humanheartedness' (*ren*) and concern for others.

Given the scope and complexity of the moral/political/ideological climate of the PRC over the last three decades, the Lei Feng lens provides a useful means through which to view the issues. During his heyday, Lei Feng represented a proletarianized version of earlier Confucian prototypes. The virtues that were cultivated by learning from Comrade Lei Feng were essentially the same — loyalty, filial piety, self-cultivation, modesty, frugality, diligence and benevolence (humanheartedness) — as those of his Confucian predecessors, although the social manifestation of these virtues was quite different.[4]

The patterns of the campaigns to 'Emulate Comrade Lei Feng' which began in 1963 indicate he served as an 'all-purpose model' for multiple political and ideological agendas.[5] Not only did he serve as a tool for the political socialization of Chinese children, youth[6] and adults, but he also had a role in political legitimization. Party leaders demonstrated their loyalty to Chairman Mao and to socialist/communist ideals by following in the Chairman's footsteps and writing calligraphy in praise of the fallen hero/model. In the process they basked in the reflection of Lei Feng's simple virtues. Nevertheless, there were people who doubted. Interviews conducted by the author (1987–90) with Chinese students in the PRC and the USA revealed serious critiques of the revolutionary hero. Some even raised doubts as to whether he ever existed. Critiques of Lei Feng reflected changing political, social and economic values, but they also revealed serious concerns about corruption in the CCP and a general resistance to political manipulation. The critiques fall into four general categories.

Critics
1. focus on Lei Feng as a political tool for manipulating the people;
2. see the Lei Feng message as anachronistic and incompatible with the times;
3. view Lei Feng as too 'saintly' a figure to aspire to; or
4. question Lei Feng's character and motives.[7]

Over several decades there were changes to the original Lei Feng story, more in terms of emphasis than in actual content. For example, in the books written for children and for political study, Lei Feng's slavish loyalty to Chairman Mao was played down, and his good deeds and service to the people were emphasized. But these changes were minor in comparison to changes in the social context. A story which sounded inspiring and could move people to tears in 1963 sounded somewhat foolish a generation later when changing economic and social circumstances caused people to re-evaluate their earlier beliefs and values. Students constructed their own understandings of what Lei Feng represented. They took the official story and extracted the attributes that they saw as valuable and desirable, and ignored the parts that did not coincide with their notions of what made a good person. In this process some people rejected or ignored Lei's unquestioning obedience to the CCP and focused on his 'humanheartedness'. Traits like his diligence and self-cultivation were seen as less important while his concern for other people made him worthy of admiration and emulation. This emphasis on 'serving the people' and caring for others occurs in the 1980s and 1990s when people are particularly concerned about the deteriorating moral climate in the PRC.

MORAL CLIMATE OF THE REFORM ERA

Since the early 1980s the Chinese news media have been replete with lamentations about the negative social effects of economic liberalization. Articles concerned about the unwanted consequences of reform like corruption, bribery, selfishness, prostitution and hooliganism have filled the pages of Chinese print media for the last two decades. Students are by no means exempt from these problems. A commentary in *Renmin Ribao* reminded readers that universities, like other social institutions, are subject to corrosion from 'extreme individualism, pleasure seeking and money worship'.[8]

The reform process has created a more permissive environment which provides greater options for individuals to pursue materialistic goals and alternative routes to upward mobility.[9] An analysis of large-scale surveys conducted in the 1980s suggests that there had been an increase in social options for Chinese youth due to the market economy. Along with a greater number of options came greater freedom to choose among the available options. This came about as a result of weakening government control over the process of social change. In turn, this has had an impact on the traditional institutions of upward mobility, the CCP, the military, state enterprises and schools, forcing them to rethink their methods of political socialization to suit a new social climate. The inevitable result of this process is a general decline in the concern for politics to the extent that, rather then being a vehicle to success, CCP membership sometimes follows economic, academic or professional success.[10]

Moral decline was a concern expressed in a poll conducted in 1994 which surveyed 7000 youths between the ages of 14 and 34. This survey, conducted by the China Youth Studies Centre, looked at the impact of 15 years of reform. The results were published in the January 1995 issue of *China Youth (Zhongguo Qingnian Bao)*.[11] Youths in ten provinces and provincial-level municipalities (Beijing, Shanghai, Guangdong, Shandong, Liaoning, Henan, Sichuan, Shaanxi, Gansu and Guizhou) were polled about their views on reform, and the results were compared with earlier data which was reported in 1988 and 1991. The survey indicates that while the youths are more positive than negative about the social developments that have occurred over the last 15 years, official honesty, public ethical practice and public order were ranked the most problematic areas. The analysts note,

> This poll found that nearly 60% of youth (57.65%) acknowledge the phenomenon of a 'moral decline' during our social change-over period. This fact proves that the social and psychological grounds for a 'moral reconstruction project' exist, so that a golden age for such a project has arrived.[12]

The article indicates that questions which related to 'material civilization' received high positive ratings, while questions which looked at the social impact of reform on 'spiritual civilization' received lower ratings.[13] This analysis is in keeping with the CCP's concerns about moral decline and its position that individuals place too much emphasis on 'material civilization' at the expense of 'spiritual civilization'.

Similarly, a group of graduate students who were surveyed for this chapter,[14] generally agreed that the moral climate had worsened over the last decade. Like the youths in other studies, the graduate students in 1996 were mostly concerned about crime, selfishness, overindulgence, a focus on money, cheating in business and a general lack of integrity. The most interesting finding was in the minority of dissenting voices who said that the moral climate was improving. They cited greater tolerance, openness and freedom to speak out as positive qualities of the present moral climate.

One graduate student wrote, 'The moral climate in China at this time is real and true and not distorted compared with previous decades.' This respondent felt that the new openness of Chinese society permitted greater honesty in communication and less political posturing. These minority views are significant because they include liberal democratic principles as part of spiritual civilization.

Has Lei Feng disappeared?

Where does Lei Feng fit in the present moral schema that Chinese youth use to make sense of the world, and how useful is he as a role model for higher education students? Student attitudes regarding these questions understandably shift as the social economy moves towards marketization. They are also influenced by current events and media campaigns. Several studies conducted in the PRC have raised questions about the efficacy of the Lei Feng model and give an indication of student views.

A 1990 study reported that 95% of military cadets saw a need to launch an 'emulate Lei Feng movement and expressed a willingness and readiness to learn from Lei Feng's example'.[15] The researchers also noted that 'the outlook [regarding Lei Feng movements] is neither as optimistic as publicized and propagandized in certain journals and newspapers nor as pessimistic as projected by certain people'.[16] This study was conducted in the context of the military, which is one of the most ideologically controlled segments of the youth population. While the high percentages present a favourable picture of Lei Feng movements, the text which accompanies these figures is careful to raise significant dissenting opinions. Indeed, it thoroughly deconstructs the Lei Feng model of the 1960s form and raises serious questions about its viability in the 1990s. Although the study attempts to counter its own critique by making a series of suggestions about how to implement future campaigns, ironically, this survey is among the most thorough critiques of Lei Feng published in the PRC.[17]

Research conducted in 1990 in the aftermath of the events of 4 June 1989[18] — a period of nationwide revival of Lei Feng — inevitably produced different results from studies half a decade later. After Tiananmen, the CCP revived Lei Feng, although largely unsuccessfully, in an attempt to restore faith in the military and in its own socialist moral agenda and possibly as a diversion. The year 1996 saw no such revival. In fact, the media did not produce a flood of Lei Feng material around the 5 March anniversary of the appearance of Chairman Mao's famous calligraphy exhorting the country to 'learn from Comrade Lei Feng' as was customary in the past. Commentaries were generally limited to two newspapers.[19]

A 1994 survey found that 82% of Beijing youth felt that the Lei Feng spirit was 'not outdated' (*meiyou guoshi*).[20] Although this high percentage is somewhat suspect[21] and leads us to question the survey methods and results, it is worth noting that questions on Lei Feng are still being asked in the 1990s.

Is Lei Feng a good model in the 1990s? The graduate students in the 1996 study were divided, with two-thirds dismissing the soldier as an outdated model. They felt the new economic conditions did not favour people of little education whose time was consumed with selfless acts that did not promote economic progress. He was also seen as 'outdated' in another respect: the diversity and maturity of present-day Chinese youth and the fact that they 'have their own ideas'. A role model promoted by the mass media was not seen as appropriate to the times. As one respondent put it, 'There are many ways to be good in a society.' Some also noted that a 'good manners machine' made people uncomfortable and that Lei Feng was too elevated. Students who saw the value of Lei Feng as a model for today's youth touted his loyalty, good character, unselfishness and respect for the older generation as traits that should be promoted. Lei was seen as helping to promote qualities that are absent in today's PRC. According to one respondent, 'When people lose interest in the collective, there is a greater need for somebody to advocate collectivism and altruism.' Thus, for some students Lei Feng still serves as a possible corrective, an antidote, to present social ills.

On the contrary, in a study of Shandong soldiers, only 8% mentioned Lei Feng as the most admired person in their lives.[22] The other 92% looked up to scientists, writers, reformers, performing artists or athletes. Likewise, when questioned about what role models the younger generation follows, the 1996 graduate students listed scholars, entrepreneurs, self-made people, pop singers, movie stars, managers, tycoons and millionaires. Fifty-four characteristics were cited as ingredients making up a good role model; the most prominent were being helpful to others, honest and kind. Frequently cited virtues included responsibility, independence, diligence, success and bravery. Descriptors mentioned by more than one respondent included intelligent, loving, well-educated (knowledgeable, learned), capable of earning enough money and optimistic. The wide-ranging list of characteristics includes values that could be identified as traditional Confucian, socialist or capitalist and is indicative of the growing plurality of thought in Chinese society. This is the inevitable result of opening the system to alternatives.

New role models

In response to the changing social and economic landscape and the growing political tensions in the hinterland, the CCP has designated new models that reflect contemporary concerns. The sacrifice of Gong Fansen, the CCP cadre who obeyed the Party's call and left his ageing mother, wife and three children to serve the Tibetan masses, was remembered in calligraphy written by Jiang Zemin.[23] Xu Hu, a model for ordinary workers, gained fame by his diligent attention to unblocking toilets, doing electrical work and inventing a new tool to do his work more efficiently.[24] Chen Guanyu, a native of Shenzhen, who strives to be 'Lei Feng's little sister', has gained her model status by remaining immune to the temptations of bribery. Serving the Party and the people, resisting the temptations of the new affluent society, discovering innovative ways to perform tasks, and sacrificing personal comforts are characteristics of some of the new models promoted by the CCP. The revival of spiritual civilization at a time when the collective consciousness has been focused on material civilization is a daunting task for the CCP, which sees its influence deteriorating. The revival of old models, the creation of new ones to carry on the revolutionary lineage, and an increased focus on patriotism and morality are familiar tools resurrected to bring about patriotism and morality.

Patriotism and morality

One of the purposes of higher education since the founding of the PRC has been to create citizens who are both 'red' and 'expert'. The balance of these two attributes has fluctuated in relation to the political fervour of the times; but whether the emphasis was on 'red' or 'expert', the ultimate purpose was to serve the needs of the motherland. This is an unquestioned moral imperative which still exists, at least in terms of official rhetoric. The connection between morality and patriotism is made in official commentaries where the effort to build 'spiritual civilization' is seen as an ideological education process in which patriotism is an essential element.[25]

A political commentary in *Renmin Ribao* directed at higher education students encourages them to 'combine [their] own destiny and future with the nation's destiny and future'.[26] Students are reminded that they must not focus on 'self-perfection' alone, but must consider also 'the nation's prosperity, national development and social progress' as well. According to this article, '[i]deological and political work and education in moral standards in universities should centre on education on the outlooks on life and the world and should try to achieve pragmatic results'.[27] Reminders like this are indicative of growing concerns that students will ignore their public responsibilities in pursuit of their personal goals. The job of moral/ political education at the university level is to remind students that these are inextricably interlinked.

Since 1989 (post-Tiananmen) a renewed effort has attempted to promote patriotism in the PRC. Education on patriotic devotion is the first of the 'Four Educations' which Chinese leader Jiang Zemin has been encouraging since 1995. The other three 'educations' are: education on a revolutionary outlook on life, education on respect for officers and love for soldiers, and education on hard struggle and plain living.[28] All of these characteristics were earlier embodied in the Lei Feng model, and images of the frugal, diligent, patriotic and human-hearted socialist revolutionary are easily conjured up by these categories. This suggests a natural relationship between patriotism and morality, a relationship that was expressed by a student who had returned to the PRC from study in the USA:

> Strictly speaking, patriotism is not a political concept: it is an ethical concept. It is an expression of a special kind of human moral phenomenon. That is, it is a kind of ethical attitude based on the socialized citizens' common identity and common sentiment toward their national community (not just one nationality) which is formed gradually and then turned into a tradition. The moral character of this kind of ethical attitude is positive, self-contained and shared by all.[29]

The clear relationship between morality and patriotism was not evident to all of the 1996 graduate students, however. About one-third of the students saw no connection at all between the two concepts, or they saw them as totally independent of each other. The two-thirds who saw them as related perceived the connections in very different ways. A sample of the responses follows:

- Patriotism is an invariable part of virtue.
- Morality includes patriotism. If a person is not a patriotic person, he will have no morality.
- They are quite different concepts. A person with good morals will unvariably (sic) love his/her own country, but a person who is a patriot is not always a good person in morals.
- There is no tight relationship between them. A real good person loves people all over the world, he will not be limited by his own country.
- They are different. Morality is a basic value guiding people's behaviour, while patriotism is a feeling of unity.
- It seems to me that morality has a loose relationship with patriotism, in a certain sense. Within China, morality is becoming bad, but patriotism still remains. On the other hand, the deteriorating morality is consuming patriotism.

- Everyone loves his country, but not everyone can behave completely morally.
- In my opinion, patriotism should be an important characteristic of a moral person.

These responses reveal a diversity of opinions regarding the relationship between morality and patriotism which is indicative of the plurality and depth of reflection that these issues generate. It also suggests that the official linkage between morality and patriotism that characterizes official pronouncements is not necessarily reflected in the thinking of all university students in the period of reform. If this is the case, it provides a rationale for students who can continue to see themselves as moral people, even if their studies are serving personal rather then patriotic ends.

EDUCATIONAL CHALLENGES FOR A CHANGING SOCIETY

Deng Xiaoping's introduction of the 'responsibility system' in 1978 was one of the first steps towards making 'choice' an operative factor in modern Chinese society. Choice among competing social options has not been an operative concept in the PRC until relatively recently. The nation's schools prepare students to become choice-makers only to a limited degree.[30] Chinese education, in fact, is designed to prepare children to function as part of a group, not to make individual choices. The introduction of 'choice' into the system necessitates a form of education that helps children learn how to choose among competing options, and this is a process that must be introduced early in the educational system and nurtured at every step of the way.

In higher education, job choice upon graduation from the university was essentially thrust upon students who were unprepared to 'market' themselves or make decisions about alternative futures. The government set up job fairs and talent fairs to link job seekers with potential employers, and to facilitate the transition from school to work. But for young people who are not educated to make choices, the process is a daunting one.

Along with 'choice', which involves carefully balancing public responsibility with individual interest, 'money' is the most powerful of all the factors which are influencing modern Chinese values. In newspaper articles, commentaries, surveys and interviews, 'money' is noted as the force which undermines socialist values and leads people astray. But the ability to make money and live a comfortable life is also one of the characteristics which makes a person worthy of emulation. It is an educational challenge to balance these two viewpoints. Another aspect of

the relationship between money and education is important to consider —
its influence upon the educational opportunity structure. Although there
were instances of support from private sources and from work-units before
1994, some students began officially paying all or part of their own tuition
in that year. According to *Xinhua*, 245 colleges carried out this reform in
1994. As of autumn 1996, half of all colleges and universities in China
charged students fees,[31] thereby greatly altering the educational opportunity
structure. As the rules of the game change, the educational challenges
become greater. Students quickly adapt to the new technology and the new
social norms, but moral/political/ideological education becomes
increasingly problematic.

Moral / political education: 1990s style

Classes that focus on Marxism, Leninism and Mao Zedong Thought
continue to be regular fare for college students, but politics is no longer the
central theme around which life is organized in the PRC. Courses tend to
be less infused with moral and political content but, while the general trend
is towards depoliticization, there are always periods of retrenchment. One
such example occurred in the wake of Tiananmen when there was a
resurgence of emphasis on military training. Students at universities in
Beijing were required to take a year out of their university programme for
training. Military training, in one form or another, is part of the university
experience for students across the country. Informants have indicated that
this training takes a variety of forms and is interpreted by the students in
different ways. One informant said they had no textbook for their course
in military science, but had a series of speakers come into the classroom to
talk about a variety of topics including military rules and regulations,
military equipment (guns, tanks, aeroplanes, personnel carriers, explosives
and missiles), survival techniques and strategic weapons deployment. A
university professor felt that among her students, the boys in particular
enjoyed the course as they 'like the subject matter'. Learning 'about' the
military and studying it through a textbook or lectures in a classroom is a
qualitatively different experience from actual military training which was
part of the experience of many university students in China. A university
graduate said that during her first year of university in Wuhan the entire
freshman class spent a month at a military base in the country living the
frugal life of a military recruit. She reported that they drew water from the
well, learned how to use rifles, engaged in hard labour and sang songs.
She commented that even though they were only at the military base for a
month, the memory of that month made a strong impression which she

vividly recalled five years later. She remembered that they had no hot water to bathe with and said, 'We could not get clean but when we finished we were very strong and healthy. In the beginning, when we had to stand for a long time some students fainted because they were weak. They taught us how to stand putting the weight on the front of our feet so we would not fall down.' She commented, 'We learned to sing very loud. We had to sing as loud as possible. It's difficult but the loud singing makes your spirit strong.' Her direct reference to the connection between singing and spiritual strength suggests that the moral content of the experience was made explicit to the students. Significantly, she also noted that one political benefit of such a course is to build strong bonds between the students and the military. As evidence of this bond she said that letters were exchanged long after the students returned to campus in Wuhan.

The experiential component in the field was complemented with lectures delivered by military instructors. She says, 'We were very quiet. We just listened to everything and did what they told us.' This attitude of quiet compliance did not continue throughout her university education, however. In her third year of university the students studied from a text entitled *Chinese Socialist Construction*. She described the instructor's difficulty in teaching the course.

> This was a hard course to teach because the teacher had to know something about economic issues and controversial issues in the society. The other courses were easy to teach because the students just had to learn the material, but this course was difficult for the teacher. The students asked a lot of questions. Because they were third-year students they had their own ideas and asked questions.

Although course titles and texts for courses related to moral/political education look similar from one university to another, differences in instructional methods and the introduction of experiential components affect the experience.

Relatively new courses like the one on socialist construction are facilitated by the Chinese textbook industry which is accustomed to printing large numbers of texts at low costs and has a well-articulated distribution mechanism in place. Less hampered by the complex legal and marketing issues faced in other countries, textbooks can move from the conceptual stage into print and on to the shelves with great speed.[32]

Political study meetings

One essential element of ideological education has been the regular political study meetings. These meetings are still a regular part of university life in the PRC as they were in the past. It is important to note, however, that the content, atmosphere and nature of these meetings vary widely even at the same institution. An informant notes that when she was in her first and second years of university in Wuhan (1991 and 1992) she and her fellow students attended the political study meetings regularly. The meetings were somewhat formal and students were compelled to sit, listen and engage in dialogue concerning issues which were raised by the meeting's organizer. Often the subject matter was a discussion of new Party directives or topics related to moral education. She noted that it was important to have an opinion, and silences were greeted with embarrassment and sympathy for the meeting's organizer who tried to encourage lively discussion with the help of a class monitor. She reported that by her third and fourth years, students were not so docile and compliant, the meetings were less formal and more time was spent planning picnics and dance parties. This suggests that the definition of political study is flexible and dependent upon a number of factors, like the age and interests of the students, the conscientiousness of the organizers and, perhaps most importantly, the political tone of the times. In the past when politics permeated every aspect of life, political study sessions were an integral part of a tightly woven moral/political/ideological framework. As the system relaxed, the general tone of political study often became less rigid. As with other aspects of university life in a time of reform and change, political study sessions are being restructured and refocused.

CONCLUSION

In a study cited above, Beijing students were asked what aspect of life they regarded as most precious. The top five answers were health, moral character, knowledge, career and family. According to this survey, money, power, fame, wealth and pleasure were 'quite low on the list'.[33] The authors note the great discrepancy between the ethical values that students purport to have and the social reality. Efforts to move reality closer to the ideal are described in the political literature as 'moral reconstruction'. For higher education students this entails a renewed emphasis on the importance of cultivating a 'correct outlook' as a means to stem present excesses and provide a balanced development of material and spiritual civilization. According to exiled Chinese literary critic Liu Zaifu, this can come about in the PRC through 'reconstruct(ing) the *liangzhi xitong* (conscience system)'.[34]

The pattern of loosening and tightening (*fangshou*) which has characterized Chinese politics and educational practices for several decades is once again moving towards a tightening in an effort to curb the effects of 'creeping capitalism'.[35] Internal and external forces are at work pressing Chinese society towards another period of constraint. One example of this is a ¥1.2 million campaign to promote communist ideology (moral and political education) over three years on the campus of Shenzhen University. This plan, which was announced by the local government shortly after a visit from Jiang Zemin,[36] appears to be part of a nationwide trend towards ideological retrenchment,[37] an inevitable occurrence at the beginning of a new political era, following the death of Deng Xiaoping. Such a retrenchment poses a particular problem for students who, on the one hand, are being encouraged to take responsibility for financing their education and conducting their own job searches — activities which demand greater autonomy, personal initiative, habits of choice-making and entrepreneurialism — but, on the other hand, are being forced to comply with an increasingly restrictive ideological education which demands compliance to a narrow set of politically correct thoughts and behaviours. The obvious disjuncture between these two conflicting messages could lead to a psychological 'double bind' which is potentially explosive. Negotiating the paths among these conflicting values is problematic. One of the graduate students surveyed described the moral climate of the PRC as in a transitional period. With the boom of the domestic economy and the Open Door policy old moral values are being challenged, while new market-oriented ones have not been established. There is a mixture of both.

The tension between material and spiritual civilization is always present and meaning is continuously being renegotiated in relation to competing social, political and economic factors. In this time of reform and transition when the social impetus is towards greater pluralism, it is significant that Lei Feng is still part of the conversation about values. Within the confines of the military and in educational settings with younger children, the message still has some usefulness. For adults and for university students, however, the Lei Feng message is too simplistic. But since it is not clear what direction the new drive towards 'moral reconstruction' will take, and since the general thrust of reform is towards plurality, it is premature to suggest that the values that the Lei Feng model represents are expendable.

NOTES

1. There were two sayings which were commonly heard: *Lei Feng shushu bu jianle* (Uncle Lei Feng has disappeared) and *Lei Feng shushu sile* (Uncle Lei Feng is dead).

2. This has been described as 'virtuocracy'. See Shirk, 1982.
3. See Sklair, 1994.
4. Reed, 1995.
5. Reed, 1991.
6. 'Youth' is a broadly applied term in China, often meaning people between the ages of 14 and 34.
7. Reed, 1991, pp. 190–200.
8. 'Setting correct outlook on life requires guidance and help', *Renmin Ribao*, 12 December 1995, p. 5, translated in FBIS–CHI–96–015, 23 January 1996, pp. 20–1.
9. Rosen, 1990.
10. Rosen, 1990.
11. See Wang Xiaodong and Wu Luping, 1995, translated in FBIS–CHI–95–050, 15 March 1995, pp. 43–9.
12. Wang Xiaodong and Wu Luping, 1995, p. 45.
13. Wang Xiaodong and Wu Luping, 1995.
14. In 1996, 29 graduate students from work-units around the country who were attending graduate school at a prestigious university responded at length in English to a series of open-ended questions related to the moral climate of the PRC. These students were part of an advanced English class and had academic backgrounds in social science and the humanities. The purpose of this research was to illuminate points and delve more deeply into issues which were touched upon in official country-wide surveys conducted in the PRC during the 1980s and '90s. The respondents' approach to answering the questions revealed a willingness to consider alternatives and look at the issues from multiple perspectives.
15. Li Kaicheng and Geng Yansheng, 1991. The authors, staff of the Political Department, General Headquarters of Chief of Staff, PLA questioned 454 students and cadets in ten military colleges.
16. Li Kaicheng and Geng Yansheng, 1991. From the translation, p. 23.
17. Another critique is provided in a study conducted by a member of the Organization Department of Troop 54685, Laiyang Municipality, Shandong province, which questioned 675 soldiers. See Wang Guisheng, 1990.
18. See Chapter 19 by Teresa Wright in this volume for a detailed account of the development of the student movements and the events in and around Tiananmen Square on 4 June 1989.
19. 'Learn from Lei Feng spirit, carry forward healthy tendencies of times', *Jiefangjun Bao* (People's Liberation Army Newspaper), 5 March 1996, p. 3, translated in FBIS-CHI-96-058, p. 21. See also Xie Qing, 1996, p. 1. Articles also appeared in the *Zhongguo Qingnian Bao* (China Youth Newspaper).
20. Survey conducted by the Beijing Municipal Society for Youth Studies. See Tian and Zhang, 1995.
21. Chinese survey methods and results are highly suspect. See Rosen, 1987.
22. See Wang Guisheng, 1990.
23. Bonnin, 1996, pp. 11–2.
24. Bonnin, 1996, p. 13–4.
25. For example, a 1995 political policy statement which discusses peasant ideological education focuses on three interrelated areas: (1) conducting peasant

ideological education which emphasizes socialism, collectivism and patriotism; (2) a better education in regard to correct outlook on life, values and moral concepts; and (3) better peasant education in changing existing habits and customs. Botou Municipal CCP Committee, Hebei province, 1995.

26. 'Setting correct outlook on life requires guidance and help', *Renmin Ribao*, 12 December 1995, p. 5, translated in FBIS-CHI-96-015, 26 January 1996, pp. 20–1.

27. See note 26.

28. 'Matter of great importance to units' political building — first comment on more thoroughly and more effectively conducting the Four Educations', *Jiefangjun Bao*, 27 February 1996, p. 1, translated in FBIS-CHI-96-061, 28 March 1996, p. 22.

29. Wan, 1995.

30. Comparative research on preschool education suggests children in the PRC have been socialized into a world of few choices. See Tobin, Wu and Davidson, 1989.

31. This policy was announced at the 1996 National Education Working Conference, *Xinhua*, 22 January 1996, translated in FBIS-CHI-96-017, 25 January 1996, p. 14. See Chapter 12 by Zhang Minxuan in this volume.

32. Reed, 1992.

33. Tian and Zhang, 1995, p. 59.

34. This concept is discussed at some length in Lin Tongqi, 1994.

35. Hertling, 1996, p. A43.

36. Hertling, 1996, p. A45.

37. Another sign of this retrenchment was that the CCP Central Party School began publication of a new bimonthly theoretical journal in early 1996. According to its editor, the journal will offer 'scientific theoretical guidance for the realization of China's trans-century development goals'. *Xinhua*, 15 April 1996, translated in FBIS-CHI-96-074, 16 April 1996, p. 38.

19

The Limits of Political Loosening: CCP Restraints on Student Behaviour in the Spring of 1989[1]

Teresa WRIGHT

INTRODUCTION

In many ways, CCP control over college campuses decreased in the 1980s. Indeed, the CCP's Education Reform Document of 1985 expressly stated that the PRC's educational problems derived from 'excessive government control'.[2] A major component of the CCP's proposed solution was decentralization; specifically, universities were given more power over curricula and teaching methods.[3] In addition, political education in CCP ideology was de-emphasized as the goal of education shifted from the production of loyal communists to the production of 'advanced specialists' fit to serve the Four Modernizations.[4] Concomitantly, political education became less doctrinaire and more tolerant of individual beliefs.[5]

Yet, as evident in the 'anti-spiritual pollution' campaign of 1983 and the 'anti-bourgeois liberalization' campaign of 1987, events of the spring of 1989 again illustrate that the post-Mao decrease in CCP control over education is neither cumulative nor irreversible. Indeed, the events of the spring of 1989 demonstrate that despite the educational reforms of the Deng era, the CCP continues to exert a profound influence over student life. This chapter provides a detailed description of this influence by illustrating the specific ways in which student behaviour and organization in the spring of 1989 were shaped by continued CCP domination of the political structure, the media and the campus. In particular, student activities at Beijing University (Beijing Daxue, hereafter Beida) and Beijing Normal University (Beijing Shifan Daxue, hereafter Shida) will be emphasized.[6]

As will be shown, fear of repression was a major consideration in virtually all student actions and decisions throughout the movement. Importantly, this fear-laden environment rendered student decision-making and organization increasingly anarchic. First, in this risky situation, students were extremely fearful of infiltration and thus tended to trust only those with whom they were well acquainted prior to the movement. Second, as the risks involved in student miscalculation were quite high, student leaders found it difficult to compromise with one another. Many students feared that yielding to the will of the majority could result in an action which would incur the wrath of the authorities. Consequently, dissenting student leaders often opted to 'exit' the group, rather than bow to majority rule or negotiate a compromise.

The culture of fear also largely explains why the two campus movement organizations at Beida and Shida initially were formed by only a handful of students. In an environment where all student activities were closely scrutinized by campus authorities and where any autonomous student organization would be likely to meet with oppression, few students dared to step forward publicly and establish a non-Party student protest group. After these few students made this dangerous step, many others joined and supported these groups. However, very few were willing to risk being charged with initiating such an action. More importantly, those who were willing to take this first step earned an enormous amount of respect from their fellow, less courageous, students. This trend continued as the movement progressed. In such a perilous atmosphere, those students willing to take the greatest risks received the most respect and enjoyed the most legitimacy, whereas those calling for moderation were branded cowards lacking true devotion to the cause. Consequently, this fear-laden environment engendered a radicalizing trend in student behaviour.

Further, student demands reflected the continued dominance of the CCP. Throughout the movement, student activists did not question single-party communist rule. At no point did student activists call for the establishment of alternative political parties or for the overthrow of the CCP. Instead, student demands consistently reflected a desire to *reform* the existent single-party political system. For example, many student complaints revolved around Party corruption; the students' proposed solution to this problem was not to eliminate the CCP, but rather to 'clean it up'. Similarly, throughout the movement students consistently called for 'dialogue' with the CCP, thus implicitly assuming that the CCP could ameliorate their dissatisfaction. Finally, student activists demanded that the government acknowledge that the movement was a patriotic and loyalist expression of the wishes of the people. Thus, rather than questioning the fundamental legitimacy of CCP rule, the students consistently sought its validation.

PRECURSORS TO THE 1989 MOVEMENT

Continued CCP control over the college campus was also evident in student dissident activities at Beida and Shida in the period immediately preceding the movement of 1989. Indeed, pressure from the authorities was often so great that some of these earlier groups existed for only a few days before they were forced to disband. In consequence, these earlier student activists were shown that despite the educational reforms, independent student organizations and activities would be closely monitored and typically punished.

The 'Wednesday Forum' at Beida was the first group established by students who would later play a part in the organization of the movement of 1989. This group was established early in the 1987–88 institution year. Its core included fewer than ten students. Although Wang Dan and Yang Tao were the most active in the group, it was quite informal and had no clear organizational structure. The group enlisted guest speakers such as US Ambassador Winston Lord and prominent dissident physicist Fang Lizhi. Every Wednesday, a speech was given on the grassy hill surrounding the Cervantes statue at Beida. Anyone interested in attending was welcome; thus, when more famous speakers came to lecture, fairly large numbers of students attended. These gatherings quickly elicited the ire of campus authorities, however, and, after only a few months, campus authorities forced the group to disband.[7]

Next, on 4 June 1988, the 'Committee of Action' was established at Beida. This group was formed following a typical discussion gathering at the Beida 'Triangle' (Sanjiao), a popular meeting place near the cafeteria. After realizing a common interest, 11 students met to found the 'Committee of Action'. As part of the founding, the students compiled a list of their names and signatures to demonstrate their commitment to publicly support the group. The Committee was composed mainly of graduate students, and many (such as Wang Dan and Yang Tao) had been key figures in the 'Wednesday Forum'.[8] The only undergraduate was Shen Tong, a first-year student. The group succeeded in appealing to a sympathetic professor and was granted the use of an office at the Philosophy Department's branch of the

Communist Youth League. Soon thereafter, the Committee published a leaflet announcing its formation, feeling that it would be best to always air its demands through proper legal channels, so as to lessen the likelihood of government repression. Members of the Committee soon decided to schedule a rally for 8 June, and drafted a list of demands for the government.[9]

Before the scheduled rally was held, however, the Committee dissolved. Group members had been watched closely since the founding of the group. Then, on 7 June, the Committee was expelled from its office by representatives of the Communist Youth League. Later that day, an announcement was broadcast on campus that 'a small group' was manipulating students and 'creating chaos'. Under fear, the group met one final time and disbanded. In fact, the pressure from institution authorities was so intense that the members decided to suspend all contact with each other. Shortly thereafter, institution authorities forced the group's members to write self-criticisms.[10]

In the middle of the autumn semester of 1988, however, these students and others again began to form autonomous organizations. Yet, the continued environment of Party penetration of the campus, coupled with the previous experience of repression, caused these students to be quite cautious in their activities. Perhaps most importantly, these organizations explicitly claimed to be academic rather than political entities, so as to avoid pressure from institution authorities.

In the autumn of 1988, the 'Olympic Institute' and the 'Democracy Salon' were formed almost simultaneously at Beida. The 'Olympic Institute', founded by Shen Tong and composed of seven members, met at various places to discuss academic and scientific matters. The group also researched and wrote essays, which were then sent to various newspapers and official organs. Perhaps most notably, the group submitted an essay on educational reform to the National People's Congress (NPC).[11] The 'Democracy Salon', founded by the familiar duo of Wang Dan and Yang Tao, was a more political organization and functioned in a way similar to the 'Wednesday Forum', inviting speakers to come lecture at the May Fourth Monument at Beida. A few weeks after their formation, the 'Olympic Institute' and the 'Democracy Salon' held a joint meeting, where it was decided that the two groups would remain separate yet cooperate on all events. The members also discussed important anniversaries which were coming up in the spring and summer (such as the 70th anniversary of the May Fourth Movement and the bicentenary of the French Revolution), as well as possibilities for student activities.[12]

Another important group founded at this time was the 'Beida Education

Society'. This group, led by Chang Jin, had around 50 active members and worked to organize students to participate in educational reform. Its specific activities included conducting surveys on rural education and sending letters to the NPC.[13] These groups, as well as several others, continued to function throughout the autumn, winter and early spring of 1988–89.[14]

Interestingly, however, when students began to take to the streets in the wake of former CCP General Secretary Hu Yaobang's death on 15 April 1989,[15] the first extra-Party student group to form at Beida to guide these student activities did not arise through the concerted efforts of the various existing autonomous groups there. Indeed, the organizations which first formed to guide student actions at both Beida and Shida in the wake of Hu's death had quite a haphazard start.

BEIDA AND SHIDA AUTONOMOUS UNIONS

Campus autonomous groups at Beida and Shida were established a few days after the death of Hu Yaobang. Yet, they did not represent the first student activity undertaken following Hu's death. Indeed, many thousands of students participated in marches and demonstrations prior to the establishment of these groups. Immediately following the announcement of the death of Hu Yaobang on 15 April, big-character posters (*dazibao*) began to appear on Beijing campuses to mourn the dead leader, who had been widely regarded as one of the CCP's staunchest supporters of intellectual freedom and political reform. Two days later, the first student marches to Tiananmen Square occurred. On 18 April, students from several institutions again marched to Tiananmen Square and many students began a sit-in in front of the Great Hall of the People. Yet these activities fundamentally were displays of mourning for Hu and were not overtly political in nature. At Shida, for example, a 3000-person march to Tiananmen on 17 April included Party officials, members of the Communist Youth League and members of the official student union (*Xueshenghui*). Similarly, on 17 April money was collected at Beida to purchase a floral wreath to bring to Tiananmen to memorialize Hu.

Further, between 15 April and 18 April, no clear student organization or leadership was operating. As one student activist notes, during this period, 'everyone was playing by their own rules, making their own rules ... people just did things, organized things'.[16] Similarly, a student who helped lead the Beida contingent to the Square on 17 April acknowledges that '[w]e hadn't planned what to do once we arrived at the Square'.[17] In short, between 15 April and 18 April, student actions were spontaneous and haphazard. Realizing the dangers of such unorganized activities, by 19 and 20 April, students at Beida and Shida separately began to organize autonomous campus groups.

On the morning of 19 April, an anonymous poster appeared at the Beida Triangle. The poster announced that a meeting to discuss the establishment of an autonomous campus organization would be held that night. By dusk, hundreds of students had gathered at the Triangle. A few spoke of the need to organize. Most, however, were afraid to speak. Then, a student named Ding Xiaoping asked people to volunteer to be leaders in the new organization. Yet, all of the students were profoundly aware that any persons willing to volunteer would likely be punished by the authorities, as it was probable official spies were in their midst. Consequently, according to one witness, Ding 'three times called on people to come forth to lead, but each time received no answer. Then he said, "OK, do we want to recall the official student union?" The crowd roared, "Yes!" Ding continued, "After its recall, what should be done? Do we want to establish our own organization?" Again the resounding reply was "Yes!"'[18] Yet still no one volunteered. Finally, Ding suggested that those who had spoken earlier be the leaders. As a result, those who had spoken previously had no choice but to back up their words and step forward.[19] Finally, the nine students who had spoken earlier volunteered.[20]

In this way, the Beida Autonomous Union (BdAU) was established. From the start, however, the group was plagued with divisions and discontent, for many of the students who had 'volunteered' to lead the group were not well acquainted with one another. Although some of the volunteers had been involved in previous autonomous organizations, few had been involved in the *same* previous autonomous organizations. As a result, many of the volunteers lacked trust in the competence and dedication of the others, or feared that some of them might be CCP infiltrators. Consequently, the group would be plagued by almost continual infighting throughout the first three weeks of the movement, causing some of the original leaders to desert the group.

At the same time that the BdAU was forming, a similar autonomous student group was formed at Shida. Unlike at Beida, however, the autonomous group at Shida was not formed through any sort of public meeting or discussion. Rather, it was the work of three close friends who had not been part of any previous autonomous groups — Wu'er Kaixi, Liang Er and Zhang Jun. Early in the morning on 20 April, these three students decided to form an autonomous group.[21] To do so, the three simply wrote a big-character poster announcing the formation of the group. The poster read:

1. Students at Shida no longer acknowledge the leadership of the official campus student government and have thus formed the Shida Autonomous Union.
2. Departments not yet registered with the autonomous union should do so at Northwest dorm room #339.
3. Wu'er Kaixi has been elected the president of the union, the general secretary is Zhang Jun and deputy general secretary is Liang Er.[22]

The poster represented the unilateral declaration of these three students and had no basis in reality. There had been no elections for the three union offices; the three leaders had appointed themselves to these positions. The 'union office' (room #339) was Wu'er Kaixi's dormitory room. No department had yet registered with the union, because no Shida students would have heard of the Shida Autonomous Union (SdAU) until they had read the poster.[23]

Nonetheless, the claims made in the poster soon became a reality. Upon reading the poster, students were greatly impressed by the courage of the three students who had publicly posted their names as founders of the illegal group. Moreover, the vast majority of the student body agreed with the sentiment of the poster. Ultimately, students proved to be much less afraid of *joining* the illegal group than they were of *initiating* such an action. Consequently, students not only began to organize and register with the group, but they did so in great haste, apparently because they became concerned that their department would be the last to register with the group (and therefore be the least worthy of respect). Thus, by 6 p.m., students from virtually every department on campus had sent a representative to room #339 to register with the autonomous campus union.[24]

Although the members of this group had no connections with any previous autonomous groups, and despite the fact that the group was not initiated by any sort of public discussion, the SdAU proved to be very effective and stable. While the BdAU was plagued with conflict and divisions throughout the movement, the leadership of the SdAU remained virtually constant, and decisions were reached quite smoothly. Moreover, when an overarching all-Beijing student autonomous federation was formed on 21 April to unite dissident students from all Beijing campuses, it was Shida that took the lead while Beida remained mired in its own organizational conflict.

ALL-BEIJING STUDENTS AUTONOMOUS FEDERATION

Calls for an all-Beijing student autonomous group had been raised by various students from the onset of the movement. However, it was not until 24 April that the federation formally was established. The federation was formed largely under the initiation of the SdAU.[25] Specifically, the three students who had written the poster announcing the formation of the union (Wu'er Kaixi, Zhang Jun and Liang Er) also composed another poster which announced that the 'All-Beijing Students' Autonomous Federation' had been formed and that the first gathering of the Federation would be at 6:30 p.m. on 21 April, at the soccer fields of Shida.[26]

By 5 p.m., the soccer fields at Shida were packed. By 6 p.m., Shida mathematics students calculated that some 60 000 students had gathered. In the meantime, the authorities were searching for Wu'er. First, Wu'er's father was located and brought to the campus to 'talk some sense' into his son. Wu'er, however, remained hidden, moving to different spots as students warned him of the location and direction of his pursuers. Finally, at 8 p.m. Wu'er emerged from hiding and walked in front of the group. He was stunned by the size of the crowd. The three poster-writers had expected only around 1000 students to show up and thus had not acquired any sound equipment. Consequently, Wu'er made only a short speech, announcing the establishment of the 'Temporary Student Federation of Beijing'. Three days later, representatives from all of the universities in Beijing attended a second meeting, where the Federation was formally established.[27]

The BdAU had no involvement in the founding of the Federation. Moreover, it never became a formal part of the Federation. Some Beida students did attend the original gathering of the Federation, as well as the first formal representative meeting, but they did so as individuals and were not under the sponsorship of the BdAU.[28] Ironically, the autonomous student union at Beida, Beijing's most reputable university, with the greatest history of prior agitation and organization,[29] was essentially uninvolved in the creation and maintenance of the first all-city student group autonomous of CCP control to appear in the PRC. Instead, cognizant of its own flawed and weak organization, the BdAU informed the Federation that it would be unable to join the group until it could work out its own campus-level organizational problems.[30]

The Federation met again on 25 April, this time at the University of Politics and Law.[31] The Standing Committee was to meet at 5 p.m., prior to a general meeting scheduled for 6 p.m. However, at 4 p.m. the Central People's Radio broadcast the text of the *Renmin Ribao* editorial which was to be published the next day. Those who heard the broadcast suggested that both meetings be postponed for one hour, so that all members could listen to a repeat broadcast, to be aired at 5:30 p.m. The editorial was entitled, 'It is Necessary to Take a Clear-Cut Stand Against Turmoil'. It read:

> During the past few days, a small handful have engaged in creating turmoil ... some shouting, 'Down with the CCP'... beating, looting, and smashing ... [and] calling for opposition to the leadership of the CCP and the socialist system. In some universities, illegal organizations have formed to seize power from student unions; some have taken over broadcasting systems, and begun a class boycott... If we tolerate this disturbance, a seriously chaotic state will appear, and we will be unable to have reform, opening, and higher living standards... Under no circumstances should the establishment of any illegal organizations be allowed. We must stop any attempt to infringe on the rights of legal organizations... [32]

The Federation Standing Committee meeting which followed the second broadcast of this editorial was filled with intense emotion and debate. All felt that the situation was now critical and that the group's next move could have serious consequences.

27 April demonstration

After the meeting reconvened, a heated debate erupted. Some argued that it would be dangerous and irresponsible to engage in provocative activity, following such an unequivocal and threatening government statement. Others, however, argued that as an illegal organization, the Federation had to strengthen its position vis-à-vis the Party, by demonstrating that despite its illegal status, it had great popular support. Proponents of this view suggested that the Federation organize a major demonstration, initially scheduled to be held on 28 April. In the final vote, these two opinions tied, 3–3 (one member abstained). It was decided to leave the question to the general meeting.[33] When the motion to organize another demonstration was put forth, almost all were in favour of the action. In fact, the group decided to hold the demonstration one day earlier than had been suggested.[34] A draft of the resolution was subsequently drawn up and sent to every university in Beijing.[35]

Proponents of the less confrontational approach were not completely vanquished, however. Pointing out that the editorial claimed that some had shouted 'Down with the CCP' in previous demonstrations, these Standing Committee members convinced the general body to chant 'Long live the CCP' during the 27 April demonstration.[36] In this way, the words of the Party-dominated media clearly influenced the strategy choice of the Federation.

The following day, 26 April, much confusion erupted surrounding the impending demonstration. Under great pressure from the authorities and in the tense atmosphere created by the publication of that day's *Renmin Ribao* editorial, nearly every major student leader voiced second thoughts about holding the demonstration. At Beida, two members of the BdAU met with institution administrators on the morning of 26 April. The authorities said that if students refrained from demonstrating, there would be a good chance for a dialogue. The BdAU later held a meeting, and through a vote of 3–2 decided to cancel the demonstration. Fearing that this decision would cause the Union to lose legitimacy, the group then presented the motion to the general student body at Beida. The students, however, remained determined to demonstrate and voted down the motion.[37] In the end, a compromise was reached. Beida students would participate in the demonstration, but would turn back at the Third Ring Road, rather than continue to Tiananmen Square.[38]

At Shida, student leaders were under similar pressure to cancel the demonstration. One prominent Shida student, for example, reports that at 5 p.m. he was called to the Chancellor's office and told that the primary school across the street contained 1000 soldiers waiting to meet any protesters.[39] Feeling a 'very heavy responsibility', this student met with departmental leaders to express his confusion and fear.[40] He then went to Beida to persuade student leaders to call off the demonstration. Yet, upon hearing that Beida students could not be thus convinced, he returned to Shida.[41]

Almost simultaneously, further confusion erupted: on the evening of 26 April, Federation President Zhou Yongjun (who had been elected two days previously, defeating Wu'er Kaixi) unilaterally announced that, due to extreme danger, the Federation had decided to cancel the demonstration. In actuality, Zhou had consulted no one before announcing this change of plan.[42] Apparently, he too had been under immense pressure from institution and government authorities, and he felt that he could not bear the responsibility for placing students' lives in danger.[43] Zhou's announcement created further turmoil. First, as the announcement contradicted the decisions made by various campus autonomous committees, many students were confused as to which direction they should follow. Moreover, although most of the larger institutions eventually heard of Zhou's announcement and began to demobilize, many smaller institutions were completely unaware of the change in plan.[44] These contradictory and incomplete messages angered many students. For example, one Beida leader complains that '[w]hen we later heard that the Federation had changed its mind on the march, we felt mad ... we had already been preparing, making pamphlets, etc'.[45] Similarly, a Central Nationalities Academy (*Zhongyang Minzu Xueyuan*) student reports that 'on the dawn of 27 April, we went to our institution gate ... then [a student representative from the Central Nationalities Academy] came and said that the Federation had decided to have a sit-in [rather than a street march]... After this, I felt that the Federation didn't have much use'.[46]

Yet, despite this confusion, fear and anger, the demonstration was held. Moreover, student participants generally felt that it was an overwhelming success: over 100 000 students, representing every higher education institution in Beijing, marched for hours, passing through numerous police blockades, to Tiananmen Square.[47] Students from Beida spontaneously changed their plan to turn back at the Third Ring Road and continued on triumphantly to the Square. Hundreds of thousands of city folk lined the streets to watch and express their support. As students marched, the tension and uncertainty of the prior two days turned into exultation as students realized that their action would not be repressed. As one participant relates,

> This hugely successful demonstration was one of the greatest events in history... During the demonstration, we received tremendous help from the Beijing city people. The route ... was mostly on Second Ring Road ... Second Ring Road has seven overpasses and every time the students went through one, people were all over shouting 'Long Live the Students', 'Long Live Democracy'. The students got especially excited every time this happened and walked in an even more orderly manner. I still get very excited talking about this today. Approximately one million people greeted us. We were out marching [all day] and were constantly surrounded by people supporting us. The government was extremely embarrassed. It was a huge, amazing success.[48]

The Federation met again at the University of Politics and Law on the following day, 28 April. Although the mood was triumphant, many had been angered by Zhou's attempt to cancel the demonstration. Thus, as the first order of business, Zhou was forced to resign from the presidency (although he remained on the Standing Committee).[49] Wu'er Kaixi was elected in his stead. In addition, the power of the president was degraded, as Standing Committee members felt that this power had been abused and that this abuse had endangered the movement. Finally, the group decided to hold its next demonstration on 4 May, the 70th anniversary of the May Fourth Movement of 1919.[50]

4 May demonstration

On the afternoon of 3 May, the Federation held a special general meeting at Shida to discuss tactics for the 4 May demonstration. To guard against infiltration by Party spies, and also to discourage official claims that the movement was being directed by a 'small handful' of non-students (as had been alleged in the 26 April *Renmin Ribao* editorial), participants were strictly checked for their representative qualifications before being allowed to enter the meeting.[51] At the meeting it was decided that while marching to the Square on 4 May, students would hold hands to further ensure and demonstrate the 'purity' of their ranks.

The 4 May demonstration was successful in bringing over 100 000 students to the Square, but it lacked the same sense of triumph that the 27 April demonstration had engendered. Inasmuch as the demonstration marked the 70th anniversary of the May Fourth Movement of 1919, it was meaningful to the students, as well as the general populace. Yet, the demonstration itself was rather uninspiring and unorganized. One participant notes, 'just after noon the different institutions began converging in the Square. We didn't know where to go or where to stand; many of the institution groups had already scattered'.[52] Amidst this chaos, Wu'er Kaixi read aloud the 'New May Fourth Declaration'. The declaration recalled the spirit of the May Fourth Movement and urged renewed emphasis on the 4 May demands for 'science and democracy'. Yet, the declaration was rather long and dry and did not succeed in capturing the attention of the students.[53] Moreover, many participants did not even hear the declaration.[54]

HUNGER STRIKE AND GORBACHEV'S VISIT

By 10 May, students had become frustrated with the movement's loss of momentum and its inability to influence the government. At the same time, many students remained highly agitated and were determined to restore vigour to the movement. Suggestions that the students heighten pressure on the government by beginning a hunger strike had been raised prior to 10 May, but these suggestions had not received widespread support, as many felt that such an action should be undertaken only as a 'last-ditch' strategy.[55] However, during this 'low point' in the movement in early May, certain influential student leaders began to advocate this strategy seriously. The most enthusiastic proponents of the hunger strike were students from Beida and Shida. On the night of 11 May, six student leaders from these two institutions met at a small restaurant, where the idea was discussed.[56] At a BdAU meeting the following morning, Wang Dan and two others[57] proposed that the group prepare to begin a hunger strike the following day. Wang noted that this would be two days before the planned visit of Soviet President Mikhail Gorbachev, and thus would give the government enough time to respond. Wang also announced that they already had discussed the idea with two prominent Shida student leaders,[58] and had received their agreement.[59]

The BdAU, however, did not unanimously agree to the proposal. Indeed, at a meeting a few days prior, the group had discussed the possibility of a hunger strike but decided that it should be used only as a 'last-moment' strategy.[60] At the 12 May meeting, the committee became divided over the issue. Finally, Wang Dan, Chai Ling (the wife of BdAU member Feng Congde) and the others in favour of a hunger strike declared that they would begin a hunger strike, regardless of the decision of the Union. Indeed, they stated that they would bypass the committee and initiate a hunger strike in the name of the student masses.[61] This action threatened to undermine completely the legitimacy of the BdAU, for these members of the BdAU were arguing that they had no need for an official sanction from the committee — or, in fact, any organization. Thus, these students felt that it was more important to proceed with the 'correct' strategy than it was to bow to institutionalized majority rule. Faced with this ultimatum, the Union decided that it would support the hunger strikers as individuals, and would allow them to use committee broadcast and communication equipment, but that it would not officially sanction the strike.

The decision of these few leaders to begin a hunger strike also caused conflict with the Federation. On the night of 11 May, the Federation issued a decision stating that it opposed large-scale activities at present and would focus on small-scale actions. The following morning, 12 May, the Federation Standing Committee met again. Shortly after the meeting began, Yang Zhaohui entered the meeting and announced that students at Beida planned a hunger strike scheduled to begin the following morning. Presenting the decision as a *fait accompli*, Yang told the group, 'We want to hunger strike; the Federation must support us! ... We want to go to Tiananmen to hunger strike and we demand that the Federation send people to protect us.'[62] Upon hearing this, some Standing Committee members erupted in anger, declaring that these students had no right to use the Federation's resources to engage in such an unsanctioned action.[63] Yang Zhaohui returned to Beida with this news and subsequently brought Chai Ling back to the Federation meeting. Upon arriving at the meeting, Chai Ling defiantly told the group, 'The hunger strike is a spontaneous movement of students; you do not have the ability to lead us... No matter what you say, Beida has already agreed on a hunger strike and we will do it.'[64]

After listening to Chai Ling's words, the Standing Committee members began to realize that the group risked a great loss in legitimacy should it criticize or censure those who undertook a hunger strike. As one Standing Committee member states, 'we felt that the hunger strike was inevitable, so we had no choice but to write a statement of sympathy and support.'[65] Finally, after great debate regarding the content of the statement, the group decided on a policy similar to that of the BdAU: although the Federation

would not officially sanction the strike, it would support those who
individually chose to engage in such an action.[66] Once again, those students
who believed that a hunger strike was the correct policy felt that
compromise would only destroy the movement; and, as a result, they
believed it necessary to ignore the dictates of majority rule.

Following these meetings, those committed to the hunger strike
displayed a poster at the Beida Triangle. Throughout the day, hundreds of
students gathered to read and discuss the poster.[67] Yet by nightfall, only 40
students had signed up to join the hunger strike.[68] Concerned with this
lack of enthusiasm, Chai Ling made a rousing and emotional appeal to the
students gathered at the Triangle, emphasizing that students must have
the courage and devotion to sacrifice their lives in order to see 'the true
face of the government' — its support of or opposition to the people.[69] The
speech deeply affected the students, who listened intently to Chai Ling's
words and erupted in applause and excited speech when she finished. By
the end of the night, 200 students had pledged to join the hunger strike.[70]

At noon on 13 May, the hunger strikers from Beida met at the May
Fourth Monument on campus, and the hunger strike statement was read.
Following this, some Beida professors treated the hunger strikers to a last
meal at a campus restaurant. Around 3 p.m., the hunger strikers set off on
foot for Tiananmen Square.[71] When Shida received news that the Beida
hunger strikers were preparing to leave, the Shida hunger strikers gathered
and prepared to join the Beida contingent.[72] The group arrived at the Square
around 5 p.m. and settled at the base of the Monument to the People's
Heroes. The hunger strikers had a nucleus of about 800, although there
were many onlookers standing nearby.[73] At 5:20 p.m., Wang Dan read the
hunger strike statement and announced that the strike had officially begun.[74]
As the day passed and news of the hunger strike spread, contingents of
hunger strikers from other institutions joined the students from Beida and
Shida at the base of the Monument.

At this time, there was no definite command or organization in control
of the hunger strikers. This did not really concern participants, however.
As Chai Ling notes, 'We had a basic recognition that the government would
likely make known its position before 15 May [the date of Gorbachev's
arrival]; we didn't think the hunger strike would continue for an unlimited
period of time.'[75] Thus, until 15 May, it was felt that little organization was
necessary.

On 14 May, it appeared that the hunger strikers' expectations might be
correct, as the Party initiated a dialogue (*duihua*) with the students. With
Soviet leader Gorbachev due to arrive in less than two days, some Party
élite seemed to have hoped to pacify the students and convince them to

withdraw from the Square. Further, as hundreds of international reporters would soon converge on the capital, Party leaders hoped to avoid any embarrassing foreign media coverage. Before the meeting began, student representatives (which included members of the Federation, as well as hunger strike participants) insisted that the meeting be broadcast live on the central television station. After some waffling, government representatives compromised, assuring the students that the meeting would be audiotaped and broadcast over loudspeakers at Tiananmen Square within one hour after the dialogue began. The talks then began. Before any progress was made, however, the dialogue ended in mayhem as a large group of hunger strikers burst into the room, and demanded that the negotiations halt, as the dialogue had not been broadcast as promised.[76]

Back at the Square, chaos reigned as word of the failed dialogue spread. As one student leader notes, 'Because originally we thought the hunger strike would end on 15 May, when the 14 May dialogue failed, the movement suddenly became unclear.'[77] Not having previously discussed what to do should the government continue to evade student demands, students now argued over the proper course of action. As dawn broke, thousands of students remained in the Square. The planned gala welcoming ceremony for Gorbachev at the Square had to be cancelled. Instead, Gorbachev was welcomed quietly by a small group of CCP officials at the Beijing airport, located miles from the city centre in a sparsely populated region. After being greeted, Gorbachev was whisked to the city centre in an official car, which silently entered the back gate of the Great Hall of the People.

As Gorbachev's arrival passed without any Party compromise, student leaders were faced with the prospect of a prolonged occupation of Tiananmen Square. Consequently, some of the hunger strike participants began to realize the need to establish some sort of organization to attend to the needs of the hunger strikers. However, due to the hunger strikers' belief that their participation in the movement was fundamentally an individual and spontaneous act, the organization which arose to 'lead' them was exceedingly weak. Indeed, even those who became leaders of the new organization proclaimed that no individual hunger striker would be expected to abide by the decisions of the group or its leaders. As a result, this effort to organize the hunger strikers did little to restore order to the Square or direction to the movement. Coupled with the increasingly negative attitude of the Party towards the student protesters, an unfavourable end to the movement became highly likely.

On the early morning of 15 May, Chai Ling gave a speech discussing the situation and asking for volunteers to help organize the hunger strike.

Many were moved to tears, and over ten students came forward to be members of the command.[78] Around 8 a.m., Chai Ling gave a speech formally establishing the 'Hunger Strike Command' (*Jueshituan Zhihuibu*). The group had no legitimacy or structure at this time, however; it had simply been declared to be in existence and was composed of only volunteers.

To address these problems, the group announced that each institution's hunger strike contingent should send representatives to discuss the basic workings of the group.[79] Approximately 40 institutions sent representatives, and each representative was required to show student identification prior to entry.[80] Once the representatives were assembled, Chai Ling opened the meeting and immediately introduced Li Lu, a newly arrived Nanjing University student, whom most students had not previously seen. She then suggested that Li chair the meeting. As chair of the meeting, Li described the nature of the command group. He announced that the sole purpose of the group was to protect the lives of the hunger striking students; the command would have no authority to force decisions on them.[81] Moreover, Li declared that any hunger striking student had the right to participate in the Hunger Strike Command and to call a meeting to recall any Hunger Strike Command leader.[82] In explaining this stance, Li states, 'as the students were risking their lives in hunger striking, we had no power to ask them to heed our views.'[83]

The group immediately set about its self-designated task of protecting the students. First, a security line was established around the four sides of the memorial, with volunteer student security marshals standing guard.[84] A security pass system also was created to ensure that only students with proper credentials could enter the hunger strike area. Then, an aisle (dubbed a 'lifeline') was created, leading from the Monument to the outside of the Square, to ease the passage of sick students to hospital.

Despite these efforts, by 17 May the Square was in crisis. As news of the hunger strike spread, thousands of students from outside Beijing poured into the Square and hundreds of new students joined the hunger strike. In addition, the hot days and cold nights had taken their toll on the hunger strikers; by 17 May, close to 1000 students had collapsed. The hunger strike leaders were also in a greatly weakened physical condition; indeed, many had already collapsed on at least one occasion.[85]

Given this crisis-ridden and confused situation, the Hunger Strike Command convened a meeting of institution hunger strike representatives to decide on a proper course of action. Approximately 50 students attended the meeting. No attempt was made to check representative credentials. In the meeting, debate was intense.[86] One of the meeting attendees, Zhou Yongjun, was particularly vociferous in advocating withdrawal from the

Square. However, he was later ejected from the meeting when four students from the University of Politics and Law entered and said he was not a University of Politics and Law representative. Finally, a vote was taken: 70%–80% opposed leaving the Square, arguing that the government had not adequately addressed student demands.[87]

4 JUNE

On the afternoon of 19 May, news arrived that the army was beginning to surround the city. At midnight Premier Li Peng announced the imposition of martial law. Soon thereafter, the army began to enter the city. Yet, in a spontaneous movement, hundreds of thousands of citizens filled the streets of Beijing to block its entrance. As morning broke, students and citizens looked about in jubilation; the efforts of the people seemed to have been successful — army troops had not entered the city. Great questions remained, however: What should be the next step for the movement and who should lead it? For, despite this victory, student leadership remained deeply divided, while dominant members of the CCP remained determined to bring the movement to an end.

As martial law progressed, fears rose among those involved in the movement. Stakes were now perceived to be extremely high: a bad decision could have devastating consequences for the movement. As Li Lu describes the atmosphere at this time,

> How can we continue the movement? What can be done about the government's hard-heartedness? What can be done about the army? In this period ... we discussed these things intensely. This was the most emotional period. ... Contradictions were completely white hot; this seemed to be the final battle. Everyone seemed to be making a final fight against death.[88]

Consequently, student leaders became even more hesitant to compromise with students holding views different from their own.

On 27 May, an important meeting was held to attempt to ameliorate this dangerous situation. Representatives of all the major factions and groups that had formed during the movement were in attendance.[89] The meeting lasted six hours, but, in the end, all agreed to withdraw from the Square on 30 May.[90] This date was chosen because it was ten days after the start of martial law and thus symbolically would show that the movement had 'broken' martial law. Further, it was agreed that it would be best to 'self-end' the movement before the authorities arrived to crush it. Thus, the group decided that on 29 May, Wang Dan, Wu'er Kaixi and Chai Ling would act as representatives of all protesting students and announce the

30 May withdrawal.

However, in the interim, Chai Ling and other hunger strike 'leaders' reconsidered this decision. Li Lu describes this change of position as follows:

> On 27 May, Feng Congde and Chai Ling came back and told me of the proposal to withdraw on the thirtieth. I asked, 'Where did this proposal originate?' [Feng] said, 'At the joint meeting.' I asked, 'How did the joint meeting make this decision? Did they discuss it with the [former hunger striking students]?' After I asked these things, Feng Congde and Chai Ling changed their minds. I asked, 'How should we make this decision?' I said, 'The highest authority here are (sic) the [former hunger striking students] ...'[91]

Thus, Li Lu argued that decisions reached by all factions of protesting students could, and should, be bypassed. Consequently, that night a meeting of all former and continuing hunger striking students was held to discuss the proposal. After much discussion, the proposal was voted down. Instead, it was agreed that these students would remain at the Square until 20 June.[92]

Unaware of this change of plan, on 29 May, Wu'er Kaixi and Wang Dan arrived at the Square to announce the withdrawal. Chai Ling then informed them of the hunger strikers' veto of the proposal. In consequence, when Wang and Wu'er took the microphone, they could only 'suggest' that the students withdraw. Immediately following this statement, Zhang Boli announced that the Hunger Strike Command had decided to remain at the Square.[93] Thus, confusion over movement leadership continued, and many students remained at the Square.

By 1 June, news of an impending army take-over had reached the Square. Li Lu reports,

> On 1 June, news came ... that the army was already preparing to enter the city. Although we had no clear idea of what measures [the army] would take after entering, this report was clearly more serious than what we had heard before. [The report] included news that the army ... had been cut off from connection with the outside world, and was now already coming out [from underground, where the soldiers had been hidden], and was waiting at the street [subway] entrances.[94]

By the morning of 2 June, student leaders at the Square began to receive reports that soldiers had been captured and weapons confiscated by students and citizens. The Hunger Strike Command immediately sent representatives to persuade the captors to release the soldiers. The representatives also questioned each captured soldier about his orders. The meaning of these developments was clear to the student leaders. As Li Lu states, 'I felt this was the first wave of a large operation ... a preview... The atmosphere became increasingly intense.'[95]

Li Lu was correct. Yet it was not until 3 June, when the first reports of bloodshed reached the Square, that the students finally agreed to follow some semblance of democratic rule. Just minutes before the army reached the Square, the Hunger Strike Command called upon all remaining students to gather at the Monument to the People's Heroes and stand shoulder-to-shoulder, holding hands. There, the remaining 5000 students stood in fear and confusion.

Finally, a voice vote was held to decide on whether or not to withdraw. Unfortunately, Feng Congde recalls, 'The "yeas" and "nays" were equally large.'[96] Yet, Feng relates, 'I believed there were more who wanted to leave. So we announced withdrawal.'[97] With that, the group began to form an orderly line and, led by Feng, Chai and Li, marched out of the Square. The group soon encountered a contingent of soldiers, who encouraged the group's peaceful retreat.[98]

Thus, the movement ended. Within days, a 'Wanted' list was distributed nationally, listing the names and photographs of 21 of the top students and intellectuals who had been involved in the movement.[99] Many of these dissidents went into hiding and eventually succeeded in fleeing the country. Others were not so lucky. Moreover, hundreds, if not thousands, had been killed during the army take-over. Yet, the official government assessment of the movement remained virtually unchanged from that expressed in the *Renmin Ribao* editorial of 26 April. On 3 June, the first two pages of *Renmin Ribao* stated,

> The 26 April *Renmin Ribao* editorial ... explicitly called for taking a clear-cut stance in opposing and halting turmoil... Above all, we want to say that the Party and the government have fully confirmed the patriotic passion of the large number of students all along and never said they were stirring up turmoil... [Yet,] under the agitation of an extremely small number of people, some people have ... without approval ... organized marches, demonstrations, sit-ins and hunger strikes at will, and have occupied Tiananmen Square for a long period of time... Is it possible that all these acts still do not constitute a serious upheaval? Under such a highly chaotic situation ... if [the government] did not take decisive measures ... there would be even greater turmoil in the capital and pandemonium in the country.[100]

Following the army crack-down, the official interpretation of the movement became even less favourable. In reports by various high-ranking leaders after 4 June, the movement was described as a 'shocking counter-revolutionary rebellion',[101] which had fomented a 'struggle involving the life and death of the Party and the state'.[102]

CONCLUSION

In sum, the power and influence of the CCP over university students remains great. Indeed, virtually every student action and decision during the spring of 1989 was influenced by consideration of likely Party responses. Most importantly, the fear-laden atmosphere resulting from these considerations engendered a radicalizing trend in student behaviour, as students vied for respect by undertaking extreme actions. Similarly, students increasingly refused to compromise with majority decisions, or respect representative movement organizations, feeling that in such a perilous situation, it was simply more important to embark on the 'correct' strategy than to abide by democratic procedures. In addition, the events of the spring of 1989 leave no doubt the CCP is determined to squelch any student activities which threaten its control. Further, the CCP clearly considers independent student organizations to be one such activity. In fact, the CCP never considered recognizing the legitimacy of the Federation, or any of the campus autonomous groups. Indeed, these activities consistently were denounced in official propaganda throughout the movement.

Of course, the demonstrations of 1989 were partially the result of official policies of political loosening. Yet, what the movement of 1989 demonstrates above all is that this loosening is not irreversible, and will be allowed to proceed only under the instigation and guidance of the CCP. In fact, this protest movement seems to have broken the cycle of political loosening and repression that was evident throughout the first ten years of Deng's rule. Instead, for the past seven years, the Party has allowed virtually no relaxation of control over political expression, and the streets of urban China have been undisturbed by any large-scale political protests. If anything, CCP control over educational and political spheres has increased following the movement of 1989, along with the risk involved in voicing political dissent. Indeed, it appears that the current regime is convinced not only that economic liberalization *may* progress without political liberalization, but also that it *must*. In the long run, whether or not the PRC's current leaders are correct in this assessment remains to be seen. However, in the short run it appears certain that the CCP will continue to loom large over the political lives of the citizens of the PRC.

NOTES

1. This chapter derives from field research for the author's doctoral dissertation. Research included interviews of approximately 20 student leaders and intellectuals who played a major role in the student movement. The majority

of these interviews were conducted in the United States, as the current situation in the PRC precludes fruitful interviews with major movement participants still living there. In addition, this research involved the reading of virtually all student-produced documents from the movement (the majority of which may be found in an archival collection edited by Robin Munro, housed in institutes such as UC Berkeley's Center for Chinese Studies Library). Finally, crucial information regarding student strategy and organization was found in an important transcription of a meeting of many important movement leaders, in which these individuals discussed in detail their motivations and actions during the movement. The transcripts of this meeting were published as *Huigu Yu Fansi*, German Rhine Writers Association, 1993.

2. Hayhoe, 1991, p. 114.
3. Hayhoe, 1991, p. 115. See also Morey and Zhou, 1991, p. 75.
4. This shift in focus was announced in 1977. It was later re-emphasized in the Education Reform Document of 1985 (see, for example, Hayhoe, 1991, p. 130; Morey and Zhou, 1991, p. 74).
5. Hayhoe, 1991, p. 128.
6. Many factors justify this choice of institutions. First, Beida and Shida were two of the first campuses to organize autonomous campus groups. Each of these groups was organized spontaneously, with no guidance from outside groups or organizations. Second, the autonomous groups at Beida and Shida were the strongest and most influential of the campus groups which were formed during the movement. Third, the two groups provide a clear contrast with regard to their background, establishment and functioning. Fourth, each had an important, yet contrasting, relationship with the all-Beijing Students Autonomous Federation. Similarly, each had a unique relationship with the Hunger Strike Command.
7. Shen Tong, 1990, p. 135.
8. Feng Congde, later a key figure in the 1989 movement, attended the first meeting of the 'Committee for Action', but subsequently withdrew, as he felt that the group was unduly secretive. See German Rhine Writers Association, 1993, p. 20.
9. The demands drawn up by the Committee of Action for the planned 8 June 1988 demonstration were: 'a free press, human rights for all, freedom of thought, pay raises for teachers and intellectuals, educational reform and open debate of the legality of the ban on demonstrations that had been put in place after the 1986 movement'. See Shen Tong, 1990, p. 136.
10. Shen Tong, 1990, p. 139.
11. Even more notably, the group's submission received a positive response: several congressmen signed the article and sent it on to the state council and the National Science Association. Shen Tong, 1990, p. 157.
12. Shen Tong, 1990, pp. 148–60.
13. Interview 12.
14. Interestingly, virtually no independent student organization seemed to have been functioning at Shida immediately prior to the movement. According to one interview, some Shida students had tried to form a kind of salon in 1986, but the group was quickly disbanded by campus authorities, and its leader expelled from school. Apparently, following this event, few dared to attempt

to organize at Shida (Interview 7).

15. Hu had been deposed from this position in 1987, due to his alleged leniency towards student protesters in the winter of 1986–87.

16. Interview 7.

17. Zhang Boli, in German Rhine Writers Association, 1993, p. 50.

18. Chai Ling, in German Rhine Writers Association, 1993, p. 3.

19. Interview 12.

20. The group included Wang Dan, Chang Jin, Feng Congde, Ding Xiaoping, Zhang Boli, Guo Haifeng, Yang Tao, Xiong Yan and Zhang Zhiyong.

21. Interview 10.

22. Interview 7.

23. Interview 7.

24. Interview 7.

25. Liang Er, in German Rhine Writers Association, p. 31.

26. Interview 7.

27. Interview 7.

28. For example, Wang Dan did attend the first meeting, but at the time, his connection with the BdAU was tenuous. Shortly after the original meeting of the BdAU, Wang was forced to resign from the group, as other members felt that he was spending an undue amount of time attending press conferences (Interview 12).

29. Most notably, students, faculty members and administrators at Beijing University initiated the famous 'May Fourth Movement' of 1919 and were later key in the formation of the CCP in 1921. Moreover, since Mao's death, Beijing University has continued to be a focal point of dissent, particularly in the 'April Fourth Movement' of 1976 and the demonstrations of 1986–87.

30. See Feng Congde, in German Rhine Writers Association, p. 25; and Wang Chaohua in German Rhine Writers Association, p. 37.

31. Apparently, students from the University of Politics and Law had promised to provide the group with food, so the group changed its meeting location (though the food never actually appeared) (Interview 7).

32. 'It is necessary to take a clear-cut stand against turmoil', *Renmin Ribao*, 26 April 1989. Reprinted in Oksenberg, Sullivan and Lambert, 1990, pp. 207–8.

33. By this point, the general body represented about 40 institutions.

34. Interview 7.

35. Interview 10.

36. Interview 7.

37. Feng Congde, in German Rhine Writers Association, 1993, p. 27.

38. Shen Tong, 1990, pp. 196–8.

39. Interview 7. Apparently, this threat was a fabrication, as these soldiers did not appear the following day.

40. Interview 7.

41. Shen Tong, 1990, pp. 200–1.

42. Interview 10.

43. Interviews 7 and 10. See also Wang Chaohua, in German Rhine Writers Association, 1993, p. 44.

44. Interview 10.

45. Feng Congde, in German Rhine Writers Association, 1993, pp. 62–3.

46. Liu Yen, in German Rhine Writers Association, 1993, pp. 65–6.
47. According to participants, the police 'blockades' broke up without force as students simply continued to walk towards them.
48. Interview 7.
49. Interview 7.
50. Interview 7.
51. Forty-seven institutions had representatives in attendance.
52. Shen Tong, 1990, p. 221.
53. Interview 7. For the text of the declaration, see the Robin Munro Collection, Section XIII, Document 7.
54. Shen Tong, 1990, p. 221.
55. Apparently, the idea was previously put forth in many different arenas. For example, it is reported that on 9 May some graduate students in Building #46 at Beida displayed a poster calling for a hunger strike (Feng Congde, in German Rhine Writers Association, 1993, p. 124). In addition, Zhang Boli earlier had suggested an on-campus hunger strike, noting that this way protesters actually could 'sneak' some food into campus bathrooms (Chai Ling, in German Rhine Writers Association, 1993, p. 89). Further, on 8 May, Wu'er Kaixi made a speech to the Chemistry Department at Shida, in which he expressed his desire to begin a hunger strike. See Liang Er, in German Rhine Writers Association, 1993, p. 127.
56. Liu Yan, in German Rhine Writers Association, 1993, p. 123. The six students were Wu'er Kaixi, Wang Dan, Wang Wen, Cheng Zhen, Ma Shaofang and Yang Zhaohui.
57. The other two were Wang Wen and Yang Zhaohui.
58. The two were Wu'er Kaixi and Ma Shaofang.
59. Chai Ling, in German Rhine Writers Association, 1993, p. 89.
60. Interview 12.
61. Chang Jin, in German Rhine Writers Association, 1993, p. 93.
62. Yang Chaohui, as quoted in German Rhine Writers Association, 1993, pp. 94–5.
63. Wang Chaohua, in German Rhine Writers Association, 1993, p. 95.
64. Chai Ling, in German Rhine Writers Association, 1993, p. 90.
65. Liang Er, in German Rhine Writers Association, 1993, p. 97.
66. Interviews 7 and 10.
67. Interestingly, administration officials did not tear the poster down. As they undoubtedly were aware of its existence, their lack of action indicated sympathy with the students.
68. Shen Tong, 1990, p. 235.
69. Shen Tong, 1990, p. 237. Also Interview 12.
70. Interview 12. See also Chai Ling, in German Rhine Writers Association, 1993, p. 92. A handbill printed on 12 May presented the list of demands: dialogue and 'a truthful assessment of the movements as patriotic and democratic' (source: Tiananmen Archive, Columbia University, Document H-18). These demands were really no different from those of the other student movement groups.
71. Shen Tong, 1990, pp. 238–9.
72. Wang Chaohua, in German Rhine Writers Association, 1993, p. 99.
73. Feng Congde, in German Rhine Writers Association, 1993, p. 130.

74. Feng Congde, in German Rhine Writers Association, 1993, p. 130.
75. Feng Congde, in German Rhine Writers Association, 1993, p. 131.
76. Interviews 7 and 11. It is not clear how much time actually had passed before the dialogue was broken up.
77. Li Lu, in German Rhine Writers Association, 1993, p. 135.
78. Chai Ling, in German Rhine Writers Association, 1993, p. 144.
79. Li Lu, in German Rhine Writers Association, 1993, p. 136.
80. Li Lu, in German Rhine Writers Association, 1993, p. 171.
81. Li Lu, in German Rhine Writers Association, 1993, p. 136.
82. Li Lu, in German Rhine Writers Association, 1993, p. 171.
83. Li Lu, in German Rhine Writers Association, 1993, p. 137.
84. Li Lu, in German Rhine Writers Association, 1993, p. 137.
85. Chai Ling collapsed on the morning of 16 May and at noon on 17 May; Wu'er Kaixi collapsed on the afternoon of 16 May; and Li Lu collapsed on the afternoon of 17 May (Chai Ling, in German Rhine Writers Association, 1993, pp. 148–9; Li Lu, in German Rhine Writers Association, 1993, p. 140).
86. Li Lu, in German Rhine Writers Association, 1993, p. 142.
87. Li Lu, in German Rhine Writers Association, 1993, p. 142. The Hunger Strike Command announced that the hunger strike would end that evening (19 May), but Feng Congde and others argued for its continuation. Some students continued their hunger strikes, but most students ceased.
88. Li Lu, in German Rhine Writers Association, 1993, p. 223.
89. Feng Congde, in German Rhine Writers Association, 1993, p. 271.
90. Feng Congde, in German Rhine Writers Association, 1993, p. 271.
91. Feng Congde, in German Rhine Writers Association, 1993, p. 238–9.
92. Feng Congde, in German Rhine Writers Association, 1993, p. 239.
93. Adding to the confusion was the various changes of names. The 'Hunger Strike Command' was changed to 'Temporary Command' and then 'Headquarters to protect Tiananmen Square' and became a standing committee in charge of the 'Campground Joint Conference' (Yingdi Lianxi Huiyi).
94. Li Lu, in German Rhine Writers Association, 1993, p. 305.
95. Li Lu, in German Rhine Writers Association, 1993, p. 306.
96. Feng Congde, in German Rhine Writers Association, 1993, p. 318.
97. Feng Congde, in German Rhine Writers Association, 1993, p. 318.
98. Apparently, the army had been ordered to refrain from using violence against the students in the Square.
99. These 21 individuals have met various fates. Those who chose to remain in the PRC (or were unable to escape) were arrested, are under police surveillance or went into hiding. The majority of those who escaped are currently living in Western Europe (mainly Paris), the USA (mainly the Northeast and California) and Taiwan. Some continue to press for reform in the PRC while others have turned to different pursuits.
100. 'Recognize the essence of turmoil and the necessity of martial law', Renmin Ribao, 3 June 1989, pp. 1–2.
101. Yuan Mu (news conference), Beijing Television Service, 6 June 1989; FBIS, 7 June, p. 12.
102. Chen Xitong, 1989, p. 3.

PART 7
CONCLUSIONS

Editors' Conclusion — The State of Chinese Higher Education Today

Michael AGELASTO and Bob ADAMSON

INTRODUCTION

In designing this volume, the editors intended to compare the planned goals of Chinese higher education reform with the experienced reality. This proved a task more easily contemplated than accomplished. As we reviewed the literature and gathered prospective authors, we quickly realized that a lack of data presented a major obstacle to achieving our intended analysis. At one level, plenty of data exist. The SEdC is vigilant in the collection, assembly and publishing of statistics. Numbers alone, however, do not give a 'feel' for education. For a look at campus life, one often turns to the Chinese media, where frequent articles on higher education reveal government concerns (perhaps more so than they offer accurate description and analysis). An especially effervescent source of news is the nation's English-language newspaper, *China Daily*, a purpose of which is to tell the foreign audience what the Chinese government wants it to hear. Triumphs are trumpeted and selected shortcomings acknowledged. One 1996 article lamented that university students shun exercise, '...that more than half of Chinese university students take no exercise whatsoever'.[1] Another praised *gaoxiao* in northeast China for running successful sideline businesses.[2] A third lauded an effort in Zhejiang province to send 600 'excellent' graduates to countryside areas.[3] Journalism, of course, is no substitute for scholarship, but it continues to remain a primary, rather than secondary, source of information on Chinese higher education.

Facts and figures, as well as journalistic accounts, only hint at the phenomenal diversity that characterizes *gaoxiao*. The wide-ranging chapters in this volume provide a richness of data usually not available in studies on Chinese education. Unfortunately, omissions have been unavoidable. As noted in the Introduction, subject areas in higher education for which we were unable to receive manuscripts that met our needs and deadlines include ethnic minorities, overseas students, and participation by multinationals and bilateral organizations. Perhaps empirical scholarship in these areas will become available in the future. Like so much of the Chinese higher education literature, this edited volume invariably focuses on *formal* higher education in the *public* sector (discussed respectively in the chapters by Xiao Jin, and Mok Ka-ho and David Chan). In doing so, the editors do not intend to lessen the importance of the non-formal sector nor to diminish the growing importance of the private sector. Some developments in these areas will be discussed briefly in this chapter. Notwithstanding the limitations of this volume, our purpose in this chapter is threefold: to summarize the successes of the reform programme; to identify the key tensions that have emerged; and to survey, briefly, the journey that lies ahead.

SUCCESSES

There is an old story of a traveller who, lost in the countryside, stops a villager to enquire the way to the city. 'Well,' says the villager, 'if I were you, I wouldn't start from here.' Looking back at the initiation of the reform programme in the PRC, it is obvious that the Cultural Revolution was not a good foundation, although its negative outcomes provided the impetus for change. The reconstruction of the nation's social, economic and educational structures through the reforms has been on the rubble of ten years' anarchy, and incorporates a faultline in human resources that runs through all the systems. There has also been the psychological price: the fear of chaos; the sense of deprivation and inferiority complex of those whose education was disrupted; and the loss of confidence in the official ideology.

Despite the weak foundations, the reform programme in higher education has clearly achieved notable successes. Higher education has expanded tremendously. Statistics for the period 1990–95 show a 16.3% increase in undergraduate enrolment (from 2.1 to 2.9 million students). Enrolment of postgraduates has expanded by an impressive 56.3%.[4] Other statistics which use broader definitions of both student and institution (for example, including part-time and fee-paying students enrolled in non-formal higher education) put the student population in higher learning in 1995 at 5.15 million, a 17.1% increase over 1994.[5] In all, about 5.7% of the country's population between ages 18 and 21 are in some sort of *gaoxiao*, which altogether receive somewhat over one-fifth of public budgeted educational funds.[6]

Another success is the longevity of the reform programme despite the controversial nature of some goals, including the loosening of central control and state planning, the synthesis of foreign ideas and practices, and the move away from traditional ways of teaching and learning. Although the success in achieving some of these goals is highly questionable, the fact that they have survived as goals is noteworthy in itself. The early history of the PRC is characterized by jerky shifts from political to economic orientations in education, but the essential thrust of the Dengist reforms has remained intact despite emergent tensions: traditionalists and hard-liners have been appeased and those who pushed for greater liberality have been suppressed.

KEY TENSIONS

As well as the major achievements and minor successes, the sweeping changes to Chinese society in the reform period have also brought disasters and problems, anticipated or unforeseen. With no state religion or strong indigenous philosophy since the dethroning of the last emperor and the demise of Marxism-Leninism-Mao Zedong Thought, the PRC appears to have embraced the economic order and values that predominate in the West, which some might argue to be a capitulation to the historical demands of the barbarians at the gate. National leaders can only appeal to 'Asian values' and patriotism to maintain social cohesion, which has been threatened directly and indirectly by the reforms.

The reform of Chinese higher education in the post-Mao era has also been an expedition into the unknown.[7] The reform programme has contributed to, and been affected by, the larger changes in Chinese society, and has not been immune from significant problems. In this section we identify four major areas of tension that have emerged:
1. Divisions and power-sharing;
2. How best to educate;
3. Politicization of education; and
4. Research.

Divisions and power-sharing

Most types of economic and administrative reforms in the PRC over the past two decades have led to decentralization and the granting of semi-autonomy to lower administrative levels. Education is a clear example of this trend. Divisions that existed before decentralization have continued and in some cases been exacerbated. Efforts to include women and minorities have had some positive results, but deep divisions still exist in higher education. The largest divide is one of quality: the élite versus the non-élite institutions (now to be exacerbated by Project 211) and regular versus irregular higher education. These divisions coexist with an urban/rural stratification.

Divisions and power-sharing in Chinese higher education are very clearly evident in irregular educational institutions and private universities and colleges. The following case study of Radio and Television Universities (RTVUs) serves to illustrate these tensions. RTVUs were first established in the PRC as part of the Great Leap Forward. They reopened after their closure during the Cultural Revolution and a national system of radio and television universities was founded in 1979. The system has been administered in a hierarchical fashion, with Beijing's Central RTVU (which itself has no students) at the top, followed by 44 provincial universities, 715 prefectural branch schools, 1500 district and county workstations and 13 045 classes offering 468 different courses.[8] From 1987 to 1994, enrolment in full-time all-subject courses decreased by about 5%, but single-subject, non-credit enrolment increased by a factor of ten. This change reflected explicit policy, enunciated in the television university reforms of 1986 and 1987, to de-emphasize undergraduate training in favour of specialized and technical short-cycle courses and continuing education.[9] It also indicated a preference by television students away from comprehensive education towards specialization. These changes were in line with a policy initiative towards decentralizing the system. From 1987, provincial television universities were individually given the right to develop 40% of all courses; the remaining 60% continued to be the reserve of the Central RTVU in Beijing.[10] Over the 1987–94 period, the number of universities has increased by 10%, while the number of branch schools and district workstations has been halved.[11] Ironically, this decentralization reform of removing the middle elements of the hierarchy could possibly lead to an increased degree of centralization in an already centralized system. Decentralization and granting autonomy to lower-level educational units are a major theme of reform, to be discussed below.

RTVUs have the potential to provide cost-efficient mass education in the PRC. They can educate students at 40% of the cost incurred at conventional universities. They are suited for mass education, able to be more flexible than regular institutions in their course offerings. While regular universities provide the core of the PRC's professional manpower with most graduates employed by state companies or administrative departments at various government levels, RTVUs turn out qualified technicians for industry, rather than professionals. They illustrate the distinction — which serves as a theme throughout this chapter — between 'regular' and 'irregular' education. The difference is purposeful, set by years of government policy and perceived by the population as one of élite versus mass education, prestigious versus commonplace, and quality versus inferior. This dualism is often referred to as education's 'walking on two legs' and has characterized learning at various levels during the post-1949 period.[12]

Before the 1986–87 reforms directionally shifted television universities away from mass higher education, RTVUs in the PRC suffered from an inferiority complex. Rather than taking advantage of their open and flexible structure which could allow them a unique niche in the educational structure, they tried to mimic the formal tertiary sector. Instead of allowing students to proceed at their own pace through individualized learning, RTVUs set up classrooms and group discussions rather than face-to-face individualized tutorials. They followed an exam orientation, with both standardized entrance tests (made compulsory nationwide in 1986) and exams upon course completion. Indeed, the RTVU system 'bought the technology of distance education without adopting the philosophy of this reformed mode of education'.[13] This points out another theme in this conclusion: the inability of Chinese higher education during the reform period to develop alternative pedagogies to the exam-based, 'all-classmates-must-do-the-same-thing' form of learning that is historically so deeply rooted in China. Although institutions of higher education are themselves diverse and individualized, the pedagogy within their walls is quite uniform. The case of RTVUs indicates a failure in pedagogic reform. A 1983 survey which solicited television students' views on their education found that students recognized and valued the importance of self-study and linked it with their own independent thinking.[14] The students interviewed entreat the RTVU to develop materials unique to their needs and study conditions; tutorials should complement and support the other media, rather than replicate them. Instead of following these recommendations which might have led to a strengthened role for television in mass higher education, policy-makers removed RTVUs from the competition altogether. Regular *gaoxiao* under policy articulated in the late 1980s will continue to define the élitist nature of higher education in the PRC.

The 'marketization' of higher education

Private universities are undergoing a revival in the PRC (see Chapter 14 by Mok Ka-ho and David Chan). Many are located in the economically developed coastal rim of China where they address excess market demand for higher education (in part the result of the unavailability of television studies for undergraduates). These institutions offer 'market-oriented' curricula, such as business studies, and reflect the utilitarian trend that Liu Yingkai reports for Shenzhen University, itself a public university with private characteristics. Other private institutions are located in the rural areas, attracting students who cannot study in urban areas for various reasons, especially a lack of resources. The urban/rural divide (along with gender inequality) is a component of stratification, a theme that runs throughout this volume, most notably in Chapters 9, 11, 12, 13 and 15 by Greg Kulander, Vilma Seeberg, Zhang Minxuan, Michael Agelasto and Carol C. Fan respectively.

The future for private universities remains uncertain. Some argue that 'private higher education will progressively shift from being the supplement to [being] the competitor of the public system'.[15] Private *gaoxiao* can educate more efficiently: unencumbered by tradition, mandated (and often outdated) state curriculum plans or tenured dead wood. They can obtain as contract teachers retired professors who are still in their intellectual prime but have been forced out of the public system by the PRC's mandatory retirement rule. Most importantly, private institutions are unburdened by the additional (costly and non-productive) non-academic line of authority resulting when the Communist Party provides a bureaucracy that shadows presidential administration. For private institutions to succeed, they must first address questions of educational quality — a theme of this volume to be discussed below — or private institutions will remain but the crippled leg of a two-leg system. Fieldwork like Mok and Chan's is starting to provide detailed data (for example, gender enrolment ratios, tuition fees, curricula and pedagogy, staff qualifications, etc.), which in time should allow scholars to assess quality of education.

Private universities are but the tip of a massive marketization iceberg adrift in the PRC's educational sea. The term *marketization* is problematic, given that the PRC's economy cannot yet be accurately described as capitalist, free market or even market-oriented. The term serves as a synonym for *metamorphosis*, which best characterizes the fundamental changes that higher education experiences as its socialist system implodes and is reconstructed into an entity that is just now taking shape. These changes under the guise of marketization include teacher moonlighting, emergence of fee-paying students, partnership with industry, market influences on curriculum and market influences on management.[16] Given the metamorphosis of the public sector, its distinction from the growing private sector is quite blurred. Neither sector assigns jobs; both charge tuition, although the state sector is concerned with equity considerations, as Zhang Minxuan points out in his chapter.

In part, the marketization phenomenon in higher education is a response to several distinct situations. First, a demand for post-secondary instruction is not being satisfied through regular channels, the *gaoxiao*. Programmes that admit through the college entrance exam have places for only the top 20% of secondary school students. Students who score below the 80th percentile must turn elsewhere to pursue advanced education. Since the late 1980s television universities have shut out potential undergraduates, who have turned to the private sector or to those regular universities that offer short-cycle, non-degree courses (*zhuanke*). Here demand has forced supply. Second, a permissiveness by the state — intentional or not — has allowed these educational businesses to develop in an unregulated fashion. Non-regulation encourages supply as entrepreneurs find selling education easier and more lucrative than selling other commodities. Third, the perception of decreasing government participation in the tertiary sector forces universities to change their demeanour from being academies for learning to enterprises for education.

Is the Chinese government in fact disinvesting from higher education? National policy avers quite the opposite.[17] This is confirmed by the state's own data that show a 87.7% increase in higher education budgeted allocations from 1990 to 1994. Yet, the *proportion* of state educational funds spent on higher education decreased by 7.8% over the same period, as the secondary and preschool educational sectors expanded and the elementary sector declined slightly.[18] Furthermore, as indicated above, tertiary enrolment swelled, but without a corresponding adjustment in academic staffing, which increased by only 1.3% during the five-year period.[19] Therefore, in absolute terms, the state's tertiary funding has increased; however, it has decreased in per capita terms, either per student or per teacher (but not per institution).

The perception of government disinvestment is abetted by continuous official statements that the government *should* spend less on the tertiary sector. Officials offer the rationale for disinvestment, rather than the reasons. The latter are financial and budgetary, and concern priorities set by the state among competing needs for money. Around the globe, when schoolbooks compete with missiles, politicians choose the latter.

An articulate spokesman for the rationale for disinvestment is Min

Weifan, vice-president of Beijing University and a Ph.D. holder from
Stanford University.[20] Arguing that the PRC is now conforming to the new
educational world order, Min defends the PRC's 'state supervision' policy
which has replaced the model of 'state control' in higher education.
Universities in the USA (he cites University of California, Berkeley, in
particular) have survived government cut-backs which have, quite
positively, forced them to develop multiple channels for money. What is
good for the USA, the argument implies, is good for the PRC. Moreover,
institutions should be responsible for their own budgets as they adopt 'cost-
sharing' and 'cost-recovery'.

> Before the mid-1980s 20% of state funds to education went for subsidies
> for poor students and their accommodation. This was not fair for the
> country because the government is doing too much for too few. If the
> university pays less, it can afford to help more students.[21]

Forcing universities to find their own funding will better integrate the
gaoxiao into society and this will force them to design more market-oriented
education that better meets the needs of the economy. Prior to reforms the
state decided what skills society needed and it assigned graduates to jobs
(see Michael Agelasto's chapter); the market-place can make better
decisions.

Clearly, the reforms of the 1980s and 1990s have redefined Chinese
higher education. It is no longer seen by the state as a *public good*, which
economists describe as something uniquely valuable and costly (like
national defence) with benefits that accrue to society at large. Individual
consumers are not expected to pay individually for public goods. Everyone
benefits; the state pays. In the PRC's education sector, nine-year compulsory
education is a public good; higher education is not. The new direction was
adopted without much analytical scrutiny and was forced on the
intellegentsia as a *fait accompli*. These changes are discussed among the
PRC's educationalists at conferences and in journal articles *post factum*, with
much enthusiasm and little voiced dissent.

How best to educate

Despite their outward appearances — with small vendors and various
enterprises clogging college campuses that were built for much smaller
(and more academic and less entrepreneurial) communities than those they
now accommodate — Chinese universities are still foremost about learning.
The Chinese tertiary education system has developed over the century and,
as this volume suggests, continues to develop. What is happening in terms
of pedagogy, quality and evaluation of education, and moral education?

ALTERNATIVE PEDAGOGIES

Educational reform among *gaoxiao* has for the most part focused on two ends: efficiency and the raising of teacher qualifications. These elements of reform, although expensive, have been fairly straight forward: increase qualifications by awarding more degrees; award more degrees by building more universities, classrooms, laboratories, etc. In turn, the execution of these elements has encouraged changes in certain policy dimensions.[22] Institutions increased in size, raising internal efficiency by taking advantage of economies of scale. Institutional merger or consolidation has also occurred, and in some cases, neighbouring institutions have undertaken joint production.[23] Most importantly, there has been a rationalization of specializations and units within institutions to meet the needs of changing times. In the past, the Soviet-inspired system of degree specialization dovetailed with the state's manpower planning system. For example, the PRC's rail system was expected to need a certain number of new staff in hydraulics systems. The new recruits, who majored in hydraulics, would come from universities under the Railway Ministry; they would be hydraulics majors. But the policy wind shifted in the late 1970s. In adhering to state dicta that moved the PRC towards an economy controlled largely by market mechanisms, educational planners abolished job assignment; they argued that a free job market was the best means of allocating qualified talent. The 'market', they said, preferred graduates with foundation skills who could shift jobs according to the economy's needs. It was no longer good for graduates to be 'locked into very narrow fields of specialization'.[24]

While to some extent curriculum is being influenced by market demands, pedagogy seems not to have been greatly affected. Classrooms are still places that encourage neither critical nor creative thinking. In the worst scenario, the teacher enters the classroom and opens a book. The bell rings. The teacher proceeds to read. Some students pay attention, anticipating that the material may be included in the examination. Other students doze off or chat among themselves, knowing they can read the text when they cram several nights before the exam. The final bell rings. The teacher closes the book. What substitutes for learning and teaching has closed another session.

Test-directed studying is not unique to China and indeed characterizes most Asian education. Achievements in international tests impress American educators.[25] The deficiencies of exam-based learning, however, concern many regional educators. But in the PRC the national college entrance exam contributes to the continuity of political centralism, while at the same time ensuring merit selection criteria for university admission.[26]

Similarly, exams in college courses serve as a threat that extracts student discipline. In other words, exam-based learning in the PRC has less to do with pedagogy than with political control. Moreover, given that uniform testing helps stem corrupt practices by closing (if not locking) back-door admission, reformers are reluctant to advocate its removal.

Journal articles by Chinese educationalists are sometimes critical of the old-fashioned pedagogy that characterizes the nation's higher education.[27] Indeed, at all levels, education — learning Chinese characters is no exception — emphasizes skill training, which often requires practice and memorization. It is assumed that once skills are acquired, creativity may follow.[28] Although educators lament the lack of critical and creative thinking in the classroom and work-unit leaders lament the absence of these qualities among graduates they employ, few criticize the pedagogy that is responsible. Whether creativity must follow skills acquisition is open to debate, yet in the PRC there is little empirical research to shed light on the issue. Skills acquisition remains the priority. Students' acquisition of critical and creative thinking is a welcome by-product of the education system; to what extent and under what conditions it occurs remain unknown.

Quality and evaluation

Educational evaluation, especially as practised in Western countries, is relatively new to the PRC. In the past, there was little need for evaluation. Institutions were (and still are) classified into a hierarchical system. Key schools run by the central authorities — the SEdC and ministries — are by definition in the first class. Their performance *ipso facto* is the best among Chinese institutions. The next stratum includes institutions under provincial authority. Finally, in the bottom class are colleges and universities run by municipal governments. Before taking the college entrance exam, secondary school students put down their preferences according to the three categories. Selection is made by test scores; indeed, the highest-stratum institutions get the best secondary school students. In the past, university faculties were mostly composed of graduates from their own institutions. Invariably, the students who performed best academically were chosen to continue with their studies, and the best of the best were hired by the institution. In this way the highest-ranked institutions acquired the highest-ranked graduates. The system experienced a trickle-down process: an unimpressive Beida graduate (whom Beida does not accept on its own staff) might be hired by a lower-ranked institution. In sum, quality in higher education (at least as perceived in academia) mostly related to student intake. For individual institutions, evaluation did not go below the surface. Shifting policies during the period from 1950 to 1980 at times evaluated the entire system as deficient, but individual *gaoxiao* were not often treated individually.[29] In the jargon of social scientists, the 'unit of observation' was the entire system.

The review of a particular institution's operations usually entailed a visit from officials in the governmental unit — state, provincial or municipal — that managed the school. These 'inspection tours' were often ritualistic in nature and included banquets and gift-giving. From the 1980s the granting of semi-autonomy to institutions has not diminished the importance of these inspections, but now *gaoxiao* are required to devise and execute their own evaluation plans that examine virtually all aspects of their education. The results of these evaluations are then discussed with higher-level authorities. Evaluation was specifically designed around inspection tours; no ongoing systems were in place.

Recent reforms have mandated ongoing evaluation systems for SEdC-supervised institutions, and other *gaoxiao* have followed the lead of the élites.[30] Conferences on evaluation are frequently held; a Society for Higher Education Evaluation Research in China has been established. By the mid-1990s, institutions are still trying to figure out how to evaluate themselves. The index system has been a frequently employed mechanism. Scores for disparate variables, such as those that relate to facilities (size of library, number of computers, etc.) and teaching quality (based on degree qualifications and even student assessment), are weighted and then summed to give departments in the institution a score.[31] Here, the unit of observation is usually the academic department.

A trend emerging in the mid-1990s is a move away from using evaluation as a grading method towards using it as a way to identify weaknesses and develop corrective strategies. Clothing themselves in the rhetoric heard in American educational circles 25 years ago, Chinese educators are promoting 'process evaluation' over 'summative evaluation'.[32] They argue that evaluation should be both qualitative as well as quantitative; it should specifically address the needs of the individual institution.[33]

For its part the government is undertaking two major evaluations in higher education. One is an accreditation of the approximately 400 institutions established after the reforms began. This primarily involves an inspection tour from an ad hoc SEdC delegation which reviews the institution's self-evaluation; students are often given tests in subjects they are studying. The second evaluation effort is Project 211, so-named to select 100 world-class universities for the twenty-first century. This élitist group will comprise comprehensive universities as well as scientific research centres, and local funding would be matched by the state. Those institutions selected are expected to grow into mega-universities to help the PRC compete on the world stage. This is an indication of the concentrating of resources into the élite and further illustrates, as discussed above, the state's move away from mass higher education. On the positive side, Project 211 has attracted private investment to higher education, has shifted the 'hot topic' from money-making to educational quality and has provided non-key provincial universities an opportunity for fair competition.[34]

Quality is never easy to evaluate. In the case of Chinese higher education, the task is made more difficult because the system is the product of factors not associated with Western higher education, where most evaluation models are developed. Chinese characteristics include emphasis on human relations and moral performance, cult for conformity and uniformity, emphasis on effort and disregard of innate abilities, and neglect of relevance of the curriculum.[35] Above all else, Chinese higher education's primary mission is to create human resources for the state's economy. Put bluntly, '...the value of schooling is none other than the degree higher institutions suit and meet the need of the society'.[36] Educating an individual 'to be a whole person', 'to be enriched' or 'to achieve his/her full potential' are phrases associated with Western, not Chinese, education. In de-emphasizing the individual, the Chinese system is so radically different from that elsewhere that the evaluation system that emerges will likely be different, also. Looking at the Western model may not be as instructive as it first appears.

Moral and civic education

As noted above, moral and civic education are important components in Chinese education, especially in higher education. Generally, morality and good citizenship in the PRC are taught by example. As Gay Garland Reed points out in her chapter, changing times require changing role models. In post-Mao China, however, no model has emerged to replace the people's hero Lei Feng. A model is especially necessary because the CCP has lost much of the legitimacy and respect it had in the early decades following the Revolution. The public's loss of confidence in politics, coupled with the state's emphasis on political correctness and its intolerance for dissent, creates a tensioned cynicism among intellectuals. Throughout China's history intellectuals have played a vital role (and have often suffered for their participation). The market economy now 'allows the intelligentsia, through their multiple involvements with it, to escape from the ancient binary alternative: either to enter politics or do nothing'.[37] There is growing anecdotal evidence that university academics are disengaging from scholarship (*xia hai*), jumping into the sea of business. If they disinvest from politics, who will replace them? Who will keep the politicians intellectually honest?

A major consequence of Chinese reforms over many fields is the granting of freedom. Institutions are given more autonomy; students are 'free to choose' their jobs. Along with choice comes individualism, a cultural attribute not generally considered part of China's collective nature.[38] Classroom pedagogy may remain anti-individual and fettered, but other aspects of the campus are indeed emancipated. Intended or not, freedom is a major repercussion of reform, one so dynamic that educational planners are hard-pressed to deal with it, much less foresee its consequences. University students relish their freedom although they are often unprepared to handle it, as Teresa Wright suggests in her chapter. *China Daily* can only bemoan students' lack of interest in physical exercise; education officials seem powerless to devise solutions to change young people's newly acquired habits. Campus crimes abound.[39] Attitudes on sexual mores have changed extremely fast in the past decade, apparently closely approximating what exists in other parts of the world.[40] Attitudinal data collected on undergraduates in 1986 indicated that the state had been successful in transferring central values to these young adults.[41] Even in the early years of reform, education approximated what educational planners wanted; it reflected state values. But as reform has progressed, Chinese characteristics as defined by the state have become increasingly difficult to discern in Chinese higher education. A replication of the 1986 study today would certainly reach an opposite conclusion.

Politicization of education

As noted above, over the history of the PRC, educational policy at the macro-level has shifted with political winds, directed at different times by radical and moderate groups.[42] At the institutional level, factional politics sometimes prevailed during the Cultural Revolution, but since the initiation of Dengist reforms, factions have been relatively less important.[43] Now, '[c]onsensus building, negotiation and persuasion are central features of much of the education policy process. It is an interactive process vertically and one that requires inter-sectoral cooperation'.[44] When there is consensus, reforms move with speed. The Visiting Scholars Programme, discussed in Michele Shoresman's chapter, was put in place within one year; many reforms in faculty development (see Cao Xiaonan's chapter) also moved ahead quickly.

But consensus does not always materialize. Policy documents flow down the hierarchy, but bureaucrats at lower levels of government can exercise veto powers over policy handed down to them.[45] Because of this *de facto* veto power, educational reforms have moved at a slower pace than many educational officials would have liked. The view of obstructionists from below is expressed in the Chinese idiom, 'they have their measures; we have our countermeasures' (*shang you zhengce, xia you duice*). Such is the case with the tuition and student loan policy, which Zhang Minxuan writes about, and changes in the job allocation system (see Michael Agelasto's chapter) which moved at a snail's pace for more than a decade. Often, officials wait for the results of 'experiments' which test a model. Some of these, as in manpower planning, are quite formal. Others result when higher-level leaders indulge their hierarchical subordinates. If an experiment is successful, it may become a candidate for nationwide adoption. If not (often judged on criteria of political correctness), it will be abandoned. Maria Jaschok's chapter describes the unfortunate closing of one such impressive experiment. This practice of relying on pioneering experimentation to handle policy issues has been described as *mosuo* ('management by groping' or cautiously feeling one's way).[46]

Bureaucratic bottlenecks also occur inside institutions, where decision-making is complex because the Party apparatus forms a shadow authority to the president-headed administrative structure, as discussed above. Officially, *gaoxiao* operate under the 'president responsible' system, but often a conservative Party Secretary can obstruct and delay reform; this can happen at the departmental level.[47] In cases where the CCP leaders are reform-minded, unnecessary delays may be avoided.

The importance of individual leaders (*lingdao*) is reinforced in a hierarchy. Often, in the PRC, the person is more important than the office. Connections (*guanxi*) are necessary for moving policy successfully through an institution's bureaucracy. Although *guanxi* can move reform along, it can also slow progress. This prospect will remain for as long as education is so influenced by personal relations that can negate regulations. Politics, however, does not equate to connections. Taiwan's higher education system has undergone a depoliticizing process,[48] but connections still remain strong. Taiwan can offer the PRC valuable instruction through the island's experience in lessening political influence over education.

Research

This volume has focused on empiricism, with several chapters presenting case studies. Most required extensive field research. They present an array of theories from economics, sociology, anthropology, political science and education. All chapters have found a nexus between theory and data, one of the indicators of quality research. Sadly, however, they are not representative of the type of scholarly research that appears in education journals published in the PRC.

Academic work in the PRC continues to be strongly influenced by politics. Mainland scholars still do not feel free to analyse, much less criticize, state policies on which the government holds strong views. Once a policy goes out of favour, academics rush in to offer their opinions. Would not these opinions have been valuable during the policy conception or implementation phase?

In handling research Chinese universities are starting to resemble their counterparts in developed countries. The rapid development of a national research establishment is most impressive (see Cong Cao's chapter). Quality of teaching and research is definitely improving, in large part due to academic exchanges, such as the one Michele Shoresman writes about, in which developed educational systems can help train Chinese scholars.

Chinese academics have difficulty in publishing abroad for various reasons (see Wenhui Zhong's chapter). Indigenous educational research published in the PRC does not much resemble academic scholarship in the West. Different modes of analysis exist. A study on the nature of articles that were published in the prestigious journal *Jiaoyu Yanjiu* (Educational Research) found the most frequent categories to be philosophical analysis, meeting/activity reports, collation/state-of-the-art, address/editorial, and policy advocacy, survey/quantitative study, experiments, and ponderings/impressions.[49] Case studies and policy studies only rarely occurred. Quantitative research, especially survey analysis, does not meet standards of reliability and validity practised in the West.[50] In general, mainland scholarship lacks objectivity and empiricism; research tends to be highly prescriptive and philosophical. It is infested with 'ponderings' and opinions unsubstantiated with data or theory. More problematic is the absence of research in key areas such as creativity, as mentioned above.

THE FUTURE OF CHINESE HIGHER EDUCATION

The objective of the reform journey appears to be to establish higher education 'with Chinese characteristics' — at least this is something viewed as highly desirable by many Chinese educational authorities. But what exactly is it? Chinese essence or 'characteristics', however defined, change over time. Indeed, post-Mao reforms are changing the very nature of education, just as Maoist reforms turned the system on its head during the Cultural Revolution.

One way to define it is to include those elements that reform reinforces as well as those that persist despite reform. The former category encompasses élitism. For centuries Chinese educational policy at all levels has subscribed to the idiom *ti gang xie ling*, the meaning of which relates to grasping an issue by first taking the most important part. Lifting an overcoat, for example, involves hooking it by the tag in the collar. But what, if at some point, the tag becomes more important than the entire garment? What happens if so much attention is given to the tag that the cloth itself deteriorates?

An element that persists despite reform is the continued politicization of education. This point is subtly made in a recent World Bank study[51] and evidence is reported throughout the chapters of this volume. There is little confirmation that the CCP plays a very positive role at present. While the PRC's policy-makers desire the state role to be one of macro-management, some local Party functionaries at the institutional level prefer micro-management. In certain institutions the CCP is no more than a bureaucratic nuisance; in others it impedes quality education. The role of the CCP in higher education needs to be defined in a way that produces administrative efficiency and enhances educational quality.

Future progress towards quality in research depends upon a change in the leadership's attitude to intellectuals. The current attempts to minimize the effects of Westernization have led to differential treatment of scholars in the natural sciences and technology from those in the social sciences, arts and the humanities. After all, too much freedom in the latter areas may cause dissent and encourage questioning of the regime's legitimacy. Liberalization would necessarily bring risks, but the real potential for Chinese scholarly productivity and contributions to the world knowledge system could come about only when the restrictions are lifted.

Pedagogy is another element that seems to be reform-resistant. Many educationalists ponder this problem. The great wall that prevents reform in this area is expressed in the idiom: *zhongxue weiti, xixue weiyong* or 'Chinese learning as the essence, western learning for its utility'. This xenophobic phrase relates empty words. Learning from foreign experience will continue to help *gaoxiao* develop Chinese characteristics. Once again, there might be a political price to be paid, as any changes to the exam-driven, duck-stuffing pedagogy to one that encourages creativity and individualism would weaken a main artery for state ideological control.

Realistically, one cannot foresee the CCP willingly surrendering its grip on power in the cause of economic modernization — as the events of 1989 proved graphically. Instead, it would appear that gradualism, with cautious, groping steps which balance rather than topple the competing interests, will continue to characterize the progress of higher educational reform in the PRC.

NOTES

1. *China Daily*, 'Survey says university students shun exercise', 26 April 1996.
2. *China Daily*, 'Liaoning college students learn the value of a yuan', 2 June 1996.
3. Zhou Weirong, 1995.
4. National Centre for Educational Development Research, 1996, p. 4.
5. Wang Jisheng, 1996.
6. Wang Jisheng, 1996, p. 13.
7. For a comparative view on the experiences of educational reform, see Fullan, 1993.
8. Fu, 1996. See also Fu, 1992.
9. Ma Weixiang and Hawkridge, 1995.
10. Ma Weixiang and Hawkridge, 1995.
11. Compare Fu, 1996 and Howells, 1989.
12. Pepper, 1996; also, J.C. Robinson, 1991.
13. Fu, 1996, p. 3.
14. McCormick, 1985.
15. Yin Qiping and G. White, 1994, p. 242.
16. Yin Qiping and G. White, 1994, pp. 217–37.
17. Wang Xianming and Hu Yanpin, 1994.
18. National Centre for Educational Development Research, 1996, p. 13. Interestingly, the SEdC in its biannual array of statistics gives scant attention (three pages) to public expenditure on education. For higher education they disclose only that from 1990 to 1991 capital outlay from budgetary allocations increased slightly (below 1%), hardly enough to keep up with the nation's double-digit inflation. *Education statistics yearbook of China 1990–1991*, p. 127.
19. *Education statistics yearbook of China 1990–1991*, p. 4.
20. Min, 1996. See also Min, 1994, pp. 106–27.
21. Min, 1996.
22. See Tsang and Min, 1992.
23. 'Education reforms put learning on higher plane', *China Daily*, 27 September 1995. But see also, Cai Hong, 1994.
24. Min, 1997a.
25. See, for example, Stevenson and Stigler, 1992.
26. Yuan Feng, 1995.
27. Huang Quanyu, 1993.
28. Gardner, 1989.
29. Most evaluations used criteria of political correctness. See Pepper, 1996.
30. SEdC, 'Temporary regulations on education evaluation of higher institution', issued October 1990.
31. See Cui, Gao, Su and Xu, 1996; and Wang and Lin, 1996.
32. See Bloom, Hastings and Madaus, 1971.
33. Li Yong, Cui Junling and Zhang Xing, 1996; and Feng Zhiguang, 1996.
34. X.D. Cheng and Zhou Chuan, 1995.

35. Cheng Kai-ming, 1994d, p. 82.
36. Wang Hui, 1996.
37. Chen Yan, 1996.
38. See generally, Cheng Kai-ming, 1994d.
39. 'China cracks down on Campus crimes', *CND-Global*, no. 162, 15 November 1996.
40. '69 percent of couples had pre-marital sex, survey says', *CND-Global*, no. 160, 11 November 1996.
41. Hu Xiaolu and Korllos, 1995.
42. Shen Jianping, 1994. For a somewhat different perspective, see Sautman, 1991.
43. A case where factional politics prevailed is reported in Agelasto, 1996a.
44. Paine, 1992b, p. 210.
45. Shirk, 1993, pp. 116–28.
46. Paine, 1992b.
47. See Chapter 16 by Maria Jaschok and Chapter 8 by Bob Adamson in this volume for instances of CCP obstruction.
48. Law, 1995.
49. Cheng Kai-ming, 1994d.
50. Rosen, 1987.
51. See Appendix for the Executive Summary of this report.

Appendix
Executive Summary of
China: Higher Education Reform.
A World Bank Country Study[1]

THE MACRO CONTEXT

The economy of China is one of the fastest growing in the world, with an annual average Gross Domestic Product (GDP) growth rate of 9.8 percent in real terms between 1978 and 1994. According to the Ninth Five-Year Plan (1995-2000), the Government's target for GDP in 2000 is to quadruple that in 1980, and that for GDP in 2010 is to double that in 2000. This entails an average annual growth rate of 8 percent between 1995 and 2000, and over 7 percent between 2000 and 2010. Given the momentum of China's historical growth rate, it is realistic to expect the GDP to continue to grow at an annual average rate of 7-9 percent in real terms over the next 25 years. If the population growth rates are held down, its GDP per capita would be $600-$700 (as in 1996 constant terms) by 2000; $1,100-$1,600 by 2010; and $2,100-$3,500 by 2020, according to this study's projection. In other words, in five years' time, China would be on its way to becoming a lower-middle-income country, and in 25 years' time, it would be poised to join the league of upper-middle-income countries. To sustain these economic growth rates, the demand for well-educated personnel is likely to be high.

Chinese higher education institutions play two key roles in sustaining economic growth rates and in facilitating socially and environmentally responsible development in the country. First, they prepare citizens to fill high-level scientific, technical, professional and managerial positions in the public and private sectors. Second, in their capacities as repositories, generators, and communicators of knowledge, they underpin internal technological advancement, particularly in transforming research and development results for industrial productivity, and provide access to and adaptation of ideas from elsewhere in the world.

These tasks of educating the leadership and generating/utilizing knowledge for China's development effort present major challenges. Destroyed by the Cultural Revolution (1966-76), China's higher education system was rebuilt only in the late 1970s as one element of a strategy to modernize the country. The 1978-94 period witnessed remarkable proliferation of public regular higher education institutions from 598 to 1,080, and extension of enrollment from 0.86 million to 2.8 million full-time students in undergraduate and short-cycle courses, at an annual growth rate of 7.7 percent. Graduate enrollment rose from zero to 0.13 million. While this achievement was impressive, the proportion of the appropriate age cohort enrolled in regular higher education institutions was only 2.4 percent in 1994, barely above that in 1960. When enrollment in all adult tertiary institutions is considered, it amounts to just over 4 percent of gross enrollment in higher education. This ratio is low in comparison not only with other fast-growing East Asian countries [for example, 10 percent in Indonesia, 19 percent in Thailand, 20 percent in Hong Kong, 39 percent in Taiwan (China), and 51 percent in Republic of Korea], but also with India, which had a per capita GNP of $300 in 1993, lower than China's $490, and yet had an enrollment rate of 8 percent in higher education.

According to the UNESCO Statistical Yearbook (1995), only about 2 percent of the Chinese population over the age of 25 have had postsecondary education, compared to 11 percent in Hong Kong, 14 percent in Republic of Korea, 21 percent in Japan, 14 percent in the former USSR, and 45 percent in the United States. The US National Science Foundation estimated that in 1990, only 5.6 scientists and engineers engaged in research and development per 10,000 persons in the work force in China, compared to 30 in Singapore, 38 in Taiwan (China), 37 in Republic of Korea, 75 in Japan, and 75 in the United States. Emerging evidence of growing economic returns to higher education and increased wage inequality in Hong Kong, Taiwan (China), Malaysia, Indonesia, and Chile indicates that fast-growing economies can face skill scarcity if supply of well-educated people is unable to keep pace with demand. Given China's small stock of highly educated people, skill scarcity would reduce China's attractiveness to foreign investment, particularly in the medium-to-high technology areas, limit the options for industrial upgrading, undermine the institutional capacity in all sectors, and exacerbate income inequality in a more liberalized labor market.

The Chinese government invested heavily in universities and research laboratories prior to 1980. Significant technological achievements have been made by the sector, but transforming research and development results into increased productivity has been limited. In 1991, only 6.2 percent of domestic technology trade originated in universities and colleges.[2] As world trade expands, China will face increasingly competitive pressure from lower-wage economies (such as Vietnam and Bangladesh). The increasing integration of the world economy and the global acceleration of technological change would make the reliance on low-skilled labor-intensive production a nonviable option for future development. For China to speed up its development and to raise her living standards in the 21st century, it is imperative that the manufacturing of medium-skilled products be mastered and a move toward production of high-technology goods and services be fostered.

Since 1978, the Chinese Government has placed priority within the education sector upon rapid expansion and improvement of higher education to help reduce the serious human resource constraints on the country's economic and social development. In 1985, the Government adopted the document *Decision on Education Reform*, which aimed at providing the mix of skills of a rapidly changing society; to improve efficiency, quality and equity; and releasing resources required to develop and enhance education at lower levels. More recently, in order to speed up nationwide transformation from a planned economy to a market economy, the Government in its *Guidelines of China's Educational Reform and Development* advocates changes at two levels: chiefly, governmental policy and institutional practice.[3] The major strategic approach is that of decentralization in institutional management and administration while maintaining managerial oversight at the macro level. Devolution of power and responsibilities to institutions has brought new challenges to the higher education sector. **The purpose of this report is to review China's higher education reform efforts over the last 10 years in relation to goals delineated in the 1985 document, with the objective of providing advice for continuation of reforms over the next 25 years.**

THE HIGHER EDUCATION SYSTEM

The Chinese higher education system is dominated by 1,080 regular public universities and colleges that are under the jurisdiction of and obtain their funding from one of three administrative authorities: (a) State Education Commission (SEdC) in the central government, (b) central ministries, and

(c) provinces and municipalities. In 1994, there were 1,080 such institutions. The distribution of their enrollment was: 11 percent in 36 national key universities funded by SEdC, 34 percent in 331 ministry-funded institutions, and 55 percent in 713 provincial and municipal institutions. Of the total student body in these public institutions, 52 percent enrolled in degree-earning undergraduate studies, 44 percent in short-cycle, nondegree programs, and 4 percent in postgraduate studies. These institutions employed 1.04 million staff, of whom 38 percent had teaching responsibilities, 44 percent were administrative and support staff, and 18 percent were employed in organizations affiliated with universities (such as factories, enterprises, and research institutes). Of the total staff, only 2 percent held a doctorate degree, 19 percent with a master's degree, 49 percent with a bachelor's degree, and 30 percent with short-cycle diplomas or without a degree but finished degree course work. How to expand the capacity of these regular public institutions, in quantitative and qualitative terms, is the focus of this study.

There are, in addition, 1,172 public adult education institutions at postsecondary levels, including radio and television universities, schools for workers, peasants, and cadres, pedagogical colleges, independent correspondence colleges, and correspondence or evening courses run by regular higher education institutions. In 1994, these institutions enrolled 2.35 million students on a part-time basis and employed 0.21 million full-time staff (of which 45 percent were teachers) and 0.03 million part-time teachers. About 90 percent of enrollees were in short-cycle programs, and only 10 percent in regular undergraduate studies. Although these adult education institutions are not the focus of this study, they are taken into consideration in some of the recommendations for improving cost-effectiveness, quality and equity of the higher education system in this report.

Furthermore, over 800 private postsecondary institutions have been in operation (enrolling about 1 to 5 percent students in addition to those in the regular public institutions). However, only 16 of these institutions have been accredited by the government. Since no official data have been collected systematically on them, these private institutions are beyond the scope of this study, but the recommendations in this report take their potential contribution into account.

Since 1981, eight Bank projects totaling $910.4 million have been undertaken in China in such fields as science and engineering, economics and finance, agriculture, medicine and education in support of the government's aim to increase the quantity and quality of high-level skilled manpower. The Bank's first sector report (1986) looked at key issues in management and financing of higher education, which became significant components in subsequent projects.[4] The overall impact of the higher education projects has been on enrollment expansion, improved quality of instruction, strengthened research capacity, improved management and curricular reform. Important lessons were learned from these projects with respect to faculty and curriculum development, as well as managing and developing university-based research. Beginning with the prestigious key universities, assistance was spread to provincial normal (teacher training) universities, universities under line ministries — agriculture and forestry, public health — and short-cycle vocational universities. A significant tier that has not been included in any of the projects is a range of nonspecialized universities under provincial jurisdictions, which are the main concern of this study.

CHALLENGES CONFRONTING INSTITUTIONS

The fundamental challenge of current economic and educational reform is to orient institutions to a more open labor market as well as to a more open society. Regular higher education institutions were established with the aim of meeting the skill requirements of a centrally planned economy and funded according to State planning. The operating environment in the recent past and the next two decades might be characterized in the following way: from a command economy to a socialist market economy; from the practice of job assignments and lifelong employment in one institution to increasing choice and mobility of the labor market responsive to changes in skill requirements; from a system that derives all directives for policy and action from the center to a more managerially and financially decentralized one, characterized by increasing autonomy; from a situation that isolates the subsector to one that sees higher education as fundamentally linked with government, business, and the local community, and with national and international institutions. Overall, the entire system in the country might shift from an input- and supply-driven model to an output- and demand-driven one, effecting wide-ranging changes in management, faculty, students, and academic programs.

The key issues confronting institutions are: (a) lack of clarity regarding respective roles and powers of SEdC, central ministries, and provincial and municipal governments; (b) ineffective management and administrative structures and processes; (c) inefficiency in the use of scarce resources for qualitative improvement and quantitative expansion; (d) inappropriate resource allocation system for improving operational efficiency and institutional quality; (e) difficulties relating to a balance between market-oriented programs of study and basic disciplines; and (f) uneven distribution of managerial, financial, academic, and technical capabilities and capacities among regions, provinces and institutions.

In the context of this operating environment and these challenges, the report's recommendations are organized around four core themes crucial to reform goals: (a) the changing role of government in relation to higher education institutions; (b) the implications of reforms for institutional management; (c) the diversification of structure and sources of financial support and its utilization; and (d) quality improvement in higher education with particular emphasis on staffing and curricular issues. Identification of core themes and subthemes of the report was guided by SEdC's verification of the issues posed by the reform goals to the system as a whole, to institutions in particular, and to their prioritized problem areas.

RECOMMENDATIONS

Education is a key element of China's strategic initiative to reach international competitive standards in economic and social terms by the 21st century. In order to achieve this goal, this report recommends that the following overarching *principles* be observed and reinforced in the implementation of reforms:

a) the role of the State be clearly that of policy and standard-setting, monitoring and regulating;

b) the State creates an "enabling environment" in which institutions can have greater financial and managerial autonomy; and

c) the State provides leadership for increasing institutional capability to handle such autonomy by establishing a national body to give advice to individual universities and provinces or municipalities.

This report finds an uneven picture of the impact of reforms on higher education institutions across the country. Except for those institutions that are well-funded by the government, have a well-developed tradition of scholarship and research, and are located in or close to areas of socioeconomic change, the majority of higher education institutions do not have the managerial, financial, academic and technical expertise to contribute to economic stabilization and long-term growth nor to the development of an open and civic society. These disparities may in themselves become the seeds of destabilization. To meet the developmental needs of the higher education system and to address its internal disparities, this report *recommends* that:

a) the role of the State be defined unambiguously vis-à-vis universities within the framework of the new Higher Education Law, which should provide definitions of the respective roles, responsibilities and powers of the national, provincial and municipal authorities and the universities themselves;

b) effective funding and policy-making bodies be established with defined functions within post-reform structures; the principle of autonomy be strengthened in the devolution of new managerial, administrative and academic responsibilities and powers to institutions;

c) universities be empowered through training and exposure, nationally and internationally, to prepare and implement their own strategies for development and to strengthen their managerial capacity. A National Higher Education Management Center should be established to assist individual institutions, provinces and municipalities;

d) a sound information base be established by designating an agency to be responsible for collection, processing and publishing data that emphasize indicators of performance and achievement;

e) nongovernmental or private institutions be encouraged and accreditation procedures and support facilities be expedited to maintain national standards;

f) critical assistance be provided to provincial institutions in poor areas that are resource-starved and have little access to professional and technological support;

g) funding methodologies for both recurrent and capital funding be reviewed so as to reward efficiency and encourage expansion at below cost;

h) policies and programs be developed that encourage universities to generate further income from the provision of short-term training, professionally-managed enterprises and donations or endowments from all sources;

i) policies of cost sharing through tuition fees be continued and student loan schemes (initiated by financial capital from government sources) along with other financial assistance programs be put in place to protect poor, minority and female students;

j) funding policies for research and training be refined in order to rectify the balance among institutions, among discipline areas, while observing gender and ethnic priorities;

k) financial and nonfinancial incentives be established and clearly spelled out in order to move institutional practices such as better research and publication outputs toward qualitative goals;

l) accreditation procedures and structures be extended and accelerated, accompanied by training using both local and international expertise, spearheaded at provincial level by the establishment of "quality centers" whose sole task would be to institutionalize accreditation procedures, working with national and provincial bodies; and

m) "centers of excellence" be established serving provinces or regions, building on institutional excellence in specified cognate areas. Their function would be to provide and coordinate degree-level and nondegree training for ongoing professional development of faculty; and to stimulate and coordinate research and publication activities.

This report suggests five approaches that may assist the government in its gradualist and selective path of reform in the subsector. First, there should be wide participation in the planning of change to win support and to provide legitimacy. Second, the outcomes of participatory planning should become visible as concrete and realizable targets for action. The development of appropriate monitoring indicators should be included in the exercise. Third, the government needs to orchestrate efficient information flows without which planning becomes a futile exercise. Fourth, while national standards are set by the center, specific provincial and institutional targets should vary according to capacity and capability. National standard setting does not imply uniformity. Finally, reform targets should be based on carefully focused reward and incentive mechanisms that will induce institutions to move toward local and national goals.

RELATIONSHIPS BETWEEN UNIVERSITIES AND THE STATE

Context

Since the early 1980s the government has been gradually moving away from a centralist model in which it controlled the detailed operations of higher education institutions. This was originally applied by central control of five key functions: provision of core funding, setting student enrollments for each institution, approving senior staff appointments, authorizing all new academic programs and managing the student assignment process. As the numbers of institutions and students grew, it became increasingly difficult for State bodies to exercise this control in a way that was compatible with the needs of the rapidly growing socialist market economy. As a result, the government began consultations on the legal framework that will designate universities as independent legal entities and establish the mechanism on which the university's managerial autonomy will rest. The legal framework will allow universities to set their own strategic goals, define their own academic focuses ("specialties") in order to respond to local and provincial needs, and control their resources.

Although the State will still continue to provide core funding, it recognizes that it can no longer provide all the funds itself. As a result, it has set up the China Education and Scientific Trust Investment Corporation, which acts as a commercial banker specializing in the education sector. It provides short-term loans to institutions, secured on their assets, for their buildings and equipment. It has been unclear, however, whether poorer institutions will have the necessary collateral to access such financing. Some initial steps have been taken to encourage the development of nongovernment (or "minban") institutions of higher education. The minban universities usually use staff from nearby State-financed universities. Although it is clear that there are significant economies of scale and relatively few risks of poor-quality teaching in the early stages, the advantages could disappear as the nongovernment sector grows, requiring quality-control procedures to be set up by government. National accreditation activities which could expedite these procedures are moving slowly.

Issues

The gradualist approach to introducing change is pragmatic and careful, but involves a judgment by a central authority as to whether a level of management is considered "ready" to acquire new responsibilities. As a result, there is sometimes resentment among some universities at the slowness with which freedoms are accorded or power delegated. Another predictable consequence of the pragmatic, selective introduction of new freedoms is that because of the variation within the system, different decisions about provinces by SEdC and about universities' capabilities by provinces are resulting in a sometimes confused, uneven picture.

A direct consequence of the change in the national funding flows appears to be an increase in the influence of the provincial governments in higher education compared to SEdC. It is still a fluid situation that also varies according to the wealth of the province and the importance it places on higher education. Moreover, economic pressures are threatening to distort the balance of courses offered. Universities are finding it increasingly hard to maintain some core academic disciplines for which students do not enroll. The number applying for the basic sciences and humanities subjects are far below what is considered efficient for comprehensive universities.

China is in the midst of moving from a "state-control model" to a "state-supervising model" (in current terms from "macrocontrol" to "macromanagement") as regards the relationship between universities and government. There are difficult questions to answer about the respective roles and powers of SEdC, central ministries and provincial/municipal governments. What could be the split of powers and control that would still allow the State to fulfill its "macromanagement" function and yet at the same time unleash the latent energy and enthusiasm within institutions?

Recommendations

A program of action has been suggested as a possible response to the above issues. In order to achieve the program's objectives, the capacity of the center needs to be greatly enhanced. The operative principles underlying the proposed program are: (a) that the role of the State should be to monitor and regulate, rather than exercise detailed control; (b) that the State should create an "enabling environment" in which universities can plan their own destiny within State-set policy frameworks or efficiency targets; and (c) that universities should be encouraged to develop individual strategic plans showing how they aim to serve their specific province or community.

IMPACT OF CHANGES ON UNIVERSITY MANAGEMENT

Context

Universities are presently operating in a policy environment in which the management role of university presidents should be strengthened. However, there is continuing evidence that presidents are still subject to the direction of the Party Secretary although university presidents do appear to maintain academic autonomy. Moreover, many universities have established Boards of Trustees in order to develop links with society and local enterprises. The roles of these Boards vary tremendously. Some Boards provide contacts with a wide range of commercial enterprises and their funds, some stress involvement of provincial or municipal government officials in university activities while others are actively involved in the actual internal management of the institutions. University organizations' structures are changing but most new structures seem to be very flat with a relatively large number of people reporting directly to the president.

Issues

As Boards of Trustees and Councils become a more integral part of the university, there will be a need to define precisely the respective roles of SEdC, the Governing Council/Board of Trustees and the President. Many presidents are also experiencing a conflict between their roles as manager/fund-raiser and academic leader. Senior academic staff have not been trained to take on management tasks and they have had difficulty reconciling the two disparate functions.

The management of university enterprises is assuming growing importance as financial pressures increase and enterprises are seen as one of the principal sources of additional finance This raises two management issues: (a) whether they can continue to serve dual academic and financial objectives given the basic conflict between using a company as a research test bed and teaching forum and using it to generate profits; and (b) whether it is right that teachers who are appointed on essentially academic criteria should be expected to manage industrial holding companies in an increasingly competitive environment.

One main task of university presidents is to improve institutional efficiency. However, presidents feel constrained in their freedom to make major changes in the staff structure of their universities. They do not have the power to dismiss unproductive or ineffectual teachers. As long as society expects them to provide a total package of care for their employees, regardless of the level of the individual's contribution to the university, the universities will not become fully efficient.

University presidents are also unable to obtain adequate information support. The present management information systems (MIS) are unable to meet the needs and demands for appropriate information in relation to decision-making. There is a massive task of training ahead in all aspects of designing and implementing integrated management information systems.

Recommendations: Government Actions

A professionally enhanced center can assist in strengthening the internal management of institutions by the following government actions: (a) including guidance about the role and composition of the university Governing Body or Council in its legal framework; (b) clarifying the position of universities with regard to their tax free status; (c) modifying its encouragement of the expansion of university enterprises so as to make clear the options for managing or holding investments in them; (d) encouraging universities to prepare strategic plans that are linked to the annual funding process; and (e) encouraging universities to collaborate in the costs of developing computerized management information systems.

Recommendations: universities

For their part, universities need to: (a) develop strategic plans of action that assess their options in the context of their history, academic strengths and potential local and regional markets; (b) develop action plans for improving management efficiency as an important element of strategic plans; (c) request university councils to review current practices of managing their enterprises; and (d) formulate a strategy for computerizing their administrative systems.

FINANCING HIGHER EDUCATION: DIVERSIFICATION OF RESOURCES

Context

Since China embarked on economic reform in 1978, the GDP has grown by an impressive 9.8 percent per year in real terms, from ¥1,006 billion to ¥4,501 billion in 1994 (in constant 1994 prices). However, the growth rate of government revenue fell far behind that of GDP, increasing at an annual average of only 2.6 percent over the period. This resulted from decentralization and from permitting production units to retain much of their earnings without simultaneously putting in place a national tax administration until 1994. The revenue-to-GDP ratio declined from 34 percent in 1978 to 13 percent in 1994. Government expenditures, nevertheless, increased at 3.3 percent per year and were higher than its revenue, resulting in budget deficit in all but one year. Between 1987 and 1993, the public sector deficit hovered around 11-12 percent of GDP and was a key factor underlying inflationary pressures in the economy. In 1994, the public sector deficit declined to 9.9 percent.

Public expenditure on education increased from ¥21 to 98 billion (in constant 1994 prices), by an annual average of 10 percent between 1978 and 1994, far exceeding the respective growth rates of the total government revenue and expenditure. As the overall public spending shrank over the years, public expenditure on education as a percentage of total government expenditure rose from 6.2 percent in 1978 to 17 percent in 1994. However, public expenditure on education as a percentage of GDP rose from 2.1 percent in 1978 to the height of 3.1 percent in 1989, and then fell back to 2.2

percent in 1994. This level of public spending on education is low in comparison with least-developed countries' average of 2.8 percent, developing countries' average of 4.1 percent, and developed countries' average of 5.3 percent.

Total public allocation to higher education grew from ¥4.2 to 18.6 billion (in constant 1994 prices), by an annual average of 9.7 percent between 1978 and 1994. Public spending on higher education increased from 20 percent of total public expenditure on education in 1978 to the peak of 29 percent in 1984, then declined to around 17 percent between 1989 and 1992, and climbed back to 19 percent in 1994. Since under 2 percent of the age cohort were enrolled in higher education in much of the 1980s, the high share of public spending devoted to them reflected the effort to rebuild the higher education system.

At the same time, given the very low enrollment ratio in China, public spending on higher education was high by international comparison. For example, Indonesia, Malaysia, Thailand, Taiwan (China), Republic of Korea, and Japan, which had a much higher enrollment ratio in higher education, spent only 11 to 17 percent of their respective total public education expenditure on higher education, and mobilized the rest of the resources from private resources; the rest of their public expenditure was spent on lower levels of education. In 1980, China spent 27 percent of its public education expenditure on the primary level, 34 percent on the secondary level, 0.5 percent on preprimary education, and 18 percent on others. By 1993, the share of primary education went up to 34 percent and that of secondary education to 38 percent, while preprimary and other types of education claimed 1.3 and 9 percent, respectively. Since the lower levels of education are where the poor have access to, whereas middle- and upper-class students tend to be overrepresented in universities, allocating more public resources to lower levels of education is more equitable. In China, in 1990, public spending per-student in higher education was 193 percent of GDP per capita, that in secondary education was 15 percent, and that in primary education was 5 percent. In 1994, this was 175 percent. While improvement has been made, this percentage is still considerably higher than the 1990 average of 98 percent in East Asian countries. The relatively low per-student spending at the tertiary level in East Asia was made possible by the relatively large enrollment in higher education and efficient use of resources, resulting in reduced unit cost.

The public allocation per student in real terms peaked in 1984, and then went on a decline with year-on-year fluctuations. The increasing share of university-generated income and student fees made up for the shortfall. In 1994, the total allocation per student amounted to ¥8,168 of which ¥6,645 were public allocation and ¥1,515 were allocated from university-generated resources. In other words, in spite of rapid enrollment expansion, the total public and institutional allocation per student maintained the average unit allocation at a relatively stable level for higher education.

Issues

The central government and line ministries have delegated financial responsibilities to provincial governments for higher education. However, the financial capacity varies from province to province. Regional disparities in funding of higher education have serious implications for the ability of poorer provinces to attract and retain capable faculty members and to provide quality education. Even within a province, disparity is evident in the resources available for provincial universities and national universities.

In conjunction with financial decentralization, the nonfungible line-item budget was replaced with a block grant allocation from the State to the university. In addition, the incremental approach to allocating recurrent funds was replaced with a formula approach, with the major allocation parameter being the number of full-time equivalent students enrolled. Although this has improved the transparency in resource allocation, it does not provide incentives to improve efficiency or quality. This is due in large part to the fact that the national norms for allocating public funds are extremely generous.

The reforms have also given higher education institutions more autonomy to generate their own revenues. In 1992, public allocation accounted for 81.8 percent of total revenue in public higher education institutions, income generated by universities themselves for the rest. The main independent sources of income (1992 figures) are from: (a) university enterprises that provide approximately 3.7 percent of higher education revenue. However, not all institutions have the relevant management expertise and not all investments produce positive returns; (b) commissioned training for enterprises that constitutes the second largest (2.3 percent) independent share of revenue. Commissioned training has potential to generate further income; but the potential for rural universities may be limited; (c) income from other educational services was 1.1 percent; (d) research and consultancy that accounts for approximately 1.3 percent. This also has limited potential for provincial colleges and teacher colleges, where the research budget is very small and research and consultancy is limited; (e) income from logistic services (dining halls, etc.) was 0.7 percent; (f) income from other funded activities was 3.7 percent; (g) donations that contribute 0.8 percent of income. Once again, small provincial universities in the interior are rarely the recipients of donations, which heightens the disparity between national universities and the others; and (h) student tuition fees contribute 4.6 percent. The total amounts to 18.2 percent of universities' funding for 1992.

The former student stipends system, which distributed funds equally to all students, was changed into a new system of merit scholarship and loans for needy students in 1988. Currently, these scholarships cover between 50 and 80 percent of students. The sums awarded are very small, ranging from ¥60 to 300 per year, which was equivalent to 1.2 to 6.1 percent of state allocation per student in 1992, and was hardly adequate support.

The report's analysis of the reforms for diversifying sources of funding and changing patterns of expenditure has found that part of the financial difficulties experienced by institutions stems from disparities in their natural endowment and location, part is due to the funding mechanism that does not provide incentives for efficiency improvement, and part stems from the welfare burden that the socialist system requires institutions to bear. Since most provincial universities are much more disadvantaged than national universities (and yet enroll over 50 percent of students), their financial plight has serious implications for the higher education system as a whole. Changing the funding mechanisms may improve efficiency and reduce some disparity in natural endowment, but systemic change is required to reduce the welfare burden.

Recommendations

To enable higher education institutions to expand enrollment under conditions of public resource constraints, three policies need to be pursued simultaneously. First, the **operating efficiency of the system needs to be improved** by: (a) containing staff growth; (b) encouraging the growth of existing public institutions in size through expansion or merger, and the expansion of private universities; (c) devising funding mechanisms that encourage efficiency and reward cost-effective provision; (d) reviewing the norms and space formulae for allocating capital funding; (e) allowing for flexible duration of study as long as course requirements are fulfilled; and (f) making better use of educational technology to reduce cost and assure minimum quality. Second, institutions can **enhance their capacity for resource generation** by: (a) conducting short-term training for industries, governmental agencies, and communities using new technology in management/administration; (b) increasing income from research development-related research, and consulting activities; (c) ensuring that university enterprises are managed professionally; and (d) effectively mobilizing donations from enterprises, Chinese citizens and overseas Chinese. Third, **cost-recovery policies** should be continued and monitored, complemented by strong provision of a **financial assistance** system.

QUALITY IMPROVEMENT IN INSTRUCTIONAL PROGRAMS

Context

Striking changes have taken place during the 1980s in China's higher education curriculum with adjustments in enrollment that reflect both personal needs and rising social demand, relaxation of central control over content, movement toward more broad-based structures of knowledge and experimentation with course organization and delivery methods. Moreover, university based research has been recognized as a necessary foundation for curriculum development in new fields, good graduate study and teacher preparation in all subject areas. These changes have put considerable demands on the faculty in Chinese universities. The demands are different by field, region and level of institution. However, the most important differences exist between faculty in terms of their geographical location, in the center of economic growth or at the periphery, and of the level of their institutions, i.e., at the national, provincial or local level of institution.

There have been solid achievements in faculty development since 1980. During the 1980s, the promotion processes changed from being based on age and seniority to evaluation of teaching quality and research. Significant investment has been made in training, both domestic and overseas. China recognizes the long-term benefits contributed by overseas research and study experience to updating and revitalizing the higher education curriculum; and to research and publication advances in many specialist areas. Current policies to improve the quality of teachers are aimed at raising the formal qualifications of faculty under 40 to graduate level and new promotion requirements are based on these qualifications. Considerable efforts have also been made to attract and retain young teachers within the system.

China also began a step toward quality assurance in 1985. Common to all quality assurance practices are: (a) the development of standards; (b) the application of those standards to a program or institution by third parties for the purposes of assessment and enhancement; and (c) the subsequent improvement of the education entity. However, accrediting activities in Chinese higher education are still very modest.

Issues

In the curricular change process over the decade, universities and their faculty have had increasing freedom to shape their own programs. As institutions take on greater managerial, professional and academic responsibilities, they are called upon to make decisions for which they have little training and experience. An appropriate balance needs to be found between (a) consideration of maintaining academic standards and the constant upgrading of the knowledge content; (b) concerns about the macroregulation of emphasis on various fields in relation to national needs; and (c) concerns about providing a foundation of knowledge and nurturing a professional attitude, which fosters abilities for an ongoing self-development process that goes beyond immediate market demands.

Despite the fact that absolute levels of research have increased, more appropriate balance is required (a) between institutes; (b) between discipline areas; and (c) between basic and applied research. Research findings need to be fed into curriculum, faculty development, and industrial innovations. Increasing investment in higher education and national research and development has become an important element in economic growth strategies. Recent studies indicate that the social rate of return from investments in new industrial technology in developed countries seems to be high. Technological change in many industries and increased output of society have been based on recent academic research.

The key to curricular change is the people who make it happen — the teachers. While changes have taken place in the character and definition of instructional programs and in making them more flexible, broad-based and overtly market-oriented in terms of content/knowledge, there has been less change in teaching methods and fundamental pedagogical approaches. This opens up questions of effective change. There is great variation across provinces and their institutions according to available human, financial and material resources. Priority policies for institutions, particularly those in the interior provinces, would include the creation and implementation of favorable working conditions; insisting on high academic qualifications; investing in inservice graduate study; and implementation of national policies on better living conditions.

Recommendations

While priorities in quality improvement would depend on each institution's unique needs and be expressed in its strategic plan, the recommendations in this section focus on four key aspects in the quality improvement strategy:

curriculum, teaching and research, quality assurance, and educational inputs and facilities. In order to maintain systemic and institutional quality in both government and nongovernment institutions, a nationwide system of accreditation should be supported, building on achievements made in this area and strengthening existing training providers. It will entail the setting up of a National Steering Committee and Secretariat; identification, training and organization of accreditation bodies; and establishment of staff development and support mechanisms in the form of "quality assurance centers" and "centers of excellence."

NOTE

1. This is the Executive Summary of *China: Higher Education Reform. A World Bank Country Study* (International Bank for Reconstruction and Development/World Bank, 1997), and is reproduced with permission.
2. World Bank, 1995.
3. CCP Central Committee and the State Council, 1993.
4. World Bank, 1986.

Glossary

Most Chinese nouns do not have different singular and plural forms.

Hanyu pinyin	Simplified characters	Gloss
211 gong cheng	211 工程	Project 211
bai qian wan gong cheng	百千万工程	'Hundred, Thousand and Ten-Thousand' project
baochan daohu	包产到户	privatization of communes to individual families
baosong shangxue	保送上学	privileged access to higher education enrolment
beishu	背书	'back to the book' ; rote learning
benke	本科	Bachelor's degree
bianzhi	编制	official staff strength
binggui	并轨	'merging the tracks' ; combining different funding systems
biyesheng fenpei	毕业生分配	graduate job allocation

daguofan	大锅饭	'eating from the common pot' ; egalitarian social security
daipei	代培	commissioned training/contract study : student is contracted to work for sponsoring company upon graduation
danwei	单位	work-unit
daxue	大学	university
dazibao	大字报	big character poster
dingxiang	定向	student commissioned to work in a specified area upon graduation
dingxiang jiangxuejin	定向奖学金	scholarship to prepare students commissioned to work in a specified area upon graduation
dingxiang zhaosheng	定向招生	scholarship programme for student commissioned to work work in a specified area upon graduation
diqu	地区	prefecture
dongshou nengli cha	动手能力差	'unable to use one's hands' ; not using what one has learnt
duanceng	断层	'faultline' ; shortage of trained personnel caused by the Cultural Revolution
duikou	对口	job specific training
duli	独立	independence
duo qudao chouji zijin	多渠道筹集资金	diversification of funding
fangfalun yanjiu	方法论研究	way of conducting research
fangwen xuezhe	访问学者	visiting scholar
fei	费	fee
fengxian jingshen	奉献精神	being prepared to take risks

fenpei	分配	job assignment system
fenshuxian	分数线	cut-off score
fenshuizhi	分税制	system of tax classification
fenzao chifan	分灶吃饭	'eating in separate kitchens' ; diverse economic rewards
fuboshi	副博士	candidate degrees
fujiaoshou	副教授	associate professor
funü huijia lun	妇女回家论	socio-economic conditions that force women to stay at home
funü yanjiu	妇女研究	women's studies research
gaige	改革	reform
gaizao	改造	transformation
ganbu	干部	state cadre
gaokao	高考	examination for university entrance
gaoxiao	高校	tertiary institution
gaozhong	高中	senior secondary school
geren fazhan	个人发展	individual development
gongjian	共建	collaboration in building an institution
gongxiao jianmian	供销见面	supply and demand interviews
gongxu jianmian	供需见面	job placement system arranged by universities and prospective employers
guanli	管理	administration
guanxi	关系	connections, network
gugan jiaoshi	骨干教师	core faculty members
guojia fuwu	国家服务	national-unified examination tuition-waiver scholarship

guojia jihua sheng	国家计划生	state-plan student
hege	合格	professionally qualified
hong yu zhuan	红与专	red-and-expert
hukou	户口	permanent residence registration
jiancha	检查	inspection visit
jiangshi	讲师	lecturer
jianku hangye	艰苦行业	professions with recruitment difficulties
jianzhi	兼职	secondary employment
jiaofei sheng	缴费生	tuition-paying students
jiaoshou	教授	professor
jiaoyu zhang	教育长	academic dean
jiceng danwei	基层单位	grass roots unit
jichuke	基础课	basic/foundation courses
jihua	计划	state plan
jihuawai	计划外	outside the state plan
jingshen wuran	精神污染	spiritual pollution
jingzheng jizhi	竞争机制	competition
jinqin fanzhi	近亲繁殖	'in-breeding' ; staff recruitment from own graduates
jintie	津贴	bonus
jiuye	就业	job arrangement
ke jiao xing nong	科教兴农	'Vitalizing Agriculture with Science and Education'
keji kaifa	科技开发	science and technology development
kua shiji youxiu rencai	跨世纪优秀人才	'Across-Centuries Leading Scholars Project'

lilun yanjiu	理论研究	theoretical research
lingdao	领导	leaders
lishixue yanjiu	历史学研究	historical research
liushi	流失	brain drain
liushi fen wansui	六十分万岁	'Long live 60!'; exam-passing mentality
minban	民办	collective, private
minjian	民间	non-governmental
mosuo	摸索	management by 'groping' or cautiously feeling one's way
mu jie	母机	maternal institution
nüquan	女权主义	the women's rights movement
nüren	女人	woman
peixun	培训	training
peiyang	培养	training, cultivation and development
pizhun	批准	official approval
qingnian jiaoshi	青年教师	young staff members
qingong jianxue	勤工俭学	work-study programmes
qu	区	district
ren	仁	humanheartedness
rencai shichang	人才市场	job market
renmin jiangxuejin	人民奖学金	People's Scholarship
sange mianxiang	三个面向	'Three Orientations'; dictum that education should be oriented to modernization, the future and the outside world
shehui fazhan	社会发展	societal development

shehui shijian	社会实践	social practice
shehui zhaosheng	社会招生	students admitted through informal channels
shehui zhuyi gaizao	社会主义改造	socialist transformation
shijian	实践	practically experienced
shixi	实习	student practice
shizi peiyang he guanli	师资培养和管理	faculty development and management
shuangxiang xuanze	双向选择	two-way choice: employers and graduates have choice over employment
shuyuan	书院	private academies of learning
suzhi	素质	essential nature, quality
tekun buzhu jijin	特困补助基金	Special Subsidy Fund for Exceptionally Disadvantaged Students
ti dui jian she	梯队建设	'echelon formation'
tongkao gongfei	统考	national-unified examination tuition-waiver scholarship
tongkao shangxue	统考	the national-unified examination system
weituo peiyang	委托培养	commissioned scholarship
wenhua yanjiu	文化研究	cultural research
wenping	文凭	Bachelor of Arts degree
wuzhi wenming, jingshen wenming	物质文明 精神文明	material improvement and moral civilization
xia hai	下海	'jumping into the sea of business'; becoming an entrepreneur
xian	县	county
xian neizhu	贤内助	inside assistance

xiandai nüren	现代女人	modern woman
xiang	乡	township
xiaoban chanye	校办产业	university-run enterprises
xuebu	学部	academic departments
xuebu weiyuan	学部委员	department membership
xueli	学历	credentials
xuesheng	学生	student
xueshenghui	学生会	student union
xuewei	学位	diploma
yi dao qie	一刀切	single standard applied to all students
yilaixing	依赖性	dependency
yixiao duozhi	一校两制	one-school, multi-system administration
youxiu xuesheng jiangxuejin	优秀学生奖学金	excellence scholarship for talented students
yuanshi	院士	academicians of the CAS
yuanxi tiaozheng	院系调整	readjustment of colleges and departments
yufenzhi	预分制	employment arrangement made before graduation
yusuan baogan, jieyu liuyong	预算包干, 结馀留用	one-line budget, with institution allowed to retain any surplus
yusuannei	预算内	budgeted item
yusuanwai	预算外	non-budgeted item
zai jiaoyu	再教育	re-education
zhengshu	证书	certificate
zhi cheng feng	职称	having a professional title

zhongdian	重点	key
zhongdian daxue	重点大学	key universities
Zhongguo	中国	China
zhongxue weiti, xixue weiyong	中学为体，西学为用	Chinese learning as the essence, Western learning for its utility
zhongzhuan	中专	vocational secondary school certificate
zhuanke	专科	non-degree undergraduate course
zhuanmen rencai	专门人才	qualified personnel
zhuanye jiangxuejin	专业奖学金	speciality-major scholarship
zhuanye jichuke	专业基础课	speciality course
zhujiao	助教	teaching assistant
zhujiao jinxiu ban	助教进修班	special training programme
zifei	自费	self-supporting, fee-paying
zijue	自觉	self-awareness
ziyou	自由	independent-minded
zizhu zhiye	自主择业	finding a job by oneself

Select Bibliography

YEARBOOKS, CHRONOLOGIES AND STATISTICAL COMPILATIONS

These entries are listed alphabetically by English title. Specific year of publication is given in the relevant chapter endnote.

Academic department membership of the Chinese Academy of Sciences (Zhongguo Kexueyuan xuebu weiyuan). Zhejiang: Zhejiang Science and Technology Publishing House.

Achievement of education in China: statistics 1949–1983. Ministry of Education, 1984. Beijing: People's Education Press.

Achievement of education in China: statistics 1980–1985. State Education Commission, 1986. Beijing: People's Education Press.

Agricultural yearbook of China (Zhongguo nongye nianjian). Beijing: China's Agricultural Press.

Book of major educational events in China 1949–1990 (Zhongguo jiaoyu dashidian, 1949–1990). Liu Yingjie, ed. 1993. Hangzhou: Zhejiang Education Press.

China development report. State Statistics Bureau. Beijing: China Statistics Press.

China education yearbook (Zhongguo jiaoyu nianjian). State Education Commission. Beijing: People's Education Press.

China education yearbook 1949–1981. Beijing: China Encyclopedia Publishing House, 1984.

China education yearbook 1982–1984. Shanghai: China Encyclopedia Press, 1985.

China science and technology statistics yearbook (Zhongguo kexuejishu tongji nianjian). State Statistics Bureau and State Science and Technology Commission. Beijing: China Statistics Press.

China statistics yearbook (Zhongguo tongji nianjian). State Statistics Bureau. Beijing: China Statistics Press.

Chinese Academy of Sciences yearbook (Zhongguo Kexueyuan nianjian). General Office of the Chinese Academy of Sciences. Beijing: Chinese Academy of Sciences.

Education statistics of the Republic of China. Taipei: Ministry of Education.

Education statistics yearbook of China (Zhongguo jiaoyu tongji nianjian / Zhongguo jiaoyu shiye tongji nianjian). State Education Commission. Beijing: People's Education Press.

Elite in Chinese science (Keyuan yinghua lu). Beijing, Popular Science Press.

Essential statistics of education in China. Beijing: State Education Commission.

Guangdong yearbook (Guangdong nianjian). Guangdong: Guangdong Yearbook Press.

Index on Education Statistics of the Republic of China. Taipei: Ministry of Education.

Shenyang Agricultural University yearbook (Shenyang Nongye Daxue nianjian). Shenyang: Shenyang Agricultural University.

Statistical yearbook of the Republic of China. Directorate-General of Budget, Accounting and Statistics. Taipei: Executive Yuan.

Statistics yearbook of Anhui (Anhui tongji nianjian). Anhui Statistics Bureau. Beijing: China Statistics Press.

Statistics yearbook of Gansu (Gansu tongji nianjian). Gansu Statistics Bureau. Beijing: China Statistics Press.

Statistics yearbook of Heilongjiang (Heilongjiang tongji nianjian). Heilongjiang Statistics Bureau. Beijing: China Statistics Press.

Statistics yearbook of Shaanxi (Shaanxi tongji nianjian). Shaanxi Statistics Bureau. Beijing: China Statistics Press.

UNESCO statistical yearbook. Paris: UNESCO.

Zhejiang yearbook (Zhejiang nianjian). Zhejiang Provincial Party Committee and Zhejiang Government.

BOOKS, ARTICLES AND CHAPTERS

These entries are listed alphabetically by author. Multiple entries for an author are listed chronologically, but publications within the same year are listed alphabetically.

Adamson, B. 1995. The 'Four Modernizations' in China and English language teacher education: a case study. *Compare* 25, no. 3, pp. 197–210.

Adamson, B. and P. Morris. 1997. The English curriculum in the People's Republic of China. *Comparative Education Review* 41, no. 1, pp. 3–26.

Agelasto, M. 1996a. Politics in charge: politically correct higher education in the PRC. *Education Journal* 23, no. 2, pp. 65–84.

———. 1996b. *Social relationships and job procurement by graduates: case study of a Chinese university.* Ph.D. thesis, University of Hong Kong.

———. 1996c. Educational transfer of sorts: the American credit system with Chinese characteristics. *Comparative Education* 32, no.1 pp. 69–93.

Alexander, K. 1982. Concepts of equity. In *Financing education: overcoming inefficiency and inequity*, eds. McMahon, W.W. and T. G. Geske, pp. 193–214. Urbana, Illinois: University of Illinois Press.

Altbach, P. G., ed. 1977. *Comparative perspectives on the academic profession.* New York: Praeger.

———. 1978. Scholarly publishing in the Third World. *Library Trends 26*, pp. 489–503.

———. 1987a. *The knowledge context: comparative perspectives on the distribution of knowledge.* Albany, New York: State University of New York Press.

———. 1987b. The knowledge networks in the modern world. *Canadian and International Education 16*, no. 2, pp. 73–88.

Andors, P. 1983. *The unfinished liberation of Chinese women, 1949–1980.* Bloomington: Indiana University Press.

Arnon, I. 1989. *Agricultural research and technology transfer.* London and N.Y.: Elsevier Applied Science.

Bai Yu. 1994. *Quanguo jiaoyu gongzuo huiyi zai jing zhaokai* (National education conference opens in Beijing). *Shen Zhou Xue Ren* 53, no. 7.

Bai Zhou. 1993. *Guanyu dangqian gaoxiao shizi duiwu xianzhuang de diaocha baogao* (Survey report on the current conditions of faculty in higher education). *Zhongguo Gaodeng Jiaoyu* 142, no. 12, pp. 21–2.

Baldwin, R.G. and R. T. Blackburn, eds. 1983. *College faculty: versatile human resources in a period of constraint.* San Francisco: Jossey-Bass.

Barlow, T.E. 1994. Politics and protocols of *funü*: (un)making national woman. In *Engendering China*, eds. Gilmartin, C.K., and G. Hershatter and L. Rofel and T. White, pp. 339–59. Cambridge, MA: Harvard University Press.

Barr, N. 1989. *Student loans: the next steps.* Aberdeen: The Aberdeen University Press.

Bartlett, W. 1993. Quasi-markets and educational reforms. In *Quasi-markets and social policy*, eds. Le Grand, J. and W. Bartlett, pp. 125–53. London: Macmillan.

Bauer, J. *et al.* 1992. Gender inequality in urban China. *Modern China* 18, no. 3, July, pp. 347–9.

Beck, E.T. 1990. To make of our lives a study: feminist education as empowerment for women. In *Storming the tower: women in the academic world*, eds. Lie, S.S. and V.E. O'Leary, pp. 211–23. New York: Nicholas/ GP Publishing.

Beck, R. 1985. Personnel management. In *Universities: the management challenge*, ed. Lockwood, G. and J. Davies, chapter 11. UK: SRHE & NFER-Nelson.

Beers, D. and J. Ellig. 1994. An economic view of the effectiveness of public and private schools. In *Privatizing education and educational choice*, eds. Hakim, S., P. Seidenstat and G. W. Bowman, pp. 19–38. Westport: Praeger.

Bei Nong Gong qingnian jiaoshi peiyang ketizu (Training of Young Teachers Research Group at Beijing Agricultural Engineering College). 1990. *Renqing jiaoshi duiwu xianzhuang, jiaqiang qingnian jiaoshi peiyang* (Recognize the situation of the teaching corps and strengthen training of young teachers). *Gaodeng Nongye Jiaoyu* no. 5, pp. 18–21, 64.

Ben, Y.Y. 1985. The contribution of female labour to economic development: a case study of Taiwan. Paper presented at the Conference on the Role of Women in the National Development Process in Taiwan, Taipei: National Taiwan University, Population Studies Center.

Bennett, M.C. 1992. The foreign teacher in China: expectations and realities. Paper presented at the Beijing International Symposium on Teaching English in China.

Bian Yanjie. 1994. *Work and inequality in urban China*. Albany: State University of New York Press.

Blaug, M. 1967. Approaches to educational planning. *Economic Journal* 77, pp. 262–87. Reprinted in *The economics of education and the education of an economist*, Blaug, M., 1987, pp. 50–75. Aldershot, UK: Edward Elgar Publishing.

Bloom, B., J. T. Hastings and G.F. Madaus. 1971. *Handbook on formative and summative evaluations of student learning*. New York: McGraw Hill.

Bonnin, M. 1996. When the saints come marching back. *China Perspectives* 5, no. 5, May/June, pp. 11–2.

Botou Municipal CCP Committee, Hebei province. 1995. A problem that cannot be ignored — discussion of peasant ideological education under the new circumstances. *Qiushi* (Seeking Truth), 16 October, no. 20, pp. 38–41. Translated in FBIS-CHI-96-021, 31 January 1996, pp. 13–7.

Bray, M. 1996. *Privitisation of secondary education: issues and policy implications*. Paris: UNESCO.

Bridges, D and T.H. McLaughlin, eds. 1994. *Education and the Market Place*. London: Falmer.

Brinkman, P.T. and L. L. Leslie. 1986. Economies of scale in higher education: sixty years of research. *The Review of Higher Education* 10, no. 1, pp. 1–28.

Broaded, C.M. 1993. China's response to the brain drain. *Comparative Education Review* 37, no. 3, pp. 277–303.

Brown, F. 1995. Privatization of public education: theories and concepts. *Education and Urban Society* 27, no. 2, February, pp. 114–26.

Bulbeck, C. 1991. Hearing the difference: First and Third World feminisms. *Asian Studies Review* 15, no. 1, pp. 77–91.

Bunting, A.H. 1991. The role of universities in national agricultural research systems of developing countries. Paper presented to the Expert Consultation on the Role of Agricultural Universities in National Agricultural Research Systems, Rome, 19–22 March.

Cai Hong. 1994. College mergers may only be in title. *China Daily*, 30 March, p. 4.

Cai Jie and Deng Haiyun. 1992. *Beijing Nong Da zhuzhong peiyang qingnian jiaoshi* (Beijing Agricultural University stresses training of young teachers). *Guangming Ribao*, 10 February, p. 1.

Cao Cong. 1996. From an academic leadership title to an academic honor — the academicianship system of the Chinese Academy of Sciences. Paper presented at the Eighth International Conference on the History of Science in East Asian (Seoul, Korea, 26–31 August).

Cao Xiaonan. 1987. *The restructuring of the academic profession in higher education*. M. Phil thesis, University of London.

———. 1990. *Gaodeng xuexiao shizi peiyong gongzuo* (Faculty training in higher education). In *Zhongguo jiaoyu nianjian 1989* (China education yearbook), ed. State Education Commission, pp. 162–4. Beijing: People's Education Press.

———. 1991a. *Zhongguo gaodeng xuexiao jiaoshi peixun tixi de lishi yange he fazhan* (History of faculty development in higher education in China. *Gaodeng Jiaoyu Xuebao* 26, no. 3, pp. 63–9.

———. 1991b. Policy-making on the improvement of university personnel in China under the national reform environment. *Studies in Higher Education* 16, no. 2, pp. 103–15.

Cao Xiaonan, *et al*. 1991. *Guanyu dangqian gaodeng xuexiao jiaoshi duiwu jianshe jige wenti de sikao* (Present problems in building teaching staff in colleges and universities). *Gaodeng Shifan Jiaoyu Yanjiu* (Teacher Education Research) 13, no. 1, pp. 52–8.

Castells, M. 1978. *City, class and power*. London: Macmillan.

CCP Central Committee. 1984. *Zhonggong zhongyang guanyu jingji tizhi gaige de jueding* (Decisions of the CCP Central Committee on the reform of economic structures). Beijing: People's Press.

———. 1985. *Zhonggong zhongyang guanyu jiaoyu tizhi gaige de jueding* (Decisions on restructuring the education system by the CCP Central Committee). In *Education system in reform: practice and experience in China*, State Education Commission. Beijing: Higher Education Press.

———. 1994. *Guowuyuan guanyu 'Zhongguo jiaoyu gaige he fazhan gangyao' de shishi yijian* (Recommendations of the State Council for the implementation of the 'Programme for educational reform and development in China). *Zhongguo Gaodeng Jiaoyu* 151, no. 10, pp. 10–6.

CCP Central Committee and the State Council. 1981. *Guanyu jiaqiang zhigong jiaoyugongzuo de jueding* (Decisions on strengthening employee training). CCP Central Committee Document no. 8, 20 February.

———. 1993. *Zhongguo jiaoyu gaige he fazhan gangyao* (Programme for educational reform and development in China). *Zhongguo Gaodeng Jiaoyu* 135, no. 4, pp. 8–17 and *Zhongguo Jiaoyu Bao* 27 February 1993. Translated in Summary of World Broadcasts: Far East/1629 B2/6 Article 18 (5 March).

Chait, R. and A.T. Ford. 1982. *Beyond traditional tenure*. San Francisco, CA: Jossey Bass.

Chang Chin-fen. 1994. A comparison of employment and wage determination between full-time working men and women in Taiwan. Paper presented at the Family, Human Resources and Social Development Conference, Taipei: National Cheng-chi University.

———. 1995. The analysis of female working struggle. In *White Book of Women's Status in Taiwan: 1995*, ed. Liu, Y.S., pp. 147–80. Taipei: Shier Bao Cultural Co.

Chang, F.C.I. 1995. *How and to what extent are women and men treated differently in faculty hiring in Taiwan?* Ph.D. thesis, Stanford University.

Chen Dongcheng. 1995. *Waimao yingyu chuyi* (My comment on the teaching of English for foreign trade). In *Shenzhen Daxue gaodeng jiaoyu yanjiu lunwenji* (Collected papers on higher education research of Shenzhen University), eds. Higher Education Research Institute and the Academic Affairs Office, Shenzhen University, p. 48. Shenzhen: Shenzhen University.

Chen Hao. 1984. *Gaoxiao qingnian jiaoshi peiyong he guanli gongzuo huiyi shuping* (Reflections from the conference on training and management of junior faculty in higher education). *Zhongguo Gaodeng Jiaoyu* 31, no. 2, pp. 12–4.

————. 1988. *Zai lilun yu shijian jinmi jiehe shang yantao shizi guanli gaige* (Studying faculty administration by combining research and practice). *Zhongguo Gaodeng Jiaoyu* 78, no. 2, pp. 21–2.

Chen, K.C. 1993. Legal independence of women under current Republic of China laws. Paper presented at the International Conference on Women, Taipei.

Chen Lifu. 1986. *The Confucian way*. London: KPI.

Chen Shaoxiong. 1990. *Xian zhen nü qingnian jiuye nan wenti* (The problem of employment of youth in rural areas) *Qingnian Yanjiu* (Youth Studies), no. 1, pp. 39–41.

Chen Xitong. 1989. Report on checking the turmoil and quelling the counter-revolutionary rebellion. Beijing: New Star Publishers, 1989.

Chen Yan. 1996. Intellectual trends in China since 1989. *China Perspectives*, no. 7, pp. 6–12.

Chen Yangjin. 1994. *Yang wei zhong yong, cu wo fazhan* (Borrowing good experience from overseas to develop our country). *People's Daily* (overseas edition), 24 December, p. 6.

Chen Yuanhui, *et al.* 1981. *Zhongguo gudai de shuyuan zhidu* (China's ancient system of academics). Shanghai: Shanghai Jiaoyu Chubanshe, pp. 86–7.

Chen Ziju. 1984. *Yuanyin zai nar? Chulu hezai?* (What is the reason? Where is the job?). *Qingnian Bao*, 14 September, p. 1. Translated as: What is the reason and solution for the disproportionate enrolment of male and female students at Shanghai's technical schools? *Chinese Sociology and Anthropology* 20, no. 1, Autumn, 1987, pp. 62–4.

Cheng Chu-yuan. 1965. *Scientific and engineering manpower in Communist China 1949–1963*. Washington, DC: National Science Foundation.

Cheng Kai-ming. 1986a. China's recent education reform: the beginning of an overhaul. *Comparative Education Review* 22, no. 3, pp. 255–69.

————. 1986b. Reforming China's higher education for qualified manpower. *China News Analysis*, no. 1314, 15 July.

————. 1991. *Planning of basic education in China: case study of two counties in Liaoning*. Paris: UNESCO.

————. 1994a. Development of higher education: Hong Kong and China. Paper presented at the Symposium on The Future Development of Higher Education in Hong Kong, Hong Kong, 26 January.

————. 1994b. Educational research in mainland China: views from the fence. Paper presented at the Chinese Education for the 21st Century Conference, Shanghai.

————. 1994c. Issues in decentralizing education: what the reform in China tells. *International Journal of Educational Research* 21, no. 8, pp. 799–808.

———. 1994d. Quality of education as perceived in Chinese culture. In *Quality of education in the context of culture in developing countries*, ed. Takala, T. Tampere: Tampere University, pp. 67–84.

———. 1994e. Young adults in a changing socialist society: post-compulsory education in China. *Comparative Education Review* 30, no. 1, pp. 63–74.

———. 1995a. Decentralisation and the market. In *Social change and social policy in contemporary China*, eds. Wong, L. and S. MacPherson, pp. 70–87. Aldershot, UK: Avebury.

———. 1995b. *Financing higher education in China*. Unpublished manuscript.

———. 1996a. China's educational reforms: efficiency at the expense of equity. *China Development Briefing*, no. 1, March, pp. 8–11.

———. 1996b, Markets in a socialist system: reform of higher education in China. In *Educational dilemmas: debate and diversity, vol. 2: reforms in higher education*, eds. Watson, K., S. Modgil and C. Modgil, pp. 238–49. London: Cassell.

Cheng, X.D. and Zhou Chuan. 1995. Global impact of China's higher education 'Project 211'. *Asia-Pacific Exchange* (Electronic Journal) 2, no. 1.

Cherrington, R. 1991. *China's students: the struggle for democracy*. London: Routledge.

Cheung Kwok Wah and Iu Pui To. 1995. Power negotiation between the centre and locale: development of higher education policy in Guangdong in the 1980s. In *Development in Southern China: a report on the Pearl River Delta including the Special Economic Zone*, eds. Cheng, J. and S. MacPherson, pp. 139–52. Hong Kong: Longman.

Chiang, N.L.H. and Y.L. Ku. 1985. *Past and current status of women in Taiwan*. Taipei: National Taiwan University, Population Studies Center, Monograph #1, Women's Research Program.

China National Institute of Educational Research. 1995. *A study of NGO-sponsored and private higher education in China*. Beijing: UNESCO.

Chon Sun Ihm. 1995. Korea. In *Education and development in East Asia*, eds. Morris, P. and A. Sweeting, pp. 125–48. New York: Garland.

Chou Chuing P. 1992. *Gender differences in the academic reward system: a nation-wide study of university faculty members in Taiwan*. Ph.D. thesis, University of California, Los Angeles.

Chow Rey. 1993. *Writing diaspora: tactics of intervention in contemporary cultural studies*. Bloomington: Indiana University Press.

Christiansen, F. 1996. Devolution in Chinese higher education policy in the 1990s: common establishment and the '211' Programme. *Leeds East Asia Papers*, no. 36. Leeds: Department of East Asian Studies, University of Leeds.

Chu, G.C. and Ju Yanan. 1993. *The Great Wall in ruin*. New York: SUNY Press.

Clark, B. R., ed. 1987. *The academic profession*. Berkeley, CA: University of California Press.

Clark, B. R., and G. R. Neave, eds. 1992. *The encyclopedia of higher education*. Oxford: Pergamon Press.

Cleverley, J.F. 1987. Enterprise and the Chinese university: a cautionary tale of profit and loss. Paper presented at the annual meeting of the Comparative and International Education Society, Washington, D.C. (March).

Cohn, E. and T. G. Geske. 1990. *Economics of education*, 3rd ed. Oxford: Pergamon Press.

Cole, J.R. and S. Cole. 1973. *Social stratification in science*. Chicago: The University of Chicago Press.

Crane, D. 1965. Scientists at major and minor universities: a study of productivity and recognition. *American Sociological Review* 30, pp. 699–714.

————. 1969. Social class origin and academic success: the influence of two stratification systems on academic careers. *Sociology of Education* 42, pp. 1–17.

Croizier, R. 1993. A bridge rebuilt: artistic interchange between China and the West in the 1980s. In *Knowledge across cultures: universities east and west*, ed. R. Hayhoe, pp. 333–47. Toronto: OISE Press.

Cross, K.P. and A-M McCartan. 1984. *Adult learning: state politics and institutional practices*. Washington D. C.: Association for the Study of Higher Education/ERIC Learninghouse on Higher Education.

Cui Yanfang, Gao Junshan, Su Chuihan and Xu Ming. 1996. Practice and inquiry on teaching quality assessment for teachers. Paper presented at the International Conference on Quality Assurance and Evaluation in Higher Education, Beijing.

Dai Nianzhu. 1982. *Wulixue zai jindai Zhongguo de licheng* (The development of physics in modern China). *Zhongguo Kexue Jishu Shiliao* (Historical Materials of Chinese Science and Technology), no. 4, pp. 10–8.

Dai Nianzhu and Wang Bin. 1993. *Yinglun: Zhongguo jindai wulixue shi gaishu* (Introduction: the development of physics in contemporary China). In *Ershi Shiji Shangbanye Zhongguo Wulixuejia Lunwen Jicui* (A source book of Chinese physicists' papers in the first half of the 20th Century), eds. Dai Nianzhu and Wang Bin, pp. 1–16. Changsha, Hunan: Hunan Educational Press.

Dai Shujun. 1990. *Woguo gaodeng zhiye jishu jiaoyude fazhan* (The development of higher vocational and technical education in China). In *Jinling zhiye daxue xuebao* (Journal of Jinling Vocational University), ed. Dai Shujun, no. 1.

Dai Weidong. 1993. *Shiying shichang jingji, shenhua waiuu jiaogai* (Adapt to the market economy and deepen language education reform). *Waiyujie* (Journal of The Foreign Language World), no. 3 (September), p. 5.

Dalian Shi Wei. 1986. *Dalian shi gaoxiao kaizhan xiaoji xianzuo huodong de diaocha* (Report of the co-operation among higher learning institutions in Dalian City). *Zhongguo Gaodeng Jiaoyu* 63, no. 10, pp. 23–5.

Davis, D. 1990. Urban job mobility. In *Chinese society on the eve of Tiananmen: the impact of reform*, eds. Davis, D. and E.F. Vogel, pp. 98–9. Cambridge, MA: Harvard University Press.

Davis, D.E. and H. S. Astin. 1990. Life cycle, career patterns and gender stratification in academe: breaking myths and exposing truths. In *Storming the tower: women in the academic world*, eds. Lie, S.S. and V.E. O'Leary, pp. 89–107. New York: Nicholas/GP Publishing.

DeAngelis, R. 1996. The last decade of higher education reform in Australia and France: different constraints, differing choices in higher education politics and policies. Paper presented at the 9th World Congress on Comparative Education, Sydney.

De Beauvoir, S. 1974. *The Second Sex*. New York: Vintage Books.

Delany, B. and L.W. Paine. 1991. Shifting patterns of authority in Chinese schools. *Comparative Education Review* 35, no. 1, pp. 23–43.

Delman, J. 1993. *Agricultural extension in Renshou County, China. A case-study of bureaucratic intervention for agricultural innovation and change.* Hamburg: Institut für Asienkunde.

Deng Xiaoping. 1993. *Deng Xiaoping wenxue dierjuan* (Selected Works of Deng Xiaoping, vol. 2). Beijing: People's Press.

Department of Education and Science. 1988. *Top-up loans for students.* London: HMSO.

Dernberger, R.F. 1982. The Chinese search for the path of self-sustained growth in the 1980s: an assessment. In *China under the Four Modernizations, part 1*, Joint Economic Committee, Congress of the United States, pp. 19–76. Washington, DC: US Government Printing Office.

Ding Gang and Liu Qi. 1992. *Shuyuan yu Zhongguo wenhua* (Academics and Chinese culture). Shanghai: Shanghai Jiaoyu Chubanshe.

Documents of the Thirteenth National Congress of the Communist Party of China. 1987. Beijing: Foreign Languages Press.

Du Fangqin. 1990. *Zhen yin daode zongheng tan* (Discourses on double morality). In *Huaxia nüixing zhimi* (The enigma of Chinese womanhood), ed. Li Xiaojiang, pp. 87–123. Beijing: Sanlian Shudian Chubanshe.

Du Ruiqing. 1992. *Chinese higher education: a decade of reform and development (1978–1988)*. London: Macmillan.

Dudley, J. 1996. Globalization and higher education policy in Australia. Paper presented to the 9th World Congress on Comparative Education, Sydney.

Dzau, Y.F. 1990. How English is taught in tertiary educational institutes. In English in China, ed. Dzau, Y.F., pp. 41–58. Hong Kong: API Press.

Educational Fund Research Group, State Education Commission, ed. 1988. *Educational fund and teachers' salaries*. Beijing: Jiaoyu Kexue Chubanshe.

Educational Research Institute, Sichuan Normal University. 1986. An investigation report on female science teachers. *Research in Educational Science* no. 4, 19 December, p. 17.

Edwards, T. *et al.* 1985. Private schools and public funding: a comparison of recent policies in England and Australia. *Comparative Education Review* 21, no. 1, pp. 29–44.

Eisemon, T.O. and C. H. Davis. 1989. Publication strategies of scientists in four peripheral Asian scientific communities: some issues in the measurement and interpretation of non-mainstream science. In *Scientific development and higher education: the case of newly industrializing nations*, eds. Altbach, P.G. *et al.*, pp. 325–75. New York: Praeger.

Elton, L. and K. Simmonds, eds. 1977. *Staff development in higher education*. UK: Society for Research in Higher Education.

Engels, F. 1975. Anti-Duhring. In *Karl Marx and Friedrich Engels Collected Works, vol. 25*. London: Lawrence and Wishart.

Epstein, I. 1983. The politics of curricular change. In *Education and social change in the PRC*, ed. Hawkins, J.N., pp. 77–96. New York: Praeger.

Fan, C.C. 1992. Modernization, Christianity, and higher education: Ginling Women's College. In *Jidujiao daxue jiaoyu zai Zhongguo xiandaihua guocheng zhong suo banyan de jiaose jiqi yingxiang* (The influence and contributions of Christian colleges in the modernization of China), ed. Lin, Chih-ping, P., pp. 119–39. Taipei: The Cosmic Light Publishing Company.

———. 1996. Feminist movement in China. *Literary East-West* 12, September, pp. 15–28.

Fan Shenggen and P.G. Pardey. 1992. *Agricultural research in China: its institutional development and impact*. The Hague: International Service for National Agricultural Research.

Feeney, T. 1994. Why educational choice: the Florida experience. In *Privatizing education and educational choice*, eds. Hakim, S., P. Seidenstat and G. W. Bowman, pp. 39–58. Westport: Praeger.

Fei, J.C., T.W. Tsau and C.C. Lai. 1982. *A study on sex discrimination and wage inequality*. Taipei: Academia Sinica, Institute of the Three Principles of the People, Monograph #10.

Feng Kaiwen. 1994. *Zhongguo minguo jiaoyu shi* (The history of education in Republican China). Beijing: People's Press.

Feng Zhiguang. 1996. Process evaluation of university teaching. Paper presented at the International Conference on Quality Assurance and Evaluation in Higher Education, Beijing.

Feuchtwang, S., A. Hussain and T. Pairault, eds. 1989. *Transforming China's economy in the eighties: vol. 1 the rural sector, welfare and employment*. Boulder CO: Westview Press.

Fewsmith, J. 1994. Reform, resistance, and the politics of succession. In *China briefing 1994*, ed. Joseph, W.A., pp. 7–34. Boulder, Colorado: Westview Press.

Finance Department, State Education Commission. 1995. *Daxue shoufei yu xuesheng zizhu zhengce* (Documentary collection on tertiary tuition fees and student financial support policies). Beijing: Higher Education Press.

Finance Department, State Education Commission and Shanghai Institute of Human Resource Development. 1994. *Yijiujiusan nian Zhongguo jiaoyu jinfei niandu fazhan baogao* (Annual report on development of Chinese educational expenditure 1993). Beijing: Higher Education Press.

————. 1997. *Yijiujiuliu nian Zhongguo jiaoyu jinfei niandu fazhan baogao* (Annual report on development of Chinese educational expenditure 1996). Beijing: Higher Education Press.

Finkelstein, M.J. ed. 1985. ASHE reader on faculty and faculty issues in colleges and universities. Lexington, MA: Ginn Press.

Fox, M.F. 1984. Women and higher education: sex differentials in the status of students and scholars. In *Women: a feminist perspective*, 4th ed., ed. Jo. Freeman, pp. 220–61. Mayfield.

Frame, D. 1985. Problems in the use of literature-based S & T indicators in developing countries. In *Science and technology indicators for development*, ed. Morita-Lou, H., pp. 117–22. Bolder, CO: Westview.

Fu Sin Yuen-ching. 1992. *China's radio and television universities: policies, problems and prospects*. Ph.D. thesis, University of Calgary.

————. 1996. The RTVU system: China's response to market demand. Unpublished manuscript. Chinese University of Hong Kong.

Fullan, M. 1993. *Change forces: probing the depths of educational reform*. London: Falmer.

Gale, B.N. 1978. The concept of intellectual property in the PRC: inventors and inventing. *China Quarterly*, no. 74, p. 34.

Gao Baoli and Zhang Tiegun. 1985. The Second National Symposium on the college entrance examination. *Jiaoyu Yanjiu* (Education Research), no. 5, pp. 78–80. Translated in JPRS-CPS-85-090, 11 September, pp. 16–7.

Gao Xiaoxian. 1994. China's modernization and changes in social status of rural women. In *Engendering China*, eds. Gilmartin, C.K., and G. Hershatter and L. Rofel and T. White, pp. 80–97. Cambridge, MA: Harvard University Press.

Gao Yi. 1993. *Gaodeng jiaoyu miandui jichang de kunhuo yu tangsuo* (Confusions and experiments in facing marketization in higher education). *Zhongguo Gaodeng Jiaoyu* 139, no. 9, pp. 36–9.

Gardner, H.W. 1989. *To open minds: Chinese clues to the dilemma of contemporary education*. New York: Basic Books.

Garfield, E. 1983. Mapping science in the Third World. *Science and Public Policy 19*, no. 3, p. 114.

———. 1987. How to boost world science. *The Scientist* 1, no. 14, p. 9.

Gaston, J. 1970. The reward system in British science. *American Sociological Review* 35, pp. 718–32.

Geiger, R.L. 1987. *Private sectors in higher education, structure, function and change in eight countries*. Ann Arbor: University of Michigan Press.

George, V. and P. Wilding. 1994. *Welfare and ideology*. Hemel Hempstead: Harvester Wheatsheaf.

German Rhine Writers Association, 1989 Student Research Group, ed. 1993. *Huigu Yu Fansi* (Review and reflect). Essen Germany: Deguo Laine Bihui Yashen Bejiu Xueshe.

Glennerster, H. 1991. Quasi-markets for education? *Economic Journal* 101, pp. 1268–76.

———. 1995. *British social policy since 1945*. Oxford: Blackwell.

Gong Danshen *et al.* 1995. *Guanyu bufen nonglin yuanxiao qingnian jiaoshi xiankuang de diaocha baogao* (An investigative report concerning the situation for young teachers at a segment of agricultural and forestry colleges). *Gaodeng Nongye Jiaoyu* no. 6, p. 24.

Green, K.C. and D. T. Seymour. 1991. *Who's going to run General Motors?: what college students need to learn today to become the business leaders of tomorrow*. Princeton: Peterson's Guides.

Gu Ning, 1995. *Zhongguo funü jiaoyu dashi nianbiao* (A chronicle of Chinese women's education). Beijing: Chinese Academy of Social Sciences, Institute of World History publication.

Guangzhou Foreign Language Institute. 1987. *Lizu yu xuyao, fangyan yu weilai* (Base ourselves on the needs and have the future in view). *Xiandai Waiyu* (Journal of Modern Foreign Languages), supplementary issue (December), p. 18.

Habermas, J. 1976. *Legitimation crisis*. London: Heinemann.

————— . 1984. *The theory of communicative action*. Boston: Beacon Press.

Hakim, S., P. Seidenstat and G.W. Bowman, eds. 1994. *Privatizing education and educational choice*. Westport: Praeger.

Han Changxian. 1988. *Woguo funü de wenhua suzhi yu chengcai zhilu* (The means through which Chinese women can raise their educational level and become successful. *Renkou yu Jingji* (Population and Economics), no. 5, May, p. 41.

Hannagan, T.J. 1992. *Marketing for the non-profit sector*. London: Macmillan.

Hargens, L.L. and W.O. Hogstrom. 1982. Scientific consensus and academic status attainment patterns. *Sociology of Education* 55, pp. 183–96.

Harlow, B. 1989. Commentary: 'All that is inside is not center': responses to the discourses of domination. In *Coming to terms. Feminism, theory, politics*, ed. Weed, E., pp. 162–79. New York, London: Routledge.

Harmer, J. 1985. *The practice of English language teaching*. Harlow: Longman.

Harvey, P. 1985. A lesson to be learned: Chinese approaches to language learning. *English Language Teaching Journal* 39 (3), pp. 183–6.

Hayhoe, R. 1984. Chinese-Western scholarly exchange: implications for the future of Chinese education. In *Contemporary Chinese education*, ed. Hayhoe, R., pp. 205–29. London and Sydney: Croom Helm.

————— . 1989a. *China's universities and the open door*. New York: M.E. Sharpe.

————— . 1989b. China's scholars returned from abroad: a view from Shanghai (part one). *China Exchange News* 17, no. 3, pp. 3–8.

————— . 1990. China's returned scholars and the democracy movement. *China Quarterly*, 122 (June), pp. 293–302.

————— . 1991. The tapestry of Chinese higher education. In *Chinese education: problems, policies, and prospects*, ed. Epstein, I., pp. 109–44. New York: Garland.

————— . 1996. *China's universities 1895–1995: a century of cultural conflict*. New York and London: Garland.

Hayhoe, R. and Sun Yilin. 1989. China's scholars returned from abroad: a view from Shanghai (part two). *China Exchange News* 17, no. 4, pp. 2–7.

He Dongchang. 1988. *Nongcun jiaoyu zhuyao wei dangdi jianshe fuwu* (Rural education should principally serve local development). *Renmin Jiaoyu* (People's Education), no. 3, pp. 2–4.

He Jinqiu. 1992. *Huigu yu zhanwang* (Return and future). *Shen Zhou Xue Ren* (China's Scholars Abroad) 34, no. 6, pp. 8–9.

Henze, J. 1992. The formal education system and modernization: an analysis of developments since 1978. In *Education and modernization: the Chinese experience*, ed. Hayhoe, R., pp. 103–39. Oxford: Pergamon Press.

Hertling, J. 1996. A crash course in communism: China tries to promote conservative political ideology on its campuses. *The Chronicle of Higher Education*, 3 May, p. A43.

Hinton, W. 1983. *Shenfan: the continuing revolution in a Chinese village*. New York: Random House.

Hong Fuzeng. 1994. *Shiying nongcun jingji fazhan xuyao, gaige he fazhan gaodeng nongye jiaoyu* (Adapt to the needs of rural economic development, reform and develop higher agricultural education). *Gaodeng Nongye Jiaoyu* no. 1, pp. 12–7.

Honig, E. and G. Hershatter. 1988. *Personal voices*. Palo Alto, CA: Stanford University Press.

Hooper, B. 1991. Gender and education. In *Chinese education: problems, policies, and prospects*, ed. Epstein, I., pp. 352–74. New York: Garland.

Howe, C. 1987. China and the World Bank: review of World Bank's China long term development issues and options, 1985. *China Quarterly*, no. 109, pp. 110–5.

Howells, G. 1989. Distance teaching in China. *Journal of Educational Television* 15, no. 2, pp. 79–85.

Hsieh Hsaio-chin. 1995. Education: from paternal reproduction to women's liberation. In *White Book of Women's Status in Taiwan: 1995*, ed. Liu, Y.S., pp. 183–218. Taipei: Shier Bao Cultural Co.

Hu Menghao. 1989. Unite and strive for the building-up of a foreign language university with multi-disciplinary applied humanities. *Journal of Foreign Language*, no. 4 (August), p. 3.

Hu Mingzheng. 1984. Patent law encourages Chinese and Foreign investors. *Beijing Review* 27, no. 15 (9 April), p. 23.

Hu Ruiwen. 1982. *Gaodeng jiaoyu tizhi gaige de yige changshi — Shanghai shoufei zoudu dazhuanban banxue qingkuang de diaocha* (A pilot of higher education system reform: a survey of the running of the certificate course for self-supporting and commuting students in Shanghai). *Shanghai Higher Education Research*, no. 6, pp. 102–6.

Hu Xiaolu and T.S. Korllos. 1995. Development of moral character in the People's Republic of China: some implications for educators. *International Review of Education* 41, nos. 1–2, pp. 59–72.

Hua Xue. 1987. *Qinghua yuan zhuru xinxian xueye* (New blood on Qinghua campus). *Shen Zhou Xue Ren* 1, no. 5, pp. 25–7. Translated in *Chinese Education* 21, no. 1, 1988, pp. 73–81.

Hua Yi. 1989. *Jiaoshi duiwu 'da huan xue' qian de sikao* (Reflections before the 'big' staff replacement). *Gaojiao Yanjiu Yu Tansuo*, nos. 2 and 3, pp. 33–8.

Huang Quanyu. 1993. *Conceptual perplexity and analysis in Chinese education*. Ph.D. thesis, Miami University, Ohio.

Huang Yisi. 1992. Making the best use of foreign experts. Paper presented at the Beijing International Symposium on Teaching English in China.

Human Resources Research Institute, State Science and Technology

Commission. 1986. Voices of women in scientific and technical fields. *Rencai Tiandi* (The World of Qualified People), no. 3, pp. 3–5.

Hunter, J.M., M. E. Borus and A. Mannan. 1974. *Programs of studies in nonformal education.* East Lansing, MI: Institute for International Studies in Education, Michigan State University.

Institute for Scientific Information, USA. 1990. *Science citation index.* Philadelphia: Institute for Scientific Information.

Institute of Population Studies, Chinese Academy of Social Sciences. 1994. *Sampling survey data of women's status in contemporary China.* Beijing: International Academic Publishers.

Institute of Scientific and Technological Information of China (ISTIC). 1990. *Statistics and analysis of Chinese scientific and technical papers: 1989 annual research report.* Beijing: The Institute of Scientific and Technical Information of China.

Ishikawa, S. 1967. *Economic development in Asian perspective.* Tokyo: Kinokuniya Book Store.

———. 1983. China's economic growth since 1949: an assessment. China Quarterly, no. 94, pp. 242–81.

Jackson, P.W. 1986. *The practice of teaching.* New York: Teachers College Press.

James, E. 1986. The private, non-profit provision of education: a theoretical model and application to Japan. *Journal of Comparative Economies* 10, pp. 255–76.

———. 1992. Why do different countries choose a different public-private mix of educational services? *The Journal of Human Resources*, June, pp. 571–92.

Jamison, D. and J. Van Der Gaag. 1986. Determinants and economic consequences of school participation in China. Paper given at International Conference, Dijon, France (23–25 June), p. 4.

Jaschok, M. 1995. On the construction of desire and anxiety: contestations over female nature and identity in China's modern market society. In *Women and market societies*, eds. Einhorn, B. and E. J. Yeo, pp. 114–28. Aldershot, UK: Edward Elgar.

Ji Ping. 1994. *Dui jinqi woguo putong gaodeng jiaoyu shiye fazhan sudu de zai sikao* (Reviewing the development speed of higher education in China). *Zhongguo Gaodeng Jiaoyu* 153, no. 12, pp. 10–1.

Jiang Naiyong. 1988. *Nü daxuesheng fenpei weihe nan* (The plight of job placement for female college students), *Funü* (Women), no. 5, May, pp. 12–3. Translated in *Chinese Education and Society* 25, no. 1, 1992, p. 49.

Johnson, D. 1987. *Private schools and state schools: two systems or one?* Open University Press.

Johnson, N. 1990. *Reconstructing the welfare state*. Hampstead, Harvester Wheatsheaf.

Josselyn, J.E. and Wang Xingguo. 1992. East/West realities: teaching English in China. Paper presented at the Beijing International Symposium on Teaching English in China.

Juan Chi-hung. 1987. Graduates' current class will first be assigned to grass roots. *Wen Wei Po*, 1 July, p. 2. Translated in FBIS-CHI-87-126, 1 July, p. K5.

Kelly, G.P. 1991. Women and higher education. In *International higher education: an encyclopedia*, ed. Altbach, P.G., pp. 297–323. New York: Garland.

Kexuejia Zhuanji Dacidian Bianjizu (Editorial group of *The biographical dictionary of scientists*) eds. 1991–94. *Zhongguo xiandai kexuejia zhuanji* (Biographies of contemporary Chinese scientists), 6 volumes. Beijing: Science Press.

King Yeo-chi, A. 1991. Kuan-shi and network building: a sociological interpretation. *Dædalus* no. 120 (spring), pp. 63–84.

Kinoshita, J. 1995. Incentives help researchers resist lure of commerce. *Science* 270 (November), pp. 1142–3.

Klatt, W. 1983. The staff of life: living standards in China 1977–81. *China Quarterly*, no. 93, pp. 17–32.

Knowles, M.S. 1984. *Andragogy in action: applying modern principles of adult learning*. San Francisco: Jossey-Bass.

Kong Shenggen, ed. 1993. *Shanghai zhuliu* (Polluted water in the commercial sea). Beijing: Tuanjie Chubanshe.

Korzec, M. and M.K. Whyte 1981. Reading notes: the Chinese wage system. *China Quarterly*, no. 86, pp. 248–73.

Kulander, G. and J. Delman. 1993. Getting to the grassroots: human resource development for agricultural extension in China. *Journal of Extension Systems* 9, no. 2, pp. 87, 122–5.

Kuo, S.W.Y. 1993. The social and economic participation of women in the Republic of China, Taiwan. Paper presented at the International Conference on Women, Taipei.

Lamontagne, J. and Ma Rong. 1995. The development of education in China's cities and countries. In *Social change and educational development: mainland China, Taiwan and Hong Kong*, eds. Postiglione, G.A. and Lee Wing On, pp. 153–73. Hong Kong: Centre of Asian Studies, The University of Hong Kong.

Lampton, D. 1986. *A relationship restored — trends in U.S.-China educational exchanges, 1978–81*. Washington, D.C.: National Academy Press.

Lardy, N. 1983. *Agriculture in China's modern economic development*. New York: Cambridge University Press.

Lauglo, J. 1995. Forms of decentralization and their implication for education. *Comparative Education Review* 31, no. 1, pp. 5–29.

Law Wing-wah. 1995. The role of the state in higher education reform: mainland China and Taiwan. *Comparative Education Review* 39, no. 3, August, pp. 322–55.

Le Grand, J. 1983. Privatization and the social services. In *Socialism in a cold climate*, ed. John, G., pp. 65–80. London: Allen and Unwin.

———. 1991. *Equity and choice*. London: Harper Collins.

Le Grand, J. and W. Bartlett, eds. 1993. *Quasi-markets and social policy*. London: Macmillan.

Le Grand, J. and R. Robinson, eds. 1984. *Privatisation and the welfare state*. London: George Allen and Unwin.

Legge, J. tr. 1935. *The Chinese classics vol. 2*. Oxford: Oxford University Press.

Leung Yat Ming. 1995. The People's Republic of China. In *Education and development in East Asia*, eds. Morris, Paul and Anthony Sweeting, pp. 203–42. New York: Garland.

Levy, D.C. 1996. *Higher education and the state in Latin America: private challenges to public dominance*. Chicago: University of Chicago Press.

Lewin, K. and Xu Hui. 1992. Higher education in transition: some strategic planning issues in China and Britain. Keynote paper presented to the Sino-British Conference on Recent Development in Higher Education, Conference Proceedings, University of Hangzhou, March 1992.

Lewin, K. M., Xu Hui, A.W. Little and Zheng Jiwei. 1994. *Educational innovation in China: tracing the impact of the 1985 reforms*. Harlow, Essex: Longman.

Li Chao. 1988. Job markets proposed for skilled workers. *China Daily*, 14 December, p. 3. Reprinted in FBIS-CHI-88-240, 14 December, p. 27.

Li Kaicheng and Geng Yansheng. 1991. On the upsurges in the 'Emulate Lei Feng' movement and some sober reflections. *Qingnian Yanjiu* (Youth Studies), no. 1, January, no. 147, pp. 26–33. Translated in *Chinese Education and Society* 20, January-February 1993, no. 1, pp. 23–47.

Li Kwok-sing. 1995. *A glossary of political terms in the People's Republic of China*. Hong Kong: The Chinese University Press.

Li Lianchang *et al.* 1993. The reform of agricultural education in China through cooperative education strategies: the evolution of the Shanxi Agricultural University experience. *Journal of Cooperative Education* 29, no. 1, pp. 61–5.

Li Peishan. 1993. The introduction of American science and technology to China before 1949 and its impact. In *The U.S. and the Asia-Pacific Region in the Twentieth Century*. Beijing: Modern Press, p. 605.

Li Peng. 1986. *Gaige chengren jiaoyu, fazhan chengren jiaoyu* (Reform adult education and develop adult education). Translated as 'Vice premier addresses adult education conference', Foreign Broadcast Information Service, 22 December, p. K19.

Li Ping. 1990. The labour service market in China. *China Report* 26, no. 1, pp. 467–71.

Li Shouxin and M. Bray. 1992. Attempting a capitalist form of financing in a socialist system: student loans in the People's Republic of China. *Higher Education* 23, pp. 375–87.

Li Tieying. 1992a *Gaodeng jiaoyu tizhi gaige yu zhengzhi, jingji, keji tizhi gaige* (The relationships of the reforms between higher education and politics, economics, and science and technology). *Zhongguo Gaodeng Jiaoyu* 131, no. 12, pp. 2–5.

———. 1992b *Zongjie jingyan, wanshan zhengce, ba chuguo liuxue gongzuo zuo de geng hao* (Reviewing and improving the policies on study abroad). *Shen Zhou Xue Ren* 34, no. 6, pp. 3–6.

Li Xiaojiang. 1994. Economic reform and the awakening of Chinese women's consciousness. In *Engendering China*, eds. Gilmartin, C.K., and G. Hershatter and L. Rofel and T. White, pp. 360–82. Cambridge, MA: Harvard University Press.

Li Xing. 1990. Three testing days in July. *China Daily*, 13 July, p. 2.

Li Yanqing. 1995. *Renli ziyuan kaifa yu chengren gaodeng jiaoyu* (Human resource development and higher adult education). *Chengren Gaocheng Jiaoyu Yanjiu*, no. 75, pp. 10–3, 31.

Li Yong, Cui Junling and Zhang Xing. 1996. A theoretical study on the formative evaluation for higher institutions in China. Paper presented at the International Conference on Quality Assurance and Evaluation in Higher Education, Beijing.

Li Yongzeng. 1984. Reform revitalizes Jiaotong University. *Beijing Review* 34 (20 August), pp. 19–20.

Li Yuzheng and Zhao Zhenghua. 1987. *Poxi shengyuan buzu de yuanying* (Analysis of the reasons for insufficient in-takes). *Chengren Gaocheng Jiaoyu Yanjiu*, no. 29, pp. 32–5.

Li Zhenping. 1994. *Guojia jiaowei zhuren fangwenlu* (Interview with the chairman at the State Education Commission). *Shou Zhen Xue Ren* 58, no. 12, pp. 2–3.

Li Zhenzhen. 1992. *Zhongguo Kexueyuan xuebu de choubei he jianli* (The preparation and establishment of the academic departments of the Chinese Academy of Sciences). *Ziran Bianzhengba Tongxun* (Journal of Dialectics of Nature), no. 4, pp. 40–50.

Li Zhongyun and Xia Hongsheng. 1991. *Gaoxiao jiaoshi duiwu 'duanceng' wenti yanjiu* (A study of the problem of a 'faultline' among the teaching corps in institutions of higher education). *Gaodeng Nongye Jiaoyu*, no. 1, pp. 29–33.

Liang Ying. 1993. *Zhujiang sanjiaozhou gaodeng jiaoyu de hongguan fenxi ji fazhan duice* (Macroanalysis and development strategies of higher education in the Pearl River Delta). In *Gaige dachao zhong de zhujiang sanjiaozhou jiaoyu* (Education in the Pearl River Delta amidst tides of reform), eds. Huang Jiajiang *et al.*, pp. 22–31. Guangdong: Gaodeng Jiaoyu Chubanshe.

Liao Deqiang. 1993. The forms of cooperative education and their key elements. *Journal of Cooperative Education* 29, no. 3, pp. 53–60.

Lieberthal, K. 1995. *Governing China*. New York: W.W. Norton & Company.

Lieberthal, K and M. Oksenberg. 1988. *Policy making in China: leaders, structures, and processes*. Princeton, N.J.: Princeton University Press.

Lievrouw, L.A. 1990. Reconciling structure and process in the study of scholarly communication. In *Scholarly communication and bibliometrics*, ed. Borgman, Christine L., pp. 59–69. London: Sage Publications.

Lilu Shangguan. 1988. *The cumulative effects as in an inferior position: a social-psychological analysis of the distribution of women in the field*. Unpublished Master's thesis. Chinese Academy of Sciences, Graduate Division.

Lin Feng. 1958. *Guanyu dangqian gongguanqiye zhigongjiaoyu zhong jige wenti de baogao* (Concerning a few problems of workers' education in enterprises). CCP Central Committee Document.

Lin Guojun *et al.* 1988. What are the working conditions of Shanghai personnel who have returned from overseas study? An investigative report. *Chinese Education* 21, no. 1, pp. 85–96.

Lin Nan and Bian Yanjie. 1991. Getting ahead in urban China. *American Journal of Sociology* 97, no. 3, pp. 657–88.

Lin Nan and Xie Wen. 1988. Occupational prestige in urban China. *American Journal of Sociology* 93.

Lin Sha and Zhang Zhenkun. 1988. *Guanyu woguo chengren jiaoyu de touzi yu xiaoyi wenti* (On investment and efficiency of adult education in China). *Chengren Gaocheng Jiaoyu Yanjiu* (Higher Adult Education Research), no. 33, pp. 5–9.

Lin Tongqi. 1994. Search for China's soul. In *China in transformation*, ed. Tu Wei-ming, pp. 171–85. Cambridge: Harvard University Press.

Link, P.E. 1992. *Evening chats in Beijing: probing China's predicament*. New York: Norton.

Liu Bohong and Sung Rong. 1995. Moving towards the market: Chinese women in employment and their related rights. In *Women and market societies*, eds. Einhorn, B. and E. J. Yeo, pp. 193–204. Aldershot, UK: Edward Elgar.

Liu Dachun and Wu Xianghong. 1995. *Xinxue ku lu* (A hard journey for new science). Nanchang: Jiangxi University Press.

Liu Daoyi. 1988. E.L.T. in schools in China. Project document. Beijing: People's Education Press.

Liu Hongren. 1994. *Jiasu qingnian jiaoshi peiyang, zhangwo gaodeng jiaoyu shiye de zhudongquan* (Speed the training of young teachers, grasp the initiative in higher education). *Gaodeng Nongye Jiaoyu*, no. 4, pp. 8–10.

Liu Jiannan, *et al.* 1992. *Gaodeng jiaoyu gailun* (Introduction to tertiary education). Beijing: Beijing Radio Institute Press.

Liu Jinxiu. 1991. *80 niandai funü minjian zuzhide xingqi yu fazhan* (Rise and development of the women NGOs of the eighties). In *Funü yanjiu zai Zhongguo* (Women's Studies in China), vol. 1, eds. Li Xiaojiang and Tan Shen, pp. 106–17. Zhengzhou: Henan Renmin Chubanshe.

Liu Runqing, *et al.* 1989. *Gaoxiao yingyu benke jiaoyu chouyang diaocha baogao* (A sample survey of ELT in Chinese tertiary education). *Waiyu Jiaoxue yu Yanjiu* (Foreign Languages Teaching and Research), no. 3, p. 3.

———. 1990. *Gaoxiao yingyu benke jiaoyu chouyang diaocha baogao — III* (A sample survey of ELT in Chinese tertiary education, part 3). *Waiyu Jiaoxue yu Yanjiu* (Foreign Languages Teaching and Research), no. 1, p. 14.

Liu Xiuwu, R. 1996. *Western perspectives on Chinese higher education.* London: Associated University Press.

Liu Xuehong, *et al.* 1991. *Shangziqi xia de Yidianyuan* (Eden under the flag of commerce). Tianjin People's Press.

Liu Yingkai. 1994. *Shenda yingda shouxian xing 'da'* (Shenda should first be a university). *Shenzhen University Journal*, no. 1, p. 18.

Liu Zhenhui. 1994. *Dali kaizhan hengxiang lianhe banxue, bokuan chengren gaodeng jiaoyu xin lu* (Open up a new kind of adult higher education through the development of horizontally linked programmes). *Gaodeng Nongye Jiaoyu*, no. 3, pp. 59–61.

———. 1984a. Primary education: a two-track system for dual tasks. In *Contemporary Chinese Education*, ed. Hayhoe, R., pp. 47–64. London: Croom Helm.

Lo, B.L.C. 1984a. Primary education: a two-track system for dual tasks. In *Contemporary Chinese Education*, ed. Hayhoe, R., pp. 47–64. London: Croom Helm.

———. 1984b. Teacher education in the 1980s. In *Contemporary Chinese Education*, ed. Hayhoe, R., pp. 154–77. London: Croom Helm.

Löfstedt, J–I. 1980. *Chinese educational policy.* Stockholm: Almqvist and Wiksell International.

Lu, H.L. 1986. *A study on the academic reward structure in Taiwan's Universities.* Ph.D. thesis, National Cheng-chi University, Taipei.

Lugones, M. C. and E.V. Spelman. 1990. Have we got a theory for you! Feminist theory, cultural imperialism and the demand for 'The Woman's Voice'. In *Hypatia reborn: essays in feminist philosophy*, eds. al-Hibri, A.Y. and M. A. Simons, pp. 18–33. Bloomington and Indianapolis: Indiana University Press.

Lutz, J.G. 1971. *China and the Christian Colleges 1850–1950*. Ithaca: Cornell University Press.

Ma Chuanpu, Liu Yan and Yu Changzhi. 1994. *Gaodeng nongke jiaoxue de jiben tedian* (The basic characteristics of higher agricultural science teaching). *Gaodeng Nongye Jiaoyu*, no. 1, pp. 39–42.

Ma Chuanpu and Yang Siyao. 1995. *Lüe lun gaodeng nongye jiaoyu jiben tedian* (A brief account of the basic characteristics of higher agricultural education). *Gaodeng Nongye Jiaoyu*, no. 2, p. 23.

Ma Weixiang and D. Hawkridge. 1995. China's changing policy and practice in television education, 1978–1993. *International Journal of Educational Development* 15, no. 1, pp. 27–36.

MacAulay, J.B. 1985. *Indicator of excellence in Canadian science*. Ottawa: Statistics Canada.

Maley, A. 1990. Xanadu — 'A miracle of rare device': the teaching of English in China. In *English in China*, ed. Dzau, Y.F., pp. 95–105. Hong Kong: API Press.

Matthews, M. 1982. *Education in the Soviet Union: policies and institutions since Stalin*. London: George Allen and Unwin.

McCormick, B. 1984. Prospects and problems for China's RTVUs. *Media in Education and Development*, September, pp. 136–9.

———. 1985. Students' views on study at the Radio and Television Universities in China: an investigation in one local centre. *British Journal of Educational Technology* 16, no. 2, pp. 84–101.

McMahon, W., E. Yates, *et al.* 1987. Economic analysis of human resource development. In *Malawi Institutional Development Project Paper*, eds. McMahon, W., E. Yates, *et al*, p. 23. Washington, D.C.: USAID.

McMahon, W.W. and T. G. Geske, eds. 1982. *Financing education: overcoming inefficiency and inequity*. Urbana, Illinois: University of Illinois Press.

Menge, J. 1994. The evaluation of the New Hampshire plan: an early voucher system. In *Privatizing education and educational choice*, eds. Hakim, S., P. Seidenstat and G. W. Bowman, pp. 163–82. Westport: Praeger.

Merton, R.K. 1973. The normative structure of science. In *The sociology of science: the theoretical and empirical investigations*, Merton, R.K. (ed. N.W. Storer), pp. 267–78. Chicago: University of Chicago Press.

Mi Lu and Hong Xin. 1989. *Gaoshao yingjie biyesheng xia jiceng duanlian shi peiyang ganbu de zhongyao cuoshi* (Subjecting new university graduates to training at the grassroots level is an important measure to nurture cadres). *Liaowang*, no. 47, pp. 27–9.

Miao Sufei. 1994. *Cong wuchang jiaoyu dao youchang jiaoyu* (From free education to fee-paying education). Chengdu: Sichuan Education Press.

Min Weifan. 1994. People's Republic of China: Autonomy and accountability: an analysis of the changing relationships between the government and universities. In *Government and higher education relationships across three continents: the winds of change*, eds. Neave, G. and F. A. van Vught, pp. 106–27. Oxford: Pergamon.

———. 1996. Worldwide trends of higher education development and China's practice in higher education reform. Paper presented at Toward the 21st Century: The Trends in World Education Development and China's Education Reform Conference, Washington, D.C.

———. 1997a. China. In *International handbook of higher education in Asia*, eds. Postiglione, G.A. and G. Mak. Hong Kong: Greenwood Press.

———. 1997b. Major strategic issues for Chinese higher education development for the twenty-first century. Paper presented at the Conference on Chinese Education towards the twenty-first century, 13 August.

Min Weifang and Chen, X.Y. 1994. *Gaodeng jiaoyu de jingfei xuqiu yu touzi tizhi de geige* (Reform in funding demand and investment system for higher education). *Gaodeng Jiaoyu Luntan* (Forum of Higher Education), no. 1, pp. 1–12.

Ministry of Education. 1980. *Jiaoyubu guanyu dali fazhan gaodeng xuexiao hanshou jiaoyu he yedaxue de yijian* (Suggestions on developing higher correspondence and evening universities), State Council Document No. 228, 5 September.

———. 1983. *Guanyu banfa putong gaodeng xuexiao benzhuanke xuesheng renmin zhuxuejin zanxing banfa he putong gaodeng xuexiao benzhuanke xuesheng renmin jiangxuejin sixin banfa de tongzhi* (Circular on the provisional regulations governing the People's Grant and the People's Scholarship). Beijing: Ministry of Education.

Ministry of Labour. 1985. *Labour and wage statistics in China 1949–1985*. Beijing: China Statistics Press.

Mok Ka-ho. 1996. Marketization and decentralization: development of education and paradigm shift in social policy. *Hong Kong Public Administration* 5, no. 1, March, pp. 35–56.

———. 1997a. Private challenges to public dominance: the resurgence of private education in the Pearl River Delta. *Comparative Education* 33, no. 1, pp. 43–60.

———. 1997b. Retreat of the state: marketization of education in the Pearl River Delta. *Comparative Education Review* 41, no. 3, pp. 260–76.

Mok Ka-ho and D. Chan. 1996. The emergence of private education in the Pearl River Delta: implications for social development. In *Social and economic development in South China*, eds. MacPherson, S. and J. Cheng, pp. 242–65. London: Edward Elgar.

Moravcsik, M.J. 1985a. Applied scientometrics: an assessment methodology for developing countries. *Scientometrics 7*, pp. 165–75.

——. 1985b. *Strengthening the coverage of Third World science*. Eugene, OR: International Task Force for Assessing the Scientific Output of the Third World.

Morey, A. and Zhou Nanzhao. 1991. Higher education in mainland China: an overview. In *Education in mainland China*, eds. Lin Bih-jaw and Fan Li-min. Taipei: Institute of International Relations, National Chengchi University.

Muhammad Shamsul Huq. 1975. *Education, manpower, and development in South and Southeast Asia*. New York: Praeger.

Naismith, D. 1994. In defense of the educational voucher. In *Education and the market place*, eds. Bridges, D and T.H. McLaughlin, pp. 34–9. London: Falmer.

Nanjing College of Chemical Engineering. 1980. *Renmin Zhuxuejin zanxing guiding* (Provisional regulations on the People's Grant). Internal document.

National Association of Faculty Administration in Higher Education, ed. 1985. *Gaoxiao shizi guanli yantaohui lunwenji* (Studies on university faculty administration). Shanghai: East China Normal University Press.

National Center for Education Statistics, US Department of Education. 1995. *Digest of education statistics 1995*. Washington, DC: Government Printing Office.

National Centre for Educational Development Research. 1996. *Development and reform of China's educational system in the 1990s*. Beijing: New Star Publishers.

National People's Congress. 1982. *The constitution of the People's Republic of China*. Beijing: Foreign Languages Press.

Nee, V. 1989. A theory of market transition: from redistribution to markets in state socialism. *American Sociological Review 54*, no. 5, pp. 663–81.

Niklasson, L. 1996. Quasi-markets in higher education: a comparative analysis. *Journal of Higher Education Policy and Management 18*, May, pp. 7–22.

Oatey, H. 1990. Developments in the training of English teachers, 1979–1989. In *English in China*, ed. Dzau, Y.F., pp. 203–21. Hong Kong: API Press.

O'Connor, J. 1973. *The fiscal crisis of the state*. New York: St. Martin Press.

Offe, C. 1982. Some contradictions of the modern welfare state. *Critical Social Policy* 2, no. 2, pp. 7–17.

Oksenberg, M., L. Sullivan, and M. Lambert, eds. 1990. *Beijing Spring, 1989; confrontation and conflict; the basic documents*. Armonk, NY: M.E. Sharpe.

O'Leary, V.E. and J. M. Mitchell. 1990. Women connecting with women: networks and mentors in the United States. In *Storming the tower: women in the academic world*, eds. Lie, S.S. and V.E. O'Leary, pp. 58–73. New York: Nicholas/GP Publishing.

Ono, K. 1989. *Chinese women in a century of revolution: 1850–1950*, ed. and trans. Fogel, J.A. Palo Alto CA: Stanford University Press.

Organization for Economic Corporation and Development. 1977. *Learning opportunities for adults*, vol. 1. Paris: OECD.

Orleans, L.A. 1987. Soviet influence on China's higher education. In *China's education and the industrialized world: studies in cultural transfer*, eds. Hayhoe, R. and M. Bastid, pp. 184–98. Armonk, N.Y.: M.E. Sharpe.

———. 1989. China's changing attitude toward the brain drain and policy toward returning students. *China Exchange News* 17, no. 2, pp. 2–5.

Ou Fangqing. 1990. *Guanyu gaoshiyuanxiao zhaosheng, biye fenpei gongzuo gaige zhi wojian* (My opinions on reform of admissions and job allocation of tertiary normal schools. *Fujian Shifan Xueyuan Xuebao* (Fujian Normal College Journal), no. 4, pp. 66–70. Reprinted in *Gaodeng Jiaoyu*, no. 11, pp. 21–5.

Ou Qing. 1991. *Gaoxiao keji duiwu de xianzhuang fenxi yu jianshe de jianyi* (Analysis of the current situation of research staff in higher education). *Zhongguo Gaodeng Jiaoyu* 116, nos. 7 and 8, pp. 39–42.

Paine, L. 1992a. Teaching and modernization in contemporary China. In *Education and modernization: the Chinese experience*, ed. Hayhoe, R., pp. 183–209. Oxford: Pergamon Press.

———. 1992b. The educational policy process: a case study of bureaucratic action in China. In *Bureaucracy, politics and decision-making in post-Mao China*, eds. Lieberthal, K. and D. M. Lampton, pp. 181–215. Berkeley, CA: University of California Press.

Parish, W.L. 1984. Destratification in China. In *Class and social stratification in post-revolution China*, ed. Watson, J.L., pp. 84–120. New York: Cambridge University Press.

Peng Yusheng. 1992. Wage determination in rural and urban China: a comparison of public and private industrial sectors. *American Sociological Review* 57, pp. 198–213.

Pennycook, A. 1994. *The cultural politics of English as an international language*. Harlow: Longman.

People's Education Press. 1982. *English language syllabus*. Beijing: People's Education Press.

———. 1993. *English language syllabus.* Beijing: People's Education Press.

Pepper, S. 1990. *China's education reform in the 1980s: politics, issues, and historical perspectives.* Berkeley, CA: University of California Institute of East Asian Studies.

———. 1995. Regaining the initiative for education reform and development. In *China Review 1995,* eds. Lo Chi Kin *et al.,* pp. 18.1–18.49. Hong Kong: The Chinese University Press.

———. 1996. *Radicalism and education reform in 20th-Century China: the search for an ideal development model.* Cambridge: Cambridge University Press.

Piper, D. W. and R. Glatter. 1977. *The changing university.* UK: NFER.

Policies and Law Department, State Education Commission. 1993. Law and regulation on basic education of the People's Republic of China. Beijing: Beijing Normal University.

Price, D.J. 1986. *Little science, big science. . . and beyond.* New York: Columbia University Press.

Pring, R. 1987. Privatization in education. *Education Policy* 2, no. 4, pp. 289–99.

Psacharopoulos, G. 1979. Synthetic approaches in manpower planning. *Comparative Education* 16, no. 2, pp. 159–69.

Psacharopoulos, G. *et al.* 1983. *Manpower issues in educational investment.* Washington: World Bank, Staff Working Paper 624.

Pu Yi, Aisin-Guoro. 1964. *From emperor to citizen.* Beijing: Foreign Languages Press.

Pye, L.W. 1988. *The mandarin and the cadres: China's political cultures.* Ann Arbor: The University of Michigan.

Qian Linzhao and Gu Yu. 1994. *Zhongguo Kexueyuan* (Chinese Academy of Sciences). 3 vols. Beijing: Contemporary China Press.

Qinghua University. 1994. *Qinghua daxue xuesheng guanli tiaoli* (A collection of student affairs documents). Beijing: Qinghua University.

Qu Shipei. 1993. *Zhongguo daxue jiaoyu fazhan shi* (A developmental history of university education in China). Taiyuan, Shanxi: Shanxi Educational Press.

Qu Tiehua. 1996. A brief description of current private school development in China. *Chinese Education and Society* 29, no. 2, pp. 34–5.

Ranson, S. and J.D. Stewart. 1994. *Management for the public domain.* Houndmills: Macmillan.

Reed, G.G. 1991. *The Lei Feng phenomenon in the PRC.* Ph.D. thesis, University of Virginia.

———. 1992. Materials for political socialization and moral education in the PRC. In *Proceedings: Chinese Education for the 21st Century,* eds. Hackett, P., Yu Xiaoming and Liu Zhang, pp. 65–8. Chinese Education for the 21st Century Project.

———. 1995. Moral/political education in the People's Republic of China: learning through role models. *The Journal of Moral Education* 23, no. 2, pp. 99–111.

Rehak, J. and A.Wang. 1996. Washington Utilities and Transportation Commission. *New Telecom Quarterly* 4, no. 1.

Ren Gaoshi. 1991. *Qiwu qijian quanguo gaoshi shizi peixun gongzuo de huigu* (Review of teacher training in the sector of teacher education in higher education during the Seventh Five-Year Plan). *Zhongguo Gaodeng Jiaoyu* 114, no. 5, pp. 28–30.

Ren Shi Bu. 1990. *Quanguo liuxue huiguo renyuan zhuangkuang jiqi chengjiu* (Current status and achievement of returnees in the country). *Shen Zhou Xue Ren* 20, no. 4, pp. 22–3.

Ren Zhong, 1987. *Jilin sheng gaodeng jiaoyu kelei jiegou de yanjiu* (Study on the structure of higher education in Jilin Province). In *Zhongguo gaodeng jiaoyu jiegou yanjiu* (Studies on higher education structure in China) eds. Hao Keming and Wang Yongquan, pp. 178–84. Beijing: People's Education Press.

Richards, J.C. and T.S. Rogers. 1986. *Approaches and methods in language teaching.* Cambridge: Cambridge University Press.

Robinsohn, S. B. 1992. *Comparative education: a basic approach.* Jerusalem: The Magnes Press.

Robinson, J.C. 1991. Stumbling on two legs: education and reform in China. *Comparative Education Review* 35, no. 1, pp. 177–89.

Robinson, S.N. 1975. *A comparative study of women and the modernization process in Taiwan and Japan.* Ann Arbor, MI: University Microfilm International.

Rogers, D.C. and H. S. Ruchlin. 1971. *Economics and education: principles and applications.* New York: The Free Press.

Rosen, S. 1984. New directions in secondary education. In *Contemporary Chinese Education*, ed. Hayhoe, R. pp. 65–92. London: Croom Helm.

———. 1987. Survey research in the People's Republic of China: some methodological problems. *Canadian and International Education* 16, no. 1, pp. 190–7.

———. 1990. The impact of reform policies on youth attitudes. In *Chinese society on the eve of Tiananmen: the impact of reform*, eds. Davis, D. and E.F. Vogel, pp. 283–305. Cambridge: The Council on East Asian Studies/Harvard University.

———. 1992. Women, education and modernization in *Education and modernization: the Chinese experience*, ed. Hayhoe, R., pp. 155–284. Oxford: Pergamon Press.

———. 1994. Chinese women in the 1990s: images and roles in contention.

In *China Review 1994*, eds. Brosseau, M. and Lo Chi Kin, pp. 17.1–17.28. Hong Kong: The Chinese University Press.

Ross, H. 1992. Foreign language education as a barometer of modernization. In *Education and modernization: the Chinese experience*, ed. Hayhoe, R., pp. 239–54. Oxford: Pergamon Press.

Ruttan, V. 1993. *Agricultural research policy*. Minneapolis: University of Minnesota Press.

Sautman, B. 1991. Politicization, hyperpoliticization, and depoliticization of Chinese education. *Comparative Education Review* 35, no. 4, pp. 669–89.

Schnepp, O. 1989. The impact of returning scholars on Chinese science and technology. In *Science and Technology in Post-Mao China*, eds. Simon, D.F. and M. Goldman, pp. 175–95. Cambridge, MA: Harvard University Press.

Scott, J.W. 1990. Deconstructing equality-versus-difference: or, the uses of poststructuralist theory for feminism. In *Conflicts in feminism*, eds. Hirsch, M. and E. Fox Keller, pp. 134–48. London: Routledge.

Scovel, T. 1983. The impact of foreign experts, methodology and materials on English language study in China. *Language Learning and Communication* 2, no. 1, pp. 83–91.

Seeberg, V. 1990. *Literacy in China: the effect of the national development context and policy on literacy levels, 1949–79*. Bochum: Brockmeyer University.

————. 1993a. Access to higher education: targeted recruitment reform under economic development plans in the People's Republic of China. *Higher Education* 25, pp. 169–88.

————. 1993b. Stratified access to higher education: a profile of the growing middle class in post-Mao China. Paper presented at the annual meeting of the American Educational Research Association, Atlanta GA.

Seeberg, V. and Wang Xu 1991. Targeting recruitment for economic development in the People's Republic of China, 1985–90: countering the internal brain drain. Paper presented at the annual meeting of the Midwest Comparative and International Education Society, The Ohio State University, Columbus, OH.

Seldon, A. 1990. *Capitalism*. Oxford: Blackwell.

Serageldin, I. and B. Li. 1983. *Tools for manpower planning: the World Bank models*. Washington: World Bank, Staff working papers 587–590.

Shang Zhi. 1989. *Shilun chengren gaodeng jiaoyu de faige he fazhan* (On reform and development of higher adult education). *Chengren Gaocheng Jiaoyu Yanjiu*, no. 37, pp. 12–4.

Shanghai Education Commission. 1995. *Guanyu gaoxiao zhaosheng binggui hou shixin zuigao shoufei biaozhun kongzhi de tongzhi* (Circular on the control of maximum tuition scales in the track-merged higher education institutions in Shanghai). Shanghai: Shanghai Education Commission.

Shanghai Financial Bureau. 1995. *Guanyu benshi gaoxiao zhaosheng binggui hou shixing zuigao shoufei biaozhun kongzhi de tongzhi* (Circular on the control of the tuition fee scale in 'merged tracks' institutions). Shanghai: Shanghai Financial Bureau.

Shanghai Higher Education Bureau. 1992. *Guanyu chongxin heding gaojiao xitong shoufei xiangmu he biaozhun de tongzhi* (Circular on reratification of the fee items and scales in higher education). Shanghai: Shanghai Higher Education Bureau.

Shao Daosheng. 1995. *Zhongguo shehui de kunhuo* (Perplexities in the Chinese society). Beijing: Social Sciences Literature Press.

Sheehan, J. 1973. *The economics of education*. London: Allen and Unwin.

Shen Jianping. 1994. Educational policy in the PRC: a political influence perspective. *Journal of Educational Policy* 9, no. 1, pp. 1–13.

Shen Tong. 1990. *Almost a revolution*. Boston: Houghton-Mifflin.

Sheng Shihan *et al.* 1990. Participation of women in higher education in China. In *Women's participation in higher education: China, Nepal and the Philippines*, pp. 14–64. Bangkok: UNESCO.

Sheridan, S. and J.W. Salaff, eds. 1984. *Lives: Chinese working women*. Bloomington: Indiana University Press.

Shi Zi and Xiao Ya. 1988. *Dui gaoxiao jiaoshi zhiwu pinren gongzuo jige wenti de renshi* (Comments on the faculty appointment system in higher education). *Zhongguo Gaodeng Jiaoyu* 80, no. 4, pp. 23–4.

Shirk, S. 1982. *Competitive comrades: career incentives and student strategies in China*. Berkeley: University of California Press.

———. 1993. *The political logic of economic reform in China*. Berkeley: University of California Press.

Shoresman, M. 1989. *Returns to education: the University of Illinois — People's Republic of China Visiting Scholars Program*. Ph.D. thesis, University of Illinois at Urbana-Champaign.

Shu Zijia. 1989. *Qingnian jiaoshi canjia shehui shijian* (Social practice for junior faculty in higher education). In *Zhongguo jiaoyu nianjian 1988* (China education yearbook 1988), ed. State Education Commission, pp. 236–8. Beijing: People's Education Press.

Si, S. 1988. *Kexue jiaoyu bixu mianxiang shijie* (Science education must be geared to the world). *Guangming Ribao*, 25 January.

Sklair, L. 1994. The culture-ideology of consumerism in urban China: some findings from a survey in Shanghai. In *Consumption in marketizing economies*, eds. Belk, R.W. and C. Schultz. Greenwich, CT: JAI Press.

Smith, J. 1982. *Manpower planning and higher education: national policy in the United States and England*. Ph.D. thesis, University of Arizona.

Smith, K. 1988. Chinese science and education. *China Exchange News* 16, no. 3 (September), p. 16.

Song, G. and X. Kong. 1991. *Kexue jijiushi zhujinle jicu yanjiu* (The system of science funds has promoted basic science research). *Renmin Ribao* (People's Daily), 24 January.

Song, L. 1990. Convergence: a comparison of township firms and local state enterprises. In *China's rural industry: structure, development, and reform*, eds. Byrd, W.A. and Lin Qingsong, pp. 392–412. London: Oxford University Press.

Song, Y.H. 1996. Electricity systems in China. *Power Engineering Journal* 10, no. 2 (April), pp. 60–3.

Song Zhenneng. 1990. *Zhongguo Kexueyuan xuebu jianshi gaikuang* (Brief history of the academic departments of the Chinese Academy of Sciences). *Zhongguo Kexueyuan Yuankan* (Bulletin of the Chinese Academy of Sciences), no. 3, pp. 272–80.

Sontheimer, K.C. 1994. Privatizing higher education. In *Privatizing education and educational choice*, eds. Hakim, S., P. Seidenstat and G. W. Bowman, pp. 145–62. Westport: Praeger.

Stacey, J. 1983. *Patriarchy and socialist revolution in China*. Berkeley: University of California Press.

State Council. 1986. *Pizhun guojia jiaoyu weiyuanhui, caizhengbu guanyu gaige xianxing putong gaodeng xuexiao renmin zhuxuejin zhidu baogao de tongzhi* (Circular on the approval and transition of the report on reforming the People's Grant in regular institutions of higher education by the State Education Commission and Ministry of Finance). Beijing: State Council.

————. 1988. *Gaodeng jiaoyu zixue kaoshi zanxing tiaoli* (Temporary regulations for self-learning for the higher education examination). State Council Document no. 5.

State Education Commission, 1985. *Jiaoyu tizhi gaige wenxian xuanbian* (Selected works on reforms of the education system). Beijing: Education Science Press.

————. 1987a. *Decisions on the reform and development of adult education*, 12 March.

————. 1987b. *Guanyu shehui liliang banxue de ruogan zanxing guiding* (The provisional regulations on social forces running schools). Beijing: State Education Commission.

————. 1989a. *Education in China, 1978–1988*. Beijing: State Education Commission.

————. 1989b. *Guanyu putong gaodeng xuexiao shouqu xuezifei he zhusufei de guiding* (Regulations on tuition fees and accommodation fees in regular higher education institutions). Beijing: State Education Commission.

———— . 1990a. *The development of education in China, 1988–1990*. Geneva: UNESCO.

———— . 1990b. *Putong gaodeng xuexiao zhaoshou zifeisheng zanxing guiding* (Provisional regulations on the enrolment of self-supporting students in regular higher education institutions). Beijing: State Education Commission.

———— . 1992. *1949–1952 wenxian huibian* (Documentary collection 1949–1952).

———— . 1993a. *Gaigezhong de Zhongguo jiaoyu: Zhongguo de jiaoyu fazhan gaige de shijian yu jingyan* (Education reform in China: experience and lessons of reform and development). Beijing: State Education Commission.

———— . 1993b. *Guanyu dui gaodeng xuexiao shenghuo tebie kunnan xuesheng jinxing zizhu de tongzhi* (Circular on the provision of special subsidies for exceptionally disadvantaged students in higher education institutions). Beijing: State Education Commission.

———— . 1993c. *Minban gaodeng xuexiao shezhi zanxing guiding* (Provisional regulations for the establishment of people-run schools for higher education). In *A study of NGO-sponsored and private higher education in China*, China National Institute of Educational Research, 1995, pp. 57–60. Beijing: UNESCO.

———— . 1993d. *Guanyu putong gaodeng xuexiao zhaosheng he biyesheng jiuye zhidu gaige de yijian* (Opinions on reform in admission and job assignment for college students), Document no. 4. Translated in *Chinese Education and Society 27*, no. 3, pp. 11–8.

———— . 1994a. *Guanyu jinyibu gaige putong gaodeng xuexiao zhaosheng he biyesheng jiuye zhidu de sidian yijian* (Suggestions on the further reform of student enrolment and graduate employment systems in higher education institutions). Beijing: State Education Commission.

———— . 1994b. *Guanyu zai putong gaodeng xuexiao sheli qingong zhuxue jijin de tongzhi* (Circular on the establishment of the foundation of work-study in regular higher education institutions). Beijing: State Education Commission.

———— . 1995. *Guanyu yijiujiusi nian jiaoyu shiye fazhan de tongji gongbao* (Statistics bulletin on educational development, 1994). *Zhongguo Jiaoyu Bao* (China Education Daily), 29 March.

———— . 1996. *Guanyu "binggui" yuanxiao shoufei biaozhun de tongzhi* (Circular on the Scale of Tuition Fees in "Merged-track" Institutions).

State Education Commission and Shanghai Institute for Human Resources Development. 1993. *Zhongguo jiaoyu jingfei niandu fazhan baogao 1993* (Annual development report of education funds in China). Beijing: Higher Education Press.

Stevenson, H.W. and J.W. Stigler. 1992. *The learning gap: why our schools are failing and what we can learn from Japanese and Chinese education*. New York: Summit Books.

Stimpson, C.R. 1987. Women's studies: the idea and the ideas. *Liberal Education* 73, no. 4, September/October, pp. 34–8.

Student Affairs Department, State Education Commission. 1994. *Yijiujiusi nian zhaosheng 'binggui' gaige qingkuang* (Situation of the reform of 'merging the tracks' in 1994). Internal document.

Su Guilin. 1989. A preliminary probe into the difficulties college women encounter in job placement. *Jiaoxue Yanjiu* no. 2, 1988. Translated in *Chinese Education*, summer 1989, pp. 89–96.

Sun Jian, 1980. Population and education. *Ziran Bianzheng fa Tongxun (Journal of Dialectics of Nature)*, no. 3, pp. 1–3.

Sun Xiang. 1991. *Qinqie guanhuai, juda de guwu — Jiang shuji wei nongye jiaoyu tici: fazhan quanguo nongye jiaoyu, wei ke jiao xing nong zuochu gongfu* (Profound concern and tremendous inspiration — Secretary Jiang Zemin's inscription for agricultural education: Develop our country's agricultural education and make contributions to the vitalization of agriculture with science and education). *Gaodeng Nongye Jiaoyu*, no. 6, pp. 3–4.

Sun Xiaobing. 1991. *Guanyu dangqian gaoxiao jiaoshi duiwu de suowei 'duanceng' wenti* (The current 'faultline' issue of faculty in higher education). *Gaodeng Jiaoyu Xuebao* 26, no. 3.

Sunderland, J. 1990. 'Doing what the Romans don't do': advanced teacher training courses in China. In *English in China*, ed. Dzau, Y.F., pp. 222–49. Hong Kong: API Press.

Suttmeier, R.P. 1969. *The Chinese Academy of Sciences: institutional building in a research oriented organization*. Ph.D. thesis, Indiana University.

——— . 1974. *Research and revolution*. Lexington, MA: D. C. Heath and Company.

Tam, T. 1989. More on new rules for graduate employment. *Hong Kong Standard*, 23 August, p. 6. Reprinted in FBIS-CHI-89-163, 24 August, pp. 19–20.

Tan Shen. 1994. A study of women and social changes. *Social Sciences in China* 15, no. 2, summer, pp. 65–73.

Tang, A.M. and B. Stone. 1980. *Food production in the People's Republic of China*. IFPRI Research Report No. 15. Washington, DC: International Food Policy Research Institute.

Tao Chunfang *et al.* eds. 1993. *Zhongguo funü shehui diwei gaiguan* (An overview of status of Chinese women). Beijing: Zhongguo Funü Chubanshe.

Taylor, R. 1981. *China's intellectual dilemma: politics and university enrolment 1949–1978.* Vancouver: University of British Columbia Press.

Teather, D.C.B., ed. 1979. *Staff development in higher education: an international review and bibliography.* London: Kogan Page.

Teng Ssu-yü and J. K. Fairbank. 1979. *China's response to the West.* Cambridge Massachusetts: Harvard University Press.

Tian Kewu and Zhang Yue. 1995. Beijing youth: present situation and thoughts. *Renmin Ribao,* 11 February, p. 11. Translated in FBIS-CHI-95-054, 21 March, pp. 58–60.

Tilak, J. B.G. 1991. The privatization of higher education. *Prospects* 21, no. 2, pp. 227–39.

Tobin, J.J., D.Y.H. Wu and D. Davidson. 1989. *Preschool in three cultures: Japan, China, and the United States.* New Haven: Yale University Press.

Treiman, D.J. 1977. *Occupational prestige in comparative perspective.* New York: Academic Press.

Tsang Mun, C. 1987. The impact of underutilization of education on productivity: a case study of the U.S. Bell companies. *Economics of Education Review* 6, no. 2, pp. 239–54.

Tsang Mun C. and Min Weifang. 1992. Expansion, efficiency, and economics of scale of higher education in China. *Higher Education Policy* 5, no. 2, pp. 61–6.

UNESCO Division of Educational Policy and Planning. 1983. Education, training and employment. In *Training materials in educational planning, administration and facilities, module II.* Paris: UNESCO Division of Educational Policy and Planning.

Vijaykumar, P. 1978. *Manpower planning analysis and educational planning in selected states in American higher education.* Ph.D. thesis, State University of New York, Buffalo.

Walder, A.G. 1983. Organized dependence and cultures of authority in Chinese industry. *Journal of Asian Studies* 43, no.1, pp. 51–76.

————. 1986. *Communist neo-traditionalism: work and authority in Chinese society.* Berkeley, CA: University of California Press.

————. 1990. Economic reform and income distribution in Tianjin, 1976–1986. In *Chinese society on the eve of Tiananmen,* eds. Davis, D. and E.F. Vogel, pp. 135–56. Cambridge, Mass: Harvard University Press.

Walford, G. 1990. *Privatization and privilege in education.* London: Routledge.

Walker, A. 1984. The political economy of privatization. In *Privatisation and the welfare state,* eds. Le Grand, J. and R. Robinson, pp. 19–44. London: George Allen and Unwin.

Walsh, K. 1995. *Public services and market mechanisms.* Houndmills: Macmillan.

Wan Junren. 1995. What kind of national concept should we hold? *Zhongguo Qingnian Bao* (China Youth Magazine), 26 September, p. 7. Translated in FBIS-CHI-96-056, 21 March 1996, pp. 26–8.

Wang Guisheng. 1990. Some thoughts on the problem of the weakening of the model effect of Lei Feng. *Qingnian Yanjiu* (Youth Studies), no. 3, March, no. 138, pp. 42–5. Translated in *Chinese Education and Society* 20, January-February 1993, no. 1, pp. 48–59.

Wang Hongyi. 1995. *Zongjie jingyan, jinyibu shenhua gaodeng nongye yuanxiao zhaosheng jiuye zhidu gaige* (Consolidate experiences and progressively deepen the reform of the enrolment and employment system for agricultural colleges). *Gaodeng Nongye Jiaoyu*, no. 1, p. 3.

Wang Hui. 1996. Schools developing properly. *China Daily*, 24 January.

Wang Jingsong. 1994. *Gaodeng nong lin jiaoyu zai huhuan* (Higher agricultural and forestry education is calling out). *Guangming Ribao* (27 April 1994), p. 1.

Wang Jisheng. 1996. The position and function of higher institution, society and government in higher education evaluation. Paper presented at the International Conference on Quality Assurance and Evaluation in Higher Education Beijing (translation grammatically edited).

Wang, S.M. and W. Zhou 1993. *Zhongguo putong gaodeng jiaoyu jingfei bokuan tizhi* (The system of funding for general higher education in China). Unpublished appendix to policy document.

Wang Wenyou. 1988. *Luelun fazhan putong gaodeng jiaoyu de san ge jiben tiaojian* (Three conditions for developing higher education). In *Zhongguo jiaoyu fazhan wenti yanjiu* (Studies on educational development in China), ed. Li Shouxin, pp. 109–26. Beijing: Zhongguo Jihua Chubanshe.

Wang Xianming and Hu Yanpin. 1994. Policies, achievements and new measures for investment in education in China. *Social Sciences in China* 15, no. 4, pp. 47–55.

Wang Xiaodong and Wu Luping. 1995. Young urban Chinese evaluate the year 1994 (edited by Ma Mingjie). *Zhongguo Qingnian Bao* (China Youth), 21 January, p. 2. Translated in FBIS-CHI-95-050, 15 March, pp. 43–9.

Wang Xiaoquan. 1993. *Guanyu gaodeng xuexiao faren diwei wenti de guandian zhongshu* (Discussions on the issue of legal status of higher learning institutions). *Zhongguo Gaodeng Jiaoyu* 133, no. 2, pp. 35–6.

Wang Yaonong. 1995. *Zhongguo chengren gaodeng xuexiao de xianzhuang jiqi fazhan zhengce* (The current status of China's higher adult education and strategies for development). *Higher Adult Education Research*, no. 75, pp. 20–7.

Wang Zhanjun and Lin Mengquan. 1996. Study on evaluation index system of graduate school in institutions of higher learning in China. Paper presented at the International Conference on Quality Assurance and Evaluation in Higher Education, Beijing.

Wang Zhongli and Wu Zhenrou. 1993. *Mianxiang 21 shiji, zhongdian jianshe yipi gaodeng xuexiao he zhongdian xueke* (Facing the 21st century, building key universities and key disciplines). *Zhongguo Gaodeng Jiaoyu* 138, nos. 7 and 8, pp. 8–9.

Watson, J. ed. 1984. *Class and social stratification in post-revolution China.* Cambridge: Cambridge University Press.

Wei Qinxian and Chen Jiacai. 1991. *Jiaqiang guonei fangwen xuezhe de peixun gongzuo* (Strengthening the domestic visiting scholar training programme). *Zhongguo Gaodeng Jiaoyu* 112, no. 3, pp. 30–1.

Wei Yitong and Zhang Guocai. 1995. A historical perspective on non-governmental higher education in China. Paper presented at the Regional Seminar on Private Higher Education in Asia and the Pacific, Xiamen, October/November, pp. 7–8.

White, G. 1981. *Party and professionals.* New York: M.E. Sharpe.

White, L. 1978. *Careers in Shanghai.* Berkeley: University of California Press.

Whyte, M.K. and W. Parish. 1983. *Urban life and contemporary China.* Chicago: University of Chicago Press.

Wilding, P. 1990. Privatization: an introduction and a critique. In *Privatization*, ed. Pring, R. London: Jessica Kingsley.

Williams, G. 1987. The OECD's Mediterranean regional project. In *Economics of education: research and studies*, ed. Psacharopoulos, G., pp. 335–6. Oxford: Pergamon Press.

Williams, R.H. 1982. *Dream worlds, mass consumption in late nineteenth-century France.* Berkeley: University of California Press.

Williamson, O.E. 1975. *Markets and hierarchies: analysis and antitrust implications.* New York: The Free Press.

Woodhall, M. 1993. *Financial diversification in higher education: a review of international experience.* Unpublished manuscript.

World Bank. 1986. *China: Management and Finance of Higher Education.* Washington: World Bank.

———. 1988. *Education in sub-Saharan Africa: policies for adjustment, revitalization and expansion.* Washington: World Bank.

———. 1991. *China: provincial education planning and finance — sector study.* Washington: World Bank.

———. 1995. *Technology Development Project.* Washington: World Bank.

Wran, N. 1988. *Report of the committee on higher education funding* (The Wran Report). Canberra: Ministry of Education, Training and Employment.

Wu Fanghe. 1994. *Gaocenci rencai peiyong zhong de wenti yu duance* (Issues and strategies in cultivating high-level personnel). *Zhongguo Gaodeng Jiaoyu* 146, no. 4, pp. 3–4.

Wu Jingyu. 1983. *Quchang buduan* — a Chinese view of foreign participation in teaching English in China. *Language Learning and Communication* 2, no. 1, pp. 111–6.

Wu Zhong. 1994a. *Shenda huhuan xueshu yishi* (Shenda should call for academic consciousness. *Shenzhen University Journal*, no. 4, pp. 17–8.

——— . 1994b. *Shenbao '211 gongcheng': biyaoxing, kexingxing, chaju ji duice* (Application for entering 'Project 211': necessity, feasibility, gap and countermeasures). *Shenzhen University Journal*, no. 3, p. 14.

Xia Hong. 1994. Graduates working in remote areas. *China Daily*, 29 June, p. 3.

Xiao Jin. 1989. Adult education in China: its development and challenges. Paper presented at the Midwest Conference on Asian Affairs, Michigan State University, 29 October.

——— . 1996. Relationship between organizational factors and the transfer of training in the electronics industry in Shenzhen, China. *Human Resource Development Quarterly* 7, no. 1, pp. 55–73.

Xiao Jin and Tsang Mun C. 1994. Costs and financing of adult education: a case study of Shenzhen, China. *International Journal of Educational Development* 14, no. 1, pp. 51–64.

Xie Qing. 1996. PLA General Political Department issues circular requiring whole army to conduct activities in learning from Lei Feng, heroes, and models in greater depth. Translated in FBIS-CHI-96-064, p. 34.

Xie Yu. 1989. *The process of becoming a scientist*. Ph.D. thesis, University of Wisconsin-Madison.

——— . 1992. The social origins of scientists in different fields. *Research in Social Stratification and Mobility* 11, pp. 259–79.

Xin Yutang. 1992. *Beijing gaoxiao shizi duiwu jianshe de jiben silu yu cuoshi* (Strategies of faculty building in Beijing's higher learning institutions). *Zhongguo Gaodeng Jiaoyu* 130, no. 11.

Xiong Minan. 1983. *Zhongguo gaodeng jiaoyu shi* (History of higher education in China). Chongqing: Zongqin Press.

Xu Guangchun. 1985. Today's education is the productive force of tomorrow. *Liaowang*, no. 1 (1 January), pp. 10–2. Translated in JPRS-CPS-85-035, pp. 75–9.

Xu Min. 1993. *Zhongguo nü daxuesheng shuang chong jiao se chongtu de zhanwangxin yanjiu* (A study of Chinese female college student's dual role: conflict and prospective). In *Proceedings of the Second International Conference on Women's Studies*, pp. 94–106. Beijing: Peking University Women's Studies Centre.

Xu Tingguan and Ye Jun. 1991. *Yi xueke jianshe wei jichu, gaohao gaoxiao shizi duiwu jianshe* (Strengthening faculty by curricular development). *Gaojiao Yanjiu Yu Tansuo* no. 2.

Xu Xiu. 1992. *Dui putong gaoxiao zhaosheng fenpei zhidu gaige de sikao* (Reflections on the reform of admission to colleges and universities and the job assignment system for their graduates). *Zhongguo Gaojiao Yanjiu* (Chinese Higher Education Research), no. 4, pp. 46–8. Reprinted in *Gaodeng Jiaoyu*, no. 8, 1992, pp. 93–5; translated in *Chinese Education and Society* 27, no. 3, 1994, pp. 51–5.

Xue Huanyu. 1986. *Dui Zhongguo gaodeng jiaoyu fazhan zhanlue de xiangfa* (Considerations of development strategy of China's higher education), *Shanghai Gaojiao Yanjiu*, no. 2, pp. 40–8.

Yan Yunxiang. 1992. The impact of rural reform on economic and social stratification in a Chinese village. *The Australian Journal of Chinese Affairs* 27, pp. 1–21.

——— . 1996. *The flow of gifts: reciprocity and social networks in a Chinese village*. Palo Alto, CA: Stanford.

Yang Busheng and Peng Dingguo. 1992. *Zhongguo shuyuan yu chuantong wenhua* (Chinese academics and traditional culture). Hunan: Hunan Jiaoyu Chubanshe.

Yang Mei-hui, M. 1994. *Gifts, favors, and banquets: the art of social relationships in China*. Ithaca, NY: Cornell University Press.

Yang Qihe and Ruan Xiumei. 1990. *Gaoxiao shizi duiwu 'duanceng' wenti qian xi* (A superficial analysis of the 'faultline' problem within the teaching corps of tertiary institutions). *Zhejiang Gaodeng Nongye Jiaoyu* (Zhejiang Higher Agricultural Education) no. 2, pp. 31–5.

Yang Qinghai. 1993. *Dui waiyu yuanxiao zhuanye ji kecheng sheji gaige de sikao* (Some thoughts on the reform of foreign language majors and curriculum design). *Waiyu Jie* (Journal of The Foreign Language World), no. 3 (September), pp. 8–9.

Yang Shimou. 1995. Agricultural education, research and training in China. Unpublished manuscript written for the Ministry of Agriculture.

Yang Shimou *et al.* 1992. *Zhongguo nongye jiaoyu fazhan zhanlüe yanjiu chutan* (Research on China's agricultural education development strategy). *Gaodeng Nongye Jiaoyu*, no. 4, p. 11.

Yang Zhihan. 1988. Non-governmental higher education shows its vitality. *Guangming Ribao*, 8 January, p. 1, in FBIS-CHI-88-020, 1 February, p. 19.

Yao, E. Shu-shin Lee. 1983. *Chinese women: past and present*. Mesquite, TX: Ide House.

Yao Ruoguang. 1988. Needs assessment in the training of secondary school English teachers. Paper presented at the Symposium on Curriculum Development and Continuing Teacher Education, The University of Hong Kong.

Yao Shuping. 1989. Chinese intellectuals and science: a history of the Chinese Academy of Sciences (CAS). *Science in Context* 3, pp. 447–73.

Yao Shuping, Luo Wei, Li Peishan and Zhang Wei. 1994. *Zhongguo Kexueyuan fazhan shi* (Developmental history of the Chinese Academy of Sciences). In *Zhongguo Kexueyuan* (The Chinese Academy of Sciences), ed. Qian Linzhaoand Gu Yu, volume 1, pp. 1–65. Beijing: Contemporary China Press.

Yao Yize and Liu Hui. 1993. *Zhongguo datoushi* (Great perspective of China). Beijing: Central National Institute Press.

Yi Changfa. 1993. *Shilun woguo chengren jiaoyu fazhan de sanda qushi* (On the three trends of higher adult education development). *Chengren Gaocheng Jiaoyu Yanjiu*, no. 62, pp. 1–5.

Yin Fenghe. 1988. *Guangyu chengren gaodeng jiaoyu lianhe baixue de tantao* (On the horizontal integration of higher adult education). *Zhongguo Gaodeng Jiaoyu*, June, pp. 40–1.

Yin Qiping and G. White. 1994. The 'marketization' of Chinese higher education: a critical assessment. *Comparative Education Review* 30, no. 3, pp. 217–37.

You Changfu *et al.* 1992. *Zai shenhua jiaoyu gaige zhong zhengque fahui gaoxiao de zhineng zuoyong* (Correctly develop the role of the university function in the deepening of educational reform). *Gaodeng Nongye Jiaoyu*, no. 5, pp. 7–9.

Youdi, R.V. and K. Hinchliffe. 1985. *Forecasting skilled manpower needs: the experience of eleven countries*. Paris: UNESCO.

Young, M. B. 1973 *Women in China*. Michigan: University of Michigan.

Young Yi Rong. 1995. Taiwan. In *Education and development in East Asia*, eds. Morris, P. and A. Sweeting, pp. 105–24. New York: Garland.

Yu Bo and Xu Hongyan. 1988. *Adult higher education: a case study on the workers' colleges in the People's Republic of China*. Paris: UNESCO, International Institute for Educational Planning.

Yu Chenchung. 1984. Cultural principles underlying English teaching in China. *Language Learning and Communication* 3, no. 1, pp. 29–40.

Yuan Feng. 1995. From the imperial examination to the national college entrance examination: the dynamics of political centralism in China's educational enterprise. *Journal of Contemporary China*, no. 8, pp. 28–56.

Yuan Guanghui. 1992. *Shanxi sheng jiaowei zhongshi gaohao shizi peixun he guanli gongzuo* (Experience of the education authority in Shanxi Province on organising faculty training). *Zhongguo Gaodeng Jiaoyu* 121, no. 1.

Yuan Wei and Xu Yi. 1988. *Shanghai jiao da liuxue guiguo renyuan da xian shen shou* (Strengths of returnees at Shanghai Jiaotong University). *Shen Zhou Xue Ren* 6, no. 2, pp. 17–9.

Yuan Xiangwan and Mao Rong. 1991. *Jiaoshi duiwu de nianling 'duanceng' yu shizi guanli moshi de zhuanbian* (The 'Faultline' in the Age Structure of the Teachers' Contingent and the Change in the Pattern of Teachers' Management). *Gaojiao Yanjiu Yu Tansuo*, no. 2, pp. 16–21.

Yuan Zhengguo. 1995. Chinese higher educational changes: from 'state model' to 'social mode'. Paper presented at the International Symposium on Education and Socio-Political Transitions on Asia, Hong Kong.

Yuan Zhenguo and Wei Chengsi. 1991. *Zhongguo dangdai jiaoyu sichao* (Contemporary Trend of Education in China). Shanghai: Sanlian Shudian.

Yue Cheng. 1975. *Renzheng dushu zhuajin xuexi* (Read the works earnestly and study hard). *Hongqi* (The Red Flag), no. 3, pp. 31–5.

Zhang Bingliang. 1990. *Gaodeng xuexiao shichen gaige gongzuo* (Reform on the promotion of the academic titles in higher education). In *Zhongguo jiaoyu nianjian 1989* (China education yearbook 1989), ed. State Education Commission, pp. 165–7. Beijing: People's Education Press.

Zhang Chenxiang. 1995. *Xiaolu youxian jiangu gongping shi dui shehuizhuyi fenpei yuanze he fenpei guanxi renshi de shenghua* (Efficiency priority and equity consideration deepened the understanding on the socialist distribution principle and relations). *Dongbei Shifandaxue Xuebao* (The Journal of Northeast China Normal University), no. 2, p. 13.

Zhang Jianhua, ed. 1992. *Da zhongzhuan biyesheng tiaopei gongzuo bibei shouce* (Indispensable handbook for university and college students' allocation and transition to work). Jiangxi: Higher Education Press.

Zhang Wei. 1988. *Huazhong ligong daxue liuxue guilai jiaoshi* (Returnees at Huazhong Science and Technology University). *Shen Zhou Xue Ren* 8, no. 4, pp. 12–3.

Zhang Xiaowen. 1994. *Jiefang sixiang, zhenfen jingshen, jiakuai gaige, kaichuang gaodeng nong lin jiaoyu xin jumian* (Emancipate the mind, inspire enthusiasm, speed up reform, and develop new aspects of higher agricultural and forestry education work). *Gaodeng Nongye Jiaoyu* (Higher Agricultural Education), pp. 3–11.

Zhang Xuyi. 1993. *Wending jiaoshi duiwu, baozheng jiaoxue zhiliang* (Stabilize teaching facilities and ensure teaching effectiveness). *Waiyu Jie* (Journal of the Foreign Language World), no. 3 (September).

Zhang Yongchang. 1985. *Employee education history in China*. Liaoning: Liaoning People's Press, pp. 578–82.

Zhang Zhongliang. 1991. People and science: public attitudes in China toward science and technology. *Science and Public Policy* 18, pp. 311–7.

Zhao Hongzhou. 1988. *Lun kexue de guojixing* (On the internationalization of science). *Guangming Ribao*, 7 January.

Zhao Longqun. 1995. *Xiandai nongye tuiguang renyuan de zhishi jiegou* (The knowledge structure of modern agricultural extension personnel). In *Nongye tuiguang lilun yanjiu* (Research on agricultural extension theory), ed. Xu Wuju, pp. 70–1. Beijing: Zhongguo Nongye Chubanshe.

Zhao Qindian. 1993. *Zhongguo gaodeng jiaoyu gaige yu fazhan, 1977–1993* (Reform and development in Chinese higher education, 1977–1993). Beijing: State Education Commission.

Zhao Renwei. 1994. *Zhongguo jumin shouru fenpei fenxi yanjiu* (Analysis and research on residents' income distribution in China). Beijing: China Social Sciences Press.

Zhao Weijie. 1995. Economic development and the marriage crisis in the Special Economic Zones of China. In *Women and market societies*, eds. Einhorn, B. and E.J. Yeo, pp. 205–16. Aldershot, UK: Edward Elgar.

Zhao Y. 1988. China: its distance higher education system. *Prospects* 18, no. 2, p. 217.

Zhao Zhongjian 1994. *Zhongguo xuesheng daikuan wenti yanjiu* (Studies on student loans in China). Unpublished manuscript.

Zhe Nong Da jiaoshi duiwu yanjiu ketizu (Teaching Corps Research Group at Zhejiang Agricultural University). 1991. *Gaoxiao jiaoshi duiwu 'duanceng' ji qi duice de tantao* (A discussion of the 'faultline' in the teaching corps of institutions of higher education and strategies to resolve it). *Gaodeng Nongye Jiaoyu*, no. 1, pp. 34–8.

Zhejiang University. 1995. *Zhejiang Daxue xuesheng guanli tiaoli* (Student administration regulations of Zhejiang University). Hangzhou: Zhejiang University.

Zheng Shaolun. 1953. Higher education in new China. *The People's China*, no. 12, June, pp. 6–10.

Zhitong University. 1995. *Leaflet introducing Zhitong University*. Guangdong: Zhitong University.

Zhongguo Kexueyuan Xuebu Lianhe Bangongshi (Unified Office of the Academic Departments of the Chinese Academy of Sciences) ed. 1994. *Zhongguo Kexueyuan diqici yuanshi dahui wenjian huibian* (A documentary collection of the Seventh General Assembly of the Members of the Chinese Academy of Sciences). Beijing: Chinese Academy of Sciences.

Zhonghua Quanguo Funü Lianhehui Yanjiusuo (Institute for Research on Women, All China Women's Federation). 1991. *Zhongguo funü tongji ziliao 1949–1989* (Statistics on women in China 1949–1989). Beijing: Chinese Statistics Press.

Zhou Beilong and Zhou Chenye. 1985. Education in China by the Year 2000. In *China by the Year 2000*, ed. Mayor's Training Programmes Office, pp. 42–6. Beijing: CCP Central Committee.

Zhou Pichuang and Chen Nailin. 1988. *Gaodeng jiaoyu fazhan zhanlue zhidao sixiang de zhuanbian* (Shifting the strategic guiding ideology of higher education development). *Gaojiao Yanjiu Yu Tansuo*, no. 3, pp. 26–30.

Zhou Runsun, Mo Huilin, Xu Zhenhua and Tu Yaqin. 1992. *Gaoxiao shixing 'Dushu shoufei, bubao fenpei' gaige de kexing fenxi he shishi fang'an* (An analysis of the possibility of putting into practice 'Charging tuition and no assignment of jobs' for college students and the scheme of its implementation). *Tongji Jiaoyu Yanjiu* (Tongji Educational Research), no. 3, pp. 56–60.

Zhou Shizhen. 1995. *Shilun Shenzhen Daxue jiaoshi duiwu de jianshe* (On the set-up of the faculty of Shenzhen University). In *Shenzhen Daxue gaodeng jiaoyu yanjiu lunwenji* (Collected papers on higher education research of Shenzhen University), eds. Higher Education Research Institute and the Academic Affairs Office, Shenzhen University, pp. 102–6. Shenzhen: Shenzhen University.

Zhou Wei, Zhang Tiedao and Liu Wenpu, eds. 1994. *The plight and perspective of girls' education in western China*. Qinghai: Institute for Educational Research.

Zhou Weirong. 1995. Talent project sends graduates to towns. *China Daily*, 23 November.

Zhou Xincheng. 1989. *Daxue jiaoshi ying cong dongluan zhong xiqu shenme jiaoxun* (Lessons university staff should learn from 4 June). *Zhongguo Gaodeng Jiaoyu 97*, no. 11, pp. 11–3.

Zhou Yuliang. 1990. *Education in Contemporary China*. Changsha: Hunan Education Press.

Zhu Kaixuan. 1992. *Zai quanguo gaodeng jiaoyu gongzuo huiyi shang de jianghua* (Speech at the National Higher Education Conference). *Zhongguo Gaodeng Jiaoyu 131*, no. 12, pp. 6–14.

Zhu Qi. 1990. *Zhongguo funü canzheng yu nüxing canzheng yishi* (Chinese women's political participation and female political consciousness). In *Huaxia nüxing zhimi (The enigma of Chinese womanhood)*, ed. Li Xiaojiang, pp. 226–42. Beijing: Sanlian Shudian Chubanshe.

Zhu Wenqin. 1994. *Gaoxiao shoufei gaige yaoyou pei tao cuoshi* (Reforms in fee payment for higher education must have other policy changes to form a coordinated set). *Guangming Ribao*, 28 March, p. 1. Reprinted in *Gaodeng Jiaoyu*, no. 4, pp. 37–8.

Zhu Yimin. 1996. Overview of nongovernmental schools. Translated in *Chinese Education and Society* 29, no. 2, pp. 23–4.

Zhuang Yongling. 1985. Official of the Ministry of Education's Office of Student Affairs lists changes in college enrollment. *Renmin Ribao*, 11 May, p. 3. Reprinted in JPRS-CPS-85-069, pp. 15–7.

Ziderman, A. and D. Albrecht. 1995. *Financing universities in developing countries*. Washington DC: Falmer Press.

Zuckerman, H. 1970. Stratification of American science. *Sociological Inquiry*
    40, pp. 235–57.
———— . 1977. *Scientific élite: Nobel laureates in the United States.* New York:
    The Free Press.
Zuckerman, H. and R. K. Merton. 1973. Age, aging, and age stratification
    in science. In *The sociology of science: the theoretical and empirical
    investigations*, Merton, R.K. (ed. N.W. Storer), pp. 497–559. Chicago:
    University of Chicago Press.

Index

USA, 30, 45, 61-2, 64, 142, 146, 207, 275,
    418
    faculty with Ph.Ds., 30
USSR, 6, 31, 33, 37, 61, 62, 64, 69, 100,
    109, 143, 146, 239
    influence on Chinese education, 1, 18,
    83-4, 108, 173, 180, 282
utilitarianism, 121-40, 285

V

visiting scholars. *See* faculty,
    international exchange
vocational/technical education, 34, 292
Voluntary Service Overseas, 154

W

wage, national average, 240, 251-2
weituo peiyang. See daipei
Western influence, 106, 108, 414
    in language education, 141-64
    in publishing, 65
    lack of, agricultural universities, 173
women, 299-320, 423
    access to higher education, 299-308
    as faculty members, 310-6
    as students, 300-4, 307
    at Beijing University, 302-3
    admissions, 300-5
    benefits from modernization, 323
    cultural factors in discrimination, 304,
    308, 313, 346, 354
    dependency, 323-5, 338-9
    discrimination of graduates in labour
    force, 305-6, 309-10
    illiteracy, 306
    in CAS, 102
    in labour force, 309
    participation in higher education, 354
    politicized by CCP, 300
    politicizing educational debate, 323,
    325
    promotions, 353
    reasons for inequality in staff, 315-6

    rural reasons for student gender
    inequality, 304-8
    salary differences, 352
    spontaneous movement 1980s, 324
    survey data, 300-15
    See also Taiwan university women
work-study programme, 248
work-unit (*danwei*), 5, 322, 331, 335
workers universities, 195, 199
World Bank, 9, 42, 74, 282, 414, 420-1
    1997 Report, 417-34
Wuhan University, 42

X

Xi'an Jiatong University, 263

Z

Zhao Ziyang, 144
Zhejiang province, 252, 288, 399
Zhejiang University, 129, 246
Zhengzhou International Women's
    Institute, 321-43
    conflicting agendas, 325-9
    curriculum, 336-9
    financial woes, 327, 333
    flexible admissions, 326
    guanxi, 328, 329, 331-3
    individual agency importance, 336
    loyalties and allegiances, 334-6
    relations with ACWF, 309, 322, 324,
    427-8
    relations with Cadre School, 327
    role of *danwei*, 331-2, 335
    structural tensions in, 332-3
    women-centeredness, 330, 338
Zhenzhou University, 324
Zhitong Private University
    (Guangzhou), 285
zhongxue weiti xixue weiyong (Chinese
    conditions, Western practice), 4, 142-4,
    414
Zhou Enlai, 238, 263
Zhu Rongji, 266
zifei. See enrolment categories